1,000,000 Books

are available to read at

Forgotten Books

www.ForgottenBooks.com

Read online
Download PDF
Purchase in print

ISBN 978-1-331-11027-9
PIBN 10146126

This book is a reproduction of an important historical work. Forgotten Books uses state-of-the-art technology to digitally reconstruct the work, preserving the original format whilst repairing imperfections present in the aged copy. In rare cases, an imperfection in the original, such as a blemish or missing page, may be replicated in our edition. We do, however, repair the vast majority of imperfections successfully; any imperfections that remain are intentionally left to preserve the state of such historical works.

Forgotten Books is a registered trademark of FB &c Ltd.
Copyright © 2018 FB &c Ltd.
FB &c Ltd, Dalton House, 60 Windsor Avenue, London, SW19 2RR.
Company number 08720141. Registered in England and Wales.

For support please visit www.forgottenbooks.com

1 MONTH OF FREE READING

at

www.ForgottenBooks.com

By purchasing this book you are eligible for one month membership to ForgottenBooks.com, giving you unlimited access to our entire collection of over 1,000,000 titles via our web site and mobile apps.

To claim your free month visit:
www.forgottenbooks.com/free146126

* Offer is valid for 45 days from date of purchase. Terms and conditions apply.

English
Français
Deutsche
Italiano
Español
Português

www.forgottenbooks.com

Mythology Photography **Fiction**
Fishing Christianity **Art** Cooking
Essays **Buddhism** Freemasonry
Medicine **Biology** Music **Ancient Egypt** Evolution Carpentry Physics
Dance Geology **Mathematics** Fitness
Shakespeare **Folklore** Yoga Marketing
Confidence Immortality Biographies
Poetry **Psychology** Witchcraft
Electronics Chemistry History **Law**
Accounting **Philosophy** Anthropology
Alchemy Drama Quantum Mechanics
Atheism Sexual Health **Ancient History**
Entrepreneurship Languages Sport
Paleontology Needlework Islam
Metaphysics Investment Archaeology
Parenting Statistics Criminology
Motivational

CONTENTS.

	PAGE
EPISTLE DEDICATORY. *William E. A. Axon*	vii
LIFE AND WIT OF THOMAS FULLER. *John E. Bailey* . . .	xi

SERMONS.

1631 (circa). A Comment on Ruth [preached circa 1631]. London, 1654. 8vo **1**

1640. Joseph's Party-coloured Coat; containing a comment on [the Institution, &c., of the Lord's Supper,] 1 Cor. xi. 18–30. Together with several [eight] Sermons [under noted]. London, 1640. 4to. . . . **107**

    1. Growth in Grace : 2 Pet. iii. 18 . . . **168**
    2. How far Examples are to be followed : Ruth i. 15 . . . . **176**
    3. An ill match well broken off : 1 John ii. 15 . **185**
    4. Good from bad Friends : 2 Sam. xv. 31 . . **192**
    5. A Glass for Gluttons : Rom. xiii. 13 . . **198**
    6. How far Grace can be entailed : 2 Tim. i. 5 **205**
    7. A Christening Sermon : 2 Kings v. 14 . . **211**
    8. Faction confuted : 1 Cor. i. 12 . . . **221**

1642. A fast Sermon preached on Innocents-Day [Wednesday 28th Dec., 1642]. London, 1642. 4to. Matt. v. 9 **231**

1643. A Sermon preached at the Collegiate Church of S. Peter in Westminster, Monday, 27th March, 1643, being the day of his Majesty's Inauguration. London, 1643. 4to. 2 Sam. xix. 30 . . . . **262**

—— A Sermon of Reformation, preached at the Church of the Savoy last Fast Day July 27 [26], 1643. London, 1643. 4to. Heb. ix. 10 . . . . **289**

Following this Sermon is a reprint of Saltmarsh's "Examinations, or a Discovery of some Dangerous Positions" in the foregoing Sermon. London, 1643. 4to. To this Tract Fuller replied in :— **315–404**

Contents.

1643. Truth Maintained; or Pofitions delivered in a Sermon at the Savoy: fince traduced for dangerous: now afferted for found and fafe. Oxford, 1643. 4to. **317–404**

1644. Jacob's Vow: A Sermon preached before Charles I. and Prince Charles at St. Mary's in Oxford, Friday, May 10th, 1644, being the day of public faft. Oxford, 1644. 4to. Gen. xxviii. 20–22 . . . . **405**

1646. Feare of lofing the old Light; or, a Sermon preached in Exeter. London, 1646. 4to. Rev. ii. 5 . . . **433**

1647 (preached 1633). A Sermon of Affurance, firft preached at Cambridge in 1633. London, 1647. 4to. 2 Pet. i. 10 **459**

1648. A Sermon of Contentment. London, 1648. 12mo. 1 Tim. vi. 6 . . . . **491**

1649. The Juft Man's Funeral, lately delivered in a fermon at Chelfey before feveral persons of honour and worfhip. London, 1649. 4to. Eccles. vii. 15 . . . . **507**

PASSAGES FROM SPENCER'S "STOREHOUSE." London, 1658. . **535**
 1647. God flow to anger and of great Patience . . . **543**
 1647. God's Infinite Power in the Refurrection of the Body **543**
 1647. Riches have Wings **544**
 1647. Not to continue angry **544**
 Undated. Blafphemous Language condemned . . . **545**
 1647. The Juftice of God, what it is, and how defined . . **546**
 1647. How it is that the proceedings of God in His juftice are not fo clearly difcerned **546**
 1648. Refurection of the Body proved by a Natural Demonftration **547**
 1648. The Great Difficulty of Forgiving One Another . . **548**
 1649. Minifters to cry down the Sins of the Time . . **548**
 —— Infirmities to be in the beft of God's Children, and wherefore **549**
 —— Knowledge and Learning to be Owned wherefoever they be Found **549**
 1650. Confideration of God's Omniprefence to the Sinners Curb **550**
 —— God, a Mercifull God **551**
 —— The Several Expreffions of God in His Mercies, and why so? **552**
 —— The Generality of God's Knowledge **552**
 —— The Great Danger of Sleighting the leaft Sinne . . **553**
 1652. Graces of the Spirit to be held faft in the midft of temporal loffes **554**
 —— How to make a right ufe of the Doctrine of Predeftination **554**

To the Rev. *JOHN E. B. MAYOR, M.A.*,

Senior Fellow of St. John's College
and Professor of Latin in the
University of Cambridge.

TO whom can I so appropriately dedicate this first collected edition of the Sermons of Thomas Fuller as to you, who so worthily represent the learning, the earnestness, and that union of enthusiasm and sobriety which is the note claimed, and not without good cause, for the University of Cambridge—the alma mater of the author of the *Worthies of England*, of the *Church History of Britain*, of *Good Thoughts in Bad Times*, and of so many other contributions to the solid and enduring literature of English history and English theology.

The reputation of a wit and humourist has, with some, obscured Fuller's claims as a man of solid learning, of genuine historical temper, and of fine ethical instincts. There is nothing so permanent as the religious spirit of man, but there is nothing so fleeting and variable as the form of its expression. Each age makes its own theology, for each fresh generation is assailed by fresh temptations and has need of fresh aids and new inspiration. This explains the rapidity with which pulpit discourses, as a rule, become obsolete.

Fuller belonged to an age which caught a reflection from the glories of the Elizabethan period, and before church oratory had frozen into the decorous commonplaces that were current in the "Augustan" period of Anne and the early Georges. Yet there are many of Fuller's contemporaries, poffibly of equal or even greater contemporary popularity, whofe fermons would not bear reprinting. His, however, preferve their vitality. This is partly no doubt due to the peculiar charm of his remarkably original ftyle; the odd fancies and the daring but always reverent conceits; the entirely unexpected light in which old truths are placed and old texts frefhly illuftrated. But fomething is alfo due to his fobriety of judgment, and his conftant defire to attain the golden mean. This is in all ages an offence to the zealots of the Extreme Right and the Extreme Left, and the man who aims to walk in this middle path muft expect to be mifjudged; to be denounced by one section as an obftructive and by another as a more or lefs difguifed revolutionary. Fuller did not efcape this danger, and yet living in times when Civil War divided all England into two hoftile camps, he had the efteem of good men of all parties, and managed to retain and to ufe with franknefſe and vigour a liberty of pro- phefying which was neither a needlefs source of irritation nor a fmoothing down of the truth, as he held it, to mere com- monplace. His fermons deal with fome temporary matters, but are for the moft part concerned with the permanent elements in human nature and human life. Whoever will dig into them will find in them the folid gold of wifdom, of confolation, and of reproof.

It is ftrange that Fuller fhould have waited fo long for a biographer; it is ftrange that two centuries fhould have paffed away before his fermons were collected from the neceſſary ephemeral form of their firft publication. Either of thefe tafks might have been congenial work for one of the many fons of Cambridge, who give themfelves to the purfuits of learning and literature. Both were undertaken by a bufy Manchefter man, the late Mr. John Eglington Bailey, F.S.A. When he was attending the evening claffes of the Owens College, a cafual remark let fall by the teacher, the

Rev. William Gaſkell—(the accompliſhed huſband of that woman of fineſt genius, Mrs. Gaſkell, authoreſs of *Wives and Daughters*)—fell upon fruitful ſoil. The teacher pointed out the great intereſt and originality of Fuller's ſtyle, and the want in our biographical literature of an adequate memorial of his varied life, which was caſt in a period ſo pictureſque in aſpect and ſo profoundly important for its ſtruggle between great conflicting principles. Mr. Bailey took the taſk in hand, and his bright and ſcholarly lecture on "The Wit and Wiſdom of Thomas Fuller" became the nucleus of the ſolid and maſterly *Life of Thomas Fuller*, which appeared in 1874, and at once took its place as a ſtandard biography. The warm welcome which this book received at the hands of all competent critics encouraged Mr. Bailey to embark upon the project of collecting and editing the Sermons of Fuller. He had made conſiderable progreſs, when apparently the firſt ſymptoms of the illneſs which eventually proved fatal, cauſed him to lay it aſide. For ſeveral years it remained in an incomplete ſtate, and after his death there was nearly all the firſt volume printed and a portion of the ſecond, but neither was finiſhed. The taſk of completing the book has not been an eaſy one, as may eaſily be imagined. The fine ſeries of Fulleriana collected by Mr. Bailey were purchaſed by Meſſrs. Taylor, Garnett and Co., and by them preſented to the Mancheſter Free Library. This included his MS. materials, and theſe, of courſe, have been freely uſed. I do not doubt that there are other ſigns by which they may be diſtinguiſhed, but the introductions to the ſermons which fell to me to edit after Mr. Bailey's death, are marked with the letter A. To Mr. Bailey are due vol. i. p. 1 to p. 528; and vol. ii. p. 17 to p. 96. But vol. i. p. 529 to p. 556 had been ſet in type and only needed the final reviſion, and vol. ii. p. 1 to p. 16 was in the ſame condition. The introductory notice of Fuller is a reprint of Mr. Bailey's lecture, originally delivered more than a quarter of a century ago. At the beginning of the ſecond volume will be found a brief memorial notice of John Eglington Bailey. His premature death was a ſad loſs to Engliſh ſcholarſhip for there were few who were ſo deeply familiar with the intricate movements of theological thought and feeling in this country during the feventeenth century.

That the work as now prefented has not the form and completenefs which it might have received from the hands of the original editor, is a fact of which I am fully confcious, but the worth of Fuller's own writings, and the large amount of the editing that was done by my dead friend would give value to the undertaking, whatever might be the fhortcomings of the continuator. The tract on the Jews at the end of vol. ii., (a portion of which is taken from the *Holy Warre,*) has all the appearance of pulpit ufe. Strangely enough it had eluded Mr. Bailey's refearches and was quite unknown to him.

In you, my dear Profeffor Mayor, I am fure of a candid, a competent, and a kindly critic ; for you know that my tafk has been a labour of love and duty, profecuted amidft the urgent preffure of a bufy life, and amidft dark fhadows of domeftic forrows. Thefe volumes are to me a memorial of the beloved friend who was not permitted to end the work he had fo well begun. They have been with me in bufy Manchefter, by the fands of our Lancafhire eftuaries, by the fhores of North Wales, and by our fouthern coaft, where firft the Norman conqueror landed—with me, alas ! whilft watching dear ones fading out of life into eternity.

WILLIAM E. A. AXON.

THE LIFE AND WIT

OF

THOMAS FULLER, D.D.

BY THE LATE

JOHN EGLINGTON BAILEY.

[*This lecture was delivered before the Manchester Phonographic Union in* 1863, *and is reprinted from* Pitman's Popular Lecturer, *January,* 1864.]

IN bringing before you some remarks on the life and wit of that "reverend divine and learned historian," as his anonymous biographer terms the subject of my address, I labour under the disadvantage of having to speak of a man whose writings, once famous, are now but very little read and sparingly referred to; whose life, spent in the service of his country, is unhonoured; and whose name is vaguely and trivially spoken of, as that of one who has no special claim on our attention. I want to show you, this evening, that THOMAS FULLER was a man who *has* some claim on our gratitude; that he was no mean author, and belonged to no mean age; that at one time he occupied a very conspicuous position in English literature, and (if not a conspicuous) an important post at a critical time in English history; and that though in respect to his writings, the opinion of the world has changed, and but little attention is bestowed upon them, yet there may there be found a vast amount of shrewd common sense and old English wit, expressed in pithy and forcible language; and from his life there may be gathered lessons pregnant of good.

Like the quaint age in which he lived, Fuller's mind was most eccentric, and this has made him "the very strangest writer in our language. Perhaps no man ever excelled him in fulness and readiness of wit;" and this—added to the plain and practical sense which pervades his writings, and which is so characteristic of this nation—makes it "passing strange" that his works should be permitted to die out, and be so scarce and difficult to obtain as some of them are. But ingratitude is ever to be met with, both in contemporaries and posterity. Fuller's works were well abused, as well during his life as since; but he has occasionally met with a generous reception from some of his critics, whose references to him have helped, in some degree, to preserve his works. Coleridge said of him, after reading his *Church History*—"Next to Shakspeare, I am not certain whether Fuller, beyond all other writers, does not excite in me the sense and emotion of the marvellous;" and "Fuller was incomparably the most sensible, the least prejudiced great man, of an age that boasted a galaxy of great men." And the genial essayist, Charles Lamb, has commended Fuller's writings, and added a few specimens of his composition; which notice is sufficient to incite any lover of our English literature to take this quaint and witty author into closer companionship.

The authentic sources from which the particulars of his life are to be gathered, are very few, and those few are very dull and dreary compositions for so lively a subject. Aided, however, by these, and the references to himself contained in his works, I have (to use one of his own modest expressions) "endeavoured" his life, my remarks being taken from more voluminous notes which I have collected for a biographical memoir.

His name may be said to be both a fortunate and an unfortunate one—fortunate, as giving us the idea of substance and solidity, very appropriate to an author whose works, compared with others, are "not only *fuller* in useful matter and varied interest, but (as a punster of his own day would have said) *fuller* in spirit, *fuller* in wit, in fact, *Fuller* throughout—'Strong without rage, without o'erflowing, *full:*'" unfortunate, as when he good-humouredly but unwittingly is said to have asked one Mr. Sparrowhawk, "What is the difference between an owl and a sparrowhawk?" received for reply, "An owl is *fuller* in the head, *fuller* in the face, and *Fuller* all over!"

His lot was cast in eventful and perilous times, when England was, on a small scale, in the same state in which America is now on a great one,—devastated and cursed by the most dreadful form of war. He was born in the year 1608, and was the elder of two sons of the Rev. Thomas Fuller, rector of St. Peter's, Aldwincle,— a place also famous in giving birth to the poet Dryden. This village is situated on the river Nene, in Northamptonshire; and, says Fuller, " if that worthy county esteem me no disgrace to it, I esteem it an honour to me." At his day it was a most populous and fruitful county—" Sixteen several towns, with their churches, have at one time been discovered by my eyes, which are none of the best; and God grant," he piously and quaintly adds, " that those who are sharper-sighted may never see fewer!" On opposite sides of Aldwincle were situated the dwelling of Mr. Brown, the founder of the sect known as the Brownists, and the demesne of Francis Tresham, one of the activities in the Gunpowder Plot. Ever on the look-out for what he calls " observables " and " remarkables," Fuller learnt from this circumstance the wisdom of being moderate; he would ever try to hit the golden mean, avoiding the fanaticism of the Anabaptist on the one hand, and the fiery zeal of the Jesuit on the other. Fuller conformed his life to this decision.

He speaks of his father as a " painful [*i.e.* painsful or painstaking] preacher; " and it appears he was also a learned man. He was one who obeyed the apostolic injunction, " Live peaceably with all men," for he was careful to avoid every occasion of strife. It was under his superintendence that the education of his son was conducted— so successfully that at the age of thirteen, becoming a scholar before he was a man, young Thomas was ready for college, and to Cambridge he was accordingly sent. He was admitted into Queen's College, of which his maternal uncle, Bishop Davenant, was president. This worthy doctor took a great interest in the welfare of the boy, and it is probable that his nephew refers largely to him when he " charactered " the " Good Bishop," in his *Holy State.* Dr. Davenant was an excellent instructor of youth.

Thomas's intellect seems early to have manifested itself. If we may believe an anecdote which Aubrey has left of him, he was a very precocious and strange lad. " He was a boy of pregnant wit, and when the bishop (Davenant) and his father were discoursing, he would be by and hearken, and now and then put in, and sometimes beyond expectation or his years. He was of a middle stature, strong set, curled hair, a very working head, insomuch that walking and meditating before dinner, he would eat up a penny loaf, not knowing that he did it."

In 1629, he removed to Sidney Sussex College, and as the fruit of his studies during the past years, he received the degrees of B.A. and M.A. His success must, however, partly be attributed to the teachers who trained his mind, being very fortunate in that respect. Dr. Ward was the president of this college; and in the place accorded to him among the *Worthies of Durham*, Fuller says of this divine—" He turned with the times, as a rock riseth with the tide "—a fine and expressive simile.

Fuller was appointed, in 1630, to the curacy of St. Benet, Cambridge; and it was while here that his abilities as a preacher first shone forth, his lectures being well attended. Here he delivered his *Lectures on the Book of Ruth*, which, however, were not printed till many years afterwards.

In his twenty-third year, he was presented by his uncle with a prebendal stall in the county of Dorset: in the same year, also, appeared his first publication. His first attempt, like that of all young authors, was poetical; and in this poem appear many of the peculiarities which afterwards made him so famous. Its characteristic title was *David's Hainous Sinne; Heartie Repentance; Heavie Punishment;* and was dedicated — (dedications were both necessary and fashionable then)—to the three sons of Lord Montague, a hospitable old English baron of worshipful estate, whose family were personal and highly-valued friends of the author. This work was never re-published, and is therefore very scarce. Mr. Fuller wrote very little poetry after this. Poetry, like music, he used to say, was excellent sauce, " but they have lived and died poor who made them their meat."

Rapidly advancing in church preferment, Fuller, in 1634, collated to the rectory of Broad-Winsor, a neat and picturesque little village, near Bridport, in Dorsetshire. Here he spent some happy moments among a flock that became endeared to him, and he to them. He was an earnest pastor, and bears some resemblance to the character of " The Faithful Minister," whom he has sketched in his *Holy State*. Like "Holy George Herbert," his whole soul appears to have been in his work; and his " dear and loving charge " highly esteemed him.

In 1635, Fuller revisited Cambridge, and attained the degree of Bachelor of Divinity; but on returning home, he got rid of another kind of bachelorship in his marriage. His happiness was, however, short-lived, for after giving birth to a son, his wife died; and though this severe affliction was rendered less acute in the active discharge of his ministry, it must have preyed upon his mind, and may, ultimately, have led him to seek change of scene and forgetfulness in the stormy times which characterized London life before the breaking out of the Civil War.

At Broad-Winsor, in his leisure moments, he had diligently been occupying himself in planning for publication some of those books on which his fame chiefly rests, though the distractions of the times delayed their publication for several years. "In the amenity and retirement of this rural life," says his biographer, " some perfection was given to those pieces which, soon after, blest this age. From this pleasant prospect he drew that excellent piece of *The Holy Land*, *Pisgah-sight*, and other tracts relating thereto; so that what was said bitterly of some tyrants, that they made whole countries vast solitudes and deserts, may be inverted to the eulogy of this doctor, that he, in these recesses, made deserts—the solitudes of Israel—the frequented path and track of all ingenious and studious persons."

One of the results of his researches appeared in 1639, being a History of the Crusades, entitled *History of the Holy War*. This strange and witty history at once attracted attention, and brought fame to the author. The droll way in which the history is written, and the lively figures which his rich imagination suggested, render this work extremely amusing. Every page of it sparkles with wit, and yet it is a work of considerable research, and shows that the writer had the necessary requirements of an historian.

While residing at Broad-Winsor, Fuller published many sermons, with odd titles, as might be expected. His discourses are characterized by their practical piety, earnestness, outspokenness, benevolence, and moderation. They are not witty productions, though even here his wit occasionally breaks out, as if it could not be confined. All his works are aptly termed "quaint," in the modern acceptation of the word; but in Fuller it also had its original meaning—" scrupulously elegant or exact "—a style of composition which, with him, was not artificial (as was the case with many authors of this quaint age), but natural. " Such was his natural bias to conceits, that I doubt not," says Lamb, " upon such occasions, it would have been going out of his way to have expressed himself out of them."

In 1640, we find Fuller in London, in the midst of the strife which ushered in the Civil War. He was appointed a member of the celebrated Convocation at which the Observances were discussed, and the passing of which was followed by such opposition on the part of the Puritans and Parliamentarians. Fuller is, perhaps, the only historian who has left a minute and impartial account of this assembly. He took no active part in it, and his opinion was, that the measures adopted were far too stringent.

As soon as the position of affairs grew more serious and determined, Fuller began to use his influence to avoid the appeal to arms. Though by conviction he was a royalist, he was not a partisan, but had respect to the rights of the people. He used his influence, as befitting his profession, in favour of peace, endeavouring to calm the angry feelings which were fomented. The pulpit was then a powerful agency, and Fuller had great influence. On arriving in London, whither his fame as a preacher and author had preceded him, his discourses were attended by crowds, and he became at once " a popular preacher." He does not appear, however, to have been so weak-minded as to have been led away by popular applause : a sermon preached about this time, shows that he was alive to its dangers. Speaking of pastors whose churches are crowded by the thickest audiences, he says—" Let them not pride themselves with the bubble of popular applause, often as carelessly gotten, as undeservedly lost. Have we not seen those who have preferred the onions and flesh-pots of Egypt before heavenly manna ?—lungs before brains, and the sounding of a voice before soundness of matter ? " He usually preached at the Inns of Court, but his pulpit acquirements procured for him the lectureship at the Savoy, and the duties of this post he faithfully discharged for two years. " He had, in his narrow chapel, two audiences, one without the pale, the other within ; the windows of that little church, and the sextonry, so crowded as if bees had swarmed to his mellifluous discourse." No wonder that amidst the chaos into which the then prevalent conflicting opinions had plunged the nation, the voice of such a preacher was welcomed—welcomed as one who might prove the messenger of peace, to avert the war which all good men dreaded. Fuller's sermons form a striking contrast to those of his time, which were bigoted, intolerant, and narrow-minded, their tendency being to hasten the war. "Our English pulpits for these eighteen years," says Fuller, in one of his *Thoughts*, "have had in them too much cardinal anger, vented by snapping and snarling spirits on both sides. But if you bite and devour one another, saith the apostle (Gal. v. 15), take heed that ye be not devoured one of another."

At last the war broke out, and the king fled to Oxford with many of the nobility. On a fast-day being ordered by the parliament, Fuller preached at his chapel of the Savoy, taking as his text, "Blessed are the peacemakers." In his discourse, he exposed the unchristian character of war. The sword, he argued, was no discerner between truth and falsehood; "it may have two edges, but hath never an eye." He advised peaceable measures, the petitioning of the king and parliament to make mutual concessions, the putting aside of the party names which had sprung up, and a general repentance.

About this time (1642), Fuller published his *Holy State and Profane State*, which he had long had in hand. It was once very popular, but is now seldom read. The plan of the book has been adopted by many celebrated writers; it professes to describe the characters of various persons, such as "The Good Husband," "The Good Schoolmaster," "The Good Prince," &c. The work commences with a delineation of "The Good Wife," giving in the opening sentence one of his characteristic, droll, and ridiculous reasons for so doing:—"St. Paul to the Colossians, chap. iii. verse 18, first adviseth women to submit to their husbands, and then counselleth men to love their wives. And, sure, it was fitting that women should first have their lesson given them, because it is hardest to be learned, and therefore they need have the more time to con it. For the same reason, we begin with the character of the good wife." These delineations of character, which Fuller, an acute student of human nature, dealt with very subtilly, are each followed by examples, taken from history or the Bible. Among the characters in the *Holy State* are some essays on memory, on building, and other unlooked-for subjects; but this diversion is quite in character with the author's manner. The second part of the book—*The Profane State*—is a short one, and contains sketches of the harlot, liar, and kindred subjects. The book abounds in keen observations, and shows him to have been as well read in men as books. So multiform are the forms that his sparkling wit here takes, that he is, perhaps, the only author in whose pages may be found *all* the definitions of the "unaccountable and inexplicable ways" of wit, which Barrow has enumerated in his explanation of the word. But it is a poor commendation of an author to be simply witty; and were Fuller's writings only witty, they would be almost worthless. His wit not only answers to its present meaning, but its original and better one—that of wisdom, or understanding. Fuller was not only a jester, but a shrewd writer of common-sense; not only a punster, but a searching investigator and historian.

On the anniversary of the king's inauguration, March 27th, 1642, Fuller (still holding the lectureship at the Savoy) preached a sermon in Westminster Abbey, taking the unpalatable text—"Yea, let him take all, forasmuch as my Lord the king is come again in peace to his own house." I need not remind you that those were the days in which the divine right of kings, church and state, &c., were seriously believed in. The character of the "Good King," in his *Holy State*, Fuller commences to describe with the bald statement, "The king is a mortal god;" in which light he seems to have regarded King Charles, for he concluded the same chapter with the most fulsome praise of that monarch. It need not, therefore, be surprising, that the sermon referred to, with its courtly sentiments, and the allusions to public affairs, should have given great umbrage to the parliamentary party, involving him in much odium, and making his position among them rather anomalous. At the taking of Bristol, all hopes of peace, which he had laboured to promote, were dispelled; but on the 27th of July, another fast-day, Fuller made one more useless exhortation in favour of peace. This sermon, on publication, was attacked by a Yorkshire clergyman, whom Fuller, when on the march, found time to reply to, challenging him to an answer. This, however, the clergyman did not give, alleging that he had heard of Fuller's death at Exeter. "I have no cause," said he, in his *Worthies*, "to be angry with fame for so good a lie. May I make this true use of that false report—to die daily. See how Providence hath willed it: the dead man is still (1661) living; the then living man dead. And seeing that I survive to go over his grave, I will tread the more gently on the mould thereof, using that civility on him which I received from him."

When the Solemn League and Covenant was drawn up and subscribed to by the House of Commons and assembly of divines, Fuller was pressed to swear to it also; but he refused to do so, except with certain reservations. Whereupon he was compelled to leave London, and joined the standard of the king, at Oxford. Here he was well received, but on preaching at the court, he made the faithful mistake of preaching *to* royalty, instead of *before* it, as is usual; and his honest, plain-spoken nature pleased the royalists no better than the "roundheads." Here is a proof of his sterling honesty to principle: Mr. Worldly Wisdom would have acted somewhat differently. As at London, so at Oxford, he was called by hard names, and not liking the sentiments or company he here met with, he shortly afterwards left, having sought and obtained a chaplaincy in part of the king's army commanded by Sir Ralph Hopton—this step being, perhaps, precipitated by taunts of suspicion as to his fidelity to the king's cause.

His property met with the same fate that attended very many in that period—it was sequestered by the parliament. Though by this act he was reduced to poverty, he bore the loss with Christian resignation, cheerfully acquiescing in the decrees of Providence, who had, he considered, justly afflicted the nation for its sins. He thus alludes to his losses in his *Mixt Contemplations:*—"I have observed that towns which have been casually burnt, have been built more beautiful than before; mud walls afterwards made of stone; and roofs, formerly but thatched, afterwards advanced to be tiled. The apostle tells me that I must not think strange concerning the fiery trial which is to happen to me. May I likewise prove improved by it. Let my renewed soul, which grows out of the ashes of the old man, be a more firm fabric and stronger structure: so shall my affliction be my advantage."

Among other things, he felt very keenly the loss of his valuable library and MSS., which, Vandal-like, had been destroyed. This want, however, was partly made good, through the noble generosity of one of his patrons, Lord Cranfield, Earl of Middlesex, who gave him his father's library.

England was then scourged and wasted by the Civil War, and there are many melancholy evidences, in his writings, of its baneful effect on the nation and on individuals. One or two extracts from his *Thoughts* are here given, which will show, at the same time, his own sentiments in those hard times, and the style of the composition of his *Thoughts*, published during its progress.

"We read (Luke xiii. 11) of a woman who had a spirit of infirmity eighteen years, and was bowed together, and could in no wise lift up herself. This woman may pass for the lively emblem of the English nation : from the year of our Lord 1642 (when our wars first began) unto this present one, eighteen years in my arithmetic ; all which time our land has been bowed together, beyond possibility of standing upright. . . . A pitiful posture, wherein the face is made to touch the feet, and the back is set above the head ! God, in due time, set us right, and keep us right, that the head may be in its proper place! Next the neck of the nobility, then the breast of the gentry, the loins of the merchants and citizens, the thighs of the yeomanry, the legs and feet of artificers and day labourers. As for the clergy (here by me purposely omitted), what place soever be assigned them—if low, God grant patience ; if high, give humility unto them."

"This nation is scourged by a wasting war : God could no longer be just if we were prosperous. Blessed be His name, that I have suffered my share in the calamities of my country. Had I poised myself so politically betwixt both parties, that I had suffered from neither—yet could I have taken no contentment in my safe escaping. For why should I, equally engaged with others in sinning, be exempted above them from the punishment? It is, therefore, some comfort that I draw in the same yoke with my neighbours, and with them jointly bear the burden which our sins have jointly brought upon us."

While engaged in active service in the army as chaplain, preaching regularly on the Lord's-day, Fuller manifested that diligence which is ever to be met with in his life. For when now wandering up and down England, following the fortunes of the Royal army, he was busily employing his time in collecting materials for his most famous and greatest work — *The Worthies of England* — a work which contains, principally, short biographies of celebrated Englishmen, but also embraces a great variety of other topics. It is said, that in searching for matter for this book, he would patiently listen for hours to the prattle of old women, that he might gather, from their gossip, snatches of local history, recollections of great men, scraps of traditionary wisdom or folk-lore; and that he would reproduce the same by the aid of his wonderful memory. Like Scott's *Old Mortality,* this itinerant chaplain would, on coming into a new district, at once seek out and take notes of anything of antiquarian interest; visiting old churchyards and tombstones, and poring over musty records of the past, for anything which would be useful towards the accomplishment of his task. By this and other means, he collected a vast amount of varied information, and particulars of great men, which might otherwise have been lost. The men whose names he has endeavoured to perpetuate, are ranged under the respective counties of their birth; and he mentions also the productions, manufactures, local history, proverbs, sheriffs, and modern battles, leaving each county with an appropriate farewell. It is a work which every Englishman should be proud to own. His object in compiling it is thus candidly stated by himself:—" Know then, I propound five ends to myself in this book: first, to gain some glory to God; secondly, to preserve the memory of the dead; thirdly, to present examples to the living; fourthly, to entertain the reader with delight; and lastly (which I am not ashamed publicly to profess), to procure some honest profit to myself."

In the discharge of his duties as chaplain, he was at Basing-house during one of its sieges; where, with all the vigour of a Crusader, or Norman bishop, he incited and animated the garrison to so vigorous a defence, that the attacked became the attackers—the leader of the Parliamentary forces being compelled to retire.

When the Royal forces were driven into Cornwall, Fuller, having obtained leave of absence from Lord Hopton, took up his residence in Exeter—" one of the sweetest and neatest towns in England," says Fuller; but these adjectives do not apply now. On the queen resorting hither for refuge, Fuller was appointed tutor and chaplain, by King Charles, to her infant, Princess Henrietta, lately born here, to testify his great worth; and the king shortly afterwards gave him a patent for his presentation to the town of Dorchester, worth £400 per annum. While in this city, Fuller's society was much sought after, and he remained here till its surrender in 1646; during which time, besides continuing his literary labours, he preached regularly to the citizens. Here he put forth his *Good Thoughts in Bad Times*—a patriotic and seasonable little book, well adapted for the condition in which his country was placed. Fuller was present at the siege of Exeter, of which he relates a strange episode, which must be told in his own words:—" When the city of Exeter was besieged by the Parliamentary forces, so that only the south side thereof, towards the sea, was open unto it, incredible numbers of larks were found in that quarter, for multitude like quails in the wilderness, though (blessed be God!) unlike them both in cause and effect—as not desired with man's destruction, nor sent with God's anger—as appeared by their digestion into wholesome nourishment: hereof I was an eye and mouth witness. I will save my credit, in not conjecturing any number, knowing that herein, though I should stop beneath the truth, I should mount above belief. They were as fat as plentiful; so that, being sold for twopence a dozen and under, the poor—who could have no cheaper, as the rich no better, meat—used to make pottage of them, boiling them down therein. Several natural causes were assigned hereof. However, the cause of causes was Divine Providence."

Fuller is next met with in London, being gladly welcomed back again at the Savoy. But the troubles he had passed through, added to the distracted state of his country, had affected his mind; and, "weak in health and dejected in spirits," he repaired to the residence of his constant patron, Lord Montague, at Boughton, near Northampton. Under his hospitable roof, he wrote *The Cause and Cure of a Wounded Conscience,* and he was all the better for it. This book is distinguished by its deep thought, tinged all the way through by melancholy, showing the reality of his affliction. It is dedicated to the Countess of Rutland; and the " Christian Reader" is told in the preface that, as it was not suitable to wear wedding clothes at a funeral, he had, in that sad subject, declined all light and luxurious expressions. This, consequently, does not read like one of Fuller's works. The last dialogue—" Whether it be lawful to pray for, or to pray against, or to praise God for, a wounded conscience"—concludes with the following beautiful and much-admired sentiment:—" Music is sweetest near or over rivers, where the echo thereof is best rebounded by the water. Praise for pensiveness, thanks for tears, and blessing God over the floods of affliction, makes the most melodious music in the ears of heaven."

He again went to London, and preached wherever he was allowed; occupying, among other pulpits, that of St. Clement's,

Lombard Street, and St. Bride's, Fleet Street. He also published another volume of meditations, entitled *Good Thoughts in Worse Times*. These little manuals were very popular, and their contents show them to be the production of an ardent patriot. They consist of short paragraphs, containing personal, scriptural, and historical incidents, &c., followed by a suitable moral or reflection—much after the manner of Quarles' Enchiridion, or Æsop's Fables. Though many of the similes used by him are extremely fanciful, they are often beautiful, and contain solid and suggestive teachings. He justifies the ways of God towards his country, and urges his readers to trust in Omnipotence, who alone could restore the country to order. To reflecting minds, these little books of practical divinity, published during the war, must have come like oil on troubled waters. Truly, " meditations are like the minstrel the prophet called for (2 Kings iii. 15) to pacify his mind discomposed with passion ; " while " controversial writings (sounding somewhat of drums and trumpets) do but make the wound the wider."

The next year, the " powers that be " prohibited Fuller from preaching " till further orders ; " " wherefore," says Fuller, " I am fain to employ my fingers in writing, to make the best signs I can ! " We nevertheless find him preaching soon afterwards at Chelsea Church, under the protection of Sir John Danvers. And on the execution of Charles I., he manifested his loyalty to that unfortunate monarch, by a very hazardous but honest act—the preaching and publication of a sermon, entitled *The Just Man's Funeral*.

The attempt made to silence his voice did not cause his church preferment to cease, for the Earl of Carlisle obtained for him the perpetual curacy of Waltham Abbey ; and this was one of the means by which many eminent churchmen in those days were kept in England. Before, however, he could obtain his curacy, he had to undergo the customary ordeal before the Court of Triers, who dispossessed such as they deemed unfit for preaching—generally those who had been political offenders. There is a droll anecdote told about him, in reference to this examination. It appears he was extremely apprehensive of the result (as well he might be), and in this emergency he sought assistance of John Howe, the celebrated divine, and one of Cromwell's chaplains. Fuller said to him, " You may observe, sir, that I am somewhat a corpulent man, and I am to go through a very strait passage. I beg you would be so good as to give me a shove, and help me through." Howe, whose catholicity of spirit allowed him to overlook his party in the man, gave him the necessary advice, and he got off more frightened than hurt.

Among other things, the Triers had asked him to give them some proof of his well-known powers of memory; upon which, Fuller promised that if they would restore a certain poor sequestered minister, he would never forget that kindness as long as he lived! Fuller was charged with pretending to the art of memory, but he said it was a fancy or trick—no art. The secret of his extraordinary power lay in order and method. He says—" Marshal thy notions into a handsome method. One will carry twice more weight trussed and packed up in bundles, than when it lies untoward flapping about the shoulders. Things orderly fardled up and hanging under both heads are most portable." His writings have been charged with displaying a want of method; but this is not the case, for discursive though some of them be, they are well arranged. There is method in his madness. His numerous digressions are always so pleasant that it is easy to put up with them, and indeed the reader would not at first think they are digressions. He may be likened to a man travelling along a road, stopping to admire or examine objects on each side of him, often leaving the path, but returning to it again; and thus he goes merrily along, and ultimately arrives at the end of his journey.

Waltham, where Fuller was now quietly residing, is a place of some literary celebrity: it was here that Fox's famous Book of Martyrs, and Bishop Hall's works, were written. Fuller here spent some peaceful years, being "wedded to the embraces of a private life, the fittest wife and meetest helper that can be provided for a student in troublesome times." He completed some of his books here. His *Pisgah-sight of Palestine and the Confines thereof*, *with the History of the Old and New Testaments acted thereon*, appeared in 1650. In others' hands this might have been a geography as dull as a school-book, but Fuller's rich, lively, and exuberant imagination has scattered throughout it a lavish display of every kind of wit and facetiousness, joined to much learning and instruction, rendering even details amusing. He was a diligent student of the Bible, and was well acquainted with, and fond of commenting on, the most obscure passages in it.

He next appeared as a contributor to a series of religious biographies, which came out in 1651 ; and in the following years, besides publishing many sermons, he wrote a work on Baptism, a Register of the proceedings in Parliament of the fourth and fifth years of the reign of Charles I., and other works. In 1654 he married the daughter of Viscount Baltinglass.

One of the results of his literary toil, extending over many years, was published in 1655, in *The Church History of Britain, from the birth of Jesus Christ till the year* 1648 ; *endeavoured by Thomas Fuller*. It contains twelve books (including the *History of the University of Cambridge*), and is cut up into subdivisions and sections in a most original manner. There are upwards of fifty dedications—quaint but often beautiful compositions, but far too fulsome and complimentary for these times. It was compiled from scarce sources, and is a work of some historical value, not only on this account, but also because of its honourable impartiality and freedom from party spirit, then too common with all classes of writers. Here, as in kindred works, the gravity of the subject does not deaden his cheerful humour: all the way along the reader comes across his fantastic conceits and puns, and quips, and cranks, and quirks, and odd digressions, and quaint allusions. This mode of writing on such a subject is of course objectionable, but in Fuller's History the reader never meets with anything improper or undevout. In his *Holy State* he has spoken very solemnly on this matter: —" Jest not with the two-edged sword of God's word. Will nothing please thee to wash thy hands in but the font? or to drink healths in but the church chalice? And know the whole art is learnt at the first admission, and profane jests will come without calling."

On the first appearance of this work it was severely censured; Dr. Peter Heylin, an ill-tempered high-church divine, and a writer of some celebrity, being its chief opponent. He went to the trouble of writing a large book against it, which Fuller replied to as fully in his manly, witty, and learned *Appeal of Injured Innocence*. It is a comment on the Church History. Many of the animadversions on his work—some of them certainly uncalled for—grieved Fuller, who had been so long and " painful " in compiling it, and he very earnestly pleaded for the exercise of their charity, especially in condemning the witticisms and levities therein. " Some men," he said, "were of very cheerful dispositions, and God forbid that all such should be condemned for lightness. Oh! let not any envious eye disinherit men of that which is 'their portion in this life comfortably to enjoy the blessings thereof.'" And in another place he says—"Harmless mirth is the best cordial against the consumption of the spirit: wherefore it is not unlawful, if it trespasseth not in quantity, quality, or season." Which limits, however, Fuller did not always confine himself to. In the discussion which took place, Fuller's candour and conciliatory spirit reconciled his opponent to him.

Fuller now prepared for publication his yet greater work—*The Worthies of England*—of which I have already spoken. He did not live to print the whole of it, but it was completed by his son, in the year after his death. Nicholson, a spiteful old bishop, charged it with being huddled up in a hurry, and of consisting of nothing but old women's tales; but posterity has passed a different verdict to this upon it.

In 1658 his patron, Lord Berkeley, made him his chaplain, and presented him to the rectory of Cranford, in Middlesex; and after this time, with the course of events, his prospects became brighter. Shortly before the Restoration, he was called upon to resume his old places as Lecturer at the Savoy, and Prebend of Salisbury; and on the king's return he was made one of his chaplains, and by royal mandate created D.D. He again preached at the court, and the wit-loving king is said to have resolved upon his translation to a bishopric; but it was to no *earthly* dignity that Fuller was destined.

His living at Broad-Winsor became rightfully his own again; but he was so pleased with the preaching of the then incumbent, that he voluntarily promised not to be the cause of his removal. He wrote a joyful poetical panegyric on his Majesty's return; and in 1660 put forth his *Mixt Contemplations in Better Times*, dedicated to Lady Monck, and bearing the appropriate motto—" Let your moderation be known unto all men: the Lord is at hand."

He appears to have contracted a malignant fever—known as the "new disease"—after a journey from Salisbury to London. On his arrival, he had promised to preach a marriage sermon for a friend at his chapel of the Savoy; but while at dinner on the 12th of August, he was seized with illness, which, however, he would not allow to interfere with the approaching service. "He had got up often in the pulpit sick," he said, "and always came down well again; and he hoped he should do as well now, through God's strengthening grace. During the delivery of the sermon, it was manifest to his congregation that he was seriously ill, and he had to confess as much to them; adding—"But I am resolved, by the grace of God, to preach this sermon, though it be my last!" He managed to get through it, and it *was* his last: he may be said, therefore, to have died at his post. He was conveyed home, and his mind became affected, but on the following day his senses were restored, and he employed his remaining hours on earth with a Christian preparation for death. "Nothing but heaven and the perfections thereof, the consummation of grace in glory, must fill up the room of his capacious soul, now ready to take its flight from this world. On the morning of Thursday, the 16th of August, his sufferings were at an end, and he entered into rest."

At his own desire, Fuller was buried in his parish church at Cranford, Lord Berkeley bearing the expense. As illustrating the respect in which he was held, about two hundred clergymen attended his funeral. A monument was erected to his memory in the chancel of the church, and it contains a conceit which Fuller himself might have written. The Latin inscription reads:—"Here lies Thomas Fuller—who, while he planned to consecrate to immortality the lives of illustrious Englishmen, by a posthumous work, himself attained immortality." This is in reference to his *Worthies* which also remains as a monument to his industry and genius.

In appearance, Fuller is described as being tall, portly, and handsome, possessing curly hair and a ruddy face, with a pleasant yet serious countenance, betokening an amiable mind. On his upper lip, which could not be curled into a sneer, he wore a slight moustache, after the old English fashion. His manners were simple and unstudied, and he was uniformly courteous. His cheerful conversation was always attractive, and "much sought after; for besides the pleasantness of it, he was for information a perfect walking library." His vivacity of spirits, and sprightliness of conversation, gained for him, in every period of his life, a large circle of friends. As might be expected, he was temperate in his habits. To his home attachments he was faithful, and was careful with the education of his children. His heart was ever open to kindly influences; and his wit and facetiousness, which have delighted so many, partakes of the same nature, being devoid of sting, bite, or claws: it is never spiteful, but ever genial and good-natured. He was as faithful to the principles of his religion, as he was loyal to his king and country, and he never hesitated to give utterance to his convictions.

Of his faults, some of which have been hinted at, I cannot now speak. The remembrance of his own gentleness and charity in dealing with the faults of others, warns us to deal gently and charitably to him. The silence which surrounds his tomb, at which we have just in fancy been gazing, should hush the voice that would harshly censure him.

> "There is a spell, by nature thrown
>   Around the noiseless dead,
> Which ought to soften censure's tone,
>   And guard the lowly bed
> Of those who, whatsoe'er they were,
> Wait Heaven's unerring audit there!"

A Comment
ON
RUTH:
BY
T. F. B. D.

LONDON,
Printed for *G.* and *H. Everſden*,
and are to be ſold at the Sign of the
Greyhound in *Pauls* Church-yard.
1654.

["She stood breast-high amid the corn,
Clasp'd by the golden light of morn,
Like the sweetheart of the sun,
Who many a glowing kiss had won.

On her cheek an autumn flush,
Deeply ripen'd; such a blush
In the midst of brown was born,
Like red poppies grown with corn.

Round her eyes her tresses fell,
Which were blackest none could tell,
But long lashes veil'd a light
That had else been all too bright.

And her hat, with shady brim,
Made her tressy forehead dim;—
Thus she stood amid the stooks
Praising GOD with sweetest looks:

Sure, I said, heav'n did not mean,
Where I reap thou shouldst but glean;
Lay thy sheaf adown and come,
Share my harvest and my home."

HOOD's *Poetical Works* (Rosetti's ed.), page 307].

[Introduction.

THOMAS FULLER'S attractive *Comment on Ruth* may have formed the lectures referred to by his anonymous Biographer as "the *Primitie* of his Ministeriall Fruits, which, like Apples of Gold in pictures of Silver (sublime Divinity in the most ravishing Elegancies), attracted the audience of the University" (*Life*, 1661, page 5). The exposition of the Book, which unfortunately only extends up to the end of the second chapter, was probably given in the ancient church of St. Bene't (Cambridge), to which Fuller had been appointed Minister in or about 1630, being then of the age of twenty-two years. The reference to "young Ministers" at page 77 is therefore a personal one. The lectures were certainly preached before the end of the year 1632; for mention is made of GUSTAVUS VASA, the heroic king of Sweden (page 25), who died in November of the year named; and there are references to other contemporary events. The literary style of the addresses is in accord with the supposed period of their delivery; and justifies their assignment to this place as the earliest known specimens of FULLER's pulpit oratory. His occasional play on words and incongruous allusions, and the frequent instances of alliteration and antithesis, show that the popular curate had been somewhat affected by the school of preaching which DONNE, ANDREWES, and others, had made popular; but these mannerisms have very little detracted from the eminently practical character of his discourses. Upwards of twenty years later his maturer judgment detected "many faults" in these Sermons on *Ruth* (page v.); and yet, it is noteworthy, he refrained from revising them. They were first issued in 1654, their publication being due to the fact that some piratical printer (in league it may be with some who had heard the lectures), taking advantage of FULLER's literary popularity, had proposed to put them forth, from imperfect notes as was believed (page v.). EARLE, in his *Characters*, describes the "Collections of Studie" of "a young raw preacher" as consisting of "the notes of Sermons, which taken vp at St. *Maries* [Oxford], hee vtters in the Country. And if he write brachigraphy his stocke is so much the better. His writing is more then his reading; for hee reads onely what hee gets without booke" (*Micro-cosmographie*, ed. Arber, page 22). There is perhaps one trace of the *Ruth* Sermons having passed through the hands of a short-hand writer, viz., in the word *respectfully* (page 86, line 14), which in the original is *respectively*.

Notwithstanding FULLER's modest depreciation of the worth of the *Comment*, it will be found to have many claims on the attention. The simplicity of the Hebrew Pastoral pervades it. The preacher's "observations" are set forth with a quaintness and vigour that are worthy of the author of *The*

Holy State. He speaks under the influence of a mind that is truly devout, and of a Christianity that is eminently practical. The "plain but effectual manner" of preaching by *Uses* and *Doctrines,* very popular with the sermon--writers of the period, was taken from Musculus, a German divine; while John Udal, the Puritan divine, introduced formal *Reasons,* called by Fuller "the strength and sinews of a Sermon" (*Church-History,* Book ix. § viii. ¶ 3). Elsewhere the same authority terms the latter "the pillars of the fabric of a sermon;" *similitudes* being "the windows which give the best lights" (*Holy State,* § The Faithful Minister, ¶ 9).

Fuller seems to have fastened with the instinct of a poet upon this exquisitely beautiful story of the Gentile Ruth, who,

" When sick for home,
Stood in tears amid the alien corn."
(Keats's *Ode to a Nightingale.*)

A former industrious editor of Fuller's works, and of this *Comment* among others, was reminded, as many readers of the *Comment* will be reminded, of the picture of the Moabitish maiden given by another poet, Thomas Hood, "a man of kindred genius, who, cast in a more mirth-loving age than Fuller's, fed the public with lighter food than he did, but whose powers were really as great in serious as in comic prose and verse " (William Nichols's Edition, page 178).

The Book of Ruth had likewise attractions for Fuller as an antiquary, inasmuch as it opened up to him the peculiar fields of inquiry amidst which he loved to ramble. "It is one of those quiet corners of history," says Dean Stanley, "which are the green spots of all time, and which appear to become greener and greener as they recede into the distance " (*Lect. Hist. Jewish Church,* vol. i. page 263).

Not the least noteworthy feature of the following *Comment* are the traces to be found in it of the opinions and the anticipations of the period;—not of the days of the Commonwealth, during which the book was printed; but of the days of Fuller's early manhood during which it was written. Reflections, which come to us with all the charm of freshness, are made on the Jesuits of America (page 30); on the advent of King James I. to England (page 99); on the Pilgrims of New England (page 14); on the condition of the Palatinate (page 26); on the return of Prince Charles from Spain (page 99); on the plague of London, 1625 (page 99); on the Swedish war (page 25); &c.

Fuller's *Ruth* was popular in his own day. It is now, perhaps, one of the best known of his treatises in divinity, having been twice re_ printed within the last ten years : viz. in 1865, in 4to. (Nicol's Series of Puritan Commentaries), edited by Rev. Thomas Smith, M.A.; and in 1868, in crown 8vo., in Tegg's series of Fuller reprints, edited by William Nichols. The present reprint is taken from a copy of the original work, 8vo., in possession of the Editor. Two other Sermons (*Comfort in Calamity,* and *The Grand Assize*) were appended (in some copies prefixed) to *Ruth;* and they will be found in Volume ii. of this collection in their proper chronological places.

TO
The Right Worſhipfull,
the Lady ANNE ARCHER,
in the Countie of
WARWICK.

HE Apoſtle to the Philippians, *chap.* 4. v. 15, *giveth them this high commendation,* None communicated with me concerning giving and receiving, but ye onely. *Should I apply the ſame in relation of my ſelfe to your Ladyſhip, I ſhould be injurious to the Bountie of many my* Worthy Benefactours. *How-ever,* (not excluſively of others, but) *eminently I muſt acknowledge you a Grand Encourager of my Studies. In publique teſtimonie whereof, I preſent theſe my Endeavours to your Ladiſhips Patronage.*

Indeed they were Preached in an eminent Place, when I firſt entred into the Miniſterie, *above twentie yeares ſince, and therefore you will pardon the many Faults that may be found therein. Nor were they intended for publique view, till underſtanding the Reſolution of ſome of my Auditors to Print them* (to their Profit, but my Prejudice) *by their imperfect Notes, I adventured on this ſeaſonable prevention.*

The Lord make his Graces flow plentifully from the Head of your Family, your Religious Husband, to the loweſt Skirts thereof, the laſt and leaſt of your Relations,

Your Ladyſhips

in all Chriſtian Offices,

THOMAS FULLER.

INTRODUCTION (from page iv.)

Fuller's brief commentary had a fitting patroneſs in Lady Archer, who gave the author much aſſiſtance in his more ambitious works. She was one of the Ferrars of Tamworth Castle, Warwickshire,—a branch of the noble family of that name ; being a daughter of Sir John Ferrars, Knt., of Tamworth Caſtle, who died in 1633. To this Knight's grandſon, " John Ferrars, of Tamworth Caſtle, Eſquire" (1629—1680), is dedicated Section iv. of Book iv. of *The Church-Hiſtory*, where Fuller said that he knew that his patron was by extraction inclined to a generous diſpoſition, " as I have found by one of your neareſt *Relations*" (page 195). The reference here is to an aunt, Lady Anne Archer (Dugdale's *Antiqq. Warwickſh.*, ed. 1656, pages 820, 580; Le Neve's *Knights*, page 246). To her Fuller likewiſe dedicated, in the ſame folio, 1655, the cloſing ſection of Book ix., which contains the reign of Elizabeth, " the Honour of your ſex and our nation ;" explaining that though thus placed laſt, her ladyſhip was " the firſt and freeſt in incouraging my weak endeavours " (page 221). This literary intimacy belongs to the latter part of the author's life. The lady was the wife of Sir Simon Archer of Tanworth (1581 — 1662), the zealous Warwickshire antiquary, whoſe topographical collections were of great value to Dugdale in his admirable work on that county (ed. 1656, Dedication to the Gentry, Inſcription on the map, and page 581). Fuller dedicated to Sir Simon the account of the copies of the Roll of Battle Abbey, *Church-History*, Book ii., *ad calcem loco ad fin.*, where he makes acknowledgment of the generoſity of his antiquarian friend (page 151). On the plate of " The Knights joined with yᵉ Monkes of Ely" Sir Simon and his lady are alſo mentioned in theſe terms: " Simoni Archer, Equiti Aurato, Antiquitatis cultori, et in digmatographia exercitatiſſimo, nec non lectiſſimæ Dnæ Annæ. T.F." Here, as in the two former references to this folio, the Knight's arms are engraved, impaling thoſe of Ferrars (varry *or* and *gu.*). By his lady, Anne, he had three ſons, Humphrey, Thomas, and John; (one of whom is named in Fuller's *Worthies*, § Warwickshire, page 133 ; see alſo § Cheſhire, page 184 ; and in *Report iv. Hiſt. MSS. Commiſſion*, page 267; see alſo page 106 ;) and three daughters, Elizabeth, Penelope, and Anne.]

A Comment on Ruth.

CHAP. I.

Verfe 1: *Now it came to paffe in the dayes when the Judges Ruled, that there was a Famine in the Land.*

BEFORE we enter into thefe words, fomething muft be premifed concerning the Name, Matter, End, Author of this Book.

It hath the name from *Ruth*, the moft remarkable perfon in it, to whom God vouchfafed his Grace, not onely to write her name in the Book of Life in Heaven, but alfo to prefix her name before a Book of Life in Earth.

The Matter may be divided into thefe two Parts: The firft Chapter fheweth, *That many are the troubles of the righteous*; and the three laft do fhew, *That God delivereth them out of all*.

One of the *Ends* is, to fhew the Pedigree of our *Saviour*, otherwife *Genealogers* had been at a lofs for four or five Defcents in the deducing thereof: Another *End* is, under the converfion of *Ruth* the *Moabiteffe*, to typifie the calling of the *Gentiles*, that as he took of the blood of a *Gentile* into his body, fo he fhould fhed the blood out of his body for the *Gentiles*, that there might be one Shepheard, and one Sheepfold.

The *Authors* name (probably *Samuel*) is conceal'd, neither is it needfull it fhould be known: for even as a man that hath a piece of *Gold* that he knows to be weight, and fees it stamped with the *Kings Image*, careth not to know the name of that man who minted or coined it: So we, seeing this Book to have the superscription of *Cæsar*, the stamp of the *Holy Spirit*, need not to be curious to know who was the *Pen-man* thereof.

And now to the words.

Now it came to passe in the dayes when the Judges Ruled, that there was a famine in the Land.] Observe in the words; What? *A Famine:* Where? In the *Land:* When? *In the time that the Judges judged;* the time being set down for the better certainty of the *History*.

Question: Is this the Land whereof it is said, *Gen.* 49. 20, Asher *his bread shall be fat, and afford dainties for a King?* which is call'd, Deut. 8. 7, *A good Land of Wheat and Barley, Vineyards and Fig-trees, Oyle Olive, and Hony*, which is commended, Ezek. 20. 6, *to be a Land flowing with Milke and Hony, the glory of all Lands?* How commeth it to passe that thy Rivers of Oyl are now dammed up? thy streams of Wine drained drie? that there is no bread found in Bethlem, the house of bread?

Answer: Israel hath sinned: *a fruitfull Land maketh he barren, for the sinne of the people that dwell therein.* The peoples *hard hearts* were rebellious to *God*, and the *hard earth* proved unprofitable to them: Their flinty eyes would afford no tears to bemoan their sins, and the churlish Heavens would afford no moysture to water their earth: Man proved unfaithfull to *God* his *Maker*, the Earth proved unfruitfull to *Man* her *Manurer*.

Observation: Famine is a heavy punishment, wherewith God afflicteth his people for their sinnes. That it is an heavie punishment appeareth, because *David*, 2 *Sam.* 24. 14, chose the *Pestilence* before it; for even as *Zebah* and *Zalmunna*, *Judg.* 8. 21, chose rather to fall by the hand of *Gideon* then by the hand of *Jether* his Son, because the Childs want of strength would cause their abundance of pain: so better it is to be speedily dispatcht by a violent disease, then to have ones life in a *Famine* prolong'd by a lingring torture. That it is inflicted for their sinnes, is shewed, *Lev.* 26. 19; *Deut.* 28.

23; 1 *King.* 8. 37. And these sinnes most especially procure *Famine*: 1ly. *Idolatry*, 1 King. 17. 1; 2 King. 4. 38. 2ly. *Abuse of plenty*: the prodigall Child, *Luke* 15, from the keeping of *Harlots*, was brought to the keeping of *Hoggs*. It is just with God to make men want that to supply their necessity, which they have misspended in their nicetie. 3ly. *Shedding of Innocent blood*, 2 Sam. 21. 1. 4ly. *Oppression of the poor*, Amos 4. 6. And no wonder if men, to grind the faces of poor people, make mony to which God gave no naturall fruit, to bring forth a monstrous increase, if God cause the earth which naturally should be fruitfull, to become barren and afford no profit.

Use 1: It may serve to confute such, that when *God* doth scourge them with *Famine*, (as blind *Balaam* fell a beating of his dumb beast, when he himself was in fault,) they vent their spite in cursing and railing on the poor Creatures; whereas indeed were the matter wel weighed, they might say of all Creatures as *Judah* did of *Thamar* his daughter-in-law, *they are more righteous then we:* for locusts, mildew, blasting, immoderate drought, and moysture, are the means by which, mans sinne is the cause, for which *Famine* is inflicted. And yet in prosperity, we are commonly like Hogs feeding on the mast, not minding his hand that shaketh it down; in adversity, like Doggs biting the stone, not marking the hand that threw it.

Use 2: If any desire to prevent or remove a *Famine*, let us prevent and remove the causes thereof. First, let us practise that precept, 1 Ioh. 5. 21, *Babes keep your selves from Idols.*

2ly. Let us be heartily thankfull to God for our plenty, who by the seasonable weeping of the Heavens hath caused the plentifull laughter of the Earth, and hath sent the former *Raine* to perform the part of a *Midwife*, to Deliver the infant *Corne* out of the *wombe* of the parched *Earth*; and the latter *Raine* to doe the duty of a *Nurse*, to swell and battle the *Grain*. Let us not seeth the *Kid* in the Mothers *Milke:* let not our wanton *Pallats* spoile wholesome *Meat*, before it commeth to the just *Maturity;* neither let us cast away any good food, but, after our *Saviours* example, *Let us cause the Fragments to be basketted up that nothing may be lost.*

3ly. Let us pray with *David, Pſal.* 51. 14, *Deliver us from blood guiltineſſe O Lord:* and let us feeke that the hoary hairs may not go down to the Grave in peace of ſuch as have ſhed Innocent blood, (leaſt the perſonal offence of a private Man remaining unpuniſhed become the National ſinne of a Kingdome,) but upon the King, and upon his Seed, and upon his Houſe, and upon his Throne ſhall be Peace for ever from the Lord.

Laſtly, Let us be pittifull, and liberall to relieve the diſtreſſes of the poor; for why ſhould our dead Tables groan under the weight of needleſſe feaſts upon them, whil'ſt *Gods* living *Temples* groan under the want of neceſſary food within them? The *Athenian* women had a cuſtome to make a Picture of *Famine* every yeare, and to drive it out of their City with theſe words: *Out Famine, in Food; Out Penury, in Plenty:* but let us ſay in word, and ſecond it in deed; *Out Sin, in Sanctity; Out Prophaneſſe, in Piety:* and then we ſhall ſee that as long as our King Reigneth there ſhall be no *Famine* in our Land.

But however God ſhall diſpoſe of us for outward bleſſings, I pray God keepe us from that *Soule Famine* mentioned *Amos* 8. 12, that we living under the *Northern Heavens* ſhould wander to the *Eaſt*, and *run to and fro to ſeek the Word of the Lord, and ſhould not find it;* but may the *light* of the *Goſpell* remain with us on Earth, as long as the faithfull witneſſe endureth in Heaven!

And a certain man of Bethlehem-Judah *went to ſojourne in the Country of* Moab.

Theſe words containe a Journey or Removall, wherein obſerve, Who went? *a certain Man:* Whence? from *Bethlehem-Judah:* Whither? *to ſojourne in Moab.* We ſhall have a fitter occaſion to ſpeak of the party removing hereafter. I begin with the place from whence he went, *Bethlehem-Iudah*.

This was the place, nigh to which *Rachel* as ſhe was travelling fell into Travail, and ended her journey to *Heaven* in the midſt of her journey on *Earth:* there was another of the fame name in *Zabulon, Iofh.* 19, 15; and therefore *Iudah* is added for difference and diftinction.

Obfervation: The *Holy Spirit* defcends to our capacity, and in Scripture doth multiply words to make the matter the plainer: let this teach the Sons of *Levi*, when they deliver one doubtfull and ambiguous Doctrine which may admit of feverall conftructions, (fo that there is danger leaft that people may miftake their meaning,) to demur a while on fuch a point, and not to be niggardly of their words, till they have blotted all doubt and difficulty out of it. Herein they fhall follow God for their pattern, who, leaft *Bethlehem* in my Text fhould be confounded with *Bethlehem* in *Zabulon*, addeth for diftinction *Bethlehem-Iudah*.

Went to Sojourne in Moab.] The *Prodigall Child* complained, *Luke* 15. 11, *How many hired Servants of my Father have bread enough, and I die for hunger!* So here we fee that the uncircumcifed *Moabites*, Gods flaves and vaffals, had ftore of plenty, whileft *Ifrael*, Gods Children (but his *prodigal Children*, which by their finnes had difpleafed their heavenly Father) were pinched with penurie.

Obfervation: Hence we gather, God oftentimes denyes outward bleffings to his Children, when as he vouchfafeth them to the wicked: the wicked mans eyes ftart out with fatneffe; *Davids* bones fcarce cleave to his flefh: *Ahab* hath an Ivory Houfe; the Godly wander in *Dens* and *Caves* of the Earth: the *Rich Glutton* fareth delicioufly every day; whileft the Godly, *Pfal.* 107. 5, *were hungry and thirfty, their foul fainted in them:* He *was clothed in purple and fine linnen*, whileft the Godly *wander up and down in fheep fkins;* and well may they wear their fkins without them, that carry their innocency within them. And the reafon thereof is, *Becaufe judgement begins at the houfe of the Lord, whilft the wicked have their portion in this world*.

Ufe: Let us not judge according to outward appearance, *but judge righteous judgement*, leaft otherwife we condemn the Generation of Gods Children, if we account outward bleffings the figns of Gods favour, or calamities the arguments of his difpleafure: neither let the afflicted Chriftian faint under

Gods heavy hand; but let him know to his comfort, God therefore is angry in this world that he may not be angry in the world to come, and mercifully inflicteth temporall punishment that he may not justly confound with eternall torment.

But here ariseth a question, Whether *Elimelech* did well to go from Bethlehem-Judah into the Land of Moab? For the better satisfaction whereof, we will suppose a plain and honest Neighbour thus disswading him from his departure.

Disswasion: Give me leave, Neighbour *Elimelech*, to say unto thee, as the Angel did to *Hagar*, Whence commeft thou? and whether goest thou? Wilt thou leave that place where Gods worship is truly professed, and goe into an Idolatrous Country? *Woe is thee that must dwell in* Moab, *and be an inhabitant amongst the worshippers of* Melchom! Indeed our Father *Abraham* came out of *Ur* of the *Chaldees*, an idolatrous Country, to come into the Land of *Canaan*; but why shouldst thou go out of the Land of *Canaan* into an idolatrous Country, where thou shalt have neither *Priest*, nor *Prophet*, nor *Passeover*? Yea, what most is to be feared, your frequent conversing with the *People* of the *Country* will at length bring you into a *love* and *liking* of their *Superstitions*, and so draw Gods anger against you; wherefore reverse your intent of removing, least while thou seek'st to store thy *Body* thou starvest thy *Soul*; rather venter the breaking of the Casket then the loosing of the *Jewel*, and go not from *Bethlehem-Iudah* unto the Land of *Moab*.

Answer: To this *Elimelech* might answer: Your disswasion doth somewhat move me, but not remove my resolution; I do not forsake my Country, but am forced from it; God hath with-holden the *Wine* and the *Winepresse*, and if I stay, I am likely to starve; I conceive it therefore to be my bounden duty to provide the best means for my *Family*; and following the examples of *Isaac's* going into *Gerah*, and *Jacobs* going down into *Egypt* in the time of *Famine*, I intend to remove to *Moab*. And though I shall be divided from the visible Congregation of *Israel*, yet shall I with my *Family* still remain the lively Members of Gods true Church. For first I intend to carry with me the five books of *Moses* (they will be no great burthen, being comprised in so small a Volum), and, according to my poor ability, out of them will I instruct my *Family*, whilst my deare wife *Naomi*, and dutifull children, *Mahlon* and *Chilion*, will be diligent to heare and practise what I propound unto them. I confesse we shall have no outward sacrifices, (becaus I am not of the Tribe of *Levi*,) yet may we offer unto God prayers and praises, which God no doubt will as gracioufly accept, as of a *Bullock* that hath Hornes and Hoofes: thus hope I to have a little Church in mine own House; and I know, *where two or three are met together in the name of God, there he will be in the midst of them.* Whereas you object, I should be in danger of being defiled with their *Idolatry*, I will be by Gods grace so much the more warie, watchfull and vigilant over my wayes: we see the flesh of fishes remaineth fresh, though they alwaies swim in the brackish waters; and I hope that the same God who preserved righteous *Lot* in the wicked City of *Sodome*, who protected faithful *Joseph* in the vicious Court of *Pharaoh*, will also keep me unspotted in the midst of *Moab*, whether I intend speedily to go, not to *live*, but to *lodge*; not to *dwell*, but to *sojourne*; not to make it *my habitation for ever*, but *my harbour for a season*, till God shall visit his people with plenty, when I purpose to return with the speediest conveniency.

Thus we see *Elimelech* putting the dangers of his removall in one scale, the benefits thereof in another; the beam of his judgement is justly weighed down to go from *Bethlehem-Iudah* into the Land of *Moab*.

Observation: It is lawfull for Men to leave their *Native Soyle*, and to travell into a forraign Country; as, 1. For *Merchants*, provided alwaies that while they seek to make gainfull Adventures for their Estates, they make not *shipwrack of a good Conscience*; 2ly. For *Embassadors*, that are sent to see the Practises and Negociations in forraigne Courts; 3ly. For *private persons*, that travell with an intent to accomplish themselves with a better sufficiency to serve their King and Country.

But unlawfull it is for such to travell, which *Dinah* like go only to see the Customes of severall Countries, and make themselves the Lackies to their own humorous curiosity: hence commeth it to passe, when they returne, it is justly questionable, whether their Clothes be disguised with more foolish fashions, or bodies disabled with more loathsome Diseases, or souls defiled with more notorious vices; having learned Jealousie from the *Italian*, Pride from the *Spaniard*, Lasciviousnesse from the *French*, Drunkennesse from the *Dutch*; and yet what need they go so farre to learn so bad a lesson, when (God knows) we have too many Schooles where it is taught here at home.

Now if any do demand of me my opinion concerning our Brethren, which of late left this Kingdome to advance a Plantation in *New England*; surely I think, as St. *Paul* said concerning *Virgins*, *He had received no commandment from the Lord*: so I cannot find any just warrant to incourage men to undertake this removall; but think rather the counsel best that King *Ioash* prescribed to *Amaziah*, *Tarry at home*: yet as for those that are already gone, farre be it from us to conceive them to be such, to whom we may not say, *God speed*, as it is in 2 *Joh.* 10; but let us pitty them, and pray for them; for sure they have no need of our mocks, which I am affraid have too much of their own miseries: I conclude therefore of the two *Englands*, what our Saviour saith of the two wines, *Luke* 5. 39, *No man having tasted of the old, presently desireth the new; for he saith the old is better.*

Verses 1 and 2: *He, and his wife, and his two sons. And the name of the man was* Elimelech, *and the name of his wife*, Naomi, *and the name of his two sons*, Mahlon *and* Chilion, Ephrathites *of* Bethlehem-Judah. *And they came into the Country of* Moab, *and continued there.*

These words contain; first, The principall party that undertook the *journey*. 2ly. His company, described by their relations, *his Wife, and Children*, and by their names, *Naomi, Mahlon,* and *Chilion*. 3ly. The successe of his *journey*; *When he came into the Land of* Moab, *he continued there*.

Now whereas *Elimelech* took his Wife and Children along with him: from his practise we gather this Observation.

[1631.]   Ruth, *Chap.* i. *verf.* 1, 2.   15

Obfervation 1: It is the part of a kind Husband, and of a carefull Father, not onely to provide for himfelfe, but alfo for his whole *Family*; Gen. 2. 24, *A man fhall cleave to his wife, and they two fhall be one flefh*; Ephe. 5. 25, 29, *Husbands, love your wives*, for no man as yet hated his own flefh; 1 *Tim.* 5. 8, *If any one provideth not for his own Family, he denyeth the faith, and is worfe than an Infidell*: this made *Abraham* to take with him at his removal his meek *Sarah*; *Ifaac*, his wife *Rebecca*; *Jacob*, his fair *Rachel*, and fruitfull *Leah*; and *Jofeph*, Mat. 2. 14, took with him *Mary*, his efpoufed wife, and our *Saviour*, his fuppofed Sonne. And when *Pharaoh*, Exod. 10. 9, offered *Mofes* with all the men of *Ifrael* to go out of *Egypt*, but on condition they fhould leave their Wives and Children behind them, *Mofes* refufed the proffer: he would either have them all go out, or elfe he would not go out at all.

Ufe: It confuteth fuch cruell Husbands and careleffe parents, who if fo be *Iobs* Meffengers, they onely can efcape alone, they care not though they leave their wives and children to fhift for themfelves; like the *Oftridge*, Job 39. 14, *who leaveth her Eggs in the fand*, and so forfakes them. Surely the two *Kine* which drew the *Arke of God out of the Land of the* Philiftines *to* Bethfhemefh, 1 *Sam.* 6. 12, fhall rife up at the day of *Judgement* and condemn fuch cruell Parents: for it is faid of them, *That as they went along the high way, they did pittifully low by that querulous ditty*, as nature afforded them utterance, with witneffing and expreffing their affection to their Calves fhut up at home: O that there fhould be fuch humanity (as I may terme it) in Beafts, and fuch beaftlineffe in many men! Remember this, you that fit drinking and bezzling wine abroad, whilft your Family are glad of water at home; and think thus with your felves, *To what end is this needleffe waft? might it not have been fold for many a penny, and have been beftowed on my poor Wife and Children?*

Obfervation 2: Secondly, Whereas we find *Naomi* and her Sons going with *Elimelech*, we gather; It is the duty of a dear Wife and of dutifull Children to go along with their Husband and Parents, when on juft caufe they remove into a forraign Country. It was an unmanly and cowardly fpeech of *Barak* to *Deborah*, Judg. 4. 8, *If thou wilt go with me, then will I go; but if thou wilt not go with me, then will I not go:* but it would be a gracious refolution of a grave Matron and her Children, *Husband, if you be pleafed to depart, I will be ready to accompany you; Father, if you be minded to remove, I will attend upon you: but if you be difpofed to ftay, I will not ftir from the place where you abide:* otherwife if the wife refufeth to go along with her Hufband, what *Abraham*, Gen. 24. 8, faid to the *Servant* in another cafe, is true in this refpect; but if the Woman will not be willing to follow thee, then thou fhalt be clear from thine Oath; if the wife be fo peevifh and perverfe, that fhe will not go along with her Husband who propoundeth lawfull means unto her to relieve her wants; then is he acquitted from the Oath he made her in Marriage, when he plighted his troth unto her, in ficknefſe and in health, to maintain her.

Queſtion: But methinks I hear the Widows and Orphants crying unto me, as the Souldiers to *Iohn Baptiſt*, *But what ſhall we do? Luke* 3. 14. It is true, faith the *Widow*, that kind Husbands are to provide for their Wives; but alas we have no *Elimelech's* to carry us into a forraign Country in the time of *Famine*. Indeed, faith the *Orphant*, it is the Fathers duty to provide for his Children; but my Parents are dead long ago; I have not, as *Samuel* had, a Mother *Hannah* every year to bring me a *new coate;* what fhall we do in this our diftreſſe?

Anſwer: Uſe the beſt means you can, and for the reſt, relie on Gods providence, who is faid, *Pſal.* 10. 14, *To help the fatherleſſe and poor to their Right;* Pſal. 68. 5, *To be a father to the fatherleſſe, and to defend the cauſe of the Widow, even God in his holy habitation:* who will deale with thee as he did with *David*, *When my Mother and Father forſooke me, the Lord cared for me.*

So much for *Elimelech's* company deſcribed by their relations: we fhould come now to ſpeak of their names, where we might take occaſion to ſpeak of the Antiquity and uſe of Names, but that hereafter we fhall have better conveniency to treat thereof, in thoſe words, *Call me not* Naomi, *but call me* Marah: We come therefore to the ſucceſſe of *Elimelech's* journey.

And they came into the Country of Moab, *and they continued there.*] The meaning is, That the *Moabites* afforded them harbour without any moleſtation.

From whence the *Obſervation* is this; *We ought to be Hoſpitall and courteous to receive ſtrangers.* First, Becauſe God in ſeverall places of Scripture enjoyneth it, *Exod.* 23. 9; *Levit.* 19. 33. 2ly. Becauſe God apprehendeth all courteſie done to a ſtranger as beſtowed on himſelfe; *He that receiveth you, receiveth me, &c.; I was a ſtranger and ye harboured me,* Mat. 25. 35. And then if we entertain ſtrangers, it may be ſaid of us not onely as it is of *Lot* and *Abraham,* Heb. 13. 2, *That we entertained Angels,* but that we entertained God himſelfe unawares. 3ly. Becauſe if ſpiritually conſidered, we our ſelves are ſtrangers with the *Patriarks,* Heb. 11. 9. *We have here no abiding City, but ſeeke one from above, whoſe builder and maker is God,* Heb. 13. 14 [and 10. 11]. *I beſeech you as Strangers and Pilgrims,* 1 Pet. 2. 11. Laſtly, Becauſe of the uncertainty of our own eſtates, for thou knoweſt not what evill ſhall be upon the earth: it may be we that now relieve ſtrangers, hereafter our ſelves being ſtrangers may be relieved by others.

Uſe: Let us not therefore abuſe ſtrangers and make a prey of them, making an advantage of their unſkilfulneſſe in the language, and being unacquainted with the faſhions of the Land; like *Laban* that deceived his Nephew *Iacob* in placing *Leah* for *Rachel,* and to cloak his cheating, pleaded it was the cuſtome of the Country: wherefore rather let us be courteous unto them, leaſt the Barbarians condemne us, who ſo courteouſly intreated S. *Paul,* with his ſhipwrackt companions; and the *Moabites* in my Text, who ſuffered *Elimelech,* when he came into the Land, to continue there.

Verſes 3 to 5: *And* Elimelech Naomies *Husband dyed, and ſhe was left, and her two Sonnes, &c.*

In theſe words we have two Marriages uſhered and followed by Funeralls: I will begin there, where one day all muſt make an end, *at Death;*

And Elimelech Naomies *Husband dyed.*] I have ſeldom ſeen

a Tree thrive that hath been transplanted when it was old; the same may be seen in *Elimelech;* his aged body brooks not the forraign Aire; though he could avoid the Arrows of Famine in *Israel,* yet he could not shun the Darts of *Death* in *Moab:* he that lived in a place of *Penury,* must die in a Land of *Plenty.* Let none condemne *Elimelech's* removal as unlawful, because of his suddain death, for those actions are not ungodly which are unsuccessfull, nor those pious which are prosperous, seeing the lawfulnesse of an action is not to be gathered from the joyfulnesse of the event, but from the justnesse of the cause, for which it is undertaken.

Observation 1: Hence we observe, that God can easily frustrate our fairest hopes and defeat our most probable projects, in making those places most dangerous which we account most safe and secure, causing death to meet us there, where we think furthest to flie from it.

Observation 2: We see that no outward plenty can priviledge us from death; the sand of our life runneth as fast, though the Hour-glass be set in the sunshine of prosperity, as in the gloomy shade of affliction.

And she was left and her two Sons.] Here we see how mercifully God dealt with *Naomi,* in that he quenched not all the sparks of her comfort at once; but though he took away the stock, he left her the stems; though he deprived her as it were of the use of her own leggs by taking away her *Husband,* yet he left her a staffe in each of her hands, her two Sons to support her. Indeed afterwards he took them away, but first he provided her a gracious Daughter-in-law : whence we learn, God powreth not all his afflictions at once, but ever leaveth a little comfort, otherwise we should not onely be pressed down, but crush't to powder under the weight of his heavy hand.

And they tooke them wives of the women of Moab, *&c.*] Here we see the fashion of the world. Mankind had long ago decaied, if those breaches which are daily made by Death, were not daily made up by Marriage. But here ariseth a question, Whether these matches were lawfull? For answer whereof, we will suppose *Naomi* disswading her Sonnes on this manner.

Disswasion: What, my Sonnes? and what, persons of my wombe? and what, the Sonnes of my desire? give not your strength to strange women, and your wayes to that that destroyed men. It is not for you, O *Mahlon* and *Chilion*, it is not for you to marry *Moabites*; nor for the Sonnes of an *Israelite* to marry the Daughters of the uncircumcised. Remember, my Sonnes, what God saith by the mouth of *Moses*, Deut. 7. 3, *Thou shalt not make Marriages with them; thy Daughter shalt thou not give to his Sonne, nor take his daughter to thy Sonne; for they will turn away thy Son from following me, to serve strange Gods; so will the anger of the Lord be kindled against thee to destroy thee suddenly*. Take heed therefore least long looking on these women you at length be made blind, least they suck out your souls with kisses, and Snake-like, sting you with embraces: curb your affections untill you come into *Canaan* where you shall find varietie of wives, who as they come not short of these for the beauties of their bodies, so they farre go beyond them for the sanctitie of their souls.

Answer: To this disswasion, thus might her Childeren answer: We thank you, deare Mother, for your carefulnesse over our good; but we must intreat you not to interpret it undutifulnesse, if upon good reason we dissent from your judgement herein. In the place by you cited, *Marriages* are forbidden with such strange women as are of a stubborn, obstinate, and refractory nature, such as are likely to seduce their Husbands; whereas you see the mild, towardly, and tractable disposition of these women we meane to make our wives; we hope to plant these wild branches in Gods Vineyard, to bring these straggling sheep to his fold, to make them Proselytes to our Religion: Besides, this Marriage will be advantagious for us, thereby we shall endeare our selves into the *Moabites* affections; they will use us the more courteously, when we have married one of their own kindred.

But methinks my tongue refuseth to be any longer the advocate of an unlawfull deed, and my mouth denyeth to be the Orator of an unjust action: when I have said what I can for the defence of their Marriage, I shall but make a plaster too narrow for the fore; the breach is fo broad I cannot ftop it, though I may dam it up with untempered morter. Nothing can be brought for the defence of thefe matches; fomething may be faid for the excufe of them, but that fetcht not from pietie, but from policy; not certain, but conjecturall; yet here we may fee the power and providence of God, who made fo good ufe of thefe Mens defaults, as hereby to bring *Ruth*, firft to be a retainer to the family of *Faith*, and afterwards a joyfull Mother in *Ifrael*. This is that good *Chymick* that can diftill good out of evill, light out of darkneffe, order out of confufion, and make the crooked actions of men tend to his own glory in a ftraight line, and his Childrens good.

I fpeak not this to defend any mans folly in doing of evil, but to admire Gods wifdome, who can bring good out of evil: and furely he that will turn evill to good, will turn good to the beft.

And they dwelled there about ten years.] Here we have the term of *Naomi's* living in *Moab*, and the Families lafting in *Ifrael*, *ten years*: we read of a Famine for three years, 2 *Sam.* 21; of three years and a half, 1 *King.* 17; of feven years, *Gen.* 42, as alfo 2 *King.* 8; but this *ten years Famine* longer then any; feven yeares which *Jacob* ferved for *Rachel* feemed to him but a fhort time; but furely thofe ten yeares feemed to the afflicted *Ifraelites*, and to the banifhed *Naomi*, as fo many millions of years.

Obfervation: God doth not prefently remove his rod from the back of his Children, but fometimes fcourgeth them with long-lafting afflictions: the reafon is, becaufe we go on and perfift fo long in our finnes; and yet herein even mercy exalteth her felfe againft judgement: for if God fhould fuffer the fire of his fury to burn, fo long as the fuell of our finnes do laft, *Lord, who were able to abide?* were the dayes of our fuffering apportioned to the dayes of our living, no flefh would be faved, but for the *Elect fake* thofe dayes are fhortened.

Ufe: Beare with patience light afflictions; when God afflicteth his Children with long-lafting punifhments, mutter not for a burning Feaver of a-fortnight. What is this to the woman that had a running iſſue for twelve years? Murmur not for a twelve moneths quartain Ague: 'tis nothing to the woman that was bowed for eighteen years; nor ſeven years Conſumption, to the man that lay thirty eight years lame at the Pool of *Bethezda*.

And Mahlon *and* Chilion *died alſo both of them.*] It was but even now that old *Elimelech* was gone to bed; ſee, his Sonnes would not ſit long up after the Father; onely here is the difference, *He* like ripe fruit fell down of his own accord; they like green Apples were cudgel'd off the Tree.

Obſervation: Even young men in the prime of their age, are ſubject to death; the Sons of *Iacob* when they came to the Table of *Ioseph* ſat down, the eldeſt according to his age, and the youngeſt according to his youth; but Death obſerves not this method; ſhe takes not men in ſeniority, but ſometimes ſends them firſt to the buriall that came laſt from the birth, and thoſe that came laſt from the wombe, firſt to their winding ſheet. There were as many Lambs and Kids ſacrificed in the old Teſtament, as Goats and old Sheep; but ſurely more there be that die in infancy and in youth, then of thoſe that attain to old age.

Uſe: *Remember thy Creator in the dayes of thy youth:* you whoſe joynts are knit with ſturdy ſinews, whoſe veines are full of blood, whoſe arteries are fluſh't with ſpirits, whoſe bones are fraught with Marrow; *Obediah*-like, *ſerve God from your youth;* put not the day of death far from you; think not your ſtrength to be armour of proof againſt the darts of Death, when you ſee the Corſlet of *Mahlon* and *Chilion* ſhot through in the left; ſo *Mahlon* and *Chilion* died both of them.

And the woman was left of her two Sons and of her Husband.] Before we had the particular loſſes of *Naomi*, now we have them all reckoned up in the totall ſum; a Threefold Cable, ſaith *Solomon*, is not eaſily broken; and yet we ſee in *Naomies* threefold cable of comfort, twiſted of her huſband and her two ſonnes, broken by Death: of the two Sex, the woman is the weaker; of women, old women are moſt feeble; of old women, widows moſt wofull; of widows, thoſe that are poor, their plight moſt pittiful; of poor widows, thoſe that want Children, their caſe moſt dolefull; of widows that want Children, thoſe that once had them and after loſt them, their eſtate moſt deſolate; of widows that have had Children, thoſe that are ſtrangers in a forraign Country, their condition moſt comfortleſſe: yet all theſe met together in *Naomi* as in the center of ſorrow, to make the meaſure of her miſery preſſed down, ſhaken together, running over. I conclude therefore, many Men have had affliction, none like *Job;* many women have had tribulation, none like *Naomi.*

Verſe 6: *Then ſhe aroſe with her Daughters in law, that ſhe might returne from the Country of* Moab: *for ſhe had heard in the Country of* Moab *how that the Lord had viſited his people, in giving them bread.*

Theſe words contain two general parts. 1. Gods viſiting his people with Plenty. 2. *Naomies* viſiting of her people with her perſon.

I begin with the firſt in the Order of the words, *Then ſhe aroſe with her Daughters in law, &c.*

Obſervation: We muſt tarry no longer in an Idolatrous Land when God offereth us an occaſion to returne into our own Country: for ſo long as we tarry in an Idolatrous Land on a juſt cauſe, ſo long we are in our vocation and in Gods protection: but when God openeth us a Gap to returne, and we will not through it, we are neither in our calling nor Gods keeping, but muſt ſtand on our own adventures; and who knows not how ſlenderly we ſhall be kept, when we are left to our own cuſtody? Let not therefore *Ioſeph* with his Wife and Son, tarry any longer in the Land of *Egypt,* when he is dead that ſought the life of the Child.

Examples we have of thoſe which in the dayes of Queen *Mary* fled beyond the Seas; though they were not in a Paganiſh, onely in a forraign Country: Mr. *Scorey, Cocks, Whitehead, Grindall, Horne, Sandys, Elmore, Geſt, Jewel;* if fear lent them feet to run when they went away, joy gave them wings to fly when they came home againe: let none therefore pretend in needleſſe excuſes to linger in the Land of

Egypt, when they may return into the bony-flowing Land of *Canaan*.

For she had heard in the Country of Moab.] I suppose when any Messenger arrived in *Moab*, out of the Land of *Canaan*, *Naomie* did presently repaire unto him, and load him with questions concerning the estate of her Country: How do the *Iews* my Country-men? How faireth it with the *Bethlehemites* my Neighbours? with *Boaz* my Kinsman? What is the rate of Corne? What the price of Oyle? What the value of Wine? If there be no performance for the present, what promise is there for the future? Though things be bad now, what hope is there but they will be better hereafter? Alas! he answers little; and from his silence and sorrowfull looks, *Naomi* gathers a denial; but as *Elijah* sending his servant towards the Sea, 1 *King*. 18. 43, to see what signs there were of Raine, for six severall times together he returned this answer, *There is nothing;* but at the seventh time he brought him the tydings of a Cloud rising out of the Sea: so though for nine years *Naomi* had no news but of want and scarcity; yet the tenth yeare there came a man (probably he was a good man that brought these good tydings) who brought her word that the valleys began to laugh and sing with plentie; and so though the hope that was deferred was the fainting of the heart, yet when it came, it was the *Tree of life*. Perchance because the covetous Jews had made nine parts great for their own profit, and the tenth small to cozen God of his portion: God, quite contrary, gave them nine years of scarcity and want, and at length made the tenth of store and plenty.

Observation: The fame of remarkable Accidents will fly into forraign Countries; for if it be bad news, the wicked will be sure to tell it in the Gates of *Gath*, and publish it in the streets of *Askelon;* if it be good, the godly will proclaim it in the Courts of *Zion*, and disperse it within the walls of *Jerusalem:* whether good or bad (if it be of moment and importance) it will not be covered nor concealed.

Question: *Is it lawfull for us to lissen, hearken, and enquire after matters of forraigne Countries?*

Answer: Though I would not have men to be like the

Athenians, to hear or tell some new thing; yet it is both lawful and laudable for them to enquire after forraigne affairs, whereby they expresse the desire that they have of the welfare of their distant Brethren, the Members of the same mysticall body: Example, *Nehe.* 1. 2. And yet would I have men (though they lend their ears) not to bestow their beliefe on every groundlesse report which is blazed abroad.

1. Because Fame is often untrue, relating 2 *Sam.* 13. 32, *That all the Kings Sonnes are kil'd, when onely* Amnon *is slain.*

2. Because many there be which with the Souldiers, *Mat.* 28. 15, do nothing but invent and disperse lyes to gull over-credulous people: And as many a benighted Traveller hath wandred out of his way, whilst he followed for his lanthorn the Meteor of foolish fire; so many a man hath been deceived by embracing of lying relations, instead of true news. Yet in case that *Cushai* and *Ahimaaz* confirm the same thing, that variety of Messengers from divers places of sundry sides and severall factions all agree in materiall and substantiall points; we ought not to be like unbelieving *Thomas, to* trust no more then our eyes have seen, but may rely on the truth of such relations, and ought accordingly to be affected with sorrow if the news be bad, or joy, if the tydings tend to the Churches good and Gods glory.

That God has visited his People.] This was the priviledge of the people of the Jews, that they were styled Gods people, but now *Ammi* is made *Lo-Ammi*, and *Ruchama, Lo-ruchama;* and we the Gentiles are placed in their roome; let us therefore remember the words of St. *Paul*, Rom. 11. 20, 21, *Be not high minded, but fear; for if God spared not the naturall branches of the Olive, fear that he will not spare thee also.*

O that he would be pleased to cast his eye of pitty upon the poor Jews, which for fifteen hundred yeares and upwards have wandred without Law, without Lord, without Land, and as once they were, so once againe to make them his people!

In giving them bread.] By *Bread* is meant all sustenance necessary for the maintaining of our lives, whereof bread is the chiefest. As the Temple of *Dagon* principally leaned on two Pillars, and fell to the ground when *Sampson* took them away, so the buildings of our bodies chiefly relye on bread and water for outward sustenance, which being taken away, cannot but presently decay: let others therefore wish those dishes which curiosity hath invented rather to encrease then satisfie hunger, which are more delightsome to the eye then pleasing to the pallat; yet more pleasing to the pallat, then wholsome to the stomack; let us pray, *Give us this day our daily bread.*

Bread is a dish in every Course; without this can be no Feast; with this can be no Famine.

Observation: Gods punishments though they last sometimes long, yet alwayes they end at last: and yet sometimes for the manifestation of his power, and tryall of his Childrens patience, he suffers them to be brought into great extremities: *Abrahams* hand shall be heaved up to slay *Isaac*, before the Angell shall catch hold of it: *Lazarus* shall be three dayes dead, before Christ will rayse him; the Ship readie to sinke, before our Saviour will awake; *Peter* must be drencht in the water, before our Saviour will keepe him from drowning; S. *Paul* must be in the Lyons mouth, before he shall be delivered out of it; the Famine must last ten yeare, before God will give them Bread.

An example hereof wee have in our Neighbouring Churches of *Germanie*, which long have beene afflicted under the Tyrannie of their Oppressors; and now at length, a Sunne is risen out of the North; and after a long Night, the Morning beginneth the Day: And thou, *Swethland*, shalt not be counted the meanest amongst the Kingdomes of *Europe;* for out of thee did a Prince arise, who hath delivered the distressed Protestants; who at his first landing, seemed to his Enemies an Object fitter of their scorne then opposition. They thought our youthfull *David* too unequall a Match to coape with their Generall, who had bean a Man of Warre from his Youth. But as Veritie consisteth not in the pluralitie of Voyces, so Victorie standeth not in the multitude of Souldiers; but God so ordered it, that he that had the best Cause, had the best successe. I dare boldly say, that all the Protestant Princes and States of *Germanie* will be readie truly to say of him what *Tertullus* spake flatteringly of *Felix*, *Act.* 24. 2, 3,

Seeing that by thee we enjoy great quietneſſe, and that very worthy deeds are done unto this Nation by thy providence, we alwayes accept it, and in all places, moſt noble Prince, with all thankefulneſſe. But let us turne our prayſes of him into prayers for him, That he who hath conquered his Foes may ſubdue himſelfe, not to be puffed up with his good ſucceſſe. So let all thine enemies periſh, O Lord ; but let all them that love thee be as the Sunne when he goeth forth in his might : And as ever I have earneſtly deſired, ſo now doe I ſtedfaſtly hope to ſee the Day, when our *Naomi* (our worthy *Naomi*, more fruitfull in Miſeries then in Children, and in Vertues then in both) ſhall ariſe, to return out of the Land of *Holland*, with her Prince and Progenie, when ſhe ſhall heare that in the Land of *Holland* God hath viſited the *Palatinate*, and given them reſt.

Verſes 7, 8 : *And ſhe went out of the place where ſhe was, and her two daughters in law with her ; and they went on the way, to returne into the Land of* Judah. *And* Naomi *ſaid to her daughters in law, Goe, returne each of you to her mother.*

Theſe words containe the continuation of *Naomies* returne; wherein we may obſerve,

Firſt, the companie that went with her, *her two daughters in law.*

Secondly, the diſcourſe ſhe had with this companie, conſiſting of a Precept in the Text, *Goe, returne each of you to her mother :* and of a prayer, in the words following.

Now, whereas her daughters in law did not take their farewell of *Naomi* at the threſhold of their houſe, but went part of the way with her, we gather,

Obſervation : That all offices of kindneſſes and courteſies ought to be betwixt the mother in law and the daughter in law, I meane her ſonnes Wife. And yet looke into the world, and ye ſhall commonly finde enmitie betwixt them, as ſaith *Terence in Heſſera* [*Hecyra*, Act ii. Sc. 1, lines 4, 5] *Neque declinatam mulierem reperias ab aliarum ingenio ; itὰ adeὸ uno omnes animo ſocrus oderunt nurus :* And their fallings out chiefely proceed from theſe two cauſes :

Firſt, they contend which ſhould have the greateſt right and intereſt in the Man, who is Sonne to the one, Husband to the other. *Judah* and *Iſrael* conteſted (2 *Sam.* 19. 43) which ſhould have moſt part in King *David;* the former claiming it, becauſe he was bone of their bone ; the latter pleaded they had eleven parts in him, to *Judahs* ſingle ſhare. Thus mother in lawes and daughter in lawes uſe to fall out; the mother, becauſe her ſonne is fleſh of her fleſh, and bone of her bone, pleades it is right that he ſhould ſide and ſecond with her ; the daughter in law, becauſe he is her Husband, and therefore one fleſh, challengeth that he ſhould rather take her part: ſo betwixt them they fill the Family with all diſcord.

Secondly, they fall out about the managing of the matters in the Houſehold, after whoſe mind they ſhould be ordered: but as S. *James* ſaid in another caſe, *Beloved, theſe things ought not to be ſo;* both theſe brawles may be eaſily ended. The firſt may be taken up by the wiſdome and diſcretion of the ſonne in law, who ought ſo indifferently to poyſe his affections betwixt them both, with ſuch dutifulneſſe and reſpect to the one, ſuch love and kindneſſe to the other, that neither may have juſt cauſe to complaine. And the ſecond controverſie may thus be decided : If the mother hath the ſtate ſtill in her hands, good reaſon it is ſhe ſhould rule the Affaires, and that the daughter in law ſhould wait till her mother in lawes naturall death hath paved the ſucceſſion to the governing of the Family : but if the old woman hath reſigned her eſtate, and confined her ſelfe to an yearely penſion, then ought ſhe not to intermeddle with thoſe matters from which ſhe had willingly ſequeſtred her ſelfe. Were this obſerved, there would not ſo many daughters in law rejoyce when the day of mourning for their mother in law is come ; ſome whereof ſay as the wicked ſaid of *David,* O, *when will ſhe die, and her name periſh?*

Now to come to the diſcourſe ſhe had with them : *Goe, returne, &c.* Where ariſeth a queſtion, Whether *Naomi* did well in perſwading her daughters to goe back unto *Moab?* For the ſatisfaction whereof, I will ſet downe, firſt, what may be ſaid againſt; ſecondly, what may be brought for her defence.

Accufation: Why, *Naomi*, why didft thou quench the zeale of thy daughters which proffered themfelves fo willingly to goe with thee? Oh, rayne them not backward with diffwafions, but rather fpurre them forward with exhortations; and ftrive to bring them out of an Idolatrous Land to a place where Gods Worfhip is purely profeft: Say unto them, Hearken, O daughters, and confider, encline your ears, forget alfo your Country, and your own Mothers houfe; fo fhall the Lord your God have pleafure in you. True it is, ye have a Mother in *Moab*, but what of that? Care not for your Mother, but care for your Maker: care not for her that Conceived you, but care for him that Created you: tarry not with them, no, not fo much as to expreffe your laft love in performing their Funeralls; rather let the dead bury their dead: thofe that are dead fpiritually, let them bury fuch as die naturally, and come go ye along with me to the Land of *Cànaan*. Thus, *Naomi*, oughteft thou to have faid, and then hadft performed the part, done the duty of a Mother. If whilft thou hadft travelled with them on the way, thou hadft travelled with them till God had been formed in them; then fhouldft thou fhine as a double Sunne in heaven for faving of two fouls, whereas now thou art in a manner acceffary to their ghoftly murther in fending them back to an idolatrous Country.

Defence: To this accufation *Naomi* might juftly anfwer: It is my hearts defire and prayer to God, that I may be an inftrument of my Daughters in laws converfion; but the wifdome of the Serpent as well as the innocency of the Dove is to be ufed in all our actions, leaft we draw needleffe danger upon our felves. True it is, my Daughters in law proffer to go with me; but here is the queftion, whether this is done out of courtefie and complement, or out of fingleneffe and finceritye. Now fhould they through my perfwafions go into the Land of *Canaan*, and there live in want and penury, they will be ready to raile on me another day: We may thank *Naomi* for all this; we had plentifull provifions in our own Country, but fhe muft have us hither; fhe by her reftleffe importunitie muft wring a conftrained confent from us to come into *Canaan;* all thefe miferies are befallen upon us through her default. Yea, I am affraid, that, finding want, they again will return into their own Country to my fhame, the fcandall of our Religion, and the deeper punifhment of their own fouls. Wherefore without their minds would I do nothing, that their going might not be as it were of neceffity, but willingly. To which end I will put them to the touch-ftone, to fee whether their forwardneffe be faithfull or faigned, found or feeming, cordiall or counterfeit; I will weigh them both in the ballance, hoping that neither fhall be found too light.

Upon thefe grounds learned men have acquitted *Naomi* from any fault in managing this matter, fhe doing it onely with an intent to trie them.

Whence we may obferve, That *Pagans* that proffer them-felves to become Converts, are not without proof prefently to be received into the Church.

And here we may take occafion to digreffe a little, to fhew how Chriftians ought to behave themfelves in the converting of Infidels.

Firft, They muft ftrive in their mutuall converfing with them to feafon them with a good opinion of their honefty and upright dealing, otherwife their Doctrine will never be em-braced, whofe manners are juftly miflik't.

Secondly, Having poffeffed them with this good efteem, they ought, as occafion is offered, to inftruct them in the Rudiments of Chriftian Religion; and to begin with fuch as are plain and evident by the light of nature, and fo in due time to proceed to matters of greater difficulty.

Laftly, They are to pray to God to give his increafe to their planting and watering: for, as *Athanafius* faith, *It is a divine work to perfwade mens fouls to believe.*

But as for the ufing of tortures and of torments thereby to force them, we have no fuch cuftome, nor as yet the Churches of God: for though none come to Chrift but fuch as his Father draws by the violence of his effectuall grace; yet ought not men to drive or drag any to the profeffion of the Faith: yet notwithftanding, if after long patience and for-bearing with them and long inftructing them in the points of Religion; if ftill thefe *Pagans* continue refractary and obftinate, then surely the civill Magistrate who hath the lawfull dominion over them may severely, though not cruelly, with *Josiah*, compell them to come to Church, and to perform the outward formalities of Gods worship.

Go then, ye bloody Jesuites! boast of those many millions of *Americanes* whom you have converted, who were not converted by the sword of the mouth, gained by hearing the Gospell, but compelled by the mouth of the sword, forced by feeling your cruelty: witnesse those seventy thousand which without any catechising in the points of Religion, were at once driven to the Font like so many Horses to a watring Trough. Indeed I find my Saviour, *Iohn* 2. 15, driving the *Merchants* out of the *Temple* with a whip of cords, but never before did I read of any which against their wills drave or instructed[1] *Pagans* to the Font to be baptized.

Each to her Mothers house.] Here we see Widows if poor are to be maintained by their Parents if they be able. These widows, 1 *Tim.* 5. 16, were not to be burthensome to the Church, but to be relieved by their own Countrie. Let Parents therefore take heed how they bestow their Daughters in Marriage: for if they match them to Unthrifts and Prodigals, will it not be bitternesse in the end? The burthen will fall heavie on their backs, when their poor Daughters with their Children must be sent again to their Fathers to maintain them.

House.] Widows are to contain themselves within the *house*, not like the *Harlot*, *Prov.* 7. 12, *alwaies in the streets;* but like meek *Sarah* in the *Tent:* whereby they shal sooner gain the love and esteem of others; for let base and beggerly fellows buy that rascal ware which is hung out at the doors and windows of Shops and Stalls, whilest men of qualitie and fashion will go into the Shop to cheapen the worth of those merchandise as are therein kept secret and conceal'd. And so surely all discreet and grave men will have the highest esteem, and bear the best affection to such Women which do not gad

---

[1] [Or *instructed* should be perhaps *uninstructed*.]

abroad to be seen, but with *Ruth* and *Orpah*, being Widows, keep themselves in their Mothers house.

Verses 8, 9: *The Lord shew favour unto you, as ye have done with the dead, and with me. The Lord grant you that you may finde rest, either of you in the house of her Husband.*

Naomi being readie to take her leave of her daughters, faine she would leave them something for which they might be the better after her departure. But Gold and Silver she had none, yet such as she had she freely gave unto them (heartie prayers). Whence we learne, It is the best expression of a gratefull minde, to pray to God for the welfare of those at whose hands we have received greater courtesies then we can requite.

As ye have done.] Hence we learne, God in the rewarding of the good deeds of his servants, dealeth with them accordingly as they have done with others. Yet farre be it from us to suppose, that in our stained and imperfect works there is any meritorious vertue, which deserveth that God should proportion a Reward unto them: but this freely proceedeth from Gods favour; who to encourage us in well-doing will not suffer a *Cup of cold water* to passe without its reward. Doe we desire then to have dutifull Children, and faithfull Servants hereafter? let us be dutifull to our Parents, faithfull to our Masters. On the other side, hath God afflicted us with *Zibahs* to our Servants, and with *Absalons* to our Sonnes? let us reflect our eyes on that which is past, and call our selves to account whether we formerly have not been unfaithfull to our Masters, undutifull to our Parents: no doubt, we may then take up the Confession of *Adoni-bezek*, *As I have dealt with others, so the Lord hath done to me.*

With the dead.] *Question:* Here ariseth a Question; How can one shew favour to the dead, who being past sense are not capable of kindnesse or crueltie?

Answer: The *Papists* (who leave the soules of most men departing from hence, like *Absalon's* body, hanging betwixt

Heaven and Hell) expound it, that thefe Women did faſt and pray for the ſoules of their deceaſed Huſbands, that they might be delivered from torments, and in due time brought to happineſſe in Heaven. For the confutation of which erroneous expoſition, I need ſay no more then that the Scripture makes no mention of any ſuch middle place, wherein the ſoules of the godly ſhould be detained before they goe into Heaven; and in matters of Faith, every Chriſtian may ſafely ſay, Except I ſee in the Bible the print thereof, or can feel it deduced out of it by undenyable conſequence, I will not believe it.

It is ſtrange to ſee what impertinent places are produced by *Bellarmine*, to prove praying for the dead; as *James* 5. 16, *Confeſſe your faults one to another, and pray one for another, that ye may be healed; the effectuall fervent prayer of a righteous man availeth much.* Then he endevoureth to prove that the dead pray for the living, from the parable of *Dives*, *Luke* 16. 27, *I pray thee therefore, Father &c.*, where *Dives* was charitably ſollicitous for the good of his ſurviving *Brethren:* But let the firſt place in S. *James* be peruſed by impartiall Judgements, and it obligeth mutually the dead Saints to confeſſe to us, as well as we to them; which being impoſſible, directeth us to confine the words onely to reciprocall confeſſing and praying to and for the living.

Some will ſay, *Bellarmine* having ſufficiently proved *Purgatorie* before, (which neceſſarily inferreth prayers for the dead,) he might be the briefer in that ſubject. It is confeſſed, many arguments are alledged by him to that intent, though to ſmall purpoſe; as *Pſalme* 66. 12, *We went through fire and through water, but thou broughteſt us out into a wealthie place.* We anſwer; firſt, the living there ſpeake *de præterito*, we went; not *de futuro*, we ſhall goe. Secondly, it was literally meant of the *Children* of *Iſrael; they went through the fire*, when envaſſalled to worke in the *Egyptian Brick-kills*; and *through water*, when miraculouſly they paſſed through the *Red Sea*. Again, they went through *fire*, when, preſerved from the ſtinging of the *fierie*, they beheld the *brazen Serpent*. Thirdly, if from *fire* in this Text any can kindle a *Purgatorie*, others will quench it from the word *water*, ſeeing no *Papiſts* ever fancied a *watered Purgatorie*.

They urge the place, *Matth.* 5. 26, *Thou shalt by no meanes come out from thence till thou hast payd the uttermost farthing;* importing, say they, a possibilitie on satisfaction to be freed thence, that is, from *hell fire.*

Answer: Until there, is not taken *terminatively,* but *extensively;* equivalent to *never,* or *not at all;* paralleled to that place, *Psalme* 57. 1, *In the shadow of thy wings will I make my refuge, untill these calamities be over-past.* What, would *David* depart from God after his deliverance? Would he use him as Travellers a Bush? come under it in a storme, and leave it in fair weather? No surely, *David* would trust in God untill that time, and at that time, and in that time, and after that time, and at all times. Parallel also to that place of *Matthew* 1. 25, *And knew her not till she had brought forth her first-borne Sonne:* it being the constant Tradition of Antiquitie, according to the proportion of Faith, and embraced by the *Papists* themselves, that Chrifts Mother lived and died a spotlesse Virgin.

Much stresse he layeth on that passage of the Apostle, 1 *Corinth.* 3. 15, *He himselfe shall be saved, yet so as by fire.* This place, saith *Bellarmine,* is *locus utilissimus & difficillimus,* most profitable and most hard.

We answer, first, in general; seeing by the *Jesuit's* confession it is so hard a place, it is utterly improbable that *Purgatorie* (being of so high concernment to every soule, as *Papists* would perswade us) can be therein intended: For all matters necessarie for men to know and beleeve, wherein the safetie of every single soule is interessed (such as *Purgatorie* is pretended to be), is by the confession of all Divines expressed in plaine and pregnant Texts of Scripture; for want whereof *Bellarmine* is faine to shrowd and shelter himselfe under the most obscure places, alledging a Text most dark and difficult by his owne confession.

Secondly, that *fire* there meant by Saint *Paul,* is affliction in this life. As for such Fathers who expounded it *de igne conflagrationis,* of that *fire* which should burn up all things at the end of the world, it makes nothing for the patronizing of *Purgatorie* in the *Popish* notion thereof.

Come we now to finde an *Office*, and make an enquirie, how many things a *dying godly man* leaves behind him in this world: His *Soule* is fent before him; and, *Revel.* 14. 13, *From henceforth bleſſed are the dead that die in the Lord.* He leaveth behind him,

Firſt, his *Body*; to which we muſt be kinde, by *Buriall* and *Lamentation*.

Secondly, his *Eſtate*; to which we muſt be kinde, by carefull and faithfull *Adminiſtration*.

Thirdly, his *Children, Friends*, or *Kindred*; to whom we muſt be kinde, by *Love* and *Affection*.

Fourthly, his *Faults* and *Failings*; to which we muſt be kinde, by *Silence* and *Suppreſſion*.

Fifthly, his *Memorie* and *Vertues*; to which we muſt be kinde, by *Congratulation, Commemoration*, and *Imitation*.

Of theſe in order: For although theſe words, *Ye have beene kinde to the dead*, are capable of this found ſenſe, *You have been kinde to your Husbands, who now are dead, whileſt they were living*, yet becauſe more ſeemeth imported therein, we will proſecute the aforeſaid Particulars.

I ſay, firſt, his *Body*; to which there is due *Buriall* and *Lamentation: Buriall*, and that according to the qualitie and condition wherein he lived. We reade of King *Hezekiah*, 2 *Chron.* 32. 33, *They buried him in the chiefeſt* (in the *Hebrew*, in the *higheſt*) *Sepulchers of the ſonnes of David.* It muſt be allowed, that the Sepulcher of *David* his Father, was higher then his; and next *David, Hezekiahs.* O that heighth might be but meaſured by true holineſſe! There was an Officer amongſt the *Greekes*, whoſe place it was to meaſure *Monuments* according to the *Standard* of the mens merits therein interred: Such Officers, if uſed in *England*, would pare off great parcels from ſome *Tombes*, more proportioned to the parties *Wealth* then *Vertues*. But nothing could be abated of *Hezekiah* his *Monument*, all the *Dimenſions* whereof were due to his *Devotion*.

And *Lamentation*: Surely, of all the *godly* that ever departed this Life, Gods ſervants had the leaſt cauſe to bewayl the death of S. *Steven*: For firſt, whereas there is a three-fold degree of certaintie of falvation; firſt, that of *Hope*, which as the leaſt and loweſt, ſcarce deſerveth to be ſtyled Certaintie; ſecondly, that of *Evidence*, whereby the perſon clearely in his ſoule apprehendeth Gods favour; thirdly, that of *Viſion*, peculiar to this *Steven* alone, antedating his happineſſe with his bodily eyes, being in Heaven before he was in Heaven: ſo that as many gates in his wounded body ſtood open to let out his ſoule, he beheld alive the Heavens opened to receive it. And yet we reade, *Acts* 8. 2, *And devout men carryed Steven to his Buriall, and made great lamentation over him*. Obſerve; it was not said, *they made great lamentation for him*, but *over him*; they knew him in a happy condition: It was themſelves they bemoaned in his death, the ſight of his Corps ſharpening their ſorrow, that the *Infant-Church* had loſt one of her beſt ſwadling-clothes.

Secondly, his *Eſtate*; to which we muſt be kinde by carefull and faithfull *Adminiſtration*. *Heb.* 9. 17, *For a Teſtament is of force after men are dead*. *Gal.* 3. 15, *Though it be but a mans Covenant*, or Teſtament, *yet if it be confirmed, no man diſannulleth or addeth thereto*. No man? He muſt either be leſſe then man in knowledge, a *meere Beaſt*; or more then man in malice, a *meere Devill*. By *Teſtament* I underſtand not onely the very words thereof, but alſo what appeareth to be the *Teſtator* his Will to the Conſcience of the Executor. How many in this kinde are cruell to the dead! So that ſome of the Legacies bequeathed by them have had a *Thumbe* or a *Toe*, yea, ſome an *Arme* or *a Legge* cut off from them. Many Legacies which came *ſound* forth from the *Teſtator*, before they could get through the *Executors* have beene more *lame* and *maimed* then the Criples in the Hoſpitall to whom they have beene bequeathed.

Thirdly, his *Children*, or (becauſe *Mahlon* and *Chilion* had none of them) his *Kindred* or *Friends*; to whom the living muſt be kinde, with *Love* and *Affection*. Remember the Character of the good Wife, *Proverbs* 31. 12, *She will doe her Husband good, and not evill, all the dayes of her life*. We have many *Wives* onely negatively *good*, pleaſing and praying themſelves in this, that they doe their *Husbands* no hurt.

This will not doe the deed; they muſt be poſitively profitable. Nor is it ſaid, *all the dayes of his life*, but *all the dayes of her life*. What if he dieth, her obligation to him is not *caſſated* or *nulled*, (as many *Wives* generally conceive,) but ſtill continueth *all the dayes of her life*. True it is, ſhe is ſet free ſo farre, as ſhe may marry againe in a competent time, without the leaſt ſhadow of ſinne; yet ſo, as ſtill obliged to doe good all her life time to the *Friends*, to the *Children* (if any) of her dead *Husband;* and he, if ſurviving her, reciprocally engaged to doe the like.

Fourthly, the beſt men leave *Faults* and *Failings* behind them; to theſe the living muſt be kinde by *Silence* and *Suppreſſion*.

Firſt, of thoſe of whom thou canſt ſay no good, ſay nothing.

Secondly, of thoſe of whom thou canſt ſay ſome good, ſay no bad.

David is a moſt excellent inſtance hereof, 2 *Sam.* 1. 24. Who could more, or more juſtly have inveighed againſt *Saul* then *David?* O *ye Daughters of Israel, rejoyce for the death of ſo great a Tyrant, who killed Ahimelech the High Prieſt, and foureſcore more of Gods Prieſts, whoſe ſoules were as cleare from Treaſon as the white Linnen Ephod they wore were from ſpots: Twice I had him at my mercy, once in the Cave, once when aſleepe; yet he (notwithſtanding all his faire promiſes to the contrarie) was the more cruell to me for my kindneſſe to him.* No ſuch matter; *David* conceales what was bad, remembreth what was good in *Saul,* at leaſtwiſe what would make his memorie acceptable with the weaker Sex; namely, his making of Gallantrie faſhionable amongſt them: *Ye Daughters of Iſrael, weepe over Saul, who clothed you in Scarlet, with other delights, who put on ornaments of Gold upon your apparell.*

Fifthly, *Memorie* of his *Vertues:* To which three things are due, to make thee kinde thereunto.

Firſt, *Congratulation*. I will touch this ſtring but tenderly; not ſo much becauſe fearing mine owne fingers (as if the Leſſon ſhould be falſe I play thereon), but expecting other mens eares as ill-diſpoſed with prejudice. It is no *Poperie,* nor Superſtition, to prayſe God for the happie condition of his servants departed: the ancient *Patriarchs*, the inspired *Prophets*, the holy *Apostles*, the patient *Martyrs*, the Religious *Confessors*. When the tribe of *Ruben*, *Gad*, and halfe *Manasses*, erected the Altar ED at the passage over *Jordan*, it startled all the rest of the Tribes, as if under it they had hatched some superstitious designe; whereas, indeed, the Altar was not intended for *Sacrifice*, but was meerely an Altar of *Memorial*, to evidence to posteritie that these two Tribes and a halfe (though divided from the rest by the River of *Jordan*) were conjoyned with them in the worship of the same God. In like manner when some Ministers thank God for the departure of his servants, some people are so weake, and some so wilfull, to condemne such for passages of *Poperie*, as if superstitious prayers were made for their departure: whereas, indeed, such *Congratulation*, on the contrarie, speakes our confidence on their present blisse and happinesse, and continueth the *Church Militant* with the *Church Triumphant*, as the compleating one intire *Catholike Church* of *Jesus Christ*.

Secondly, *Commemoration* is due to the *Memories* of the deceased. Hence the ancient custome of *Funerall Orations* continued in our moderne practice, both to the honour of the dead, and profit of the living.

Thirdly, *Imitation* of their *Vertues*. It hath been a great Question amongst such who desire to expresse themselves thankfull to their dead *Ancestors*, of what *Metall* or *Matter* to make their *Monuments*, so as they may be most lasting and permanent. Wise men have generally decryed *Silver* and *Brasse*; not so much, because too costly (such may be the worth and wealth of the *Executors* and partie deceased), but too tempting to *Sacriledge* to demolish them. *Brasse* is generally subject to the same mischiefe, and *Marble Touch* and *Alablaster*, are generally used for that purpose; but the *Monument* lesse subject to Casualtie, is, to *imitate* the *Vertues* of our dead *Friends*: in other *Tombes* the dead are preserved; in these they may be said to remaine alive.

When we see a Child very like to the Father and Mother thereof, we use to say, *Thy Father will never be dead as long as thou livest*. Thus it is the best remembrance of our dead *Progenitors*, to follow their *Vertues*. S. *Paul* cannot looke upon *Timothy* but prefently calls to minde his Mother *Eunice*, and his Grandmother *Lois*, though the latter no doubt long fince departed.

The Lord grant that you may finde reft, each of you in the houfe of her Husband.] Here we may obferve, firft, that it is the part of pious Parents to pray to God for the good fucceffe of their Children, efpecially in the matter of their Marriage: example in *Abraham*, *Gen.* 24. 7. Secondly, hence we may gather, that the Life of married perfons, meeting together in the feare of God, is *Reft*.

Objection: How then commeth it to paffe that many men and women may take up the words of *Rebecca*, *Seeing it is fo, why am I thus? Gen.* 25. 22. If the married Life be *Reft*, how commeth it to prove my Purgatorie, my Hell, my caufe of reftleffe Torment? Men and women were joyned in Marriage, *Gen.* 2, to the end to be a mutuall *helpe* one to the other; but many prove fuch helpers as the King of *Afhur* did to *Ahaz*, 2 *Chron.* 28. 20, of whom it is faid, he diftreffed him, but helped him not.

Anfwer: Who can hinder it, if men of their Girdles and Garters make Halters to hang themfelves? If thofe things, which fhould be for their ftrength and ornament, be through their owne default turned to their utter undoing, the eftate of Marriage is not herein to be blamed, but the folly of fuch who out of fome finifter ends undertake it. Happily [Haply] fome chufe their Wives like as our Grandmother *Eve* did the Apple, becaufe they are pleafant to the eyes to be lookt upon: others out of a love of their Wealth, faying of their Wives what the *Sichemites* did of the fonnes of *Jacob*, *Shall not all their Heards and Cattell be ours?* Whereas if Grace and Pietie were principally refpected in their Choice (other outward accommodations in their due diftance not neglected), they would finde the truth of our obfervation, that a married Life is *Reft*. For though fome pettie Brawles may happen amongft the moft fanctified Couple, which may move their anger, yet fhall it not remove their love, if one with Chriftian difcretion beareth with the infirmities of the other. *Joab* made this compact with his Brother *Abifhai*, 2 *Sam.* 10.

11, *If the Aramite be stronger then I, thou shalt helpe me; but if the Ammonites be too strong for thee, I will come and succour thee.* Thus ought Man and Wife to make a Bargaine with their best Councell to, and prayers for each other, to assist themselves mutually against their sundry weaknesses and infirmities, which otherwise would turne their *Rest* of their Life into unquietnesse.

Verses 9 *to* 13: *And when she kissed them, they lift up their voices, and wept. And they said unto her, Surely, we will returne with thee unto thy people. But* Naomi *said, Turne againe, my daughters: for what cause will you goe with me? Are there any more sonnes in my Wombe, that they may be your Husbands? Turne againe, my daughters, goe your way, for I am too old to have an Husband: If I should say, I have hope; and if I had an Husband this night; yea, if I had borne sonnes: Would you tarry for them while they were of age? Would you be deferred for them from taking of Husbands? Nay, my daughters, for it grieveth me much for your sakes that the hand of the Lord is gone out against me.*

And when she kissed them.] Kisses was the ordinarie salutation of the *Jewes* at the meeting of acquaintance, men with men, women with women; men with women, provided that then they were of neere kindred, to avoid all suspition of unchastitie.

And they lift up their voices, and wept.] The observation here may be the same which the *Iewes* collected, *Iohn* 11. 36, which, when they saw our Saviour weepe for *Lazarus*, they said, *Behold how he loved him.* So these teares in this place were the expression of their affection. Sorrow like the River of *Iordan*, 1 *Chron.* 12. 15, *in the first moneth did overflow the bankes*, and streamed water downe their cheekes.

But Naomi *said, Turn againe, my daughters, &c.*] In these words, she disswadeth her daughters in law from returning with her; the strength of her Reason, contained in three Verses, may thus be set downe, as if she had said:

Happily [Haply], daughters, you have heard that it is the cuftome in the Land of *Canaan* for Childleffe Widowes to marry their deceafed Husbands Brothers; but if your returne be grounded hereon, know that you build your hopes on a falfe foundation, it being impoffible for me, by the courfe of Nature, to have *any more fonnes*. Who will looke that Water fhould flow from a drie Fountain, Grapes grow on a withered Vine, Fruit flourifh on a dead Figge-tree? Though *Sarah* at ninety was made a Mother, though *Aaron's* Rod did bud and bloffome when it was drie; I my felfe fhould be a Miracle, if I fhould expect fuch a Miracle: and therefore know that *there are no more fonnes in my Wombe.*

Doctrine: Now whereas *Naomi* dealeth thus plainly with her daughters, not feeding them with falfe hopes, it teacheth us this: We ought not to gull our friends with the promifes of thofe things that neither will nor can come to paffe. Otherwife we fhall both wrong our friends, who the higher they are mounted upon the Hill of feeming hopes, at length the deeper they will be caft into the Dale of reall defpaire; and alfo we fhall wrong our felves; when Time, the Mother of Truth, fhall unmaske us, we fhall prove our felves to be no better then Lyars and Cheaters.

Ufe: Let us Labour to be *Nathanaels*, true *Ifraelites, in whom there is no guile;* and as *John Baptift,* when as the *Pharifes* asked him, whether he was the Chrift, or no, he *confeffed, and denyed not,* and faid plainly, *I am not the Chrift* (*John* 1. 20): So if we neither meane to doe, nor know that fuch things cannot be done which our friends requeft of us; let us confeffe, denie not, and fay plainly that their fuites cannot, fhall not be granted; and by fuch downe-right dealing we fhall at laft get more favour from them, then they who flatter them with their tongue. Let not the Phyfician, when he reades in the Urinall thofe difmal fymptomes which are the Ufhers of Death, ftill promife Life and Health unto his Patient; but plainly tell him, that there is *Mors in olla;* that fo he may flye unto the Phyfician of the Soule for a better Life when this fhall fade. Let not the Lawyer, when he knowes the Cafe is defperate, feed his Clyent with falfe hopes to recover it, that fo from him he may be fed with Money;

but rather let him advife him to *agree with his adverfarie while he is in the way;* that though he cannot get the Conqueft, yet he may have the eafier Compofition.

For I am too old to have a Husband.] Here arifeth a Queftion.

Queftion : Is there any Age fo old, wherein a man or woman may not marry?

Anfwer : Naomies meaning was not fimply and abfolutely that fhe was too old to marry, but fhe was too old to have a Husband, and by a Husband to have Children, and that thofe Children fhould grow up and make fit Husbands for *Orpah* and *Ruth.* Yet, by the way, I would advife fuch who are ftricken in yeares, efpecially if impotencie be added unto Age, and that it may ftand with their conveniencie, to refraine from all thoughts of a fecond Marriage, and to expect that happie day, when Death fhall folemnize the Nuptiall betwixt their Soule and their Saviour. For when *Barzillai* hath counted eighty yeares, he hath even had enough of the pleafure and vanitie of the world; let him retire himfelfe to a private life, and not envie his fonne *Cimcham* to fucceed to thofe delights of which his Age hath made his Father uncapable. Yet if any ancient perfons, for their mutuall comfort and focietie (which is not the leaft end for which Marriage was ordained), are difpofed to match themfelves herein, they are blamelefle; efpecially, if they have a care to obferve a correfpondencie of Age with thofe to whom they linke themfelves. Otherwife, as our Saviour noteth, when the old Cloth was joyned to the new, it made no good medley, but the Rent was made the worfe : So when the Spring of Youth is wedded to the Winter of Age, no true comfort can arife from fuch unequall Yokes, but much jealoufie and fufpition are caufed from the fame.

Would ye tarry for them ?] That is, you would not tarry for them; or if you fhould tarry for them, you fhould wrong your felves, and doe unadvifedly; becaufe in the mean time, refraining from the ufing of Gods Ordinance, you expofe your felves to the Devill, to tempt you to incontinencie.

Therefore S. *Pauls* councell is good which he prescribes in 1 *Tim.* 5. 14, *I will therefore that the younger Women, &c.*

While they were of age.] Note from hence, that Children are not to be married in their Non-age, before they are arrived at yeares of discretion: *Thamar*, Gen. 38. 11, is to wait till *Selah* be grown up. Those Parents are therefore to be blamed, who out of by-respects match their Children in their infancie. Whence it commeth to passe, that as their age doth increase, their minde doth alter: so what formerly they did like, afterwards they do loath, such Marriages proving commonly most insuccessfull.

Nay, my Daughters: for it grieveth me much for your sakes.] As if she had said, It grieveth me much that you are already plunged into povertie; but it would add more to my sorrow, if you should increase your calamities by returning home wiht me; for mine own part, my misery troubleth me not so much because the Sun of my life is readie to set, and it mattereth not though the Ship be scanted of Victuals when it is hard by the Harbour; all my care is for you who are young women and stand upon your own preferment; it grieveth me much for your sakes.

Doctrine: See here, such is the ingenuous nature of Gods Children, that they sorrow more for others that are inwrapped with them in a common calamitie then for themselves. Example in *Elias*, 1 *King.* 17. 20. But then it goeth nearest to their heart when others are not onely afflicted with them, but also for them, when they themselves are the principall Malefactors for whose defaults others are punish't, as in *David*, 2 *Sam.* 24. 17.

Uses: It may confute the devillish nature of such who, being in Trouble, care not though they pawne their dearest friends in their stead, so be it they themselves may escape. And it may also serve to comfort those that are in distresse, when God onely layeth his punishments on them alone, and doth not involve others together with them. Art thou afflicted with povertie? Comfort thy selfe, that though thou beest poore yet thou hast undone none by Suretiship for thee.

Art thou in sickneſſe? Be glad that thy Diſeaſe is not infectious, and that thou haſt not derived the contagion to others. Doth God puniſh thee for thy ſinne with a perſonall puniſhment? Be glad that thou beareſt the weight of thine owne offence, and that thou art not the *Ionah*, for whoſe private ſinne a whole Ship of Paſſengers is endangered to be caſt away; for then their caſe would grieve thee more then thine owne calamitie.

That the hand of the Lord.] *Naomi* here taketh eſpeciall notice that her Loſſes proceedeth from no other by-cauſes, but from the hand of God. As *David* therefore aſked the Widow of *Tekoah*, 2 *Sam.* 14. 19, *Is not the hand of* Joab *with thee in all this?* So when any affliction befalleth us, let us preſently have recourſe unto God, and ſay, *Is not the hand of the Lord the principall cauſe hereof?* And not with the Prieſts of the *Philiſtims* ſay, *It was a chance that happened us.*

Is gone out againſt me.] *Obſervation:* Hence we may obſerve, every Saint of God, in a common calamitie, is to thinke, that God aimed at his puniſhment, and intended his reformation in particular. *The hand of the Lord* was gone out alſo againſt *Orpah* and *Ruth*, in taking away their Husbands; yet *Naomi* appropriateth the ſtroake to her ſelfe, *Is gone out againſt me.*

How contrarie is this to the practice of the world! Men in a publike and generall affliction, each ſhifteth it off from themſelves, and no one man will be brought to confeſſe that his ſinnes are puniſhed, or his amendment intended in particular, if the Scourge be univerſall. As the *Philiſtims*, 1 *Sam.* 5. poſted the Ark of God from *Aſhdod* to *Ekron*, from one place to another, and none would receive it: So, in a common Calamitie, none will acknowledge, that he himſelfe is eſpecially intereſted in it, but plead, *What is that to us? Let others looke unto it.* O, ſaith the people, *God hath juſtly ſent this Plague for the corruption of the Magiſtrates; It is juſtly inflicted,* ſaith the Magiſtrate, *for the diſobedience of the people:* Herein, ſaith the poore man, *God hath met with the oppreſſion and extortion of the Rich;* Herein, ſaith the rich man, *God hath payed home the muttering & the repining of the Poore*: *Now*, faith the prodigall, *God punisheth the covetousnesse of Old men*; *Now*, faith the old man, *he scourgeth the prodigalitie of such as be Young*. Farre otherwife *Naomi*, who, though the Arrowes of God did glance and rebound to the wounding of *Orpah* and *Ruth*, yet fhe thought fhe her felfe was the Mark at whom God did levell his Shafts; *The hand of the Lord is gone out against me*.

Verfe 14: *And* Orpah *kiffed her mother in law, but* Ruth *clave unto her*.

These words containe two generall parts:
Firft, A blazing Meteor falling downe out of the Ayre; *And* Orpah, &c.
Secondly, A fixed Starre fairely fhining in the Heaven; *But* Ruth, &c.

And Orpah *kiffed her mother*.] Is this fhe which even now was fo promifing in her words, and so paffionate in her weeping? See how foon a forward Profeffor may turne to a fearefull Apoftate: Though fhe ftandeth or falleth to her own Mafter, yet, as the Pfalmift faith, *I am horribly afraid for thofe that forfake thy Law;* fo have we juft caufe to fufpect the fearfull finall eftate of *Orpah*.

Kiffed her mother.] That is, gave her this laft falutation of her departure. Here we fee that thofe who want grace and true fanctitie may notwithftanding have manners and good civilitie. Now had *Orpah* changed the corporall Kiffe fhe gave to her mother, into a fpirituall Kiffe to her Saviour, *Pfal*. 2. 12, *Kiffe the Sonne, left he be angry*, her cafe had been as happie as now it may feeme to be hopeleffe. But leaving her, we come to our felves, and gather this Doctrine.

Doctrine: Thofe who at the firft were forward in Religion, may afterward altogether fall away, 1 *Tim*. 1. 20; *Heb*. 6. 4 -6; *Matth*. 13. 20-1. It may therefore ferve to abate the proud carriage of fuch, who, as if it were not enough to be fure, will alfo be prefumptuous of their falvation, and thereby take leave and libertie to themfelves to live more licentioufly.

Objection: But as once one of the Children of the Prophets cryed out to *Elifha, O man of God, there is Death in the Pot;* fo may the weak Chriftian complaine againft this Doctrine: O it is a deadly and dangerous one, containing much matter of defpaire, too bitter for the pallat of a poore Chriftian to tafte, or his ftomack to digeft; it quencheth all the fparkes of my comfort, and hacketh afunder all the finewes of my hope; I feare left *Orpah*-like I alfo fhould fall away: what fhall I doe, that I may be faved?

Anfwer: Let not the *fmoaking Flax* be difmay'd, which in time may be a *blazing flame;* nor the *bruifed Reed* be difcouraged, which may prove a *Brazen Pillar* in the Temple of God: That therefore thou mayeft finally perfevere, obferve thefe foure Rules.

1 *Rule:* Firft, utterly renounce all fufficiencie in thy felfe. Who but a mad man will now adayes warrant the PaperShields of his owne ftrength, that knowes that *Adams* compleat Armour of Original Integritie was fhot thorow in *Paradife*.

2 *Rule:* Secondly, place all thy confidence on the undeferved mercie of God: Perfeverance commeth neither from the Eaft, nor from the Weft, nor as yet from the South; but God fuffereth one to fall, and holdeth up another. The Temple of *Solomon* had two Pillars; one called *Jachin,* founding in Hebrew, *The Lord will ftablifh;* the other *Booz,* fignified, *In him is ftrength:* So every Chriftian (*the Temple of the Holy-Ghoft*) is principally holden up by thefe two Pillars, Gods Power, and Will, to fupport him. Wherefore in every diftreffe let us crie out to God, as the Difciples did to our Saviour in the midft of a Tempeft, *Helpe Mafter, or elfe we perifh.*

3 *Rule:* Thirdly, ufe all thofe means which God hath chalked out for the encreafe of grace in thee; as Prayer, Meditation, reverent receiving the Sacraments, accompanying with Gods Children, Reading, Hearing the Word, &c.

4 *Rule:* Fourthly, alwayes preferve in thy felfe an awfull feare, left thou fhouldft fall away from God: Feare to fall, and Affurance to ftand, are two Sifters; and though *Cain* faid,

he was not his *Brothers keeper*, fure I am, that this Feare doth watch and guard her Sifter Affurance : *Tantus eft gradus certitudinis, quantus follicitudinis :* They that have much of this Feare, have much certaintie ; they that have little, little certaintie ; they that have none, have none at all. It is faid in Building, that thofe Chimneyes which fhake moft, and give way to the wind, will ftand the longeft: The Morall in Divinitie is true; thofe Chriftians that fhiver for feare by finnes to fall away, may be obferved moft couragious to perfift in Pietie.

Comfort : To thofe that diligently practife thefe Rules, I will adde this Comfort : Encourage thy felfe, that God will keepe thee from Apoftafie unto the end, becaufe alreadie hitherto he hath preferved thee : For Gods former favours are pawnes and pledges of his future love. *Davids* killing of a Lyon and a Beare, were the Earnefts of his Victorie over *Goliah*. Thus S. *Paul* reafoneth, 2 *Cor.* 1: 10, *Who delivered us from so great a death, and doth deliver; in whom we truft that he will yet deliver us.* When *Rachel* bare her firft fonne, *Gen.* 30. 24, fhe called him *Joseph,* and faid, *The Lord fhall adde to me another fonne.* So, when God hath alreadie bleffed us and fupported us for the time paft, let us fay with *Rachel, Jofeph, the Lord will adde:* he will not ftay, or ftint, or ftop here ; but as he hath kept me from my mothers wombe, and ever fince I was borne, fo I truft he will not forfake me when I am aged, and full of gray haires.

But to returne to her which returned again to *Moab :* We reade in 2 *Sam.* 20. 12, that the people which paffed by the Corps of murthered *Amafa*, being moved with fuch a hideous and uncouth a spectacle, they ftood ftill : But when we reade this Booke of *Ruth*, and come to *Orpahs* Apoftafie, there let us a while paufe and demurre, to reade in her fall a Lecture of our owne infirmitie. For if we ftand, it is not becaufe we have more might in our felves, but becaufe God hath more mercie on us. Let us therefore *worke out our falvation with feare and trembling :* ever *trembling*, left we fhould be caft to Hell ; ever triumphing, that we fhall come to Heaven : ever *fearfull*, left we fhould fall; ever certaine, that we fhall ftand :

ever carefull, left we fhould be damned; ever chearfull, that we fhall be faved. Concerning *Ruths* perfeverance, we intend to treat hereafter.

Verfe 15: *And* Naomi *faid, Behold, thy fifter in law is gone back unto her people, and unto her gods; returne thou after thy fifter in law.*

In thefe words, *Naomi* feekes to perfwade *Ruth* to returne; alledging the example of *Orpah*, whom fhe faith was *gone back to her people and to her gods*.

Obfervation: Where firft we finde, that all the Heathen, and the *Moabites* amongft the reft, did not acknowledge one true God, but were the worfhippers of many gods; for they made every Attribute of God to be a diftinct Deitie. Thus in ftead of that Attribute, the Wifdome of God, they fained *Apollo* the god of Wifdome; in ftead of the Power of God, they made *Mars* the god of Power; in ftead of that admirable Beautie of God, they had *Venus* the goddeffe of Beautie. But no one Attribute was fo much abufed as Gods Providence: For the Heathen fuppofing that the whole World, and all the Creatures therein, was too great a Dioceffe to be dayly vifited by one and the fame Deitie; they therefore affigned fundry gods to feverall creatures. Thus Gods Providence in ruling the raging of the Seas was counted *Neptune;* in ftilling the roaring Winds, *Æolus;* in commanding the Powers of Hell, *Pluto:* yea, Sheepe had their *Pan*, and Gardens their *Pomona:* the Heathens then being as fruitfull in faining of gods, as the *Papifts* fince in making of Saints.

Doctrine: Now, becaufe *Naomi* ufed the example of *Orpah* as a Motive to worke upon Ruth to returne, we gather from thence; Examples of others fet before our eyes, are very potent and prevalent arguments to make us follow and imitate them: Whether they be good examples; fo the forwardneffe of the *Corinthians* to relieve the *Jews*, provoked many: or whether they be bad; fo the diffembling of *Peter* at *Antioch* drew *Barnabas* and others into the fame fault. But thofe examples, of all others, are moft forcible with us, which are set by such who are neere to us by kindred, or gracious with us in friendship, or great over us in power.

Use 1: Let men in eminent places, as Magistrates, Ministers, Fathers, Masters, and the like, (seeing that others love to dance after their Pipe, to sing after their Tune, to tread after their Tract,) endeavour to propound [to] themselves patternes of Pietie and Religion to those that be under them.

Use 2 : When we see any good example propounded unto us, let us strive with all possible speed to imitate it. What a deale of stirre is there in the World for Civill Precedencie, and Prioritie! Every one desires to march in the Fore-front, and thinkes it a shame to come lagging in the Rere-ward: Oh, that there were such an holy Ambition and heavenly Emulation in our hearts, that as *Peter* and *Iohn* ran a Race, which should come first to the Grave of our Saviour; so men would contend, who should first attaine to true Mortification! And when we see a good example set before us, let us imitate it, though it be in one who in outward respects is farre our inferiour. Shall not the Master be ashamed to see that his Man, whose place on Earth is to come behinde him, in Pietie towards Heaven to goe before him? Shall not the Husband blush to see his Wife, which is the weaker Vessel in Nature, to be the stronger Vessel in Grace? Shall not the elder Brother dye his cheekes with the Colour of Vertue, to see his younger Brother, who was last borne, first re-borne by Faith and the Holy-Ghost? Yet let him not therefore envie his Brother, as *Cain* did *Abel;* let him not be angry with his Brother, because he is better then himselfe; but let him be angry with himselfe, because he is worse then his Brother; let him turne all his malice into imitation; all his fretting at him, into following of him: Say unto him as *Gehazi* did of *Naaman*, *As the Lord liveth I will run after him:* And though thou canst not over-run him, nor as yet over-take him, yet give not over to run with him; follow him, though not as *Azahel* did *Abner*, hard at the heeles; yet as *Peter* did our Saviour, *afarre off:* that though the more slowly, yet as surely thou mayest come to Heaven: and though thou wert short of him whilest he lived, in the Race, yet thou shalt be even with him when thou art dead, at the Marke.

Ufe 3: When any bad Example is prefented unto us, let us decline and deteſt it, though the men be never fo many, or fo dear unto us. Imitate *Michaiah*, 1 *Kings* 22. 13, 14, to whom when the meſſengers, fent to fetch him, faid, *Behold now the words of the Prophets declare good to the King with one mouth: let thy word therefore, I pray thee, be like to one of them; Michaiah* anſwered, *As the Lord liveth, whatſoever the Lord faith unto me, that will I fpeake.* If they be never fo deare unto us, we muſt not follow their bad practice. So muſt the fonne pleaſe him that begat him, that he doe not difpleaſe him that created him; fo muſt the Wife follow him that married her, that ſhe doth not offend him that made her. Wherefore as *Samſon*, though bound with new Cords, fnapt them afunder as Towe when it feeleth the fire; fo rather then we ſhould be led by the lewd examples of thoſe which be neere and deare unto us, let us breake in pieces all Tyes, Engagements, Relations whatſoever.

Queſtion: Yea but one may fay, What if I finde in the Scripture an action recorded, whoſe doer is knowne to have beene a godly and gracious man; may I not, without any further doubt or fcruple, follow the fame?

Anſwer: For the better fatisfying hereof, I will ranke the actions of godly men, regiſtred in the Scriptures, into nine feverall rankes, and will ſhew how farre forth we may fafely proceed in the imitation of them.

1. We finde fome actions fet downe which are extraordinary, the doers whereof had peculiar ſtrength and difpenfation from God to doe them. Thus *Samſon* flew himfelfe and the *Philiſtims* in the Temple of *Dagon; Elias* cauſed *fire* to defcend on the two Captaines and their fifties; *Eliſha* curſed the Children of *Bethel.* Now theſe are recorded rather for our inſtruction then imitation: For when the fonnes of *Thunder* would have been the fonnes of *Lightning,* and have had *fire from Heaven* to burne the *Samaritans* which refuſed to receive our Saviour, after the example of *Elias,* Chriſt checked their ill-tempered Zeale and told them, *You know not of what fpirit you are of.*

2. Some examples are fet down which are founded in the

Ceremonial Law, as the eating of the *Paschall Lamb*, the *Circumcising of their Children* the eight daie: Now the date of these did expire at the death of Christ; the substance being come, the shadows are fled, and therefore they may in no wise still be observed.

3. Such examples as are founded in the Judicial Law, which was onely calculated for the elevation of the Jewish Commonwealth, as to put Men to death for Adulterie. Now these examples tie us no farther to imitate them then they agree with the Moral Law, or with those Statutes by which every particular Countrie is Governed.

4. Some there be founded in no Law at all, but onely in an ancient custome by God tolerated and connived at, as Polygamie in the *Patriarks*, Divorces in the *Iewes* upon every slight occasion; from these also we must in these daies abstaine, as which were never liked or allowed by God, though permitted in some Persons and Ages, for some speciall reasons.

5. Doubtful examples which may so be termed, because it is difficult to decide whether the Actors of them therein did offend or no; so that should a Jurie of learned Writers be empannelled to passe their verdict upon them, they would be puzled whether to condemn or acquit them, and at length be forced to find it an *Ignoramus*; as whether *David* did well to dissemble himselfe frantick, thereby to escape the crueltie of *Achish* King of *Gath*. Now our most advised way herein is altogether to abstain from the imitation of them, because there is a deal of difficultie and danger, and our judgements may easilie be deceived.

6. Mixt examples, which containe in them a double action, the one good, the other bad, both so closely couched together, that it is a very hard thing to sever them: thus in the unjust Steward, there was his wisdome to provide for himselfe, and his wickednesse to purloyne from his Master: the first God did commend, we may imitate; the latter he could not but loath, we may not but shun. In the *Israelitish Midwives*, Exod. 1. 19, there was *fides mentis & fallacia mentientis:* the faith of their love, and the falsenesse of their lying: the first God rewarded, and we may follow; the latter he could not but dislike, and we must detest. Behold here is wisdome, and

let the Man that hath underſtanding diſcreetly divide betwixt the Droſſe and the Gold, the Chaffe and the Wheat in theſe mixt examples, that ſo they may practice the one, eſchew and avoid the other.

7. Thoſe which be abſolutely bad, that no charitable Comment can be faſtened upon them, as the drunkenneſs of *Noah*, the inceſt of *Lot*, the lying of *Abraham*, the ſwearing of *Ioſeph*, the adulterie of *David*, the denial of *Peter*: Now God forbid we ſhould imitate theſe; farre be it from us with King *Ahaz* to take a pattern from the Idolatrous Altar of *Damaſcus*: the Holy Spirit hath not ſet theſe ſinnes down with an intent they ſhould be followed; but firſt to ſhew the frailtie of his deareſt Saints when he leaves them to themſelves; as alſo to comfort us when we fall into grievous ſinnes, when we ſee that as haynous offences of Gods ſervants ſtand upon record in the Scripture.

8. Actions which are only good as they are qualified with ſuch a circumſtance, as *Davids* eating of the *Shew-bread* provided for the Prieſts, in a caſe of abſolute neceſſitie. Theſe we may follow, but then we muſt have a ſpeciall eye and care that the ſame qualifying circumſtance be in us, for otherwiſe the deed will be impious and damnable.

9. Examples abſolutely good, as the faithfulneſſe of *Abraham*, the peaceableneſſe of *Iſaac*, the painfulneſſe of *Iacob*, the chaſtitie of *Ioſeph*, the patience of *Moſes*, the valour of *Ioſhuah*, the ſinceritie of *David*; theſe it is lawful and laudable with our beſt endeavours to imitate: follow not the Adulterie of *David*, but follow the chaſtitie of *Ioſeph*; follow not the diſſembling of *Peter*, but follow the ſincerity of *Nathaniel*; follow not the teſtineſs of *Ionah*, but follow the meekneſſe of *Moſes*; follow not the apoſtaſie of *Orpah*, but follow the perſeverance of *Ruth*, which comes in the next Text to be Treated of.

Verſes 16, 17: *And* Ruth *anſwered, Intreat me not to leave thee, nor to depart from thee; for whither thou goeſt, I will goe; and where thou dwelleſt, I will dwell: thy people ſhall be my people, and thy God my God. Where thou dieſt, will I die, and there will I be buried; the Lord doe ſo to me, and more alſo, if ought but death part thee and me.*

Here we have the refolution of *Ruth* portrayed in lively Colours: fo that if we confider her Sex, a Woman; her Nation, a *Moabite;* one may boldly pronounce of her what our Saviour did of the Centurion, *Verily I fay unto you, I have not found fo great faith, no, not in Ifrael.*

Intreat me not to leave thee.] Some reade it, *Be not thou againft me,* as it is in the Margent of the New Tranflation. Where we fee that thofe are to be accounted our Adverfaries, and againft us, who diffwade us from our Voyage to *Canaan,* from going to Gods true Religion. They may be our Fathers, they cannot be our Friends; though they promife us all outward profits and pleafures, yet in very deed they are not with us, but againft us, and fo muft be accounted of.

Where thou lodgeft, I will lodge.] A good Companion, faith the *Latine* Proverb, is *pro viatico;* I may adde alfo, *pro diverforio: Ruth,* fo be it fhe may enjoy *Naomies* gracious companie, will be content with any Lodging, though happily [haply] it may be no better then *Iacob* had, *Gen.* 28. 11. And yet we fee how fome have been difcouraged even from the company of our Saviour, for feare of hard lodging; witneffe the Scribe, to whom when our Saviour faid, *The Foxes have their holes, and the Fowles of the ayre have nefts, but the Sonne of man hath not where to lay his head:* This cold comfort prefently quencht his forward zeale, and he never appeared afterward; whereas he ought to have faid to our Saviour as *Ruth* to *Naomi, Where thou lodgeft will I lodge.*

Thy people fhall be my people.] *Haman* being offended with *Mordecai,* as if it had been but leane and weak revenge to fpit his fpight upon one perfon, hated all the *Iewes* for *Mordecai's* fake: the mad Beare ftung with one Bee, would needs throw downe the whole Hive. But cleane contrarie, *Naomi* had fo gracioufly demeaned her felfe, that *Ruth* for her fake is fallen in love with all the *Iewes.* Farewell *Melchom,* farewell *Chemofh,* farewell *Moab;* welcome *Ifrael,* welcome *Canaan,* welcome *Bethlehem:* all of a fudden fhe will turne Convert, fhe will turne *Profelyte.*

Observation: The godly carriage of one particular person may beget a love of that Countrey and People whereof he is, even in a stranger and forreiner. Doe we then desire to gaine credit to our Countrey, prayse to our People, honour to our Nation, repute to our Religion? Let us deport and behave our selves graciously if we live amongst strangers. On the other side, the base and debauched manners of some one man is able to make his Countrey stink in the nostrils of those forreiners amongst whom he lives: *Ex uno discite omnes;* in one faithlesse *Sinon* one may reade the Trecherie of all the *Grecians*.

Thy God shall be my God.] *Jehosaphat* when he joyned with *Ahab*, 1 *Kings* 22. 4, said unto him, *My people is as thy people, and my horses are as thy horses;* that is, he would comply with him in a Politike League: but *Ruth* goes further to an unitie in Religion, *Thy God shall be my God.* Yea, but one may say, How came *Ruth* to know who was the God of *Naomi?* I answer: As God said of *Abraham, I know that* Abraham *will instruct his children;* so may one confidently say of *Naomi:* I know that *Naomi* had catechised and instructed her daughter in law, and often taught her that the God of the *Israelites* was the onely true God, who made Heaven and Earth, and that all others were but Idols, the workes of mens hands: Yet as the *Samaritans* beleeved our Saviour first upon the relation of the woman that came from the Well, but afterwards said unto her, *Iohn* 4. 42, *Now we beleeve, not because of thy saying; for we have heard him our selves and know that this is indeed the Christ, the Saviour of the world:* So happily *Ruth* was induced first to the liking of the God of *Israel*, upon the credit of *Naomies* words; but afterwards her love of him proceeded from a more certaine ground, the motions of Gods holy Spirit in her heart.

Where thou diest will I die.] Here *Ruth* supposeth two things: first, that she and her mother in law should both die; *It is appointed for all once to die:* secondly, that *Naomi*, as the eldest, should die first; for according to the ordinarie custome of Nature, it is most probable and likely that those that are most stricken in yeares should first depart this Life: Yet I know not whether the Rule or the Exceptions be more generall, and therefore let both young and old prepare for death; the firſt may die ſoone, but the ſecond cannot live long.

And there will I be buried.] Where ſhe ſuppoſeth two things more: Firſt, that thoſe that ſurvived her, would doe her the favour to burie her; which is a common courteſie, not to be denyed to any: It was an Epitaph written upon the Grave of a Beggar, *Nudus eram vivus, mortuus ecce tegor.* Secondly, ſhe ſuppoſeth that they would burie her, according to her inſtructions, neere to her mother *Naomi.*

Obſervation: As it is good to enjoy the companie of the godly while they are living, ſo it is not amiſſe, if it will ſtand with conveniencie, to be buried with them after death. The old Prophets bones eſcapt a burning, by being buried with the other Prophets; and the man who was tumbled into the Grave of *Eliſha,* was revived by the vertue of his bones. And we reade in the *Acts* and *Monuments,* that the body of *Peter Martyr's* Wife was buried in a Dunghill; but afterward being taken up in the Reigne of Queene *Elizabeth,* it was honourably buried in *Oxford,* in the Grave of one *Frideſwick,* a *Popiſh* ſhee-Saint; to this end, that if *Poperie,* which God forbid, ſhould over-ſpread our Kingdome againe, and if the *Papiſts* ſhould goe about to untombe *Peter Martyr's* Wives bones, they ſhould be puzzled to diſtinguiſh betwixt this womans body and the Reliques of their Saint. So, good it is ſometimes to be buried with thoſe who ſome doe account pious; though perchance in very deed they be not ſo.

The Lord doe ſo to me, and more alſo.] To aſcertaine *Naomi* of the ſeriouſneſſe of her intentions herein, *Ruth* backs what formerly ſhe had ſaid with an Oath, lined with an execration.

Obſervation: Whence we may gather, it is lawfull for us to ſweare upon a juſt cauſe: but then theſe three Rules muſt be warily obſerved.

Firſt, that we know that the thing whereto we ſweare be true, if the Oath be aſſertorie; and if it be promiſſorie, that we be sure that it is in our intent, and in our power, God blessing us, to performe that which we promise.

Secondly, that the occasion whereupon we use it, be of moment and consequence, not trifling and trivial.

Thirdly, that we sweare by God alone, and not by any Creature. Sweare then neither by the Heaven, nor by the Earth, nor by *Jerusalem*, nor by the Temple, nor by the Gold of the Temple, nor by the Altar, nor by the Sacrifice on the Altar, but by God alone; for he onely is able to reward thee, if that thou affirmest be true; he onely is able to punish thee, if that thou avouchest be false. Yet this doth no wayes favour the practice of many now adayes, who make Oathes their language. Our Saviour said to the *Jewes*, *Many good workes have I shewed you from the Father; for which of them goe you about to stone me?* So may the Lord say to many riotous Gallants now adayes; Many good deeds have I done to thee: I created thee of nothing; I sent my Sonne to die for thee; by my providence I continually protect and preserve thee: for which of these deeds doest thou goe about by Oathes to blaspheme me?

Now whereas *Ruth* does not say, *God damne me, God confound me, I would I might never stirre;* but shrowds the execration under generall termes, *God doe so to me, and more also:* we learne, it is not good to particularize in any kinde of punishment when we sweare, but onely to expresse the Curse in generall termes, leaving it to the discretion of God Almightie, to chuse that Arrow out of his Quiver which he shall thinke most fit to shoot at us.

If ought but death.] See here the large extent of a Saints love, it lasts till death; and no wonder, for it is not founded upon Honour, Beautie, or Wealth, or any other sinister respect in the partie beloved, which is subject to Age, or Mutabilitie, but onely on the Grace and Pietie in him; which foundation because it alwayes lasteth, that Love which is built upon it is also perpetuall.

Part thee and me.] Death is that which parteth one friend from another: Then the deare Father must part with his dutifull Child, then the dutifull Child muſt forgoe his deare Father; then the kinde Husband muſt leave his conſtant Wife, then the conſtant Wife muſt loſe her kinde Husband; then the carefull Maſter muſt be ſundred from his induſtrious Servant, then the induſtrious Servant muſt be ſevered from his carefull Maſter. Yet this may be ſome comfort to thoſe whoſe friends Death hath taken away, that as our Saviour ſaid to the Diſciples, *Yet a little while and you ſhall not ſee me, and yet a little while and you ſhall ſee me againe:* ſo yet a little while, and we ſhall not ſee our friends; and yet a little while, and we ſhall ſee them againe in the Kingdome of Heaven; for, *non mittuntur, ſed præmittuntur*, we doe not forgoe them, but they goe before us.

To conclude: we ſee many women ſo ſtrangely diſguiſed with phantaſtick faſhions, as if they deſired to verifie the nickname of the Philoſopher, and to prove themſelves in very deed to be very Monſters; yea, many of them ſo affect Man--like Clothes and ſhorne Haire, it is hard to diſcover the Sex of a Woman through the Attire of a Man. But we ſee in my Text worthy *Ruth* taking upon her, not the Clothes, but the Courage; not the Haire, but the Heart; not the Attire, but the Reſolution of a Man, yea, and more then of a Man, witneſſe her worthy ſpeech, *Intreat me not to depart, &c.*

Verſe 18: *And when ſhe ſaw that ſhe was ſtedfaſtly minded to goe with her, ſhe left off ſpeaking unto her.*

Orpah and *Ruth* may be compared to two ſtrong Forts, *Naomi* to one that beſieged them, who made three ſore Aſſaults upon them: The firſt, in the eighth Verſe; which Aſſault both of them reſiſted with equall conſtancie: The ſecond, in the eleventh Verſe; to which *Orpah* baſely yeeldeth, and accepteth termes of Compoſition: The laſt, in the fifteenth Verſe; which *Ruth* moſt valiantly defeated, and ſtood upon termes of Defiance to the mention of any returne. Now as ſouldiers when they have long beſieged a Citie with the loſſe of Time, Money, and Men, being hopeleſſe to take it, they even found a Retreat, and retire home, without accompliſhing their deſire: ſo *Naomi* perceiving that all her arguments which she used to conquer *Ruth*, like Water in the Smiths Forge cast on Coales, did more intend the heat of her constancie, gives over in my Text, *And when she saw, &c.*

Which words doe probably perswade what formerly we affirmed, namely, that *Naomi* disswaded her daughter, onely to search and found her sinceritie, not with any true desire she should goe back to *Moab*. For even as it is plaine, that the Replyer in his Disputation aimeth not at the suppressing, but at the advancing of a Truth, who surceaseth and cavills no longer when he sees the neck of his argument broken with a sufficient answer; so it appeareth that *Naomi*, what she had said formerly, spake it onely to trie her daughter, because having now had sufficient experience of her constancie, she so willingly desisted. God wrestled with *Jacob*, with a desire to be conquer'd; so *Naomi* no doubt opposed *Ruth*, hoping and wishing that she her selfe might be foiled.

And when she saw that she was stedfastly minded.] The Hebrew reades it, *that she strengthned her self*; that being their phrase to expresse an Oath.

Observation: Where we observe, Oaths taken upon just occasion are excellent Ties and Bands to strengthen men in the performance of those things to which they sweare. The greater pittie it is then that a thing in it selfe so soveraigne should be so dayly and dangerously abused. Witnesse *Herod*, who by reason of a rash Oath cast himselfe into a worse Prison then that wherein he had put the *Baptist*, making that (which being well used might have confirmed in Pietie) to be a meanes to inforce him to Murther.

Use: Let this teach us, when we finde our selves to lagge and faulter in Christianitie, to call to minde that solemne Vow, Promise, and Profession, which our God-fathers in our Name made for us at our Baptisme, *To forsake the Devill and all his workes, the vaine pompes and vanities of this wicked world, and to fight valiantly under Christs Standard.* Let us remember from whence we are fallen, and doe our first worke. We need not make a new Vow, but only renew the old, and so settle and establish our selves in the practice of Pietie, as *Ruth* in my Text by an Oath strengthned her selfe.

She left off speaking unto her.] She saw she had now enough expressed and declared her integritie, and therefore she would not put her to the trouble of any farther tryall.

Observation: Hence the Doctrine is this: After proofe and tryall made of their fidelitie, we are to trust our Brethren, without any farther suspition. Not to trie before we trust, is want of wisdome; not to trust after we have tryed, is want of charitie. The Gold-smith must purifie the drosse and oare from the Gold, but he must be warie left he make waste of good Metall, if over-curious in too often refining. We may search and found the sinceritie of our Brethren, but after good experience made of their uprightnesse, we must take heed left by continuall sifting and proving them, we offend a weak Christian. Christ tryed the woman of *Syrophænicia* first with silence, then with two sharpe answers; at last finding her to be found he dismissed her with granting her request and commending of her faith. When he had said to *Peter* the third time, *Lovest thou me?* he rested satisfied with *Peters* answer and troubled him with no more questions.

Use: It may confute the jealous and suspitious mindes of such who still thinke that their Brethren are rotten at the heart, hypocritical, dissemblers, though they have made never so manifest proofe of their uprightnesse. *Thomas* would not take his Masters Resurrection on the Credit of his fellow-Apostles relation; his faith would not follow except his owne sense was the Usher to lead it the way: so these men are altogether incredulous, and very Infidels in the point of their Brethrens sinceritie, though it be never so surely warranted unto them on the words of those whom they ought to beleeve. Hence oftentimes it comes to passe, that they scandalize and offend many weake Christians, whose Graces are true, though weake; Faith unfained, though feeble: Yea, it maketh weake Saints to be jealous of themselves, to see others so jealous of them. But we must be wonderfull carefull how we give offence to any of Gods *little ones.* When *Esau, Gen.* 33. 13, would have perswaded *Jacob* to drive on faster, *Jacob* excused himselfe, saying, *That the Children were tender, and the Ewes big with young; and if they should be over-driven one day, they would die.* Thus if any would perswade us to sift and winnow, and trie the integritie of our Brethren, after long experience of them, we may anfwer, This is dangerous to be done, becaufe *fmoaking Flax* and *bruifed Reeds*, tender Profeffors, may utterly be difcouraged and dif-heartened by our reftleffe preffing and difquieting of them. Wherefore *Naomi*, having now feene the Realitie of *Ruths* Refolutions, left off from any further molefting of her.

Verfes 19 to 22: *So they went both untill they came to* Bethlehem; *and when they came to* Bethlehem, *all the Citie was moved at them, and they faid, Is not this* Naomi? *And fhe faid, Call me not* Naomi, *but call me* Marah; *for the Lord hath dealt bitterly with me. I went out full, and the Lord hath caufed me to returne emptie; why call you me* Naomi, *fithence the Lord hath teftified againft me, and the Almightie hath afflicted me? So* Naomi *returned, and* Ruth *the* Moabiteffe, *her Daughter in law, with her, when fhe came out of the Countrey of* Moab; *and they came to* Bethlehem *in the beginning of Barley Harveft.*

The holy Spirit mentioneth not what difcourfe they exchanged by the way; yet no doubt they were neither filent nor bufied in unprofitable talke.

And all the Citie was moved, &c.] See here, *Naomi* was formerly a woman of good qualitie and fafhion, of good ranke and repute; otherwife her returne in povertie had not been fo generally taken notice of. Shrubs may be grubb'd to the ground, and none miffe them, but every one markes the felling of a Cedar. Groveling Cottages may be evened to the Earth, and none obferve them; but every Traveller takes notice of the fall of a Steeple. Let this comfort thofe to whom God hath given fmall Poffeffions. Should he vifit them with povertie, and take from them that little they have, yet their griefe and fhame would be the leffe: they fhould not have fo many fingers pointed at them, fo many eyes ftaring on them, fo many words fpoken of them; they might lurke in obfcuritie: it muft be a *Naomi*, a perfon of eminency and eftate, whofe povertie muft move a whole Citie.

And they said, Is not this Naomi ?] Remarkable it is that so many people should jump in the same expression; but as *Abraham* laughed, and *Sarah* laughed, both used the same outward gesture, yet arising from different causes; his laughter from joy, her's from distrust: so all these people might meet in the same forme of words, yet farre dissent in their minds wherewith they spake them. Some might speak out of admiration: *Strange, wonderfull! Is this she who once was so wealthie? How quickly is a River of Riches drained drie! She that formerly was so faire, now one can scarce read the ruines of beauty in her face: Is not this* Naomi? Some out of exprobation: *See, see, this is she that could not be content to tarry at home to take part of the Famine with the rest of her fellows, but needs, with her Husband and Sons, must be gadding to* Moab: *see what good she hath got by removing; by changing her Country, she hath changed her Condition: Is not this* Naomi? Some might speak it out of Commiseration: *Alas, alas, Is not this that gracious woman, that godly Saint, which formerly by her Charity relieved many in distresse? How soon is a full clod turned into parched earth! one that supplied others, into one that needeth to be supplied by others!* Is not this *Naomi?*

And she said, call me not Naomi, *but call me* Marah.] *Naomi* signifieth *Beautifull*; Marah, *Bitter*, Exod. 15. 23, where we see, that the Godly in povertie are unwilling to have Names and Titles, disagreeing and disproportioned to their present estates; which may confute the folly of many, which being in distress, and living little better then-upon the alms of others, will still stand upon their points, bear themselves bravely on their birth, not lose an inch of their place, not abate an ace of their gentrie. Far otherwise was *Naomi* affected, being poor, she would not be over-named, or Title-heavie: *Call me not* Naomi, *but call me* Marah.

Observation: Here also we may see, that it was a custome of great Antiquitie in the World, that Men and Women should have severall names whereby they were called, and that for these three Reasons.

1. That they might be differenced and distinguished from others.

2. That they might be ftirred up to verifie the meanings and fignifications of their names: wherefore let every *Obadiah* ftrive to be a fervant of God, each *Nathaniel* to be a gift of God, *Onefimus* to be profitable, every *Roger* quiet and peaceable, *Robert* famous for counfell, and *William* a help and defence to many; not like *Abfalon*, who was not a Father of Peace, as his name doth import, but a fonne of Sedition; and *Diotrephes*, not nurfed by God, as his name founds, but puffed up by the Devill, as it is 3 *John* 9.

3. That they might be incited to imitate the vertues of thofe worthy perfons, who formerly have been bearers and owners of their names. Let all *Abrahams* be faithfull, *Ifaacs* quiet, *Jacobs* painfull, *Jofephs* chafte; every *Lewis* pious, *Edward* confeffor of the true faith, *William* conqueror over his own corruptions. Let them alfo carefully avoid thofe finnes for which the bearers of the Names ftand branded to pofteritie. Let every *Jonah* beware of frowardnefs, *Thomas* of diftruftfulneffe, *Martha* of worldlinefs, *Mary* of wantonneffe. If there be two of our names, one exceedingly good, the other notoriously evill, let us decline the vices of the one, and practife the vertues of the other. Let every *Judas* not follow *Judas Ifcariot*, who betrayed our Saviour, but *Iudas* the brother of *Iames*, the writer of the generall Epiftle; each *Demetrius*, not follow him in the Acts who made filver fhrines for *Diana*, but *Demetrius*, 3 *Iohn* 12, who had a good report of all men. Every *Ignatius* not imitate *Ignatius Loiola* the lame Father of blind obedience, but *Ignatius* the worthy Martyr in the *Primitive Church*. And if it fhould chance through the indifcretion of Parents and Godfathers, that a bad name fhould be impofed on any; oh let not folly be with them, becaufe *Nabal* is their name; but in fuch a cafe, let them ftrive to falfifie, difprove, and confute their names; otherwife if they be good, they muft anfwer them.

In the dayes of Q. *Elizabeth*, there was a Royall Ship called the *Revenge*, which having maintained a long fight againft a Fleet of *Spaniards*, (wherein eight hundred great Shot were difcharged againft her,) was at laft faine to yeeld: but no fooner were her men gone out of her, and two hundred frefh

Spaniards come into her, but fhe fuddenly funke them and her felfe; and fo the *Revenge* was revenged. Shall liveleffe pieces of Wood anfwer the Names which men impofe upon them, and fhall not reafonable foules doe the fame? But of all Names, I pray God that never juft occafion be given that we be Chriftened *Iccabod*, but that the glory may remaine in our *Ifrael* fo long as the faithful Witneffe endureth in Heaven. And fo much of thofe words, *Call me not* Naomi, *but &c.*

For the Lord hath dealt bitterly with me.] Afflictions rellifh foure and bitter even to the pallats of the beft Saints.

Obfervation: Now bitter things are obferved in Phyfick to have a double operation: firft, to ftrengthen and corroborate the Liver; and fecondly, to cleanfe and wipe away Choler, which cloggeth the ftomack: both thefe effects afflictions by their bitterneffe produce; they ftrengthen the inward Vitals of a Chriftian, his Faith and Patience, and cleanfe Gods Saints from thofe fuperfluous excrements which the furfeit of Profperitie hath caufed in them. It may therefore ferve to comfort fuch as groane under Gods afflicting hand, *Hebrews* 12. 11. The book which S. *Iohn* eat, *Rev.* 10. 10, was *fweet* in his mouth, but *bitter* in his belly: cleane contrarie, afflictions are bitter in the mouth, but fweet in the belly; God by fanctifying them, extracting Honey out of Gall, and Sugar out of Wormewood. And let it teach us alfo, not to wonder if the Children of God winch and fhrug, and make foure faces, when afflicted: Wonder not at *David*, if he *cryeth out* in the *anguifh of his heart*; at *Iob*, if he *complaineth* in the *bitterneffe of his foule*; at *Ieremiah*, if he *lamenteth* in the *extremitie of his griefe*: For even then they are fwallowing of a Potion which is bitter unto flefh and blood.

I went out full, and the Lord hath caufed me to returne emptie.] Here may we fee the uncertaintie of all outward wealth.

Obfervation: How quickly may a *Craffus*, or *Crœfus*, be turned into a *Codrus*; the richeft, into the pooreft of men! Whom the Sunne-rifing feeth in wealth, him the Sunne-fetting may fee in want. Set not up then your hornes fo high, neither fpeake prefumptuous words, ye wealthie men; for God, if it pleafeth him, can in a moment difpoffeffe you of all your Riches. And let us all *not lay up Treafures here on Earth, where Ruft and Mothes doe corrupt, and Theeves breake through and fteale; but lay up your Treafure in Heaven, where Ruft and Moth doe not corrupt, and Theeves doe not breake through and fteale.*

Why call you me Naomi, *fithence the Lord, &c.*] The mention of their former Wealth is grievous to the godly when they are in prefent Povertie.

Obfervation: When the Children of *Ifrael* are Captives in *Babylon*, it cuts them to the heart to be twitted with the Songs of *Sion*. And it may teach this point of wifdome to fuch as repaire to give comfort to men in affliction, not to mention that tedious and ingratefull fubject, what happineffe that partie formerly enjoyed. Summe not up to *Job* in diftreffe the number of his Camels, tell not his Sheepe, reckon not his Oxen, reade not unto him an Inventorie of thofe Goods whereof he before was poffeffed; for this will but adde to his vexation: rather defcend to apply folid and fubftantial comfort unto him.

Sithence the Lord hath teftified againft me, and the Almightie hath afflicted me?] Every affliction is a witneffe that God is angry with us for our finnes.

Obfervation: Who then is able to hold out Suit with God in the Court of Heaven? For God himfelfe is both Judge and Witneffe, and alfo the executor and inflicter of punifhments. It is therefore impoffible for finfull man to plead with him; and it is our moft advifed courfe, as foone as may be, to come to termes of compofition with him, and to make meanes unto him through the mediation of our Saviour. Now that all afflictions are immediately inflicted by God we have fhewed formerly [pages 8 *feq*., and 18].

And they came to Bethlehem *in the beginning of Barly Harveft.*] The *Iewes* had two diftinct Harvefts of Wheat and Barly, and Barly was the firft, 2 *Sam.* 21. 9. So here we fee the providence of God in ordering and difpofing the Journey of *Naomi*, to end it in the moft convenient time. Had fhe come before Harveft, fhe would have been ftraitned for meanes to maintaine her felfe; if after Harveft, *Ruth* had loft all thofe occafions which paved the way to her future advancement. God therefore, who ordered her going, concludes her Journey in the beginning of Harveft.

And thus have we gone over this Chapter. Now as *Samuel* in the firft Booke, *chap.* 7. *verf.* 12, erected an Altar, and called it *Eben-ezer*, for, faid he, *Hitherto the Lord hath helped us*: fo here may I rayfe an Altar of Gratitude unto God with the fame infcription, *Eben-ezer, Hitherto the Lord of his goodneffe hath affifted us.*

CHAP. II.

Verſes 1, 2: *And* Naomi *had a kinſman of her Husbands, a mighty man of wealth, of the Family of* Elimelech, *and his name was* Boaz. *And* Ruth *the* Moabiteſſe *ſaid unto* Naomi, *I pray thee let me go into the field, and gather ears of Corne after him in whoſe fight I find favour : and ſhe ſaid unto her,* Goe, *my Daughter.*

This firſt Verſe preſents us with two remarkable things.
 1. Poore *Naomi* was allied to powerful *Boaz*.
 2. *Boaz* was both a powerful man and a Godly man.
Of the firſt. Poore people may be allied and of great kindred to thoſe that are wealthy ; and thoſe that be wealthy, to ſuch as are poor. *Ioſeph*, though Governour of *Egypt*, had poor *Iacob* to his Father, and plain ſhepheards to his brethren. *Eſther*, though Queene to *Ahaſhuerus*, hath poore *Mordecai* for her Uncle.

Uſe 1 : Let this confute ſuch as having gotten a little more thick clay then the reſt of their Family, the getting of new wealth and honour makes them to loſe their old eyes, ſo that they cannot ſee and diſcern their poor kindred afterwards. When *Ioſeph* was Governour of *Egypt*, it is ſaid that he knew his brethren, but his brethren knew not him; but now adayes it happeneth cleane contrary. If one of a Family be advanced to great honour, it is likely that his kindred will know him, but he oftentimes comes to forget them. Few there be of the noble nature of the Lord *Cromwel*, who fitting at Dinner

E

with the Lords of the Council, and chancing to see a poor man afar off which used to sweep the Cells and the Cloisters, called for the man, and told the Lords, This mans Father hath given me many a good meale, and he shall not lack so long as I live.[1]

Use 2 : Let it teach those who are the top of their kindred, the best of their House, to be thankful to Gods gracious goodnesse who hath raised them to such a height. He hath not dealt thus with every one, neither are all of their kindred so well provided for outward maintenance. And also let them learn to be bountiful and beneficial to their kindred in distress. *Mordecai* said to *Esther*, Esth. 4. 14, *Who knoweth whether thou art come to the Kingdom for such a time?* namely, to deliver her Country-men the Jews from that imminent danger.

So who knoweth whether God hath raised thee up, who art the best of thy kindred, to this very intent, that thou mightest be the Treasure and the Storehouse to supplie the want of others which are allied unto thee? But if one should chance to be of so wealthy a stock, as that none of his alliance stood in need of his charity; let such a one cast his eye upon such as are of kindred unto him by his second birth, and so he shall find enough Widows, Orphans, and poor Christians, to receive his liberalitie.

Notwithstanding, let poor people be warie and discreet, that through their idlenesse they be not a burthen to wealthie men of their alliance. When a Husband-man claimed kindred in *Grosted Bishop* of *Lincoln*, and would fain on the instant turn a Gentleman, and to this end requested his Lordship to bestow an office upon him: the *Bishop* told him, that if his *Plough* were broken, he would mend it; if he wanted a *Plough*, he would make him a new one; telling him withall, that he should by no means leave that Calling and Vocation wherein God had set him. So ought all poor people industriously to take pains for themselves, and not to give themselves over to ease, relying and depending for their maintenance on their reference and relation to a rich kinsman.

Come we now to the second Observation, That the same

---

[1] *Fox*, page 1188.

man may be godly, and alfo mighty in wealth, like *Boaz*. Behold your Calling; not many wife, yet fome wife, as *Salomon*, and *Sergius* Deputie of *Cyprus*; not many rich, yet fome rich, as *Abraham*, *Iob*; not many noble, yet fome noble, as *Theophilus*. For it is not the having of wealth, but the having confidence in wealth; not the poffeffing it, but the relying on it, which makes rich men incapable of the Kingdome of *Heaven*: otherwife Wealth well ufed is a great bleffing, enabling the owner to do God more glorie, the Church and Common-Wealth more good.

Ufe: Let all Wealthie men ftrive to add inward grace unto their outward greatnefs. Oh 'tis excellent when *Ioafh* and *Iehoiada* meet together; when *Prince* and *Prieft*, *Power* and *Pietie* are united in the fame perfon; that fo Greatneffe may be feafoned and fanctified by Grace, and Grace credited and countenanced by Greatneffe; that fo *Kings* may be *Nurfing--Fathers*, and *Queenes Nurfing-Mothers* to Gods Church. Contrarie to which, how many be there, that thinke themfelves priviledged from being good, becaufe they are great! Confining Pietie to Hofpitals; for their owne parts they difdaine fo bafe a Companion. Hence as Hills, the higher, the barrener; fo men commonly, the wealthier, the worfe; the more Honour, the leffe Holineffe. And as Rivers, when content with a fmall Channel, runne fweet and cleare; when fwelling to a Navigable Channel, by the confluence of feverall Tributarie Rivulets, gather mudde and mire, and grow falt and brackifh, and violently beare downe all before them; fo many men, who in meane Eftates have been Pious and Religious, being advanced in Honour and inlarged in Wealth, have growne both empious and prophane towards God, cruell and tyrannicall over their Brethren.

And Ruth *the* Moabiteffe *faid unto* Naomi, *I pray thee let me goe into the field, and gather eares of Corne, &c.*] Herein two excellent Graces appeare in *Ruth*.

Firft, Obedience; fhe would not goe to gleane without the leave of her Mother in law. Verily I fay unto you, I have not found fo much dutie, no, not in naturall Daughters to their owne Mothers. How many of them now-adayes, in matters of more moment, will betroth and contract themselves, not onely without the knowledge and confent, but even againft the expreffe Commands of their Parents!

Secondly, fee her Induftrie, that fhe would condefcend to gleane. Though I thinke not, with the *Iewifh Rabbins*, that *Ruth* was the Daughter to *Eglon*, King of *Moab*; yet no doubt fhe was defcended of good Parentage; and now fee, faine to gleane. Whence we may gather, that thofe that formerly have had good birth, and breeding, may afterward be forced to make hard fhifts to maintaine themfelves. *Mufculus* was forced to wórke with a Weaver, and afterwards was faine to delve in the Ditch, about the Citie of *Strafburgh*; as *Pantalion* in his Life. Let this teach even thofe whofe veines are wafhed with generous bloud, and arteries quickned with Noble fpirits, in their profperitie to furnifh, qualifie, and accommodate themfelves with fuch Gentile Arts, and liberall Myfteries, as will be neither blemifh nor burthen to their birth; that fo if hereafter God fhall caft them into povertie, thefe Arts may ftand them in fome ftead, towards their maintenance and reliefe.

And Naomi *faid, Goe, my Daughter.*] See here how meekely and mildly fhe anfwers her. The difcourfe of Gods Children, in their ordinarie talke, ought to be kinde and courteous: So betwixt *Abraham* and *Ifaac, Gen.* 22. 7; betwixt *Elkanah* and *Hannah*, 1 *Sam.* 1. 23. Indeed it is lawfull and neceffarie for *Jacob* to chide *Rachel* fpeaking unadvifedly, *Gen.* 30. 2; for *Job* to fay to his Wife, *Thou fpeakeft like a foolifh Wife.* But otherwife, when no juft occafion of anger is given, their words ought to be meeke and kinde like *Naomies, Goe, my Daughter.*

Verfes 3 and 4: *And fhe went, and came and gleaned in the field after the Reapers; and it happened that fhe met with the portion of the field of* Boaz, *who was of the family of* Elimelech. *And behold,* Boaz *came from* Bethlehem, *and faid unto the Reapers, The Lord be with you; and they anfwered him, The Lord bleffe thee.*

Formerly we have feene the dutifulneffe of *Ruth*, which would not leave her Mother untill fhe had leave from her Mother: Proceed we now to her induftrie, and Gods providence over her. As the *Starre, Math.* 2. 9, guided the *Wife-men* to *Iudea*, to *Bethlehem*, to the *Inne*, to the *Stable*, to the *Manger*: fo the rayes and beames of Gods Providence conducted *Ruth*, that of all Grounds within the compaffe and confines, within the bounds and borders of *Bethlehem*, fhe lighted on the field of *Boaz*.

And it happened.] *Objection*: How comes the holy Spirit to ufe this word; a prophane terme, which deferves to be banifht out of the mouthes of all Chriftians? Are not all things ordered by Gods immediate Providence, without which a *Sparrow lighteth not on the ground*? Is not that fentence moft true, *God ftretcheth from end to end ftrongly, and difpofeth all things fweetly*? *Strongly*, Lord, *for thee*; *fweetly*, Lord, *for me*: fo S. Bernard. Or was the Providence of God folely confined to his people of *Ifrael*, fo that *Ruth* being a ftranger of *Moab*, muft be left to the adventure of hazard? How comes the holy Spirit to ufe this word, *Hap*?

Anfwer: Things are faid to happen, not in refpect of God, but in refpect of us; becaufe oftentimes they come to paffe, not onely without our purpofe and fore-caft, but even againft our intentions and determinations. It is lawfull therefore in a fober fenfe to ufe thefe expreffions, *It chanced*, or, *It fortuned, Luke* 10. 31. Nor can any juft exception be taken againft thofe words in the Collect, *Through all Changes and Chances of this mortall life*: Provided alwayes, that in our formes of fpeech we dreame not of any Heathen Chance. It is obferved, that τυχὴ is not ufed in all the Workes of *Homer*; but fure S. *Auftine* in the firft of his *Retractationes*, complaineth, that he had too often ufed the word *Fortuna*; and therefore in the *Pagans* fenfe thereof we ought to abftaine from it.

Obfervation: Now whereas *Ruth* by chance lighteth on *Boaz* his field, we may obferve: Admirable is the providence of God in the ordering of contingent events to his glory and his Childrens good. The Scripture fwarmeth with

Presidents in this behalfe, which at this time I surcease to recite, and conclude with the *Psalmist*; *O Lord, how wonderfull are thy workes! in wisdome hast thou made them all; the Earth is full of thy Riches.* To which I may adde; *Oh that men would therefore prayse the Name of the Lord, and shew forth the wonderfull workes that he doth for the children of men!*

And behold, Boaz *came unto his Reapers.*] He had a man over them, yet himselfe came to over-see them.

Observation: Where note: it is the part of a thriving Husband not to trust the care of his affairs to his servants, but to over-see them himselfe. *The Masters eye maketh a fat Horse:* and one asking, what was the best compost to Manure Land, it was answered, *the dust of the Masters feet;* meaning his presence to behold his own businefs. *Hushai* would not councell *Absolon* to let *Achitophel* goe with his Armie, but advised him, *Thou shalt goe to battel in thine own person.* However he herein had a secret intent, yet thus farre the proportion holds: Things thrive best, not when they are committed to Surrogates, Deputies, Delegates, and Substitutes; but when men themselves over-see them. Let Masters therefore of Families carefully attend on their own businesse; and let the Daughters of *Sarah,* whom the meekneffe of their Sex hath priviledged from following without-doors affairs, imitate the wife woman, *Proverbs* 31. 15, 27, *She rises whiles as yet it is night, and giveth her meat to her Houshold, and their portions to her Maids: She looks well to all the wayes of her Houshold, and eateth not the bread of idleneffe.* And such servants which have careleffe Masters, let them look better to their Masters estate then their Masters do to their own: let them be neither idle nor unfaithfull in their place, knowing *that though their earthly Master be negligent to eye them, yet they have a Master in heaven who both beholds and will punish, or reward them according to their deserts.* And as for the Sons of the *Prophets,* let them feed the Flock over which they are placed, and not thinke to shuffle and shift off their care to their Curates and Readers in their own unneceffary absence; and yet how many are there that Preach as seldome as *Apollo* laughs, once in the yeare: Indeed *Eliah* fasted forty dayes and forty nights in the strength of one meale; but surely these think that their people can hold out fasting a twelve-moneth. Well, let them practise *Boaz* example; as they have Curates, so had he one to care for his affairs; and yet behold in person he comes forth unto his Reapers.

And said unto them, The Lord be with you.] Observe, Curteous and loving salutations beseeme Christians: indeed our Saviour, *Luke* 10. 4, forbade his Disciples to salute any in the way; but his meaning was, that they should not lag or delay whereby to be hindred from the service wherein they were imployed; and S. *John* in his second Epistle (verse 10), saith, *That to some we must not say God speed, lest we be made partakers of their evill deeds;* but that is meant of notorious sinners, which have discovered their impious intents. It is commonly said that the *Small Pox* is not infectious untill it be broken out, so that before the time one may safely converse, eat, drinke, lie with them; but after the Pox is broken out it is very dangerous: So we may safely salute and exchange discourse with the most wicked sinners, whiles yet they smoother and conceale their bad designes; but when once they declare and expresse them, then it is dangerous to have any further familiarity with them; for such *Marcions*, the first born of the Devill, and the eldest Sonne of Satan, are salutations good enough.

Use: Those are justly to be reproved, which lately have changed all hearty expressions of love into verball Complements, which Etymologie is not to be deduced a *completione mentis*, but a *complete mentiri*. And yet I cannot say that these men lie in their throat, for I perswade my selfe, their words never came so neare their heart, but meerly they lie in their mouths, where all their promises

Both birth and burial in a breath they have;
That mouth which is their womb, it is their grave.

Yea, those words which S. *Paul* to the *Corinthians* thought to be the most affectionate expression of love, is now made the word of course, commonly bandied betwixt superficial friends at the firſt encounter: *Your Servant.* Worſe then theſe are the ambitious Saluters like *Abſolon,* 2 Sam. 15. 4, who at the ſame time, by taking his Fathers Subjects by their hands, ſtole away their hearts; and the lower his bodie did couch, the higher his mind did aſpire. Worſt of all is the treacherous ſalutation of *Judas* and *Joab,* who at one inſtant pretend lip-love, and intend heart-hatred; who both kiſſe and kill; embrace another with their hands, and imbrew their hands in his blood whom they embrace.

And they anſwered him, The Lord bleſſe thee.] When one offers us a curteſie, eſpecially being our ſuperiour, it is fitting we ſhould requite him. It is a noble conqueſt for to be overcome with wrongs; but it is a ſigne of a degenerous nature to be out-vied with courteſies; and therefore if one begin a kindneſſe to us, let us (if it lie in our power pledge) him in the ſame nature.

Verſes 5 to 7 : *And* Boaz *ſaid unto the ſervant which was appointed over the Reapers, Whose is this Maid? And the ſervant which was appointed over the Reapers anſwered and ſaid, This is the* Moabitiſh *Maid which came with* Naomi *from the Countrey of* Moab; *which came and ſaid, Let me gather I pray among the ſheaves after the Reapers; and ſo ſhe came and ſtayed here from morning untill now; onely ſhe tarried a little in the houſe.*

And Boaz *ſaid unto the ſervant which was appointed over the Reapers.*] Here we learne, that it is a part of good Husbandry in a numerous Family, to have one ſervant as Steward, to over-ſee the reſt. Thus *Abraham* had his *Eliezer* of *Damaſcus*; *Potiphar* his *Joſeph, Joſeph* his man which put the Cup into *Benjamin's* Sack; *Ahab* his *Obadiah*; *Hezekiah* his *Eliakim,* the ſonne of *Hilkiah.*

Obſervation: Let Maſters therefore, in chuſing theſe Stewards to be ſet above the reſt, take ſuch as are qualified like *Jethro's* deſcription of inferiour Judges, *Exod.* 18. 21, *men of courage, fearing God, dealing truly, hating covetousneſſe.* And how-ever they privilege them to be above the reſt of their servants, yet let them make them to know their dutie and their distance to their Masters, lest that come to passe which *Solomon* fore-telleth, *Prov.* 29. 21, *He that bringeth up his servant delicately in his youth, will make him like his sonne at the last.* Let Stewards not be like that unjust one in the Gospel, who made his Masters Debtors write down fiftie measures of Wheat, and fourescore measures of Oyle, when both severally should have been an hundred; but let them carefully discharge their Conscience in that Office wherein they are placed: whilest inferiour servants that are under their command must neither grieve nor grudge to obey them, nor envie at their honour: But let this comfort those underlings, that if they be wronged by these Stewards, their Appeale lyes open from them to their Master, who if good will no doubt redresse their grievances.

Now if Stewards be necessarie in ordering of Families, surely men in authoritie are more necessarie in governing the Church and managing the Commonwealth. If a little Cock-Boat cannot be brought up a Tributarie Rivulet without one to guide it; how shall a Caravan, a Gallioun, or Argosie, sayling in the vast Ocean, be brought into a Harbor without a Pilot to conduct it? Let us therefore with all willingnesse and humilitie submit our selves to our Superiours, that so under them we may live a peaceable life in all godlinesse and honestie.

Whose is this Maid?] *Boaz* would know what those persons were that gleaned upon his Land; and good reason: for we ought not to prostitute our liberalitie to all, though unknowne; but first we must examine who and whence they be; otherwise that which is given to worthlesse persons is not given, but throwne away. I speake not this to blunt the Charitie of any who have often bestowed their benevolence upon Beggars unknowne and unseene before; but if easily and with conveniencie (as *Boaz* could) they may attaine to know the qualities and conditions of such persons, before they dispose their liberalitie unto them.

And the servant which was appointed.] He herein performed the part of a carefull fervant, namely, fully to informe his Mafter. Servants ought fo to inftruct themfelves as thereby to be able to give an account to their Lords when they fhall be called thereunto, and give them plenarie fatisfaction and contentment in any thing belonging to their Office, wherein they fhall be queftioned. Now, whereas he doth not derogate or detract from *Ruth*, though a ftranger, but fets her forth with her due commendation ; we gather, Servants when asked ought to give the pure character of poore people to their Mafters, and no way to wrong or traduce them.

Which came and faid, Let me gather I pray.] See here *Ruths* honeftie ; fhe would not prefume to gleane before fhe had leave. Cleane contrarie is the practice of poore people now-adayes, which oft times take away things not onely without the knowledge, but even againft the will of the owners. The Boy of the Prieft, 1 *Sam.* 2. 16, when the sacrifice was in offering, used to come with a *flefh hooke of three teeth*, and ufed to caft it into the fat of the Sacrifice, making that his Fee which fo he fetcht out; if any gain-fay'd him, he anfwered, *Thou fhalt give it me now ; or if thou wilt not, I will take it by force.* Thus poore people now-adayes, they caft their hooke, their violent hands (gleaning the leane will not content them) into the fat, the beft and principall of rich mens Eftates; and breaking all Lawes of God and the King, they by maine force draw it unto themfelves. Not fo *Ruth ;* fhe would not gleane without leave.

And ftayed here from morning untill now.] See here her conftancie in Induftrie : Many are very diligent at the firft fetting forth, for a fit and a gird, for a fnatch and away ; but nothing violent is long permanent : They foone are tyred, quickly wearie, and then turne from labour to lazineffe. But *Ruth* continued in her labour *from the morning till now ;* till Night, till the end of the Harveft. O that we would imitate the conftancie of *Ruth* in the *working out of our falvation with feare and trembling!* Not onely to be induftrious in the *Morning*, when we firft enter into Chriftianitie, but to hold out and to *perfevere even to the end of our lives.*

Onely she tarried a little in the house.] No doubt some indispensable businesse detained her there; and probable it is, that a principall one was, to say her *Mattins*, to doe her Devotions, commend her selfe with fervent prayer unto the Lord, to blesse her and her endeavours the day following. *A whet is no let*, saith the Proverb: Mowers lose not any time, which they spend in whetting or grinding of their Sythes: our prayer to God in the Morning, before we enter on any businesse, doth not hinder us in our dayes worke, but rather whets it, sharpens it, sets an edge on our dull soules, and makes our mindes to undertake our labours with the greater alacritie.

And here may I take just occasion to speake concerning *Gleaning*. Consider, first, the antiquitie thereof, as being commanded by God, *Levit.* 19. 9, and 23. 22. Secondly, consider the equitie thereof; it doth the Rich no whit of harme, it doth the Poore a great deale of good. One may say of it as *Lot* of *Zoar*: *Is it not a little one, and my soule shall live?* Is it not a pettie, a small, exile courtesie, and the hearts of poore people shall be comforted thereby? *Reliquiæ Danaum, atque immitis Achillis;* the Remnant which hath escaped the edge of the Sythes, and avoided the hands of the Reapers. Had our Reapers the Eyes of Eagles, and the Clawes of Harpeyes, they could not see and snatch each scattered Eare which may well be allowed for the Reliefe of the Poore. When our Saviour said to the woman of *Syrophænicia*, *It is not good to take the Childrens Bread and cast it to the Dogs:* She answered, *Yea, Lord, but the Dogs eat of the Childrens Crummes that fall from their Table.* So, if any Misers mutter, *It is not meet that my Bread should be cast unto poore people to gleane Corne upon my Lands;* yea, but let them know that poore people (which are no *Dogs*, but setting a little thick Clay aside, as good as themselves) may eat the *falling Crummes*, the scattered Eares, which they gather on the ground.

Use: It may confute the Covetousnesse of many which repine that the Poore should have any benefit by them; and are so farre from suffering the Poore to gleane, that even they themselves gleane from the Poore, and speake much like to churlish *Nabal*, 1 *Sam.* 25. 11, *Shall I take my Wheat, my*

Rye, and my *Barley*, which I have prepared for my *Family*, and give it to the *Poore*, which I know not whence they be? Yea, some have so hard hearts that they would leave their Graine to be destroyed by Beasts and Vermine, rather then that the Poore should receive any benefit thereby. Cruell people, which preferre their Hogs before Chrifts Sheep, Mice before Men, Crowes before Christians!

But withall, Poore people must learne this Lesson, to know the meaning of these two Pronounes, *Mine* and *Thine;* what belongs to their rich Masters, and what pertaines to themselves. The Sheep which had little spots, those were *Jacobs* Fee; so the little spots, the loose straggling and scattered Eares, those are the Poores: but as for the great ones, the handfulls, the arme-fulls, the Sheaves, the Shocks, the Cocks, these are none of theirs, but the rich Owners; and therefore let the Poore take heed how they put forth their hands to their neighbours goods.

Motive: One forcible Motive to perswade the Rich to suffer the Poore to gleane, may be this: Even the greatest, in respect of God, is but a gleaner. God, he is the Master of the Harvest; all Gifts and Graces, they are his in an infinite measure; and every godly man, more or lesse, gleanes from him. *Abraham* gleaned a great gleane of Faith; *Moses*, of Meeknesse; *Joshuah*, of Valour; *Samson*, of Strength; *Solomon*, of Wealth and Wisdome; S. *Paul* of Knowledge, and the like. Now, if we would be glad at our hearts that the Lord would give us free leave and libertie for to gleane Graces out of his Harvest, let us not grudge and repine that poore people gleane a little gaine from our plentie. To conclude: when God hath multiplyed our *five Loaves*, that is, when of our little Seed he hath given us a great deale of increase, let poore people, like *Ruth* in the Text, be the *twelve Baskets* which may take up the fragments of gleanings which are left.

Verses 8 to 10: *Then said* Boaz *unto* Ruth, *Hearest thou, my Daughter? Goe to no other field to gather, neither goe from hence, but abide here by my Maidens. Let thy eyes be on the field which they doe reape, and goe after the Maidens.*

Have I not charged the servants, that they touch thee not? Moreover, when thou art thirstie, go unto the vessels, & drink of that which the servants have drawn. Then she fell on her face, and bowed her selfe to the ground, and said unto him, Why have I found favour in thy eyes, that thou shouldst know me, since I am a stranger?

Mothers and Nurses are very carefull tenderly to handle Infants, when they are but newly borne. So *Ruth*; Christ was newly formed in her, a young Convert, a fresh *Proselyte*: and therefore *Boaz* useth her with all kindnesse, both in workes and words; *Hearest thou, my Daughter?*

Observation: Aged persons may terme younger people their Sonnes and Daughters, 1 *Sam.* 3. 6. And if they were persons in Authoritie, though they were well-nigh equall in age, they used the same expression. Thus *Joseph* to his Brother *Benjamin*, *Gen.* 43. 29, *God be mercifull to thee, my Sonne.* Let young people therefore reverently observe their dutie and distance to their Seniors in Age, and Superiours in Authoritie: Yet I am afraid, men keepe not the method of *Jacobs* Children, the eldest sitting downe according to his Age, and the youngest according to his Youth; but fulfill the Complaint of the Prophet, *The young presume against the aged, and the base against the honourable.* Let aged persons strive to deserve their respect, by demeaning themselves gravely, and striving to adde gracious hearts to gray haires: otherwise, if they discover any lightnesse, loosenesse, wantonnesse in their carriage, young men will hereupon take occasion not onely to slight and neglect, but also to contemne and despise their paternall distance, and Father-like authoritie. Now as for young Ministers, they have not this advantage, to speake unto young people in the phrase of *Boaz*, *Hearest thou, my Daughter?* but must practise S. *Pauls* Precept, 1 *Tim.* 5. 1, 2, *Rebuke not an Elder, but exhort him as a Father, and the younger men as Brethren; the elder women as Mothers, the younger as Sisters, in all purenesse.*

But abide here by my Maidens.] *Observation*: Hence we gather, 'tis most decent for women to associate and accompanie themselves with those of their owne Sexe: *Miriam, Exod.* 15. 20, with a feminine Quire, *with Timbrels and Dances,* answered the men; and the Disciples wondred, *John* 4. 27, that Christ talked with a woman; shewing hereby, that it was not his ordinarie course to converse alone with one of another Sexe: For herein the Apostles Precept deserves to take place, namely, *to avoid from all appearance of evill.*

Have I not commanded the servants, that they should not touch thee?] *Boaz* had just cause to feare lest some of his servants might wrong her; to prevent which, he gave them strict charge to the contrarie.

Observation: Here we see that servile natures are most prone and proclive to wrong poore strangers. Indeed, generous spirits disdaine to make those the subjects of their crueltie, which rather should be the objects of their pittie: but it complyes with a servile disposition to tyrannize and domineere over such poore people as cannot resist them. Like pettie Brookes pent within a narrow Channell, on every dash of Raine they are readie to overflow, and wax angry at the apprehension of the smallest distast. The *Locusts, Revel.* 9. 10, had *tails* like *Scorpions,* and *stings* in their *tails;* which by some is expounded, that of those people which are meant by the *Scorpions,* the poorest were the proudest; the meanest, the most mischiveous; the basest, the bloodiest. And surely he that readeth the story of our English *Martyrs* shall find, that one *Alexander* a *Jaylor,* and one drunken *Warwick,* an *Executioner,* were most basely and barbarously cruell to Gods poor Saints.

Secondly, From these words observe; That it is the part of a good Master not onely to doe no harm himselfe, but also to take order that his Servants doe none, *Gen.* 12. 20, and 26. 11. When *Elisha* would take nothing of *Naaman,* 2 *Kings* 5. 20, *Gehazi* said; *As the Lord liveth, I will run after him and take something of him.* Thus may base Servants (if not prevented with a command to the contrary) wrong their most right and upright Masters, by taking Gifts and Bribes privately. The water (though it ariseth out of a most pure Fountain) which runneth through Mineralls of Lead, Copper,

Brimstone, or the like, hath with it a strange taste and relish in the mouth. So Justice, which should runne downe like a streame, though it ariseth out of a pure Fountaine, out of the breast of a sincere and incorrupted Judge; yet if formerly it hath passed through the *Mines* of *Gold* and *Silver*, I meane, through bad *Servants*, who have taken Bribès to prepossesse the Judge their Master with the prejudice of false informations, Justice hereby may be strangely perverted and corrupted. Many Masters themselves have been honest and upright, yet much wrong hath been done under them by their wicked Servants. It is said of Queene *Mary*, that, for her own part, *She* did not so much as bark; but she had them under her, which did more than bite; such were *Gardner, Bonner, Story, Woodroffe, Tyrrell*: Now she should have tyed up these *Bandogs*, and chained and fettered up these *Bloodhounds* from doing any mischiefe. *Camden* in his *Elizabetha*, in the yeare 1595, writeth thus of the then Lord *Chancellor* of *England*; *Ob sordes & corruptelas famulorum in beneficiis Ecclesiasticis nundinandis, ipse vir integer ab Ecclesiasticis haud bene audivit.* He ought to have imitated the example of *Boaz*, not onely to have done no harme himselfe, but also to have enjoyed the same to his servants: *Have I not commanded my servants, that they should not touch thee?*

Thirdly, in these words *Boaz* doth intimate, That if he gave a charge to the contrarie, none of his servants durst presume once to molest her.

Observation: Where we see, Masters commands ought to sound Lawes in the eares of their servants, if they be lawfull. Indeed, if *Absolon* (2 *Sam*. 13. 28,) saith to his servants, *Kill Amnon, fear not, for have I not commanded you?* this command did not oblige, because the thing enjoyned was altogether ungodly. Otherwise, men must imitate the obedience of the Centurions servants; who said to the one, *Goe, and he goeth; and to another, Come, and he commeth; and to his servant, Doe this, and he doth it.*

Corollary: Now, if we ought to be thus dutifull to our Earthly Masters, surely, if the Lord of Heaven enjoyneth us any thing, we ought to doe it without any doubt or delay. Were there no Hell to punish, no Heaven to reward, no Promises pronounced to the godly, no Threatnings denounced to the wicked; yet this is a sufficient reason to make us doe a thing, because God hath enjoyned it; this a convincing argument to make us refraine from it, because he hath forbidden it.

Then she fell on her face and bowed.] *Question:* Was not not this too much honour to give to any mortall Creature? And doth it not come within the compasse of the breach of the second Commandement, *Thou shalt not bow downe and worship them?* Especially seeing godly *Mordecai* refused to bend his knee to *Haman*.

Answer: Civill honour may and must be given to all in Authoritie, according to the usuall gestures of the Countrey: Now such *bowing* was the custome of the Easterne people, Gen. 33. 3. As for *Mordecai's* instance, it makes not against this; he being therein either immediately warranted by God, or else he refused to bow to *Haman* as being an *Amalakite*, betwixt which cursed Brood and the *Israelites* the Lord commanded an eternall enmitie.

Corollary: Now, if *Ruth* demeaned her selfe with such reverent gesture to *Boaz*, how reverent ought our gesture to be when we approach into the presence of God. Indeed, *God is a Spirit, and he will be worshipped in Spirit and Truth;* yet so that he will have the outward decent posture of the bodie to accompanie the inward sinceritie of the soule.

And said, Why have I found favour?] As if she had said: When I reflect my eyes upon my selfe, I cannot reade in my selfe the smallest worth to deserve so great a favour from thy hands; and therefore I must acknowledge my selfe exceedingly beholden to you. But principally I lift up my eyes to the providence of the Lord of Heaven; *mens hearts are in his hand as the Rivers of Water; he turneth them whither he pleaseth:* He it is that hath mollified thy heart, to shew this undeserved kindnesse unto me. Here we see *Ruths* humilitie. Many now-adayes would have made a contrarie construction of *Boaz* his Charitie, and reasoned thus: Surely he seeth in me some extraordinarie worth, whereof as yet I have not taken notice in my felfe; and therefore hereafter I will maintaine a better opinion of my owne deferts. But *Ruth* confeffeth her owne unworthineffe: And from her example let us learne to be humbly and heartily thankfull to thofe which beftow any courtefie or kindneffe upon us.

Since I am a ftranger.] She amplifies his favour from the indignitie of her owne perfon, being a ftranger.

Corollary: Oh then, if *Ruth* interpreted it fuch a kindneffe that *Boaz* tooke notice of her, being a ftranger, how *great is the love of God to us, who loved us in Chrift when we were ftrangers and aliens* from the Commonwealth of *Ifrael*! As the never-failing foundation of the Earth is firmely faftned for ever fleeting, yet fetled on no other fubftance then its owne ballafted weight; fo Gods love was founded on neither caufe nor condition in the Creature, but iffued onely out of his owne free favour. So that in this refpect we may all fay unto God what *Ruth* doth unto *Boaz* in the Text; *Why have we found favour in thine eyes, that thou fhouldeft take knowledge of us, feeing we were but ftrangers?*

Verfes 11 and 12: *And* Boaz *anfwered and faid unto her, It hath fully been fhewed me, all that thou haft done unto thy Mother in law fince the death of thine Husband; and how thou haft left thy Father and thy Mother, and the Land of thy Nativitie, and art come unto a people which thou knewest not heretofore. The Lord recompence thy worke, and a full reward be given thee of the Lord God of* Ifrael, *under whofe wings thou art come to truft.*

It hath been fully fhewed me, all.] More then probable it is, that *Boaz* had received his intelligence immediately from *Naomi*.

Obfervation: How-ever, here we may fee, the vertues of worthy perfons will never want Trumpets to found them to the world. The *Jews* were the *Centurions* Trumpet to our Saviour, *Luke* 7. 3. And the Widowes *Dorcas* her Trumpet to S. *Peter*, *Acts* 9. 39. Let this encourage men in their vertuous proceedings, knowing that their worthy deeds fhall not be buried in obfcuritie, but fhall finde tongues in their lively colours to expreſſe them. *Abſolon* having no Children, and deſirous to perpetuate his Name, erected a Pillar in the Kings Dale; and the ſame is called *Abſolon's* Pillar unto this day. But the moſt compendious way for men to conſecrate their Memories to Eternitie, is to erect a Pillar of vertuous Deeds; which ſhall ever remaine, even when the moſt laſting Monuments in the World ſhall be conſumed, as not able to ſatisfie the *Boulimee* of all-conſuming Time. And to put the worſt, grant that envious men with a Cloud of Calumnies ſhould eclipſe the beames of vertuous Memories from ſhining in the World, yet this may be their comfort, that *God that ſees in secret, will reward them openly*. Moreover, it is the dutie of ſuch who have received Courteſies from others, to profeſſe and expreſſe the ſame as occaſion ſhall ſerve; that ſo their Benefactors may publikely receive their deſerved commendation. Thus ſurely *Naomi* had done by *Ruth*; from whoſe mouth no doubt, though not immediately, her vertues were founded in the eares of *Boaz*. *It hath been fully ſhewed me, all.*

Here now followeth a Summarie, reckoning up of the worthy Deeds of *Ruth*; which, becauſe they have been fully diſcourſed of in the former Chapter, it would be needleſſe againe to inſiſt upon them: Proceed we therefore to *Boaz* his Prayer.

The Lord recompence thee.] As if he had ſaid: Indeed, *Ruth*, that courteſie which I afforded thee to gleane upon my Land without any diſturbance, comes farre ſhort both of thy deſerts and my deſires. All that I wiſh is this, That what I am unable to requite the Lord himſelfe would *recompence:* May he give thee *a full reward* of Graces internall, externall, eternall; here, hereafter; on Earth, in Heaven; while thou liveſt, when thou dieſt; in Grace, in Glory, *a full reward*.

Where firſt we may learne, that when we are unable to requite peoples deſerts of our ſelves, we muſt make up our want of workes with good Wiſhes to God for them. Indeed, we muſt not doe like thoſe in the ſecond of S. *James, verſe* 16, who onely ſaid to the Poore, *Depart in peace, warme your ſelves, and fill your bellies*, and yet beſtowed nothing upon them: We muſt not both begin and conclude with good Wiſhes, and doe nothing elſe; but we muſt obſerve *Boaz* his method:

firſt, to begin to doe good to thoſe that being vertuous are in diſtreſſe; and then, where we fall ſhort in requiting them, to make the reſt up with heartie Wiſhes to God for them.

Obſervation: But the maine Obſervation is this; *There is a recompence of a full reward upon the good workes of his ſervants,* Gen. 15. 1. *Moreover, by them is thy ſervant taught; and in keeping them, there is great reward,* Pſal. 19. 11. Verily, there is a Reward for the Righteous; doubtleſſe, there is a God that judgeth the Earth; Godlineſſe hath the promiſes of this Life, and of the Life to come.

Uſe 1: It may ſerve to confute ſuch falſe Spies as rayſe wrong Reports of the Land of *Canaan,* of the Chriſtian Profeſſion, ſaying with the wicked, *Mal.* 3. 14, *It is in vaine to ſerve God; and what profit is it that we have kept his Commandements, and that we have walked 'mournfully before the Lord of Hoaſtes?* Slanderous Tongues! which one day ſhall be juſtly fined in the Starre-Chamber of Heaven, *Ob ſcandala magnatum,* for ſlandering of Gods noble ſervants and their Profeſſion; for indeed, the Chriſtian Life is moſt comfortable, for we may both take a liberall Portion, and have a ſanctified uſe of Gods Creatures: beſides, within we have peace of Conſcience, and joy in the Holy-Ghoſt in ſome meaſure; one Dramme whereof is able to ſugar the moſt wormewood affliction.

Uſe 2: When we begin to feele our ſelves to lagge in Chriſtianitie, let us ſpurre on our affections with the meditation of that *full reward* which we ſhall in due time receive; with our Saviour, let us *looke to the Joyes which are ſet before us*; and with *Moſes,* let us have *an eye to the recompence of Reward:* Yet ſo, that though we look at this *Reward,* yet alſo we muſt look through it, and beyond it. This meditation of the *Reward* is a good place for our ſoules to bait at, but a bad place for our ſoules to lodge in: we muſt mount our mindes higher, namely, to aime at the glory of God; at which all our actions muſt be directed, though there were no Reward propounded unto them. Yet ſince it is Gods goodneſſe to propound unto us a Reward over and beſides his owne Glory, this ought ſo much the more to incite us to diligence in our Chriſtian calling: For if *Othniel, Judges* 1.13, behaved himſelfe so valiantly against the enemies of *Israel*, in hope to obtaine *Achsah*, *Calebs* Daughter, to Wife; how valiantly ought we to demeane our selves against our spirituall enemies, knowing that we shall one day be married unto our Saviour in eternall happinesse! And this is a *full Reward*.

Objection: But some may say, These termes of *Recompence* and *Reward* may seeme to favour the *Popish* Tenent, That our good workes merit at Gods hand.

Answer: Reward and *Recompence* unto our good workes are not due unto us for any worth of our owne, but meerely from Gods free favour and gracious promise. For, to make a thing truly meritorious of a Reward, it is required, first, that the thing meriting be our owne, and not anothers; now our best workes are none of ours, but Gods Spirit in us. Secondly, it is requisite that we be not bound of dutie to doe it; now we are bound to doe all the good deeds which we doe, and still remaine but *unprofitable servants*. Thirdly, there must be a proportion betweene the thing meriting, and the Reward merited; now there is no proportion betweene our stained and imperfect workes (for such are our best) and that infinite weight of glory wherewith God will reward us. It remaines therefore, that no Reward is given us for our owne inherent worth, but meerely for Gods free favour, who crownes his owne workes in us.

Under whose wings thou art come to trust.] A Metaphor; it is borrowed from an Hen, which with her clocking summons together her stragling Chickens, and then out-stretcheth the fanne of her wings to cover them. Familiarly it is used in Scripture, and amongst other places, by our Saviour, *Math.* 23. 37, *How oft would I have gathered thee together, as an Hen gathereth her Chickens under her wings, and ye would not!* And just it was with God, because the foolish Chickens of the *Iewes* would not come to Christ, the Hen, calling them, to suffer them to be devoured by the Eagle, the Imperiall Armie of the *Romans*.

Observation: Gods love and care over his Children is as great as an Hen's over her Chickens. Now the Hen's wings doe the Chickens a double good.

Firſt, they keepe them from the Kite; ſo Gods providence protecteth his ſervants from that Kite, the Devill: For as the Kite uſeth to fetch many Circuits and Circles, and long hovers and flutters round about, and at length ſpying her advantage pops downe on the poore Chicken for a prey; ſo the Devill, who, as it is *Iob* 1. 7, *compaſſeth the Earth to and fro, and walketh through it;* and at length ſpying an opportunitie pitcheth and ſetleth himſelfe upon ſome poore Soule to devoure it, if the wings of Gods providence (as the Citie of Refuge) doe not reſcue him from his clutches.

Secondly, the Hen with her wings broodes her Chickens, and makes them thereby to thrive and grow. In Summer her wings are a Canopie, to keepe her Chickens from the heat of the ſcorching Sunne; and in Winter they are a Mantle, to defend them from the injurie of the pinching cold: So Gods providence and protection makes his Children to ſprout, thrive, and proſper under it. In Proſperitie, Gods providence keepeth them from the heat of Pride; in Adverſitie, it preſerveth them from being benummed with frozen Deſpaire.

Uſe: Let us all then ſtrive to runne to hide our ſelves under the wings of the God of Heaven. Hearke how the Hen clocks in the *Pſalmes, Call upon me in the time of trouble, and I will heare thee, and thou ſhalt prayſe me!* How ſhe clocks in the *Canticles, Returne, O Shulamite, returne, returne, that we may behold thee!* How ſhe clocketh, *Math.* 7. 7, *Aske and ye ſhall have, ſeeke and ye ſhall finde, knock and it ſhall be opened unto you!* How ſhe clocks, *Math.* 11. 28, *Come unto me all ye that are wearie and heavie laden, and I will eaſe you!* Let not us now be like ſullen Chickens, which ſit moaping under a rotten Hedge, or proating under an old Wood-pile, when the Hen calleth them. Let not us truſt to the broken Wall of our owne Strength, or think to lurke under the tottering Hedge of our owne Wealth, or winde--ſhaken Reeds of our unconſtant Friends; but flye to God, that he may ſtretch his wings over us, as the Cherubins did over the Mercie-Seat. And as alwayes in Day-time, ſo eſpecially at Night, when we goe to Bed, (for Chickens, when going to Rooſt, alwayes run to the Hen,) let us commend our ſelves with prayer to his Providence, that he would be pleafed to preferve us from the dangers of the Night enfuing; *trufting*, with *Ruth* in the Text, *under the wings of the Lord God of Ifrael.*

Verfes 13 and 14: *Then fhe faid, Let me finde favour in the fight of my Lord; for thou haft comforted me, and fpoken comfortably unto thy Maid, though I be not like to one of thy Maids.* And Boaz *faid unto her, At the meale time come thou hither, and eate of the Bread, and dip thy morfell in the vineger. And fhe fate befide the Reapers, and he reached her parched Corne; and fhe did eate, and was fufficed, and left thereof.*

Boaz had formerly called *Ruth*, Daughter; now *Ruth* ftileth him, Lord. When great ones carry themfelves familiarly to meaner perfons, meaner perfons muft demeane themfelves refpectfully to great ones. Indeed, with bafe and fordid natures familiaritie breeds contempt; but ingenuous natures will more awfully obferve their diftance towards their Superiours, of whom they are moft courteoufly intreated. And if great Perfonages fhould caft up their accompts, they fhould finde themfelves not lofers, but gainers of honour by their kinde ufage of their Inferiours. Thofe Starres feeme to us the greateft and fhine the brighteft which are fet the loweft. Great men, which fometimes ftoop, and ftoop low, in their humble carriage to others, commonly get the greateft luftre of credit and efteeme in the hearts of thofe that be vertuous.

And fpoken comfortably unto thy Maid.] In *Hebrew*, *haft fpoken unto the heart*. A comfortable fpeech is a word fpoken to the heart.

Meditation: Oh that Minifters had this facultie of *Boaz* his fpeech; not to tickle the eares, teach the heads, or pleafe the braines of the people, but that their Sermons might foake and fink to the root of their hearts! But though this may be endeavoured by them, it cannot be performed of them without Gods fpeciall affiftance. We may leave our words at the outward porch of mens eares, but his Spirit muft conduct and lodge them in the Clofet of their hearts.

Though I be not like to one of thy Maids.] Meaning, becauſe ſhe was a *Moabiteſſe*, a Stranger and Alien, they Natives of the Common-wealth of *Iſrael;* in this reſpect ſhe was farre their inferiour.

Obſervation: The godly ever conceive very humbly and meanly of themſelves: *Moſes*, Exod. 4. 10; *Gedeon*, Judg. 6. 15; *Abigail*, 1 Sam. 25. 41; Eſay, 6. 5; Jerem. 1. 6; *John Baptiſt*, Math. 3. 11; [*Paul,*] 1 Tim. 1. 15. And the reaſon hereof is, becauſe they are moſt privie to and ſenſible of their owne infirmities; their Corruptions which cleave unto them are ever before their eyes. Theſe black feet abate their thoughts when puffed up with Pride for their painted Traine of other Graces. On the other ſide, the wicked ſet ever the greateſt price on their owne worth; they behold their owne ſuppoſed Vertues through magnifying Glaſſes, and think with *Haman* that none deſerves better to be honoured by the King but themſelves.

Uſe: Let us endeavour to obtain humilitie with *Ruth*, a vertue of moſt worth, and yet which coſteth leaſt to keepe. Yet notwithſtanding, it is both lawfull and needfull for us to know our owne worth, and to take an exact ſurvey of thoſe Graces which God hath beſtowed upon us. Firſt, that we may know thereby the better to proportion our thanks to God. Secondly, that we may know how much good the Church and Common-wealth expecteth to be performed by us. And laſtly, that if any ſhould baſely inſult and domineer over us, we may in humilitie ſtand upon the lawfull juſtification of our ſelves, and our owne ſufficiencie, as S. *Paul* did againſt the falſe Apoſtles at *Corinth;* always provided that we give God the glory, and profeſſe our ſelves to be but *unprofitable ſervants.*

And Boaz *ſaid unto her, At the meale time come thou hither, and eate of the Bread.*] Two things herein are commendable in *Boaz*, and to be imitated by Maſters of Families.

Firſt, That he had provided wholeſome and competent foode for his owne ſervants: ſo ought all houſe-holders to doe. And herein let them propound God for their Preſident, for he maintaineth the greateſt Family; all creatures are his servants, and *he giveth them meat in due season; he openeth his hand, and filleth with his blessing every living thing.*

Secondly, As *Boaz* provided Meat for his servants, so he allowed them certaine set convenient Times wherein they might quietly eate their Meat. But as the people of the *Jewes* pressed so fast upon our Saviour, that he had not so much leisure as to *eate Bread (Mark 3. 20,)* and take necessarie sustenance: So, such is the gripple nature of many covetous Masters, that they will so taske and tye their servants to their worke, as not to afford them seasonable Respite to feede themselves.

And dip thy morsell in the vineger.] *Observation:* The Fare of Gods servants in ancient time, though wholesome, was very homely: Here they had onely Bread and Vineger, and parched Corne. For a thousand five hundred and sixtie yeares the World fed upon Herbes; and the Scripture maketh mention since of meane and sparing Fare of many godly men. It may therefore confute the Gluttonie and Epicurisme of our Age, consisting both in the superfluous number of Dishes, and in the unlawfull nature of them. We rifle the Ayre for daintie Fowle, we ransack the Sea for delicious Fish, we rob the Earth for delicate Flesh, to suspend the doubtfull Appetite betwixt varietie of Dainties. As for the nature of them, many are meere needlesse Whetstones of Hunger, which in stead of satisfying doe encrease it. And as in the *Spanish Inquisition* such is their exquisite Crueltie, that, having brought one to the doore of Death by their Tortures, they then revive him by Cordials; and then againe re-killing him with their Torments, fetch him againe with comfortable things; thus often re-iterating their Crueltie: So men, having killed their Appetite with good Cheare, seeke with Dishes made for the nonce to enliven it againe, to the superfluous wasting of Gods good creatures, and much endammaging the health of their owne bodies. But leaving them, let us be content with that competent Foode which God hath allotted us, knowing that *better is a Dinner of Herbes with peace, then a stalled Oxe with strife;* and God, if it pleaseth him, can so blesse *Daniels* Pulse unto us, that by meane Fare we shall be made more strong and healthfull then those who surfet on excesse of Dainties.

And she did eate and was sufficed.] It is a great blessing of God, when he gives such strength and vertue to his creatures as to satisfie our hunger; and the contrarie is a great punishment: For as, (1 *Kings* 1. 1,) when they heaped abundance of *Clothes* on aged King *David*, yet his decayed body felt no *warmth* at all; so God so curseth the Meat to some, that though they cramme downe never so much into their bellies, yet still their hunger encreaseth with their Meat, and they finde that Nature is not truly contented and satisfied therewith.

And left thereof.] Hence we learne, the over-plus which remaineth after we have fed ourselves, must neither be scornfully cast away, nor carelesly left alone, but it must be thriftily kept: Imitating herein the example of our Saviour; who, though he could make *five Loaves* swell to sufficient foode for five thousand men, yet gave he command, that the *fragments* should be carefully basketted up.

Verses 15 to 17: *And when she arose to gleane,* Boaz *commanded his servants, saying, Let her gather among the sheaves, and doe not rebuke her; Also let fall some of the sheaves for her, and let it lie, that she may gather it up, and rebuke her not. So she gleaned in the field untill Evening, and she threshed that she had gathered, and it was about an* Ephah *of Barley*.

Before I enter into these words, behold an Objection stands at the doore of them, which must first be removed.

Objection: One may say to *Ruth*, as our Saviour to the young man in the Gospel, *One thing is wanting.* Here is no mention of any *Grace* she said to God either before or after Meat.

Answer: Charitie will not suffer me to condemne *Ruth* of forgetfulnesse herein: She who formerly had been so thankfull to *Boaz*, the Conduit-Pipe, how can she be thought to be ungratefull to God, the Fountaine of all favours? Rather I think it is omitted of the holy Spirit to be written downe; who, had he regiftred each particular action of Gods Saints, (as it is *John* 21. 25,) *the world would not have been able to containe the Books which should be written.*

Let none therefore take occafion to omit this dutie, becaufe here not fpecified; rather let them be exhorted to performe it, becaufe in other places it is both commanded by Precept, and commended by Practice, *Deut.* 8. 10; 1 *Cor.* 10, 31. Yea, in the twenty-feventh of the *Acts,* the Mariners and Souldiers (people ordinarily not very Religious) though they had fafted fourteene days together, yet none of them were fo unmannerly, or rather fo profane, as to fnatch any Meat, before S. *Paul* had given *Thanks.* Let us not therefore be like *Efau,* who in ftead of giving a Bleffing to God for his Pottage, fold his Bleffing to his Brother for his Pottage: but though our hafte or hunger be never fo great, let us difpenfe with fo much time as therein to crave a Bleffing from God, wherein his creatures are fanctified; as no doubt *Ruth* did, though not recorded.

And when she arose to gleane.] The end of feeding, is to fall to our Calling. Let us not therefore with *Ifrael,* fit downe to eate and to drinke, and fo rife up againe to play; but let us eate to live, not live to eate. 'Tis not matter, we need not make the Clay-Cottage of our Body much larger then it is, by immoderate feafting; it is enough, if we maintaine it fo with competent food, that God our Landlord may not have juft caufe to fue us for want of Reparations.

Boaz *commanded his fervants, faying, Let her gather among the sheaves, and doe not rebuke her.*] *Obfervation:* It is lawfull for us, according to our pleafure, to extend our favours more to one then to another. *Ruth* alone, not all the gleaners, was priviledged to gather among the fheaves uncontrouled. Give leave to *Jacob* to bequeath a double Portion to *Joseph,* his beft beloved fonne; for *Joseph* to make the Meffe of *Benjamin* five times greater then any other of his Brethren; for *Elkanah* to leave a worthier Portion to *Hannah* then to

Peninnah : the reason is, because there can be no wrong done in those things which are free favours. I am not lesse just to him, to whom I give lesse; but I am more mercifull to him, to whom I give more. Yet in the dealing and distributing of Liberalitie, let those of the Family of Faith be especially respected; and of these, those chiefly which, as the Apostle saith, are worthy of a *double honour*.

Corollarie: Shall it not therefore be lawfull for the Lord of Heaven to bestow Wealth, Honour, Wisdome, effectual Grace, Blessings outward and inward, on one, and denie them to another? You therefore, whom God hath suffered to gleane among the Sheaves, and hath scattered whole handfulls for you to gather; you that abound and flow with his favours, be heartily thankfull unto him; he hath not dealt so with every one, neither have all such a large measure of his Blessings. And ye common gleaners, who are faine to follow farre after, and glad to take up the scattered eares, who have a smaller proportion of his favour, be neither angry with God, nor grieved at your selves, nor envious at your Brethren; but be content with your condition. It is the Lord, and let him doe what is good in his eyes: shall not he have absolute power to doe with his owne what he thinketh good, when *Boaz* can command, that *Ruth*, and no other, may gleane among the sheaves without *rebuke*?

Had the servants of *Boaz*, without expresse warrant and command from their Master, scattered handfulls for her to gleane, their action had not been Charitie, but flat Theft and Robberie; for they were to improve their Masters goods to his greatest profit. On the other side, it had been a great fault, to with-hold and with-draw any thing from her, which their Master commanded them to give. Yet, as the unjust Steward in *Luke* made his Masters Debts to be lesse then they were; so many servants now-adayes make their Masters gifts to be lesse then they are, giving lesse then he hath granted, and disposing lesse then he hath directed. Men commonly pay Toll for passing through great Gates, or over common Bridges; so when the Liberalitie of Masters goeth through the Gate of their servants hands, and Bridges of their fingers, it is constrained to pay Tribute and Custome to their servants, before it commeth to thofe Poore to whom it was intended. Thus many men make the augmentation of their owne Eftates, from the diminution of their Mafters Bountie.

Queftion: But fome may fay, Why did not *Boaz* beftow a quantitie of Corne upon *Ruth,* and fo fend her home unto her Mother?

Anfwer: He might have done fo, but he chofe rather to keep her ftill a working. Where we learne, that is the beft Charitie which fo relieves peoples wants, as that they are ftill continued in their Calling. For as he who teacheth one to fwimme, though happily [haply] he will take him by the Chinne, yet he expecteth that the learner fhall nimbly ply the Oares of his hands and feet, and ftrive and ftruggle with all his ftrength to keepe himfelfe above water: fo thofe who are beneficiall to poore people, may juftly require of them, that they ufe both their hands to worke and feet to goe in their Calling, and themfelves take all due labour, that they may not finke in the Gulfe of Penurie. Relieve an Hufbandman, yet fo, as that he may ftill continue in his Husbandry; a Tradef-man, yet fo, as he may ftill goe on in his Trade; a poore Scholar, yet fo, as he may ftill proceed in his Studies. Hereby the Common-wealth fhall be a gainer. Drones bring no Honey to the Hive, but the painfull hand of each privat man contributes fome profit to the publike good. Hereby the able poore, the more diligent they be, the more bountifull men will be to them; while their bodies are freed from many difeafes, their foules from many finnes, whereof Idleneffe is the Mother. Lazineffe make a breach in our Soule, where the Devill doth affault us with greateft advantage; and when we are moft idle in our Vocations, then he is moft bufie in his Temptations. A reverend Minifter was wont to fay, that the Devill never tempted him more then on Mondayes, when (becaufe his former Weekes Taske was newly done, and that for the Weeke to come fix dayes diftant) he tooke moft libertie to refrefh himfelfe.

Since therefore fo much good commeth from Induftrie, I could wifh there were a publike *Vineyard,* into which all they fhould be fent who *ftand lazing in the Market-place till the eleventh houre of the day.* Would all poore and impotent were well placed in an Hofpitall, all poore and able well difpofed in a Work-houfe; and the common Stocks of Townes fo layd out, as they thereby might be imployed!

So fhe gleaned in the field untill evening.] The Night is onely that which muft end our labours: onely the Evening muft beg us a Play, to depart out of the School of our Vocation, with promife next Morning to returne again; *Man goeth out to his labour untill Evening.* Let fuch then be blamed, who in their working make their Night to come before the Noone; each day of their labour being fhorter then that of S. *Lucy* [Dec. 13]; and after a fpurt in their Calling for fome few houres, they relapfe againe to lazineffe.

And fhe threfhed what fhe had gathered.] The Materialls of the Temple were fo hewed and carved, both Stone and Wood, before that they were brought unto *Hierufalem*, that there was not fo much as the noyfe of an *Hammer heard in the Temple*. So *Ruth* fits all things in a readineffe before fhe goes home: What formerly fhe gleaned, now fhe threfhed; that fo no noyfe might be made at home to difturbe her aged Mother. Here we fee Gods fervants, though well defcended, difdaine not any homely, if honeft, worke for their owne living: *Sarah* kneaded Cakes, *Rebeccah* drew Water, *Rachel* fed Sheepe, *Thamar* baked Cakes. *Suetonius* reporteth of *Auguftus Cæfar*, that he made his Daughters to learne to fpinne; and *Pantaleon* relates the fame of *Charles* the Great. Yet now-adayes, (fuch is the pride of the World,) people of farre meaner qualitie fcorne fo bafe imployments.

And it was about an Ephah *of Barley.*] An *Ephah* contained ten *Omers, Exod.* 16. 36. An *Omer* of *Mannah* was the proportion allowed for a mans one day meat. Thus *Ruth* had gleaned upon the quantitie of a Bufhell; fuch was her Induftry in diligent beftirring her felfe; *Boaz* his Bountie in fcattering for her to gather; and, above all, God his Bleffing, who gave fo good fucceffe unto her. *Ruth* having now done gleaning did not ftay behind in the field, as many now-adayes begin their worke when others end; if that may be termed worke, to filch and steale; as if the darke Night would be a Veyle to cover their deedes of Darknesse: but home she hasteneth to her Mother, as followeth.

Verses 18, 19: *And she tooke it up, and went into the Citie, and her Mother in law saw what she had gathered: also she tooke forth, and gave to her that which she had reserved, when she was sufficed. Then her Mother in law said unto her, Where hast thou gleaned to day? And where wroughtest thou? Blessed be he that knew thee. And she showed her Mother in law with whom she had wrought, and said, The mans name with whom I wrought to day is* Boaz.

And she tooke it up.] See here, the shoulders of Gods Saints are wonted to the bearing of Burthens: Little *Isaac* carryed the Faggot, wherewith himselfe was to be sacrificed; our Saviour his owne Crosse, till his faintnesse craved *Simon* of *Cyrene* to be his successor. Yet let not Gods Saints be dis-heartened: if their Father hath a *Bottle wherein he puts the teares* which they spend; sure he hath a Ballance wherein he weighs the Burthens which they beare; he keepes a Note to what weight their Burthens amount, and (no doubt) will accordingly comfort them.

Those are to be confuted, who with the *Scribes*, Math. 23. 4, *binde heavie burthens, and grievous to be borne, and lay them on the backs of others; but for their owne part they will not so much as touch them with one of their fingers:* Yea, some are so proud that they will not carry their owne Provender, things for their owne sustenance; had they been under *Ruths Ephah* of Barley, with *David* in *Sauls* Armour, they could not have gone under the weight of it, because never used unto it.

And her Mother in law saw what she had gathered.] Namely, *Ruth* shewed it unto her, and then *Naomi* saw it. Children are to present to their Parents view all which they get by their owne labour; otherwise doe many Children now-adayes: As *Ananias* and *Saphira* brought *part of the Money, and deposed it at the Apostles feet,* but reserved the rest for themselves; so they can be content to shew to their Parents fome parcell of their gaines, whileft they keepe the remnant fecretly to themfelves.

Alfo fhe tooke forth, and gave to her.] Learne we from hence, Children, if able, are to cherifh and feed their Parents, if poore and aged. Have our Parents performed the parts of Pelicans to us? let us doe the dutie of Storkes to them: Would all Children would pay as well for the *partie-coloured Coats* which their Parents doe give them, as *Jofeph* did for his, who maintained his Father and his Brethren in the Famine in *Egypt*! Thinke on thy Mothers ficknefe, when thou waft conceived; forrow, when thou waft borne; trouble, when thou waft nurft: She was cold whileft thou waft warme; went whileft thou layd'ft ftill; waked whileft thou flept'ft; fafted whileft thou fed'ft: Thefe are eafier to be conceived then exprefs'd, eafier deferved then requited. Say not therefore to thy Father according to the Doctrine of the *Pharifes*, *Corban*, it is a gift, if thou profiteft by me; but confeffe that it is a true Debt, and thy bounden dutie, if thou beeft able, to relieve them: fo did *Ruth* to *Naomi*, who was but her Mother in law.

Which fhe had referved when fhe was fufficed.] *Obfervation*: We muft not fpend all at once, but providently referve fome for afterwards; we muft not fpeake all at once, without *Jefuiticall* refervation of fome things ftill in our hearts; not fpend all at once, without thriftie refervation of fomething ftill in our hands. Indeed our Saviour faith, *Care not for to morrow, for to morrow fhall care for it felfe:* but that is not meant of the care of providence, which is lawfull and neceffarie; but of the care of diffidence, which is wicked and ungodly. Thofe are to be blamed, which [say], as *Abifhai* faid to *David* concerning *Saul*, *I will ftrike him but once, and I will ftrike him no more.* So many men, with one act of Prodigalitie, give the bane and mortall wound to their Eftates: with one exceffive Feaft, one coftly Sute of Clothes, one waftfull Night of Gaming, they fmite their Eftates under the fifth Rib, (which alwayes is mortall in Scripture,) fo that it never reviveth againe. But let us fpare where we may, that fo we may spend where we should: in the seven yeares of Plentie let us provide for the seven yeares of Famine; and to make good construction of our Estates, let us as well observe the Future as the Present Tense.

Then her Mother in law said unto her, Where hast thou gleaned to day?] These words were not uttered out of Jealousie, as if *Naomi* suspected that *Ruth* had dishonestly come by her Corne; (for Charitie is not suspitious, but ever fastens the most favourable Comments upon the actions of those whom it affects;) but she did it out of a desire to know who had been so bountifull unto her. Yet hence may we learne, that Parents after the example of *Naomi* may and ought to examine their Children, how and where they spend their time: For hereby they shall prevent a deale of mischiefe, whilest their Children will be more watchfull what Companie they keepe, as expecting with feare at Night to be examined. Neither can such Fathers be excused, who never say to their Children, as *David* to *Adoniah*, *Why doest thou so?* But suffer them to rove and range at their owne pleasure. *Am I,* say they, *my sonnes keeper? He is old enough, let him looke after himselfe.*

Now, as for those *Joashes*, whose *Jehoiada's* are dead, those young men whose Friends and Fathers are deceased, who now must have Reason for their Ruler, or rather Grace for their Guide and Governer; Let such know that indeed they have none to aske them as the Angell did *Hagar, Whence commest thou, and whither goest thou?* None to examine them, as *Eliab* did *David, Wherefore art thou come downe hither?* None to question them, as *Naomi* did *Ruth, Where wroughtest thou to day?* But now, as S. *Paul* said of the *Gentiles*, that *having no Law, they were a Law unto themselves:* so must such young persons endeavour, that having no Examiners, they may be Examiners to themselves, and at Night, accordingly as they have spent their time, either to condemne or acquit their owne actions.

Blessed be he that knew thee.] The man shot an Arrow at unawares, 1 *Kings* 22. 34, yet God directed it to the Chinke of the Armour of guiltie *Ahab*: But *Naomi* doth here dart and ejaculate out a prayer, and that at Rovers, aiming at no one particular Marke; *Bleſſed be he that knew thee:* Yet, no doubt, was it not in vaine; but God made it light on the head of bountifull *Boaz*, who deſerved it.

Learne we from hence, upon the fight of a good deed, to bleſſe the doer thereof, though by Name unknowne unto us: And let us take heed that we doe not recant and recall our prayers, after that we come to the knowledge of his Name; as ſome doe, who when they ſee a laudable Work willingly commend the doer of it; but after they come to know the Authors Name, (eſpecially if they be prepoſſeſſed with a private ſpleene againſt him,) they fall then to derogate and detract from the Action, quarrelling with it as done out of oſtentation, or ſome other ſiniſter end.

And ſhe ſhewed her Mother in law with whom ſhe had wrought.] Children, when demanded, are truly to tell their Parents where they have been; rather let them hazard the wrath of their earthly Father, by telling the Truth, then adventure the diſpleaſure of their heavenly Father, by feigning a Lye. Yet as *David*, when *Achiſh* asked him (1 *Sam.* 27. 10) *where he had been?* told him, that he had been *againſt the South of* Judah, *and againſt the South of the* Jerahmeelites, *and againſt the South of the* Kenites; when indeed he had been the cleane contrarie way, *invading the* Geſhurites, *and* Gezrites, *and the* Amalekites: So many Children flap their Parents in the mouth with a Lye, that they have been in their Studie, in their Calling, in good Companie, or in lawfull Recreations; when the truth is, they have been in ſome Drinking-School, Taverne, or Ale-houſe, miſ-ſpending of their precious time. And many ſerve their Maſters as *Gehezi* did the Prophet; who being demanded, anſwered, *Thy ſervant went no whither*, when he had been taking a Bribe of *Naaman*.

The mans Name with whom I wrought to day is Boaz.] We ought to know the Names of ſuch who are our Benefactors. Thoſe are counted to be but baſely borne who cannot tell the Names of their Parents; and ſurely thoſe are but of a bafe nature who doe not know the Names of their Patrons and Benefactors. To blame therefore was that lame man cured by our Saviour (*John* 5. 13), of whom it is faid, *And he that was healed knew not the Name of him that faid unto him, Take up thy Bed, and walke.* Yet let not this difcourage the charitie of any Benefactors, becaufe thofe that receive their courtefies oftentimes doe not remember their Names; let this comfort them, though they are forgotten by the living, they are remembered in the Booke of Life. The *Athenians* out of Superftition erected an Altar with this infcription, *Unto the unknowne God:* but we out of true Devotion muft erect an Altar of Gratitude to the memorie, not of our once unknown, but now forgotten Benefactors, whofe Names we have not been fo carefull to preferve, as *Ruth* was the Name of *Boaz: And the mans Name was* Boaz.

Verfe 20: *And* Naomi *faid unto her Daughter in law, Bleffed be he of the Lord, for he ceafeth not to do good to the living and to the dead. Againe* Naomi *faid unto her, The man is neere unto us, and of our affinitie.*

Thefe words confift of three Parts. 1. *Naomies* praying for *Boaz.* 2. Her praifing of *Boaz.* 3. Her reference and relation unto *Boaz.* Of the firft:

Bleffed be he of the Lord.] The Lord is the Fountain from whom all bleffedneffe flowes. Indeed *Jacob* bleffed his Sonnes, *Mofes* the twelve Tribes, the *Priefts* in the *Law* the people; but thefe were but the inftruments, God the principall; thefe the pipe, God the fountaine; thefe the Minifters to pronounce it, God the Author who beftowed it.

For he ceafeth not.] *Obfervation:* Naomi never before made any mention of *Boaz,* nor of his good deeds; but now being informed of his bountie to *Ruth,* it puts her in mind of his former courtefies. Learn from hence, new favours caufe a frefh remembrance of former courtefies. Wherefore if men begin to be forgetfull of thofe favours which formerly we have beftowed upon them, let us florifh and varnifh over our old courtesies with fresh colours of new kindnesses, so shall we recall our past favours to their memories.

Use: When we call to mind Gods staying of his killing Angell, *Anno* 1625, let that mercy make us to be mindfull of a former; his safe bringing back of our (then Prince, now) King from *Spaine*; when the pledge of our ensuing happinesse was pawned in a forreine Country: Let this blessing put us in mind of a former; the peaceable comming in of our Gracious Soveraigne of happie Memory, when the bounds of two Kingdoms were made the middle of a *Monarchy*: Stay not here, let thy thankfulnesse travell further; call to minde the miraculous providence of God in defending this Land from Invasion in '88. On still: be thankfull for Gods goodnesse in bringing Queene *Elizabeth* to the Crown, when our Kingdome was like the Woman in the Gospell, *troubled with an issue of blood* (which glorious Martyrs shed), but stanched at her ariving at the *Scepter*. We might be infinite in prosecution of this point; let present favours of God renew the memories of old ones, as the present bounty of *Boaz* to *Ruth* made *Naomi* remember his former courtesies: *For he ceaseth not to doe good to the living and the dead.*

He ceaseth not.] Our deeds of Piety ought to be continued without interruption or ceasing. Some men there be whose charitable deeds are as rare as an Eclipse, or a Blazing-Starre; these men deserve to be pardoned for their pious deeds, they are so seldome guiltie of them: With *Nabal* they prove themselves by excessive prodigalitie at one Feast; but he deserves the commendation of a good house-keeper, who keepes a constant Table, who with *Boaz ceaseth not to doe good*.

To the dead.] The meaning is, to those who now are dead, but once were living; or to their Friends and Kindred. Whence we learne, Mercie done to the Kindred of the dead, is done to the dead themselves. Art thou, then, a Widower, who desirest to do mercie to thy dead Wife; or a Widow, to thy dead Husband; or a Child, to thy deceased Parent? I will tell thee how thou mayest expresse thy selfe courteous: Hath thy Wife, thy Husband, or thy Parent any Brother, or

Kinſman, or Friends ſurviving? be courteous to them; and in ſo doing, thy favours ſhall redound to the dead: Though old *Barzillai* be uncapable of thy favours, let young *Kimham* taſte of thy kindneſſe: Though the dead cannot, need not have thy mercie, yet may they receive thy kindneſſe by a Proxie, by their Friends that ſtill are living.

Mercie, then, to the dead makes nothing for the *Popiſh Purgatorie*; and yet no wonder if the *Papiſts* fight for it. 'Tis ſaid of *Sicily* and *Ægypt*, that they were anciently the Barnes and Granaries of the Citie of *Rome*: but now-adayes *Purgatorie* is the Barne of the *Romiſh* Court, yea, the Kitchin, Hall, Parlour, Larder, Cellar, Chamber, every Roome of *Rome*. *David* ſaid, 2 *Sam*. 1. 24, *Ye Daughters of* Iſrael, *weepe for* Saul, *which clothed you in Skarlet with pleaſure, and hanged ornaments of Gold upon your apparell*: But ſhould *Purgatorie* once be removed, weep Pope, Cardinals, Abbots, Biſhops, Fryers; for that is gone which maintained your exceſſive pride. When *Adonijah* ſued for *Abiſhag* the *Shunamite*, *Solomon* ſaid to his Mother, *Aſke for him the Kingdome alſo*. But if once the *Proteſtants* could wring from the *Papiſts* their *Purgatorie*, nay, then would they ſay, Aske the Triple Crowne, Croſſe-Keyes, S. *Angelo*, *Peters* Patrimonie, and All: in a word, were *Purgatorie* taken away, the Pope himſelfe would be in *Purgatorie*, as not knowing which way to maintaine his expenſiveneſſe.

The man is neere unto us, and of our affinitie.] *Naomi* never before made any mention of *Boaz*: ſome, had they had ſo rich a Kinſman, all their diſcourſe ſhould have been a Survey and Inventorie of their Kinſmans goods; they would have made an occaſion at every turne to be talking of them. Well, though *Naomi* did not commonly brag of her Kinſman, yet, when occaſion is offered, ſhe is bold to challenge her intereſt in him.

Obſervation: Poore folks may with modeſtie claime their Kindred in their rich alliance: Let not therefore great Perſonages ſcorne and contemne their poore Kindred. *Cambden* reports of the Citizens of *Corke*, that all of them in ſome degrees are of kindred one to the other: but I thinke, that all wealthie men will hook in the Cousin, and draw in some alliance one to other; but as they will challenge Kindred (where there is none) in rich folkes, so they will denie Kindred where it is in poore; yet is there no just reason they should doe so: All mankind knit together in the same Father in the Creation, and at the Deluge; I know not who lay higher in *Adams* Loynes, or who tooke the Wall in *Eves* Belly. I speake not this to pave the way to an *Anabaptisticall* paritie, but onely to humble and abate the conceits of proud men, who look so scornfull and contemptuous over their poore Kindred.

Use: Let such as are allyed to rich Kindred, be heartily thankfull to God for them; yet so as they under God depend principally on their owne labour, and not on their reference to their Friends; and let them not too earnestly expect helpe from their Kindred, for feare they miscarry. A Scholler being maintained in the Universitie by his Uncle, who gave a Basilisk for his Armes, and expected that he should make him his Heire, wrote these Verses over his Chimney:

Falleris aspectu Basiliscum occidere, Plini,
Nam vitæ nostræ spem Basiliscus alit.

Soone after it happened that his Uncle dyed, and gave him nothing at all; whereupon the Scholler wrote these Verses under the former:

Certè aluit, sed spe vanâ; spes vana venenum;
Ignoscas, Plini, verus es historicus.

So soone may mens expectations be frustrated who depend on rich Kindred: Yea, I have seene the twine-thred of a Cordiall Friend hold, when the Cable-Rope of a rich Kinsman hath broken.

Let those therefore be thankfull to God, to whom God hath given meanes to be maintained of themselves, without dependance on their Kindred: better it is to be the weakest of Substances, to subsist of themselves, then to be the bravest Accidents, to be maintained by another.

Verse 21: *And* Ruth *the* Moabitesse *said, He said unto me alſo, Thou ſhalt keep faſt by my young men, untill they have ended all my Harveſt.*

He ſaid unto me alſo.] *Ruth* perceiving that *Naomi* kindly reſented *Boaz* his favour, and that the diſcourſe of his kindneſſe was acceptable unto her, proceeds in her relation.

Doctrine: People love to enlarge ſuch diſcourſes which they ſee to be welcome to their audience.

What maketh *Tale-bearers* ſo many, and their *Tales* ſo long, but that ſuch perſons are ſenſible that others are pleaſingly affected with their talke? Otherwiſe, a *frowning looke*, Prov. 25. 23, will ſoone put ſuch to ſilence. When *Herod* ſaw, *Acts* 12. 3, that the killing of *James* pleaſed the *Jewes*, he proceeded farther, to take *Peter* alſo. *Detractors*, perceiving that killing of their *Neighbours Credits* is acceptable to others, are encouraged thereby to imbrew their *Tongues* in the murthering of more Reputations.

Secondly, Whereas *Ruth* candidly confeſſeth what favour ſhe found from *Boaz*, we learne, we ought not ſullenly to conceale the bountie of our *Benefactors*, but expreſſe it to their honour, as occaſion is offered. The *Giver* of *Almes* may not, but the *Receiver* of them may, *blow a Trumpet*.

This confuteth the ingratitude of many in our Age; *clamorous* to beg, but *tongue-tyed* to confeſſe what is beſtowed upon them. What the *ſinne againſt the Holy-Ghoſt* is in *Divinitie*, that *Ingratitude* is in *Moralitie*; an Offence unpardonable. Pittie it is, but that *Moone* ſhould ever be in an *Eclipſe*, that will not confeſſe the beames thereof to be borrowed from the *Sunne*. He that hath a *Hand to take*, and no *Tongue to thanke*, deſerves neither *Hand* nor *Tongue*, but to be *lame* and *dumbe* hereafter.

Obſerve by the way, that *Ruth* expreſſeth what tends to the prayſe of *Boaz*, but conceales what *Boaz* ſaid in the prayſe of *her ſelfe*. He had commended her, *verſe* 11, for a *dutifull Daughter in law*, and for leaving an *Idolatrous Land*. But *Ruth* is ſo farre from commending *her ſelfe in a direct Line*, that ſhe will not doe it by reflection, and at the *ſecond hand*, by reporting the commendations which others gave her.

Doctrine: Let another prayſe thee, and not thine owne mouth.

How *Large* are the *Pen-men* of the Scripture in relating their owne faults! How *concise* (if at all) in penning their owne prayses!

It is generally conceived that the Gospel of S. *Marke* was indited by the Apostle *Peter*; and that from his mouth it was written by the hand of *John Marke*, whose Name now it beareth. If so, then we may observe, that *Peters denying of his Master*, with all the circumstances thereof, his *Cursing* and *Swearing*, is more largely related in the Gospel of S. *Marke* then in any other: But as for his *Repentance*, it is set downe more shortly there then in other Gospels: *Mathew* 26. 75, *And he went out and wept bitterly*; *Luke* 22. 62, *And* Peter *went out and wept bitterly*; but *Marke* 14. 72, it is onely said, *When he thought thereon, he wept*.

So short are Gods servants in giving an account of their owne Commendations, which they leave to be related by the mouthes of others.

Thou shalt keepe fast by my young men.] *Objection*: Here either *Ruths* memorie failed her, or else she wilfully committed a foule mistake. For *Boaz* never bad her to *keepe fast by his young men*, but, *verse* 8, *Abide here fast by my Maidens*. It seemes she had a better minde to Male-companie, who had altered the Gender in the relating of his words.

Answer: Condemne not the *Generation of the Righteous*, especially on *doubtfull evidence*. Boaz gave a Command, *verse* 15, *to his young men* to permit her to *gleane*: she mentioneth them therefore in whom the authoritie did reside, who had a *Commission* from their *Master* to countenance and encourage her in her *extraordinarie gleaning*, which Priviledge his Maidens could not bestow upon her.

Verse 22: *And* Naomi *said unto* Ruth *her Daughter in law, It is good, my Daughter, that thou goe out with his Maidens, that they meet thee not in any other field*.

And Naomi *said unto* Ruth, *her Daughter in law*.] *Doctrine*: It is the bounden dutie of Parents, to give the best counsell they can to their Children: As *Naomi* here prescribes wholsome advice unto her Daughter in law.

It is good.] That is, it is better. It is ufuall both in the *Old* and *New Teſtament* to put the *Poſitive* for the *Comparative* in this kinde. Luke 10. 42, Mary *hath choſen that good part;* that is, the *better part.* *It is profitable for thee that one of thy members periſh, and not thy whole body,* Math. 5. 29 ; *profitable,* that is, *more profitable ;* and as it is expounded, Math. 18 .8, *better. It is good for a man not to touch a woman,* 1 Cor. 7. 1 ; that is, *it is better ;* it is more convenient, and freer from trouble, in time of perſecution. *It is good for thee, that thou goe out with his Maidens ;* that is, *it is better.*

Doctrine : Maids are the fitteſt companie for Maids; amongſt whom, a chaſt Widow, ſuch as Ruth was, may well be recounted: *Modeſtie* is the *Life-guard* of *Chaſtitie.*

That they meet thee not in any other field.] Here ſhe rendreth a Reaſon of her *Councell,* becauſe *Ruth* thereby ſhould eſcape ſuſpition, or appearance of evill.

Objection : What hurt or harme had it been, if they had met her *in another field ?* She might have been met there, and yet have departed thence as *pure* and *ſpotleſſe* as ſhe came thither.

Answer : It is granted. Yet, being a *ſingle woman,* ſlanderous Tongues and credulous Eares meeting together had ſome colour to rayſe an ill Report on her Reputation. Beſides, being a *Moabite,* ſhe ought to be more cautious of her Credit; leſt, as ſhe was a *ſtranger,* ſhe might be taken for a *ſtrange woman* in *Solomon his ſenſe.* And therefore *Nimia cautela non nocet.* In ſome eares it is not enough to be honeſt, but alſo to have *teſtes honeſtatis ;* many a Credit having ſuffered, not for want of cleareneſſe, but clearing of it ſelfe, ſurprized on ſuch diſadvantages.

Verſe 23 : *So ſhe kept faſt by the Maidens of* Boaz, *to gleane unto the end of Barley Harveſt and of Wheat Harveſt ; and dwelt with her Mother in law.*

So ſhe kept faſt by the Maidens of Boaz.] Here was good Counſell well given, becauſe thankfully accepted and carefully practiſed.

Doctrine : It is the dutie of Children to follow the advice of their Parents.

We meet with two Examples in wicked perſons, which in this reſpect may condemne many *undutifull Children* of our dayes. The one *Iſmael;* who, though he be charactered to be a wild man, *Gen.* 16. 12, *His hand againſt every man, and every mans hand againſt him :* yet it ſeemes his hand was never againſt his Mother *Hagar,* whom he obeyed in matters of moſt moment ; in his Marriage, *Gen.* 21. 21, *His Mother tooke him a Wife out of the Land of Ægypt.*

The ſecond is *Herodias;* of whom no good at all is recorded, ſave this alone, That ſhe would not beg a Boone of her Father *Herod,* untill firſt ſhe went in to her Mother *Herodias,* tok now what ſhe ſhould aske. How many now-adayes make *Deeds of Gift* of themſelves, without the knowledge and conſent of their *Parents !*

Unto the end of Barley Harveſt.] Commendable is the conſtancie and the continuance of *Ruth* in labour. Many there are who at the firſt have a *ravenous appetite* to worke, but quickly they *ſurfet* thereof. *Ruth* gleanes one day, ſo as ſhe may gleane another ; it is the conſtant pace that goeth fartheſt, and freeſt from being tyred : *Math.* 24. 13, *But he that ſhall endure unto the end, the ſame ſhall be ſaved.*

And dwelt with her Mother in law.] It was Chriſts counſell unto his Diſciples, *Math.* 10. 11, *to abide in the place wherein they did enter,* and not to goe from houſe to houſe. Such the ſetledneſſe of *Ruth ;* where ſhe firſt faſtned, there ſhe fixed : *She dwelt with her Mother.* *Naomi* affords *Ruth* Houſe-room, *Ruth* gaines *Naomi* Food ; *Naomi* provides a Manſion, *Ruth* purveyes for Meat ; and ſo mutually ſerve to ſupply the wants of each other.

If *Envie,* and *Covetouſneſſe,* and *Idleneſſes* were not the hinderances, how might one *Chriſtian* reciprocally be a helpe unto another ! All have ſomething, none have all things ; yet all might have all things in a comfortable and competent proportion, if ſeriouſly ſuting themſelves as *Ruth* and *Naomi* did, that what is defective in one, might be ſupplyed in the other.

FINIS.

[" Within that order which the third feats make
    Is feated Rachel, lower than the other,
    With Beatrice, in manner as thou feeft.
Sarah, Rebecca, Judith, and her who was
    Anceftrefs of the Singer, who for dole
    Of the mifdeed faid, *Miferere mei*,
Canft thou behold from feat to feat defcending."
            Dante's *Paradifo*, Longfellow, xxxii. 7-13.]

IOSEPH'S PARTY-COLOVRED COAT,

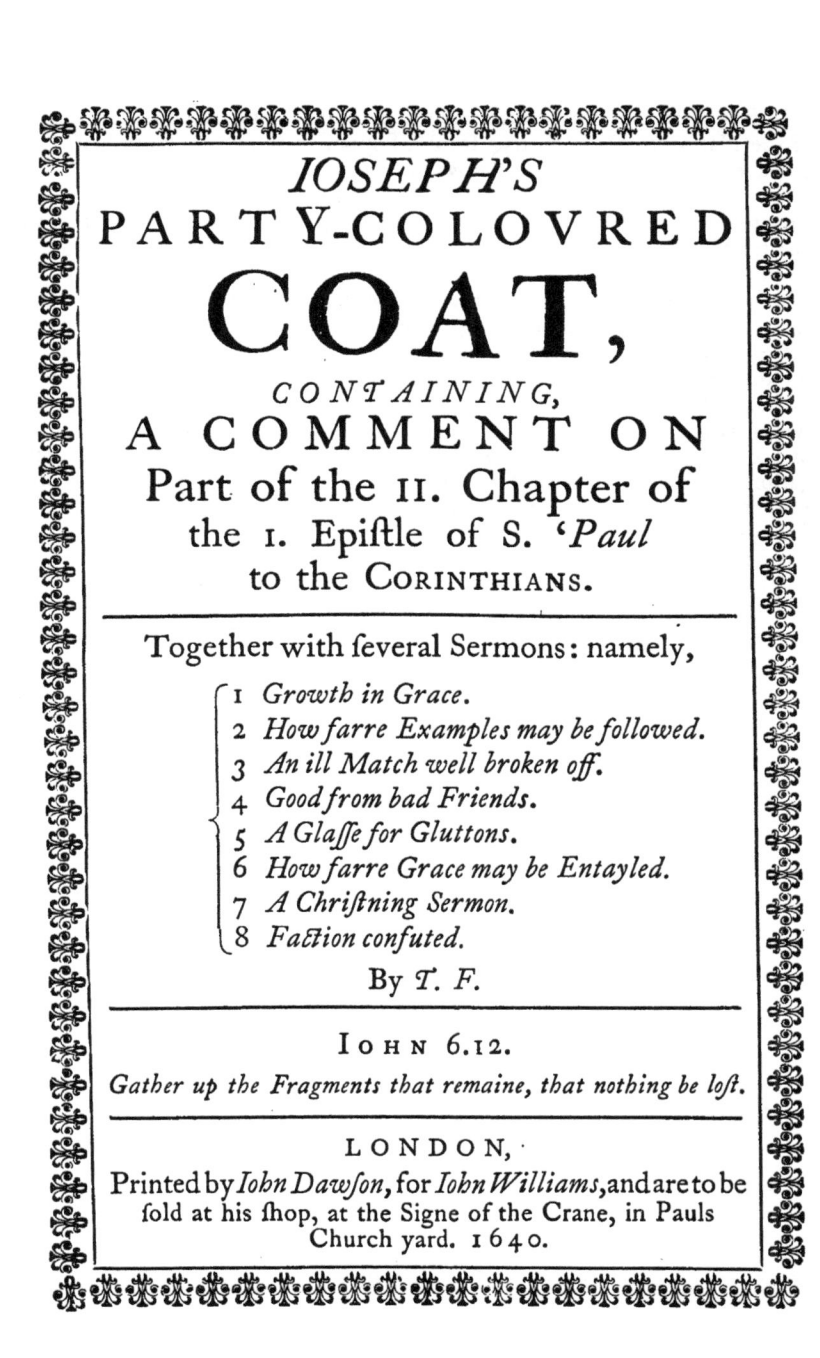

CONTAINING,
A COMMENT ON
Part of the 11. Chapter of
the 1. Epistle of S. *Paul*
to the Corinthians.

Together with several Sermons: namely,

1. *Growth in Grace.*
2. *How farre Examples may be followed.*
3. *An ill Match well broken off.*
4. *Good from bad Friends.*
5. *A Glasse for Gluttons.*
6. *How farre Grace may be Entayled.*
7. *A Christning Sermon.*
8. *Faction confuted.*

By *T. F.*

Iohn 6.12.
Gather up the Fragments that remaine, that nothing be lost.

LONDON,
Printed by *Iohn Dawson*, for *Iohn Williams*, and are to be sold at his shop, at the Signe of the Crane, in Pauls Church yard. 1640.

["But after the manducation of the Paschal Lamb, it was the custom of the Nation to sit down to a second Supper in which they ate herbs and unleavened bread; the *Major-domo* first dipping his morsel, and then the family; after which the Father brake bread into pieces, and distributed a part to every of the Guests, and first drinking himself, gave to the rest the chalice filled with wine, according to the age and dignity of the person; adding to each distribution a form of benediction proper to the mystery, which was Eucharistical and commemorative of their Deliverance from *Egypt*. This supper *Jesus* being to celebrate, changed the forms of benediction, turned the Ceremony into Mystery, and gave his Body and Blood in Sacrament and religious configuration; so instituting the venerable Sacrament, which from the time of its institution is called *the Lord's Supper;* which Rite *Jesus* commanded the apostles to perpetuate in commemoration of him their Lord untill his second coming. And this was the first delegation of a perpetual Ministery which *Jesus* made to his apostles, in which they were to be succeeded to in all the generations of the Church."— JEREMY TAYLOR's *Great Exemplar of Sanctity*, &c.; part iii. sect. xv. page 350, ed. 1702.]

TO

The Right Worſhipfvl,

the Lady IANE COVERT,

of Peper Harrow

in SURRY.

MADAM,

CVSTOME hath made it not only pardonable, but neceſſary to flatter in Dedicatory Epiſtles: Epitaphs, and Dedications, are credited alike.

But I will not follow the ſtreame herein: Firſt, becauſe I account it beneath my calling to ſpeake any thing above the truth. Secondly, becauſe of you it is needleſſe: Let deformed Faces be beholding to the Painter; Art hath nothing to doe, where Nature hath prevented it.

Wherefore I will turne my prayſing of you, into prayer for you, deſiring God to ſtrengthen and increaſe all goodneſſe in you, and give you perſeverance (that golden Claſpe) which joynes Grace and Glory together.

Thus deſiring to ſhroud my weake labours under your favourable Patronage, I reſt

Your Ladiſhips in all ſervice,

T. F.

[Introduction.

THIS quaintly-entitled collection of sermons connects itself with the preacher's Dorsetshire cure, and his Salisbury canonry,—"*none of the worst Livings*, and *one of the best Prebends in England*," as he termed them (*Appeal of Iniured Innocence*, 1659, part i. page 2). The Prebendal stall of Netherbury-in-Ecclesia, near Beaminster, had, 18th June, 1631, been bestowed upon the young divine by his uncle DAVENANT, Bishop of Salisbury, who moreover had in 1622 advanced the elder THOMAS FULLER to the Prebend of Highworth, Wilts., in the same Church. The son had afterwards occasion to remind his opponent, Dr. HEYLIN, who had imputed to Fuller disloyalty to his Church, that his "*Extraction* who was *Prebendarius Prebendarides*, and *relation* (as the *Animadvertor* knows) to two no meane Bishops, my Uncles" (TOWNSON and DAVENANT), might clear him from any episcopal antipathy (*Appeal*, part iii. page 47). Picturesque and instructive details of cathedral-life at Salisbury at this time have (as if to compensate for the disfavour shown to literary inquirers at the Episcopal registry) been given to the public in the *Fourth Report of the Royal Commission on Hist. MSS.* This Blue-book contains the detailed replies to Archbishop LAUD's Visitation-Articles of 1634, from the original documents in the House of Lords (pages 127 *seq.*). FULLER's name is not found amongst the printed answers (they belong to May, 1634) of the Prebendaries, perhaps because, not being a Canon-residentiary, his visits to the cathedral were infrequent. On two other occasions only does he himself refer to his position at Salisbury, viz., in *Good Thoughts in Bad Times*, § Mixt Contemplations, No. xxii. page 241 (ed. 1645); and in the *Worthies*, § Wilts., page 145. Certain of his cousins and connections, who were likewise non-resident, are, however, named in the *Report*, as giving joint or particular replies to some of the twenty-nine articles of inquiry. Dr. EDWARD DAVENANT, his cousin (formerly his college-tutor, but then holding preferment in Wiltshire, Somersetshire, and Berkshire), makes four answers, and then adds: "To the rest of the articles given in charge, I, being only a prebend at large, and not resident among them who have the immediate care and government of the Church, am able to say nothing;" and their relative John TOWNSON (who was then holding the stall of the elder FULLER) is similarly reticent (page 132). The longer and more interesting replies definitely indicate at once the duties and defaults of the canons. According to a statute made "by the now Lord Bishop" (Dr. DAVENANT), and the Dean (Dr. MASON) and chapter seven in number, the Prebendaries were to preach in their own turn in the Cathedral, on Sundays and holydays, and they were to wear the surplice and the square cap (according to the canon and ancient cuftoms of the Church) ; but if unable to perform their duty, fome other Prebendary or able preacher might do it upon the Dean and Chapter being acquainted beforehand; "yet this good ordinance hath ben broken by many" (page 128). Some of the replies in the documents which admit that in the Church there was "a faction againft the Church," are of a recriminatory nature ; and they all reveal a remiffnefs in duty and a ftate of diffenfion that muft have haraffed the prefiding bifhop, who was, fays his nephew, "happy to die before his order for a time died, April, 1641" (*Worthies*, § London, page 207). Like this "Good Bifhop," the "fecond JEWELL of Salifbury," FULLER kept ftrictly to the Canonical regulations of JAMES I.'s reign ; and he could therefore appeal, as his compurgators in an unjuft accufation that was afterwards made againft him of being "carelefs of furplice, hood, and band," to "fuch as knew my conformity in the Colledge Chappel, Country Parifhes,. and Cathedral of Sarum" (*Appeal*, part ii. page 80). It is, however, afferted in one of the Vifitation-replies that furplice and hood were then feen in the cathedral fcarce once a quarter (page 131).

About three years after this laft preferment, FULLER was appointed by his uncle to the Rectory of Broadwindfor, near Beaminfter, Dorfetfhire. The living was then in the diocefe of Briftol ; and hence arofe the election of FULLER, then a Bachelor of Divinity, as a Proctor for that diocefe, in the famous Convocation of 1640. The ftate of ecclefiaftical matters in the thriving villages of the weft took their complexion from the towns. In the "Remembrancer" that accompanies the documents relating to the Vifitation of the diocefe, it is faid that "in moft parifhes in Wiltfhyre, Dorcetfhyre, and the Wefterne partes, there is ftill a puritane and an honeft man chofen churchwardens together. The puritane alwayes croffes the other in repayres and adorning the church, as alfo in the prefentments of vnconformtyes, and in the iffue putts fome trick or other vpon the honeft man, to putt him to fue for his charges hee hath been at for the church. Y^u fhall find it at this inftant in the parifh of Beaminfter in Dorfettfhyre, between CRABB and ELLERY. The fuit now pending" (page 131). The firft of thefe litigants was the Rev. JOSEPH CRABB, M.A., one of CALAMY's ejected minifters (i. 176, ed. 1802), but who died Vicar of Axminfter in 1699. CRABB was, with WILL. BALL and THO. LYE (who alfo belonged to the Weft), concerned in fetting forth *Eighteen Sermons preached* (by Archbifhop USSHER) *in Oxford* in 1640 (4to. 1660), —thefe three editors being perhaps the note-takers mentioned in the Epiftle as "fuch who had the pens of ready writers." The Rev. STANLEY GOWER of Dorchefter wrote the preface to this volume.—With reference to ELLERY, the troublefome Churchwarden, there is an aifle in Beaminfter Church, built by the ELLERY or HILARY family, of Meerhay, between whom and the Vicar for the time being there was a continual feud.

The religious queftions which had in FULLER's time entered into difcuffion, were not a little heightened by the political fituation of the country. Of thefe troubles the only indication in the following Sermons is perhaps found in certain paffages in the laft of the feries, called *Faction Confuted*. An air of peace feems, indeed, to pervade the Church-life of the preacher, his connection with his benefice and cathedral being the "fimple annals" of a good parson. That he ranked high in the opinion of his ruftic parifhioners is fhown by an anecdote related in his anonymous *Life*, 1661, pages 9, 10; and none the lefs exemplary was his intercourfe with his fellow-canons, among whom are to be found the names of fome who became as famous as himfelf.

The fermons show that the author's churchmanfhip was of a found kind, being as far removed from the high Anglicanism that was affuming authority, as from the fimple ritual of the Anabaptifts. He was emphatically a moderate Divine. Hence his warning to kill the itch of novelty, and to keep to the old paths (page 122); his plea for the "decent garnifhing" of churches (page 113); his objection to general cenfures (page 116); &c.

As in the former addreffes, we have here a running commentary on the paffage which deals with the diffenfions in the Corinthian affemblies, and with the Lord's Supper (1 Cor. xi. 18–30). The nature of the fubject draws the preacher into deeper and more debateable topics, which are reverently handled. His knowledge of the human heart is feen in his remarks on worthinefs in receiving the Sacrament (pages 151 *seq.*), on felf-examination (pages 155 *seq.*), &c.; while his acquirements in hiftorical divinity may be gathered from the difcuffion of tradition (pages 135 *seq.*), transubstantiation (pages 142 *seq.*), &c.

Amongft many noticeable paffages is the character of the Founder of a herefy (pages 120 *seq.*), which is equal in finifh to any of the portraits in *The Holy and Profane State*. This fketch was perhaps the original of The Heretic in that work (ed. 1652, page 378).

There are copies of *Jofeph's Party-colovred Coat* differing from others in respect of corrections of certain errors of the prefs. The uncorrected copies have no border round the title-page. This book has been reprinted once only, viz. in 1867 (London, 8vo. Tegg), edited by William NICHOLS.

Lady JANE COVERT, the patronefs of this volume (*anteà*, page cix.), was the eldeft daughter and co-heirefs of Sir JOHN SHIRLEY, of Isfield, co. Suffex, Knight, where fhe was baptized, 3rd January, 1596-7. She was thrice married. Firft, to Sir WALTER COVERT of Slougham, Suffex, Knight, 22nd Auguft, 1616. She was next united to Sir JOHN FREAKE of Cerne, co. Dorfet, Knight, about 1632-3. Her abode in this county explains her connection with thefe fermons; and FULLER addreffes her, as was cuftomary, by her old title. The lady's third hufband was DENZELL HOLLES, firft Baron HOLLES (married 12th March, 1641-2), to whom fhe was fecond wife, and who furvived her. Her will, dated 31st July, 1658, was proved 13th April, 1667. In this document fhe defcribes herfelf as "Dame JANE COVERT, of Cerne Abbas, co. Dorfet," mentioning her jointure-houfe at Pepper Harrow. She was buried at Iwerne Courtnay, co. Dorfet, 25th April, 1666.]

A Comment
on 1 Cor. 11. 18. &c.

Verſe 18: *For firſt of all when you come together in the Church, I heare there be diviſions among you, and I partly beleeve it.*

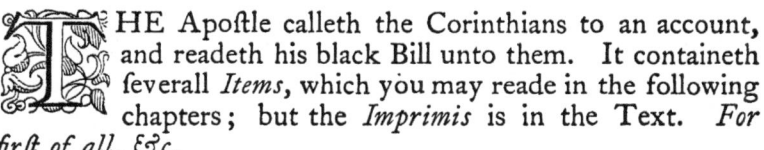

THE Apoſtle calleth the Corinthians to an account, and readeth his black Bill unto them. It containeth ſeverall *Items*, which you may reade in the following chapters; but the *Imprimis* is in the Text. *For firſt of all, &c.*

When you come together in the Church, &c.] *Obſervation:* Even in the non-age and infancy of Chriſtianity, there were Churches appointed for Gods holy ſervice. True, ſome take *Church* here, *pro cœtu fidelium*; yet *Theophylact* and all Greeke Writers generally expound it, the materiall place of meeting.

Two things then were chiefly aymed at in Churches: 1. Receipt, that the place were capable to containe the people. 2. Privacie.

Being then under perſecution they built not their Churches to be ſeene, but not to be ſeen; and then were as plaine in their houses as in their dealing. Beauty and Magnificenſe were of later date in Chriſtian Temples, when Religion grew acquainted with peace and proſperity; and good reaſon Gods houſe now ſhould bee decently garniſhed: Some, ſhunning whoriſh gaudineſſe, leave the Church to ſluttiſh naſtineſſe; the Font (our Iordan) having more mud than water in it; the Communion-table unſeemingly kept.

H

Caution: Withall let us take heed left as it hath been obferved in England, that great Houfe-building hath beene the bane of good Houfe-keeping: So let us take heed left piety in us bee fo much the worfe, by how much our Churches are better then they were in the time of Saint *Paul:* What a fhame would it be, if there fhould be more light in the Church windows than in our underftanding, more pious fentences written in their wals than in our hearts, more uniformity in the building than in our behaviours!

I heare there be divifions among you.] *Queftion:* How came Saint *Paul* by this intelligence? Was not hee at Philippi when hee wrote this Epiftle, (as appears by the Poftfcript), which was many miles from Corinth? How heard the Apoftle of thefe divifions at fuch a diftance?

Anfwer: Saint *Paul* was cunning in a kind of Chriftian and lawfull Magick. All the world was his circle; (for fo he faith of himfelfe, *The care of all Churches lyeth upon me*, 2 *Cor.* 11. 28;) and fome faithfull friends in every Church were his familiar Spirits in this circle, to inform him of all confiderable paffages. So that Saint *Paul* was at Corinth, when hee was not at Corinth; abfent in perfon, prefent by his Proxies, thefe Intelligencers which kept correfpondencie with him.

Doctrine: Men in authority have quick eares to heare at a great diftance. The mutterings of Malefactors are hollowings to Magiftrates, who heare diftinctly what offenders but whifper to themfelves.

Ufe: Let none therefore be encouraged to finne through a confidence to be concealed: What though Sinners be the fervants of the Prince of darkeneffe, and therefore hope to obtain from their Lord and Mafter a protection that no punifhment may arreft them? yet let them know, that though the place wherein they fin feeme to them as darke as Egypt, it is as light to men in authority as the land of Gofhen: Lyons fleepe with their eyes open; Magiftrates with their eyes both open, and feeing: when wee thinke them blind, they *Behold:* when deafe, with Saint *Paul* they *Heare.*

Queftion: Did thefe men (whofoever they were) well in telling Saint *Paul* thefe difcords of the Corinthians? Had they not better have gone backward, and covered the nakednesse of their neighbours with the cloake of silence? Pitty it is but that his tongue should bee for ever bound to the peace, who will prate of every fault hee finds in another; and at the best they are but clacks and tel-tales for their paines.

Answer: Had they told it to some scoffing *Cham* or mocking *Ismael*, who would have made musick to himselfe of the Corinthians discords, then they had been faulty in relating the faults of others: *Tell it not in Gath, nor publish it in Askalon, lest, &c.* 2 *Sam.* 1. 20; but it being told to S. *Paul,* who would not mock, but bemoan, not defame, but reform these offenders, it was no breach, but a deed of charity, and the doers hereof benefactors herein to the Church of Corinth.

Doctrine: It is both lawfull and laudable to discover the faults of our dearest friends, to those who have power and place to reforme them. Thus *Ioseph* brought to his father *Iacob* the evill deeds of his brethren, *Gen.* 37. 2. Indeed the Devill is called the Accuser of the brethren, *Revel.* 12. 10; but he accuseth them often without cause, even without charity, who since hee hath been cast into hell knowes no other heaven then to doe mischiefe. But for a man to open the sins, the wounds of his neighbour, not with desire to put him to torment, but that the Chyrurgion may search and salve them, is an action most charitable.

There are divisions.] *Objection:* But did not Saint *Paul* in the second verse of this Chapter prayse the Corinthians? *Now I commend you brethren, that you remember me in all things, and keepe the Ordinances as I delivered them to you.* Were they growne so bad since the beginning of this Chapter? or doth Saint *Paul* with Saint *Augustine* write a retractation of what hee had written before? Is this faire dealing, that hee who formerly had by his commendations given the Corinthians a generall Acquittance from all their faults, should now come over them with an after-reckoning, and charge them with the sin of divisions?

Answer 1: Some answer, [1]*Omnia, id est, pleraque omnia.*

---

[1] Cornelius à Lapide *on the Text* [*i.e.* on verse 2, Ed. Paris, 1638, page 283].

So that all the ordinances are to be expounded the greatest part of them.

2. Others by Ordinances understand onely certaine Ecclesiasticall [1]Rites and Ceremonies, touching the discipline of the Church, which had no necessary influence, either on doctrine or manners; so that the Corinthians might be observant of all these, and yet peccant both in life and beliefe.

If this bee the meaning, then let us take heed that though we be whole in discipline, wee be not halting in Doctrine; though found in ceremonies, not sick in manners; there being no such inseparable connexion betwixt the one and the other, but that a man may observe all orders in Church service, and yet be disorderly in his life and conversation. Lightning oft times breaks the sword, yet bruises not the scabard; so error and vitiousnesse may breake all piety and religion in us, though in the mean time the sheath of Religion (formall decency and outward conformity) remaine in us found and entire.

Calvins [2]opinion is that the Apostle commending the Corinthians, meaneth the maine and general body of the Church, though there might be many straglers justly to be reproved, confessing *Laborasse quidem alios alijs vitijs: Interea tamen ab universo corpore retentam fuisse formam quam commendaverat.* That Church therefore is, and is to be counted and commended for a good Church, whose head is whole, heart healthful, all vital parts entire, though having a lame leg, a bleared eye, a withered hand, some bad and vitious members, belonging unto it.

And I partly beleeve it.] That is, I beleeve some of you are guilty of this fault, though others be innocent.

Doctrine: Generall censures condemning whole Churches are altogether uncharitable. Angle out the offenders by themselves, but take heed of killing all with a Drag-net: And grant many, yea, most to be faulty, yet some may be guiltlesse. Wickednesse was not so generall a Rule in Sodome, but that righteous *Lot* was an exception from it. See *Obadiah* (as a

---

[1] Thom. Morton *in his Comment upon the* 1 Cor. 11.
[2] Cal[vin, on] 1 Cor. 11. 2 [*Com. in omnes Pauli Apostoli Epistolas*, Ed. Geneva, 1600, page 192].

Iewell in the head of a Toad) Steward of *Ahabs* wicked houfhold. Yea, feeing Impiety intrudes it felfe amongft the thickeft of Gods Saints, (even drowning *Cham* in *Noahs* Arke,) juft it is that God fhould have fome names even where the throne of Satan is erected.

Let us therfore follow the wary proceedings of *Iehu*, 2 *Kings* 10. 23, who being about to kil *Baals* Priefts, caufed a ftrict fearch before to be made: *Search and look that there be here with you none of the fervants of the Lord, but the fervants of Baal only.* So when wee are about with cenfuring, to murder the credits of many together, let us take heed that there be not fome Orthodoxe amongft thofe whom we condemn al to be Hereticks; fome that defire to bee peaceable in this our Ifrael, amongft thofe whom wee condemne for all factious Schifmaticks.

But thefe words (*I partly beleeve it*) may thus alfo be expounded, as wel of the faults, as of the perfons, as if he had faid, I beleeve thefe accufations only in part, and hope they are not fo bad as they are reported.

Doctrine: When Fames are brought unto us from good hands, let us not be fo incredulous as to beleeve no part of them; nor fo uncharitable as to beleeve all; but with Saint *Paul* partly beleeve it. The good man carrieth a Court of Chancery in his owne bofome, to mitigate the rigour of common reports with equall and favourable interpretations.

Reafon 1: Becaufe Fame often creates fomething of nothing, always makes a great deale of a little. 'Tis true of Fame what is faid of the Devill: It has beene a Lyar from the beginning. Yea, and fometimes a Murderer. *Abfalom* flew one of *Davids* fonnes, and Fame killed all the reft, 2 *Sam.* 13. 30.

2. Becaufe men in reporting things often mingle their own interefts and ingagements with their Relations, and making them better, or worfe, as they themfelves ftand affected: Water refembleth both the tafte and colour of that earth through which it runneth; fo reports rellifh of their Relators, and have a blufh and a fmack of their partiall difpofitions, and therfore fuch Relations are not to be beleeved in their full latitude, extent, and dimenfion.

It confutes (1) Thofe that will beleeve nothing of what they heare reported, though warranted by never so good witnesses. Though they be perswaded, they will not be perswaded, and will not credit any accusations though never so just. Yea, sometimes are so farre from trusting the tongues of others, that they wil not trust their owne eyes: I beare them witnesse these men have charity, but not according to knowledge.

(2) But where too much charity hath slaine her thousands, too little hath slaine her ten thousands. More men there be who take all reports upon the credit of the Relators, and never weigh them in the scales of their owne judgements to see if they bee too light or no: Yea, some are so excessive in this kind, their beliefe out-stretcheth the report: what is told them to be done out of ignorance, they beleeve to be out of knowledge; what is told them to be done out of infirmity, they beleeve to bee done out of presumption: they need not say with the man in the Gospel, *Lord, I beleeve, helpe my unbeleefe*; but, Lord, pardon my too much beliefe, pardon my over-credulity, in that I beleeve all, and more than all reported.

To conclude, let not our beliefes be altogether of clay to receive any impression, nor altogether of Iron to receive none at all. But as the toes in the Image of *Nebuchadnezzars* Dreame were partly iron and partly clay: So let our beliefes be composed of charity mixt with our credulity; that when a crime is reported wee may with Saint *Paul* partly beleeve it.

Verse 19: *For there must be also heresies among you, that they which are approved may be made manifest among you.*

Ere Saint *Paul* argueth *a minore ad majus*, being the more easily induced to beleeve there might be divisions among them, becauſe alſo there muſt be Hereſies.

Doctrine: *Hereſies are worſe than Schiſms, falſe doctrines more dangerous than diviſions.* The former ſinnes againſt Faith; the later, againſt Charity; and though theſe two Graces be ſiſters and twins, yet Faith is the eldeſt and choyceſt.

However, as children uſe to ſay, they love Father and Mother both beſt: So let us hate Hereſies and Schiſms both worſt. The rather becauſe ſchiſme is a fit ſtock to graft

Heresie on; yea, of their owne accord, old Schismaticks ripened with age, grow young Heretikes: witnesse the Donatists, who (as Saint [1]*Augustine* saith) were but pure Schismaticks at first, and turned Heretikes afterwards.

Question : What is a Heresie? A demand very important to be answered, seeing Saint *Paul* saith, *Acts* 24. 14, *After the way which they call Heresie, so worship I the God of my Fathers.*

Answer: Heresie is an errour in the fundamentals of Religion, mayntayned with obstinacy. It must be in the fundamentals. In the Primitive Church many were too lavish in bestowing the name of Heretike on those which dissented from the Church, in (as I may say) Veniall errours. A charitable man would have been loath to have beene of the Jury, to condemne *Iovinian* for an Heretike on no other evidence than that hee mayntayned marriage in merit to be equall with Virginity. As therefore by those many Kings mentioned in the old Testament, thirty and one in the little land of Canaan, *Josh.* 12. 24, is meant onely Toparchs, not great Kings, but Lords of a little Dition and Dominion; So in the ancient Catalogues of Heretikes (especially of that which [2]*Phylaster* made) we may understand in some of them onely erroneous persons, swarving from the truth.

The next thing necessary in an Heresie is that it be maintained with obstinacy, which is the dead flesh, making the greene wound of an errour fester into the old soare of an Heresie. Those two hundred men of Ierusalem, 2 *Sam.* 15.11, who followed *Absolom* to Hebron in their simplicity, and knew not any thing, cannot properly be counted Traytors or Rebels: No more can people purely erroneous, who doe not bolt and barre their eyes against the beames of truth, but willingly would imbrace it if delivered unto them, and maintaine an errour out of conscience, not knowing the truth, be accounted Heretikes. Charitable therefore was the cautiousnesse of *Epiphanius*, who would not condemne the Anthropomorphites for Heretickes, (who, mistaking some places of

---

[1] Libro *de Hæresibus ad quod vult Deum.*
[2] S. Aug[ustine] *loco prius citato* saith of him, *Hæreses quidem ipse commemorat, sed mihi appellandæ hæreses non videntur.*

Scripture which speake of Gods eyes, feet, and hands, conceived him to bee of a bodily substance,) but rather imputed it to their simplicity than obstinacy, *Rusticitati eorum tribuens.*

Question: Whether doth every Heretike maintain that which in his owne conscience he knowes to be false?

Answer: No: perchance some Heretikes at first may strive to defend errors, even against the reluctancies of their own judgements, and God may afterwards justly take from them that light which they thrust from themselves: and as great Lyars tell lyes so long till at last they themselves beleeve them to bee true: so many Heretikes so long mainetaine falshoods against their judgement, till at last, being delivered up to a Reprobate Mind, they beleeve their very errours to be truth.

And wee will take just occasion to describe those qualities which dispose a man to bee a Father and Founder of an Heresie.

1. He must be abominably proud: Pride is the key of the worke, especially spirituall pride. When one is elated with conceited sanctity above others, chiefly he wil snarle with his Superiours, and quarrel with men in authority, that those are before him in place, which are behind him in piety. 2. To pride add discontentment, that his preferments bare not proportion to his supposed deserts; thus *Arius* would be an Arian, because he could not bee a Bishop. 3. Learning void of humility. *The Serpent was the subtilest of all the beasts in the field,* Gen. 3. 1: in this kind a Dunce is no dish for the Devils tooth. But in default of learning, good naturall parts will serve the turne, especially Memory (which is θαυματουργός, a Wonder-working facultie) and a fluent expression: so that when hee calleth for words, *Gad: Behold, a Troope commeth.* If both learning and natural parts bee wanting, yet (as when the golden shields were taken away, *Rehoboams* brazen Shields did the deed, and made as much glittering, 2 *Chron.* 12. 10) boldnesse and brazen-fac't impudence will supply the place, especially if hee trades with the Vulgar, broaches dregs, and founds a dull and sottish Heresie which hath no affinity with Learning. [4.] To varnish all these there must bee pretended Piety and Austerity of life, and how fowle or filthy soever

the Posterne or Back doore be, the door which opens to the street must be swept and garnished. Put all these together, Pride, Discontent, Learning (at least-wise good parts, or impudency), pretended sanctity; and they spel together *Hæresiarcham*, one cut and carved out to be Ring-leader and Captaine of an heresie.

To prevent these mischiefes, let such men pray to God for Humility, (that vertue which is most worth, yet costeth the least to keepe it,) and beware of spirituall pride, which is the Hectick Fever of the soule, feeding on the very moisture of the heart of Piety. Let them beware of discontentment, which is a direct quarrelling with God, who is the fountaine of all preferment, though men may be the channell; and hee who hath the least from Him, hath more than he deserveth: And grant preferment is denyed thee, bee not so childish to cast away a Crowne, because thou canst not get a counter; willingly throw away thy soul, and foolishly revenge the fault of the times (as thou countest it) upon thy selfe. Lastly, if God hath bestowed good parts upon thee, pray to him to sanctifie them to thee; otherwise the greatest memory may soone forget it selfe, and a fluent tongue may cut his throat that hath it.

So much for the Character of an Arch-Heretike. But those whose barren wits want pregnancy to be the Mothers of Heresies, may notwithstanding serve for dry Nurses to feed and foster them; and to this purpose the Devil will make use of them.

A plaine Follower of an Heresie may bee thus described: First, he must be ignorant, for hee that knowes nothing will beleeve any thing. These bee Maidens for their Religion; and therefore the opinion which first woed them first wins them, first come first served. Old Sèducers, as it is 2 Tim. 3. 6, 7, *Creepe into houses, and leade captive silly women laden with sinnes, led away with divers lusts, ever learning, and never able to come to the knowledge of the truth.* Secondly, desirous of Novelty: It is an old humour for men to love new things, and in this poynt even many Barbarians are Athenians Lastly, (what resulteth from the two former,) they must have the persons of men in much admiration, doting on some fancied mans parts and perfections, and entertayning anything he saith, becauſe he ſaid it.

To prevent theſe miſchiefes, that men may not be Followers of Hereſies, let the meaneſt-parted labour to attaine to ſome competent meaſure of knowledge in matters of ſalvation, that ſo hee may not truſt every ſpirit, but be able to try whether he bee of God, or no. Beleeve no man with impliciete faith in matters of ſuch moment; for hee who buyes a Iewell in a caſe, without ever looking on it, deſerves to be couzened with a Briſtoll Stone, in ſtead of a Diamond. Secondly, kill the itch of novelty in thy ſoule, practiſing the Prophets Precept, *Jer.* 6. 16, Thus ſaith the Lord, *Stand yee in the wayes, and ſee, and aske for the old pathes, where is the good way, and walk therein, and yee ſhall find reſt for your ſoules.* Laſtly, love and admire no mans Doctrine for his perſon, but rather love his perſon for his Doctrine.

And now to returne to the very words of the Text.

There muſt be alſo Hereſies.] There is a double Muſt, or a two-fold neceſſity of things being: firſt, an abſolute neceſſity; when the thing hath in it ſelfe the cauſe of its neceſſary being: Thus God alone *Muſt Be:* (for what can bee, if being it ſelfe be not?) and muſt bee good, and muſt bee true. Secondly, a conditionate *Muſt*, or a neceſſity, *ex hypotheſi*, which muſt needs bee if ſuch a thing be granted before. As, ſuppoſe the Sun be riſen, and it muſt bee day. Such a conditionate neceſſity is this in the Text: For upon the preſuppoſition of theſe two things which cannot be denyed: that the Devill goeth about like a roaring Lyon ſeeking whom he may devoure; and that the fleſh luſteth againſt the ſpirit, making men prone to all wickedneſſe: hence it followeth ther muſt be hereſies. Thus he that beholdeth a family, and findeth the Maſter to be careleſſe, the Miſtris negligent, the ſons riotous, the ſervants unfaithfull; hee may ſafely conclude that family cannot be ſafe, but muſt be ruined; *There muſt be hereſies*: paralel to that, Luke 17. 1, *It is impoſſible but that offences ſhould come.* But farre bee it from us to conceive that God impoſeth a fatall neceſſity, or by the irreſiſtableneſſe of his Decree urgeth or enforceth any to bee Heretikes: their badneſſe he wiſely permits, but in no wiſe is the cauſe or Author thereof.

Among you.] You Corinthians, though men of excellent parts and endowments, are not priviledged from having hereſies among you; yea, happily [haply] becauſe of your excellent naturall gifts, are more diſpoſed thereunto. Or take it generally, Among you Chriſtians, for properly hereſies have their riſe and originall out of the Church, and iſſue thence, according to the 1 *Iohn* 2. 19, *They went out from us, but they were not of us; for if they had, &c.* I ſee not therefore how *Epiphanius* can well make Platoniſts and Pythagoreans to bee Heretikes, (the latter for their opinion of Tranſanimation,) ſeeing neither of theſe were ever of the Church.

That they which are approved may be made manifeſt among you.] That they whom God from all eternity in his ſecret councell hath approved, may have their Epiphany and manifeſtation unto the world; that, thus diſcovered, they may receive from men a Teſtimoniall of their ſoundneſſe and ſincerity. Not that God hereby gaineth any acceſſion of knowledge (*fore-knowne unto God are all his workes from the beginning of the world, Act.* 15. 18), but others hereby are certified and aſſured of that which was doubtfull before: Thus often times Gold-ſmiths, though they themſelves bee ſufficiently ſatisfied of the goodneſſe of the gold, yet *put it to the touch* to content the Beholders.

And hereby alſo thoſe which are not approved are made manifeſt. Many who doe εὐπροσωπῆσαι ἐν σαρκί, make a brave ſhew in the fleſh, and carry it in a high tryumphant way, wil prove but baſe when brought to the tryal. Whilſt many unknowne men, of whom the world tooke no notice, not ſuſpected for any worth, ſhall acquit themſelves valiant and appeare glorious to God and all good men: Many a bright candle formerly hid under a buſhell, of a private and obſcure life, ſhall then be ſet on a Candleſtick and ſhine forth to the world: And ſhall cauſe,

1. Glory to God, who ſhall be honoured and prayſed in

these his servants, and, as it is *Matth.* 9. 8, *The multitudes will marvell, and glorifie God which hath given such power unto men.*

2. Honour to these his Champions of the truth. Never had *Athanasius* so answered his name and beene so truly immortall in his memory, but for opposing of the Arrians. Never had Saint *Augustine* been so famous but for quelling of Manicheans, Pelagians, Donatists, and whom not? for all his Heretikes lay pat for his hand to dash them in peeces.

3. Clearing to the Truth: her old Evidences which have layd long neglected wil then be searched and found out; her rusty Arguments will be scoured over and furbished up. Many will run to and fro, and knowledge shal be increased. Those which before shooting at the Truth, were over, under, or wide, wil now, with the left handed Gibeonites, hit the mark at an haires bredth, and faile not: Many parts of true Doctrine have bin but slenderly guarded, till once they were assaulted by Heretikes; and many good Authors in those points which were never opposed, have written but loosely, and suffered unwary passages to fall from their posting pens. But when theeves are about the countrey, every one will ride with his sword and stand on his guard: when Heretikes are abroad in the world, Writers weigh each word, ponder each phrase, that they may give the enemies no advantage.

4. Confirmation to weak Christians. Many, whose hearts and affections were loyall to the Truth, but likely to be overborne by the violence of the opposite party, will hereby be strengthened and established in the Right.

5. Those will bee reduced, who (as *Agrippa* said of himselfe, *Act*. 26. 28, *That hee was almost a Christian*) are almost Heretikes, not as yet *Formati et Radicati Hæretici*, but such as well going (or rather ill going) that way will plucke one foot out of the snare, and will returne to the bosome of the Church.

6. Lastly, the Hardned will bee made unexcusable, who obstinately persist in their errours: They cannot plead they lost their way for want of Guides, but for meere wilfulnesse. And thus God is so good, hee would suffer no Heretikes to

bee in the World; were hee not alſo ſo ſtrong and ſo wiſe that hee can extract thus many goods by permitting them.

Verſes 20, 21: *When you come together therefore into one place, this is not to eate the Lords Supper. For in eating, every one taketh before other his own Supper; and one is hungry, and another is drunken.*

OF the ſenſe of the firſt of theſe verſes are many and different opinions, both what is meant by *This is not to eate*, and *the Lords Supper*. Omitting varietie of Interpretations, we wil embrace that which we conceive the beſt.

This is not to eate the Lords Supper.] As if hee had ſaid: True it is, yee Corinthians, when yee come together to one place, you *eate the Lords Supper;* (meaning the body and blood of Chriſt in the Sacrament, ſo expounded by [1] Saint *Auguſtine*, and *Ambroſe*, with many other Latine Writers;) and yet though *you eate it*, you doe not eate it. You perform the materiall part of the action, but leave out the life and ſoule thereof, not doing it legally and ſolemnely according to Chriſts Inſtitution. Such is your want of charity and exceſſe of riot in your *Love-feaſts* (which you eate before the Sacrament), whereby your ſoules are diſturbed, diſtempered, and quite put out of tune to eate the *Supper of the Lord*, as yee ought.

Doctrine: A duty *not done as it ought to be done, is in effect not done at all*. Eſay 64. 7: *There is none that calleth upon thy name, that ſtirreth up himſelfe to take hold of thee*. Not that the true Church of God, in whoſe perſon it is ſpoken (as Antiquity expounds it, and may bee demonſtrated by unanſwerable Arguments), do any times wholly neglect, though too often negligently performe their calling on God; not doing it with that faith and conſtancy, care and fervencie, devotion and diligence, as they ought, and God requires;

---

[1] *Epiſt*. 118. *ad Ianuar*. cap. 5. *Ipſam acceptionem Euchariſtiæ, cœnam Dominicam vocat.*

they did not call on God, in the fame fenfe as Saint *Paul* fpeaketh, *This is not to eate.*

Vfe: It will abate their pride who reft on *Opus operatum,* as bad Divinity as Latine. For a deed done is a deed not done, where the manner of the doing confutes and confounds the matter of the deed. Yea, in the beft of Gods children; as *Gideons* Army of two and thirty thoufand did fhrinke to three hundred, *Iudg.* 7. 6 ; So it is to bee feared, that their fo many Sermons heard, prayers made, Almes given, which they fcore up to themfelves, and reckon upon, will fhrinke in the tale when God takes account of them; and prove Sermons not heard, prayers not made, Almes not given, becaufe not done in forme as he requires.

Yet it is fome comfort unto us, if all our actions proceed from faith, and ayming at Gods glory ; fo that the faylings be rather in the branches and leafes than in the roots of our performances. As for the Vnregenerate, they fo remayning have in them *læfum principium* of all true pious workes: all their divine actions are none at all; it being true of their whole lift, what [1] one writes of the yeare of our Lord, 903, *Annus fua tantum obfcuritate illuftris,* famous only for this, that nothing famous was done in it, and the whole ftory thereof a very *Blanke.*

For in eating every one taketh before other his owne Supper.] Herein the Apoftle reproveth their abufes in their LOVE-FEASTS, whofe Inftitution, Declination, and Corruption, we will briefly defcribe.

Their Inftitution: Love-feafts were founded on no expreffe command in Holy Write, but only on the Cuftome of the Church, who immediatly before the receiving of the Sacrament, as appears both by the Text and Saint [2]*Auguftines* Comment on it, (though Saint *Chryfoftome* makes thefe *Love-feafts* to bee after the taking of the *Euchariſt,*) ufed to have a great Feaft, to which all the poore people were invited, on the charges of the rich. This they did partly in

---

[1] Spondanus, *Annal. Eccles.* [*Baronii*] *in anno* 903 [Ed. Paris, 1639, part ii. page 329].
[2] *Loco prius citato.*

imitation of our Saviour, who inftituted the Sacrament after a full Supper; and partly in expreffion of their perfect love and charity towards all men.

Their Declination: But the number of the rich men encreafed not proportionably with the poore: 1 *Cor.* 1. 26, *Behold your calling, that not many wife men after the flefh, not many mighty, not many noble are called.* The Church (in time of perfecution, efpecially) is like a Copfe, wherein the underwood growes much thicker and fafter than the Oakes. Hence came it to paffe, that there were few Hofts, many Guefts; few Inviters, many to be invited; and the burden growing heavie, lying on few backs, they wholly omitted the poor, who loath to come without any invitation, (the warrant to keepe a Gueft from trefpaffing on good manners,) were excluded from their Feafts.

Their Corruption: Thus love to men in want, was quickly turned into want of love, *Mare Euxinum* into *Mare Axinum*, *Love-feafts* into *No-love-fafts*. (Thus too often Charity is changed into bargaining; *Hofpitals* turned into *Exchanges*, wherein thofe are taken in, that can give; and thofe left out, that have nothing.) The poore people in Corinth did fee and fmell, what the rich men tafted, *Tantalizing* all the while, and having their penury doubled by the *Antiperiftafis* of others plenty; yea, ryot and exceffe; for fome of them were drunken.

Yet marke by the way that Saint *Paul* doth not plant his Arguments poynt-blanke to beat thefe *Love-feafts* downe to the ground, wholly to abrogate and make a nullity of them, but onely to correct and reforme the abufes therein, that there might be leffe ryot in the Rich and more charity towards the poore.

Ufe: Let not things fimply good in themfelves, be done away for their abufes; *Abraham* faid unto God, *Gen.* 18. 25, *To flay the Righteous with the wicked, that be farre from thee;* and farre be it from us to cafheare the good ufe of a thing with the ill abufes annexed thereunto. Hee is a bad hufband that having a fpot in his coat will cut out the cloath, not wafh out the dirt. Wherefore in matters of a mixt nature, wherin good and bad are confufedly jumbled together, let us with the fire of judgement try the droffe from the gold; and with the fanne of difcretion winnow the chaffe from the corne.

For in eating every one taketh, &c.] By *Every one*, underftand not every particular perfon in the Church of Corinth (for then how could fome bee *hungry?*) but every divifion: the faction of *Paul* a part, of *Apollo* a part, the fect of *Cephas* by it felfe.

His owne Supper.] Meaning that *Love-feaft*, or plentifull Supper, whereof formerly, therefore called their *Owne*, both becaufe feverally provided for their *Owne* faction, as alfo in diftinction of the *Lords Supper* which they tooke afterwards.

And one is hungry.] Here is nothing in the poore to be condemned. For that they were hungry, was no finne in them, but their punifhment; Gods pleafure, and the rich mens fault. *Obfervation: Poverty fometimes keeps men innocent, while abufed wealth makes rich men to offend.*
Something is here in the poore to be commended, that they would be *hungry*. Our age affords fuch unmannerly *Harpies*: they would have fnatched the meat out of the rich mens mouthes. Some will not want a fire if there be fewell in their neighbours yard: But O let us not unlawfully *remove the Land-mark* of our eftates! Let us rather trefpaffe againft modefty than honefty, goe naked, than fteale clothes; be hungry and faft, than feaft on forbidden food.

And another is drunken.] *Queftion*: Is it credible that any of the Corinthians, being about to receive the Sacrament, would be fo farre overtaken, as to *be drunken?*
Anfwer: Surely not fo drunken as he, *Prov.* 23. 35: *They have ftricken mee, faid hee, and I was not ficke; they have beaten me, and J felt it not.* They pronounced not *Siboleth* for *Shiboleth;* fo that it might have beene faid to them, as it was to Saint *Peter, Thy very language betrayeth thee.* Sure their tongues, eyes, and feet, were loyall enough to preferve their Mafters credit. So then by *Drunken* here, underftand the higheft flight and pitch of mirth. And as hearbs hot in

the fourth degree are poyſon; ſo *Summa hilaritas* is *Ima ebrietas*, the higheſt ſtaire of mirth is the loweſt ſtep of drunkenneſſe.

Doctrine: There is a concealed Drunkenneſſe, which no Informer can accuſe, no witneſſe can teſtifie, no earthly Iudge can puniſh; yet is it lyable to a cenſure in the Court of Heaven, and counted Drunkenneſſe in the eyes of God. And though others cannot perceive it in us, wee may take notice of it in our ſelves, eſpecially if wee examine our ſelves: 1. By our unaptneſſe to ſerve God in our generall or particular callings. 2. By the quantity of the liquor wee have drunke. 3. By the company with whom wee drinke. For as ſome who of themſelves never take notice of their owne faſt going, yet are ſenſible of it when they heare ſome of their company, whoſe legs are not ſo long and ſo ſtrong, begin to complaine: ſo though of our ſelves we find no alteration in our owne temper; yet if any of our Companions in drinking, who ſtarted from the ſame place and ran the ſame pace with us, begin to be tyred, let them bee our Monitours that it is high time, *claudere jam rivos*, to leave off our courſe, as being already drunkenneſſe before God.

Vſe: Let us not walke to the utmoſt bounds of what we may, nor take ſo much liquor as perchance we may juſtifie. It was permitted to the Iewes to beat a Malefactor with *forty ſtripes*, *Deut.* 25. 3; yet they never exceeded nine and thirty, as appeares by their ſcourging Saint *Paul*, to whom no doubt they uſed their greateſt cruelty, 2 *Cor.* 11. 24. Let us not ſtretch our Chriſtian Liberty to the utmoſt: *he that never will drinke leſſe than he may, ſometimes will drinke more than hee ſhould*.

Queſtion: But why is here mention of Drunkenneſſe onely, and not of Gluttony, ſeeing probably at ſuch great *Feaſts* theſe twin-vices goe together?

Anſwer: The Apoſtle only inſtanceth in that ſinne which is moſt obvious and appearing to ſight: Gluttony is ſcarce diſcernable in him that is guilty of it; *Quia per eſum neceſſitati voluptas miſcetur, quid neceſſitas petat, et quid voluptas ſuppetat, ignoratur*, ſaith [1]*Gregory*, Neceſſitie in eating ſo incorporates

---

[1] *Moralia in Expoſ. Beati Iob*, cap. 39. ver. 7] lib. 30. cap. 28 *ante medium* [¶ 62].

it selfe with delight, that they are hardly to be distinguished. Besides, as thunder and lightning, though they come together, yet lightning first arriveth to our sight: So though probably at the Corinthians Feasts, Gluttony and Drunkennesse were both joyned together in the same person, yet Drunkennesse was soonest and easiest discerned.

Verse 22: *What! have yee not houses to eate and drinke in? or despise yee the Church of God, and shame them that have not? What shall I say unto you? shall I prayse you in this? I prayse you not.*

MVST you needs make the house of God the place of your feasting? If you be disposed to bee merry, have yee not houses wherein yee may doe it with more privacie and lesse offence? or *despise you the Church of God?* Doe you under-value the place set apart for Gods service, to convert it into an ordinary Banquetting-house? This is the exposition of all Greeke Writers, who expound it the Materiall Church; and their opinion is much favoured by the Antithesis and opposition in the Text betwixt *Church* and *Houses.* Hence it appeares, that these *Love-feasts* (which of late by the rich mens covetousnesse were inclosed into a private courtesie, which at the first were a common Charity) were to their greater abuse kept in the Church or place of publike meeting.

Only duties pious and publike are to be performed in the Church. Duties publike and not pious more befit a Guildhall or Towne-house; duties pious and not publike more become a Closet: *Psalme* 4. 4, *Commune with your heart in your Chamber, and be still;* whilst duties publike and pious beseeme a Church, as proper thereto.

Vse: Too [to] blame those that turne the Church into a Counting-house, there to rate their neighbours, both to value their estates, and too often to revile their persons. Others make it a Market-place, there to bargaine in; yea, some turne it into a Kennell for their dogs, and a Mew for their Hawkes, which they bring with them. Surely if Christ drove out thence sheep and doves, the emblems of Innocencie, he would not have suffered these Patterns of cruelty to have abide in his Temple.

But most Latine Writers expound these words, *Or despise yee the Church of God?* of the spirituall Church. The rich Corinthians in not inviting the poore made Balkes of good ground, chaffe of good corne; yea, Refuse of Gods Elect.

Objection: But not inviting the poore, was not despising them. A Free-will-offering is no debt. *In gratuitis nulla est injustitia.* Seeing therefore it had beene no sin in the Corinthians wholly to have omitted their Feasts (as being not commanded by Gods Word), it could bee no offence to exclude any Guests at their pleasure.

Answer: This is true of civill and ordinary entertainements: But these being entitled *Love-feasts*, and Charity pretended the maine Motive of them, poore people were the most proper, should have beene the most principall Guests. Besides, if not Christianity, yet Civility; if not grace, good nature; might have moved them, whilst they gorged themselves, to have given something to the poore which stood by. To let them look on hungry was a despising of them in an high degree, a *Scandalum Magnatum*, censurable in the *Star-chamber* of Heaven: Thus to wrong their Peeres in Grace here and glory hereafter.

Doctrine: Hee that despiseth the poore, despiseth the Church of God. Whereof they are a member inferiour to none in piety; (*God hath chosen the poore of this world to be rich in faith, Iames* 2. 5;) superiour to all in number. Now he that pincheth the little toe paineth the whole body; the disgracing any member is the despising the whole Church. Let us beware of affronting those in want, upbrayding their rags with our silkes; setting our meat before their eyes only to raise their appetites. He that hath the things of this World, and seeth his Brother to want, how doth the love of God dwell in him?

And shame them that have not.] Not, that have not houses, though perchance but homely and hired; but μὴ ἔχοντες, those that have not wealth and substance to pay the shot, and goe to the cost to invite you againe.

What shall I say? shall I prayse you in this?] Doctrine: *Pastours may and must prayse their people wherein they doe well.* Reasons: 1. Hereby they shall peaceably possesse themselves of the good-wils of their people, which may much advance the power and efficacie of their preaching. 2. Men will more willingly digest a Reproofe for their faults, if prayfed when they doe well. 3. Vertue being commended doth increase and multiply; Creepers in goodnesse will goe, Goers run, Runners fly.

Use: Those Ministers to bee blamed which are ever blaming, often without cause, alwayes without measure; whereas it is said of God, *hee will not be alwayes chiding*, P*s*ame 103. 9. These Preachers use their reproofes so commonly, till their Physicke turnes naturall, and will not worke with their people.

Doe any desire to heare that which *Themistocles* counted the best Musicke; namely, themselves commended? On these conditions, wee Ministers will indent with them: Let them find matter, wee will find words; let them doe what is commendable, and blame us if we commend not what they doe. Such work for us would be Recreation; such employment, a pleasure, turning our most stammering tongue into *the pen of a ready Writer*. To reprove is prest from us as Wine from Grapes; but prayses would flow from our lips as water from a Fountaine. But alas! how can we build when they afford us neither *brick*, nor *straw*? how can wee prayse what they doe when they will not doe what is to bee prayfed? If with *Ahab* they will doe what is evill, then with *Micaiah* wee must always prophesie evil unto them.

In this I prayse you not.] Doctrine: *Ministers must not commend their people when they doe ill.*

Reasons: 1. Dishonourable to God. 2. Dangerous to the Ministers. That Embassadour, who being sent to proclaime warre pronounceth peace to Rebels, (*There is no peace, saith my God, to the wicked*, Esay 57. 21,) deserves at his returne to bee preferred to the Gallowes. 3. Dangerous to the people, who are footbed in their sinnes: Honey-dewes, though they be sweet in taste, doe black and blast the corne: So those who prayſe their people without cauſe are cruelly kind unto them: it is pleaſant to the pallate of fleſh, but deſtroyeth and damneth the ſoule.

Vſe: It were to be wiſhed that as thoſe that live under the Equinoctiall at Noon-day have no ſhadowes at all; ſo great men ſhould have no ſhadowes, no Paraſites, no Flatterers to commend them, when they leaſt deſerve it.

Objection: But why doth Saint *Paul* deale ſo mildly with the Corinthians, *I prayſe you not?* Me thinkes hee ſhould have made his little finger as heavie as his loynes: O yee Corinthians, I excommunicate every mothers child of you; I damne you all to the pit of hell, and deliver you to Satan for your ſinne of Drunkenneſſe at the receiving of the Sacrament, never to be abſolved but on your moſt ſerious and ſolemne repentance. Otherwiſe, conſidering the corrupt humour in the Corinthians, the Apoſtles purge was too gentle for them.

Anſwers: 1. *Theophylact* anſwers, that Saint *Paul* reproves the rich men the more mildly, leſt otherwiſe they ſhould be implacably incenſed againſt the poore, fretting againſt them as the cauſers of the Apoſtles anger.

2. It was the firſt time hee told the Corinthians of their fault, and therefore uſed them the more gently on hope of their amendment. This corrupt humour in the Corinthians was not as yet growne tough, bak't and clodded in them by cuſtóme, and therefore the eaſier purged and removed.

Obſervation: Miniſters muſt uſe mildneſſe, eſpecially at their firſt reproving of a ſinne. Yea, God ſo bleſt the mild ſeveritie of Saint *Paul* that the Corinthians reformed all their errours; for no fault reprehended by the Apoſtle in them in this firſt Epiſtle is taxed againe in the ſecond Epiſtle; a very ſtrong preſumption that all thoſe faults were amended.

Now whereas wee find ſuch abuſes in the Church of Corinth preſently after it was newly planted: we may learne

Doctrine: Corruptions will quickly creepe into the beſt Church. Thus Saint *Paul* no ſooner went back from the Galatians, but they went back from his Doctrine, *Gal.* 5. 7: *Yee did run well; who did hinder you?* And as we reade of *Mezentius,* a cruell Tyrant, who joyned dead corpes to living men, and so killed them with lingering torments: So some Seducers in the Church of Galatia sought to couple the lively grace of God and active faith with the dead Letter of the Law, and old legall Ceremonies long since dead, buried, and rotten, in the Grave of our Saviour.

Vse: *If it be done thus to the greene Tree, what shall be done to the dry?* If Primative Churches, whilst the Apostles which planted them were alive to pruine them, had such errours in them, no wonder if the Church at sixteene hundred yeares of age may have some defaults. *Moses* said unto the Israelites, *Deut.* 31. 27, *Behold while I am alive with you this day, yee have beene rebellious against the Lord; and how much more when J am dead?* So if, while Saint *Paul* survived, Churches were so prone to decline, what can be lesse expected in our dayes? It was therfore well concluded in the thirty-ninth Session of the Councell of [1]*Constance* [A.D. 1414-18]: That every ten yeare at the farthest there should bee a Generall Councell held to reforme such errours in the Church as probably in that time would arise.

Verse 23: *For I have received of the Lord that which J also delivered unto you, that the Lord Iesus, the same night in which he was betrayed, took bread.*

AFTER hee had fully reproved the corruptions of their *Love-feasts*, commeth he now to reduce the receiving of the Sacrament to the first Institution of Christ. *Observation*: It is the safest way to correct all the Errata's *in the Transcript according to the Originall Copie*: Thus did Christ in the matter of Divorce, *Mat.* 19. 8, *But from the beginning it was not so.* Excellently, Saint *Cyprian*: *Wee must not heed what others did who were before us, but what Christ did who was before all.*

Vse: Were this used betwixt us and the Papists, to cleare the streame of Gods service by the Fountaine of its first Institution, how soone would seven Sacraments shrinke to two! How quickly would Creame, Oyle, and Spittle, fly out

---

[1] Fox, *Martyrol.* page 594. [Ed. 1641, i. 784; Ed. 1855, iii. 420.]

of Baptisme, and leave nothing but faire water behind! How soone, &c.

For I have received of the Lord.] Question: How could Saint *Paul* receive it of the Lord, with whom hee never vers't in the flesh, being *one borne out of time*, as he confesseth of himselfe?
Answer: He received it, 1. Mediately by *Ananias*, who began with him where *Gamaliel* ended. [2.] Besides, (left the Corinthians should say that they received it likewise at the second hand, as well as Saint *Paul*,) he had it immediately from God, *Gal.* 1. 12: *For I never received it of man, neither was I taught it, but by the Revelation of Iesus Christ.*

I also delivered unto you.] The Greeke is παρέδωκα ὑμῖν. Latine, *Tradidi vobis*, English it as you please, I traditioned it unto you. *Nota* (saith *A Lapide* on this place) *hunc locum pro traditionibus quas Orthodoxi verbo Dei scripto adjungendas docent.* *Bellarmine* also starts Traditions out of the same place. What eye-salve are their eyes anoynted with, that can see unwritten Traditions here, when the Apostle delivereth nothing but is recorded in three Evangelists, *Mathew, Marke, Luke*?

However, hence we will take occasion briefly to speak of unwritten Traditions; the Church of Rome maintayning that the Scriptures of themselves are too scant to salvation, except the course lift of unwritten Traditions be cast in to make measure; and this they will have of equall authority with the written Word.

Marke by the way *Four Observables concerning Traditions*:
1. This is the Reason why Romanists are so zealous for Traditions; for finding themselves cast by the Scriptures, they would faigne appeale to another Judge: yea, hereon are founded those points which get them their gaine, as Purgatory and the Appurtenances thereof. Hath not *Demetrius* then reason to stand for *Diana* (*Acts* 19. 25,) when his goods and her Godship must go together?
2. Though they lock up the Scriptures in an unknowne language and forbid the Laity to reade them, yet they suffer

Traditions to bee preached and publifhed to all in generall. Such woodden Daggers will never hurt Popery to the heart; and therefore they fuffer their children to play with thefe dull tooles, though not to handle the *two-edged Sword of Gods Word.*

3. Romanifts will never give us a perfect Lift and Catalogue of their Traditions, that we may know their fet number, how many there be of them; but ftill reckon them up with an *Et Cætera,* leave ftill a *Plus ultra* to place more in if need require. And as the Athenians for feare they fhould omit any Deity erected an Altar *to the unknowne God:* So the Papifts in fumming up their Traditions will not compleat their number, but are carefull to leave Blankes and void places for a Refuge and Retreating Place, that, in cafe they be preft in Difputation and cannot prove their point by places of Scripture, they may ftill plead it is a *Tradition.*

4. Whereas the word *Tradition* is taken in feverall fenfes, and there be many kinds of them, Papifts jumble and confound them together. As Cheaters ufe to caft their counterfeit coyne amongft good gold, hoping fo to paffe it away currant and undifcovered: So they fhuffle falfe and true Traditions together in one heape, that the bad may goe off under the countenance and protection of the good. Wee will marre their Mart, by forting them into thefe feverall Rankes.

1. *Traditions* in a generall fenfe are taken for things delivered, though in Scripture, by Chrift and his Apoftles; thus Saint [1]*Bafil* cals Baptifing in the name of the Father, Son, and Holy Ghoft a *Tradition*.

2. For fuch matters of Faith which are not found in Scripture *totidem verbis,* in the words and found; but yet in the fame fenfe and fubftance, or at leaft may by faithfull confequence bee thence deduced; as the Trinity of Perfons, two wils in Chrift, his Confubftantiality with God the Father: Thus *Lindan* a Papift cals Originall finne a *Tradition.*

3. For fuch opinions againft which nothing appeares in Scripture, and the Church in all times and ages have maintained them, condemning the Oppofers for erroneous: As that the Mother of Chrift was ever a Virgin.

---

[1] Lib. 3. *contra Eunomium* [page 84, Ed. Paris, 1618].

4. For such Rites and Ceremonies of the Church (no matters of Faith) which therein have beene used from great Antiquity; and therefore probably might have their Original from the Apostles: As *Fasting* in Lent, though the manner, time, and continuance in keeping it was very different in severall Churches.

Take *Traditions* in the first and second acception, wee account them to have equal force and authority with the Written Word. In the third sense we honour and embrace them as true. In the last Acception wee approve and practise them as decent and ancient; provided alwayes they be not obtruded as things necessary to salvation, but indifferent in their nature.

But all this makes nothing for the blacke Guard of *Romish Traditions* which lag still behind: some of them frivolous; as [1]this Apostolical Tradition, That a Priest if against their wils they receive any money from wicked men they must in no case expend it on meat, but to buy wood and coals. Some impious and blasphemous; worshipping of Images, prayers to Saints, the Sacrifice of the Masse, Purgatory, &c., having nothing for them, much against them, in Gods written Word.

To draw to a conclusion. Scriptures besides many others have two most principall priviledges above *Traditions*:

First, their Infallibilitie, as being inspired by the Spirit of God, 2 *Pet.* 1. 20: *So that yee first know this, that no prophecie of the Scripture is of any private Interpretation.* Verse 21: *For the Prophecie came not in old time by the will of man; but holy men of God spake as they were moved by the Holy Ghost.* As for the authors of *Traditions*, they might both *falli* and *fallere*, be deceived themselves, and deceive others. They might be deceived themselves, either by mis-understanding the Traditions delivered unto them, or by mis-remembring, or by mis-relating them againe. They might deceive others, either unwillingly by these fore-named slips and infirmities, or else willingly and wittingly by venting those things as received from the Apostles, which they had not received from them. And by usurpation intitling the fancies of your [their] owne heads to bee Apostolicall Precepts.

---

[1] Clemens Rom. lib. [sect.] 40. cap. 10, *Apost. Constit.* [Ed. Whiston, 1711.]

2. The Providence of God plainly appeares in his preserving of the Scriptures against all oppofitions. *Many a time from my youth up,* (*may* the Scriptures *now say,*) *yea, many a time have they fought againſt me from my youth, but they could not prevaile againſt me.* Neither *Antiochus* before *Chriſt*, nor *Iulian* the Apoſtate fince him, nor the force of Tyrants, nor the fraud of Heretikes (though the world of late hath fcarce yeelded a wicked fharpe wit that hath not given the Scriptures a gafh) could ever fuppreffe them. Their treading on this Cammimell made it grow the better; and their fnuffing of this candle made it burne the brighter. Whereas, on the other fide, the Records of *Traditions* are loft, and thofe bookes wherein they were compiled and compofed, *Aut incuria hominum, aut injuria temporis,* or by fome other finifter accident, are wholly mifcarried, and no where appeare. *Papias* is reported by [1] *Eufebius* in five bookes to have contained all the Apoftolicall Traditions, which they call the Word not written, by *Bellarmine* himfelfe confeffed that thefe are loft. Likewife *Clemens Alexandrinus* (as the fame [2] *Eufebius* ftorieth it) wrote in a booke thofe Traditions which hee received from the Elders, and they from the Apoftles; which booke the Papifts themfelves at this day cannot produce.

I will conclude all with *Gamaliels* words, *Acts* 5. 39, *But if it be of God, yee cannot deftroy it.* Had thefe bookes beene infpired by Gods Spirit, no doubt the fame Providence would have watched to preferve them which hath protected the Scripture. Let us therefore, leaving uncertaine Traditions, ftick to the Scriptures alone; truft no Doctrine on its fingle band, which brings not Gods word for its fecurity. Let that Plate be beaten in peeces which hath not this *Tower-ſtampe* upon it.

That the Lord Jeſus, the ſame night wherein he was betrayed.] Obfervation: *Chriſt beſtowed the greateſt courteſie on mankind, when hee foreſaw that hee ſhould receive the greateſt cruelty from them.* O that wee were like minded with our Saviour, to move faſteſt in Piety when wee draw

---

[1] Lib. 4, *Hiſt.* cap. 8. [This chap. is about Hegefippus, and his Five Books; for Papias, fee lib. iii. cap. 39.]   [2] Lib. 6, *Hiſt.* cap. 11.

neereſt the Center of Death ; and then chiefly to ſtudy to faſten favours on our Enemies!

Queſtion: Why did Chriſt inſtitute it then, and not before?

Anſwer 1 : Becauſe dying men bequeath not their Legacies till they make their wils, nor departing friends beſtow their tokens till they take their farewell.

2. Becauſe till then the Paſſeover (a Sacrament in the ſame kind) did continue in full force, and the Lords Supper was not to bee lighted, til the Paſſeover was firſt fairly put out.

Queſtion: Seeing Chriſt appoynted it a Supper, how comes it now to be a Dinner?

Anſwer: God hath intruſted the diſcretion of his Church on juſt occaſion to alter ſome circumſtances in the Sacrament. True it is, ſuch circumſtances as are Sacramental, not only of the *Commiſſion at large*, but alſo of the *Quorum nomina*, whoſe abſence or alteration maims and mangles the Sacrament, are unchangeable. But *Common* and ordinary circumſtances (ſuch as is the *Time, Place, Kind* of Bread and Wine) the Church hath power to alter by vertue of a *Warrant* left to it by Chriſt. Let all things be done decently, and in order.

Reaſons of the change : It was turned into a dinner: 1. To avoid the Inconveniencies which a full ſtomake ſurfetted and ſurcharged will bring, as in the Corinthians.

2. That our bodies, which are like new barrels whiles we are faſting, may firſt bee ſeaſoned with the liquor of Chriſts blood.

Let us thanke God that we are not neceſſitated to receive the Communion in the night, as in the Primitive Church, in time of Perſecution, when Chriſtians to drink Chriſts blood did adventure the looſing of their owne.

Tooke Bread.] *Queſtion:* Why did Chriſt chooſe ſo cheap and common a thing to exhibite his body in?

Anſwer 1 : Herein he graciouſly provided for the poor. Had he appoynted ſome rich and coſtly receit, the eſtate of the poore could not procure it for themſelves, and the charity of the rich would not purchaſe it for others.

2. Had he inſtituted it in ſome dear and precious element, happily [haply] people would have imputed the efficacie thereof to its natural worth and working, not to Chriſts Inſtitution.

Chrift therefore choofeth plaine bread; a thing fo meane in it felfe, it is not within fufpition to eclipfe God of his glory; none can be fo mad as to attribute to plaine Bread it felfe fuch fpirituall Operation.

Let us take heed how we take fnuffe at the fimplicity of Gods Ordinance. Say not with *Naaman: Is not Abanah and Pharphar, &c.* Is not the Bread in the Bakers panniers and the Wine in the Vintners cellar, as good as that which is propounded in the Sacrament? And farre be it from us to feeke with our owne inventions to beguard that which God wil have plaine; rather let us pray that our eyes may be anoynted with that eye-falve, to fee Majefty in the meaneffe, and the ftate in the fimplicity of the Sacraments.

Queftion: But amongft fuch variety of others, fuch cheape Elements to reprefent Chrifts body in, why was bread preferred above all?

Anfwer: To fhew our bodies can as well fubfift without Bread, as our foules without à Saviour. It is called *the ftaffe of Bread* [*Life*]: other meats are but as pretty wands to whifk in our hands. *Without Bread no Feaft, with Bread no Famine.*

Verfe 24: *And when hee had given thankes, hee brake it, and fayd, Take, eate, this is my body, which is broken for you; this doe in remembrance of mee.*

AND when he had given thanks: Εὐχαριστήσας.] So it is *Luke* 22. 19. But Saint *Matthew*, chap. 26. 26, hath it εὐλογήσας, *hee bleffed.* Yet let not thefe two words fall out, for they are Brethren, of affinity in fenfe and fignification: At this day εὐχαριστήσας, *Hee gived thankes,* hath chriftned the whole fervice of the *Eucharift.*

Doctrine: *Whenfoever wee are to receive any food, wee are to give God thankes, but efpecially at Sacrament.*

Reafon 1: It is our duty. God the Lord Paramount of the World, though hee hath made us in Chrift Free-holders of all his creatures, yet hath referved thankes as a quick Rent for himfelfe.

2. It is profitable for us, 1 *Tim.* 4. 4, 5 : *For every creature of God is good, and nothing to be refused, if it be received with thankesgiving ; for it is sanctified by the Word of God and Prayer.* Yea, thankfgiving makes every creature both chew the cud, and cleave the hoofe. The Phyfician may forbid one meat, the Divine cannot; it may bee againft ones health, not ones confcience. True, the Jewes life was a conftant *Lent,* from much forbidden meat; but Chriftians, paying thankes to God, buy a *Licenfe* to eate any thing.

Hee brake it.] To fignifie how his body fhould bee broken for mankind. Whilft therefore the Prieft in the Sacrament breaketh the Bread, let the peoples meditation attend his Action, and conceive they fee Chrifts head, backe, hands, feet, fide, broken with the thorns, whips, nailes, fpeare. And hence it appeareth, that the celebrating of Chrifts body in broken bread is more naturall to Chrifts Inftitution, and more expreffive in it felfe, than as the Church of Rome doth in a whole and entire Wafer.

And faid unto them, Take.] That is, take it in their hands and put it to their mouth, not as the cuftome lately induced in the Romifh Church, for the Prieft to put it in the mouth of every Communicant.

Objection : But it is pleaded for the Popifh cuftome that it is unmannerly for Lay-men to handle Chrifts body ; and therefore it is moft reverence to take it with their mouthes.

Anfwer 1 : There is no fuch Clowne in Chriftianity as he who will bee more mannerly than God will have him : It is moft reverence for us to doe as God commands us. *Ahaz* tempted God in faying he *would not tempt him,* when God bid him *afke a figne, Efay* 7. 12. Thofe do little better who more nife then wife ftraine courtefie not to take Chrifts body in their hands, when hee reaches it.

2. Take it ftrictly, and our mouthes are as unworthy as our hands to receive Chrifts body. No more fanctity in the one than in the other, being both made of the fame lump of flefh : But feeing it is Chrifts pleafure to come under the roofe of our mouth, let him alfo paffe through the porch of

our hands. The rather because it seemeth that wee entertaine Chrifts body in more ftate and with more obfervance towards it, when the more fervants attend it, the more members of our body, ufing their fervice in receiving it.

3. Laftly, the Romifh cuftome in putting it into their mouthes loofeth the expreffion and fignificancie of the hand of faith. The taking Chrifts body in our hands mindeth us fpiritually by faith to apprehend and lay hold on his mercies and merits.

T[homas] C[artwright's] needleffe cavill. And here let us take notice of the needleffe cavill of fuch as fnarle at the practife of our Englifh Church. Becaufe whereas Chrift faid in a generality, once for all to his Difciples, *Take and eate;* our Church fpeaketh it to every particular perfon.

Wee anfwer, this is no confiderable variation from Chrifts form ; for firft, it appeares not in the Text to the contrary but that Chrift might fpeake thefe words feverally to each Apoftle, though it be not expreffed, becaufe Hiftories truffe up things in bundles, and omitting particulars fet downe only the totall fumme. Secondly, God hath intrufted the Minifters of his Church to fpin out his univerfall Precepts and promifes into particulars. Thus *Mat.* 28. 19, Chrift faith, *Teach all nations, baptizing them in the name of the Father, &c.* Which the Prieft by the confent of all Churches applyeth to each Infant, *I baptize thee, &c.*

This is my body.] That is, that which fignifies, fignes, and prefents my body, and facramentally is my body, and which received with faith feales to thee all the benefits of my death and paffion, not tranfubftantiated into my body, according to the Popifh opinion, whereof briefly.

The Doctrine of *Tranfubftantiation* was firft occafioned by the unwary fpeeches of *Damafcen* and *Theophylact*. Thefe feeing no prefent, and forefeeing no future errours about the Sacraments, were too tranfcendent and hyperbolicall in their expreffions about the reall prefence of Chrift in the Sacrament: Thus as oftentimes *Lafcivia calami*, the dafhes and florifhes of a Scrivener over-active with his pen, have afterwards beene miſtaken to bee Letters really intended: So the witty extravagancies and Rhetoricall phraſes of theſe Fathers were afterward interpreted to be their diſtilled doctrinall poſitions: ſo dangerous it is for any to wanton it with their wits in myſteries of Religion. But *Tranſubſtantiation* was never made an Article of faith till the [fourth] Councell of Lateran [A.D. 1215]; no penalty impoſed on the Maintainers of the contrary, till the Councell of Trent [1545-63]. But let us heare ſome of their Arguments.

Argument 1: The Text ſaith, *this is my body*, and therefore it is ſo plainely to bee underſtood. For Scripture admits of a figurative ſenſe as its *Refuge*, not as its *Choyce*; onely *ſe defendere, to ſhield and ſhelter* it ſelfe from non-ſenſe and contradictions; otherwiſe the literall ſenſe is to bee embraced. And therefore the Holy Spirit is ſo here to be underſtood, this is truly my body.

Anſwer: From the literall underſtanding of theſe words flow many abſurdities, and therefore wee are forced to fly to a figurative meaning. Philoſophy brings in an Army of Impoſſibilities; as that the ſame body at the ſame time ſhould be in ſeverall places; that accidents ſhould ſubſiſt without a ſubſtance; &c. To wave theſe, the Antiquity of faith excepts againſt it, it deſtroyes the nature of a Sacrament; the ſame thing cannot bee the ſigne and ſeale of Chriſts body, and the very body in ſubſtance.

Argument 2: Wee are not to meaſure Gods Arme by our eye, his power by our underſtanding; Wherefore, *non obſtante* all pretended impoſſibility, God doth turne the bread into his ſonnes body; for nothing is impoſſible unto him.

Anſwer: Were it expreſſed in Scripture, that it were Gods will to turne the Bread into Chriſts fleſh, wee would worke our ſelves to beleeve it, and make Reaſon ſtrike ſayle to Faith: So it is not Gods power wee queſtion, but his will and pleaſure.

Argument 3: But he ſaith, *totidem verbis, this is my body*; and dying men uſe to ſpeak moſt plainely; with them figures are out of date, the flowers of Rhetoricke fade; eſpecially they write without welt or Guard in their wils and Teſtaments.

Anfwer: A familiar Trope or Figure is as plain as no figure: Even a child in age is man enough to underftand, *Coole the Pot, Drinke off that Cup.* Yea, many fpeake figures, who know not what figures meane: Befides, Chrift at his death fpake no other language then what his tongue and his Difciples eares were ufed to in his life time: *I am the Vine, I am the Way, I am the Doore.* Hee who is fo fottifh as to conceive that Chrift was a materiall Doore fheweth himfelfe to be a Poft indeed.

Which is broken for you.] The flefh of Chrift was afterwards on the Croffe literally broken; there was *folutio continui*, with the nayles in his hands and feet: As for his bones, *John* 19.36, *Not a bone of him was broken* in the literall fenfe. But vertually and eminently, in the fame meaning wherein it is faid a *Broken Heart, all his bones were broken,* that is, contrited and grinded with griefe and forrow.

Doe this.] In Latine, *hoc facite,* which the Papifts expound facrifice: this according to [1]*Virgils* verfe:—

Cum faciam vitula pro frugibus ipfe venito.

So much is the Church of Rome beholding to this Poet, both for the facrifice of the Maffe out of his Eclogs, and *Limbus Patrum* out of the firft [sixth] booke of his Æneads. But feeing this action, *Doe this,* is injoyned as wel to the people as the Prieft; and feeing none but the Prieft could offer *Proprij nominis facrificium;* it plainely appeares this cannot here be a proper facrifice.

In Remembrance.] *Doctrine:* Wherein this Doctrine is intimated: *Men are prone to forget Gods favours unto them, except they be minded of them.* The Ifraelites had not this great goodneffe in remembrance; but *were difobedient at the Sea, even at the Red-fea, Pfalme* 106. 7. Who would have thought that the deliverance at the Red-fea would fo foon have beene drowned in a deeper Sea of Oblivion?

[[1] Bucolica, Ecloga, iii. 77. See alfo *Iliad,* i. 444]

Reasons of our Forgetfulnesse. *Reason* 1 : The Devils malice, who whilst we sleep in Idlenesse, and negligence, stealeth into the memory, the Muniment house of the soul, and embezileth and purloyneth from thence the Records of most moment and importance.

2. But not to play the Devill with the Devill, not to accuse him falsely, hee is not the principall cause of our forgetfulnesse, which floweth chiefly from the corruption of our nature; which like a Bolter lets all the floore [flour] passe, and keeps only the bean behind.

But here wee must not understand the bare naked and empty *Remembrance* of Christs death, the calling to mind the History of his passion; (which the Devils can doe, and the worst of men;) thus to remember Christ were but to forget him: But a remembrance *cum effectu*, the relying on his death with a lively faith, and applying his merits to our soules. Whereof more largely hereafter.

Of mee] Incarnated, *of me* borne, *of me* circumcised, *of me* baptized, *of me* tempted, *of me* scourged; but especially *of me* crucified, and also *of me* ascended and now glorified.

Verse 25 : *After the same manner also hee tooke the Cup, when hee had supped, saying, This Cup is the new Testament in my blood, this doe yee, as oft as yee drinke it, in remembrance of me.*

FOLLOWETH now the other part of the Sacrament instituted in the Wine. He doubleth the elements to shew that in Christ is not only necessary and sufficient, but also plentifull and abundant, with assured Redemption.

Too too blame then the Church of Rome, whose Levites are guilty of that fault whereof *Benjamin* was taxed: they *have stolne away the Cup.* If *to steale the Chalice* be the phrase whereby men expresse the highest sin, what sacriledge is it to steale the *Wine* of the *Chalice*, from whom it belongeth? But it is a wonder if old Theeves be taken without an excuse; let us heare what these Romanists plead for themselves.

Objection 1: Nature hath so put flesh and blood in a joynt Patent, that they goe always together. Where there is one, there are both; and where not both, neither. It is superfluous therefore to give the Laity the blood the second time, who by concomitancie had received it before.

Answer 1: Indeed flesh and blood like loving Playmates were together in Chrifts body, till torments forced them to part asunder: Now we are to receive Chrifts blood *Shed*, not as it was at home, housed in heavinesse; but as payne banished it abroad and powred it out. Wherfore what God hath put asunder to bee taken severally and distinctly, let no man joyne together.

Objection 2: But there be many Inconveniences, yea, mischiefes, attend the Layeties receiving of the Wine, as its sticking in their beards, spilling of it, &c.

Answer 2: *Non debemus esse sapientiores legibus.* God in the Omnisciency of his wisedome surveyed the latitude of all occurrencies; yet beholding all future Inconveniences present, hee appoynted the Laity to drinke of the cup. Wine was then as subject to spilling; it hath not since gotten a more liquid or diffusive quality.

Objection 3: But in severall places of Scripture no mention is made of wine, but of bread onely, as *Acts* 2. 42, and the 46: *Continued breaking of bread from house to house. Acts* 20. 7: *Met together to breake bread.*

Answer 3: Either bread by a Synecdoche is here put for Bread and Wine, or else that phrase importeth their ordinary meetings and civill feasts. But a Cart-load of these exceptions, *Tekel*, are *weighed in the ballance, and found too light* to out-poyse Chrifts Institution. The wise Shunamite woman, 2 *Kings* 4. 30, was not content with the company of *Elisha's* staffe and servant; but, *as the Lord liveth* (saith she) *and as thy soule liveth, I will not leave thee;* she would not leane on the staffe, but on the staffs Master, and would have him with her: So let us not be so foolish to depart from Gods written Word in the Sacrament, concerning giving the Laity the Cup, for the company of humane Arguments on our side; but let us stick close to our Commission, and then wee need not feare a *Premunire*, so long as wee have the Letter of Gods Law on our side.

When hee had supped] Chrift did therefore inftitute this Sacrament after Supper, to fhew that herein hee chiefly aymed not at the feeding of our bodies, but the refreshing of our foules. We are not to bring our devotion in our guts, and to come to the Communion for Belly-cheare; like thofe that followed our Saviour, *John* 6. 26, *Becaufe they had eaten of the Loaves, and were filled.* No, wee are to come with more refined thoughts, and as for matter of bodily meat, containe ourfelves as after Supper.

This Cup is the New Teftament in my blood.] *This Cup*, that is, the wine in *this Cup*. Wee cannot fcarce ftirre a pace in Scripture, without meeting with a figure, even in thefe Teftamentary Expreffions of our Saviour. Why then doe the Papifts make fuch newes, yea, wonders at Figures, then which nothing is more common? *Is the New Teftament in my blood;* that is, the wine therein contained figneth unto you the New Covenant of Grace, which is ratified and confirmed in my blood; that is, by my death. For indeed it is the death of the Teftator that giveth life to the Teftament; and the will, though fealed, is not fealed in effect till the Maker of the fame be dead.

But why is it called the New Teftament, feeing it is an old one and the fame which was made to *Adam*, (*The feed of the Woman fhall breake the Serpents head*,) often reiterated and confirmed to *Abraham*, *David*, and others?

Indeed it was old in the Promife, new in the Performance; old *quoad fubftantiam et materiam fœderis*, new *quoad modum clarioris manifeftationis*. It is faid of thofe that live within a mile or two of *Olympus*, that they are under a conftant and continued fhade, which the height of the Mountaine cafteth upon them: So the Jews and al the Church of God before Chrifts comming lived in conftant umbrages, and fhadows, of Types, Figures, Ceremonies, and Reprefentations; al which were taken away when our Saviour, *the Sun of Righteoufnes*, did appear. Therefore it is faid in *My Blood*, as in oppofition to the blood of Kids, Calves, Goats, facrificed in the Temple.

Other parts of the verfe are expounded in the former.

Verse 26 : *For as often as yee eate of this Bread, and drinke this Cup, yee doe shew the Lords body [death] till hee come.*

UNDER *as often*, is *often* included ; whence we gather, *Wee must frequently celebrate the Lords Supper.* In the ¹Primitive Church it was done every day ; and fit it was the *Aqua Vitæ* bottle should ever be at their nostrils, who were sounding every moment ; and they needed constant cordials, who ever and anon had the Qualmes of temptation in the time of Persecution. This frequencie soone abated when peace came into the Church ; which makes Saint ²*Ambrose* reprove the negligence of the Easterne Churches, who received it but once a yeare : At this day our Mother-Church of England, seeing her childrens backwardnesse herein, by canon compelleth them to receive at the least thrice a yeare ; such is the necessity to force them by Law to come to a Feast, and to make a statute for hungry men to eate, and sicke folke to take Physicke. But heare the Arguments of some to the contrary ; that it is to be but seldome received.

Objection 1 : The Passeover was celebrated but once a yeare, in whose place (for Sacraments never dye without heirs) the Lords Supper succeeds.

Answer 1 : The Passeover by God was stinted to bee used no oftner ; in the Lords Supper we are left to our own liberty. Finding therefore our continuall sinning, and therefore need thereof to strengthen us in our grace, we may, yea, must oftner use it, especially seeing all services of God under the Gospel ought to bee more plentifull and abundant than under the Law.

Objection 2 : Things done often are seldome done solemnely. Manna, if rayned every day, is not dainty. The frequent doing of it will make men perfunctory and negligent therein.

Answer 2 : Necessary duties are not to be left undone for the Inconveniences, which, *per accidens*, through humane cor-

---

¹ Eusebius, lib. 1, *Demonst. Evan.*, cap 10 [Ed. Paris, 1628, p. 34].
² Lib 5, *De Sacramentis*, cap. 4 [Ed. Paris, 1690, ii. 376].

ruption may follow thereon: Then Sermons should be as seldome as *Apolloes* smiles, *semel in anno*; and prayers should not be presented to God every day, lest the commonnesse of the duty should bring it into contempt. Rather Ministers are to instruct their people to come with reverence; notwithstanding their frequent repayring thereunto.

Objection 3: But long preparation is requisite to this Action; and therefore this Sacrament cannot often be received.

Answer 3: After the first *Grand Preparation*, where by faith and repentance wee are first estated in Gods favour, other preparations are not so difficult in doing, or tedious in time, as being but the reiterating of the same againe. The good Huswife which scoureth her Plate once a weeke hath lesse worke than she that doth it but once in Twelve-moneth. Often preparing makes the worke easie, and fits men the sooner for the Sacrament: though I am not altogether of Saint [1]*Ambrose* his opinion, that *Qui non meretur quotidie accipere, non meretur post annum accipere*.

Question: Whether is it of absolute necessity that a man on his Death-bed should receive the Sacrament?

Answer: Hee is as weake in Iudgement as the dying man in body, who conceives it so. It is not the bare Absence, but the neglect and contempt of the Sacrament, which is dangerous. Besides, that surely is not by God made absolutely necessary to salvation, which in some cases is impossible to bee had. As in sudden death, when the sicke man is gone before the Priest can come; in infectious diseases, when the Priest cannot bring Christs blood without the hazarding of his owne; not to speake of the Inconveniencie of giving it to those who goe out of the world for pain to bring others into it.

Yea, of such persons who desire the Sacrament, I find three sorts. Some doe it out of meere fancy, who desire it because they desire it; (like *Davids* longing for the water of the Well of *Bethlem*;) can give no account of their humour therein. A second sort, out of superstition. A third, out of a true faith, and feeling of their infirmity. Now *Charity thinketh no ill; hopeth all things*. We Ministers beleeve all

---

[1] Loco prius citato.

to be of the later fort, and will not think much of our paines to tender our fervice unto them when fent for: But bē it betwixt God and their confciences; let them take heed how they abufe Gods Ambaffadours, and caufe us to come on foolifh occafions to feed their owne fancies.

You doe fhew forth the Lords body.] Doctrine: *The Sacrament folemnly celebrated doth reprefent and fet forth the death and Paffion of Chrift.* This is the meaning of Saint *Paul*, Galat. 3. 1 : *O foolifh Galatians, who hath bewitched you, that you fhould not obey the truth; before whofe eyes Iefus Chrift hath beene evidently fet forth, crucified among you?* That is, Chrift was fo powerfully and pathetically pieached unto them in the word, his Death fo done to the life in the folemne, decent, and expreffive Adminiftration of the Sacrament, that the tragedy of Chrifts death nigh *Ierufalem* was re-acted before them.

Vfe: Say not then in thine heart, how fhall I get to Ierufalem, to fee the place of Chrifts fuffering? See, Faith can remove Mountaines; Mount *Calvary* is brought home to theε; and though there be μέγα χάσμα, a great Gulfe, or diftance of ground, betwixt England and Paleftine, yet if thou beeft a faithfull Receiver, behold Chrift Sacramentally crucified on the Communion-Table. Say not in thine heart, how fhall I remember Chrifts Paffion; it was *Time out of mind*, sixteen hundred yeares ago? Chrift here teacheth thee the art of Memory; what fo long was paft is now made prefent at the inftant of thy worthy receiving. Stay, Pilgrims, ftay! (would your voyages to the Holy Land had beene as farre from fuperftition as hitherto from fucceffe!) go not you thither, but bring Paleftine hither, by bringing pure hearts with you when you come to receive the Sacrament, for there *the Lords body is fhewed forth,* as on the Croffe.

Till I come.] Obfervation: *God till the Worlds end, when hee commeth to judgement, will have a Church on Earth, wherin Paftors fhall adminifter, and people receive the Sacrament.* Witneffe his promife before his death, Mat. 16. 18, *And the Gates of hell fhall not prevaile againft it;* and another after his Refurrection, Mat. 28. 20, *And loe, I am with you alway unto the end of the world;* with you in your felves and fucceffours, perfons and pofterity. Indeed the Church may want things of Lufter, never of Effence: It may want a glorious being, never a being; *Deus non deerit in neceffarijs:* The Church is like the funne, which may be clouded and eclipfed, yet ftil remaineth, *Pfal.* 89. 37, *A faithfull witneffe.* Befides, Churches may fall away, but the *Church* cannot; the fetting of the Gofpel in one place will bee the rifing of it in another: This is meant, *Rev.* 2.5: *I will remove thy Candlefticke out of his place;* not I will quench, or put out thy Candle, but I will remove it, fo that it fhal ftill remaine in one place or other, *Till I come.* And then Sacraments fhall be celebrated no more, but types fhall give place to the truth, and fhadowes fhall yeeld to the fubftance: Then all the weeke fhall be one conftant Sabbath, and yet therein no Sermons preached, nor prayers made, but all our Lyturgie fhall be praifing of God. And now what remaineth, but that we cry from our hearts with the Saints, *Come, Lord Jesus, come quickly?*

Verse 27: *Wherefore whofoever fhall eate this Bread and drinke this Cup of the Lord unworthily, fhall be guilty of the body and blood of the Lord.*

LOE, thefe words prefent us with two principall parts:
1. The finne. 2. The finfulneffe of the finne.

[I.] The finne is the unworthy eating and drinking of the Bread and Wine of the Lord.

Queftion: Is any man fo wel ftored with grace that he can eate thefe Sacraments worthily?

Anfwer: Three-fold worthineffe. One may doe an action worthily in a three-fold refpect.

[1.] Firft, worthily, *Dignitate æqualitatis,* as *the Labourer is worthy of his hire, Luke* 10. 7. This exact worthineffe may claim and challenge a reward due unto it, and the Denier or Detayner doth this worthy party wrong and injury: Now no Saint can receive with this Gods juftice-proofe worthineffe, as appeares by their humble confeffions, not out of complement, but confcioufneffe of their faults: *Iacob, Gen.* 32. 10; *Iohn Baptift, Mat.* 3. 11.· Yea, this worthineffe is waved by our Church Liturgy, at the Communion, both (as I may fay) in our Grace before meat: *Wee be not worthy fo much as to gather up the crums under thy Table*; and in our Grace after meat: *and though wee bee unworthy through our manifold fins to offer unto thee, &c.*

2. The fecond is, worthily *Dignitate convenientiæ, aptitudinis,* or *decentiæ*; which confifts, though not in a perfect and exact proportion, yet in fome fitneffe, meetneffe, and likeneffe unto that which is required; fuch phrafes are frequent in Scripture. *Mat.* 3. 8: *Bring forth therefore fruits worthy of Repentance*; that is, fuch as bear no open repugnancy and contradiction to the repentance you profeffe, but in fome fort meet and agreeing thereunto. So, *Walke worthy of the Lord, Col.* 1. 10; *worthy your calling, Ephef.* 4. 1; *worthy the Gofpel, Phil.* 1. 27. That is, let not your life fhame your beliefe, break not the Commandements againft the Creed; let not your practice bee ἀσύστατος with your profeffion. And wee muft know, that *Peccata furreptitia*, finnes of infirmity (not through their want of wickedneffe, but Gods ftore of mercy) may ftand and fubfift with this worthineffe of conveniencie. In this acception wee underftand in my Text to eat worthily; that is, fo fitted and prepared as may beare fome refemblance and agreement to the folemnity of the worke wee goe about.

3. There remayneth a third kind of Worthineffe, which is *Dignitas dignationis*, the worthineffe of acceptance, when God for Chrifts fake is pleafed to take our actions in good worth. That is well fpoken which is well taken, and that man is worthy who by God is accepted fo to bee. Indeed if bafe and ignorant people fhould cry one up to bee worthy, and prize pebles to bee pearles, hee is no whit the better for the over-valuing of him; but if God pleafeth to efteeme men worthy, things are as they are accounted by him; his valuing of them puts worth into them: *I have bleffed him*; (faith *Ifaac* of *Iacob, Gen.* 27. 33;) *Yea, and hee fhall be bleffed*: God hath accounted them worthy; yea, and they fhall be worthy, as it is *Rev.* 3. 4, *They fhall walke with me in white; for they are worthy.* Let us when wee come to the Sacrament bring with

us the worthineffe of fitneffe, and convenience ; and God of his goodneffe will be pleafed to reward us with the worthineffe of acceptance.

Two forts of people, then, doe eate and drinke unworthily. Firft, the Vnregenerate, thofe which, as it is *Heb.* 6. 1, *Have not as yet laid the Foundation of Repentance from dead workes, and faith in Chrift,* but remaine ftill in their pure, impure naturals, not ingrafted into Chrift. Without this foundation, the faire fide-wals of a good nature, and the proud roofe of all morall performances, will both totter and tumble to the ground. Secondly, the Regenerate, but guilty of fome finnes unrepented of, who eate unworthily till they have fued out a fpeciall pardon out of the Court of Heaven.

[II.] Come wee now to the finfulneffe of the fin : *fhall bee guilty of the body and blood of the Lord ;* that is, they are offenders in the fame forme with *Iudas* and the Iewes, guilty of fhedding the blood and wounding the body of Chrift : For as thofe that deface the ftamp, or abufe the Seale of a King, are entituled to be traytors ; fo the unworthy receivers of thefe elements, which perfonate and reprefent Chrifts body, are interpreted to fin againft the body of Chrift it felfe. Some Proteftants have by Gods Providence efcaped in their perfons, and yet the papifts to manifeft their fpite have burned their pictures at a stake : Chrifts perfon is fhot-free from any mans malice, out of the reach of your cruelty, fitting at the right hand of God in Heaven ; as for his Picture, it is with us in the Sacraments ; and unworthy Receivers fhew to the fhaddow what they would doe to the fubftance if it were in their power ; they pufh as farre as their fhort hornes will give them leave.

Objection : But may one fay ; Grant unworthy Receiving bee a grievous finne, yet me thinkes too heavy an accent is put upon it to equalize it with the murthering of Chrift. *Jonathan* faid, 1 *Sam.* 14. 43, *J did but tafte a little honey with the end of my Rod, and loe, I muft dye ;* but more juftly and grievoufly may the wicked Communicant complaine ; I did but eate a morfell of Bread and dranke a Draught of wine, and loe, I muft dye here, hereafter, temporally, and eternally ;

yea, my finne is heigthned to be even with the finne of *Iudas* and the Iewes, who wilfully embrued their hands in Chrifts blood.

Anfwer: However humane corruption may bee the Advocate to plead herein, yet wee muft count finnes to be fo great as God efteemes them to be. *Hee feeth not as man feeth,* nor judgeth he as man judgeth : Hee will judge that to be pride which wee count to be good carriage; that luft, which wee count love ; that drunkenneffe, which wee [call] good fellowship; and unworthy receiving, which we perchance efteeme a fault, but not of the firft magnitude, hee judgeth it the higheft of any pardonable finne, even guiltineffe of Chrift blood it felfe. Learne wee from hence to meafure and furvey a fin in the true heigth, length, and bredth thereof. Hearken not to the partiality of thine owne flefh, which wil make thine offences in number lefs, in nature lighter; liften not to the fuggeftions of Satan, which will never fuffer us to fee our finnes truely, but is alwayes in the exceffe or defect : When wee goe on in a finfull courfe, hee beares us in hand that our finnes are fmall ; and when we are toucht in confcience he feeks to perfwade us that they are too great, Mountaines too big to bee drowned in the Ocean of Gods mercy ; but let us meafure them by the fquare of Gods Word, an infallible rule that will not deceive us.

To conclude, men generally hate *Pilate* and *Iudas :* if wee fee them but in Pictures our blood rifeth at them, we could fcratch them out with our nayles ; being more angry with them then *David* with the rich man that tooke away the poore mans Ewe Lambe; whereas in fome fenfe it may bee faid of many of us, *Thou art the man.* Yet as for thofe which hitherto have not taken notice of the haynoufneffe of this finne, and through the want of confideration, have beene *guilty of the body of Chrift ;* let mee fay to them what Saint *Peter* doth, *Acts* 3. 17, 19, *And now brethren, I wot that through Ignorance you did it : Repent therefore, and bee converted, that your finnes may bee blotted out.* And let us all pray with *David, Pfalme* 51. 14, *Deliver us from bloodguiltineffe, O God,* but efpecially from being guilty of the body and blood of thy Sonne.

Verse 28: *But let a man examine himselfe, and so let him eate of this Bread and drinke of this Cup.*

LET us know that some make these words (*Let a man examine*) to be a bare permission and concession, that if they wil they may doe it. Others make it a councell or advice, that according to the rule of Prudence or discretion they should doe it. A third sort, and that the truest, make it a mandate or command, that wee must doe it; and the seeming indifferency in the English tongue is necessitated in the Greeke, Δοκιμαζέτω.

Reasons of the necessity. 1. The first is taken from the Majesty of that God to whose presence wee approach. Lord, what prodigious state did *Ahashuerosh*, an earthly Prince, stand upon, *Esther* 1. 12! The woman that was thought fit to bee his wife, must bee purified twelve monethes before, six monethes with the oyle of myrrhe, and six monethes with sweet odours: *Behold, a greater than Ahashuerosh is here;* and therefore those that come to his Table must seriously examine and prepare themselves before.

2. From the great profit which we receive thereby, if we come prepared.

3. From the grievousnesse of the punishments, if we be unworthy Receivers: The Sacrament is not like to those harmlesse Receits, (as innocent as the Prescribers are simple,) which some good old women give sick people, which, if they doe no good, do no harme; but this is a true maxim, *To him to whom the Sacrament is not Heaven, it is hell:* If it brings not profit and spirituall grace, it drawes great plagues and punishments on us.

Examine himselfe.] A Christians eyes ought to be turned inward, and chiefly reflected on himselfe: yet how many are there whose home is to be always abroad! It is a tale of the wandring Iew, but it is too much truth of many wandring Christians, whose thoughts are never resident on their own souls, but ever searching and examining of others: These say not with the souldiers, *Luke* 3. 14, *And what shall we do?*

but are queftioning alwayes, as S. *Peter* is of *Iohn*, *Ioh*. 21. 21, *And what fhal this man do?*

Yet a mans examining of himfelfe excludes not his examination of thofe who are committed to his care and charge; as Paftors examining such young people as according to the orders of the Church they are to catechife. As for that Father who trieth his wife and children, he ftill examineth himfelfe.

Two forts of people are unfit to receive. 1. Thofe that wilfully wil not examine themfelves. 2. Thofe that cannot by reafon of their want of age, or fome other impotency.

Yea, children which are old enough to conceive the words of a Minifter, yet as yet not of age to partake of the Sacrament: Thinke not that the Church maketh cyphers of you, and efteemeth you of no account; you are heires apparent to the Sacrament of the Lords Supper; none can hinder you from it; yet during your minority the Church is your Guardian, and carefully keepes that treafure for you till you come of age, provided you carefully learne your Catechifme, to be able to anfwer your Minifter. But I will turne my Precepts to you into prayers for you, and fo *wifh you good fucceffe in the name of the Lord.*

In examining of this word *Examine*, learned men run in three feverall ftreames. Some profecute the Metaphor of a Gold-fmith, fearching the purity of his gold, Δοκιμάζειν being a proper word to them in their myfterie: 1 Pet. 1. 7, "Ἵνα τὸ δοκίμιον ὑμῶν τῆς πίστεως πολὺ τιμιτώερον χρυσίου, *That the tryall of your faith, being much more precious then of gold that perifheth, though it be tryed with fire, might bee found unto praife, &c.* Others, becaufe bread and wine to bee taken in the Sacrament are both food and phyfick, pleafe themfelves beft to infift on the fimilitude of a Phyfician, giving preparatives to his patients before he receives the phyficke. A third fort make *Examine* here to bee *Verbum forenfe et juridicum*, as Magiftrates queftion offenders; and therefore chufe to follow that refemblance: *David* was in a great ftrait, betwixt three evils; I am in a ftraight betwixt three goods, not knowing which to chufe: however, wee will follow the latter as moft confonant to the Apoftles fenfe.

A man in examining himfelfe muft perfonate three, and act three feverall parts. 1. The part of the Offender. 2. Of the Accufer. 3. Of the Iudge. The part of the Accufer may be wel performed by that faculty of the foul which is called *Confcience;* for, befides her office to be the Regefter and Recorder of the foule, and Remembrancer of the acts thereof, it is alfo the *Atturney Generall* of the King of Heaven in our hearts, to prefs the evidence againft us after the inditement. As for our reafon and judgement, that muft supply the office of a Iudge, *Et fecundum allegata et probata,* acquit or condemne us.

But here it is to be feared, men will be partiall to themfelves in two refpects. 1. Firft, in not giving their confcience fair play: they will not give it that liberty *Agrippa* granted to S. *Paul, Acts* 26. 1, *Thou art permitted to fpeak for thy felfe;* but what in whol they cannot filence, they wil in part difturb and interrupt. 2. It is to be feared our judgement wil not be upright; but as S. *Peter* faid to our Saviour, Ἴλεώς σοι Κύριε, *Mafter, fpare thy felfe, Propitius tibi fit, Mat.* 16. 22: So our judgement will be partiall and favourable to us, as foundred feet will never tread hard.

Wherfore becaufe of this double fufpition of partiality, this is a found and fafe Rule: Let us account our felves to be worfe than upon examination wee find our felves to be: Thus did Saint *Paul,* 1. *Cor.* 4. 4: *For I know nothing by my felfe; yet am I not hereby juftified; but he that judges mee is the Lord.* That is, fince his converfion, his confcience accufed him of no great finne unrepented; and yet hereupon he durft not pronounce himfelfe to be innocent, for *God judgeth not as man judgeth, neither feeth as man feeth;* but thofe who are acquitted by themfelves, may be condemned by him.

Seeing thus, as it is faid, a man is to act three parts, by the way wee may obferve:

Doctrine: A Chriftian, though alone may make company for himfelfe. Pfalme 4. 4: *Commune with your hearts in your Chamber, and be ftill.* Pfal. 43. 5: *Why art thou fo heavy O my foule? why art thou, &c.* One, (as wee have faid,) may make himfelfe three, Offender, Accufer, Iudge; fo that hee fhould never be leffe alone then when alone, being alwayes in the company of heavenly Difcourfers in himfelfe: Had men the art of thefe felfe-examinations and Soliloquies, they need not (to put away melancholly, as they pretend, and to avoid folitarineffe) repair to the fchools of drunkenneffe, there to feeke for bad company, that there (to ufe their owne expreffion) they may drive away the time. Fools! to drive away that which is winged, and which though they fhould ftrive to stay, they cannot.

Now the Interrogatories, wherupon every man is to be examined, are thefe.

1. Whether doft thou repaire to receive the Sacrament with a competent meafure of knowledge?

2. Whether doft thou come with unfained Repentance for thy finnes paft? which Repentance confifteth not fo much in outward forrow (for their faces may be flints, whofe hearts may bee Fountaines; their foules may drop blood, whofe eyes cannot fhed teares) as in the inward contrition and hatred of finne, and fhunning of it in the fequell of our lives.

3. Whether doft thou come with a lively faith, relying upon God in Chrift for the pardon of thy finnes?

4. Whether doft thou come with love undiffembled, freely from thy heart to forgive all injuries committed againft thee? Some when they are to partake of the Sacrament fay to their malice, as *Abraham* did to his two fervants, *Gen.* 22. 5, *Abide you here, and I will goe yonder and worfhip, and come againe to you.* They leave their injuries at the Church doore, till they have received the Lords Supper, and then returning make a refumption of them againe: But let us not onely lop the bowes, but grub up even the roots of our malice; not only fufpend the act, but depofe the habit of our hatred.

And here as God faid to the Iewes, *Ezek.* 18. 3, that they fhould have no occasion any more to ufe that Proverbe in Ifrael, *The Fathers have eaten fower Grapes, and the childrens teeth are fet on edge;* in like manner I could wifh no occafion that the Englifh by-word be any more ufed, *I forgive him, but I will not forget him.* Such people, I dare fay, neither forgive nor forget; like fluts, they fweepe the houfe of their heart, but leave all the duft ftil behind the doore; but let us not only breake the teeth of our malice in forgiving, but alfo pluck out the sting, which is still behind in the tayle, and labour fully to forget.

To these Interrogatories, some have added these additionals which vertually are contained in the former: Whether dost thou come with an earnest desire and longing to be made partaker of these heavenly mysteries? Whether dost thou come with thankfulnes to the God of heaven for this his great blessing?

Hereon let every one examine himselfe. I dare boldly say, none can decline the answering to these interrogatories; not that common evasion, *Non tenetur respondere*, as if they were not absolutely pertinent to the matter in hand; but it concernes every one of us to make a punctuall and direct answer thereunto.

Vpon examination all will confesse themselves guilty, except a dumbe Devill or a Pharisaicall spirit hath possessed any. Yet are there degrees of guiltinesse: Some are guilty that they have not these graces at all, but the opposite vices in stead of them; in stead of knowledge ignorance. All the reason *Laban* could render *Iacob* in cozening him with the elder sister for the younger, was but pleading the custome of the countrey, *Gen.* 29. 26. And this is the best account some can give why they receive the Sacrament: It is an old ceremony, a fashion of their Fore-fathers, a custome of the Church, that young men and maidens at such an age use to receive. And so of the rest: in stead of repentance, obstinacy in sin; in lieu of faith, unbeliefe; in place of charity, malice; an indifferency for desire, and ingratitude for thankfulnesse. These in no case must presume to receive, but tarry till these vices are amended, and graces in some degree begotten in them.

Others are guilty, that though they have them in sincerity, yet they have them not in perfection. These are bound to come to Gods table; his dainties are provided properly for such guests; and by his blessing these holy mysteries may worke in them what is wanting, and strengthen what is weak. And, to conclude, as the father of the lunatick child cryed out, *Mark* 9. 24, *Lord, I beleeve, help my unbeliefe*; so may the best of us all, when we come to communicate, call out with teares, Lord, I come with knowledge; helpe my want of knowledge: Lord, I come with repentance; help my want of repentance: Lord, I come with faith; helpe my want of faith: Lord, I come with love; help my want of love: Lord, I come, &c.

Verse 30: *For this cause many are weake and sicke among you, and many sleepe.*

RIGHT at this time, there raged and raigned in the Church of Corinth an Epidemicall disease; and my Apostle in my Text tels them the Fountaine from which it flowed, namely from the unprepared and unreverent receiving of the Sacrament. The words containe the punishment, and the cause thereof. I must confesse, in the Heraldry of nature, the cause is to be handled before the effect; but because the punishment, being the effect, discovered it selfe first, while the cause was yet unknown, we will first treat thereof. The punishment containes three steps to the Grave: 1. Weaknesse. 2. Sicknesse. 3. Temporal death called *sleep*.

Learne, *God inflicteth not the same punishment for all, but hath variety of correction*. In his Quiver some Arrowes are blunt, some sharpe; and of these some he drawes halfe way, some to the head. And the Reason is, because there are divers degrees of mens sinnes: some sinne out of Ignorance, others out of Knowledge; some out of Infirmity, others of Presumption; some once, others often; some at the seducing of others, others seduce others. God therefore doth not like the unskilfull Empiricks, who prescribe the same quantity of the same receit at all times, to all ages, tempers and diseases; but wisely he varieth his physick, *few stripes* to those that knew not his will, and *many stripes* for them who knew his wil, and did it not. Sometimes hee shooteth halfe canon, weaknesse; sometime full canon, sicknesse; sometimes murthering Peeces, death it selfe.

Use 1: Let us endeavour to amend when God layeth his least judgement upon us; let us humble our selves with true Repentance under his hand, when hee layeth his *little finger* upon us, lest we cause him to lay his *loynes* on us: let us be bettered when he *scourgeth us with rods*, left we give him occasion to *Sting us with Scorpions*, for light punishments neglected wil draw heavier upon us.

Vse 2: Let Magistrates and men in authority mitigate or increase the punishment, according to the nature of the offence. Let there be as well the stocks for the Drunkard, the house of correction for the idle Drone; the whip for the petty Lassoner, as the brand for the fellon, and the Gallowes for the Murtherer. Let mercy improve it selfe to obtaine, if not a pardon, yet a lighter punishment for those in whose faces are read the performance of present sorrow, and promise of future amendment. Let severity lay load on their backs which are old and incorrigable sinners, so that there is more feare of their perverting others than hope of their converting. Then shal the gods in earth be like to the God in Heaven, and Magistrates here imitate the patterne which God setteth in my Text. For probable it is, that those Corinthians who are least offenders in the irreverent receiving of the Sacrament, were punished with weaknesse; the greater with sicknesse; the greatest of all with death temporall, called *Sleepe* in my Text.

The death of the Godly, in Scripture language, is often stiled *sleepe*. And indeed sleepe and death are two twins: sleepe is the elder brother, for *Adam* slept in Paradise; but death liveth longest, for *the last enemy that shall bee destroyed is death*. But some will object, Was Saint *Paul* so charitably opinioned to these Corinthians, as to thinke that they, some whereof were drunken at the receiving of the Sacrament, that they *slept*; that is, dyed and went to Heaven? me thinkes so strong a charity argues too weake a judgement. I answer, the Apostle had perceived in these mens lives the strength of unfained piety; and though God suffered them to fall into a sin of so high a nature as this must be confest to be, yet Saint *Paul* did Christianly beleeve that this sinne, by Repentance and faith in Christ, was pardoned, and their soules eternally saved. Let us measure the estates of men after death by the rule of their lives; and though wee see some commit grievous sinnes, yea, such sinnes for which they are brought to exemplary death (perchance by the orderly proceeding of the

Law), yet withall, if wee had knowne that the drift and scope of their lives had beene to fear God, we may and must charitably conceive of their finall estate, and that, with the Corinthians in my Text, they are fallen asleepe.

So much for the punishment: wee come now to the cause. *For this cause many are weake.*

All sicknesses of the body proceed from the sinne of the soule: I am not ignorant that the Lethurgy ariseth from the coldnesse of the braine; that the dropsie floweth from waterish blood in an ill affected Liver; that the spleen is caused from melancholly wind, gathered in the mindriffe; but the cause of all these causes, the Fountaine of all these Fountaines, is the sinne of the soule. And not onely the sinnes, which wee have lately committed and still lye fresh bleeding on our consciences, but even those which wee have committed long agoe, and which processe of time hath since scarred over: *Iob* 13. 26, *For thou writest bitter things against me, and makest me possesse the sinnes of my youth.* So that *Iob* being gray is punished for *Iob* being greene; *Job* in the autumn of his age smarts for what he hath done in the spring of his age: and as those which have beene given to violent exercises in their youth, when they are old, reade the admonitions of their former folly in the aches of their bones; so they who have prodigally ryoted their youth out in vitious courses, in their old age find the smart of it in their weak and diseased bodies. Doe wee then desire to lead our old age in health? know, no better preservative or dyet drinke can bee prescribed then in our youth to keepe our soules from sin; for now wee sow the seeds of health or sicknesse, which perchance wee shall reape twenty yeares after.

Question: But how came Saint *Paul* to know that this sicknesse of the Corinthians proceeded from the irreverent receiving of the Sacrament, especially sithence there were for [four] other grand sinnes which then raigned in their Church, each whereof upon hew and cry might be taken as suspitious to be the cause of this disease? 1. Factious affecting of one Minister above another, to the disgrace of God and the Gospel: 1 *Corinthians*, 1. 12, *Now this I say, that every one of you saith, I am of* Paul, *I am of* Apollo, *I am of* Cephas, *and I am of* Chrift. 2. Suffering an *inceftuous perfon*, hufband to his mother, and fonne to his wife, to live amongft them without publike penance and punifhment: For though this inceft, as it was committed but by one man, was but a particular and perfonall fin, yet as it was connived at and not punifhed, it began gangreen-like to fpread, and leaving its nature of perfonality, it intituled it felfe to be a publike generall Church-fin of the Corinthians. 3. Going to law one with another under heathen Iudges: 1 *Cor.* 6. 1, *Dare any of you, having bufines againft another, be judged by the unjuft, and not by the Saints?* 4. Denying the Refurrection of the body: 1 *Cor.* 15. 12, *How fay fome among you, that there is no Refurrection of the dead?* Sithence therefore at the fame time the Corinthians were guilty of factious affecting of their Minifters, going to law under Pagan Iudges, fuffering an inceftuous perfon to live amongft them unpunifhed, denying of the Refurrection of the body; why might not Saint *Paul* thinke that any one or all of thefe might be the caufe of this difeafe in the Church of Corinth, as well as the irreverent receiving of the Sacrament?

Anfwer 1: Becaufe this finne was the finne paramount, like *Saul, higher then his fellowes, from the fhoulders upwards.* The other for [four] finnes were fellony, robbing God of his glory; but the irreverent receiving of the Sacrament was high treafon againft the perfon of Chrift, and fo againft God himfelfe. The other for fins were Tetrarchs raigning over the Corinthians; but this was as *Auguftus* the Emperour ove the Tetrarchs, more confpicuous then any of the reft. Lear we then, that though God of his goodneffe may be pleafed gracioufly to pardon and paffe by fins of an inferior nature and meaner alloy, yet he wil not hold them guiltleffe and let them efcape unpunifhed, who irreverently receive the body and blood of his Sonne. This ftentor fin fhouts in Gods ears for revenge. Saint *Anfelme* faith, that many difeafes that raigne in the fummer (though Phyficians may impute them to other fecond caufes) proceed from peoples irreverent receiving the Sacrament at Eafter.

Anfwer 2: Becaufe the Apoftle perceived fome refemblance betwixt the fin committed and the punifhment inflicted. For as a Phyſician when he comes to his Patient and finds him ſtrangely affected, ſo that the diſeaſe puzles al his rules of art to reduce it to ſome naturall cauſe, then he will be ready to ſuſpect that his Patient hath eaten ſome poyſon which hath ſtrangely invenomed the eſtate of his body; ſo Saint *Paul*, ſeeing the Corinthians to be puniſhed with a ſtrange and unuſuall ſickneſſe (ſome conceive it was the plague), preſently ſuſpected that they had eaten ſome poyſenous thing, and on inquiry he finds that it was the Sacrament irreverently received: It being juſt with God to turne that which was appoynted to bee preſervative for the ſoule, to prove poyſon to the body, being not received with due preparation.

And here I may adventure upon a profitable diſ-courſe, how a man in· his ſickneſſe may come to know the very particular ſin for which God hath inflicted that ſickneſſe upon him. It is not a meer curioſity, which will afford the ground work of much good meditation; nor an impoſſibility, though a difficulty to arrive at the knowledge of it: Wherefore let a man in ſuch a caſe ſummon all his great ſins to make a perſonall appearance in his memory, and not onely thoſe of the laſt edition, but even thoſe whoſe impreſſion is almoſt out of the date of his memory, ſuch as were committed long agoe in his youth: This done, all the matter will bee to find out which is the verieſt ſinne for which God puniſheth him at that time; and here I muſt confeſſe my candels to be but dim, but I will light the more of them.

Reason 1: Firſt, ſee to which ſin the puniſhment thou ſuffer-eſt bears the moſt proportion of reſemblance; for God commonly puniſheth like with the like. Thus one may ſee Gods hand in the cutting of one of *Adonibezecks* fingers, he being ſerved, as hee had ſerved ſeventy-two Kings. And thus King *Ioram*, who had cruelly ſlaughtered his brethren on a ſtone [with the ſword, 2 Chron. xxi. 4], was troubled with an incurable diſeaſe, that his bowels fell out; and juſt it was that he ſhould have no bowels, that had no compaſſion.

2. See if thou canſt not find ſome proportion in the diſproportion, and likeneſſe in the unlikeneſſe of ſome ſin to this puniſhment; God oft times puniſhing by the contrary.

Thus those who out of nicenesse and curiosity have tooke more then comes to the share of a corrupt creature, are commonly sent to their graves by some nasty and loathsome disease; as for proud *Herod*, whom the wormes, impatient to stay so long till death had dished him for their palate, devoured him alive.

3. Something may be gathered from the place or part wherein the disease lieth. For, if it be in eyes, it is probable its inflicted for the shooting out of lustfull and lascivious glances, or looking with envious and covetous sight on the means of others; if in the eares, for giving audience to wanton sonnets, or for being over credulous in the hearing ill reports of others; if in the tongue, for lying, swearing, &c.

4. See whether Chronology, or the time wherein the sicknesse seizeth upon thee, will not something advantage thee for the discovering the cause thereof. Thus, as one observes, the Lord *Hastings* was beheaded at London, that very selfe-same day twelve-moneth, yea the same houre, and if curiosity may goe further, the same minute, wherein he had conspired the death of the Queenes kinred at Pomfret Castle.

5. Consider what sinne it is, for the committing whereof thou hast conceived the least sorrow. For though wee can never bee condignly sorry for our least sinne, yet we may be more penitent for one sinne than for another; and that sinne which hath cost us the slightest and shallowest Repentance, is most likely to be the cause of our present sicknesse.

6. Hearken chiefly to the Inditement of thy conscience. For when wee hunt after that sin which causeth our disease, and wee find our selves to be either at a losse, or at a cold sent, if once our conscience begin to spend her open mouth, wee may certainely conclude that the game went that way, and that that is the very sin for which at that time wee are punished. Thus the Patriarks, *Gen.* 42. 21, *said one to another, We have verely sinned against our Brother, in that we saw the anguish of his soule, when hee besought us, and wee would not heare; therefore is this evill fallen upon us.* *Reuben* did not impute it to the defiling of his Fathers bed, nor *Iudah* to his Incest, nor *Simeon* and *Levi* to their murthering of the Shechemites; for these were but personall sinnes; but all joyntly agreed

that it was for their cruelty to their Brother, a fin wherein all were equally ingaged, as they were equally inwrapt in the punifhment.

If by thefe or any other meanes we attaine to the knowledge of that particular finne for which wee are punifhed, let us drown that fin in penitent teares, and in the blood of our Saviour; but if we cannot find it out, let us imitate the example of *Herod*, *Mat.* 2. 16, who, that he might make fure work to kil our Saviour, flew all the children in Bethelem, and the countrey about it, from two years old and under; a plot probable to have taken effect, if heaven had not beene too wife for hell. In like manner, let us indifferently and impartially repent for all our fins in generall: if wee know not which was the Bee that ftung us, let us throw downe the whole Hive; if wee know not which was the thorne that prickt us, let us cut downe the whole [1] hedge, and fo wee fhall bee fure that finne fhall not efcape, which hath caufed our prefent ficknefse.

Now whereas God might have tumbled the Corinthians down into hell-fire for their irreverent receiving of the Sacrament, and yet was pleafed to inflict on them bodily weakenefse and ficknefse, and death, we learn,

God oftentimes with his Saints commuteth eternall torments into temporall punifhments. Hee is therefore angry in this world, that hee might not be angry in the world to come, *Et mifericorditer adhibet temporalem pœnam, ne jufte inferat æternam ultionem.* If any object, But why will God pardon talents, and not tokens; pounds, but not pence; and for Chrifts fake forgive, and ftrike off eternall torment, and yet not crofse the fcore of temporall punifhment? I anfwer, 1. To make us take notice that wee have beene offenders. 2. That by feeling the fmart of what hee inflicteth on us, wee may bee the more fenfible of his favour, how much paine he hath forgiven us. 3. To make us more wary and watchfull in time to come. But farre bee it from us to conceive that there is any fatisfactory or expiatory power in the afflictions which wee fuffer. Satisfaction for finne could not be but

[¹ *Edge*, in other copies.]

once; and once was fully made when Christ offered himselfe upon the Crosse.

Vse: Let us therefore learne patience under Gods afflicting hand, when hee layeth any sicknesse upon us. *Solomon* said to *Abiathar*, 1 Kings 2. 26, *Get thee to Anathoth, to thine owne fields; for thou art worthy of death; but I will not at this time put thee to death, becaufe thou barest the Arke of my Lord God before* David *my Father*: Thus God dealeth with us, when hee might justly deprive us of our life, yea, of our eternall life; yet if wee have borne his Arke, if wee can plead any true reference or relation to Christ our Saviour, God will be gracioufly pleafed, not to take away our lives, but onely to send us to our *Anathoth*, to confine us to our beds, to keepe us his close Prisoners, and onely to deprive us of our health, pleasure, and delight. Let us therefore patiently endure the aking of the teeth; wee have all deserved the gnashing of the teeth. Let us patiently endure a burning Fever; for wee have all deserved Hell-fire. Let us patiently endure a bodily Consumption; for wee have deserved to bee consumed, and brought to nothing.

[The Eight Sermons which follow formed the laſt portion of *Ioſeph's Party-colovred Coat.*]

[EIGHT SERMONS, 1640.]

[1] Growth in Grace.

2 PET. 3. 18.

But grow in grace, and in the knowledge of our Lord and Saviour Iesus Christ.

PHILOSOPHERS make a double growth. One, *per aggregationem materiæ*, by gayning of more matter: Thus Rivers grow by the accession of tributary Brooks; heaps of Corne waxe greater by the addition of more graine; and thus stones grow, as some would have it, though this more properly bee termed an augmentation or increase then a growth. The other, *per introreceptionem nutrimenti*, by receiving of nourishment within, as plants, beasts, and men grow. Of the latter growth wee understand the Apostle in the Text, and will prosecute the Metaphor of the growth of vegetables, as that which the Holy Spirit seemes most to favour and intend in these expressions.

2. Here is one thing presupposed in the text and laid down for a foundation; namely, that those to whom S. *Peter* writes were already rooted in grace and goodness. There must be an Vnit at least, before any multiplication; a Basis, before any building upon it: no doubt they were such as to whom S. *Paul* writes, *Eph.* 3. 18 [of the Textus Receptus], ἐν ἀγάπῃ ἐρριζωμένοι, *Being rooted and grounded in love* [ver. 17]; such as the *Colossians* were, *Col.* 2. 7, *Rooted in Christ, and established in faith.* And such I trust you are to whom my discourse is directed; or else it were in vaine for me, or any, to give you instructions for *Growth in Grace.*

3. *Objection:* But why is it said in the Text, first *in*

Grace, and then *in Knowledge?* This feemes to be an ὕστερον πρότερον. The Lanthorne is to go firft; Knowledge is to be the Vfher of Grace: information in the underftanding muft goe before reformation in the will and affections.

Anfwer: I could anfwer, the holy Spirit is no whit curious in marfhalling thefe graces, which he putteth firft; they need no herauld to fhew their pedigree, which wil not fal out for precedency. But to the point: there is a two-fold knowledge; one precedent grace, as difpofing one therto, and making capable therof; the other fubfequent, and is an effect therof, and a reward of it through Gods mercy. Thefe that have gracious hearts do daily better and improve their knowledge in matters of falvation; and fome herein arrive at a great heigth, as *David*, *Pfa.* 119. 99, *I have more underftanding than al my teachers, for thy teftimonies are my meditation.*

4. However, fee, the Apoftle puts grace and Knowledge together: *What God hath joyned, let no man put afunder.* We muft grow according to both demenfions, both in heigth, in knowledge, and in bredth, in piety; both in head and in heart; both in fpeculation and practife; we muft not all run up in heigth, like an Hop-pole, but alfo burnifh, and fpread in bredth: then fhall we be wel proportioned and compleat. And indeed practife without knowledge is blind, and knowledge without practife is lame.

5. Three things are required to make a plant to grow. Firft, that it hath life within it. Thus the Chriftian muft have in his foul a quickning vivifying faith. Secondly, it muft be watered in a man with the dew of Gods Word: *Ifa.* 55. 10,11, *For as the rain commeth down, and the fnow from heaven, and returneth not thither, but watereth the earth, and maketh it bring forth and bud, that it may give feed to the fower, and bread to the eater; fo fhal my word be that goeth forth out of my mouth, &c.* And the fame allegory is followed by *Mofes*: *Deut.* 32. 2, *My doctrine fhal drop as the rain; my fpeech fhal diftil as the dew, as the fmal rain upon the tender herb, and as the fhowers upon the grafs.* Thirdly, the bleffing of God is requifite, without which both the former are nothing worth: *Paul may plant, and Apollo may water, but*

God giveth the increase. It was observed of Master *Greenham*, that painefull and zealous Preacher of Gods Word, that though hee was very industrious in his calling, yet his people still remayned most ignorant; and, as one saith,

> *Greenham* had Pastures green,
> But sheepe full leane.

So true it is, that Gods blessing is the Key of the worke, without which all is but labour in vaine.

6. Now wee may take notice of two remarkeables in the growth of a Christian. First, plants have their ἀκμη, their bounds, both in heigth and bredth set by nature; (*Hither shalt thou come and no further;*) to which when they have attayned they grow down-ward and waxe lesse; yea, all sublunary things, *Habent suos terminos, quo cum venerint sistunt retrocedunt ruunt.* But *growth in grace* admits of no such period, but still there is *Plus ultra:* What Saint *Paul* saith, *Pray continually; reioyce evermore,* 1 *Thess.* 5. 17, 16, is as true of spirituall growth: grow continually, encrease evermore, never stop nor stay in grace till thou commest to glory. Secondly, trees dote as well as men in their old age; yea, then they are barren, and bring forth little or no fruit; whereas Christians, on the contrary, *Psal.* 92. 13, 14, *That bee planted in the house of the Lord, shall flourish in the Court of our God; they shall still bring forth fruit in old age: They shall be fat and flourishing.* Like wine, they are best when they are oldest; like *Caleb,* able and active men, even at fourscore years of age.

7. Come wee now to set downe those things which doe either in part hinder or in whole destroy mens growth in Grace. For the first, let us take heed of *Suckers* in our soule; such superfluous excrementall sprigs, which, like so many theeves, steale away the nourishment which should maintaine the tree. By these Suckers we may understand those felonious avocations of worldly employments, which, either out of season or out of measure, busie our soules in earthly things, when they should bee employed in heavenly matters. The onely way to prevent this mischiefe is to prune and cut off these Suckers, and speedily to stop up these

Emiffaries by out-lets and private fluces, left they drain dry the very main channell of grace in our hearts.

8. As for deftroyers of grace, it is two-fold. Firft, the blighting or blafting of a confcience-wafting finne. Thus drunkenneffe and Inceft deftroyed grace in *Lot* for that very inftant, till hee recovered himfelfe againe by unfained repentance. Secondly, the drowth and fcorching heat of perfecution. How promifing a Plant! what a fhoot in Goodneffe did he give on a fudden, who faid to our Saviour, *Mafter, I will follow thee whether foever thou goeft!* But how quickly was he withered with one fcorching beame, when Chrift told him how hard fervice he muft undergoe!

9. Obferve by the way: There is a double rooting in Grace; the one a found and fure one, the other but fhallow and fuperficiall: The former rooting belongs to the Saints of God; and thefe, though they may bee blighted with finne, or fcorched with perfecution, yet ftill, as I may fay, there is a fecret fprig of life in the root, though in outward appearance the leaves and bowes may feeme quite dead; and in Gods due time they grow out of their fins by repentance, out of their afflictions by patience. Let us therefore take heed of being too tyrannicall, in paffing fentence of condemnation upon them before the time. [1]*Scotus*, that famous Schoole-man, being in a ftrong fit of an Apoplexy, was by the cruell kindneffe of his over officious friends buried before he was dead. Many, over hafty in their uncharitable cenfures, feeing one fallen into a finne, bury him alive in their judgements, counting him a Caft-away and Reprobate, when by Gods mercy and his owne repentance he may recover againe, as ftill retaining in his heart fome fparkes of fpirituall life. As for the wicked, which have onely a fuperficiall hold in grace, rather fticked than rooted in it; wee fee what our Saviour faith of them, *Mat.* 13. 5, 6: *And forthwith they fprung up, becaufe they had no deepeneffe of earth; and when the funne was up they were fcorched, and becaufe they had not root they withered away.* They were quite dryed up, and here made fuell for hell, never recovering themfelves any more; whereas the godly, though they feeme dead in the winter, they may grow againe next fpring.

---

1 Cambd[en's] *Brit[tania]*, *in Northumberland* [Holland's ed., 1610, p. 814.]

10. *Vse* 1 : This Doctrine, if applyed, ferves to confute many: Firft, thofe that grow backward in grace, and are worfe now then they were feven yeares before; like the Galatians, *You have run well; who hindred you?* Secondly, thofe who ftand ftill in goodneffe; like thofe women whereof the Apoftle complayneth that they were *Ever learning, and never come to the knowledge of the truth.* Thirdly, thofe that grow, but not proportionably to the long time wherein they have beene planted, the fat foyle wherein they have been fet. [a] The long time wherein they have beene planted, Heb. 5. 12: *For when for the time yee ought to bee teachers, you have need that one teach you againe which be the firft principles of the Oracles of God, and are become fuch as have need of milke, and not of ftrong meat.* [β] The fatneffe of the foyle wherin they have beene fet, and plenty of water powred on them; and herein no countrey comes neere to ours; and therefore wee are moft unexcufable if wee grow not in grace. Out-landifh men call our Iland the Rainy Iland, becaufe wee have fuch plenty therof, arifing of the ftore of vapours, from the vicinity of the fea. They call it alfo the Ringing lland, becaufe it hath bels fo many and fo tuneable. I am fure without flattering it may be thus called in an higher fenfe : the dew of Gods Word is no where powred more plentifully; and we have (God increafe their number) many and melodious bels, tuneable amongft themfelves, and loud-founding the Word of God to others: Moft heavie therefore will be our account if wee yeeld not fome proportionable growth in grace to thefe great means God affords us.

11. Now, in examining themfelves, I find three forts of men to be deceived. Some account themfelves to be growne in grace when they are not: others efteeme themfelves to be not growne, when they are. Of the former fome account themfelves to bee improved in goodneffe, when God takes from them the ability to commit finne they had formerly. An old man faith, I thanke God I am growne in grace. Well, how fhall this appeare? Thus, faith the old man: Twenty yeares agoe I was given to luft and wantonneffe; now I have left it. Alas! hee puts a fallacy on his owne foule; for the finne hath left him, his moyfture is fpent, his heate abated,

and hee difabled from performing the tafke of wickedneffe. So the Prodigall who hath fpent his eftate hugs himfelfe in his owne happineffe, that now hee is growne in grace, becaufe hee hath left Vanity in clothes, Curiofity in dyet, Excefliveneffe in gaming; when, alas! needs muft the fire goe out when the fuell is taken away; he is not growne in grace, but decreafed in eftate. Others conftrue it to be growth of grace in themfelves, when only God takes away from them the temptations to finne. Hee that living in a populous place was given to drunkenneffe, who now, being retyred to a private Village, takes himfelfe to bee turned very fober, Alas! it is not hee that is altered, but his place: he wanteth now (a want with gain) a crue of bad good fellows to folicite him to the taverne; but, had he the fame temptation, let him examine himfelfe whether he would not be as bad as ever hee was before. A third fort count themfelves growne in grace, when they have not left, but onely exchanged their fin; and perchance a leffe for a greater: *Thou that abhorreft Idols, committeft thou facriledge? Rom. 2. 22.* Some thinke themfelves improved in piety, becaufe they left prodigality, and reele into Covetoufneffe; left Profaneneffe, and fallen into fpirituall. Pride, or peevifh affecting of out-fide holineffe. Thus, like the Sea, what they loofe in one place, they gaine in another, and are no whit growne in Grace.

12. Others conceive themfelves not to bee growne in grace when they are growne; and that in thefe foure [five] cafes. Firft, fometimes they thinke that they have leffe grace now than they had feven yeares agoe; becaufe they are more fenfible of their badneffe. They daily fee and grieve to fee how fpirituall the Law of God is, and how carnall they are; how they finne both againft Gods will and their owne, and forrow after their finne, and finne after their forrow. This makes many miftake themfelves to be worfe than they have beene formerly; whereas, indeed, the fick-man begins to amend, when hee begins to feele his paine.

13. [Second,] Many thinke themfelves to have leffe faving Knowledge now than they had at their firft converfion; both becaufe (as we faid before of Grace) they are now more fenfible of their ignorance; and becaufe their knowledge at

their firſt converſion ſeemed a great deale, which ſince ſeemeth not increaſt, becauſe increaſt inſenſibly and by unappearing degrees. One that hath lived all his life time in a moſt darke Dungeon, and at laſt is brought out but into the twi-light, more admires at the clearneſſe and brightneſſe thereof than hee will wonder a moneth after at the ſun at noonday. So a Chriſtian newly regenerated, and brought out of the darke ſtate of nature into the life of grace, is more apprehenſive, at the firſt illumination, of the knowledge hee receives, than of farre greater degrees of knowledge which hee receiveth afterwards.

14. [Third,] Some thinke they have leſſe grace now than they had ſome yeares ſince, becauſe a great meaſure of grace ſeemes but little to him that deſires more. As, in worldly wealth,

[1]*Creſcit amor nummi quantum ipſa pecunia creſcit;*

So is there an holy, heavenly, and laudable covetouſneſſe of grace, which deceives the eye of the ſoule, and makes a great deale of goodneſſe ſeeme but a little.

15. [Fourth,] Many thinke they are growne leſſe and weaker in grace, when indeed they are aſſaulted with ſtronger temptations. One ſaith, Seven years ſince I vanquiſhed ſuch temptations as at this day foyle me; therefore ſurely I am decreaſed in grace. *Non ſequitur;* for, though it be the ſame temptation in kind, it may not be the ſame in degree and ſtrength; thou mayeſt ſtill be as valiant, yet thy enemies may conquer thee, as aſſaulting thee with more force and fury: when thou wert newly converted, God proportioned the weight to the weakneſſe of thy ſhoulders, bound up the Devill, that hee ſhould ſet upon thee with no more force than thou couldeſt reſiſt and ſubdue. Now thou haſt gotten a greater ſtock of grace, God ſuffers the devil to buffet thee with greater blows.

16. [Fifth,] Some thinke grace is leſſe in them now than it was at their firſt converſion, becauſe they find not in their ſouls ſuch violent flaſhes, ſuch ſtrong, impetuous, (I had almoſt

[[1] Juvenal, *Satira* xiv. 139. Modern editors give *crevit* for the laſt word]

said furious,) raptures of goodneſſe, and flaſhes of grace and heavenly illumination : But let them ſeriouſly conſider that theſe raptures which they then had, and now complaine they want, were but fits ſhort and ſudden, *Nimbus erat, cito præterijt,* not ſetled and conſtant, but ſuch as quickly ſpent themſelves with their own violence: Whereas grace in them now may bee more ſolid, reduced, digeſted, and concoćted: *Bos laſſus fortius figit pedem;* more ſlow, but more ſure; leſſe violent, but more conſtant. Though grace be not ſo thicke at one time, yet now it is beaten and hammered out to bee broader and longer; yea, I might adde alſo, it is more pure and refined : This we may ſee in Saint *Peter :* when hee was a young man, in a bravery, he would walk on the water ; yea and ſo daring was hee in his promiſes : *Though all forſake thee, yet will not I:* But afterwards in his old age hee was not ſo bold and daring ; experience had not only correćted the rankneſſe of his Spirit, but alſo in ſome ſort quenched, ſurely tempered, the flaſhes of his zeale for the adventurouſneſſe of it ; yet was he never a whit the worſe, but the better Chriſtian ; though he was not ſo quick to run into danger, yet hee would anſwer the ſpur when need required, and not flinch for perſecution, when juſt occaſion was offered; as at laſt hee ſuffered martyrdome glorfiouſly for Chriſt.

17. To conclude : Grace in the good Thiefe on the Croſſe, like *Ionah's* Gourd, grew up preſently ; for hee was an extraordinary example ; but in us it is like the growth of an Oak, ſlow and inſenſible; ſo that wee may ſooner find it *creviſſe* then *creſcere :* it muſt therefore bee our daily taſke all the dayes of our lives ; to which end let us remember to pray to God for his bleſſing on us. Our Saviour ſaith, *Matth.* 6. 27, *Which of you by taking care is able to adde one cubit unto his ſtature* in the corporall growth ? Much leſſe able are wee in the ſpirituall growth to adde one inch or haires bredth to the heigth of our ſoules. Then what was pride in the Builders of Babel will be piety in us, to mount and raiſe our ſoules ſo high, till the top of them ſhall reach to Heaven. Amen.

[II] How Far Examples are to be followed

R VTH. I. 15.

And Naomi *said, Behold thy sister in Law is gone backe unto her people, and unto her gods; returne thou after thy sister in Law.*

IN these words *Naomi* seekes to perswade *Ruth* to returne, alleaging the example of *Orpah*, who as she saith was *gone back to her people, and to her gods;* where, first, wee find that all the Heathen, and the Moabites amongst the rest, did not acknowledge one true God, but were the Worshippers of many gods; for they made every attribute of God to be a distinct Deity. Thus, in stead of that attribute, the wisedome of God, they fained *Apollo* the God of wisedome; in stead of the power of God, they made *Mars* the God of power; in stead of that admirable beauty of God, they had *Venus* the Goddesse of beauty: But no one attribute was so much abused as Gods Providence. For the Heathen supposing that the whole world and all the creatures therein was too great a Diocesse to bee daily visited by one and the same Deity, they therefore assigned sundry gods to severall creatures. Thus Gods Providence in ruling the raging of the seas was counted *Neptune;* in stilling the roaring wind, *Æolus;* in commanding the powers of Hell, *Pluto;* yea, sheep had their *Pan,* and Gardens their *Pomona;* the Heathens then being as fruitfull in faigning of gods as the Papists since in making of Saints.

Now because *Naomi* used the example of *Orpah* as a motive to worke upon *Ruth* to returne, wee gather from thence: Examples of others set before our eyes are very potent and prevalent Arguments to make us follow and imitate them, whether they bee good examples, fo the forwardneffe of the Corinthians to releeve the Iewes, provoked many; or whether they be bad, fo the diffembling of *Peter* at *Antioch drew Barnabas and others into the fame fault*: But thofe examples of all others are moft forcible with us which are fet by fuch who are neer to us by kindred, or gracious with us in friendfhip, or great over us in power.

Let men in eminent places, as Magiftrates, Minifters, Fathers, Mafters, (fo that others love to dance after their Pipe, to fing after their Mufick, to tread after their tract,) endeavour to propound themfelves examples of piety and religion to thofe that be under them.

When wee fee any good example propounded unto us, let us ftrive with all poffible fpeed to imitate it. What a deale of ftirre is there in the world for civill precedency and priority! Every one defires to march in the Fore-front, and thinkes it a fhame to come laging in the Rear-ward. Oh that there were fuch an holy ambition and heavenly emulation in our hearts, that as *Peter* and *Iohn* ran a race, who fhould come firft to the grave of our Saviour, fo men would contend, who fhould firft attain to true mortification! And when we fee a good example fet before us, let us imitate it, though it be in one which in outward refpects is far our inferior. Shal not our Mafters be afhamed to fee that their men, whofe place on earth is to come behind them, in piety towards Heaven to goe before them? Shall not the Husband blufh to fee his Wife, which is the weaker veffell in nature, the ftronger veffell in grace? Shall not the elder Brother dye his cheeks with the colour of vertue, to fee his younger Brother, who was laft borne, firft reborne by faith and the Holy Ghoft? yet let him not therefore envie his Brother, as *Cain* did *Abel*; let him not be angry with his Brother becaufe hee is better than himfelfe, but let him be angry with himfelfe becaufe hee is worfe than his brother; let him turne all his malice into imitation, all his fretting at him into following of him. Say unto him, as *Gehazi* did of *Naaman*, *As the Lord liveth I will run after him*: and although thou canft not over-run him, nor as yet over-looke him; yet give not over to run with him; follow him, though not as *Azael* did *Abner*, hard at the heeles; yet as *Peter* did our Saviour, *a farre off*; that though the more flowly, yet as furely thou mayeft come to Heaven; and though thou wert fhort of him while hee lived, in the race, yet thou fhalt be even with him when thou art dead, at the marke.

When any bad example is prefented unto us, let us decline and deteft it, though the men be never fo many or fo deare unto us. Imitate *Micaiah*, 1 *Kings* 22. 13, 14, to whom when the Meffenger fent to fetch him said, *Behold now, the words of the Prophets declare good unto the King with one mouth; let thy Word therefore, I pray thee, be like to one of them;* Micaiah anfwered, *As the Lord liveth, whatfoever the Lord faith unto me, that will I fpeake.* If they be never fo deare unto us, wee muft not follow their bad practife: fo muft the fonne pleafe him that begot him, that hee doth not difpleafe him that created him; fo muft the wife follow him that married her, that fhe doth not offend him that made her. Wherefore as *Samfon*, though bound with new cords, fnapt them afunder as tow when it feeleth the fire; fo rather then we fhould be led by the lewd examples of thofe that be neere and deare unto us, let us breake in peeces all their engagements, relations whatfoever.

Now here it will be a labour worthy difcourfe to confider how farre the examples even of good men in the Bible are to bee followed. For as all examples have a great influence on the practife of the Beholders, fo efpecially the deeds of good men regiftred in the Scripture (the Kalender of Eternity) are moft attractive of imitation.

Wee find in Holy Writ nine feverall kinds of examples.

Firft kind of examples. *Actions extraordinary*, the doers whereof had peculiar ftrength and difpenfation from God to doe them. Thus *Phineas* in an heavenly fury killed *Cozbi* and *Zimri*; *Samfon* flew himfelfe and the Philiftims in the Temple of Dagon; *Elias* caufed fire to defcend on the two Captains of fifties; *Elifha* curfed the children, the children of Bethel.

Vse of them: These are written for our instruction, not for our imitation. If with *Elisha* thou canst make a Bridge over Iordan with thy cloake; if with him thou canst raise dead children; then it is lawfull for thee with *Elisha* to curse thy enemies. If thou canst not imitate him in the one, pretend not to follow him in the other.

Abuse of them: When men propound such examples for their practise, what is said is imputed to *Phineas* for righteousnesse will bee imputed to us for Iniquity, if being private men, by a Commission of our own penning, wee usurpe the Sword of Iustice to punish Malefactors.

Second sort. *Actions founded in the ceremoniall Law*; as *Abrahams* circumcising of *Isaac*, *Hezekiahs* eating the Passeover, *Solomons* offering of sacrifices, &c.

Vse of them: We are to be thankful to God, that these shadowes in Christ the substance are taken away. Let us not therefore superstitiously faine that the ghosts of these Ceremonies may stil walk, which long since were buried in Christs grave.

Abuse of them: By those who still retaine them. Excellently [1]*Ignatius, Epistola ad Magnesios*, ὁ γὰρ Χριστιανισμὸς οὐκ ἔστιν Ἰουδαϊσμός. Yea, wee must forfeit the name of Christians if we still retaine such old Rites. Let those who are admitted in the Colledge of grace disdaine any longer to goe to the schoole of the Ceremoniall Law, which truly may bee called the Schoole of *Tyrannus*.

Third sort. *Actions which are founded in the Iudiciall Law*; as punishing theft with foure-fold Restitution, putting of Adulterers to death, and raising up seed to the Brother, &c.

Vse of them: These oblige men to observe them so farre as they have in them any taste or tincture of a Morall Law; and as they beare proportion with those Statutes by which every particular Countrey is governed. For the Iudiciall Law was by God calculated alone for the elevation of the Iewish Common-wealth. It suted onely with the body of their state, and will not fit any other Common-wealth, except

[1 Ed. Vossius, 1646, page 36]

it be equall to Iudea in all Dimenſions. I meane in climate, nature of the ſoyle, diſpoſition of the people, quality of the bordering Neighbours, and many other particulars, amongſt which the very leaſt is conſiderable.

Abuſe of them: When men out of an over Imitativeneſſe of Holy Preſidents, ſeeke to conforme all Countries to Iewiſh Lawes. That muſt needs breake, which is ſtretched further than God intended it. They may ſooner make *Sauls* Armour fit *David*, and *Davids* Sling and Scrip become *Saul*, then the particular Statutes of one Countrey adequately to comply with another.

Fourth ſort. *Actions founded in no Law at all, but onely in an ancient Cuſtome* by God winked and connived at, yea, tolerated, at the leaſt wiſe not openly forbidden in precept or puniſhed in practiſe. As *Poligamy*, in the Patriarkes having many wives. Indeed when God firſt made the large volume of the world, and all creatures therein, and ſet it forth, *Cum regali privilegio, Behold all things therein were very good*, hee made one *Eve* for one *Adam*. *Poligamy* is an *Erratum* and needs an *Index expurgatorius*, being crept in, being more than what was in the maiden coppy: It was the Creature of *Lamech*, no worke of God.

Vſe: We are herein to wonder at and praiſe the goodneſſe of God, who was pleaſed herein to winke at the faults of his deare Saints, and to paſſe by their frailty herein, becauſe they lived in a darke age wherein his pleaſure was not ſo plainely manifeſted.

Abuſe of them: If any in this bright ſun-ſhine of the Goſpel pretend as a plea for their luſt to follow their example.

Fifth ſort. *Doubtfull examples*, which may ſo be termed becauſe it is difficult to decide whether the Actors of them therein did offend or no: ſo that ſhould a Iury of learned Writers be empannelled to paſſe their verdict upon them, they would bee puzzelled whether to condemn or acquit them, and at laſt be forced to find it an *Ignoramus*. As, whether *David* did well to diſſemble himſelfe frantick, thereby to eſcape the cruelty of *Achiſh*, King of Gath; whether *Huſhai* did well in counterfeiting with *Abſolom,* or whether therein hee did not make Heaven to bow too much to earth, I meane Policie to entrench upon Pietie ; and ſo in this act was ſo good a Stateſman that hee was a bad man.

Vſe of them: Let us not meddle with imitation of theſe actions that are ſo full of difficulty and danger that our judgements therein may eaſily bee deceived: *The ſonnes of Barzillai,* Ezra 2. 62, 63, *becauſe their Genealogies were doubtfull and uncertaine, were put by the Prieſt-hood, till a Prieſt ſhould riſe up with Vrim and Thummim ;* by which wee may underſtand ſome eſpeciall man amongſt them, who by Gods Spirit might be able to decide the controverſies which were queſtioned in their pedigrees. So let us refraine from following theſe doubtfull examples, till (which in this world is not likely to bee) there ariſe an infallible Iudge which can determine in theſe particulars whether theſe actions were well done or no.

Abuſe of them: By ſuch who thought they have roome enough beſides, yet delight to walke on a narrow Banke neere the Sea, and have an itch to imitate theſe doubtfull Examples, wherein there is great danger of miſcarrying.

Sixth ſort. *Mixt examples,* which containe in them a double action, the one good, and the other bad, ſo cloſely couched together that it is a very hard thing to ſever them. Thus in the unjuſt Steward, there was his wiſedome to provide for himſelfe, which God doth commend ; and his wickedneſſe to purloyne from his Maſter, which God cannot but condemne. Thus in the *Hebrew Midwives, Exod.* 1. 19, when they told the lye, there was in them *Fides mentis, et fallacia mentientis,* the faithfulneſſe of their love to their Countreymen, and the falſeneſſe of their lying to *Pharaoh.*

Vſe of them: Behold, here is wiſedome, and let the man that hath underſtanding, diſcreetly divide betwixt the Gold and the Droſſe, the Wheat and the Chaffe ; what hee is to follow and imitate, and what to ſhun and avoyd. In the firſt yeare of the raigne of Queene *Elizabeth* the ſtudents of Chriſt-Church in Oxford buried the bones of *Peter Martyrs* wife in the ſame Coffin with the aſhes of *Fridſwick* a Popiſh Saint ; to this intent, that if Popery (which God forbid) ſhould ever after over spread this land, Papists should bee puzled to part the ashes of a supposed Heretike from one of their canonized Saints. Thus in some actions of Gods Saints in the Bible, which are of a mixt nature, wickednesse doth so insensibly unite and incorporate it selfe with that that is good that it is very difficult to sever and divide them without a sound and well advised Iudgement.

Abuse of them: In such as leave what is good, take what is bad, follow what is to bee shunned, shunne what is to bee followed.

Seventh sort. *Actions absolutely bad*, so that no charitable Comment can bee fastned upon them, except wee will incurre the Prophets curse and woe, *To call good evill, and evill good*: such were the Drunkennesse of *Noah*, the Incest of *Lot*, the lying of *Abraham*, the swearing of *Ioseph*, the Adultery of *David*, the Deniall of *Peter*.

Vse of them: Let us reade in them, first, a Lecture of our owne Infirmity: who dare warrant his Armour for proofe when *Davids* was shot through? Secondly, let us admire and laud Gods mercy, who pardoned and restored these men on their unfained Repentance. Lastly, let us not despaire of pardon our selves, if through Infirmity over taken, God in like manner is mercifull to forgive us.

Abuse of them: When men either make these their patterns, by which they sin, or after their sinning alledge them for their excuse and defence. Thus *Iudith* did, *Iudith* 9. 2: For whereas that murder which *Simeon* and *Levi* did commit upon the Shechemites, *Gen*. 34. 25, was cursed by *Iacob*, as a most hainous and horrible sinne; yet shee propounds it as an heroicke act, and the unworthy President for her imitation: *O Lord God of my Father Simeon, to whom thou gavest the Sword to take vengeance on the strangers, which opened the wombe of a Maid, and defiled her, &c.* Well, if the Arme of *Iudith* had beene as weake as her judgement was herein, I should scarce beleeve that shee ever cut off the head of *Holophernes*.

Eighth sort. *Actions which are onely good as they are qualified with such a circumstance*, as *Davids* eating the *Shew-bread* in a cafe of abfolute neceffity; which otherwife was *provided* for the Priefts alone. Such are the doing of fervile workes on the Lords day, when in cafe of neceffity they leave off to bee *Opera fervilia*, and become *opera mifericordiæ*.

Vfe of them: Let us be fure, in imitating of thefe, to have the fame qualifying circumftance, without which otherwife the deed is impious and damnable.

Abufe of them: In thofe which imitate the example without any heeding, that they are fo qualified, as the action requires.

Ninth fort. The ninth and laft fort remaines; and fuch are thofe which are eminently good; as the Faith of *Abraham*, the Meekneffe of *Mofes*, the Valour of *Iofhua*, the Sincerity of *Samuel*, the plaine Dealing of *Nathaniel*, &c. Follow not then the Infidelity of *Thomas*, but the Faith of *Abraham;* the Teftineffe of *Ionah*, but the Patience of *Iob;* the Adultery of *David*, but the Chaftity of *Iofeph;* not the Apoftafie of *Orpa*, but the Perfeverance of *Ruth* here in my Text.

[Note that the fubftance of this Sermon is found in the *Comment on Ruth*, anteà, pages 47—51.]

[III] An Ill Match Wel Broken Off.

1 IOHN 2. 15.
Love not the world.

THE Stoicks said to their affections, as *Abimelech* spake to *Isaac, Gen.* 26. 16, *Get you out from amongst us; for you are too strong for us:* Because they were too strong for them to master, they therefore would have them totally banisht out of their soules, and labour to becalm themselves with an Apathy. But farre be it from us, after their example, to root out such good herbes (in stead of weeds) out of the Garden of our nature; whereas affections if well used are excellent, if they mistake not their true object, nor exceed in their due measure. *Ioshua* killed not the Gibeonites, but condemned them to bee *Hewers of wood and Drawers of water for the Sanctuary.* Wee need not expell passions out of us, if wee could conquer them, and make Griefe draw water-Buckets of teares for our sinnes, and Anger kindle fires of zeale and indignation when wee see God dishonoured. But as that must needs be a deformed face, wherein there is a transposition of the colours, the blewnesse of the vines being set in the lips, the rednesse which should be in the cheeks, in the nose; so, alas! most mishapen is our soule, since *Adams* fall, whereby our affections are so inverted, Ioy stands where Griefe should, Griefe in the place of Ioy. Wee are bold where wee should feare, feare where we should be bold; love what wee should hate, hate what wee should love. This gave occasion to the blessed Apostle in my Text to disswade men from loving that whereon too many dote. *Love not the World.*

For the better underſtanding of which words, know that the Devill goes about to make an unfitting match, betwixt the ſoule of a Chriſtian, on the one party, and this world on the other. A match too likely to goe on, if wee conſider the ſimplicity and folly of many Chriſtians (becauſe of the remnants of corruption) eaſily to be ſeduced and inveagled, or the bewitching, entiſing, alluring nature of this world : But God by Saint *Iohn* in my Text forbiddeth the banes: *Love not the world.*

In proſecuting whereof, wee will firſt ſhew the worthineſſe of a Chriſtian ſoule, then wee will conſider the worthleſneſſe of the world ; and from the comparing of theſe two, this Doctrine will reſult, that

It is utterly unfitting for a Chriſtian to place his affections on worldly things.

[1.] Let us take notice of a Chriſtians Poſſeſſions, and of his Poſſibilities; what he hath in hand, and what he holdeth in hope. In poſſeſſion he hath the favour of God, the Spirit of Adoption crying in him, *Abba, father*, and many excellent graces of ſanctification in ſome meaſure in his heart. In hope and expectance he hath the reverſion of Heaven and happineſſe, (a reverſion not to be got after anothers death, but his owne,) and thoſe happineſſes which eye cannot ſee, nor eare heare, neither it can enter into the heart of man to conceive.

[2.] Now ſee the worthleſneſſe of the World. Three Load-ſtones commonly attract mens affections, and make them to love ; *Beauty, Wit*, and *Wealth*. [a] Beauty the world hath none at all. I dare boldly ſay, the world put on her Holy-day Apparell, when ſhee was preſented by the Devill to our Saviour, *Matth*. 4. 9. She never looked ſo ſmug and ſmooth before or ſince ; and had there beene any reall beauty therein, the Eagle-ſight of our Saviour would have ſeene it ; yet when all the glory of the world was proffered unto him at the price of Idolatry, hee refuſed it. Yet as old *Iezabel*, when ſhee wanted true beauty, ſtopt up the leakes of age with adulterated complexion, and painted her face ; ſo the world in default of true beauty decks her ſelfe with a falſe appearing fairneſſe, which ſerves to allure amorous fooles, and (to give the world, as well as the Devill, her due) fhee hath for the time a kind of a pleafing fafhionableneffe: But what faith Saint *Paul?* 1 *Corinth.* 7. 31: παράγει γὰρ τὸ σχῆμα τοῦ κόσμου τούτου, *the fafhion of this World paffeth away.* [β] The wit of the World is as little as her beauty, how ever it may bee cryed up by some of her fond Admirers; yet as it is, 1 *Cor. 3. 19, The wifedome of this World is foolifhneffe with God;* and *Cuilibet artifici credendum eft in fua arte;* what wifedome it felfe counts foolifhnes, is folly to purpofe. [γ] Her wealth is as fmall as either: what the world cals Subftance, is moft fubject to Accidents, uncertaine, unconftant; even lands themfelves in this refpect are moveables. *Riches make themfelves wings, and fly away;* they may leave us whilft wee live; but wee muft leave them when wee dye.

[3.] Seeing then the World hath fo little, and the Chriftian foule fo much, let us learne a Leffon of Holy Pride, to practife heavenly Ambition. Defcend not fo farre, O Chriftian, beneath thy felfe; remember what thou art, and what thou haft; loofe not thy felfe in lavifhing thy affections on fo difproportioned a Mate. There is a double Difparity betwixt thy foule and the world: firft, that of Age. Perchance the world might make a fit mate for thy old Man, thy Vnregenerate halfe, thy Reliques of finne; but to match the old, rotten, withered, worme-eaten World to thy new Man, thy new Creature, the regenerated and renewed part of thy foule, gray to green, is rather a torture then a marriage, altogether difproportionable. Secondly, that of quality or condition. Thou art Gods Free-man: *If I have freed you,* (faith Chrift) *then are you free indeed;* the world is, or ought to be thy flave, thy vaffaile. 1 *Iohn* 5. 4: *For whofoever is borne of God overcommeth the world; and this is the victory that overcommeth the World, even our faith.* Bee not then fo bafe as to make thy vaffall thy mate. *Alexander* denyed to marry *Darius* his Daughter, though proffered unto him; fcorning to bee conquered by her beauty, whofe Father hee had conquered by his valour. Let us not make the world our Miftreffe, whereof wee ought to be the Mafter, nor proftitute our affections to a flave we have conquered.

Objection: Yea, may fome fay, this is good counfell, if it came in due feafon. Alas! now it commeth too late, after I have not only long doted, but am even wedded to this world. Infant affection may be eafily crufht, but who can tame an old and rooted love? Thinke you that I have my affection in my hand, as Hunters their dogs, to let flip or rate off at pleafure? How then fhall I unlove the world, which hath been my bofome Darling fo long?

Anfwer:. Art thou wedded to the World? then inftantly fend her a Bill of Divorce. It need never trouble thy confcience; that match may be lawfully broken off, which was firft moft unlawfully made: Yea, thou wert long before contracted to God in thy Baptifme, wherein thou didft folemnely promife thou wouldft *Forfake the Devill and all his workes, the vaine pompe and glory of this World.* Let the firft contract ftand; and becaufe it is difficult for thofe who have long doted on the world to unlove her, wee will give fome rules, how it may bee done by degrees. For indeed it is not to bee done on a fudden, (matters of moment cannot bee done in a moment,) but it is the tafke of a mans whole life, til the day of his death.

Rules how to unlove the World.

1. Looke not with the eyes of covetoufneffe or admiration on the things of the world. The eye is the principall *Cinqueport* of the foule, wherein love firft arrives, *Vt vidi, ut perij.* Now thou mayeft looke on the things of the world, *Vt in tranfitu,* as in paffage (otherwife wee fhould be forced to fhut our eyes); and wee may behold them with a flighting, neglectfull, faftidious looke; but take heed to looke [againft looking] on them with a covetous eye, as *Eve* on the forbidden fruit, and *Achan* on the wedge of Gold. Take heed to looke on them with the eye of Admiration, as the Difciples looked on the Buildings of the Temple, *Matth.* 24. 1, wondring at the Eternity of the ftructure, and conceiving the Arch of this World would fall as foone as fuch ftones riveted to immortality might bee diffolved. Wherefore our Saviour checketh them, *Verely I fay unto you, there fhall not be left one ftone upon another, that fhall not bee caft downe.* Excellently *Iob, chap.* 31. 1, *I have made a Covenant with*

mine eyes, that I should not behold a woman. A Covenant? But what was the forfiture *Jobs* eyes were to pay in cafe hee brake it? It is not expreft on the band; but furely the penalty is employed [implied, *viz.*] many brackifh teares, which his eyes in repentance muft certainly pay if they obferved not the Covenant.

2. Silence, that Spokefman in thy bofome; I meane the allurements of the flefh and Devill, who improveth his utmoft power to advance a match betwixt thy foule and the world. And when any breach happens betweene thee and the world, fo that thou art ready to caft her off, the flefh in thy bofome pleads her caufe: Why wilt thou (faith it) deprive thyfelfe of thofe contentments which the World would afford thee? Why doft thou torment thy felfe before thy time? Ruffle thy felfe in the filkes of fecurity; it will be time enough to put on the Sack-cloath of Repentance when thou lyeft on thy Death-bed. Hearken not to the Flefh, her Inchantments; but as *Pharaoh* charged *Mofes* to get him out of his prefence, he fhould *fee his face no more*, *Exodus* 10. 28; fo ftrive as much as in thee lyeth to expell thefe flefhly fuggeftions from thy prefence, to banifh them out of thy foule; at leaftwife to filence them; though the mifchiefe is, it will bee muttering, and though it dare not hallow, it will ftill be whifpering unto thee, in behalfe of the world, its old friend, to make a Reconciliation betwixt you.

3. Send back againe to the world, the Love-tokens fhe hath beftowed upon thee; I meane thofe ill gotten goods, which thou haft gotten by indirect and unwarrantable meanes. As for thofe goods which thy parents left thee, friends have given thee, or thou haft procured by Heavens Providence on thy lawfull endeavours, thefe are no Love-tokens of the world, but Gods gifts; keepe them, ufe them, enjoy them to his glory. But goods gotten by Wrong and Robbery, Extortion and Bribery, Force and Fraud, thefe reftore and fend back: For the world knoweth that fhee hath a kind of tye and engagement upon thee, fo long as thou keepeft her tokens; and in a manner thou art obliged in honour, as long as thou detaineft the gifts that were hers. Imitate *Zacheus*: fee how he cafts backe what the world gave him: *Luke* 19. 8,

Behold, Lord, the halfe of my goods I give to the poore; and if I have taken any thing from any man by falfe accufation, I reftore him foure-fold.

4. Set thy affections on the God of Heaven. The beft wedge to drive out an old love is to take in a new:

[1]*Poftquam nos Amaryllis habet, Galatæa reliquit.*

Yea, God deferves our love firft, becaufe *God loved us firft*, 1 *Iohn* 4. 19. It is enough indeed to blunt the fharpeft affection, to be returned with fcorne and neglect; but it is enough to turne Ice into Ashes, to bee firft beloved by one that fo well deferves love. Secondly, his is a lafting love: *Iohn* 13. 1, *Having loved his owne that were in the world, he loved them to the end.* Some mens affection fpends it felfe with its violence, hot at hand, but cold at length; God's not fo, it is continuing. It is recorded in the honour of our [2]King *Henry* the feventh; that hee never difcompofed favorite, one only excepted, which was *William*, Lord *Stanly*; a rare matter, fince many Princes change their Favorites, as well as their clothes, before they are old: But the obfervation is true of the Lord of Heaven without any exception: thofe who are once eftated in his favour, he continues loving unto them to the end.

Hearke then how hee woes us, *Efay* 55. 1, *Hoe, every one that thirfteth, come yee to the waters, and he that hath no money, come, &c.* How he woes us, *Mat.* 11. 28, *Come unto me all yee that labour, and are heavy laden, and I will give you reft.* Love his Love-letter, his Word; his Love-tokens, his Sacraments; his Spokef-men, his Minifters, which labour to further the match betwixt him and thy foule. But beware of two things.

1. Take heed of that dangerous conceit, that at the fame time thou mayeft keepe both God and the World, and love thefe outward delights, as a Concubine to thy foule. Nay, God he is *a jealous God;* hee will have all or none at all. There is a Citie in Germany, pertaining halfe to the Bifhop

---

[1 Virgil, *Ecloga* i. 31.]
[2 Look Lord Bacon in his *Life* [Ed. 1622, page 242].

thereof, and halfe to the Duke of Saxony, who named the Citie Myndyn, that is, mine and thine; becaufe it was theirs *Communi jure,* and at this day by corruption it is called [1]*Minden.* But God will admit of no fuch divifions; hee will hold nothing in Coparceny; hee will not fhare or part ftakes with any; but hee will have all entire to himfelfe alone.

2. Take heed thou doft not onely fall out with the world, to fall in with it againe, according to that

[2]*Amantium iræ amoris redintegratio eft:*

For even as fome furious Gamefters, when they have a bad game, throw their cards out of their hands, and vow to play no more; (not fo much out of miflike of gaming as of their prefent game;) but when the cards run on their fide, they are reconciled to them againe; fo many men, when the world frownes on them and croffes them, and they miffe fome preferment they defire, then a qualme of piety comes over their hearts; they are mortified on a fudden, and difavow to have any further dealing with worldly contentments. But when the world fmiles on them againe, favours and profpers them, they then return to their former love, and doting upon it. Thus *Demas,* 2 *Tim.* 4. 10, would needs have another farewel embrace of the world, even after his folemne converfion to Chriftianity, *Demas hath forfaken me, having loved this prefent World.* But when we are once at variance with the world, let us continue at deadly eternall feuds with it; and as it is faid of *Amnon,* 2 *Sam.* 13. 15, that *the hatred wherewith hee hated his fifter Thamar, was greater then the love wherewith he loved her:* fo, (what was cruelty in him, will bee Chriftianity in us,) once fallen out with the world, let the joynt bee never fet again, that it may bee the ftronger; but let our hatred bee immortall, and fo much the ftronger by how much our love was before.

---

[1] Munfters *Cofmog*[*raphia*]: *De Germ*[*ania*], iii. *lib.*, pag. 143 [lib. iii. cap. 450, pag. 894, Ed. Bafle. 1572.
[2 Terrence, *Andria,* iii. iii. 24.]

[IV] Good from Bad Friends.

2 Sam. 15. 31.

And one told David, *saying*, Achitophel *is among the Conspirators with* Absalom.

THIS Text is a Glasse, wherein Gods Iustice is plainely to be seen. *David* had formerly falsely forsaken *Vriah*, and now God suffers *Achitophel* to forsake *David*. *Vriah* neither in loyaltie nor valour, though placed the last in the List, of the List of *Davids* Worthies, was any whit inferiour to any of *Davids* subjects. How did hee sympathize with Gods Arke, and his fellow souldiers, stayed still in the Campe, though hee was in the Kings Court, in that hee would not embrace those delights the Marriage-bed did afford him! No, though they practised upon him to make him drunke, yet in his drunkennesse, hee was so sober that all their wine washed not from him his first resolution, but hee remayned still constant. But how falsely did *David* forsake him, sending him with that Snake in his bosome which was to sting him to death; I meane the Letter, which was *Vriahs* Pasport to his own Grave! Well, *Vriah* placed much confidence in the love of *David*, who deceives him; *David* with no lesse trust relyes on the loyaltie of *Achitophel*, and see what my Text saith : *And one told David, saying, Achitophel is also among the Conspirators with Absalom.*

Observation 1 : Before we goe farther, let us learne, *when our friends forsake us, to enter into a serious scrutinie of our owne soules :* Hast thou never played foule or false with thy friend; if not in action, yet in intention ? Dost thou not mean to prove base, if put to the tryall, and if occasion be offered, to deceive him ? If so, know thy false friend hath only got the start of thee, and playd the fore-game, doing what thou meaneft to doe. Rayle not, then, on the times, nor fpeak Satyres againft the faithlefneffe of men; but, laying thy hand on thy mouth, confeffe God hath juftly found thee out, and dealt with thee as hee did with *David*.

Obfervation 2: Secondly, hence we may obferve: *The moft politicke heads have not alwayes the faithfulleft hearts.* *Achitophel* was the Iewifh Neftor, or their *Salomon* before *Salomon*, and like *the Oracle of God for his wifedom*, but like the Oracle of the devill for his deceitfulneffe; for whilft *David* fwaied the fcepter, who more loial to him than *Achitophel* ? and once when *David* is in banifhment, he fals firft to *Abfalom* ; he loved to worfhip the fun rifing ; yea, whils *David* the true fun was but over-caft with a cloud, he fals adoring that blazing ftar, that Comet only fed with the evaporations of pride and ambition, which fhined for a while, and then went out in a ftink.

Reafons why the moft politick are not alwayes the moft faithfull. 1. Becaufe that cement which conglutinates hearts, and makes true friends indeed, is grace and Goodnes, wherof many politick heads are utterly devoid: 1 *Cor.* 1. 26, *For ye fee your calling, Brethren, how that not many wife men after the flefh, not many mighty, not many noble are called.* 2. Politick men make their owne profit the rule and fquare of their loves; they fteere their courfe by the pole-ftar of their own good; and as in their actions, fo in their affections, have an invifible end to themfelves, which beginneth where that end endeth, which is apparent to others.

Vfe : Do not, then, undervalue and defpife the love of thofe who are of meane and inferior parts: wife men have made ufe of fuch fervants, and found them more manageable and more profitable; though their judgements were weaker, their affections might be ftronger, than wifer men.

Obfervation 3: Thirdly, obferve; *Falfe friends will forfake [us] in time of adverfity.* Hee that beleeveth that all thofe who fmile on him and promife faire in time of profperity will performe it in time of his want, may as well beleeve that all the leeves that bee on trees at Mid-fummer will hang there as frefh and as faire on New-yeers day.

Come wee now to confider what good ufes one may make to himfelfe from the unfaithfulneffe of friends when they forfake us.

1. Firft, confider with thy felfe whether thou haft not beene faulty in entertaining Tale-bearers, and lending a liftning eare unto them: *Solomon* faith, *Prov.* 16. 28, *A whifperer feparateth chiefe friends.* Whetherfoever hee commeth, he bringeth with him the fire, fuel, and bellowes of contention.

2. If herein thy confcience accufe thee not, examine thy felfe whether there was not a *Læfum principium* in the firft initiation of your love: How came you acquainted? whereout grew your amitie? whereon was your intimacie grounded? Didft thou not firft purchafe his favour with the price of a finne? for know, friends unjuftly gotten are not long comfortably enjoyed. Thus *Abfalom* by sordid flattery ftole the hearts of the Ifraelites, defcending too much beneath himfelfe, 2 *Sam.* 15. 5; as alwayes ambitious fpirits, when they would perfonate Humility, over-act their part, and play bafeneffe: Wee fee King *Hezekiah*, who procured *Senacharibs* love by his facriledge, enjoyed not that purchafe which he made God and his Temple pay for, 2 *Kings* 18. 16. For *Senacharib* no fooner received his money, but *hoc non obftante*, perfifted in his former enmity and hoftility againft the Iewes, and, as it followeth in the very next verfe, fent up his Captaines to befiege Ierufalem.

3. If there be no fault in the inchoation, Examine, hath there beene none in the continuance of your friendfhip? haft thou not committed many finnes, to hold in with him? If fo, then it is juft with God hee fhould forfake thee: Thus Tyrants often times cut off thofe ftaires by which they climbe up to their Throne: Yea, good Princes have often times juftly facrificed thofe their Favorites to the fury of the people, who formerly have been the active Inftruments to oppreffe the people, though to the enriching of their Princes. Haft thou not flattered him in his faults, or at leaft wife by thy filence confented to him? If fo, God hath now opened thy friends eyes, he fees thy falfe dealing with him, and hath juft caufe to caft thee out of his favour.

When *Amnon* had defiled his fifter *Thamar*, the Text faith, 2 *Sam.* 13. 15, that *the hatred wherewith hee hated her, was greater than the love wherewith he loved her.* Poore Lady, fhee was in no fault; not the caufe, but onely the object and the occafion of her brothers finne; and that againft her will, by his violence. Now to reafon, *A minore ad majus*: If *Amnon* in cold blood viewing the hainoufneffe of his offence fo hated *Thamar*, which onely concurred paffively in his tranfgreffion, how may our friends juftly hate us, if haply we have beene the Caufers, Movers, and Procurers of their badneffe! If wee have added fewell to the flame of their ryot, played the Pandors to their lufts, and fpurred them on in the full fpeed of their wantonneffe, deferve wee not (when their eyes are opened to fee what foes we have been unto them under pretended Friendfhip) to bee fpit in the face, kik't out of their company, and to bee ufed with all contumely and difgrace?

4. Haft thou not idolatrized to thy friend? hath he not totally monopolized thy foule, fo that thou haft folely depended on him, without looking higher, or further? *Tu patronus, fi deferis tu, perimus.* Thus too many wives anchor al their hopes for outward matters on their hufbands, and too many children leane all their weight on their Fathers fhoulders; fo that it is juft with God to fuffer thefe their woodden Pillars to breake, on whom they lay too much heft.

5. Haft thou not undervalued thy friend, and fet too meane a rate and low an eftimate on his love? If fo, God hath now taught thee the worth of a Pearle, by loofing it. And this comes often to paffe, though not in our friends voluntary deferting us, as *Achitophel* did *David*, yet in their leaving us againft their wils, when God taketh them from us by death.

Queftion: But here this queftion may be demanded: whether is one ever againe to receive him for his friend, and to reftore him to the old ftate of his favour, who once hath deceived and dealt falfely with him?

Anfwer: Many circumftances are herein well to bee weighed. Firft, did hee forfake thee out of frailty and infirmity, or out of meer fpight and malicioufneffe? Secondly, hath he fince shewed any tokens and evidences of unfained forrow? hath hee humbled himfelfe unto thee, and beg Gods and thy pardon? If hee hath offended mifchievoufly, and perfifts in it obftinately, O let not the ftrength of thy fuppofed charity fo betray thy judgement, as to place confidence in him! *Samfon* was blind before hee was blind; the luft of *Dalilah* deprived him of his eyes before the Philiftims bored them out, in that, once and againe being deceived by *Dalilah*, hee ftill relyed on her word. But if hee hath fhewed him felfe fuch a Penitent, and thou art verely perfwaded of his Repentance, receive him againe into thy favour. Thus dealt our Saviour with Saint *Peter, Marke* 16. 7: *But goe your way, tell his Difciples, and Peter, Peter* efpecially; *Peter* that hath finned, and *Peter* that had forrowed; *Peter* that had denyed his Mafter; but *Peter* that *went out and wept bitterly.*

6. Sixthly, and laftly, it may bee God fuffers thy friends to prove unfaithfull to thee, to make thee fticke more clofely to himfelfe. Excellent to this purpofe is that place, *Micah* 7. 5, 6, *Truft yee not in a friend, put yee no confidence in a Guide; keepe the doors of thy mouth from her that lyeth in thy bofome: For the Son difhonoureth the Father; the Daughter rifeth up againft the Mother; the Daughter in law againft her Mother in law; a mans enemies are the men of his own houfe.* But now marke what followes: *Therefore will J looke unto the Lord; I will wayte for the God of my falvation.* As if hee had faid, Is the world at this bad hand? is it come to this bad paffe that one muft bee farre from trufting their neereft friends? It is well, then, I have one faft Friend on whom I may relye, the God of Heaven. I muft confeffe thefe words of the Prophet are principally meant of the time of Perfecution, and fo are applyed by our Saviour, *Mat.* 10. 21. However they containe an eternall truth, whereof good ufe may bee made at any time. Let us therefore, when our friends forfake us, principally relye on God, who hath thefe two excellent properties of a friend: firft, he is neere to us: fo faith the Pfalmift, *Thy name is neere, and this doth thy excellent workes declare.* They have a fpeedy way of conveying Letters from *Aleppo* to *Babylon*, fending them by a winged Meffenger, tyed to the legs of a Dove; but wee have a fhorter cut to fend our

prayers to God, by fending our prayers by the wings of the Holy Spirit, that heavenly Dove, whereby they inſtantly arrive in Heaven. As God is neere to us, fo hee is ever willing and able to helpe us : On him therefore let us ever relye ; and when other Reeds bow or break, or run into our hands, let us make him to bee our ſtaffe, whereon wee may leane our felves.

[v] A Glaffe for Glvttons.

Rom. 13. 13.

Not in Gluttony [μὴ κώμοις].

THESE words are a parcell of that Scripture that converted Saint *Auguftine*. He (as hee [1]confeffeth of himfelfe) at the firft was both erroneous in his Tenets and vicious in his life. When running on in full carreare in wickedneffe, God ftopt him with his voyce from Heaven, *Tolle et lege*, take up thy Book, and reade; and the firft place which God directed his eye to was thefe words in my Text; and after this time, being reclaymed, hee proved a worthy Inftrument of Gods glory and the Churches good. Now as thofe receipts in Phyficke are beft, which are confirmed under the Broad Seale of Experience, and fet forth with the priviledge of *Probatum eft*; fo my Text may challenge a priority before other places of Scripture, becaufe upon Record it hath been the occafion to convert fo famous a Chriftian. Neither thinke that the vertue of thefe words are extracted by doing of this one Cure, or that my Text, with *Ifaac*, hath onely one bleffing for him that came firft; no, by Gods bleffing it may be cordial, for the faving of our foules. To day therfore part of *Samfons* Riddel fhall be fulfilled in your ears: *Out of the Devourer came meat: Gluttony*, that vice which confumeth and devoureth food. The difcourfe thereof by Gods affiftance fhall feed us at this time. *Not in Gluttony*.

Doctrine: *Gluttony is a dangerous fin for any Chriftian to be guilty of*.

Reafon 1: *Becaufe humane Laws hath provided no penalty for it*. Men will be afraid to commit petty Laffony, for feare of

---

[1 *Confeffions*, Bk. viii. chap. xii.]

whipping; Fellony, for feare of branding; Murther, for feare of hanging; worfe fins, for feare of having a Grave whilft living. But it is too likely that men will take leave and liberty to themfelves to be Gluttons, prefuming upon hope of Impunity, becaufe mans Laws have ordered no punifhment for it; yet as thofe offences are accounted the greateft, which cannot be punifhed by a Conftable, a Iuftice, or Iudge of Affize; but are referved immediatly to be punifhed by the King himfelfe; fo Gluttons muft needs be Sinners in an high degree, who are not cenfureable by any earthly King, but are referred to be judged at Gods Tribunal alone.

Reafon 2: *Becaufe it is fo hard and difficult to difcerne.* Like to the Hecktick fever, it fteales on a man unawares. Some fins come with obfervation, and are either ufhered with a noyfe, or, like a fnaile, leave a flime behind them, whereby they may be traced, and tracted, as Drunkenneffe. The Ephramites were differenced from the reft of the Ifraelites by their lifping: they could not pronounce *H*, which then was a heavie afpiration unto them when it coft the lives of fo many thoufands. Thus Drunkards are diftinguifh't from the Kings fober fubjects by clipping the coyn of the tongue. But there are not fuch fignes and Symptomes of *Gluttony*. This finne doth fo infenfibly unite and incorporate it felfe with our naturall appetite, to eate for the Prefervation of our lives, that, as Saint [1]*Gregory* faith, *It is a hard thing to difcerne, Quid neceffitas petat, et quid voluptas fuppetat, quia per efum voluptas neceffitati mifcetur,* what is the full charge of food which nature requires for our fuftenance, and what is that fure charge which is heaped by fuperfluity.

Reafon 3: *Becaufe of the fundry dangers it brings;* firft, to the foule: *Luke* 21. 34, *Take heed left your hearts bee oppreffed with furfetting:* And indeed the foule muft needs bee unfitting to ferve God, being fo incumbred. That man hath but an uncomfortable life, who is confined to live in a fmoaky houfe. The braine is one of thefe places of the refidence of the foule; and when that is filled with ftreames, and vapours arifing from unconcocted crudities in the ftomacke, the foule

---

[1] Lib. 30. Moral[ia in Expos. Iob, cap. 39. ver. 7], cap. 28. ante medium [¶ 62].

muſt needs *malè habitare*, dwell unchearfully, ill accommodated in ſo ſmoaky a manſion. And as hereby it is unapt for the performance of good, ſo it is ready for moſt evill; for uncleanneſſe, ſcurulity, ill ſpeaking; this being the reaſon, ſaith Saint [1] *Gregory*, why *Dives* his tongue was ſo tormented in Hell, becauſe hee, being a Glutton, with his tongue had moſt diſhonoured God.

Secondly, this ſinne empaires the health of the body: the out-landiſh Proverbe ſaith, *That the Glutton digs his Grave with his owne teeth, haſtens his death by his intemperance;* For if there were a conflict in *Rebeckaes* body, when two Twins were in her wombe, muſt there not bee a Battell and Inſurrection in his ſtomack, wherein there is meat, hot, cold, ſod, roſt, fleſh, fiſh? and which ſide ſoever wins, nature and health will bee overcome, whenas a mans body is like unto the Arke of *Noah*, containing all Beaſts cleane and uncleane; but hee the moſt uncleane Beaſt, that containes them. Our Law interprets it to bee murther, when one is killed with a knife. Let us take heed wee bee not all condemned by God for being Fellons *de ſe;* for wilfull murthering our owne lives with our knifes by our ſuperſtitious eating.

Thirdly, it wrongs the creatures that hereby are abuſed. Indeed they willingly ſerve man, ſo long as hee is a King over them; but they are loath to doe it when he turnes Tyrant: So if when the Drunkard ſings, the drinke ſighes; when the Glutton laughes, the Meate grieves to bee ſo vainely miſpent by him. God ſaith, *Hoſea* 2. 9, *That hee will recover his Flaxe and his Wooll* from the Idolatrous Jewes; *Vindicabo*, I will reſcue and recover them, as from ſlavery and ſubjection, wherein they were detayned againſt their will; and in ſuch like tyrannie are the creatures, as Bread, Wine, and Meat, tortured under the Glutton.

Laſtly, it wrongeth the poore; for it is the over-much Feaſting of *Dives* which of neceſſity maketh the Faſting of *Lazarus;* and might not the ſuperfluous Meat of the Rich bee ſold for many a pound, and given to the poore?

[[1] *Moralia in Expos. Iob*, cap. i. ver. 5.]

Come we now to confider wherein *Gluttony* doth confift. I am not ignorant of that verfe in [1]*Thomas* [*Aquin*] :

Præproperè lautè, nimis ardenter, ſtudioſè:

But I will not march in *Sauls* heavie Armour, or confine my felfe to follow the Schooles directions herein ; I will goe againft this *Goliah* of Gluttony with my owne Sling and Stone, and ufe a private and plaine Method. This finne therefore confifteth, either in the quantity of the meate, or in the quality, or in the manner of eating.

I. In the quantity: And here it is hard to define the Omer of Manna for every mans belly ; the proportion of meate for every mans ftomacke : that quantity of raine will make a claye ground drunke, which will fcarce quench the thirft of a fandy Countrey. It is thus alfo in men ; that proportion of meat furfetteth and furchargeth the ftomacks of fome, which is not enough to fatisfie the hunger of others, efpecially of thofe who being young have hot and quick difgeftion ; of thofe who living in a cold clymate, and thereby have the heat of there ftomacks intended; of thofe whofe ftomacks are ftrong, by reafon of their labour and travell. And not to fpeake of the difeafe called *Boulamya*, mens natures being thus diverfe, by what ftandard fhall I meafure them ? Let this be the rule : hee fhall be arraigned and condemned before God for *Gluttony* in the quantity of meat, who hath eaten fo much as thereby hee is difabled, either in part, or wholly, to ferve God in his generall or particular calling, be his age, clymate, or temper whatfoever.

II. In quality; and that foure ways :

1. When the meat is too young: *Exod.* 23. 19, *Thou ſhalt not ſeeth a Kid in his Mothers milke ;* that is, thou fhalt not eat it before it hath age, to bee juft and firme flefh. Circumcifion was deferred till the eighth day ; one reafon rendred by Divines is, becaufe a Child before that time is not *Caro conſolidata ;* and fure there is a time before which Beafts and Fowles are not follid, faft, and lawfull to bee eaten. I muft confeffe, wee are to live by the creatures death ; they being

---

[1 *Summa Theologiæ*, I. ii. Quæs. 72, Art. 9, Ed. Antwerp, 1585, p. 143.]

borne are condemned to dye, for our neceffity, or pleafure; and thefe condemned perfons defire not a pardon, but deferve a Reprive, that they may be refpited and referved fo long, till they bee good and wholefome food, and not clapt into the Gluttons bowels, before they be fcarce out of their Mothers belly.

Secondly, when the meat is too coftly. Thus *Cleopatra* macerated an Vnion, a Pearle of an ineftimable worth, and dranke it in a health to *Marke Anthony*; a deed of hers as vaine as the other wicked, when fhe poyfoned her felfe.

Thirdly, when the meats are onely incentives and provocations to lufts, in fome kind thereof. I could inftance were I not afraid to teach fin, by confuting it. Why is the Furnace made feven times hotter then ever it was before? Is not the Devill of himfelfe fufficiently mifchievous? Is not our owne corruption of it felfe fufficiently forward, yea, head-long to evill, but alfo wee muft advantage them by our owne folly? Have wee vowed in our Baptifme to fight againft, and doe wee our felves fend Armour and Munition to our Enemy? Yea, many fet their owne houfes on fire, and then complaine they burne:

[1]*Labor eft inhibere volantes,*
Parce, puer, ftimulis; et fortiùs utere loris.

Laftly, when the Meat is fuch as is onely to increafe Appetite; when one before is plentifully fed. Such is the cruelty of the Spanifh Inquifition, that when they have brought a man to the doore of death, they will not let him goe in; when by exquifite tortures they have almoft killed him, then by comfortable Cordials they doe again revive him: And whereas of God it is appoynted for all men once to dye, thefe mens cruelty makes men to dye often. Thus men, when they have ftabbed and killed hunger with plentifull eating, with fauce and falt meats of purpofe they reftore it againe to life; and for feverall times, according to their owne pleafures, kill and recall, ftab and revive their appetites.

III. In the manner of eating.

1. Greedily, without giving thankes to God: Like Hogs, eating up the Maske, not looking up to the hand that fhaketh

[[1] Ovid, *Metamorphofes*, ii. 128, 127.]

it downe. It is said of the Israelites, *Exod.* 32. 6, *The people sate downe to eate and to drinke*; there is no mention of Grace before Meate; *and rose up to play;* there is no mention of Grace after.

Secondly, Constantly. *Dives* fared deliciously every day; there was no Friday in his weeke, nor Fast in his Almanack, nor Lent in his yeare: whereas the Moone is not alwayes in the full, but hath as well a wayning as a waxing; the Sea is not alwayes in a Spring-tide, but hath as well an Ebbing as a Flowing; and surely the very Rule of Health will dictate thus much to a man, not alwayes to hold a constant tenure of Feasting, but sometimes to abate in their dyets.

Lastly, when they eat their meats studiously, resolving all the powers of their mind upon meat, singing *Requiems* in their soul, with the Glutton in the Gospel, *Soule take thine ease, &c.* And whereas we are to eat to live, these only live to eat.

Let us therfore beware of the sin of *Gluttony*, and that for these Motives.

Motive 1: Because it is the sin of *England;* for though, without Usurpation, we may intitle our selves to the pride of the Spanish, Jealousie of the Italian, Wantonnesse of the French, Drunkennes of the Dutch, and Lazinesse of the Irish; and though these out-landish sins have of late bin naturalized and made free Denisons of *England;* yet our ancientest Carte is for the sinne of *Gluttony*.

Motive 2: It is the sinne of our age. Our Saviour saith, *Mat.* 24. 37, 38, *But as it was in the dayes of* Noah, *so likewise shall the comming of the Sonne of Man be. They did eate and drinke, &c.* That is, excessively; for otherwise they did eate in all ages. It is said of old men, that they are twise children: the same is true of this old doting World; it doth now revert and relapse into the same sinnes whereof it was guilty in the Infancy: wee, on whom the ends of the World are come, are given to the sinnes of *Gluttony*, as in the dayes of *Noah*.

Motive 3: The third Motive is from the time. *These seven full Eares, these seven fat Kine;* these seven weekes of Feasting betweene Christmas and Shrovetide are past; these feven leane Eares, thefe feven leane Kine, the feven Fafting Weeks in Lent, are now begun: Practife therefore the counfell which *Salomon* gives, *Prou.* 23. 1, 2, *When thou fittest to eate with a Ruler, confider diligently what is before thee; and put thy knife to thy throat, if thou beeft a man given to thy appetite.* This is thy throat, that narrow paffage of Importance; guard it with thy knife, as with a Halbert, that no fuperfluous meat paffe that way to betray thy foule to *Gluttony*. But it is to be feared that wee will rather turne the backs of our knifes then the edges; I meane, we will ufe little violence to repreffe and reftraine our own Greedineffe. That our knifes may therefore bee the fharper, let thefe Whet-ftones fet an edge on them.

1. Confider the Bread that thou eateft is the Bread that perifheth: And our Saviour faith, *Labour not for the meat that perifheth, but for that which endureth to everlafting life:* Bifcate is but perifhing Bread, though it may lafte two yeares; for what is two yeares to Eternity?

2. We fhall perifh that eate the meat, but God fhall deftroy both it and that: And then the Glutton which hath playd the Epicure on meat whilft he lived, the wormes fhall play the Epicures on him when he is dead; and whilft the temperate Man fhall give them but ordinary commons, the larded Glutton fhal afford them plentifull exceedings.

To conclude this point: wary was the practife of *Job, Iob* 1. 5, *Who after the dayes of his fons feafting were gone about, offered burnt Offerings to God for them; for he faid, It may be my fonnes have finned, and curfed God in their hearts.*

So, fith *Gluttony* is fo fubtill a finne, and fo hard to be difcerned; when we have beene at a great Feaft in the day, let us facrifice our prayers to God, and fue out a Pardon from him, left peradventure in the heart of our mirth, without our knowledge, and againft our will, we have infeverably been overtaken with the fin of *Gluttony*.

[VI] How Farre Grace can be Entailed.

2 Tim. 1. 5.

When I call to remembrance the unfained faith which is in thee which dwelt firſt in thy Grand-mother Lois, *and thy Mother* Eunice; *and I am perſwaded that it is in thee alſo.*

HEN I call to remembrance.] *Obſervation* 1. It is good to feed our ſoules on the memories of pious perſons: Partly that we may be moved to prayſe God in and for his Graces given to his Saints; and partly that we may bee incited to imitate the vertues of the deceaſed. *Ahaz* was ſo taken with the Altar at Damaſcus, 2 *Kings* 16. 10, that hee would needs have one at Ieruſalem, made according to all the worke-manſhip thereof. When we call to mind the vertues of the deceaſed, and cannot but be delighted with their Goodneſſe, let us labour to faſhion our ſelves after their frame, and to erect the like vertues in our owne ſoules.

Obſervation 2: *Godly Children occaſion their Parents to bee called to memory.* Saint *Paul* beholding *Timothies* Goodneſſe, is minded thereby to remember his Mother and Grand-mother, *Eunice* and *Lois*; they can never bee dead, whiles hee is alive. Good children are the moſt laſting monument, to perpetuate their Parents, and make them ſurvive after death. Doſt thou deſire to have thy memory continued? Art thou ambitious to be revenged of death, and to out-laſt her ſpight? It matters not for building great houſes, and calling them after thy name; give thy children godly education, and the ſight of their goodneſſe will furbiſh up thy memory in the mouthes and minds of others, that it never ruſts in oblivion.

Which dwelt first.] That is, which was an Inhabitant in their hearts: Faith in temporary Believers is as a Guest; comes for a night, and is gone; at the best is but as a Sojourner, lodges there for a time; but it dwelleth, maketh her constant residence and aboad in the Saints and servants of God.

Grand-mother Lois, *and Mother* Eunice.] *Question*: Why doth not Saint *Paul* mention the Father of *Timothy*, but as it were blanch him over with silence?
Answer 1: First, it is probable that Saint *Paul* had not any speciall notice of him, or that hee was dead before the Apostles acquaintance in that Family.
 2. Likely it is, he was not so eminent and appearing in Piety. The weaker vessell may sometimes be a stronger vessell of honour: yea, the Text, *Acts* 16. 1, intimateth as much: *Behold, a certaine Disciple was there, named* Timotheus, *the sonne of a certaine woman which was a Iewesse, and beleeved; but his Father was a Greeke.* Let women labour in an holy Emulation to excell their husbands in Goodnesse; it is no trespasse of their modesty, nor breach of the obedience they vowed to their husbands in marriage, to strive to bee Superiours and above them in Piety.
 3. *Eunice* and *Lois*, the Mother and Grand-mother, are onely particularly mentioned, becaufe deserving most commendation for instructing *Timothy* in his youth; as it is in the *Chap.* 3. [Epist. 2] *ver.* 14, 15: *Knowing of whom thou hast learned them, and that from a Child thou hast knowne the Holy Scriptures.* For the same reason the names of the Mothers of the Kings of *Iudah* are so precisely recorded for their credit or disgrace, according to the goodnesse or badnesse of their sonnes. Let Mothers drop instruction into their children with their milke, and teach them to pray when they beginne to prattle.
 Though *Grace* bee not entayled from Parent to Child; yet the Children of godly Parents have a great advantage to Religion; yea, that five-fold.
 1. The advantage of the promise; yea, though they come but of the halfe blood, (much more if true borne on both

fides,) if one of their Parents bee godly. 1 *Corinth*. 7. 14 : *For the unbeleeving Husband is sanctified by the (beleeving) Wife; and the unbeleeving Wife is sanctified by the Husband; else were your Children uncleane; but now they are holy.*

2. Of good Precepts, some taught them in their Infancy; so that they can easier remember what they learned then when they learned it. *Gen*. 18. 19: *For I know Abraham, that hee will command his children, and his Houshold after him, to feare the Lord.*

3. Of good Presidents. *Habent domi unde discant:* whereas the children of evill Parents see daily what they ought to shun and avoyd, these behold what they should follow and imitate.

4. Of Correction, which though untoothsome to the palat to taste, is not unwholsome to the stomacke to digest.

5. Of many a good prayer, and some no doubt steept in teares, made for them before some of them were made. *Filius tantarum lachrymarum non peribit*, said Saint [1]*Ambrose* to *Monica*, of Saint *Augustine* her son. Disdane thou, then, out of an holy pride, to bee the vitious sonne to a vertuous Father; to bee the prophane Daughter of a pious Mother; but labour to succeed as well to the lives as to the Livings, the Goodnesse as the Goods of the Parents.

Objection: Yea, but, may the Children of bad Parents say, this is but cold comfort for us; and they may take up the words of the Souldiers, *Luke* 3. 14, *And what shall wee doe?*

Answer: First, if thy Parents be living, conceive not that their badnesse dispenceth with thy duty unto them, thou hast the same cause, though not the same comfort, with good children to obey thy Parents; this doe labour, to gaine them with thy conversation. It was Incest, and a fowle sinne in *Lot*, to bee Husband to his Daughters, and beget children on them; but it would bee no spirituall Incest in thee, to be Father to thy Father, to beget him in grace who begat thee in nature; and by the Piety and Amiablenesse of thy carriage, to be the occasion, by Gods blessing, of his Regeneration; and what *Samuel* said to the people of Israel, 1 *Sam*. 12. 23,

---

[1 Not attributed to S. Ambrose in *Confessions*, bk. iii. chap. xii.]

God forbid that I should sinne against the Lord, in ceasing to pray for you; so God forbid thou shouldest ever leave off to have thy knees bended, and thy hands lifted up, for the conversion of thy bad Father. Moreover, labour more especially to shun and avoyd those sinnes to which thy Father was addicted; and chiefly such sinnes, the Inclination whereto may depend from the temper and constitution of the body; so that a pronenesse thereto may in some sort seem to be intayled to Posterity. Was thy Father notorious for wantonesse? strive then to be noted for chastity. Was hee infamous for Pride? labour thou to be famous for Humility. And though thou must not be dejected with griefe at the consideration of the badnesse of thy Parents; yet mayest thou make a Soveraigne use thereof, to bee a just cause of Humiliation to thy selfe.

If thy Parents bee dead, and if thou canst speake little good of them, speake little of them. What Sullennesse did in *Absolon*, 2 *Sam.* 13. 22, *Hee spake to his Brother* Amnon, *neither good nor bad;* let Discretion do in thee: seale up thy lips in silence; say nothing of thy Parents. He is either a Foole, or a mad man, who being in much company, and not being urged thereunto, by any occasion will tell others, My Father lyes in the Fleet; my Father lyes in Prison, in the Counter. More witlesse is hee who will speake both words Vncharitable and Vnnaturall concerning the finall estate of his Father, in an eternall bad condition.

And I am perswaded, there is a three-fold kind of Perswasion, whereby one may be perswaded of good in another man.

1. The perswasion of Infallibility; and this onely God hath. *Acts* 15. 18 : *Knowne unto God are all his workes from the beginning of the World.* Hee alone *searcheth and tryeth the hearts and reines.* And they also have it to whom God immediately reveales it. Thus *Ananias* knew that *Paul* was a true servant of God, after it was revealed to him, *Acts* 9. 15 : *For hee is a chosen Vessell unto me, to beare my name, before the Gentiles, and Kings, and the children of Israel.* And in this sense of infallible perswasion we may understand Saint *Paul* in the Text, because it is said, 1 *Tim.* 1. 18, *This Commandement write I unto thee, sonne* Timotheus, *according to the prophecies*

which went before upon thee, that thou by them shouldst fight a good fight.

2. The perswasion of Charity; and this I must confesse is but weake, and rather a presumption than a perswasion. *Charity,* 1 *Corinth.* 13. 5, 7, *Thinketh no evill; it beleeveth all things, hopeth all things;* and in this kind of Perswasion wee conceive that all men have faith dwelling in them, of whom wee know no just reason to conceive the contrary.

3. The Perswasion of a well and strong grounded opinion; to make which, these three things must concurre. First, the party that conceives this opinion must have a good judgement and discerning Spirit, well to dive and pierce into the natures and dispositions of men. Secondly, He must be long acquainted with that person, of whom hee hath such an opinion, that faith dwelleth in him. Too bold are these men, who upon a superficiall knowledge and short conversing with any, dare peremptorily pronounce, that such an one hath saving grace and sanctity in him. These are Professors of spirituall Palmestry, who thinke that upon small experience they can see the Life line (the Line of Eternall life in the hands of mens souls); whereas for all their skil they often mistake the hands of *Esau* for the hands of *Iacob.* Lastly, they must have intimate familiarity with them, and be not onely their acquaintance [at] large, but in Ordinary:

[1] *Te intus et in cute novi.*

Put all these three together, that one hath a discerning Spirit, long and intimate acquaintance with one; and hee may arrive at Saint *Pauls* perswasion in my Text, to be perswaded of faith dwelling in him, with whom hee hath beene thus long and intimately acquainted. And in this sense (though it may bee of the infallible Perswasion by Revelation) understand wee that 2 *Kings* 4. 1: *Now there cryed a certaine Woman of the Wives of the sonnes of the Prophets unto* Elisha, *saying, Thy Servant my Husband is dead; and thou knowest that thy Servant did feare the Lord.*

Yet for all this wee may set this downe for a true Position;

[[1] Persii *Satira* iii. 30]

that the wifeſt of men eaſily may and ſometimes are deceived in counting them good which are very counterfeits; and eſpecially in theſe caſes.

1. Firſt, in cloſe natured men, ſuch as lye in at a cloſe Guard, and offer no play; whoſe Well is deepe, and men generally want Buckets to meaſure them; ſo that one may live twenty yeares with them, and bee never a whit the wiſer in knowing their diſpoſition.

2. In various and inconſtant men, which like *Proteus* never appeare twiſe in the ſame ſhape, but differ as much from themſelves as from other men, and are onely certaine in uncertainty; ſo that one can build no certaine Concluſion on ſuch floting, flitting Sands; and even know not what to make of them.

3. In men of an excellent nature, ſuch as *Titus Veſpatian*, [who] was called *Deliciæ humani generis*. This *Euphuia* preſents it ſelfe in all outward ſignes and Symptomes; So like to Grace that it is often miſtaken for it. Whereas, on the other ſide, men of a rugged, unbruſht nature, ſuch as were never lickt, hewen, or poliſht, may bee ſlaundered in many mens judgements, to bee altogether devoyd of Piety.

4. In affected Diſſemblers, Hypocriſie is as like Piety as Hemlocke to Parſley; and many one hath beene deceived therein.

To conclude: if wee deſire to paſſe a rationall Judgement on Faith in others, and Piety in their hearts, let us firſt labour to have true Sanctity in our owne. One complayned to a Philoſopher that it was an hard thing to find a wiſe man. It is true, ſaid hee; for hee muſt firſt bee a wiſe man that ſeekes him, and knowes when hee hath found him: So that, on the matter, it is not one wiſe man, but two wiſe men, muſt meete together. So it is an hard thing to know true Sanctity in another man; becauſe hee muſt have true Piety in himſelfe that knowes it, or elſe hee is an Incompetent Iudge to paſſe a Verdict on another. Let us therefore labour firſt to have true Grace in our hearts, that ſo with Saint *Paul* we may bee perſwaded of Grace that dwels in another.

[VII] A Christning Sermon.

2 Kings 5. 14.

Then went hee downe and dipped himselfe seven times in Iordan, *according to the saying of the man of God; and his flesh came againe, like to the flesh of a little child; and he was cleane.*

IN this Chapter, *Naaman* the Syrian coms hurrying with his Horses, and ratling with his Chariot to the doore of the Prophet *Elisha*, to be cured of his Leprosie. Now hee said in his heart, (I could not have told his thoughts, except first hee had told them mee,) He will surely come out to mee, and stand and call on the name of the Lord his God, and strike his hand over the place, and recover the Leper: Thus hee thought that the very noyse of the wheels of his Chariot should call *Elisha* to come to him; because hee was Captaine of the Hoast of Syria, hee thought to be Commander of Gods Prophet; and hee expected a great deale of service from him. And truly hee might expect it: For the Prophet beate him at his owne weapon, outshot him in his owne bow, out-stated him in statelinesse it selfe.

1. *Called him not in, but let him stand at doore.*
2. *Came not to him in his person, but by a Proxie.*
3. *Sent him a plaine and cold answer: Wash seven times in Iordan.*

By the way, I dare boldly say, *Elisha* in himselfe was not proud at other times; hee could fare hardly on Barley Loaves, and feed hungerly on plaine pottage; but at this time his affecting of state was both lawfull and necessary.

Firſt, it was the fight of *Naamans* ſhoe, which made *Eliſha* ſo high in the Inſtep; with the ſtately, hee would be ſtately; the rather becauſe hee did perceive that *Naaman* muſt bee humbled before hee could bee healed, and the proud fleſh firſt taken out of his heart, ere the putrid fleſh could bee cured in his body. Secondly, *Naaman,* though hee was a Prince, yet hee was but a Pagan; and in this reſpect the loweſt Hebrew was higher than hee. *Eliſha* therefore would teach him to learne himſelfe; that hee was not proper to receive ſo great favours, as being but a Goat, and no loſt ſheepe of the Fold of Iſrael. Laſtly, *Eliſha* was an extraordinary man: hee might well ſtand upon termes of double diſtance, who had a double portion of *Elijah's* Spirit.

You, my Brethren of the Miniſtery, let us know that wee ſucceed to the office, but not to the Eminencies, to the place, but not to the perſonall perfections of the Prophet *Eliſha*. And let us know that Humility is our Honour and Crowne; ſo that except wee be forced unto it againſt our wils, *Se defendendo,* to maintaine the Honour of God and our office, to ſtand upon our points, let us leaving the Patterne of *Eliſha's* ſtatelineſſe rather follow the preſident of Saint *Pauls* Humility: *I was made all things to all men, that by all meanes I might gaine ſome.*

To returne to *Naaman:* The mention of the water put him into a fire; hee burneth with Choler and Paſſion: Are not *Abanah* and *Pharpar,* Rivers of *Damaſcus,* better than all the waters of Iſrael? May I not waſh in them, and be cleane? So he turned and went away in a rage. Well, his ſervants come to him, to perſwade him, and bring with them good Logick and Ethicks, good Arguments and good manners. Good Logick: reaſoning *a minori ad majus: If the Prophet had bid thee doe ſome great thing, wouldeſt thou have not done it? How much rather then, when he ſaith to thee, Waſh and be cleane?* Good Ethicks: *my Father. My*; All ſpeaking in one perſon, ſo unanimouſly they conſented in one opinion. *Father;* as if they had ſaid, Wee confeſſe thou art wiſer then wee are, of more age, of more honour; yet you are neere unto us, you are deare unto us, wee wiſh your weale and welfare: O what a deale did they ſpeake in a little, and how many sentences are comprised in this one word, Father! These words so wrought on *Naaman*, that the Lyon became a Lambe; hee that formerly had conquered his foes, now subdues himselfe; down came he in his stomacke, and downe comes hee in his person.

Then went hee downe, &c.] These words contain a Cure most strange, most true; wherein observe:

1. *The time wherein it was wrought, Then.*
2. *The sick man, or, if you please, since his servants have perswaded him, the Patient.*
3. *The Disease, Leprosie.*
4. *The Physitian, the Man of God,* Elisha.
5. *The Physicke,* { Quid, *Washing in* Iordan; Quoties, *seven times.*
6. *The Effect and Operation thereof: And his flesh came againe, like the flesh of a little Childe, and he was cleane.*

But as *Gideon* had too great an Army for his use, and therefore sent most of his Souldiers away; so the time commands me, to dismisse most of these points, and onely to retaine such with me as are most pertinent to the present occasion. I begin with the time wherein the Cure was wrought: *Then.*

Then: When? After his servants had perswaded him: Whence observe,

Wise men must sometimes follow the counsell of their Inferiours, as Naaman *did of his servants.* The reason is, that wise men may bee deceived in those actions wherein they themselves are parties and interested. It is possible that Passion, Prejudice, and Partiality, one or all of these, like so many Pearles, may blind the eyes of your Iudgement. Whereas such as looke on may see more then those that play the game; and though in other respects their judgements be farre inferiour, yet herein they may be more cleare, because lesse ingaged. Yea, *Salomon* himselfe, though the wisest of Kings, had a Counsell of aged men, that stood before him. And though this might seeme but the lighting of so many Candles to the Sun, yet no doubt hee knew wifely to make ufe of them, who in wifedome were farre beneath him. I have feene a dull Whet-ftone fet an edge on a Knife: yea, the wifeft of men need not thinke fcorne to learne of the worft of men, when we may be taught not to take carking care by the Lillies, and yet providently to provide from the Pifmire.

But then efpecially are wee to liften to the counfell of Inferiours, whofe advife we know proceeds from a loving heart, and is aymed and levelled at our good; efpecially if they be fuch that our credit and profit is imbarked in the fame bottome with theirs; together they finke, and together they fwim; fo that wee cannot fufpect, dare not deny, and muft confeffe, that their advife lookes ftraight forward at our good, and fquints not afide at any finifter refpect. Wherefore, fometimes let *Abraham* hearken to *Sarah* his wife; *Mofes* the Iew, to *Iethro* the Gentile; *David* the Soveraigne, to *Ioab* the fubject; yea, let not *Apollo*, though eloquent and mighty in Scripture, thinke fcorne to learne his Chrift-croffe from *Aquila* and *Prifcilla*.

Yet when Inferiours prefume to commend their counfell to their Superiours, let it be qualified with thefe cautions.

1. Let them doe it feafonably, in a fit opportunity. Now opportunity is the Spirits of time extracted, or the quinteffence of time at large, diftilled; and fuch an opportunity muft he waite for, who hopes to doe any good by his advife to his betters. *Abigail* was excellent hereat, 1 *Sam.* 25. 36: *Shee told her Husband* Nabal *nothing, leffe or more, untill the Morning light*: Either becaufe fhee would not caft the pearle of her good counfell before a Swine, wallowing in Drunkenneffe; or becaufe fhee thought her phyficke would worke the better with him, if fhee gave it him fafting.

2. It muft be done fecretly. An open reproofe of our betters is little better than a Libell. True it is, wee Minifters may publikely (when occafion is offered us) reprove the vices of thofe who in outward refpects are far our Superiours; yet we muft doe it Publikely, Secretly; publikely for the place, fecretly for the manner. We are not to make in the Pulpit fuch an Hue and Cry after the Offender, that the capacity of the meaneft may take him on fufpition whom we meane.

No; let us deliver our doctrine in common, and let the guilty conscience inclose it to it selfe.

3. They must doe it with all reverence and humility, as the servants of *Naaman* in my Text. A Wool-packe doth conquer the strength of an Ordnance, by yeilding unto it: so there may be many natures which will be led, but may not be drawne, or dragged; and these may be broken with faire usage, that cannot be bowed with forcible dealing.

4. Let them pray to him, who hath the hearts of all men in his hand: like the Rivers of water, hee turneth them whether he pleaseth: that he would be pleased to prepare, and mollifie their hearts, to whom they are to addresse their counsell; that he would bow their eares to heare, their heads to conceive, and their hearts to practise, that advise which shall be commended to them for their good. And so much for the time.

Come we next, in the second place, to the Physick prescribed, Water of *Iordan*. Whence observe,

God appoints weake meanes, by the vertue of his Institution, to accomplish great matters. Take a survey of all the parts of Gods service, and we shall find this true. Begin at the Font: there is plaine water of *Iordan*; yet, by the vertue of Gods Ordinance, it washeth away originall sin. Passe from the Font to the Ministers Pue: there is stil plain water of *Iordan*, the weaknesse of the Word, and the folly of Preaching; yet Gods wisdome and power, to make the Goat a Sheep, the Lyon a Lamb, the Wanton chaste, the Passionate patient; yea, to revive such as are dead in trespasses and sins. Looke on the Minister: here is still plaine water of *Iordan*, earthen vessels, men loaden with infirmities, like the rest of their Brethren; yet are they Dispensers of the mysteries of God. Proceed to the Communion-Table: there is still plaine water of *Iordan*, a morsell of Bread and a Draught of Wine; yet these worthily received signe and seale unto us the body of Christ, and the benefits of his Passion.

Vse: Let us take heed, that wee take not exception at the simplicity of Gods Ordinance. A Spanish *Don* having heard much of the fame of *Calvin*, travelled to Geneva to see him;

where finding him both plaine in perſon and poore in apparell, hee repented himſelfe of his paines; and whom his eare did admire at diſtance, his eye did contemne, when preſent. Juſt ſuch Valuers are carnal men of Gods Ordinances; they gueſſe the Jewell by the Caſe, and thinke nothing can be good which is not gawdy. But ſurely were our eyes anointed with that Eye-ſalve, mentioned *Revel.* 3. 18, then (as Heraulds account the plaineſt Coats the moſt ancient, better then thoſe of a later Edition, which are ſo full of filling that they are empty of honour) wee ſhould ſee the inward ſtate in the outward ſimplicity, and inward Majeſty in the outward meanneſſe of Gods Ordinance. When one of his Courtiers ſhewed the Great Turke the Sword of *Scanderbeg:* I ſee, ſaid he, no ſuch miracles in this ſword rather then in any other, that it ſhould atchieve ſuch victories: Yea, but, ſaid one that ſtood by, if you had ſeene alſo *Scanderbegs* Arme, with what a mighty force hee wielded this Sword, you then would change your reſolution. So, many ſay, they can ſee nothing in the water of Baptiſme more then in ordinary well water; they can ſee nothing in the world in the Bread and Wine in the Communion [more] then in that in the Bakers panniers, or Vintners Cellar; no more in a Sermon than in a civill Oration in a Guild-hall of the ſame length. But if they ſaw the Arme of God, with what a mighty ſtrength hee enforceth theſe Ordinances, and how his inviſible Grace attendeth them, they would be of another mind. Gaze then no longer on *Ehuds* hand, for that was lame; or on his Dagger, for that was ſhort; but looke on Gods finger in *Ehuds* hand, and that can worke wonders. Looke not on the Ordinance, but on the Ordainer; [not] on the meanes, but on the Meanes-maker; neither be offended at the meanneſſe of the one, but admire the Majeſty of the other.

Vſe: It confutes the Papiſts, who diſpleaſed, as it were, at the ſimplicity of the Sacraments, as God hath inſtituted them, ſeeke to better and amend them by their owne additions: Thus they account plaine water in Baptiſme too meane; and therefore they mingle it with Creame, Oyle, Spittle, and other Ingredients, which I as little know what they be as they know why they uſe them. Yea, all their ſervice of God is not onely made sweet, but luscious to the palate of flesh; and they plainely shew by their baits what fish they angle to catch; namely, rather to get mens senses then their soules, and their eyes then their judgements. Not that I am displeased with neatnesse, or plead for nastinesse in Gods service. Surely God would have the Church, his Spouse, as not an Harlot, so not a slut; and indeed outward Decencie in the Church is an Harbinger to provide a lodging for inward devotion to follow after. But wee would not have Religion so bedaubed with lace, that one cannot see the cloath; and Ceremonies which should adorne, obscure the substance of the Sacraments, and Gods worship. And let us labour to be men in Christianity, and not only like little children to goe to Schoole, to looke on the guilt and gaudy Babies of our Bookes, and to be allured to Gods service by the outward pomp and splendor of it. But let us love religion, not for her clothes, but for her face; and then shall wee affect it, if shee should chance (as God forbid) to bee either naked through poverty, or ragged through persecution. In a word, if God hath appointed it, let us love the plainenesse of his Ordinance, though therin there be neither warm water, nor strong water, nor sweet water, but plaine water of Iordan.

Come we now to the *Quoties*, how often? He dipped himselfe seven times; that is, hee went in, and washed himselfe, and came out againe; and went in, and washed himselfe, and came out againe; and so till the seventh time. Thou, therefore, whosoever thou art, who art afflicted in body or mind, or any other way, doe not grudge against God, and grieve in thy selfe, if thy paine be not eased in an instant, if thy malady bee not removed in a moment: O tarry the Lords leisure; (the Lords pleasure is the Lords leisure;) waite and attend his time: Thinke not that thou shalt not be cured at all, because thou art not all cured at once. *Naaman* himselfe was not compleatly cleansed at the first entrance into *Jordan*, but it cost him seven times washing.

The number of seven is most remarkeable in Holy Writ, and passeth for the Emblem of perfection, or compleatnesse; as well it may, consisting of an Vnity in the middle, guarded and attended with a Trinity on either fide. Once, I muft confeffe, I find this number of feven to be defective, and too little; and yet the correction and fupplying thereof ftill runs on a feptinary number: *Shall I forgive my Brother feven times? Yea, faid our Saviour, feventy feven times.* If any afke, why God pitched on this number, and impofed [it] on *Naaman;* the beft anfwer I can make fhall be in the words of our Saviour, *Matth.* 11. 26: *Even fo, Father, becaufe it pleafed thee well.* Naaman was bid to wafh feven times, and hee did wafh feven times: Hence obferve,

Doctrine: We muft obferve Gods Commandements, both in matter and manner, both in fubftance and circumftance. But fome will fay, Had *Naaman* wafhed once more or leffe, under or over feven times, would fo fmall a matter have broken any fquares? and would God have impofed any penalty on fo fleight a forfeiture? I anfwer, Things that are fmall in themfelves fwell great, when they are either forbidden or commanded by God: Looke upon *Lots* Wife, looking backe with carnall eyes, and it will feeme a fmall offence: O how flefh and blood could eafily be her Advocate, to plead for her! What if fhe did look back? Shee did no more, and could doe no leffe, and be a Mother: Would you have her to bee a Pillar of ftone, before fhee was a Pillar of falt? I meane, fo hard, fo remorfeleffe, as not to fend one farewell glance to that unfortunate Citie, wherein fhee had fo much kindred and acquaintance? Well, however, we muft know, the Offence was moft hainous, by the heavineffe of the punifhment inflicted upon her.

And as it is thus in fmall things forbidden, fo is it in fmall things commanded. They muft bee precifely obferved. In thofe generall Maps of the world which are ufually made in a fheet of paper, the leaft prick or poynt which can bee made with a pen, extends to five mile at the leaft: But I fay, the fmalleft Deviation and Declination, the leaft imaginable Deflection, from the commanded will of God, is an infinite diftance from it, as breaking the command of an infinite God, and deferveth infinite punifhment. Obferve, therefore, not onely all things confiderable, but all things in Gods will: For indeed all things therein are confiderable; not onely every

Syllable, but every *Iota*, the leaſt Letter; yea, every Prick, Comma, and Accent, hath his Emphaſis, and muſt bee pronounced in our practiſe. As *Moſes* therefore in making the Tabernacle, made it in all things alike to the Patterne hee ſaw in the Mount; not a Knop, or a Bole, or an Almond, in the Candleſtick, under or over; not a Bell, or a Pomegranate in *Aarons* Coat, more or leſſe; but *Concordat Copia cum Originali*, the tranſcript agreed with the Originall in all things: ſo let us preciſely follow the inſtructions God giveth us; let us not willingly bee *Hetroclites* from his will; either Defectiues, to doe too little, or Redundants, to doe too much; but let us bee truely regular; not waſhing more than ſeven times with the ſuperſtitious man; nor leſſe then ſeven times with the prophane man; but with *Naaman* in my Text, juſt ſeven times.

When I compare our preſent occaſion with this Hiſtory wee have treated of, I find a great Reſemblance betwixt them. Here is a little Child to bee cured of a Leproſie: For ſo may Originall Corruption fitly bee called: Firſt, for the Hereditarineſſe of it; it is a ſucceſſive diſeaſe, entayled from Father to Child, ever ſince the fall of our firſt Parent *Adam*. Secondly, from the over-ſpreading nature thereof; the Infection defiling all the powers of our ſoules and parts of our bodies. Here alſo is the water of *Iordan* to waſh it away. Since Chriſt waſhed *Iordan* by being waſhed in it, hee hath given it a power to cleanſe our Originall Corruption. Some Theeves have eat off their Irons and fretted off their Fetters with Mercury water; but there is no way to worke off the Chaines of our Naturall Corruption, whereby our feet are hurt in the Stocks, the Irons have entred into our ſoules; but onely by the Water in Baptiſme. Onely the Maidenhead and Virginity of the water, in the Poole of *Betheſda*, was medicinall to cure Diſeaſes: hee that came firſt was cured; the ſecond got no profit. But in our *Jordan*, our Water in the Font, the vertue thereof is not leſſened in the uſing; the Child that is laſt baptized ſhall receive as much benefit as that which is firſt waſhed therein.

But herein, I muſt confeſſe there is a difference on the

cure of *Naaman*, and this Child: he was totally and perfectly cleansed from his Leprosie; but this Child is wash't but in part, so farre as is Gods pleasure. The condemning power of Originall Corruption is drowned in the Font; but though the bane be removed, the blot doth remaine; the guilt is remitted, the blemish is retayned; the sting is gone, the staine doth stay; which if not consented to, cannot damne this Infant, though it may hereafter defile it. Secondly, the finall peaceable-commanding power is washed away in the Laver of Regeneration; though afterwards it may dwell in us, it shall not domineere over us; it may remaine there as a slave, not as a Soveraigne, sure not as a lawfull one, be he ever resisted, often subdued, though never expelled.

These things deserve larger Prosecution; but this is none of *Ioshua's* day, wherein the Sunne standeth still; and therefore I must conclude with the time.

[VIII] Faction Confvted.

1 COR. I. 12.

Now this I say, that every one of you saith, I am of Paul, *and I am of* Apollo, *and I am of* Cephas, *and I am of* Christ.

SVCH is the subtilty of Satan, and such is the frailty of the flesh, though things be ordered never so wel, they wil quickly decline. Luther was wont to say, hee never knew a good order last above fifteene yeares: This speedy decaying of goodnesse you may see in the Church of *Corinth*, from which S. *Paul* was no sooner departed, but they departed from his Doctrine. Some, more carried by fancy then ruled by reason, or more swayed by carnall Reason then governed by Grace, made choyse of some particular Pastor, whom they extoll'd, to the great disgrace of his fellow Ministers, and greater dishonour of God himselfe. Now Saint *Paul, not willing to make* these Ministers *a publike Example*, concealeth their persons, yet discovereth the fault; and, making bold with his Brethren, *Apollo* and *Cephas*, applyeth to them and himselfe what the Corinthians spake of their fancied Preachers. *Now this I say, that every one of you saith, I am of* Paul, *and I am of* Apollo, *and I am of* Cephas, *and I am of Christ*.

Objection: But the Apostle herein hath made no good choyce, to mention *Cephas*: for hee was onely knowne to the *Corinthians* by his fame, not by his person, seeing it appeares not, either in Scripture or Ecclesiasticall Story, that ever *Cephas* (that is, Saint *Peter*) was ever at *Corinth*.

Answer: This hinders not the Application of the Apostle, granting Saint *Peter* was never there; for many Ministers are most admired at distance, [1]*Major è longinquo reverentia*: Like

---

[1] Tacitus. [*Annales*, i 47.]

some kind of stuffe, they have the best Glosse a good way off, more then a *Prophet in his owne Countrey*. Thus the good esteeme which Forrainers have conceived of the Piety and Learning of the *Geneva* Ministers, hath been the best stake in the hedge of that *State*.

I need not divide the words, which in themselves are nothing else but division, and containe foure sorts of people, like the foure sorts of Seed, *Mat.* 13. The three first bad, the last only, (*I am of Christ*,) being good and commendable.

I am of Paul; as if they had said, There is a Preacher called *Paul*; his matter is so powerful, his Methods so pleasing, his Doctrine so sound, his Life so sincere; his Preaching I affect, or his person I preferre; *I am of Paul*. Tush, saith another, what talke you of *Paul*? *Indeed his Epistles are powerfull and strong, but his bodily presence is weake, and his speech of none effect*. There is one *Apollo*, an *eloquent man, and mighty in the Scriptures*; hee stands highest in my esteeme; *I am of Apollo*. Fie, saith a third, why name you *Apollo*, one that learnt the best part of his Divinity from *Aquila* and *Priscilla*, a Lay-man and a weake woman? There is one *Cephas*, that caught three hundred soules at the preaching of one Sermon; that is the man for my money: I will say of him, as *Gehazi* did of *Naaman*, *As the Lord liveth I will run after him*. *I am of Cephas*. Well, saith a fourth, *Paul* I know, and *Apollo* I know, and *Cephas* I know; men endowed with great Grace, and eminent Instruments of Gods glory; I acknowledge them as the Channell, but on God alone as the Fountaine of Faith and Conversion, and doe attend on him alone in these his Instruments; *I am of Christ*.

Doctrine: The Staple Doctrine herein to be observed is this: *The factious affecting one Pastor above another is very dangerous*. Indeed wee may and must give a *famous part* of Reverence, and a *Benjamins Portion* of respect, to those who (*Data paritate in ceteris*) excell in age, paines, Parts and Piety. 1. In Age: for hee is a Traytor against the Crowne of old Age, who payeth not the Allegeance of respect due thereunto. Such Reverence the hoary haires of *Gousartius* did deserve, when for more than fifty yeares hee had beene a Preacher in

Geneva. 2. In Paines: being such as have borne the beate of the day; so that the stresse of the Ministery hath layen heaviest on their shoulders. Such an *Elder is worthy of double honour.* 3. In Parts: being stars of the first Magnitude, brightly shining with their rich endowments. 4. In Piety: which setteth a lustre on all the former. But the factious affecting of Ministers, lavishing *by whole sale* all honour on one, and scarce *Retaliating* out any respect to the other; raysing high Rampires to the prayse of the one, by digging deepe Ditches to discredit and disgrace an other, is that which Saint *Paul* doth reprove in my Text, and wee must confute at this time.

Foure great mischiefes will arise from this practise.

Mischief 1: First, it will set enmity and dissension betwixt the Ministers of Gods Word.

I confesse, wee that either have or intend to take on us the high calling and holy Function of the Clergy, ought to endeavour by Gods Grace so to qualifie our selves that our affections never mistake the true object nor exceed their due measure. But alas! such is our misery (rather to bee bemoaned then amended; the perfect removing whereof is more to be desired then hoped for) that as long as wee carry Corruption about us, wee are men *subject to like Passion with others.* Hence is it come to passe, that as the Grecians, *Acts* 6. 1, murmured against the Hebrewes, *because their Widdowes were neglected in the daily Ministration:* So Ministers will find themselves agrieved, that people in the partiall dispencing of their respect passe them by unregarded. Perchance the matter may fly so high as it did betwixt *Moses* and *Aaron*, Numb. 12. 2: *And they said, Hath the Lord indeed spoken onely by Moses? Hath hee not spoken also by us?* It will anger not only *Saul*, a meere carnall man, but even those that have degrees of Grace: *Hee hath converted his thousands, but such a one his ten thousands.* These discords betwixt Ministers, I could as heartily wish they were false, as I doe certainly know they are too true.

Mischief 2: It will set dissention amongst people, whilst they violently engage their affections for their Pastors: The woman that pleaded before *Salomon*, 1 *Kings* 3. 22, *The living Child is mine*, said shee, *but this dead Child is thine: Nay* said the other, *but thy sonne is dead, and my sonne is the living*. Thus will they fall out about their Pastors. The living Minister is mine; he that hath life, spirit, and Activity in the manner and matter of his Delivery; but the dead Minister is thine; flash in his matter, confused in his Method, dreaming in his utterance; hee commeth not to the quicke; hee toucheth not the conscience; at the most with *Ioash*, King of Israel, 2 *Kings* 13. 18, *He smites the Aramites but thrice;* leaves off reproving a vice before people bee fully reformed. Nay, saith the other, my Minister is the living Minister, and thine is the dead one: Thy Pastor is like the fire, 1 *Kings* 19. 12, flashing in the flames of ill tempered and undiscreet zeale; *but the Lord was not in the fire:* or like the Earthquake, shaking his Auditors with ill applyed terrors of the Law; *but the Lord was not in the Earth-quake:* whilest my Minister is like to a *still voyce; and the Lord was in the still Voyce;* stanching the Bleeding hearted Penitent, and dropping the Oyle of the Gospel into the wounded Conscience.

Mischief 3: It will give just occasion to wicked men to rejoyce at these dissentions, to whose eares our discords are the sweetest Harmony. O then let not the Herdsmen of *Abraham* and *Lot* fall out, whilst the Canaanites and Peresites are yet in the Land. Let us not dissent, whilest many Adversaries of the truth are mingled amongst us, who will make sport thereat.

Mischief 4: Lastly, it will cause great Dishonour to God himselfe; his Ordinance in the meane time being neglected. Heare is such doting on the Dish, there is no regarding the Dainties: Such looking on the Embassadour, there is no notice taken of the King that sent him. Even *Maries* Complaynt is now verified: *They have taken away the Lord, and placed him I know not where.* And as in times of Popery *Thomas Becket* dispossessed our Saviour of his Church in Canterbury (instead of Christ's Church, being called Saint *Thomas* Church): And whereas rich Oblations were made to the Shrine of that supposed Saint, *Summo Altari nil*, nothing was offered to Christ at the Communion-Table: So whilest some Sacrifice the Reverence to this admired Preacher, and others almost adored this affected Pastor, God in his Ordinance is neglected, and the Word, being the savour of life, is had in respect of persons.

To prevent these mischiefes, both Pastors and people must lend their helping hands. I begin with the Pastors; and first with those whose Churches are crowded with the thickest audience.

Let them not pride themselves with the bubble of popular applause, often as causelesly gotten as undeservedly lost. Have wee not seene those that have preferred the Onions and Flesh-pots of Egypt before heavenly Manna, Lungs before Braynes, and sounding of a voyce before soundnesse of matter? Well, let Princes count the credit of their Kingdomes to consist in the multitude of their Subjects: Farre bee it from a Preacher to glory when his Congregation swels to a Tympany, by the Consumption of the Audience of his Neighbour Minister.

Yea, when Pastors perceive people transported with an immoderate Admiration of them, let them labour to confute them in their groundlesse humours. When Saint *Iohn* would have worshipped the Angel, *See thou dost it not* (saith hee); *worship God*. So when people post head-long in affecting their Pastors, they ought to wave and decline this popular honour, and to seeke to transmit and fasten it on the God of Heaven. Christ went into the Wildernesse when the people would have made him a King: Let us shun, yea, fly such dangerous Honour, and teare off our heads such wreathes as people would tye on them, striving rather to throw Mists and Clouds of Privacy on our selves then to affect a shining appearance. But know, whosoever thou art, who herein art an Epicure, and lovest to glut thy selfe with peoples applause, thou shalt surfet of it before thy death; it shall prove at the last pricks in thy eyes and thornes in thy side, a great affliction, if not a ruine unto thee; because sacrilegiously thou hast robbed God of his Honour.

Let them labour also to ingratiate every Pastor, who hath tolerability of desert, with his owne Congregation. It was the boone *Saul* begg'd of *Samuel, Honour me before my people:* And surely it is but reason wee should seeke to grace the Shepherd in the presence of his Flock: though perchance privately wee may reprove him, disgrace him not publikely before those that are under him.

I am come now to neglected Ministers, at whose Churches *Solitudo ante ostium*, and within them too; whilst others (perchance lesse deserving) are more frequented.

Let not such grieve in themselves, or repine at their Brethren. When Saint *Iohn Baptists* Disciples told him that all flock't to Iesus, whom hee baptized beyond *Iordan: I must decrease*, (answered hee,) *and hee must increase.* Never fret thy selfe or vexe out thy soule if others bee preferred before thee: they have their time; they are *Crescents* in their waxing, full Seas in their flowing: Envie not at their Prosperity. *The Starres in their course did fight against Sisera;* thy course of credit may chance to bee next; thy turne of Honour may chance to come after. One told a Grecian *Statist*, who had excellently deserved of the Citie hee lived in: That the Citie had chosen foure and twenty Officers, and yet left him out. I am glad, (said hee,) the Citie affords twenty foure abler than my selfe. So let Ministers triumph and rejoyce in this, that the Church yeilds so many men better meriting then themselves, and be farre from taking exception thereat.

And let us practise Saint *Pauls* Precept, by Honour and Dishonour, by good Report and Disreport: Seven yeares have I served God in good esteeme, and well respected; by the time I have served God so long in disgrace and reproach, perchance the Circulation of my credit may returne, and with patience I may regaine the esteeme I have lost. And if otherwise, let him say with *David, Lord, here I am; doe with thy servant as thou pleasest.*

By this time, mee thinkes, I heare the people saying unto mee, as the Souldiers to *Iohn Baptist*, But what shall wee doe? Now the Counsell I commend to you, is this.

Remedy 1: First, ever preserve a reverent esteeme of the Minister whom God hath placed over thee. For if a Sparrow lighteth not on the ground without Gods especiall Providence, surely no Minister is bestowed in any Parish without a more immediate and peculiar disposing of God; and surely their owne Pastor is best acquainted with their diseases, and therefore best knoweth to apply spirituall Physicke thereunto. And as Gods Word hath a generall Blessing on every place, so more particularly is it sanctified and blessed there, to those Parishioners, from the mouth of their lawfull Minister. Let not therefore the Sermon of a stranger, who perchance makes a Feast of set purpose to entertaine new Guests, be preferred before the paines of thy owne Minister, who keeps a constant house and a set Table, each Lords day, feeding his owne family. Wherefore, let all the Ephesians confine themselves to their *Timothy;* Cretians to their *Titus;* every Congregation to their proper Pastor. And I hope Pastors, considering the solemne oath they tooke at their Institution, and the profit they receive from their people, and how irrationall it is to take wages and doe no worke, and the heavie account they must make at the day of Iudgement, will provide Milke in their brests for those who must suck of them. As for those whose necessary occasions doe command their absence from their Flocks, let them be Curats of their Curats; over-see such whom they appoynt to over-see their people. *Columella* gives this counsell to Husband-men: Never keepe a horse to doe that worke which may be done by an Asse; both because Asses are of a lower price, and cheaper kept: But God forbid Ministers should observe this Rule, and so consult with their profit as to provide unworthy Substitutes, to save charges.

Remedy 2: Let them not make odious comparisons betwixt Ministers of eminent parts: It is said of *Hezechiah,* 2 Kings 18. 5, That *after him, was none like him, of all the Kings of Iudah, neither any that were before him.* It is said also of King *Iosiah,* 2 Kings 23. 25, *And like unto him, there was no King before him, that turned to the Lord with all his heart, and with all his soule, and with all his might; neither after him rose up any like him.* The Holy Spirit prefers neither for better, but concludes both for best; and so amongst Ministers, when each differs from others, all may bee excellent in their kinds. As in comparing severall handsome persons, one surpasseth for the beauty of a naturally painted face; a second, for the feature of a well proportioned body; a third, for a grace of Gesture and Comelinesse of carriage: so that Iustice it selfe may bee puzled, and forced to suspend her Verdict, not knowing where to adjudge the Victory: So may it bee betwixt severall Pastors. Ones Excellency may consist in the unsnarling of a knowne controversie; an other, in plaine expounding of Scripture, to make it portable in the weakest memory. One, the best *Boanarges;* an other, the best *Barnabas.* Our Iudgements may bee best informed by one; our Affections moved by a second; our lives reformed by a third. I am perswaded there is no Minister in England, for his Endowments, like *Saul, Higher then his Brethren, from the shoulders upwards;* but rather some hundreds like the Pillars in *Salomons* House, all of a height. But grant some in parts farre inferiour to others: was not *Abishai* a valiant and worthy Captaine, though hee attayned not to the Honour of the first three? And may not many bee serviceable in the Church, though not to bee ranked in the first forme, for their sufficiencie?

Let them entertaine this for a certaine truth, That the Efficacy of Gods Word depends not on the parts of the Minister, but on Gods blessing, on his Ordinance. Indeed there is a Generation of Preachers that come upon the Stage before ever they were in the Tyring-house, whose backwardnesse in the Vniversity makes them so forward in the Countrey; where what they lack in Learning, they supply in boldnesse. I could wish, that as, *Gen.* 21. 19, *When Hagars Bottle of Water was spent, God opened her eyes, and shee went to the Fountaine againe;* So when these Novices have emptied their store of set Sermons they brought with them, that their Parents would remit them backe to the Vniversity, the Fountaine of Learning and Religion, to furnish themselves with a better stocke of sufficiencie. Such Ministers as these, I account as none at all; but as for those that have the *Minimum ut sic,* the least degree of tolerability, to enable them in some measure to discharge their Office, God may bee, and often is, as effectuall in and by them as by *Rabbies* of farre greater parts.

To conclude: let us, with one mind and one mouth, advance the Glory of God, that thereby the Gospel may bee graced; wicked men amazed; some of them converted, the rest of them confounded; weake Christians confirmed, to the griefe of Devils, Ioy of Angels, Honour of God himselfe. Amen.

FINIS.

Imprimatur,
Thomas Wykes,
May 30. 1640.

A FAST SERMON PREACHED

On Innocents day

BY
THOMAS FVLLER, B.D.
Minister of the *Savoy*.

---

2 Sam. 2. 26.
Then Abner called to Joab, and said, Shall the sword devoure for ever? knowest thou not that it will be bitternesse in the latter end? How long shall it be then, yer thou bid the people returne from following their brethren?

LONDON,
Printed by L.N. and R.C. for JOHN WILLIAMS
at the signe of the Crowne in Saint *Pauls*
Church-yard, 1642.

["THE foules of thefe Children are charitably conceived by the Primitive Church all marched to heaven, as the *Infantry of the noble Army of Martyrs.*"—*A Pifgah-Sight of Paleftine*, 1652, book ii. chap. xiv. § 19.

"DEUS auctor pacis et amator, quem noffe vivere, cui fervire regnare eft ; protege ab omnibus impugnationibus fupplices tuos ; ut qui in defenfione tua confidemus, nullius hoftilitatis arma timeamus. Per Jefum Chriftum Dominum noftrum. *Amen.*"—Gelafii Sacramentarium, Muratori's *Liturgia*, vol. i. page 727 ; Blunt's *Annotated Book of Common Prayer*, 1872, page 254.]

[Introduction.

THE Sermons here beginning, and extending to 1650 (embracing, roughly speaking, the period of the Civil war), form a distinct group. They are of the highest importance by reason of the light they throw as well on the times as on the life of the preacher.

This Sermon on Peace was delivered at the Savoy Chapel, which was at that time attended by the courtiers and the nobility, whose residences were along or near the Strand. FULLER's presence at the Convocation of 1640, where he had taken part in framing some ill-advised ecclesiastical Canons, had introduced him to "most of the voyced pulpits of London," his attractive manners and earnest aims proving acceptable to his audiences. Upon his final removal to London he preached at first at the Inns of Court; but about six months before the date of the *Sermon of Reformation* (viz. 26th July, 1643), he received the appointment of Lecturer or Curate to the parish-church of St. Mary-le-Savoy at the hands of the Master, Dr. BALCANQUAL, and of the brotherhood (four in number) of the Foundation of the Savoy; "as well as earnestly desired and intreated by that small parish" (*Life*, 1661, page 14). Of the Lecturer's connection with the parishioners some important particulars will be found at page ccxci. *et seq. posted*, which in turn give value to the very interesting letter to his "Deare Parish" at page 331.

FULLER's pulpit ministrations were welcome to an audience made up for the main of moderate Royalists. He was regarded with considerable favour, and he attained to a position of influence in his own and the adjoining parishes. His biographer thus quaintly pictures his popularity (*Life*, 1661, page 15): "He had in his narrow Chappel two Audiences, one without the pale, the other within; the windows of that little Church and the Sextonry so crowded as if Bees had swarmed to his mellifluous discourse."

In the opening paragraph of the following Sermon the conflict between the old and new authority is made manifest. On that Wednesday, 28th December, 1642, a fast and a feast "jostled together." In the Sermon, indeed, the preacher gives prominence to the former as most suitable to the exigencies of the time; but on his title-page he boldly stands by the ecclesiastical day. At least two of FULLER's Sermons were connected with these parliamentary fast-days. These fasts began in London towards the close of the year 1641, having derived their origin from the shocking massacre of the Irish Protestants, which broke out on the 23rd October, 1641. The matter of the appointment of the fast was introduced into Parliament on the 14th December, and by ordinance dated Friday, the 17th, faſt-days were fixed as follows : "*Wedneſday* next for both Houſes of Parliament, and *London; Thurſday* next for the City of *Weſtminſter;* and *Thurſday* come Month for the whole Kingdom" (Nalſon's *Impartial Collection*, vol. ii. page 754). To this national faſt, and its origin, FULLER has made the following alluſion : " Our general *Faſt* was firſt appointed to bemoane the maſſacre of our Brethren in *Ireland*" (*Good Thoughts in Worſe Times*, 1647; Scripture Obs., No. ix. page 72). This original intention of the faſt was preſent in his mind when in his Sermon (¶ 11) he drew attention to the diſtreſſing condition of the ſiſter iſland. The Proclamation which made this ſpecial faſt-day into a general faſt-day, ſtatedly kept, is dated 8th January, 1641-2. The firſt faſt under this new arrangement was appointed for the 20th of that month. It is then added :—

" And His Maieſtie doth further by this His Proclamation ſtraitly charge and command that a Generall, Publike, and Solemn Faſt be kept and holden as well by abſtinence from Food as by publike Prayers, Preaching, and Hearing of the Word of God and other Sacred Duties, in all Cathedrall, Collegiate, and Pariſh Churches, and Chappels within this Kingdom of *England* and Dominion of *Wales* (without any exception) on the laſt Wedneſday of the moneth of February next following the date hereof, and from thenceforth to continue on the laſt Wedneſday of every moneth during the Troubles in the ſaid Kingdom of *Ireland*. All which His Maieſtie doth expreſſly charge and command ſhall be reverently and devoutly performed by all His loving ſubjects, as they tender the favour of Almighty God, and would avoid His juſt indignation againſt this Land, and upon pain of ſuch puniſhments as His Maieſtie can juſtly inflict upon all ſuch as ſhall contemn or neglect ſo religious a Work" (Husbands' Quarto *Collections*, p. 49.)

The picture of the evils of war preſented by the preacher in the earlier portion of the Sermon (¶¶ 6 *seq*.) has not been overdrawn, although he was not at this time as afterwards a ſpectator of the actual fighting. But already many of the ſad effects of the internecine warfare were apparent. In the far north a Scotch divine, ROBERT BAILLIE, whoſe viſit to England in 1640-1, as one of the Scottiſh Commiſſioners to London, had intereſted him in its politics, was watching the courſe of events with the eagerneſs of a patriotic Engliſhman ; and early in 1643 he was acquainting a correſpondent with the poſture of affairs, the ſurpriſing accuracy of his information betokening the keenneſs of his intereſt in the ſtrife.

" That countrie," he writes, "is in a moſt pitifull condition ; no corner of it free from the evills of a cruell warre. The caſe is lyke the old miſeries of the Guelphs and Gibelines. Everie ſhyre, everie citie, manie families, divided in this quarrell ; much blood and univerſall ſpoyle made by both where they prevaill. Beſyde the maine armies, which hes made their marches to and fro from Wales to London, there hath been in the north all this winter on foot Newcaſtle and Cumberland, and now King, for the King ; Fairfax, Hotham, and Chomley, for the Parliament. In the In-ſhyres Derby for him, others for them. In Cornwall Hoptoun for him, and Stainfoord for them, betuixt which there hath been continuall skirmishing, let be plundering and sessing. Of these evills great appearance of increase with the Spring. We might have been happie instruments of accommodation, had not the willingness of both parties goeing about in a circle, upon their apprehension of their advantage, made them both, bot by turnes, untractable, and our own unhappie divisions made us less considerable mediators" (*Letters & Journals*, vol. ii. page 57).

In a later portion of this Sermon (¶ 29) the preacher is led to contrast our Civil war with the wars that had been raging in Germany, his opinion being that if England had evinced a more practical sympathy on behalf of the Palatinate, it had not itself suffered as deeply as it had. In his proverb-like phrases, "winter fights, woeful fights;" "sabbath wars, sorrowful wars," there is particular reference to the engagement at Edge-hill, fought on Sunday, 23rd October, 1642, the evening being frosty. On that day, the first anniversary of the dreadful insurrection in Ireland, RICHARD BAXTER was preaching for his reverend friend, Mr. SAMUEL CLARK, at Alcester, a town in the neighbourhood of Kineton, Warwickshire; and during the sermon the congregation heard the cannon playing on the battle-field (*Life*, ed. 1696, I. i. 43). One of the chaplains present called the fight, in bitterness, "a goodly Sabbath-day's work." The accounts of the attacks on Gloucester, Manchester, Bradford, and elsewhere, shew that Sunday was not an exceptional day for such warfare. Upon a later Sabbath, 13th November, the King's army, after having attacked and taken Brentford, stood all day long watching the army of the Parliament, until the resolute attitude of the latter, reinforced by the train-bands under SKIPPON, caused the former to retreat and ultimately to take up quarters in Oxford. The anxiety of that day was long remembered in London. In the circumstances of the attack on Brentford an explanation is found of what FULLER alludes to (¶ 25) as a "great gulf" between London and the King. "This action of the King in the time of a treaty," says WHITELOCK, "was so ill-resented by many men that they spoke very hardly of it; and the Parliament voted that they would have no accommodation" (*Memorials*, fo. ed. page 66; ed. 1853, vol. i. page 193).

It remains to show that this Sermon illustrates a certain phase in the position of affairs, and that in common with several of the succeeding discourses it has a distinct historic value. The events of December, 1642, and of the next two or three months, have been unaccountably overlooked by most of the modern historians. In spite of the disfavour with which the King was regarded on account of the affair at Brentford, a party came into notice made up of those who did not belong to the more pronounced of the Royalists, and whose humane feelings were roused at the prospect of civil strife in or near a populous city. In Parliament their representatives comprised amongst others D'EWES, WHITELOCK, and MAYNARD. To this moderate party FULLER attached himself (¶ 38). When, therefore, peace-overtures were in a short time renewed from Oxford, the moderates urged that the message should be favourably entertained, and they laboured to create a feeling that would give hopes of the desired consummation. Under the influence of the views of this party, even the city of London was moved to frame a petition for the King's return (*Lords' Journals*, vol. v.

page 511*b*) ; and an order was given to allow fome of the petitioners to have accefs to the King. Weftminfter was much more zealous, its loyalty being quickened in no fmall degree by the injury which its trade had received in confequence of the exodus of the Court (¶ 23). In the Weft-end parifhes, accordingly, peace-petitions to the King found more favour. A petition of the inhabitants of the liberties of Weftminfter and the Duchy of Lancafter, urging the Parliament to a fpeedy accommodation with the King, is mentioned in the Journals of the Houfe of Lords feven days before the delivery of FULLER's Sermon (*Journals*, v. 503*b*, 507*b*; *Report V. Hift: MSS. Commiffion*, page 61). This petition is remarkable for the abfence of ariftocratic fignatures. Thofe of the clergy who were ftill in poffeffion of their city livings entered into the prevailing feeling, but none, perhaps, more heartily than the author of the *Innocents-Day Sermon* (see ¶ 25). His anonymous biographer relates that "his exhortations to peace and obedience were his conftant fubjects in the church ; (all his Sermons were fuch Liturgies ;) while his fecular daies were fpent in vigouroufly promoting the King's affairs, either by a fudden reconciliation or potent affiftance" (page 16). He has himfelf left it upon record that in all his Sermons at the Savoy he would by leave of his text introduce a paffage in the praife of peace (fee page 332, *poftea*.) His advice to petition for peace has an intimate relation with the peace-petition to his Majefty, which was printed in the writer's *Life of Thomas Fuller, &c.* (pages 267-9). That document is defcribed as emanating from the City of Weftminfter, and from the contiguous parifhes of St. Clement Danes and St. Martin's-in-the-Fields. (FULLER's curacy of St. Mary-le-Savoy adjoined the parifh of St. Clement Danes.) Thefe parifhes, fays CLARENDON, "always underwent the imputation of being well affected to the King" (*Hiftory of the Rebellion*, book vi. page 333, ed. 1843). They unitedly expreffed themfelves as "oppreffed with all the calamities that can be ;" that they were grieved principally at the long abfence of the King (who had left Whitehall with his court on the 10th January, 1642) ; that they were "afflicted at the afflictions of our brethren," having "a fellow-feeling of their fufferings, who in the countries round about us groan under the heavy burden of a civil war, their houfes plundered, their goods taken away, and their lives in daily danger ;" and that they lamented efpecially the decreafe of bufinefs confequent upon the abfence of the "families of fuch of the nobility and gentry as inhabited the Strand and the adjacent places." It can now be fhown that the "Doctor FULLER," whofe name, with three others, was attached to the printed copy of this petition (*Life of Fuller*, page 267), was the author of the following Sermon. The difcourfe, it has been feen, was preached on Wednefday, 28th December. On that day the petition was in active preparation, being brought before the notice of the congregation at the Savoy by the preacher, who in an apparently ironical ftrain, which elfewhere breaks out in this Sermon, afferted that the Houfe, "that High and Honourable Court," expected their fervice to petition for peace (¶23). The fignificance of the petition attracted attention ; and a deputation was appointed to wait upon the Houfe ot Lords for permiffion to take it to Oxford with fuch equipage as was fitting.

On the subsequent Monday, 2nd January, 1642-3, six gentlemen accordingly presented themselves to their Lordships. The Lords who were present on that day, and who seem to have entered into the spirit of the petition, were (according to the Minute-book of the House) the following : " E. Manchester Sp., E. Rutland, E. Exon., E. Saru'., E. Holland, E. Nottingham, E. Warwick, E. Bolingbroke, E. Bedford, E. Northumb'land, E. Pembroke ; Vic. Sayelsb.; L. Lovelace, L. Howard de Esc, L. Grey de Wot., L. Newenham, L. Brook." In the course of the proceedings of the sitting, the following entry occurs :—

Westm: Peticon passe. "ORDERED That severall of the Inhabitants of Westm̄. and others shall have a Passe to goe to the King wth their Peticon. Coaches Servants Horses &c."

The applicants for the Pass were the six following gentlemen. Sir EDWARD WARDER was one of the Officers in the Exchequer, his son of the same name being Clerk of the Pells. In March or early in April Sir EDWARD abandoned his office, "to the great disservice of the Commonwealth" (*Lords' Journals*, vi. 41*b*), and betook himself to Oxford, whither his wife, by a pass from the Lords, dated 11th April, followed him (*Ibid.* v. 710). WARDER lodged at Lincoln College, where also FULLER himself was sheltered a few months later. The Knight died in 1645, and his lady in 1652 ; both being buried in All Saints' Church, hard by Lincoln College.—JOHN CASTLE, Esq. (called erroneously *Sir* JOHN CASTLE and in the printed petition *Dr.* CASTLE) ; and JOHN CHICHLEY, Esq., were possibly gentlemen of position in one or other of the parishes named, who had not rendered themselves obnoxious to the King.—LAWRENCE LISLE, gentleman, was originally "an honest Bookseller." In his later years he became a farmer of the revenues, the Impost on tobacco and tobacco-pipes brought into Ireland having been granted to him by the King ; but by the obstruction of this Impost he lost £12,000. In the civil war he was an adherent of the King ; and his daughter said that his large losses were due to his loyalty. His two sons were in the King's service : one, Major FRANCIS LISLE, was slain at Marston Moor ; and the other, Sir GEORGE LISLE, who had been knighted (21st December, 1645) for his bravery at the second battle of Newbury, and who had been Master of the King's household, was " cruelly sentenced and shot to death," with Sir GEORGE LUCAS, at Colchester, 28th August, 1648. LISLE referred to his father and mother just before his execution. Both parents were, however, dead when in 1660 MARY, the only survivor of the family, petitioned for a compensation of £2,000 : "her two brothers were slain fighting for the late King, and her parents died of grief for their loss." After two years' delay the sum was paid as the King's bounty. The elder LISLE left no will (Lloyd's *Worthies*, 478-9, 698 ; Fuller's *Worthies*, § Essex, 347 ; *Calendar State Papers*, Dom. Ser., 1660, page 173, 1662, pp. 259-60, 277 ; *Hist. MSS. Com. IV. Report*, pages 58, 110).—Dr. RICHARD DUCKSON was Rector of St. Clement Danes, 1634-1678. He and his Curate Mr. SMITH had been summoned, 4th July, 1642, for reading a King's declaration. When the Doctor was questioned by the Speaker of the House of Commons on the 13th he "did moſt infolently prevaricate with the Houſe; and gave nothing but ſhuffling Anſwers." For this, as well as for "laying an Aſperſion on a Member of this Houſe" he was committed to the Gate-houſe, whence after eight days he was releaſed on his "humble petition" (*Commons' Journals*, ii. 650*b*, 669*b*, 683*b*; Walker's *Sufferings*, pt. i. p. 56, ii. 167 ; D'Ewes's *Journal*, fo. 655*a*; *Faſti Oxon*. ii. 85, 100). THOMAS FULLER, the laſt on the liſt, was the ſoul of the party, and admirably fitted both by his manners and his profeſſion to be a pacificator.

The paſs was promptly given. The formal entry stands thus in the original Journals (No. 25 : this is not the ſame book as the Minute--book above-mentioned) :—

Edward Warden, } ORDERED that S[this letter is erased] Edward Warder, Sir John Caſtle } Kt. Jo. Caſtle Esq. John Chichley Esq. Laurance Liſle gent. Richard Dickſon D[r] in Diuinity, Tho: Fuller Batchiler in Diuinity wth 2 Coaches wth 4 horſes or 6 horſes for each coach and Saddles for 8 or 10 ſervants ſhall have a paſſe to goe to Oxford to preſent a Peticon to his Ma[ty.]"

The foregoing entry is given in the printed copy of the *Lords' Journals* in the following form (vol. v. page 523*b*), thus :—

Die Lunæ, viz., 2° Januarij, 1642-3 :—" ORDERED, That Sir *Edward Warder* Knight, *Jo. Caſtle* Eſquire, *John Chichley* Eſquire, *Laurance Liſle*
Sir Edw. Warder, Sir John   Gentleman, *Richard Dukeſon* Doctor in Divinity,
Caſtle, &c. a Paſs to Oxford, to   *Tho. Fuller* Batchelor in Divinity, with Two
preſent a Petition to the King.   Coaches, with Four Horſes or Six Horſes for each Coach, and Saddles for Eight or Ten Servants, ſhall have a Paſs, to go to *Oxford*, to preſent a Petition to His Majeſty."

The like impoſing equipage was allowed when later the ſame month WHITELOCK and the other Parliamentary Commiſſioners were deſpatched to Oxford to negotiate peace : "The Commiſſioners were admitted by the lords, two with each lord in their coaches, which were with ſix gallant horſes in every coach, and a great number of their ſervants on horſeback to attend them. In this equipage we came to Oxford" (Whitelock's *Memorials*, fo. ed. page 67 ; ed. 1853, vol. i. page 195).

FULLER and his party ſtarted on their winter's journey on Wedneſday, 4th of January, and all went well until they reached Uxbridge, fifteen miles from the metropolis. At the town mentioned, a well-guarded Parliamentary outpoſt, ſome officer (perhaps Sir SAMUEL LUKE ; see *Lords' Journals*, v. 632), armed perhaps with ſecret inſtructions from the Commons, challenged the party, and ſpite of the Lords' order, detained it. The reſult may be gathered from the Parliamentary minutes :—

Houſe of Commons, *Die Jovis*, viz. 5° January, 1642-3 :—"Mr. *Whittacre* is appointed to go to the Lords, to deſire a Conference concerning the Stay of ſome Perſons going to *Oxon*, by Virtue of a Paſs from the Lords" (*Journals*, vol. ii. page 915*b*).

On the same day (5th) in the House of Lords the following entry stands in the original minutes :—

"A message was brought from the H. C. by Mr Whitaker. That they have receved Informacon of 2 Coaches & 12 horses wth Men; which are stayed at Uxbridge going towards Oxford, & upon their stayeing they produced a warrant for their passage under the Clarkes hand of this house; And being searched there is found amongst them one Dr Dukes & some Clarkes of the Privy Signett, and there is found about them 2 scandalous bookes arraigneing the proceedings of Parliam^t, and letters wth Ciphers t^o Lo: Visc. ffalkland, & the Lo: Spencer; The house of Comōns thinke it that they should be stayed, but in regard they have, their lo^{ps} passe, they thought good to acquainte their Lo^{ps} first wth it.—Ordered that these p'sons that are stayed, shall be sent for backe."

[Message from the H.C. about staying some Clerks of the Privy Seal who had a Pass to Oxford, on whom were found Two scandalous Books against the Parliament, and Cyphers to Lord Falkland : *Jour*.v. 529*b*, 530*a*].

The House of Commons asked by their messenger for the concurrence of their Lordships in this order, and the following answer was sent :—

"That this house doth owne the warrant wch these p'sons have, but seing they have abused their lib'ty, this house concurrs wth the H. C. in sending for them backe. After that this house agrees wth the H. C. in the orders now brought up" (Original Journals, No. 25).

House of Commons, the same day :—" Mr. *Whittacre* reports, That he had acquainted the Lords that some Gentlemen had been examined, that were going to *Oxon*; and with them was found a scandalous Book intituled, *A Complaint to the Commons*, and other Letters and Matters concerning the Signet: That they had been stayed, had they not produced their Lordships Warrant : The Lords did own the Warrant ; but, in regard they had abused it, they were willing to withdraw it, and that they might be sent for back.— Ordered, That the Serjeant send a Man forthwith to stay Sir *Edward Wardour*, Dr. *Dukeson*, and the rest, notwithstanding the Lords Order" (*Journals*, vol. ii. 915*b*).

Stay of Persons going to Oxford.

House of Commons, *Die Veneris*, 6° Januarii, 1642-3 :—" Resolved, That Sir *Edward Wardour*, Dr. *Dukeson*, and the rest that were going down to *Oxon*, stayed and brought up by Order of this House, do continue in the Serjeants Custody, till the House take further Order" (ii. 917*a*).

House of Commons, *Die Sabbati*, 7° Januarii, 1642-3 :—" Ordered, That the Examination of the Matters concerning the Prisoners that were stayed going to *Oxon*, and now in the Serjeant's . . . . . . be referred to the Committee for Examinations, where Mr. *Whittacre* has the Chair : And they are to fit upon it this Afternoon" (ii. 918*b*).

House of Commons, *Die Mercurii*, 11° Januarii, 1642-3 :—" Ordered, That Mr. *Whittacre's* Report be re-committed, upon Information given, That some of these Ministers did in the Churches publish a Summons, and Notice for the Parishioners to meet to subscribe the Petition" (ii. 921*a*).

Unfortunately, none of thefe matters relating to FULLER's imprifonment are alluded to in *D'Ewes's* valuable MS. volumes of the proceedings of Parliament: otherwife the epifode would have received further illuftration. The filence of the induftrious note-taker is explained by the following entry made at the end of the journal for 26th December: "I went out of towne vpon tuefday Dec. 27, 1642, & returned againe into the Howfe vpon Friday, Jan. 13, $\frac{1642}{1643}$" (*Harl. MS.* 164, fol 1074*b*).

Parliament was more cautious in regard to other paffes to Oxford. On the 10th January an application was received by the Houfe of Lords from Mrs. USSHER who wifhed to go to her husband, the Archbifhop of ARMAGH: and it was given with the provifo that fhe could "go quietly" (*Journals*, v. 542*b*). The Commons, on the fame day, granted an order for Lady SYDENHAM to go thither "with fuch numbers of Servants and Horfes as fhall be expreffed in the Warrant; provided that they carry no Letters nor anything elfe that may be prejudicial to the State" (*Journals*, ii. 921*a*). For further fecurity the names of fervants were added in the warrants.

It does not appear how the Petition which FULLER and his friends were taking to Oxford ultimately reached the King, but that it was done fecretly by one or more of the deputation immediately afterwards there cannot be a doubt. According to the printed copy of the Petition it was prefented on the 7th January (Saturday), 1642-3; and it was printed in London and circulated there about a year afterwards. In 1659 FULLER made a diftinct reference to his connection with this hiftoric Petition. PETER HEYLYN had taunted him with coming to Oxford when he was never fent for. FULLER replied that HEYLYN had not heard of all that was done, adding: "I was *once* fent up thither from *London*, being *one* of the *Six*, who was chofen to carry a Petition of Peace to his Majefty, from the *City* of *Weftminfter* and the Liberties thereof, though in the way remanded by the Parliament" (*Appeal of Injur'd Innocence*, Part ii. pages 46-7; ed. 1840, page 444).

The *Innocents-Day Sermon* was not entered at Stationers' Hall; and the date of its publication is not therefore to be obtained from that fource. There is, however, in the Britifh Mufeum a copy (E. 86. 16) to which the date "Jan. 26" has been added with a pen.

It was reprinted in octavo in 1654 by Will. Bently for John Williams, together with the *Inauguration Sermon* preached on the 27th March, 1643, but the latter is erroneoufly placed firft. The *Innocents-Day Sermon* has no title-page, the regifter continuing from c 2; but the paging re-commences (1-37). A copy of the firft edition of 1642 in poffeffion of the Editor is taken as the bafis of the following text; but corrections have been made with the help of the 8vo. copy, fome of the more noticeable differences in the orthography, &c., of the latter copy being placed in the foot-notes.]

A FAST SERMON
Preacht on Innocents day.

MATTH. 5. 9.

Bleſſed are the Peace-makers.

1. ON this day a Faſt and Feaſt do both juſtle together; and the queſtion is, which ſhould take place in our affections. I pray let *Solomon*, the wiſeſt of Kings and Men, be made Doctor of the Chaire to decide this controverſie: *Eccleſ.* 7. 2, *It is better to go to the houſe of mourning* [1] *then to goe to the houſe of feaſting: for it is the end of all men, and the living will lay it to his heart.* Let us therefore diſpenſe with all mirth for this time, and apply our ſelves to lamentation.

2. Wee reade, *Ezra* 3. 11, 12, that when the foundation of the ſecond Temple was laid by *Zerubbabel*, the young men ſhouted for joy: *But many of the Prieſts and Levites, and chiefe of the fathers, who were ancient men, that had ſeen the firſt houſe; when the foundation of this houſe was laid before their eyes, wept with a loud voice, and many ſhouted aloud for joy.* Thus, what if young men be ſo addicted to their toyes and Chriſtmas ſports, that they will not be weaned from them: O let not old men, who are or ſhould be wiſer, and therefore more ſenſible of the ſinnes and ſorrowes of the State; let not us who are Prieſts, whoſe very profeſſion doth date us ancient, be tranſported with their follies, but mourne whileſt they are in their mirth. The French Proverb ſaith, *They that laugh on Friday, ſhall cry on Sunday.* And it may pleaſe God of his goodneſſe ſo to bring it to paſſe that if we keep a ſad Chriſtmas, we may have a merry Lent.

---

[1] than, *throughout the Sermon.*

3. This day is called *Innocents* or *Childermas* day; a day which superstitious Papists count unluckie and unfortunate, and therefore thereupon they will begin no matter of moment, as fearing ill successe should befall them. Indeed I could willingly have sent their follies in silence to Hell, left by being a Confuter I become a Remembrancer of their vanities, but that this fond conceit must be rooted out of the minds of the ignorant people. Why should not that day be most happy, which in the judgement of charity (charity which though not starke blind with *Bartimeus*, with *Leah* is alwaies tender eyed) sent so many Saints by *Herods* cruelty to Heaven, before they had committed any actuall sinne? Well, out of sacred opposition and pious crossing of Popish vanities, let us this day begin, and this day give good handsell of true repentance. *To the cleane all things are cleane:* To the good all dayes are good. We may say of this day as *David* of *Goliahs* sword, 1 *Sam.* 21. 9, *There is none like that; give it me.* No day like this day for us to begin our sanctified sorrow, and to hearken to Gods word, *Blessed are the Peace-makers.*

4. In this and the two next Chapters, Christ having a Mountain for his Pulpit and the whole Law for his text, seeks to clear it from those false glosses (corrupting the Text) which the Priests and Pharisees had fastened upon it; and shewes that Gods Law was not to be narrowed and confined to the outward act alone, but according to the will of the Law-giver (the Surveyour that best knew the latitude thereof) is to bee extended to the very thoughts of the heart, and takes hold of mens wicked inclinations, as breaches thereof and offences against it. We use to end our Sermons with a Blessing; Christ begins his with the Beatitudes; and of the eight my Text is neither the last nor the least: *Blessed are the Peacemakers.*

5. Observe in the words the best worke and the best wages: the best worke, *Peace-makers;* the best wages, *They are blessed.*

I begin with the worke, which shall imploy my paines and your attention this day. Now the goodnesse of peace will the better appeare if we consider the misery of warre. It is said,

Gen. 12. 11, *And it came to paſſe when* Abraham *was come neere to enter into* Egypt, *that hee ſaid unto* Sarai *his wife, Behold, now I know that thou art a faire woman to looke upon.* Why Now *I know thou art a beautifull woman?* Did *Abraham* live thus long in ignorance of his wives beauty? Did he now firſt begin to know her handſomneſſe? Learned [1]*Tremelius* on the place ſtarts and anſwers the objection: *Now,* that is, when *Abraham* came into Egypt; as if he had ſaid, When I ſee the tawny faces and ſwarthy complexions of the ſun-burnt Egyptians, thy face ſeemeth the fairer, and thy beauty the brighter in mine eyes. I muſt confeſſe, I ever prized Peace for a pearle; but we never did or could ſet the true eſtimate and value upon it till this interruption and ſuſpenſion of it. *Now* we know, being taught by deare experience, that peace is a beautifull bleſſing: And therefore we will conſider warre, firſt, in the wickedneſſe, then in the wofulneſſe thereof.

6. Firſt, warre makes a Nation more wicked. Surely, ſwearing and Sabbath-breaking do not advance the keeping of the firſt Table. And as for the ſecond Table, how hard is it in theſe diſtracted times to be practiſed! Yea, it is difficult to ſay the Lords Prayer, the Creed, or ten Commandements: The Lords Prayer for that Petition, *And forgive us our treſpaſſes, as wee forgive them that treſpaſſe againſt us;* the Creed for that Article, *The Communion of Saints,* which doth tye and [2]obliege us to the performance of all Chriſtian offices and charitable duties to thoſe who by the ſame Chriſt ſeeke ſalvation, and profeſſe the ſame true Chriſtian Catholike faith with us; the ten Commandements for that precept, *Thou ſhalt not kill:* and though men in ſpeculation and ſchoole diſtinctions may ſay that all theſe may be eaſily performed in the time of war; yet our corrupt nature, which is ſtarke nought in time of peace, is likely to be far worſe in warre; and if theſe times continue, I am afraid wee ſhall neither ſay the Lords Prayer, nor beleeve the Creed, nor practiſe the Commandements. And as hard it will be preparedly and profitably to receive the Sacraments, when wee ſhall drinke

---

[1] [Tremellii et Junii *Teſt. Veteris Bib.*, ed. 1607, p. 16.]   [2] oblige.

Chrifts bloud as on to day, and go about to fhed our brothers bloud as on to morrow.

7. Secondly, let us confider the wofulneffe of war, and that both in its felfe, and in its attendance. See a Map of war drawne by a holy hand, *Pfal.* 78. 63, 64 : *The fire confumed their young men, and their maidens were not given to marriage; their Priefts fell by the fword, and their widowes made no lamentations.* *The fire confumed the young men :* Wee behold with contentment ripe fruit to drop downe to the ground ; but who will not pity greene apples when they are cudgelled downe from the tree? *And the maidens were not given in marriage :* So that the faireft flowers of virginity were faine to wither on the ftalke whereon they did grow, for want of hands to gather them. *The Priefts were flaine with the fword. Sed quid cum Marte Prophetis?* Well then, there they were, though they were none of the beft of the Priefts, being lewd *Hophnee* and *Phyneas*, and there they were killed: for ought I know, if thefe times hold, Gods beft *Samuels* muft goe the fame way. *And their widowes made no lamentation :* You will fay, The more unnaturall women they. O no; *they made no lamentation* either becaufe their griefe was above lamenting, fuch as onely could be managed with filence and amazement ; or elfe becaufe they were fo taken up with deploring the publike calamity, they could fpare no time for private perfons to bemoane their particular loffes.

8. But warre is not fo terrible in it felf as in its attendants. Firft, the Plague, which brings up the reare of war ; the Plague, I fay, which formerly ufed to be an extraordinary embaffador in this Citie of *London*, to denounce Gods anger againft it ; but is of late grown a conftant legier, and for thefe many late yeares hath never been clearly removed from us : furely fome great unrepented fin lyes on this City, that this conftant punifhment doth vifit us, which will be more terrible when it fhall be extended over the whole Realme.

9. Secondly, Famine, a waiter in Ordinary on Warre. Truly it may feeme a riddle, and yet it is moft true, that *Warre makes both leffe meat and fewer mouthes :* Firft, becaufe in time of war none dare attend hufbandry, wherewith,

Solomon faith, *The King himself is maintained.* Secondly, becaufe Souldiers fpoile more out of prodigality then they fpend out of neceffity. When our Saviour multiplied loaves and fifhes, there were thofe appointed who tooke up the twelve bafkets of fragments; but, alas! no fuch care is taken in fouldiers feftivals. Hitherto indeed wee have had plenty enough, and as yet in this City [1]are not fenfible of any want. But, you know, next [2]*Pharaohs* full eares came *Pharaohs* blafted ears; next *Pharaohs* fat kine came *Pharaohs* lean kine; and I pray God poor people for this years ftore be not next year ftarved.

10. Thirdly, wilde beafts. See Gods foure cardinall punifhments reckoned up, *Ezechiel* 14. 21 : *For thus faith the Lord God, for [how] much more when I fend my foure fore judgements upon* Jerufalem: *the fword, and the famine, and the noyfome beaft, and the peftilence, to cut from it man and beaft?* Some perchance wil fay that there is [no] more danger of wilde beafts in our [3]Iland, which is invironed with water. Truely there need no other wilde beafts then our felves, who are Lions, Beares, Boares, Wolves, and Tygers one to another. And though as yet wee were never plagued with wilde beafts, yet wee know not how foone God may hiffe for them over, and for our new and ftrange fins caufe new and ftrange punifhments. Now conceive a City as bigge as your thoughts can imagine, and fancy the Sword marching in at the Eaft-gate, and the Plague comming in at the Weft-gate, and Famine entring in at the North-gate, and wilde beafts paffing in at the South-gate, and all meeting together in the Market-place, and then tell me how quickly will your voluminous Citie be abridged to a poor pittance.

11. But hitherto wee have only fpoken of the miferies of War in generall; but the worft is ftill behind, for we are afflicted with Civill war. Many warres have done wofully, but this furmounteth them all. In Civill war nothing can bee expected but a ruine and defolation. What faid *Mordecai* to *Hefther?* Hefther 4. 13: *Think not with thy felfe that thou fhalt efcape in the Kings houfe more then all the Jewes.*

---

[1] we are.   [2] *Pharaoh's* (quater).   [3] Iſland.

So let none in what houfe foever, in the Kings Houfe, or Houfe of Lords, or Houfe of Commons, or ftrongeft Caftles, or walled Towns, or fenced Cities, flatter themfelves with a fond conceit of their fafety; for if Civill warres continue long, they muft expect as well as others to bee devoured; yea, none can promife great Perfons fo much happineffe as to bee laft undone: For, for ought any knowes, it may come to their turnes to be the firft, as being the faireft markes to invite envy and malice againft them. Meane time poore *Ireland*, which as the man in the vifion cryed to Saint *Paul, Come over into* Macedonia *and helpe us,* which hath fo long, fo often, fo earneftly intreated, implored, importuned our [1]affiftants, muft be loft *of courfe.* The Proteftants there, which have [2]long fwom againft the tide till their armes are weary, muft at laft of neceffity even give themfelves over to bee drowned: That Harpe, which when it was well tuned made fo good muficke, muft now and hereafter for ever *bee hung upon the willowes,* a fad and forrowfull tree; and our diftraction will haften their finall deftruction. Wee reade, *Deut.* 28. 56, That in a great Famine *the eye of the mother fhall be evill towards her fon and towards her daughter;* fhee fhall grudge every morfell of meat which goes befides her owne mouth, preferring nature before naturall affection. If thefe times doe continue, *London* will grudge *London-derry* her daughter; and *England,* Mother generally of *Ireland* (as a Colony deduced from it), will grieve to part with the leaft meat, money and munition to it.

12. But all thefe Mifchiefes are nothing in refpect of the laft; namely, the fcandal and difhonour which hereby will redound to the Proteftant religion, whereof a true Chriftian ought to be more tender and fenfible then of any worldly loffe whatfoever: *Tell it not in* Gath, *nor publifh it in* Afcalon, *left the daughters of the* Philiftims *rejoyce, left the daughters of the uncircumcifed triumph.* O what mufick doth our difcord make to the Romifh adverfaries! We reade, *Genef.* 13. 7, 8, *And there was a ftrife between the heard-men of* Abrams *cattel, and the heard-men of* Lots *cattell, and the* Cananite

---

[1] affiftans. [2] fo long.

and the Perizite *dwelled then in the Land. And* Abram *said unto* Lot, *Let there be no strife, I pray thee, between my &c.* Wherein obferve that the *Canaanites* and *Perizites* being there in the Land, is mentioned as a motive with *Abraham* to make him make the fpeedier accommodation with *Lot*, left the true religion and fervice of God fhould fuffer in the cenfure of Pagans by their difcords, being Uncle and Nephew, ingaged in a brawle by their fervants diffention. How many *Canaanites* and *Perezites* behold our bloudy differences, and clap their hands to fee us wring ours, yea, infult and rejoyce to fee us fheath our fwords in one anothers bowels! Wee ufed formerly to tafke the Papifts of cruelty to Proteftants; but hereafter, as *Abner* faid to *Afahel*, 2 Sam. 2. 22, *How then shall I hold up my face to* Joab *thy brother?* So how fhall we looke in the face, from this day forwards, of our Romifh adverfaries? Tell them no more of their cruelty to the Proteftants at *Hedlebergh*, of their cruelty to Proteftants of *Magdenbergh*, of their cruelty to the Proteftants at *Rochel*; for if thefe wars continue, wee are likely not onely to equall, but to outdoe thefe cruelties one to another; fo that difcharging this accufation of bloudineffe againft them, it will rebound and recoile in our own faces. Put all thefe together; that warre makes a Land more wicked, makes a Land more wofull, is bad in it felfe, is worfe in its traine, deftroyes Chriftian people, and difgraces Chriftian profeffion; and then will all have juft caufe to fay as is it in my Text, *Bleffed are the Peace-makers.*

13. If any object that Peace alfo hath her mifchiefes which attend thereupon; for it brings plenty, and plenty brings pride, and pride brings plagues upon it; peace makes men pampered, and with *Jeffurun* to kick againft God. War indeed brings *cleanneffe of teeth*, whileft peace brings *fulneffe of bread*, which is as bad and worfe, making men prefumptuoufly to rebell againft God. The anfwer is eafie: woes may come from peace, but they muft come from warre; miferies arife from the very ufe of warre, which come but from the abufe of peace, being effentiall to warre, but accidentall to peace, inherent alwaies in the one, adherent too

often to the other : in a word, in war calamities proceed from the thing it felfe, in peace from men abufing it.

14. *Objection:* But peace without truth is rather poyfon then a cordiall: O let us not be like the thirfty traveller, who fo long longs for water that at laft he drinkes mud and water together, not only without diftinction or diftafte, but even with delight! O let us not with *Sampfon* fo dote on the *Dalilah* of peace as to get her love to betray truth, wherein our ftrength lyes! Some perchance would propound peace unto us, but on fuch fervile conditions as *Naafh* the *Ammonite* offered a truce to the men of *Jabefh-Gilead*, 1 Sam. 11. 2: *On this condition will I make a covenant with you, that I may thruft out all your right eyes, and lay it for a reproach upon all* Ifrael. And fo if we will give in truth to boot, and put out our owne eyes into the bargaine; forfeit the true faith and knowledge of God, with the purity of his fervice; then perchance a peace may be proffered us; but as *Peter* faid to *Simon Magus*, Acts 8. 20, *Thy money perifh with thee;* fo let fuch a hellifh peace perifh with thofe that feek to promote it.

15. In the anfwering of this Objection, give me leave, as *Peter* faid, *Acts* 2. 29, *Men and brethren, let me freely fpeake unto you of the Patriarch* David; fo let me boldly and fully fpeak in anfwer to the objection: If leave be denied mee: I know whence my commiffion is derived; I am an Embaffadour for the God of Heaven; if I fpeake what is falfe, I muft anfwer for it; if truth, it will anfwer for me. And what I have to fay, I will divide into foure Propofitions.

16. Propofition 1: *Curfed be hee that feekes to divide Peace from Truth.* I muft confeffe I was never bred upon Mount Ebal, neither did ever my tongue take delight in curfing. The rather becaufe we may obferve, *Deut.* 27. 12, that the moft eminent Tribes from which the Princely and Prieftly men defcended, [as] *Levi, Iudah, Ephraim* [*Iffachar,*] and *Benjamin*, took their ftation in Mount *Gerafin*, to fhew that Magiftrates and Minifters are principally to inure their mouths to bleffing. And yet for thofe that feek to fever peace from truth, I cannot refrain my felf, but muft fay, *Curfed be they in the city, and curfed be they in the field; curfed be they in*

their basket and in their store; cursed be they in the fruit of their body, and in the fruit of their land, in the increase of their kine, and in the stock of their sheep; cursed shall they be when they come in, and cursed shall they be when they go out.

17. Proposition 2: *Before this warre began, wee had in England truth in all essentiall to salvation.* Wee had all necessary and important truths truly [1]compiled in our thirty-nine Articles. We had the word of God truly [2]preacht (I could wish it had been more frequently and generally), the Sacraments duly administred; which two put together doth constitute a true Church. S. *Paul*, 1 *Cor.* 15. 18, being to prove the resurrection of the dead, presseth the Corinthians with this among other Arguments, *Then they also which are fallen asleep in Christ are perished.* Putting them a most uncharitable absurdity, that in case the dead arise not againe, they must be bound to confess that all the Saints formerly deceased were perished. And surely, such as deny that *England* before this warre began had all essentiall truth to salvation, must of necessity split themselves on the same uncharitable rocke, and passe a sentence of condemnation on all those which dyed in our Church before these two yeares last past.

18. Proposition 3: *Many errors in Doctrine and innovation in Discipline did creepe fast into our Church.* Arminian positions, Tenents, Treason to Gods grace, invaded the truth of the Word in many places. One Ceremony begat another, there being no bounds in will-worship, wherewith one may sooner be wearied then satisfied. The inventors of new Ceremonies endeavouring to supply in number what their conceits wanted in solidity; and [3]God knowes before this time where they had been if they had not been stopt.

19. *Proposition* 4: The best and onely way to purge these errors out, is in a faire and peaceable way; for the sword cannot discerne betwixt [4]truth and errour; it may have two edges, but hath never an eye. Let there on Gods blessing be a Synode of truely grave, pious, and learned Divines; and let them both fairely dispute and fully decide, whats true, whats false; what Ceremonies are to be retained, what to be rejected;

---

[1] compiled .... truly, *omitted by an error of the press.*   [2] preach'd.
[3] God *omitted.*   [4] truth, error, and falshood.

and let civill authoritie ſtampe their command upon it, to be generally received under what penaltie their diſcretion ſhall think fitting. But as long as Warre laſts, no hope of any ſuch agreement: this muſt be a worke for Peace to performe. So then under the notion of Peace, hitherto we have and hereafter doe intend ſuch a Peace as when it comes we hope will reſtore truth unto us in all the accidentall and ornamentall parts thereof; and adde it to that truth in eſſentialls to ſalvation, which we enjoyed before this Warre began; and in this ſence I will boldly pronounce, *Bleſſed be the Peace-makers.*

20. Come we now to conſider what be the hindrances of Peace. Theſe hindrances are either generall or particular. The generall hindrance is this: The many nationall ſinnes of our kingdome being not repented of. I ſay, of our kingdome, not of one Army alone. Thinke not that the Kings Army is like *Sodome,* not ten righteous men in it; (no, not if righteous *Lot* himſelfe be put into the number;) and the other Army like [1]*Syon* conſiſting all of Saints. No; there be drunkards on both ſides, and ſwearers on both ſides, and whoremungers on both ſides; pious on both ſides, and prophane on both ſides: like *Jeremies* figges, thoſe that are good are very good, and thoſe that are bad are very bad in both parties. I never knew nor heard of an Army all of Saints, *ſave the holy Army of Martyrs;* and thoſe, you know, were dead firſt; for the laſt breath they ſent forth proclaimed them to be Martyrs. But it is not the ſinnes of the Armies alone, but the ſinnes of the whole kingdome which breake off our hopes of Peace: our Nation is generally ſinfull. The City complaines of the ambition and prodigality of the Courtiers; the Courtiers complaine of the pride and covetouſneſſe of the Citizens: the Laity complaine of the lazineſſe and ſtate-medling of the Clergie; the Clergie complaine of the hard dealing and ſacriledge of the Laity: the Rich complaine of the murmuring and ingratitude of the Poor; the Poor complaine of the oppreſſion and extortion of the Rich. Thus every one is more ready to throw durt in anothers face then

---

[1] Zion.

to wafhe his owne cleane. And in all thefe, though malice may fet the varnifh, fure truth doth lay the ground-worke.

21. Of particular hindrances, in the firſt place we may ranke the Romiſh Recufants. *Is not the hand of* Joab *with thee in all this?* was *Davids* question, 2 *Sam.* 14. 19; but is not the hand, may we all fay, of *Jefvites* in thefe diſtractions? *Many times from my youth up have they fought againſt me*, may England *now fay; yea, many times from my youth up have they vexed me, but have not prevailed againſt me.* At laſt, the Popiſh party perceived that the ſtrength of *England* confiſted in the unity thereof; (*Sampfon* is halfe conquered when it is knowne where his ſtrength doth lye;) and that it was impoſſible to conquer *Engliſh* Proteſtants, but by *Engliſh* Proteſtants. Is this your ſpite and malice, O you *Romiſh* adverfaries, becaufe you could not overcome us with *Spaniſh* Armadoes, nor blowe us up with Gunpowder Treafons, nor undoe us with *Iriſh* Rebellions, to fet our felves againſt our felves, firſt to divide us, then to deſtroy us? Well, God knowes what may come to paffe. It may be when we have drunke the top of [1]this bitter cup, the dregs may be for your ſhare; and we may all be made friends for your utter ruine and deſtruction.

22. Next the Papiſts, the Schifmatickes are the hindrances of our Peace. Thefe know their kingdome cannot be eſtabliſhed but by Warre, as affured that the wifdome of the State is fuch as will blaſt their defignes when matters are fettled. I have heard (when a childe) of a *Lawleffe Church;* fure thefe if they might have their will, would have a Lawleffe Church and a Gofpelleffe too; and yet they as falſly as fondly conceive that the State gives approbation and connivance to them. We read, *Pfalm* 50. 21, where Gods fpirit reckons up many finnes which the wicked had committed, that God faith, *Thefe things haſt thou done, and I kept ſilence; thou thoughteſt that I was altogether fuch a one as thy felfe: but I will reprove thee, and fet them in order before thine eyes.* In which place of Scripture three things are confiderable. Firſt, God is faid to keep filence when he doth

---

[1] his.

not presently and visibly punish offenders: *Psal.* 35. 22, *O Lord, keep not silence;* and so *Psal.* 83.1, *Keepe not thou silence, O God.* God, for reasons best known to himselfe, and for some known to us, namely, to make wicked men swel and break with a Timpany of good successe for the time, does not outwardly expresse the dislike of their bad courses in inflicting a suddain and sensible punishment upon them. Secondly, observe the false Logick and bad inference of wicked men; who conceive that God is altogether such an one as themselves, yea, make accessary and confederate with them; becauſe silent, therefore consenting: *Qui tacet satis laudat.* Thirdly, see time wil come when, in time best known to himselfe, he will publikely reprove them and shew not onely his free diſſent but full displeasure. Thus Schismatickes improve themselves upon the clemency and long suffering of our State. Becauſe they are taken up with matters of higher concernment, and are not at leasure to stoope to their punishment, as imployed in businesse of more present and pressing importance, Separatists and Sectaries conceive that they favour what they doe not punish. But time will come when to the glory of God and their own honour, though slowly, surely they will visit their offences, and, as the *Pſalmiſt* saith, *Set their sinnes in order before them,* who have beene the partiall cauſe of the disorder and confusion of this Kingdome.

23. Thirdly, those are enemies to Peace, whose beeing meerely consisteth by Warre and [1]discention. Indeed the truly noble English spirits desire a forraigne Foe for a marke for their Bullets; but many there be rather turbulent then valiant, *who as* Demetrius *by this craft they get their gaine,* desire a perpetuity of Warre for their posseſſion. We read in [2] *Plutarch* of one *Demades* who by profession was a maker of Coffins, and he was banished out of the city of *Athens* for wishing that hee might have good trading; that wise State

---

[1] dissention.

[2] [This anecdote, with the moral, has a place in *Things New and Old; Or, a Store-houſe of Similies,* 1658, folio, by John Spencer, of Sion College, Fuller's friend (page 107, ¶ 435*a*). The paragraph is headed "A meer Soldier, an Enemy to Peace," and is erroneously said to be taken fiom Fuller's *Holy State.* Spencer adds a reference to Plutarch's *Morals,* but does not give book or chapter.]

truly interpreting the language of his wifh, as defiring fome epidemicall difeafe; his private profit being inconfiftant with the publike flourifhing of the Common-wealth. So thofe people who are undone and cannot live but by undoing of others, certainly wifh no good to our Church and Kingdome, but muft needs be State Barrettors to keep the fore alwayes raw betwixt Prince and people.

24. Let us now come to fee the meanes wherby private perfons may and muft endeavour the obtaining of peace. The firft is prayer: *Pray for the peace of* Jerufalem: let every one in that prayer which he ufeth in his Family, or private devotions, build a roome more and inlarge it to pray for peace in our Ifraell.

25. Secondly, let us petition for peace, not only to the God in Heaven, but to the Gods on earth. Firft, to his Majeftie; but, alas! there is a great gulfe between us and him fixed, fo that they which would paffe from hence to him cannot, neither *can they paffe to us that would come from thence.* The fins of our Realm are amounted to fuch a height that we deferve this and worfe punifhment. Next, let us petition to the High and Honourable Court of Parliament, next under God and the King the hope and help of our happineffe. Let none fay it is prefumption to petition them, as undertaking to tell them of what they are ignorant, or to put them in remembrance of what they may forget; for herein we apply our felfe to them in imitation of our acceffe to God; and furely their greatneffe cannot, and their goodneffe will not be difpleafed in our compliance and conformity to fuch an Architype. True it is that God, *Matthew* 6. 8, *Our Father, knoweth what things we have need of before we aske him;* and yet it is his will and pleafure to be fought too by our prayer. And fo no doubt that High and Honourable Court, though that they know full well that peace is that we ftand in need of, yet they take delight in our duty, yea, expect our fervice herein to petition for peace, that fo our begging of peace may in effect be a modeft and mannerly expreffion of an hearty thanks for their long and conftant endeavours herein. Wherefore what *Tertullus* faid flatteringly to *Felix, Acts* 24.

2, 3, 4, we may say truly and feelingly to them, *seeing that very worthy deeds are done to this Nation by their providence, we accept alwaies, and in all places, with all thankfulnes.* Notwithstanding I pray you, that you of your Clemency would heare us a few words. And let us in all Humility, not directing but beseeching them, without a tumultuous thought, most peacable and pathetically begge of them and sue unto them to continue their care in advancing a seasonable and happy accomodation, that so the blessing pronounced in my text may lie both upon them and theirs, *Blessed are the Peacemakers.*

26. Thirdly, we must be content soundly to pay for peace. We read, *Exod.* 38. 8, *And he made the* [1]*Lever of Brasse, and the foot of it of Brasse, of the Looking-glasses of the Women assembling, which assembled at the door of the Tabernacle of the congregation.* It seemeth that the back-sides of their Looking-glasses were made of brasse, which commonly with us are made of wood, and they consigned them over for Gods service; and good reason too; for formerly they had given their ear-rings for the making of a Calfe; Justly therefore now they did pennance for their pride, as counting it Honour enough that that wherein they looked their owne faces, should make the foot of Gods [1]Leaver. But what should not people give to buy a true peace and a peace with Truth? O how many yeeres purchase is it worth! Let us not thinke much, to give all our superfluities, but to give some of our necessaries, for the advancing and obtaining of it.

27. Fourthly, let us banish out of our mouthes all words and phrases of contempt and [2]reproach, (I could instance in the word, but that it is beneath the Majesty of a Pulpit,) which the malice of men hath minted and fastned on opposite parties. O let us have no other Christian name then the name of Christians, or other surname then Christian Protestants; neither answering to, nor calling others by any term of disgrace!

28. Fifthly, let us with a speedy, serious and generall repentance, remove the crying sinnes of our Kingdome, which

---

[1] Laver. [2] reproch.

as long as they laſt wil bane all peace amongſt us. I ſay, ſpeedy, leaſt the phyſick come too late for the diſeaſe; ſerious, leaſt the tent be too ſhort for the wound; generall, leaſt the plaſter be too narrow for the ſore. Suppoſe that the Sea ſhould breake forth in this Land, as ſuch a thing may come to paſſe; *The Lord is King,* ſaith David, *let the earth rejoyce; yea, let the multitude of the Iſles be glad thereat,* Pſal. 97. 1. And good reaſon hath the Iles to be glad, as more particularly concerned; for if the water were not countermanded by Gods Prerogative Royall, it would ſpeedily recover its naturall place above the earth. [1]But ſuppoſe the Sea ſhould break into the Land, it is not the endeavours of a private man can ſtop it. What if he goes downe with a faggot on his backe, and a mattock on his ſhoulder, and a ſpade in his hand: his deſire is more commendable then his diſcretion, it being more likely the Sea would ſwallow him then he ſtop the mouth thereof. No; the whole Country muſt come in: children muſt bring earth in their hats, women in their aprons; men with handbarrowes, wheelbarrowes, carts, carres, waines, waggons; all muſt worke [2] leaſt all be deſtroyed. I rather inſtance in this expreſſion of the irruption of the Sea, becauſe I finde Gods anger ſo compared in holy writ, 1 *Chron.* 14. 11: *David ſaid, God hath broken in upon mine enemies like the breaking forth of waters.* So when a generall deluge and inundation of Gods anger feaſeth [ſeizeth] upon a whole Kingdome, it cannot be ſtopt by the private endeavours of ſome few, but it muſt be an univerſall work, by a generall repentance; all muſt raiſe bankes to bound it. Till this be done, I am afraid we ſhall have no peace; and, to ſpeak plainly, I am afraid we are not yet ripe for Gods mercy. As *Gideon,* Judg. 7. 4, *had too many men* for God to give victory to: ſo we are too proud hitherto for God to give peace to; many of us are *Humiliati,* but few of us are *Humiles:* Many by theſe warres brought [3] loe, but few made [3] loely; ſo that we are proud in our poverty;

---

[1] [This paragraph is printed, but with ſome variations, in John Spencer's *Things New and Old,* London, 1658, fo., page 68, ¶ 283. It is entitled "National Judgements call for National Repentance," with this marginal note: "T. FULLER, *ſerm. at* Westm. 1642."]

[2] leſt.   [3] lo, loly.

and, as the unjuſt Steward ſaid, *to beg I am aſhamed,* ſo we are too ſtout though halfe ſtarved on the bended knees of our ſoules, with true repentance, to crave pardon of God for our ſinnes; which till it be done, we may diſcourſe of peace and ſuperficially deſire it, but never truely care for it, or can comfortably receive it.

29. And indeed wee may take forcible motives from our owne miſeries to endeavour peace by all poſſible meanes; for look upon the complexion of the warre, and doth it not look of a moſt ſtrange and different hue from other warres? The wars of *Germany* (which, give me leave to ſay, if we had pittied by the proxie of a true [1]Simpathy, we had never ſo ſoon ſuffered them in our owne perſon) were far lighter affliction then ours. [1,] In *Germany* people when hunted with warre took covert in their fenced Citties. But here in *England* we have no guard againſt wars blow, but lye open to plundering and deſtruction. [2,] *Germany* was a great Continent bearing ſix hundred miles ſquare; ſo that whilſt one part thereof was mowed downe with warre, the other, enjoying peace, might grow up in the meane time. But little *England* (great onely in her miſeries, ſevered by the Sea from other Countries, and by diviſions parted from her ſelfe) is a morſell which civill warre will quickly devoure. Thirdly, in *Germany* commonly they lay in Garriſon in winter and fought in ſummer. We read, 2 *Sam.* 11. 1 : *And it came to paſſe at the time when Kings goe forth to battell.* This all Comments generally expound of the ſpring time. But, alas! if we in our woes were *Antipodes* to all others, our miſeries begin when others end, in the winter time. *Pray* (ſaith our Saviour) *that your flight be not in the winter, nor on the Sabboth-day*: winter fights woful fights, Sabboth wars ſorrowful warres; and yet ſuch are theſe in our Kingdome. Laſtly, in *Germany* Papiſts did fight againſt Proteſtants, whereas our inteſtine wars are againſt thoſe that profeſſe the ſame Religion.

30. It hath been a great curſe of God upon us, to make a conſtant miſunderſtanding betwixt our King and his Parlia-

---

[1] Sympathy.

ment; whileſt both profeſſe to levell at the ſame end. I cannot compare their caſe better than to the example of [1]*Ruben* and *Judah*, *Gen. 37*. There *Ruben* deſired and endeavoured to preſerve the life of his brother *Joſeph*, and *Judah* deſired and endeavoured to preſerve the life of his brother *Joſeph*; and yet theſe two imbracing different meanes, did not onely croſſe and thwart, but even ruine and deſtroy the deſires of each other; for *Ruben* moved and obtained that *Joſeph* might not be killed, *verſe* 22: *And* Ruben *ſaid unto them, ſhed no blood, but caſt him into this Pit that is in the wilderneſſe, and lay no hand upon him; that he might rid him out of their hands, to deliver him to his Father againe.* *Judah* alſo deſired the ſame; but being not privie to *Rubens* intents, and to avoid the cruelty of the reſt of his Brethren, propounded and effected that *Joſeph* might be ſold to the [2]*Medianitiſh* Merchants, meerly ſo to preſerve his life; and thereby he did unravell all the web of *Rubens* deſignes, and fruſtrated his endeavours. Thus when God will have a people puniſhed for their ſinnes, hee will not onely ſuffer, but cauſe miſtakes without mending, and miſpriſions without rectifying, to happen betwixt brethren who [3]meane and really intend the ſame thing; ſo that they ſpeake the ſame matter in effect, and yet be Barbarians one to another, as either not or not right underſtanding what they ſay each to other. Thus, the maintaining of the Proteſtant Religion in the purity thereof; the vindicating of the lawfull Prerogative of the King; the aſcertaining of the juſt rights and priviledges of the Parliament; the defending of the dues and properties of the Subject are pleaded and pretended on both ſides as the ultimate ends they aime at. Well, as our Saviour ſaid to the blinde man, *Mat. 9. 29*, *according to your faith be it unto you:* ſo, according to the ſincerity and integrity of their hearts, whom God knowes means moſt ſeriouſly, be it unto them; *we wiſh them good victory in the name of the Lord:* and yet even herein a friendly peace were as much better then victory it ſelfe as the end is better then the means; for, *bleſſed are the Peace-makers.*

---

[1] *Reuben* throughout the paragraph.
[2] *Midianitiſh.*
[3] meane, and *omitted.*

31. *Objection:* But may some say, though we doe never so much desire peace, we shall not obtaine that blessing, which is pronounced in my text, for the Peace-makers are to be blessed. And it is to be feared, that our breaches are too wide to be cured, and Gods justice must have reparation upon us.

32. [*Answer:*] By Peace-makers, Peace-endeavourers are to be understood; not only the Effectours of Peace, but even the Affectours of Peace shal be blessed. *Rom.* 12. 18: *If it be possible, as much as in you lyeth, live peaceably with all men.* God out of his goodnesse measures mens reward not by their successe, but desires: 2 *Cor.* 8. 12, *For if there be first a willing minde, it is accepted according to that a man hath, and not according to that he hath not.*

33. And yet I am not out of heart, but that there is hope of Peace, and that as yet our sinnes are not swel'd so high, but that there is mercy with God for our nation. First, my hope is founded on the multitude of good people in this land, which assault and batter Heaven with the importunity of their prayers. We [1]read of *Ptolomeus Philadelphus*, King of *Egipt*, that he caused the Bible to be translated by seventy Interpreters; which seventy were severally disposed of in seventy severall Cels, unknown each to other; and yet they did so well agree in their several translations that there was no considerable difference betwixt them in rendering the text; an argument that they were acted with one and the same spirit. Surely it comforts me when I call to minde, what shall I say? seventy? nay seven times seventy, yea, seventy hundred, yea, seventy thousand, which are peaceable in Israel, which on the bended knees of their souls daily pray to God for peace. These though they know not the faces, no, not the names one of another; nay, have neither seen nor shall see one another till they meet together in happinesse in Heaven; yet they unite their votes and centre their suffrages in the same thing, that God would restore Peace unto us, who no doubt in his due time will heare their prayers.

---

[1] [This paragraph is found, with a few slight alterations, in Spencer's *Things New and Old*, page 109, ¶ 440. It is entitled "Prayers of the Godly, the unanimity of them," and is said to be from "T. FULLER. *Ser. at* Savoy, 1642." Spencer has added this historical reference: "Conrad. Zuingerus, *ex citat. variarum.*"]

34. The second thing that comforts mee is, when I looke on Gods proceedings hitherto in our Kingdome, his judgements seeme to be judgements rather of expostulation then of exterpation: we read, *Exod.* 4. 24, that God being angry with *Moses* for not circumcising his Sonnes, *It came to passe by the way in the Inne that the Lord met him, and sought to kill him.* Sought to kill him? strange: did God seeke to kill him, and not kill him? Speake, Lord, speake to the Fire, and it shall with flashes consume him; to the Ayre, and with pestilent vapours it shall choake him; to the Water, and with deluges it shall over-whelme him; to the Earth, and with yawning chops it shall devoure him. Well, the meaning is this; God sought to kill him, that is, in some outward visible manner whereof *Moses* was apprehensive; God manifested his displeasure against him, that so *Moses* might both have notice and leisure to divert his anger, with removing the cause thereof. He that saith to us, *Seeke and yee shall finde,* doth himselfe seeke and not finde; and good reason too, for he sought with an intent not to finde. Thus I may say that for these last foure yeeres God hath still *sought* to destroy the Kingdome of *England;* manifesting an unwillingnesse to doe it, if in any reasonable time we would compound with him by serious repentance. Thus the loving Father shakes the rod over his wanton childe, not with an intent to beat him, but to make him begge pardon; and such hitherto hath beene Gods dealing with our Nation, that he even courts and [1] woes us to repentance, as [2] loath to punish us, if wee would understand the signes of his anger, before it breake out upon us.

35. But if all faile, yet those that are Peace-makers in their desires doe enter a caveat in the Court of heaven, That if warres doe ensue, yet for their part they have laboured against it. If a man slaine were found in the field, and it not knowne who slew him, God provided, *Deut.* 21. 7, 8, That the Elders of the next City should wash their hands in the blood of an Heifer, and say, *Our hands have not shed this blood, neither have our eyes seen it. Be mercifull, O Lord, unto thy people*

---

[1] woos.   [2] loth.

Israell, whom thou hast redeemed, and lay not innocent blood unto thy people of Israels charge; and the blood shalbe forgiven them. So this one day will be a comfort to the consciences of godly minded men, that they may appeale to the God of heaven, how they have prayed heartily for peace, have petitioned humbly for Peace, have been contented to pay deerly for peace, and to their powers have endevoured to refraine themselves from sinnes, the breakers of peace; and therefore they trust that Christian *English* Protestant blood, which shall be shed, which hath beene and hereafter may be shed in these wofull warres, shall never be visited on their score or laid to their charge.

36. But if all faile, and if we must be involved in a finall desolation, then let us goe to the *Assurance Office* of our soules, and have peace of conscience with God in our Saviour. It was wont to be said *A mans house is his Castle;* but if this Castle of late hath proved unable to secure any, let them make their conscience their castle; if beaten from all our parapets and outworkes, let us retire to this strength for our defence. It may seem, be it spoken with all reverence, a blunt expression of the holy spirit, *Luke* 12. 4, *Be not afraid of them that kill the body, and that have no more that they can doe.* Yea, but one may say, they may kil me with torment and with torture, make me drop out my life by degrees; why, the totall some of their malice is but to kill the body, *and then they have no more that they can doe.* But they may forbid my body Christian buriall; herein they do not do but suffer, for the living will be more troubled then the dead, if thy corps be not committed to earth; so that this in effect is just nothing. Then let Drums beat, and Trumpets sound, and Banners be displaid; let swords clash, and pikes push, and bullets flye, and Cannons roare; warre, doe thy worst; Death, doe thy worst; Devill, doe thy worst; their souls shal be happy that sleep in the Lord, for they rest from their labours. However, if it be possible, and if so great mercy be stored up in God for us, we would rather have peace in this world; and on the promoters thereof let the blessing in the light and rest, *Blessed are the Peacemakers.*

37. And now as I began with the mention of the Faſt, ſo to conclude with the ſame: let us keep this day of humiliation holy to the Lord. Some perchance may make this but a mock-faſt, and faſt for ſome private and ſineſter ends; but every one that will may make it a true faſt to himſelf, therin to be grieved for the miſery of Gods Saints. God complaines, *Amos* the [1]ſixt, of the gluttonie of the Iſraelites; wherein wee finde the compleat Character of an Epicure, making wantons of his five Sences: entertaining their eyes with *bedſteads of Ivory*, verſe 4, curious to behold for the milk-whiteneſſe thereof; pleaſing their feeling, *they ſtretch themſelves on Couches*; courting their eares, *they chant to the Violl*, verſe 5; contenting their taſte, and making that ſence a Pander both to gluttony and drunkenneſſe, *they eate the fat of Lambes, and drinke Wine in boules*, verſes 4 and 6; delighting their ſmell, *and annoynt themſelves with the chiefe oyntments*; and then concludes all with this ſharpe cloſe, *but they are not grieved for the affliction of Joſeph*. Wherein the Prophet alludes to the ſtory of *Joſeph*, *Geneſ.* 37. 24, who was put into a pit without water (except ſuch as flowed from his eyes) where he muſt either dye for want of meat, or dye for being meat to wilde Beaſts; and yet in the meane time his Brethren, though they ſaw the anguiſh of his ſoul, *Geneſ.* 42. 21, (made viſible and tranſparent through the windowes of his weeping eyes, bended knees, begging tongue, folded hands,) did moſt barbarouſly *ſit down to eate*. I dare boldly ſay, they ſaid no grace with a good heart, either before meate or after.

38. Juſt ſuch is the cruelty of many of us (who profeſſe Chriſtianity) to our Brethren in the Countrey, becauſe as yet the City of *London* is as the Land of *Goſhen*, being light when all the reſt is darkned with miſeries: they lay not to heart the afflictions of *Joſeph*, which our Countrey-men do ſuffer. Where is the man that founds a retreat to his ſoul when he feeles it marching too faſt in [2]myrth, who abates a diſh of his Table out of principles of Conſcience, though perchance many doe out of reaſons of thrift, and I am afraid all ſhortly muſt doe out of neceſſitie? Well, if we be not the more penitent, it

---

[1] ſixth.   [2] mirth.

may come to passe that that sad dance which hath beene led all over the Kingdome will come to us to this City at last, and God grant we pay not the [1]Musique for all the rest.

39. Remember *Vriah* who kept a Campe in the Court, and would not enjoy those pleasures the marriage-bed reached unto him. Thinke of *Mephibosheth*, lame but loyall, who went not out with *David* in his person, but attended him with his affections, and during the Kings absence, *dressed not his feet* (enough to gangrene them), as not caring for his owne feet, whilest his [1]Soveraignes head was in danger. Seriously consider *Nehemiah*, who sympathized with the calamities of *Jerusalem*, which sadded his countenance even in the presence of the King. Two things onely can make a Courtier sad: sicknesse (which cannot be dissembled), and his Princes displeasure. *Nehemiah* had neither of these; he was in perfect health; and he stood *rectus in curia*, right in his [2]Soveraignes esteeme, as appeares, *Nehemiah* 2. 2, by the Kings favourable and familiar questioning him, *Why is thy countenance sad, seeing thou art not sicke?* So then, it was nothing else but the impression of the suffering of Gods Saints, which clouded the brightnesse of his countenance with sadnesse. And God grant we having the same cause, we may have the same compassion with him. Amen.

---

[1] Musick.   [2] Sovereigns.

FINIS.

A SERMON PREACHED

AT
THE COLLEGIAT
Church of S. *Peter* in *Westminster*,
on the 27. of March, being the day
OF
HIS MAJESTIES
INAUGURATION.

By *Thomas Fuller*, B.D.

LONDON,
Printed for *John Williams*, at the signe of the Crowne
in Saint Pauls Church-yard, 1643.

["THE Synode taking into confideration the moft ineftimable benefits which this Church enjoyeth under the peaceable and bleffed government of our dread Sovereign Lord King CHARLES; And finding that afwell the godly Chriftian Emperours, in the former times, as our own moft religious Princes fince the Reformation, have caufed the dayes of their Inaugurations to be publikely celebrated by all their Subjects, with Prayers and Thanksgiving to Almighty God; and that there is a particular form of Prayer appointed by Authority for that day and purpofe; And yet with all confidering how negligent fome people are in the obfervance of this day, in many places of this Kingdom; Doth therefore decree and ordain, that all manner of perfons within the Church of *England*, fhall from henceforth celebrate and keep the morning of the faid day in coming diligently and reverently unto their Parifh Church or Chappell at the time of Prayer, and there continuing all the while that the prayers, preaching, or other fervice of the day endureth; in teftimony of their humble gratitude to God for fo great a bleffing, and dutifull affections to fo benign and merciful a Sovereign. And for the better execution of this our Ordinance, the holy Synode doth ftraitly require and charge, and by Authority hereof enableth all Archbifhops, Bifhops, Deanes, Deanes and Chapters, Archdeacons, and other Ecclefiafticall perfons, having exempt or peculiar jurisdiction; as alfo all Chancellors, Commiffaries, and Officials in the Church of *England*, that they enquire into the keeping of the fame in their Vifitations, and punifh fuch as they find to be delinquent, according as by Law they are to cenfure, and punifh thofe who wilfully abfent themfelves from Church on Holydayes. And that the faid day may be the better obferved, We do enjoyn that all Church-wardens fhall provide at the Parifh charge, two of thofe books at leaft, appointed for that day, and if there be any want of the faid book in any Parifh, they fhall prefent the fame at all Vifitations refpectively."
—§ ii. of *Conftitutions and Canons Ecclefiafticall Treated upon by the Archbifhops of Canterbury and York, Prefidents of the Convocations for the refpective Provinces of Canterbury and York, and the reft of the Bifhops and Clergie of thofe Provinces; And agreed upon with the Kings Majefties Licence in their feverall Synods begun at London and York.* 1640. *In the yeer of the Reign of our Sovcraign Lord Charles, by the grace of God, King of England, Scotland, France, and Ireland, the Sixteenth. And now Publifhed for the due obfervance of them, by His Majefties Authority under the Great Seal of England. London: Printed by Robert Barker, Printer to the Kings Moft Excellent Majeftie: And by the Affignes of John Bill.* 1640. 4to.]

[Introduction.

THE following remarkable Sermon, preached on the Anniverfary of the Coronation of CHARLES I., definitely marks a point in the decline of the Royal intereft in the metropolis, and as fuch is of importance to the hiftorian. From it alfo may be derived an illuftration of the moral heroifm of the preacher, who was at the time one of the very few Royalift clergymen left in London. The occafion caufed many of them to declare themfelves to be "Cavalier parfons." At Cambridge, as Vice-chancellor of the Univerfity, BROUNRIG, bifhop of Exeter, was on the fame day preaching the Inauguration-Sermon of the King, "wherein many paffages were diftafted by the Parliament party": he was in confequence banifhed the Univerfity and deprived of his office there (Fuller's *Hiftory of the Univ. Camb.* § 9, ¶ 39). The ejections of the London clergy had, indeed, for fome time been actively profecuted; but a "great and general purgation" took place during two or three months preceding the date of FULLER's Sermon. The fequeftered livings were occupied without lofs of time by Parliamentary adherents, who were chiefly taken, the Church-Hiftorian avers, from the ranks of young ftudents from the Univerfities, "whofe orders got the fpeed of their degrees;" it being deemed neceffary that all pulpits "muft be made, like the whole earth before the building of Babel, of one language and of one fpeech" (Book xi. § ix. ¶¶ 32, 34). Under fuch circumftances the delivery of a Royalift fermon, upon a date which did not fall upon a faft day, was fomewhat anachronous. The Editor was once in doubt of the real date of the difcourfe; becaufe when the 1654 edition of fome of thefe Sermons was reiffued, FULLER or his publifher placed it before that delivered upon Innocents-day, and the anonymous biographer (page 16) gave to it the date of 1642, in which year Coronation-day, falling on a Sunday, was pretty generally obferved in the city. But internal evidence makes it clear that the difcourfe belongs to the *nineteenth* anniverfary of the King's acceffion, Monday, 27th March, 1643. As to the origin of thefe fervices, fee Lathbury's *Hiftory of the Book of Common Prayer*, 1858, pages 123 *feq.* and 158. The annual obfervances formed a fubject of inquiry in the Vifitation Articles of fome of the diocefes. The obfervance of the day, which had in fome places fallen into neglect even before the civil troubles began, had been difcuffed at the firft Convocation of the year 1640; and the fecond of the Canons of that affembly had enjoined the better keeping of the day (see page cclxiv. *anteà*); but the injunction fared none the better on account of the illegal Canons which accompanied it. The events of the year 1642 had, however, produced in

London a change of feeling in regard to the cuftomary fervice. The Prayer-book was not yet abolifhed by ftatute, although, as FULLER ftates, it had been taken away out of moft places (¶ 8); and the attacks upon it were unchecked. The King was regarded with a growing disfavour; and already the unfavourable omens attending the firft Coronation-day of the "White King" were being recalled by the fuperftitious. Peace-negotiations, it is true, were ftill under difcuffion (¶ 27); but the breach between the King and his people had grown too wide to be healed. One of the Chaplains avowed that there "was as much difference between the treaty and peace as between heaven and hell!" (*Athen. Oxon.* iii. 279.)

In the Journals of the Parliament, fome light is thrown upon the obfervance of this critical Coronation-day. From that fource the firft intimation of the neglect of the cuftomary celebration may be obtained. The matter gave rife to two divifions in the Lower Houfe, for the fecond of which, to judge from the large numbers of votes, there was a "whip." In the Lords' Houfe on Friday, 24th March, 1642-3, it was ordered, "That the King's Mafter-gunner fhall have Powder allowed him to charge the Ordnance at the *Tower*, to fhoot off at the Coronation-day, according to the ufual Manner" (*Journals*, v. 667b). On the felf-fame day, in the Commons' Houfe, an explicit order to the contrary was given: "That the Lieutenant of the *Tower* be required and enjoined not to fire the Ordnance in the *Tower* nor the Chambers upon *Tower Hill, London*, on *Monday* next; in regard of the great Expence it will caufe of Powder, and the great Concourfe of People: And the Committee for the *Tower* is to take care that this Order be obferved." It is noticeable that thofe who fupported this meafure were extreme politicians of the "pious and movement party," viz., Sir ROBERT HARLEY, Sir NEVILLE POOLE, Sir WALTER EARLE, Mr. STRODE, &c. A motion the next day for the reconfideration of the order was moved by members of the moderate party, amongft whom were Mr. HOLLES, Sir PETER WENTWORTH, and Sir JOHN EVELYN of Surrey; and the order was in confequence revoked by 75 votes againft 57. It was then refolved that a proportion of powder not exceeding twenty barrels fhould be taken from the ftores in the Tower for the purpofe required (*Journals*, iii. 16b, 18a). It is noticeable that Good Friday, which fell five days later (31ft March), was not kept as heretofore, for both Houfes of Parliament fat; and that the preceding Chriftmas of 1642, falling upon a Sunday, had prepared the way for neglecting the next public obfervance of the hallowed feftival. In that year 1643 Chriftmas-day fell upon Monday; and the day was difregarded chiefly through the influence of the Scotch Commiffioners. In the following year Chriftmas-day was ordered to be kept as a faft:—

> "Gone are the golden days of yore,
>   When Chriftmas was an high day,
> Whofe fports we now fhall fee no more:
>   'Tis turned into Good Friday."

By this time all were more eager to keep up the anniverfary of their entering into the Solemn League and Covenant as "England's Coronation-day" (See Heyricke's *Harmonious Confent of the Minifters* . . . . *of Lancafhire*, 1648, 4to., page 19).

In admirable adaptation to the fentiments of this Coronation Sermon was the Abbey in which it was preached. Although the difcourfe has not come under the notice of the picturefque pen of the prefent diftinguifhed Dean (*Memorials of Weftminfter Abbey*, 3rd ed., page 502 ; but fee page 687), it is unqueftionably one of the great Sermons connected with a critical period in the hiftory of the venerable pile. After this occafion no other difcourfe as full of loyalty to the throne was preached until the cuftom was revived when, eighteen years afterwards, Divine Providence (to ufe FULLER's words) affigned to England another King (*Church-Hiftory*, Book xi. § 1, ¶ 31). Upon the Anniverfary of 1644, the war was raging more keenly, and FULLER was amidft it ; the day, moreover, was the monthly Wednefday faft ; and if in the difcourfes in the Parliament's quarters on that occafion the Coronation-day was named at all, it was as a fuperftitious obfervance of the paft.

On the delivery of the prefent Inauguration Sermon, to a congregation largely compofed of moderate Royalifts, the hiftoric glories of the Abbey were unbroken and unobfcured. The foundation ftill had its Chapter. The Dean had, indeed, in the middle of the former year, abandoned his Deanery for his Archbifhopric, where the King was then quartered. But the fub-Dean, Dr. NEWELL, ftill held a nominal fway ; and in his hands the felection of the Preachers would lie. As a confequence of the confufion in ecclefiaftical affairs, no record of FULLER's Sermon appears to have been preferved. There is a blank in the Chapter-book from 1642 to 1660. In the Muniment-room at Weftminfter Abbey, however, are feveral documents relating to the payment of preachers during the civil war ; but FULLER's name is not met with. One fuch lift begins in February, 1643-4, and extends up to 1ft December, 1645. On 27th March, 1644, the following entry occurs :—

"ffaft daie { Forenoone | Afternoone } £01. 00. 00."
              Dr. SMITH   Dr. SMITH

This paper fhows that minifters preached fermons as follows : Dr. SMITH preached 179 fermons ; Mr. BELL, 21 ; Mr. JACKSON, 25 ; Mr. THACHE, 13 ; Mr. GOODWIN, 1 ; Mr. TINSLEY, 1 ; Mr. LATHUM, 1 ; Mr. DACIE, 3 ; Dr. TATE, 2 ; Mr. NYE, 15.

After the delivery of FULLER's Sermon, changes in the Abbey rapidly took place. It was in the fucceeding month that the Committee was appointed, with the well-known iconoclaft Sir ROBERT HARLEY for its chairman, for the purpofe of demolifhing any "monuments of fuperftition or idolatry in the Abbey Church at Weftminfter or the windows thereof" (*Commons Journals*, 24th April, iii. 57*b* ; alfo 63*a*). On the 29th April Mr. WHITE, "one of the finging men of the Abbey," and therefore, it may be affumed, one of FULLER's moft enthufiaftic hearers, was fent a prifoner to Winchefter Houfe, for "feveral contempts committed by him" againft the Houfe of Commons, "in reading of Declarations, and fixing up of Proclamations" (*Ibid.* iii. 64*a*). It was in the fucceeding Auguft that the Houfe of Commons made an order that the fub-Dean and Prebends were to give up the ufe of their pulpit every Sunday afternoon for fuch minifters as were appointed by the Houfe (*Ibid.* 21ft Auguft, iii. 213*a*).

FULLER had often entered the Abbey, "an acre fown with royal feed," and thoughtfully gazed on the evidences of piety and mortality (see *Worthies of England*, § Hartfordfhire, page 20); and when fhut up in beleaguered ftrongholds in the Weft, would direct his thoughts to the national Sanctuary as naturally as the Ifraelite in a ftrange land turned to Zion. In one of his meditations he utters a prayer with reference to Henry VII.'s chapel : " God grant I may once again see it with the Saint who belongs, our Soveraign, there in a wel-conditioned Peace !" (*Good Thoughts in Bad Times*, § Mixt Contemplations, No. vi. page 205, ed. 1645.)

In ¶ 16 of the Sermon there is a reference to the battle of Edge-hill. As to the prefence of CHARLES I. in that engagement, FULLER is perhaps referring to a fentence in the King's Declaration to his Subjects, in which he attributed the protection of himfelf and children to the mercy and goodnefs of Almighty God. The following details are given by the hiftorian ECHARD :—

"The King Himfelf was in no fmall Danger, together with the two young Princes, who were on Horfe-Back on each fide of him. His Majefty feeing his Troops give way, mov'd to fuftain them, and the two Princes with him, when he was advif'd to leave the Field, and no longer expofe his Perfon. He thought the Advice good as far as it refpected his Children, but look'd upon it as Unprincely to forfake them who had forfaken all to ferve him. He propofed it therefore to the Duke of *Richmond* to conduct them up the Hill, but that loyal Lord excus'd himfelf, begging leave not to abandon his Majefty ; who next apply'd Himfelf to the Earl of *Dorfet* for the fame purpofe, but was anfwer'd in his accuftom'd jocofe Manner, *That all the Kings in the World fhou'd not make him retire when he was to fight.* At laft the two Princes retired by the Affiftance of one of the Gentlemen Penfioners, not without eminent Danger of being taken in an Ambufh by the Way. In the mean while the King led on his Party with Sword in Hand, and his Prefence giving his Troops frefh Vigour, the Royal Standard was retaken by the valiant Captain *John Smith*, who for that great Action was made a Knight Banneret in the Field, and honour'd with bearing that Standard he had fo bravely recover'd." (*Hiftory of England*, vol. ii. page 352.)

This difcourfe deals in part with the fubject of the foregoing Sermon, viz. Peace. An accommodation, as is feen by the numerous petitions prefented early in the year, was regarded with general favour : " in truth," fays SANDERSON (*Hiftory of King Charles*, 1658, page 609), " honeft men were weary of war." In the interval between the delivery of the two fermons, the bafis of a peace-negotiation had been difcuffed, and the preliminary arrangements were at length drawing to a succefsful end. On the very day, indeed, when FULLER was expatiating on what he expreffively calls " the fubftance of earthly bleffings, the fhadow of heavenly happinefs " (¶ 12), a treaty was beginning. This treaty was one of the moft earneft and important that had yet been entered upon. The Commiffioners who had gone to treat with the King were ALGERNON, Earl of NORTHUMBERLAND, WILLIAM PIERREPOINT, Esq. (who was afterwards one of FULLER's patrons), Sir WILLIAM ARMYN, Sir JOHN HOLLAND, and BULSTRODE WHITELOCK, Efq.

To the Reader.

SERMONS have their Doomes, partly according to the capacities, partly according to the affections of the Hearers. *Some said of our Saviour, He is a good man. Others, Nay, but he deceiveth the People.* The bitter Health which my Master began, is now come to mee (the lowest at his Table) to pledge. I am therefore enforced to print my poore paines, not to get applause, but to assert my Innocency; and yet indeed he gaineth that can save in this Age. Reade with Judgement; censure with Charitie. As for those who have unmercifully pre-sentenced me, my Revenge is in desiring that they may be forgiven. I count their words spoken in passion, and (according to a Doctrine in this Sermon [¶ 11] delivered) such Speeches must be favourably interpreted. Meane time, let me say with SAMUEL, *God forbid that I should sin against the Lord in ceasing to pray* (such an omission of Pietie were a commission of Profanenesse) for the blessed and happy agreement of the King and Parliament, and desire thee to joyne with mee, whosoever shall reade this weake worke of

Thine in Christ Jesus,
THOMAS FULLER.

cclxx   INTRODUCTION (from page cclxviii.)

They all feem to have been actuated by a real defire to bring about an honourable fettlement. On the bafis of the propofitions which had been exchanged the treaty itfelf began. It lafted "twenty Days, according to Agreement, from the 27th of March to the 15th of April. And yet in all this Time, though there were many Conferences and Debates, only the firft Propofition on both Sides was fully canvaffed and difcuffed" (Echard, *Hiftory of England*, ii. 398). A fummary of all the proceedings, with obfervations upon the carriage of the Commiffioners, will be found in WHITELOCK (pages 68 *feq.*), who regrets that their labours and hazards were of no effect: "All good Englifhmen, lovers of the peace of their country, were troubled and difappointed." Various opinions were expreffed as to the caufe of the failure of thefe negotiations. WHITELOCK afcribes it to the King being fo unhappy as to have a better opinion of others' judgments than his own, though they were weaker than his own; "and of this we had experience to our great trouble." MAY more juftly afcribes it to a mutual difinclination to make conceffions: "In vaine was this Treaty: fo high the demands were judged to be on both fides that there feemed no poffibility of ever meeting. Where the fault lay I judge not; but the Parliament after many Meffages between *London* and *Oxford*, at laft fent for their Commiffioners home again, who returned to London upon the 17 of April; upon which the Lord Generall advanced with his Army (as aforefaid) to befiege *Reading*" (*Hiftory of the Parliament*, lib. iii. cap. ii. p. 37). ECHARD (ii. 400-1) refers to large promifes that were privately made to the King if he would but at prefent comply with "the unhappy circumftances;" but he adds that if the nature of the propofitions fubmitted to the King, as degrading as any fent before, were confidered,— "their fequeftering of the Bishops Lands, their rifling of *Somerfet-Houfe*, which belonged to the Queen, and other Acts both of Power and Refentment, during the very Time of this Treaty"—it could hardly be thought that any compliances on the King's side could have produced a peace.

The *Inauguration Sermon*, which has never been reprinted fince FULLER's day, is here taken from a 4to. copy in the Editor's poffeffion (pp. iv. + 26), the title-page of which has been copied at page 263.

There was alfo another 4to. edition (pp. and title-page as before) with frefh fetting up and different fignatures. Copies of this edition may be diftinguifhed by the preacher's name on the title-page being placed between two lines.

In 1654 a 12mo. edition (pp. iv. + 30) appeared: "*London*, Printed by *Will. Bently* for *John Williams* at the Crown in S. *Pauls* Church-yard. Anno Dom. 1654." On the title-page was the oval device of the Sun in an efcutcheon encircled by the legend "Deus · eft · nobis · fol · et · scutum," which is often found on the title-pages of WILLIAMS's books. There are many variations in fpelling, &c., between this and the former copies. Some of the principal differences in this 12mo. edition are placed in the foot-notes.]

A SERMON

Preached at the Collegiat Church of S. PETER in WESTMINSTER,

on the 27. of *March*, being the day of His MAJESTIES Inauguration.

2 SAM. 19. 30.

Yea, let him take All, forasmuch as my Lord the KING *is come againe in peace unto his owne Houſe.*

1. IT is as naturall for malicious men to backbite as for dogs to bite, or ſerpents to ſting. See this in *Ziba*, who raiſed a falſe report on his Maſter *Mephiboſheth*, and accuſed him to *David* (when he departed from Jeruſalem) of no leſſe then high Treaſon, as if in *Davids* abſence he affected the Kingdom for himſelf. Well was *Ziba* ſtudied in the Art of ſlandering, to charge home, and draw his arrow to the head; for in hainous accuſations, when the wound is cured, the very ſcarre will kill; and though the innocence of the party accuſed may chance to cleare the main debt, yet the arrerages of the ſuſpition will be enough to undoe him. But I wonder not at *Ziba's* accuſing *Mephiboſheth*; I wonder at *Davids* beleeving *Ziba*, at the firſt information, of a ſingle witnes, and him a ſervant againſt his maſter, without further proofe, as hearing both parties. To proceed to cenſure and fine *Mephiboſheth* with the loſſe of his lands was a piece of unjuſt juſtice wherein *David* cannot be excuſed, much leſſe defended. All that can be ſaid for him is this, That not *David*, but *Davids* diſtractions paſſed this ſentence, ſo that, being in feare and fright and flight, it can ſcarce be accounted his deliberate Act: once *he*

said in his haste All men are lyars, and now being on the spurre in his speed he beleeves *Mephibosheth* was a Traytor.

2. But it pleased Gods providence that in this Chapter the tide was turned, and *David* returned to Jerusalem, where *Mephibosheth* meeting him was admitted to speake in his owne behalfe, and makes a plaine and pithy narration of the matter. Innocence hath so clear a complexion that she needs no painting; and a good cause consisting in matter of fact, when it is plainly told, is sufficiently pleaded. He shewes how that *violenta detentio* withheld him from attending on *David*, being no lack of his loyalty, but the lamenesse of his legs, which might and should have been helpt, had not *Ziba* hindred it on purpose in refusing to saddle his Asse: And thus having wrong'd his master at home, he then traduced him abroad, transferring his own guile to make it become the others guiltinesse. Soon did *David* perceive his errour, and to make amends did order, That the lands should be held in Copartnership betwixt them; *Mephibosheth* have one moiety, and *Ziba* the other: *Why speaketh thou any more of thy matters? I have said it, Thou and* Ziba *divide the lands*.

3. This did not satisfie *Mephibosheth*, not becauſe it was too little, but becauſe it was too much: Hee now needs nothing, seeing his [1]Soveraign is returned in safety: and therefore desires that *Ziba* may have All, according to *Davids* former appointment, *Yea, let him take All*. This he did partly perchance to assert the Honour of *David*. It should never be said that *David* said any thing, and it was not done; what grants he made, *Mephibosheth* would make good, though with the losse of his lands. It beares no proportion to the greatnesse of Princes, nor stands with the statelinesse of States, to say and unsay, doe and undoe, order and disorder againe; whose first resolutions are presumed to bee grounded on so good reason, they shall need no revocation. But chiefly he did it to shew the Hyperbole of his happinesse and Transcendency of his joy, conceived at *Davids* safe return; joy which sweld up him in full meaſure, *pressed downe, shaken together, and running over*. Yet, left the leaſt drop of so precious a

---

[1] Sovereign *throughout*.

[1643.] *Inauguration.* 2 Sam. xix. 30.

liquor as this was (being the spirits of loyalty distill'd) should be spilt on the ground, let us gather it up with our best attention, and powre it in our hearts to practise it as it flowes from the Text, *Yea, let him take All, &c.*

4. The words contain a large Grant, and a just consideration moving thereunto. The large Grant, *let him take All:* wherein observe the Granter, *Mephibosheth:* The Grantee, *Ziba:* and the thing Granted, *All* (*i.e.* house, and lands, and rents, and profits, and emoluments, and obventions, and hereditaments, with the appendants and the appurtenances thereunto belonging). What the warinesse of moderne men deviseth in many words, and all twisted together (few enough to hold in this litigious age, wherein a span of land cannot be conveyed in lesse [1]then a span of parchment), see all these words summ'd up in this one word *All* in my Text: *let him take All.*

Secondly, Here is the consideration of the Granter, which consisteth not in any mony paid, or service perform'd by the Grantee; but onely in respect of a generall good which God hath bestowed on *David*, and in him on all Israel: *Forasmuch as my Lord the King is come in Peace to his owne House.*

5. In prosecuting which parts I could desire that my discourse might have been open and champion to proceed in an even and continued style; but my Text is incumbred with so many difficulties that my Sermon must rise and fall into hills and dales of Objections and Answers, which Answers, as so many fruitfull vallies, shall afford us plentifull store of profitable observations.

6. *Objection:* The first hill which we are to climbe is an objection, if not within the walls, yet surely in the suburbs of my Text. Why? (may some say;) me thinks *David* doth *Mephibosheth* justice but by [2]halfes; For when his Innocence so plainly appeared, the slanderer should have been soundly punished: *Thou and Ziba divide the land:* He should rather

---

[1] than *throughout the Sermon generally.*   [2] half.

have divided *Ziba's* head from his shoulders; or of all the land leave him only one Tree, wherein hee ſhould be juſtly executed as a land-mark to [1]forwarne all deceitfull ſervants how they tread on ſo unwarrantable wayes. What hope was there he would hereafter prove faithfull to his Prince that was falſe to his Maſter? Yea, this was contrary to the fundamentall lawes of *Davids* family: *Pſal.* 101. 5, *Who ſo privily ſlandereth his neighbour, him will I cut off:* Whereas *Ziba* here was ſo far from being cut off that he was both freely forgiven and fairly rewarded for the malicious diſſervice he had done his maſter.

7. *Reſponſe:* I anſwer, wee muſt conſider that *Ziba* was a conſiderable man in his tribe of *Benjamin*, and probably might make a great impreſſion on the people: Beſides, great was his experience, being an old Courtier of *Sauls*, greater the [2]allyance to him, and dependance on him, having fifteen ſonnes and twenty ſervants (all now officiouſly attending on King *David* at his return, as it is in the ſeventeenth verſe of this chapter). Greateſt of all was his will and skill to doe miſchief; and therefore no wonder if *David* was unwilling to offend him. Secondly, conſider *David* was at this time in the *Non-age* (not to ſay Infancy) of his new-recovered Kingdome. Wary Phyſitians will not give ſtrong purges to little children; and *David* thought it no wiſdome at this time, on theſe termes, as matters ſtood with him, to be ſevere in his proceedings; but rather by all indeerments to [3]tye and oblige the affections of his people the faſter unto him. We may ſee this in the matter of *Shimei*, which immediately concerned *David* himſelfe: Yea, when by *Abiſhai* he was urged and preſt to puniſh him, *Shall not* Shimei *be put to death for this, becauſe he hath curſed the Lords annointed?* Yet *Davids* policie was ſo farre above his revenge that he not onely flatly rejected the motion, but alſo ſharply reproved the mover: *What have I to doe with you, yee ſonnes of* Zerviah, *that yee ſhould this day be adverſaries unto me? Shall there any man be put to death this day in* Iſrael? *for doe I not know that I am this day King over* Iſrael? He would not have the conduits run bloud on the day of his new

---

[1] forewarne. [2] alliance. [3] tie.

Coronation, nor would he have the firſt page in the ſecond Edition of his Soveraignty written in red letters, but rather ſought (*by all acts of grace*) to gaine the good will of his Subjects. Hence wee obſerve,

8. Magiſtrates ſometimes are faine to permit what they cannot conveniently puniſh for the preſent. Thus ſometimes Chirurgions leave their ulcers unlaunch't, either becauſe they are not ripe, or becauſe perchance they have not all their neceſſary inſtruments about them. And indeed, if Statiſts perceive that from the preſent removing of an inconvenience, a greater miſchief will inevetably follow, 'twere madneſſe to undoe a ſtate for the preſent, for feare it will be undone hereafter. Perchance the wiſdome of our Parliament may ſuffer in the cenſures of ſuch who fathome myſteries of ſtate by their owne ſhallow capacities, for ſeeming to ſuffer Sectaries and Schiſmaticks to ſhare and divide in Gods ſervice with the *Mephiboſheths*, the quiet and peaceable children of our Church. And indeed ſuch Sectaries take a great ſhare to themſelves, having taken away all the Common Prayer out of moſt places, and under pretence to aboliſh ſuperſtition, have almoſt baniſh't decency out of Gods Church: But no doubt the Sages of our State want not will, but wait a time when with more conveniency and leſſe diſturbance (though ſlowly, ſurely) they will reſtraine ſuch turbulent ſpirits with *David* in my Text, who was rather contented then well pleaſed to paſſe by *Ziba* for the preſent.

9. *Objection*: Yea, but (may ſome ſay) this ſpeech of *Mephiboſheth* cannot be allowed either in piety or policie: For if he ſpake true, then he was a foole; and if he ſpake falſe, then he was a flatterer. If he ſpake true, then he was a foole: for what wiſe man would at once give away all that he hath? Charity may impart her branches, but ſhee muſt not part with her root: The wiſdome of our grand Charter hath provided, That no offender (though for an hainous fault) ſhould be ſo heavily amerced, but alwayes [1]*ſalvo ſuo ſibi contenemento*: What favour is afforded to malefactors, Charity

---

[1] [Stubbs's *Select Charters*, page 291.]

surely should give to ¹it felfe, as not thereby to prejudice and impaire her owne livelihood. I commend the well bounded and well grounded bountie of *Zacheus*, Luke 19. 8 : *Behold, Lord, halfe of my goods I give to the poore:* But with *Mephibosheth* to give All his goods, and that not to the poore, but to a couzening cheating fervant, was an action of madneffe. How would he doe hereafter to fubfift ? Did he expect hereafter to bee miraculoufly fed with *Manna* dropt into his mouth ? Or in his old age would he turne Court almef-man, and live on the bounty of others ? And grant he could fhift for himfelfe, yet what fhould *Micah* his fonne doe, and his future pofteritie ? If he fpake falfe, then hee was a flatterer : and faid it onely to footh *David*, when hee meant no fuch matter : But Court-holy-water never quenched any thirftie foule. Flatterers are the worft of tame beafts, which tickle Princes even to their utter deftruction.

· 10. *Refponfe:* I anfwer, He was neither foole nor flatterer, but an affectionate Subject, and at the prefent in a mighty paffion of gladneffe. But firft, we muft know that it ²behooved *Mephibosheth* to do fomething extraordinary ; and in his expreffions to exceed the fize and ftandard of common language, were it only to unftain his credit from the fufpition of difloyalty *Ziba* had caft upon him. Secondly, *Mephibosheth* was confident and well affured that whatfoever *David* did for the prefent, yet hereafter, when fufficiently informed of *Mephibosheths* innocence, he would make not only competent, but plentiful provifion for him. But laftly and chiefly, we muft know that thefe words of *Mephibosheth* were fpoken in a great paffion of joy ; and paffionate fpeeches muft alwayes fue in Chauncery, and plead to have the equitie of a candide and charitable conftruction allowed them. Let us not therefore bee over-rigid in examining his words when we knew his meaning, that hee was affected with an unmanageable joy at *Davids* fafe return : Rather hence let us learne,

11. Speeches fpoken in paffion muft not be ftretcht fo farre as they may be ftrain'd, but have a favourable interpretation ; for fuch is the very nature of paffion that it can fcarce doe

---

¹ its felfe *in the other* 4to. *ed.*   ² behoved *in the other two editions.*

any thing but it muft over-doe. Seeft thou then the foule of a man fhaking with feare or foaring with joy, or burning in anger, or drowning in griefe? meet his words with a charitable acception of them, and [1]defalke the extravigancies of his expreffions: *The wringing of the nofe bringeth forth bloud,* faith wife *Agur, Prov.* 30. 33. And he who fhall preffe and wrack and torture fpeeches fpoken in paffion, may make a bloudy conftruction thereof, befides, beyond, againft the intent of him that fpake it: But let us content our felves that we know their meaning, and not profecute (much leffe perfecute) their words too farre, as here in my Text, wee know the mind of *Mephibofheth* was to fhew That hee was foundly, fincerely, and from the ground of his heart glad when he faid, *Yea, let him take All, forafmuch as, &c.*

12. Come we now to the confideration of the Grant: *Forafmuch as my Lord the King is come in peace unto his owne houfe.* Behold in the words a confluence of many joyes together. Firft, *The King:* there is matter of gladneffe for all Subjects in generall. Secondly, *My Lord the King: Mephibofheth* was *Davids* fervant in Ordinary, or rather his extraordinary Favorite, and this made his joy to be greater. Thirdly, *Is come againe:* is come back, is returned, and therefore more welcome after long wanting: The interpofing of the night renders the arifing of the funne more defired: Princes prefence after fome abfence more precious. Fourthly, *To his owne houfe.* Why? were not all the houfes in Ifrael *Davids* houfes? Are not Kings alwaies at home whilft in their Kingdom? True, all the houfes in Ifrael were *Davids* owne, not by his private ufe, but Paramount [2]Soveraignty over them; whereas his Palace in Jerufalem was peculiarly his owne, by his particular poffeffion thereof, and proper refidence therein. Fifthly and laftly, *Come in Peace:* in Peace, which is the fubftance of all earthly bleffings, and the fhadow of heavenly happineffe.

13. *Objection:* Yea, but (may fome fay) *Mephibofheth* doth not meafure out [3]*Davids* happineffe to the beft advantage, nor

---

[1] defalk. [2] Sovereignty. [3] *David's* (ter).

doth hee give the true Emphasis to his honour; for *David* returned with victory. Had hee not gotten a glorious conquest under the conduct of *Joab*, in the forrest of *Ephraim*, over all his enemies? Twenty thousand slaine by the sword, more devoured with the wood, the rest routed, their Captain kill'd, and all with a losse [1]of so little on *Davids* side that none at all is mentioned: But *Mephibosheth* takes no notice of *Davids* Trophies and Triumphs, but either out of envie, or ignorance, or both, concealing his conquests, huddles all up under the name of Peace: *Forasmuch as my Lord the King is come to his owne house in Peace.*

14. I answer, *Mephibosheth* therefore suppresseth victory, and mentioneth Peace only, because victories are not valuable in themselves but in order and tendencie as they conduce to the attaining of Peace. Excellently doth the Apostle argue the distance and dignity of men above women, from the end and intent of their creation, 1 *Corinth.* 11. 9: *Neither was the man created for the woman, but the woman for the man*: so Peace was never made for victory, but victory for Peace; as all Meanes, even by Indentures drawne by nature, are bound Apprentices to serve the End their Master. Let not therefore the maid grow so proud as to strive for equipage, much lesse for priority with her Mistresse: victory doth the work for Peace, and therefore Peace alone is mentioned by *Mephibosheth*.

15. *Responce:* Secondly, I answer, If *Davids* conquests had atchieved against the *Edomites, Amonites,* or *Amorites,* or *Moabites,* or *Midianites,* or *Syrians,* or *Sidonians,* or *Egyptians,* or *Philistines,* or any [2]forraine foe, *Mephibosheth* no doubt would have made mention thereof to the purpose: But *David* was thus unhappy in his very happinesse, That this victory was gotten over his owne Subjects. The ribs of *Jacob* did grate one against the other, and in that civill--uncivill warre many worthy men lost their lives unworthily. Whose lives there prodigally spent, had they been thriftily expended in a [1]forraine designe, had been sufficient to have purchased *David* another Kingdome: Say not that such as

---

[1] of *omitted in the other* 4to. *ed.*   [2] forraign.

were flain were none of *Davids* Subjects, but Traytors and Rebels, which did oppofe their Prince and refift their ¹Soveraigne. For here we muft know that they were *Davids* Subjects. Firft, *de jure*, they ought to have been his Subjects; and a joynt, though out of joynt, is a joynt ftill, though diflocated out of its proper place. Secondly, fome of them were *Davids* Subjects *de facto*: *Two hundred men went out of* Jerufalem *to* Hebron *in their fimplicity, and they knew not any thing*, Chap. 15. 11 ; onely their innocence was practifed upon by the policie of *Abfolom*. Thirdly and laftly, they were all prefum'd his Subjects *de futuro*: when their eyes were opened and they faw their owne errours, they would either return of themfelves, or be eafily reduced to their former obedience. Wifely therefore did *Mephibofheth* wave the mention of victory, which very word would have been a fad remembrancer to call to *Davids* mind the loffe of his Subjects; and rather folds up all under the notion of Peace, as a cover (if leffe gaudy, furely more pleafing): *Forafmuch as my Lord the King is come in peace to his own houfe.*

16. Pious Princes can take no delight in victories over their own Subjects. For when they caft up their Audits, they fhall find themfelves lofers in their very gaining. Nor can they properly be faid to have *wonne the day*, which at the beft is but a twilight, being benighted with a mixture of much forrow and fadneffe. For Kings being the Parents of their Country, muft needs grieve at the deftruction of their children. Who knowes the love of a Parent, but a Parent? Maidens are incompetent Judges of Mothers affections. How doth the affectionate Father when hee beats his child firft feele the blowes ftruck through himfelfe? I dare boldly fay, that in that unhappy *Aceldama,* wherein the perfon of our Soveraigne was prefent, *A fword did pierce through his owne heart,* in the fame fenfe as it is faid of the Virgin *Mary, Luke* 2. 35. For though (thankes be to God) divine providence did *cover his head in the day of battell,* as it were miraculoufly commanding the bullets, which flew about and refpected no perfons, *not to touch his Annointed;* yet notwithftanding his foule was fhot through with griefe to behold a

---
¹ Sovereign *throughout.*

field fpread with his Subjects corpfes, that fcarce any paffage but either through rivelets of bloud, or over bridges of bodies. And had he got as great a victory as *David* got in the forreft of *Ephraim*, yet furely hee would have preferred Peace farre before it. Well did *Mephibofheth* know *Davids* dyet, who to pleafe his pallate makes mention onely of Peace and fuppreffeth victory: *Forafmuch as my Lord the King is come to his owne houfe in peace.*

17. But the maine [1]of Doctrine is this: All loyall Subjects ought to be glad when their Soveraigne is returned in peace. The fweeteft mufick of this Doctrine is in the clofe thereof, *in peace;* for nothing is more wofull than warre. [2] The *Lacedemonians* were wont to make their fervants drunke, and then to fhew them to their children, that they then beholding their frantick fits and apifh behaviour, once feeing might ever fhun that beaftly vice. Our fins have made this Land, which formerly was our faithfull fervant, drunke with bloud: I hope our children, feeing the miferable fruits and effects thereof, will grow fo wife and wary by their fathers follies as for ever to take heed how they ingage themfelves in fuch a civill warre againe. But why doe I compare warre to drunkenneffe? which far better may be refembled to the Devill himfelfe, feeing all thofe fymptomes that appeared in the poffeffed man, *Marke* 9, fhew themfelves too evidently in all places where warre comes: *And wherefoever he catcheth him, he teareth him, and he fometh and gnafheth with his teeth, and pineth away. And oft-times it hath caft him into the fire, and oft-times into the water to deftroy him.* Wherefoever war feizeth on City, Caftle, Town, or Village, he teareth it, making both breaches in the houfes with batteries, and fractions in mens hearts with divifions, till the place pine away, having all the marrow and moifture of the wealth thereof wafted and confumed; oft-times cafting it into the fire, burning beautifull buildings to afhes; and oft-times into the water, drowning

---

[1] main Doctrine.

[2] [This fentence with the next is in Spencer's *Store-houfe of Similes*, page 67, ¶ 279. It is entitled "Others Harms to be our Arms," and faid to be from "T. Fuller's *Ser. on K. inaugurat. at* Weftm. 1644"; and the reference is added "Juftin. *Hift.*"]

fruitfull medowes with wilfull inundations. Yea, if thefe times long continue, one of thefe two mifchiefes will inevitably come to paffe: Either (which is moft probable) both fides being fo equally poyfed, will doe as the twelve Combatants *in the field of ftrong men*, 2 Sam. 2. 16, *thruft their fwords in each other, and fo fall downe both together;* or if one party prove victorious, it will purchafe the conqueft at fo deare a price as the. deftruction of the Kingdom, which will be done before. And what is faid, *Matth.* 24. 22, of the fiege of Jerufalem, is as true of our miferable times: *And except thofe dayes were fhortened, there fhould no flefh be faved:* Would to God I could as truly adde the words that follow: *But for the Elects fake thofe dayes fhall be fhortened!* However in my Doctrine there remaines an eternall truth, that all loyall Subjects ought to be glad when their Soveraign returneth in peace.

18. Yea, may fome fay, *David* deferved to be welcommed indeed, and at his return to be entertained with all poffible expreffions of gladneffe; for he brought true religion along with him, and fetled Gods Service in the puritie and precife- neffe thereof. But now adayes all crie to have Peace, to have Peace, and care not to have Truth together with it. Yea, there be many filly *Mephibofheths* in our days that fo adore Peace that to attaine it they care not what they give away to the malignant *Ziba's* of our Kingdome. Thefe fay, *Yea, let them take All*, Lawes, and Liberties, and Priviledges, and Proprieties, and Parliaments, and Religion, and the Gofpell, and godlineffe, and God himfelfe, fo bee it that the Lord our King may come to His houfe in Peace. But let us have Peace and Truth together, both or neither; for if Peace offer to come alone, we will doe with it as *Ezechiah* did with the brazen Serpent, even breake it to pieces, and ftampe it to powder, as the dangerous Idoll of ignorant people.

19. I anfwer, God forbid, God forbid wee fhould have Peace, and not Truth with it; but to fpeak plainly, I would to God men did talk leffe of Truth and love it more, have it feldomer in their mouthes, and oftner, yea, always in their heads and hearts, to beleeve and [1]practife it. Know then that the word *Truth* is fubject to much *Homonymie*, and is taken in

---

[1] practice *in the other 4to. edition.*

feverall fenfes, according to the opinions, or rather humours of thofe that ufe it. Afke the Anabaptift what is Truth, and hee will tell you, Truth is the maintaining that the dominion over the creatures is founded in grace; and that wicked men (whereby they meane all fuch whom they fhall be pleafed to account and call fo) neither ufe the creatures right, nor have any right to ufe them, but may juftly be difpoffeffed of them. It is Truth that all goods fhould bee common, that there fhould be no civill Magiftrate, that there ought to be no warres but what they make themfelves, for which they pretend infpiration; that children ought not to be baptized till they could give a reafon of their faith, and that fuch as have been formerly, muft be rebaptized Again. Afk the Separatifts what is Truth, and they will tell you that the further from all ceremonies (though ancient and decent) the nearer to God; that it is againft the liberty of a Chriftian to be prefs'd to the forme of a fet prayer, who ought only to be Voluntaries, and follow the dictate of the fpirit; that the Minifters made in our Church are Antichriftian; with many more. Ask the Schifmaticks of thefe times what is Truth, and they will bring in abundance of their own opinions, which I fpare at this time to recite; the rather, becaufe when the wheele of their fancie is turned about, another fpoak may chance to be verticall; being fo fickle in their Tenents that what they account truth now will perchance not be counted truth by them feven yeares hence.

20. To come clofe to the anfwer, I fay that fome of their pretended truths are flat falfities, and others meere fooleries: as it is eafie to prove in time and place convenient. Secondly, Grant fome of them be truths, yet are they not of that importance and concernment as to deferve to imbroyle a Kingdome in bloud to bring them in. *David* longed for the waters of the Well of Bethlehem, 2 *Sam.* 23. 17; *but when it was brought him,* hee checkt his owne vanitie, *and would not drinke it, becaufe it was the bloud of men that went in jeopardie of their lives.* But with what heart as men, or confcience as Chriftians, can Sectaries feek to introduce their devices with fuch violence ¹unto the Church, when they know full well that

---
¹ into.

it will coft blood before it be fetled? and if it ¹e're be done, *non erit tanti*, it will not quit coft, being in themfelves flight, matters of mean confequence. Thirdly, Grant them not onely true, but important, if they be fo defirous to have them introduced, the way moft agreeable to Chriftian proceedings is to have them fairely debated, freely difputed, fully decided, firmly determined by a ftill voyce; and not that their new Gofpell fhould be given as the Law, with thundering and lightning of ²Cannon, fire and fword. Fourthly, Bee it affirmed for a certain truth, that formerly we had in our Churches all truths neceffary to falvation. Of fuch as deny this, I ask *Jofephs* queftion to his Brethren, *Is your father well? the old man, is he yet alive?* So, how fares the foules of their Sires, and the ghofts of their Grand-fathers? are they yet alive? do they ftill furvive in bliffe, in happineffe? Oh no; they are dead, dead in foule, dead in body, dead temporally, dead eternally, dead and damned, if fo be wee had not all truth neceffary to falvation before this time. Yea, let thefe that cry moft for the want of truth, fhew one rotten kernell in the whole Pomegranet, one falfe Article in all thirty-nine. Let them fhew where our Church is deficient in a neceffary truth. But thefe men know wherein their ftrength lyeth, and they had rather *creep into houfes and leade away captive filly women laden with infirmities* then to meddle with men and enter the lifts to combate with the learned Doctors of the Church.

21. But, it is further objected, *David* brought home a true Peace with him, which long lafted firm, the fhowre of ³*Abfolom's* rebellion being afterward quickly blown over. But we have caufe to fufpect our Peace will not be a true Peace; and an open wound is better then a palliate cure. Would you have us put off our Armour to be kill'd in our clothes? and bee furprized with warre on a fudden, when it will be paft our policie to prevent, or power to refift it?

22. *Anfwer*: There muft at laft be a mutuall confiding on both fides, fo that they muft count the honefty of others their onely hoftages. This the fooner it be done, the eafier it is done. For who can conceive that when both fides have

---

¹ ere.   ² Canon.   ³ *Abfaloms* (*Ziba's* in the other 4to. ed.).

suffered more wrongs they will sooner forgive, or when they have offered more wrongs be sooner forgiven? For our Kings part, let us demand of his mony what Christ ask'd of *Cæsars* coine: *Whose image is this?* CHARLES'S. And what is the superscription? RELIGIO PROTESTANTIUM, LEGES ANGLIÆ, LIBERTATES PARLIAMENTI; and hee hath caused them to be cast both in silver and gold, in pieces of severall sizes and proportions; as if thereby to shew that he intends to make good his promise both to poore and rich, great and small; and we are bound to beleeve him. Nor lesse faire are the professions of the Parliament on the other side; and no doubt but as really they intend them. But these matters belong not to us to meddle with; and as for all other politick objections against Peace, they pertain not to the Pulpit to answer. All that wee desire to see is the King re-married to the State; and we doubt not but as the Bridegroome on the one side will bee carefull to have his portion paid, *His Prerogative;* so the Brides friends entrusted for her will be sure to see her joynter setled, *the liberty of the Subject.*

23. Come wee now briefly to apply our Text to the time. And wee begin first with *the King*, as this day doth direct us; and truly he may bee called so emphatically, for his goodnesse. We may observe in our Saviour, *Mat.* 11. 7, that he spake nothing in the praise of *John Baptist* whilst the Disciples of *John Baptist* were in his presence, lest perchance he might have incurred the suspition of flattery, to commend the Master before the Servants: but the *Text* saith, *as they departed Jesus began, &c.*, to speak largely in *Johns* commendation. Seeing now the servants of our Soveraign are generally gone hence to wait on their Lord, we may now boldly, without danger to make them puft up with pride, or our selves suspected for flattery, speak that in praise of their Master which malice it selfe cannot deny. Look above him; to his God, how [1] he is pious! Look beneath; to his Subjects, how he is pitifull! Look about him; how hee is constant to his wife, carefull for his children! Look neare him; how hee is good to his

---

[1] is he *in all the instances, in the 4to. editions.*

fervants! Look far from him; how he is juft to forraigne Princes! We may fee in our Catalogue of Kings that we fhall fcarce find any but, befides the common infirmities attending on mankind, were branded with fome remarkable eye-fores. WILLIAM, a Conqueror, but cruell. RUFUS, refolute, but facrilegious. HENRY the firft, learned, but unnaturall to his Brother. STEVEN ftout, but an ufurper. HENRY the fecond, wife, but wanton. RICHARD the firft, undaunted, but undutifull to his parents. IOHN, politique, but a great diffembler. HENRY the third, of great devotion, but of fmall depth. EDWARD the fecond, beautifull, but deboift. RICHARD the fecond, well natur'd, but ill manner'd. HENRY the fourth, fortunate, but having a falfe title. HENRY the fifth, a victorious King, but formerly a riotous Prince. HENRY the fixth, Saint-like, but very fimple. EDWARD the fourth, fortunate, but perjur'd: to proceed no further. But let malice it felf ftain our Soveraign with any notorious perfonall fault; for to wifh him wholly without fault were in effect to wifh him dead. Befides this, confider him as a King, and what favours hath he beftowed on his Subjects! and then, that his curtefies might not unravell or fret out, hath bound them with a ftrong border and a rich fringe, a Trienniall Parliament. *When God brought againe the captivity of Sion, then were wee like unto them that dreame, Pfa.* 126. 1. The Jewes would not beleeve their owne happineffe, it was fo great, fo fudden. But when wee confider fo many favours conferred upon us by our King in fo few yeares: Ship-money condemned, Monopolies removed, Star-chamber it felfe cenfured, High-commiffion levelled, other Courts regulated, offenfive Canons declined, burdenfome ceremonies to tender confciences profer'd to bee abolifhed, Trienniall Parliaments fetled and the prefent indefinitely prolonged: we have caufe to fufpect with our felves, are we awake? Doe wee not dreame? Do I fpeake? Doe you heare? Is it light? Doe wee not deceive our felves with fond fancies? Or are not thefe Boones too bigge to begge? too great to be granted? Such as our Fathers never durft defire, nor Grand-fathers hope to receive? O no; it is fo; it is fure, it is certaine we are awake; wee doe not dreame; if any thing be afleepe it is our ingratitude, which is so drowsie to returne deserved thankes to God and the King for these great favours. And so much for the first, *the King*.

24. Next to the King, comes *my Lord the King*; and this peculiarly concernes the Courtiers, and such *Mephibosheths* as eat bread at his Table, who under God owe their being to his bounty, and whose states are not onely made, but created by Him. These indeed of all other are bound most to rejoyce at their Soveraignes returne, being obliged thereunto by a three-fold tye: Loyaltie to a Soveraigne, dutie to a Master, and gratitude to a Benefactour: except (as some fondly hold, that a letter seal'd with three seales may lawfully be opened) any conceive that a three-fold engagement may the easiest be declined.

25. Next, we insist on *His own house*; wherein this City is particularly pointed at. For if *London* be the *Jerusalem* of our *David*, then certainly *Westminster* is His [1]*Sion*, where He hath His constant habitation. Here is the principall Palace of His residence, the proper seat of His great Councell, the usuall receipt of His Revenues, the common Courts of Justice, the ancient Chaire of His Enthroning, the Royall Ashes of His Ancestours, the fruitfull Nursery of His Children. You therefore, the Inhabitants of this Citie, have most reason to rejoyce.

26. But alas! What have I done that I should not? Or rather, what have I to do that I cannot, having invited many guests now to a Feast, and having no meat to set before you? I have called Courtiers and Citizens to rejoyce, and still one thing is wanting, and that a maine materiall one, the founder of all the rest: the King is not returned in Peace. Thus the Sunne is slipt out of our Firmament, and the Diamond dropt out of the ring of my Text. I pretended and promised to make an application thereof to the time; and must I now be like the foolish Builder in the Gospell, begin and cannot finish? *Owne house*: that is the bottom of the Text; but this stands empty. *My Lord the King*: and that is the top of the Text; but Hee is farre off: and the words which are the side-walls to joyne

---

[1] *Zion.*

them together, *He is come home in Peace*, thefe, alas! cannot be erected: In this cafe there is but one remedy to help us, and that prefcribed by our Saviour himfelfe: *Joh.* 16. 23, *Whatfoever yee afke the Father in my Name, he will give you.*

27. Let us pray faithfully, pray fervently, pray conftantly, pray continually. Let Preacher and People joyne their prayers together that God would be pleafed to build up the walls and make up the [1]breaches in the Application, that what cannot be told, may be foretold for a truth; and that our Text may be verified of *Charles* in Prophefie, as by *David* in Hiftory. Excellently Saint *Auftin* advifeth that men fhould not be curious to enquire how *Originall fin* came into them, but carefull to feek how to get it out. By the fame fimilitude (though reverfed) let us not be curious to know what made our King (who next to God I count our *Originall good*) to leave this City, or whether offences given or taken mov'd Him to His departure; but let us bend our braines, and improve our beft endevours to bring him fafely and fpeedily back againe. How often herein have our pregnant hopes mifcarried, even when they were to be delivered! Juft as a man in a ftorme fwimming [2]thorow the fea to the fhore till the oares of his faint armes begin to faile him, is now come to catch land, when an unmercifull wave beats him as far back in an inftant as he can recover in an houre: Juft fo when our hopes of a happie peace have been ready to arrive, fome envious unexpected obftacle hath ftarted up, and hath fet our hopes *ten degrees backwards, as the fhadow of the Sun-diall of Ahaz.* But let us not hereat be difheartened, but with blind *Bartimeus* the more we are commanded by unhappy accidents to hold our peace, let us cry the louder in our prayers. The rather, becaufe our King is already partly come, come in his offer to come, come in his tender to treat, come in his proffer of Peace. And this very day being the beginning of the Treaty, I may fay he fet his firft ftep forward: God guide his feet, and fpeed his pace! [3]O let us thriftily hufband the leaft mite of hopes that it may increafe, and date our day from

---

[1] breach. [2] through. [3] Oh.

the firſt peeping of the morning Star, before the Sun be riſen! In a word, defiſt from ſinning, perſiſt in praying, and then it may come to paſſe that this our Uſe may once be antidated, and this dayes Sermon ſent as a Harbinger before-hand to provide a lodging in your hearts for your joy againſt the time that *my Lord our King ſhall returne to his owne houſe in peace.*

FINIS.

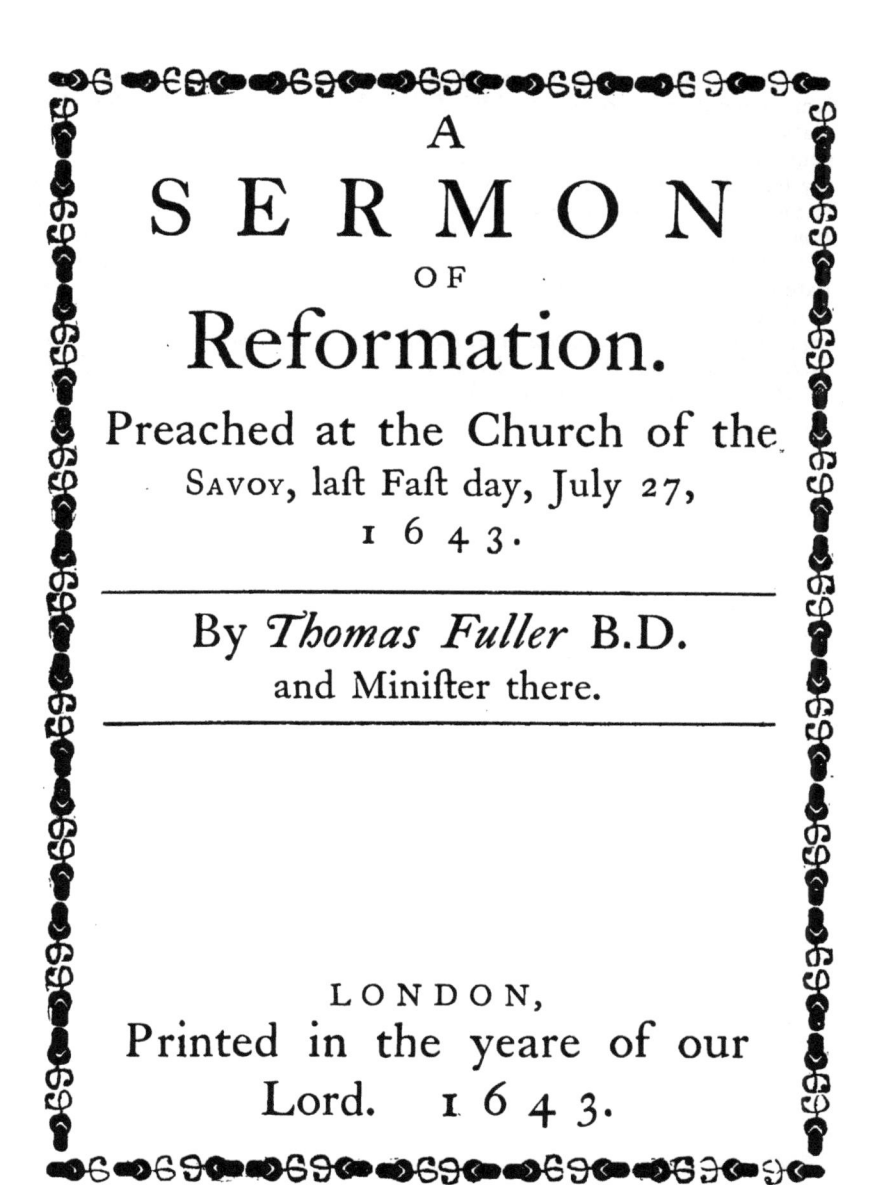

A SERMON OF Reformation.

Preached at the Church of the Savoy, laſt Faſt day, July 27, 1643.

By *Thomas Fuller* B.D. and Miniſter there.

LONDON,
Printed in the yeare of our Lord. 1643.

["... . Thus have I recited to you (Reverend Fathers, and right famous men) the particulars which I thought fit to be spoke for the reformation of Ecclesiastical affairs. I trust you will take all (out of your gentleness) in good part. If peradventure it be thought that I have passed my bounds in this Sermon, or have said anything out of temper, forgive it me; and ye shall forgive a man speaking out of meer zeal, a man *heartily* lamenting the decay of the Church: and consider the thing it self, not regarding any foolishness. Consider the miserable condition and state of the Church, and endeavour your selves with all your souls and abilities to reform it."—Pp. 27-28 of *A Sermon of Conforming and Reforming: made to the Convocation at S. Pauls Church in London, By John Colet, D.D., Dean of the said Church: upon Rom. xii. 2. 'Be ye reformed,' &c. Writ an hundred and fiftie years since.* Cambridge, 1661, 8vo.]

[Introduction.

THIS important Sermon, which gave rife to a controverfy that attracted confiderable notice, was preached on the ufual monthly Parliamentary Faft-day (*anteà*, page ccxxxiii.), Wednefday, 26th July, 1643; but by a fingular error, which is detected by a reference to one of the "late reformed almanacks" of the time, and to the title-page of Saltmarfh's *Examinations* (page cccxv. *poftea*), the date on the title-pages of the two editions of the difcourfe has been put one day too far in advance (fee pages cclxxxix. and ccxcvi.). It was one of feveral sermons on the fame fubject; and the preacher was at the time labouring under the imputation of being "one extremely difaffected to the Parliament" (Herle's *Ahabs Fall*, 4to., 1644, Dedication to Fuller).

It was preached at the Savoy Chapel in the Strand, now the only relic of "Old John of Gaunt's" Palace. For upward of a century after the time of that Duke of LANCASTER, the Savoy lay in ruins; but HENRY VII. rebuilt and endowed it as a collegiate foundation for the relief of one hundred poor people; and the hofpital-chapel was confecrated about 1516. When the Protector SOMERSET demolifhed the parifh-church of St. Mary-le-Strand, the parifhioners began to worfhip at the Savoy Chapel. The old Foundation was revived by Queen MARY, but it fubfequently became "a nurfery of rogues and mafterlefs men,"—a notoriety which it kept up till its diffolution in the year 1702. As regards the Chapel, in the reign of Queen ELIZABETH a new parifh was formed out of St. Clement Danes parifh and the royal Precinct, the name of the old parifh church being perpetuated in the name commonly applied to the new one, viz. St. Mary Savoy (fee page 331), or St. Mary-le-Savoy (Newcourt's *Repertorium*, i. 696). But the Chapel itfelf is dedicated to St. John the Baptift, accefs to it being obtained, as is often ufual in churches whofe patron Saint is the Baptizer JOHN, by defcending fteps. The Savoy in its double capacity of hofpital-chapel and parifh-church has been the fcene of fome noteworthy events in the ecclefiaftical annals of the fixteenth and feventeenth centuries, and feveral famous preachers have been connected with it. (See an article on "Dr. Fuller and the Savoy," in the Rev. W. J. Loftie's *In and Out of London*, 8vo., London, 1875, pages 135 *feq*.)

The *Reformation-Sermon* is the firft of feveral difcourfes preached by THOMAS FULLER at this chapel. His appointment to the parifh has already been noted, page ccxxxiii. *anteà*. NEWCOURT (*Repertorium*, i. 697) mentions one RIC. BARKER as Curate in 1640; but the names of the four Lecturers in FULLER's time have been loft fight of. It feems, however, that the parifhioners (including the inhabitants of the Precinct) interfered with the appointments. According to the *Journals of the Houſe of Commons*, 30th May, 1642, certain of the pariſhioners requeſted through Sir ROBERT HARLEY, the foremoſt of the "deforming reformers," that a "Mr. T.HO. GIBBS ſhall be recommended to the Savoye to be a Lecturer there;" "and that the Doctor there [*i.e.* BALCANQUAL, who had with ſome the reputation of "a vile man," *Baillie*, i. 286] be required to ſuffer . . . the Lecturer there accordingly" (vol. ii. 595*a* : the blank is in the original). The petition does not ſeem to have been received with the favour of the Houſe ; for on the 15th of the next month the following entry is met with : "The humble Petition of the Tenants of the *Savoye*, together with the major Part of the Pariſhioners of *St. Mary le Strand*, was this day read ; and nothing done upon it" (*Journals*, ii. 625 *b*). Influence at that time was at work on behalf of FULLER, a more exact date to whoſe actual appointment can now be obtained.

Under the firſt of the dates ſupplied by the *Commons Journals* there are no particulars on the matter in Sir SIMONDS D'EWES's valuable manuſcript journal (Harl. MS. 163, ff. 526*b*, 527*ab*); but in the ſecond caſe ſome details can be added to the circumſtances already known. After Mr. OLIVER CROMWELL had moved (Wedneſday, 15th June : folio 548*b*) that the Juſtices of the Peace in Yorkſhire who had any of the Armes of the Papiſts in their cuſtodie ſhould not deliver them to any perſon whatſoever, but by authoritie from his Majeſtie ſignified unto them by both Howſes of Parliament, and after it had been ordered accordingly,—Sir JOHN NORTHCOTE, Baronet, Member for Aſhburton, ſpoke in favour of the appointment of THOMAS FULLER, as one of the Lecturers of the Savoy. It is preſumed that the Baronet, from his Weſt-country aſſociations, would be acquainted with FULLER. Sir SIMONDS's important note on the ſubject is as follows :—

"Sʳ John Norcot moued that the petition of the greater part of the pariſhioners of the Savoy might bee read which was done accordingly and therein it appeared that ſome 14 or 15 of them had before petitioned for on Mr. Gibbs to bee a Lecturer there and that now neare vpon ſix ſcore of the ſame pariſh had petitioned for one Mr. ffuller to bee the Miniſter there which place had beene formerly ſupplied by the ſaid Mr. Gibbs under the name of a Lecturer and ſo deſired that the ſaid order touching the ſaid Mr. Gibbs might bee vacated but vpon Sʳ Robert Harleys iuſtifying his delivering in the former petition vpon which the ſaid Mr. Gibbs was allowed the howſe would at this time meddle noe further with the buſines but proceeded to matter of more publike concernment." (Harl. MS. 163, folio 549, or 162 in pencil.)

Soon after the delivery of the Sermon, FULLER, "for the preſent diſtreſs," went away from London. Upon the 30th September the Houſe of Commons reſolved to prefer Mr. JOHN BOND "to the Sequeſtration of the *Savoy*, to preach there" (*Journals*, iii. 259*b*) ; *i.e.* moſt probably to FULLER's vacated poſition. BOND was of Dorcheſter, being the ſon of a member for that town, and pupil of "Patriarch" WHITE. One of his Sermons, preached on the 27th March, 1644, is dated from his ſtudy at the Savoy, and on the title-page he was faid to be then preacher there; fhowing that he had promptly taken up quarters that were indeed always earneftly coveted. To BOND, therefore, FULLER refers in his letter to the Parifhioners, page 332 *poſteà;* "Doctor" being there ufed for *teacher*, in antithefis to doctrine. On the 10th April, 1644, Sir BENJAMIN RUDYARD moved for conferring the place of Mafter of the Savoy upon Mr. PATRICK YOUNG, celebrated as the tutor of MILTON; and it was decided that both YOUNG and BOND fhould be confidered of in relation to that place (*Commons' Journals*, iii. 455). After confiderable delay the latter was appointed; and he was to be efteemed Mafter "as if he were chofen and elected by the Chaplains of the faid perpetual Hofpital of the Savoy." The tenants, however, made fo many excufes from paying the new Mafter any rents, &c., that a refolution of the Parliament (2nd Nov., 1644) was paſſed to eftablifh his right to all the profits "in as full and ample a manner as Doctor BALCANQUAL, late Mafter thereof." BOND was confirmed in the poffeffions of BALCANQUAL'S lodgings, as alfo in his fequeftered goods, valued at £97 6s. od. (*Commons' Journals*, iii. 684-5 *et feq.; Lords' Journals*, vii. 59 *et feq.*)

The fubject of the Sermon, the Reformation of the Church, is characterifed by FULLER's biographer as a "frequent and thumbed fubject." It had gradually been affuming importance fince the complication in Scotch politics, 1638-40. Side by fide with the "Interfeits of Arms" went on a vigorous "Exchange of Pens." In reply to the arguments of the Scotch, Bifhop HALL "afferted" his *Epifcopacie by Divine Right* (London, 1640, 4to.). In the firft recefs of the Long Parliament, Lord BROOKE "opened" *The Natvre of that Epifcopacie, which is exercifed in England* (London, 1641, 4to.), a difcourfe in which "with all humility are reprefented fome confiderations tending to the much defired Peace, and long expected Reformation, of This our Mother Church." PRYNNE, "late (and now againe), an Utter-Barefter of Lincolnes Inn," wrote in the fame intereft *The Antipathie of the Englifh Lordly Prelacy both to Regall Monarchy, and Civil Unity* (London, 1641, 4to.). On the other fide "Theophilus Churchman" (HEYLYN) put forth his *Hiſtory of Epifcopacy* (London, 1641, 4to.), and JEREMY TAYLOR, concerned for the fate of Laud, "afferted" Epifcopacy "againft the Aerians and Acephali New and Old" (Oxford, 1642, 4to.). The advocates for reformation had for their champions the SMECTYMNUANS, MILTON, and a hoft of pamphleteers. For the chief literature of this prolific controverfy, fee HEYLYN's *Cyprianus Anglicus* (Life of LAUD), ed. 1671, book v. page 465; MASSON's *Life of John Milton*, vol. ii. pages 213 *feq.*, 356 *feq.;* and feveral paffages in vol. i. of the *Letters* &c. of BAILLIE, who with his fellow-Commiffioners interefted themfelves in fome books againft "his little Grace," as he termed LAUD. It is very noteworthy that one of MILTON's three anonymous pamphlets in this difcuffion had already come under FULLER's cenfure in his *Holy and Profane State*. Profeffor MASSON has thus referred to the circumftance : "There was enough in the pamphlets themfelves to caufe an inquifitivenefs refpecting their author among both friends and foes of his principles. Proof of this as refpects foes of his principles might be produced in the form of angry allusions to the pamphlets occurring in contemporary writings. One instance of the kind may be given. There was not a better soul breathing, and certainly not a more quiet and kindly English clergyman, than THOMAS FULLER, Rector of Broad Windsor, Dorsetshire, but now much in London and known as a preacher there. He was exactly of MILTON's own age; he had been MILTON's coeval at Cambridge, and, like MILTON, he was destined to be remembered in the world of English letters. His greater historical works which were to preserve the memory of his industry, his moderation and candour, his lucid intelligence, and his quaint and delicious wit, were yet to come; but he had published one or two things, including his *History of the Holy War*. As a work to follow that, he had been engaged since 1640, partly in his Dorsetshire Rectory, and partly in London, on the collection of short essays and popular biographic sketches now known as his *Holy and Profane State*. This work was not published till 1642, when it appeared as a folio volume, with cuts, from the Cambridge press; but it had been in manuscript nearly a year before it was published, and therefore the allusion made in one of the sketches in it to MILTON's maiden-pamphlet, *Of Reformation and the causes that hitherto have hindered it*, may be considered as the earliest recognition of that pamphlet by any critic of note to us now. Whatever FULLER may have thought of the pamphlet as a whole, there were passages in it that shocked him. More particularly he was shocked by those passages in which MILTON, in his zeal against bishops, had not hesitated to speak irreverently even of such Bishops as CRANMER, LATIMER, and RIDLEY, fathers and martyrs of English Protestantism though they were. So much had this grated on the good FULLER that, in his little sketch called *The Life of Bishop Ridley*, he cannot forbear bringing the pamphlet and its anonymous author (though FULLER may have known who he was) sharply to book. 'One might have expected,' he says, speaking of the martyr-bishops of MARY's days, 'that these worthy men should have been re-estated in their former honour; whereas the contrary has come to passe. For some who have an excellent facultie in uncharitable synecdoches, to condemne a life for an action, and taking advantage of some faults in them, do much condemn them. And one lately hath traduced them with such language as neither beseemed his parts (whosoever he was) that spake it, nor their piety of whom it was spoken. If pious Latimer, whose bluntness was incapable of flattery, had his simplicity abused with false informations, he is called *another Doctour Shaw to divulge in his Sermon forged accusations*. CRANMER and RIDLEY, for some failings, styled *the common stales to countenance with their prostituted gravities every politick fetch which was then on foot, as often as the potent Statists pleased to employ them*' [*Holy State*, ed. 1652, p. 279]. Here, after a further quotation or two from the impious pamphleteer, who is referred to in a note as 'Authour of the book lately printed of *Causes Hindering Reformation in England*, lib. i. pag. 10,' FULLER holds up his hands in pious sorrow" (*The Life of John Milton*, 1871, vol. ii. pages 359, 360). In connection with this interesting passage, the reader will not fail to remark FULLER's more earnest commendation of the reformers in ¶ 25 of the following Sermon (page 307 *posteà*), and his prayer at page 350 that the very Doctrine of martyrdom be not martyred. See also *Worthies*, chap. iii. page 9.

Several schemes of Church-reformation were put forth by moderate Churchmen whose names carried weight. FULLER himself had hazarded a basis of agreement (see *Innocents-Day Sermon*, ¶ 19, page 249); but Anabaptism (¶ 23, page 307 *posteà*), Millenarianism (¶ 33, pages 311-2), and the multitude of other sects, the adherents of which were eager for their own reformations, was already bringing so much disrepute on the Protestant religion (*Truth Maintained*, page 354 *posteà*,) that he was drawn closer to the "old paths." The hope to which he had given expression, that the delusive anticipations of the sectaries were being tolerated by the Parliament only for a time (*Innocents-Day Sermon*, ¶ 22, page 252 ; *Inauguration-Sermon*, ¶ 8, page 275), is of course a touch of satire. The schemes of ecclesiastical reform that were advanced by all these parties suggested the ridicule of BUTLER (*Hudibras*, part i. canto i. lines 201 *seq*.).

FULLER as effectively as the satirist directed strokes of humour against the "sub-de-re-reformations" of the subsequent years, until many of them were "worn quite out of fashion." An historic value attaches to the *Sermon of Reformation* from the fact that the famous Assembly of Divines had, the same month, begun its meetings with the view of resolving what system of ecclesiastical polity should replace the stately fabric recently overthrown. At the time in question the metropolis had been abandoned by the King (see ¶ 34, page 312), the nobles, several members of parliament, and the bulk of the clergy. Moreover, the Sequestrations of the remaining City benefices, in cases where the rod of sequestration was thought necessary to be applied, were under active prosecution. The delivery of the sermon—perhaps the last Royalist discourse preached in London in that excited year—is not therefore without an element of the heroic ; although the preacher, it is true, seems to be playing the part of a wary theologian. He had already acknowledged the necessity of a reformation (see *anteà*, page 249, ¶ 18), which, however, was to retain the important element hinted at in the lines of RICHARD LOVELACE ("To Lucasta : from Prison," an Epode : Ed. 1649, page 51 ; Hazlitt's ed. page 43) :—

> "A *Reformation* I would have,
> As for our griefes a *Sov'raigne* salve ;
> That is, a cleansing of each wheele
> Of State, that yet some rust doth feele."[1]

FULLER's reference to the loud noise (¶ 12, page 302) imported into the discussion is not exaggerated. The subject was debated by the Commons, who, as FULLER gives us to understand, made the subject "boil over." They received frequent petitions on the subject, large numbers of them being mentioned in the Journals of their proceedings. "No day passed," says FULLER (*Church-History*, xi. 185, § viii.), "wherein some petition was not presented. . . . In so much that the very porters (as they said) were able no longer to undergoe the burden of Episcopall tyranny, and petitioned against it." B_{AILLIE}, as well as FULLER, was amidſt theſe Reformation ſcenes; and he wrote: "The Toun of London and a world of men minds to preſent a petition, which I have ſeen, for the abolition of Biſhops, Deanes, and all their appurteanances.... Hudge things are here in working.... All here are wearie of Biſhops." "Yeſterday [11th Dec. 1640] a world of honeſt citizens, in their beſt apparell, in a very modeſt way, went to the Houſe of Commons, ſent in two Aldermen with their petition, ſubſcryved as we hear by 15,000 hands, for removing Epiſcopacie, the Service-Book, and other ſuch ſcandalls, out of the Church. It was weell received.... Never ſuch a Parliament in England: all is to be rectified; for all is much out of right" (*Letters*, &c., i. 274, 280). But theſe reforming reformers ſoon laid aſide their beſt clothes and good manners. Their conduct has fallen under the cenſure of the Parliamentary hiſtorian: "Another thing which ſeemed to trouble ſome who were not bad men was that extreame Licenſe which the Common People, almoſt from the very beginning of the Parliament, tooke to themſelves of reforming, without Authority, Order or Decency, rudely diſturbing Church-Service whileſt the Common-Prayer was reading, tearing thoſe Bookes, Surplaces, and ſuch things: which the Parliament, either too much buſied in variety of affaires, or (perchance too much) fearing the loſs of a conſiderable Party whom they might have need of againſt a reall and potent Enemy, did not ſo far reſtraine as was expected or deſired by thoſe men" (May's *Hiſtory*, 1647, Book i. chap. ix. pages 113-4). The ſupineneſs of thoſe in authority is eſpecially condemnatory in the caſe of the barbarous conduct of the ſoldiery amongſt the tombs of the Saxon Kings at Wincheſter Cathedral, at which conduct FULLER is juſtly indignant (page 354 *poſteà*).

FULLER's bold diſcourſe, which he ſays was preached at a ſhort notice, was at once committed to the preſs, being by the "Crown" publiſher, JOHN WILLIAMS, entered at Stationers' Hall on the 2nd Auguſt, under the hands of DOWNAM the Licenſer. It was publiſhed on the ſame day (manuſcript note in the Britiſh Museum copy, E. 63. 3) in 4to., with WILLIAMS's name and DOWNAM's imprimatur on the title-page (pp. ii. + 28), the ſame imprimatur being alſo repeated at the end. It was a copy of this edition that SALTMARSH criticiſed (see page 315 *poſteà*). It is noticeable that this edition, like the ſecond, gave a wrong date to the Sermon. SALTMARSH's attack as well as FULLER's reply created a demand for another edition, which was perhaps intended for circulation in Oxford, where FULLER then was. This ſecond edition (pp. 24, 4to.) was without printer's name and DOWNAM's imprimatur on the title-page, but the imprimatur was given at the end. The title-page of this latter edition is that which is given at page cclxxxix. in fac-ſimile, except that the blank ſpace is in the original taken up with a ſmall block depicting a roſe, a thiſtle, a lily, and a harp, betokening loyalty; and a floreated deſign containing the ſame devices forms the ornament at the head of the ſermon on page 297. This lateſt edition is taken as the baſis of the text; but ſome corrections are made on the authority of the firſt edition, and a few of the chief differences in the reading are indicated in the foot-notes.]

A Sermon of Reformation.

HEB. 9. 10.

Vntill the time of Reformation.

1. THOSE who live beyond the Polar circles are called *Periscii*, because they have shadows round about them. In a more myſtical meaning the Jewes before Chriſt may be ſo called, living in conſtant Umbrages of Types and Ceremonies, which were taken away when the Sunne of Righteouſneſſe did ariſe. Their ſacrificing of Lambes and Rammes, and Kids and Goats, and Calves, and Kine, and Turtle-doves, with their obſerving of Meates and Drinkes, and Dayes, [1]were, as the Apoſtle ſaith, *Coloſ.* 2. 17, *A ſhadow of things to come, but the body is of Chriſt.*

2. Yea, in ſome ſenſe I may ſafely ſay, that the very *Sanctum* and *Sanctum Sanctorum* was ſtill but the outward *Atrium*, as containing therein ſuch Types as related to a higher and holier truth. To inſtance only in the Holy of [2]Holies: herein were ſeven ſacred Utenſils, all full fraught with Heavenly Myſteries.

3. Firſt, *the Golden Cenſor*, ſignifying our prayers mingled with Chriſts merits (woefull for us if he did not give better Incenſe then we bring) which he offers up for us to his Father. Secondly, *the Arke of the Covenant overlaid round about with gold;* whileſt *Shittim* wood was in the middeſt thereof, to Typifie Chriſts humanity decked and adorned with his Godhead. Thirdly, *the Pot of Manna*, looking backwards in memoriall of the miraculous meat of the Iſraelites in the

---

[1] whereas. [2] Holieſt.

Wildernesse; and forwards to set forth Angels food in Heaven, which is neither to eat nor to drinke, but to doe Gods will, and to see Gods glory. Fourthly, *Aarons Rod which budded*, and besides the History contained therein, alluded to Chrifts Resurrection, *that Branch of Jesse* cut downe and cast out amongst the dead: which yet afterwards did revive, flourish, and fructifie. Fifthly, *the Tables of the Covenant*, wherein the Commandments were written by Gods finger, to intimate that only an infinite power can effectually print Gods Lawes in our hard and obdurate hearts. Sixthly, *the golden Cherubims* overshadowing the Mercy-Seat with their wings, and looking towards it; to shew that the mystery of Gods mercy is to be covered from the curiosity of prophane eyes, whilest the pious may with comfort behold it. Seventhly, and lastly, *the Mercy-Seat it selfe;* the Embleme of that Mercy-Seat in Heaven, to which poore penitents being cast at the Barre of Gods justice have a free and open appeale.

4. All these were of gold and pure gold, and yet Saint *Paul Gal.* 4. 9, calleth all legall ceremonies *beggarly Elements*, in comparison of Christ the Truth, in whom these did determine and expire. As the rude lines of Black-Lead wherwith the Picture is first drawne vanish away when the curious Limner layeth on the lively colours; so all these outward Ordinances had an end at the comming of Christ, being only to last *Vntill the time of Reformation.*

5. The Text is so short, it needs not to be divided, only the word REFORMATION must be expounded; a word long in pronouncing and longer in performing, as generally signifying the bettering and amending of what is amisse: In Greeke διόρθωσις, *A Through Rectifying.* However, sometimes the word *Reformation* is not opposed to things bad in their owne nature, but to things that are lesse perfect, and may be more perfected, as in the Text. For the Ceremoniall Law of the Jewes was compleat in its kinde, as given of God, and every thing made by *Him* must be like *Him* that made it, *very good.* Yet comparatively that Law was imperfect, and needed a Reformation, which was performed at Chrifts comming. Besides, though the Ceremoniall Law was good in it selfe,

yet it was bad as it was abused by the ignorant Jewes. For though the knowing Patriarks looked through and beyond the Types to the Messias himselfe; yet the dull People mistaking the Shell for the Kernell, and the Casket for the Jewell, lodged their soules where they should only have bayted, and did dote on the shadowes as on the substance it selfe; in which respect the Peoples judgements, as well as those Ceremonies, needed a Reformation.

6. The maine point we shall insist on, is this; That *Christians living under the Gospel, live in a time of Reformation*, which will appeare in severall particulars: For besides Ceremonies removed according to the principall intent of the Text, Manners are now reformed and Doctrine refined: Poligamy connived at in the Patriarks, now generally condemned, the Bill of Divorce cancelled by Christianity, which was permitted to the Jewes, not because that was good, but because they were bad, and by this Tolleration were kept from being worse. The second Table abused by the restrictive Comments of the Pharisees, confining those Lawes (which were made to confine them) onely to the outward Act, are now according to our Saviours interpretation extended to their true demention. The mistery of the Trinity clouded in the old Testament is cleered in the New. The Doctrine of Gods righteousnesse by faith, of the merit of Christ, of the spirit of Adoption, of the Resurrection of the Body, darkly delivered under the Law, are manifested in the Gospel, with many other heavenly Revelations.

7. *Use:* Let us be hartily thankfull to God, who gave us to be borne since the comming of Christ in the time of Reformation. Our Twi-light is [1]cleerer then the Jewish Noon-day. The men of *China* use to brag that they (because of their ingenious civility) have two Eyes, the Europæans one, and that all the World besides are starke blinde: more truely it may be said that the Christians had two Eyes, the Law and Gospell; the Jewes but one, the Law alone; and all people and Pagans besides sit in darknesse and the shadow of death. The Jewes indeed saw Christ presented in a land-scept, and

---

[1] now cleerer.

beheld him through the Perspective of faith, *seeing the promises a farre off*. But at this day a Dwarfe-Christian is an overmatch for a gyant Jew in knowledge, as appeareth by our Saviours Riddle, *Mat.* 11. 11 : *Among them that are borne of women there hath not risen a greater then* John *the Baptist : Notwithstanding he that is least in the Kingdome of Heaven is greater then he.*

8. Which Riddle is thus untyed : *John* Baptist was the greatest amongst the Children of Women, becaufe other Prophets forefaw Christ, He saw him; others spake of Christ, He spake to him, and had the high honour to baptize him with water, by whofe spirit he himfelfe was baptized : Yet was he the least in the Kingdome of Heaven (which properly began after Christs Afcention), becaufe though perchance acquainted with the generals thereof, the particulars of the time, place, meanes and manner were as much conceal'd from him as cleerly revealed unto us. He never knew that *Judas* should betray Christ, *Caiphas* accufe him, *Peter* deny him, *Pilate* condemne him, Souldiers crucifie him, *Nicodemus* embalme him, *Joseph* bury him. Thefe, and many more Circumstances of our Saviours Paffion, Resurrection and Afcention, now Histories to our Children, were Misteries to *John* Baptist; who, though Christs Harbinger *to prepare his way*, yet did not live to fee his Master [1]to poffeffe what he had provided for him. Wherefore if *Alexander* the Emperour did count himfelfe much indebted to the Gods that he was borne a Grecian, and not a Barbarian, how thankfull ought we to be to God, who gave us to be borne neither Jewes, nor Pagans, but Christians, fince *the time of Reformation!*

9. *Objection :* But this indeed were true, if all things in the Church continued at this time in the fame condition of Primative Purity, whereto Christ Reform'd it. But long fince that *falling away*, foretold by the Apostle, is come to paffe, and that *man of finne* hath played his part in the Church, therein deforming Manners with Vice, Doctrine with Herefie, Difcipline with Superstition. As for any Reformation which

---

[1] to *omitted.*

since hath happened in *England*, it hath been but partiall and imperfect. King *Henry* the eight brake the Popes necke, but bruised not the least finger of Popery; rejecting his Supremacy, but retaining his superstition in the six Articles. The Reformation under *Edward* the sixth was like the Reformer, little better then a childe; and he must needs be a weake *Defender of the Faith*, who needed a Lord Protector for himselfe. As Nurses to woe their Children to part from knives, doe suffer them to play with Rattles; so the State then permitted the People (infants in Piety) to please themselves with some [1]frivious points of Popery, on condition they would forsake the dangerous opinions thereof. As for Queene *Elizabeth*, her Character is given in that plaine, but true expression, *that she swept the Church of England and left all the dust behinde the doore*. Her Successors have gone in the same path and the same pace with little alteration, and lesse Addition in matters of Moment, save that besides some old errours unamended; many Innovations have broken in upon us, which might be instanced in, were it as safe as it is easie to reckon them up. We therefore desire and expect a *Through Reformation*, to see Christ mounted on his Throne, with his Scepter in his hand, in the Purity of his Ordinances, and we shall grieve and groane *untill* such *a Reformation*.

10. *Answer:* This objection containes many parts, and must be taken asunder: Some things therein are freely to be granted, and others flatly to be denied, and others warily to be qualified. We freely confesse the Deformation by Popery, as also that the Reforming [which] was by *Henry* the eight and *Edward* the sixth (good Prince, of whom I had said that he dyed too soone, but because he dyed when God would have him) were but partial and imperfect. Withall, we flatly deny that Queene *Elizabeth left the dust behinde the Doore*, which she cast out on the Dunghill, whence this uncivill expression was raked up. The Doctrine by her established, and by her Successors maintained in the thirty-nine Articles, if declared, explained, and asserted from false Glosses, have all gold, no dust or drosse in them.

---

[1] frivilous.

11. Againe, we freely confeffe that there may be fome faults in our Church in matters of Practice and Ceremonies; and no wonder if there be : it would be a Miracle if there were not. Befides, there be fome Innovations rather *in the Church* then *of the Church*, as not chargeable on the Publique Account, but on private mens fcores, *who are old enough, let them anfwer for themfelves.* Religion in *England* is like the Cloathes of the Ifraelites, *Deuteronomie* 29. 5, which for many yeeres together *waxed not old*. Alas! in fome places it is threadbare, may it have a new nappe; in more it is fpotted, may it be well fcowred; and in all places rent afunder, may it be well mended!

12. A Through Reformation we and all good men doe defire with as ftrong affections, though perhaps not with fo loud a noife, as any whatfoever. The higheft clamour doth not alwayes argue the greateft earneftneffe. But with this qualification, that by *Through Reformation* we meane fuch a one whereof we are capable, *pro ftatu viatorum*, made with all due and Chriftian moderation : That Arrow is well drawne that is drawne to the head, but it may be over-drawne cleane through the Bow, and fo doe no good. There is in like manner a poffibility of out-doing, even in the point of Reforming : And therefore how a true Through Reformation may be made, and managed long to continue, by Gods affiftance and your patience, I will take in hand to give the true Characters of fuch who are to be true and proper Reformers.

13. Firft, they muft have a lawfull calling thereunto : What better deede then to make Brothers friends, and to be an equall Umpire betwixt them ? Yet Chrift himfelfe declin'd the Imployment, as out of his Vocation, *Luke* 12. 14: *Who made me a Judge or Devider over you ?* Some good duties lye in common to all good men. Whofoever is called a Chriftian hath a juft calling to performe them : 'Tis fo farre from being a finne for any to doe them, that it is a finne for any to leave them undone. But there be other duties which God hath impaled in for fome particular perfons, fo that it is a Ryot or Trefpaffe at leaft for any other to force their Entrance into

them: Amongſt theſe Actions, Reformation of Churches is a chief, as of higheſt Honour, and greateſt concernment.

14. Now, the Supreme power alone hath a lawfull calling to Reforme a Church in thoſe reſpective places wherein it is ſupreme. Where this ſupreme power is ſeated, the Statiſts of the ſeverall places may judge; the Divine goeth no farther, but to maintaine that where the Supreme power is, there alone is the power of Reformation; as it plainely appeares by the Kings of *Judah* in their Kingdome. Two ſorts of Idolatry the Jewes therein were guilty of: The one Groſſe, the other Refined. Groſſe Idolatry againſt the firſt Commandement, in worſhipping a falſe God, as *Baal*, and the like. Refined Idolatry againſt the ſecond Commandement, in worſhipping the true God after a falſe and forbidden manner, 2 *Chronicles* 33. 17: *Nevertheleſſe the people did ſacrifice ſtill in the high places, yet unto the Lord their God onely.* Groſſe Idolatry found many Reformers, *Aſa, Joaſh, Amaziah, Vzziah, Jotham,* [1]*Manaſſeh*; whileſt onely two, *Jehoſaphat* and *Hezekiah*, endeavoured the Reforming of Refined Idolatry, and *Joſiah* alone perfected it. In both we may obſerve that the Kings were praiſed for doing ſo much, or diſpraiſed for doing no more; which plainly proves that the Reforming of the Church did properly pertaine unto them. God neither miſtakes nor confounds the good Deeds or Rewards of men, but ſets the due praiſes on the true perſons. The perſon that doth well ſhall be praiſed: the Prince ſhall not be commended for the good Deeds of the people, nor the people commended for the good Deeds of the Prince; indeed God threatens the common people of Iſrael, *Leviticus* 26. 23, with Beaſts, Warres, and many other Plagues, *if they will not be reformed.* But we never read that God reproved the people for not Reforming the Jewiſh Church from Idolatry, as a Taſke belonging to the Supreme power placed over them.

15. Meane time meere private men muſt not be idle, but move in their Spheare till the Supreme power doth Reforme. Firſt, they are dayly to pray to God to inſpire thoſe who have power and place with Will and Skill, couragiouſly to begin,

---

[1] *Manaſſe*

constantly to continue, and happily to conclude such a Reformation. Secondly, *they* are seriously to reforme themselves: He needs not to complaine of too little worke, who hath a little world in himselfe to amend. A good man in Scripture is never called Gods Church (because that is a collective terme belonging to many), but is often termed Gods Temple; such a Temple it is lawfull for every private man to Reforme: He must see that the foundation of faith be firme, the Pillars of Patience be strong, the windowes of Knowledge be cleere, the roofe of Perseverance be perfected. Thirdly, he may Reforme *the Church in his house, Philemon* 2, carefully looking to his owne Family, *Joshua* 24. 15, *that he and his house may serve the Lord*. But as for the publique Reforming of the Church in generall, he must let it alone as belonging to *the Supreme power*, to whom it is appropriated.

16. *Objection:* But seeing wee have occasion to speake of lawfull Callings, what Calling (may some say) have you to meddle with this point above your reach, and without your Compasse? Who [1]penned your Commission to take such matters in hand? Leave the describing of Reformers Characters to such who have more age, experience, and ability to performe it.

17. *Answer:* I am, or should be, most sensible of mine owne weakenesse, being ἐλαχιστότερος, the least of those that dispence the Word and Sacraments. Yet have I a calling as good as the Church of *England* could give me: And if she be not ashamed of such a Sonne, I count my selfe honoured with such a Mother. And though meere private Christians may not intermeddle with [2]publick Reforming of a Church, Gods Prophets have in all Ages challenged the privilege to tell necessary Truths unto the greatest. The tongue used to be cut out of the Roman Sacrifices and given unto their Heraulds, to shew that freedome of language was allowed them. We are Christs [3]Ambassadors, 2 *Corinthians* 5. 20, and claime the leave to speake Truth with sobernesse: And though I cannot expect my words should be *like Nailes fastened by the Masters of the Assemblies, Eccl.* 12. 11, yet I hope they may prove as

---

[1] pen'd.   [2] publique.   [3] Embassadours.

Tacks, entred by him that defires to be faithfull and peaceable in Ifrael.

18. The fecond Requifite in Reformers is Piety. The very *Snuffers* in the Tabernacle were *made of pure Gold, Exodus* 37. 23. They ought to be good themfelves who are to amend others, leaft that reproofe fall heavie on them, *Pfal*. 50. 16, 17, *But unto the ungodly* (faith God), *Why doeft thou preach my lawes, and takeft my Covenant in thy mouth? whereas thou hateft to bee Reformed, and haft caft my words behinde thee.* And though fometimes bad men may Reforme others, *by [1]vertue of their Office:* Yet when it is done by the Office of their Vertue, and efficacy of their goodneffe, it is more gracefull in it felfe, more acceptable to God, and more comfortable to the Doer.

19. Thirdly, Knowledge in a competent, yea, plentifull meafure. Dangerous was the miftake committed by Sir [2]*Francis Drake* in Eighty Eight; when negleding to carry the [3]Lanthorne, (as he was commanded) in the darke night, [he] chafed five Hulkes of the Dutch Merchants, fuppofing them to have been his Enemies of the Spaniards. Such and worfe Errors may be committed in the Reforming of a Church, good miftaken for bad, and bad miftaken for good, where the light of knowledge is wanting for direction.

20. Fourthly, true courage and magnanimity. Reformers need to be armed with a ftout fpirit Cap à Pee, which are to breake through the front of bad cuftomes long received. Such Cuftomes, as they are bad, are [4]*Vfurpers;* as they are Cuftomes, are Tyrants; and will ftickle ftoutly to ftand in their old place. [5]Saint *Matthew* faith, 27. 15, *At the Feaft the Governour was wont to releafe unto the people a Prifoner.* [6]Saint *Luke* faith, 23. 17, *Of neceffity he muft releafe one unto them at the Feaft.* What was but a Curtefie at the firft grew in proceffe of time to bee a cuftome, and at last became a neceffity. Such cuftomes made neceffary by continuance muft Reformers expect to encounter, and refolve to remove. O, Coward-lines in a Magiftrate is a great finne! Who would thinke to finde the fearfull marching in the fore-front? and

---

[1] *the vertue.*   [2] Camdens [*Annals of*] *Eliz.* p. 367 [Ed. 4to. 1625, Bk. iii. p. 270].
[3] Lanterne.   [4] *Vferpers.*   Saint *omitted.*

yet in that forlorne hope which goeth to Hell, *Revelation* 21. 8, fee them firſt named: *but the fearfull, the unbeleeving and abominable, &c.:* fo neceſſary is Chriſtian courage, eſpecially in a Reformer.

21. Fifthly and laſtly, they muſt be endued with *Chriſtian diſcretion*, a grace that none ever [1]speak againſt but thoſe that wanted it: *A good man will guide his affaires with diſcretion, Pſalme* 112. 5. I muſt confeſſe there is a diſcretion (falſely ſo called) both carnall in it ſelfe, and inconſiſtent with true Zeale, yea, deſtructive of it. Christ had two Diſciples of the ſame name, the one a true man, the other a Traytor, both *Judaſſes*. Wherefore to prevent miſtakes, the former is never cited in Scriptures, but with an addition: *Judas ſaith unto him, not Iſcariot, Lord, &c.,* John 14. 22; *Judas* the ſervant of *Jesus Chriſt*, and Brother of *James*, Jude 1. In like manner wee, here mentioning Diſcretion, call it *Chriſtian Diſcretion*, for difference thereof, that all may know we meane not that which deſtroyes Zeale, but that which directs it; not that which quencheth Zeale, but which keepes it in the Chimney, the proper place thereof; not that which makes it leſſe lively, but what makes it more laſting. This Diſcretion, though laſt named, is not leaſt needfull in the Reformers of a Church; and muſt principally appeare in two things: Firſt, the not ſparing of the Tares for the Wheats ſake. Secondly, the not [2]ſpoyling the Wheat for the Tares ſake.

22. The not ſparing the Tares for the Wheats ſake. By Tares we underſtand, not only things unlawfull in a Church, but things unexpedient and unprofitable, which alſo muſt be removed. The barren Fig-tree, *Luke* 13. 7, was condemned, not for bearing deadly or dangerous fruit, but none at all: *Cut it downe; why [3]cumbereth it the ground?* Gods Garden ought to bee ſo well dreſſed as to have nothing ſuperflous: that doth harme that doth no good therein. [4]*Hee that will not worke, neither ſhall hee eate*, 2 Theſſalonians 3. 10. [5]If ſuch Ceremonies are to be found in our Church, which will not labour, neither needfull in themſelves, nor [6]conducing

---

[1] ſpake.   [2] ſpilling.   [3] *cumbreth.*   [4] *He.*
[5] Is ſuch Ceremonies to be, &c.   [6] conducting.

to decency, let them no longer have countenance in the Church, nor maintenance from it.

23. The not ¹spoyling the Wheat for the Tares fake, and letting thofe things alone which are well ordered already. Yet is there a generation of Anabaptifts, in number fewer, I hope, then are reported, yet more, I fear, then are difcovered; people too turbulent to obey, and too tyrannicall to command. If it should come into their hands to reforme, Lord, what worke would they make! Very facile, but very foule is that miftake in the vulgar Tranflation, *Luke* 15. 8. Inftead of *Everrit domum, She fwept the houfe,* 'tis rendred, *Evertit domum, She overturn'd the houfe.* Such fweeping we muft expect from fuch Spirits, which under pretence to cleanfe our Church, would destroy it. The beft is, they are fo farre from *fitting at the Helme* that I hope they fhall ever be *kept under Hatches.*

24. Now as difcretion difcovereth it felfe in the matter of Reformation, fo alfo it appeareth in the manner thereof. Firft, it is to be done with all reverence and refpect to the ancient Fathers. Thefe, though they lived neer the Fountain of Religion, yet lived in the Marches of Paganifme; as alfo in the time wherein the *Myftery of Iniquity began to work,* which we hope is now ready to receive the wages. If therefore there be found in their practice any Ceremonies fmacking of Paganifme or Popery, and if the fame can be juftly chalenged to continue in our Church, I plead not for their longer life, but for their decent buriall.

25. Secondly, with honourable refervation to the memories of our firft Reformers. Reverend *Cranmer,* Learned *Ridley,* Downright *Lattimer,* Zealous *Bradford,* Pious *Philpot,* patient *Hooper,* men that had their failings, but worthy in their Generations: *Thefe bare the heat of the day,* indeed, which were burnt to afhes; and though we may write a fairer hand then they, yet they affixed a firmer Seal, that dyed for their Doctrine.

26. Laftly, with carefulneffe not to give any juft offence to the Papifts. Say not, we need not to feere to offend them

---

¹ fpilling.

who would confound us. We have fo long waited for their converfion, we have almoft feene our fubverfion. Indeed we are forbidden to offend Gods *little ones*, but not inhibited to offend the Devils *great ones*. And though S. *Paul* bids us to *give no offence to thofe that are without*, that is meant of pure Pagans; and therefore the Papifts being neither well *within* nor well *without*, fall not under that precept. For all thefe Expreffions favour more of *Humor* then Holineffe, of *Stomack* then the Spirit. Though Papifts forget their duty to us, let us remember our duty to them; to them, not as Papifts, but as profeffors of Chriftianity, to their perfons, not erronious opinions, not giving them any juft offence. But if they will be offended without caufe, be their amends in their own hands. If *Rebeckah* will come to *Ifaac*, fhe fhall be wellcome. But in no cafe fhall *Ifaac* go back to *Rebeckah*: *Genefis* 24. 6, *Beware that thou bring not my fon thither again*.

27. Thefe five Ingredients muft compound effectuall reformers. Where any, or all of thefe are wanting, a Reformation will either not be made or not long kept. Witneffe the pretended Reformation the Papifts fo much bragge off, in the laft of Queen *Mary*, in the Univerfity of *Cambridge*, by the *Delegates of Cardinall Poole*. Where nothing of worth was done, but many foolifh ceremonies enforced, and the Bones of *Bucer* and *Phagius* burnt. It paffeth for the expreffion of a mad man, *to beat the aire*; and it is little better to beat the *earth*. To fight (as they did) againft duft and afhes, bodies of men long before buried: except they thought by this fimilitude of burning dead bodies to worke in filly people a beliefe of Purgatory fire, tormenting foules deceafed. Now when it came into queftion whether the Ordinances and Decifions of thofe Reformers fhould be ingroffed in Parchment or in Paper, [1]Doctor *Swinborne*, Mafter of *Clare Hall*, gave his opinion that paper would doe the deed well enough, as being likely to laft longer then thofe decrees fhould ftand in force; as afterward it came to paffe, they being all refcinded in the next yeer, being the firft of Queene *Elizabeth*.

---

[1] Fox, *Acts Monum.* page 1064. [Ed. Lond. 1641, vol. iii. page 773; Ed. Lond. 1868, viii. 286.]

28. Two things more muſt here be well [1]obſerved. Firſt, that there is a grand difference betwixt founding of a new Church, and reforming of an old. For the former, Saint *Paul* outſtript all men in the World. The Papiſts bragge much of King *Edgar*, who is ſaid to have founded as many Monaſteries as there be weekes in the yeer. Surely more Churches in *Aſia* and *Europe* were built from the ground by Saint *Paul, who ſtrived to preach the Goſpel, not where Chriſt was named, leſt he ſhould build upon another mans foundation, Romans* 15. 20. But reforming of Churches is an eaſier work, as not giving a Church the life but the luſtre; not the birth but the beauty; either repairing what is defective, or removing what is redundant. Thus we acknowledge *Solomon* the ſole founder of the Temple, though *Joaſh* repaired it, amending the breaches thereof; *Jotham* enlarged it, adding the beautifull porch thereto; and *Ezechiah* adorned it, covering the pillars with ſilver therein.

29. However, it is worth our obſerving that Reformers are ſometimes ambitious to entitle themſelves to be founders, as being covetous of credit, and counting it more honour to make a thing then to mend it. Thus *Nebuchadnezzar* boaſted, *Daniel* 4. 30, *Is not this great Babylon that I have built for the houſe of the Kingdome, by the might of my power, and for the honour of my majeſty?* Whereas *Babylon* was built by *Nimrod*, or (as others ſay) *Semyramis*, many yeers before *Nebuchadnezzars* cradle was made. Yet he, no doubt, did encreaſe, ſtrengthen, and beautifie it; on which title, ſee how he engroſſeth all the glory unto himſelfe, as firſt and ſole founder! *Is not this great Babylon that I have built?*

30. Let none in like manner brag that they are now the firſt Founders of a Church in *England*, built long ſince therein, time out of minde. We deny and [2] defie ſuch Papiſts as ſay that *Auguſtine* the Monke was the firſt Apoſtle of this Iſland, where the Goſpel long before had been preached, though not to the *Saxons* our Anceſtors, yet to the *Britans* our Predeceſſors. Yea, having cauſe to ſearch who firſt brought

---

[1] Two things more I will briefly touch, and ſo conclude.   [2] defile.

Chriſtianity over into *Britanny*, my endeavours have been ſtill at a loſſe and left at uncertainty. Perchance as God, *Deuteronomie* 34. 6, buried the body of *Moſes*, That *no man knoweth the place of his* [1]*Sepulchre unto this day*, to cut off from the Jewes all occaſion of Idolatry; ſo it ſeems his wiſdom hath ſuffered the names of the firſt founders of Religion *Here* to be covered in obſcurity, to prevent poſterity from being ſuperſtitious to their Memories. However, if juſtly we be angry with the Papiſts for making the Brittiſh Church (a tall ſtripling grown) to weare ſwaddling cloathes againe: more cauſe have we to diſtaſte the pens and preachings of ſuch who make their addreſſes unto us, as unto pure Pagans where the word is newly to be planted. A [2]Moderne Author tels us a ſtrange ſtory, how the ſervants of Duke *D'Alva*, ſeeking for a Hawke they had loſt, found a new country in the Navell of *Spaine*, not known before, invironed with Mountaines, and peopled with naked Salvages. I ſhould wonder if ſuch a *Terra incognita* could be found in *England*, which (what betwixt the covetouſneſſe of Landlords and the carefullneſſe of Tenants) is almoſt meaſured to an Acre. But if ſuch a place were diſcovered, I muſt allow that the Preachers there were the firſt planters of the Goſpel, which in all other places of the kingdom are but the Continuers thereof. I hope Chriſt hath reaped much goodneſſe long ago, where theſe, now, new pretend to plant it. And if *England* hath not had a true Church hitherto, I feare it will not have a true Church hereafter.

31. The ſecond thing I commend unto you is this, That a perfect Reformation of any Church in this world may be deſired, but not hoped for. Let *Zenophons Cyrus* be King in *Plato's* Common-wealth, and Batchelors wives breed maides children in *Mores Vtopia*, whileſt Roſes grow in their Gardens without prickles, as [3]Saint *Baſil* held they did before the fall of *Adam*. Theſe phanſies are pleaſing and plauſible, but the performance thereof unfeiſable; and ſo is the perfect reformation of a Church in this world difficult to bee deſcribed,

---

[1] *Sepulture.*
[2] In a book of directions to travel [Howell's *Inſtructions for Forreine Travell*, 1642, ed. Arber, 1869, pages 51, 52]. [3] [*Opera*, Ed. Baſle, 1567, iv. 32.]

and impoſſible to be practiſed. For beſides that [1]Sathan will doe his beſt, or rather his worſt to undoe it, Man in this life is not capable of ſuch perfection. Look not to finde that in man out of Paradiſe, which was not found in man in Paradiſe, continuance in an holy eſtate. [2]*Martin Luther* was wont to ſay, he never knew good order in the Church laſt above fifteen yeares in the purity thereof; yea, the more perfect the Reformation is, the leſſe time it is likely to laſt. Mans minde being in conſtant motion, when it cannot aſcend higher, will not ſtand ſtill, but it muſt decline. I ſpeake not this to dif--hearten men from endeavouring a perfect Reformation, but to keep them from being diſ-heartened, when they ſee the ſame cannot be exactly obſerved.

32. And yet there are ſome now adayes that talke of a *great light*, manifeſted in this age more then ever before. Indeed we Modernes have a mighty advantage of the Ancients: whatſoever was theirs, by Induſtry may be ours. The Chriſtian Philoſophy of *Juſtin Martyr*; the conſtant Sanctity of *Cyprian*; the Catholick faith of *Athanaſius*; the Orthodox judgement of *Nazianzen*; the manifold Learning of *Jerome*; the ſolid Comments of *Chryſoſtome*; the ſubtill Controverſies of *Auguſtine*; the excellent Morals of *Gregory*; the humble Devotions of *Bernard*: All contribute themſelves to the edification of us, who live in this [3]later Age. But as for any tranſcendent extraordinary miraculous light, peculiarly conferred on our Times, the worſt I wiſh the opinion is this, that it were true. Sure I am that this light muſt not croſſe the Scripture, but cleere the Scripture. So that if it affirmeth any thing contrary to Gods written Word, or enforceth any thing (as neceſſary to ſalvation) not expreſt in Gods Word, I dare boldly ſay, That ſuch a light is kindled from Hell.

33. As for the opinion of Chriſts corporall viſible Kingdome, to come within few yeares, I will neither peremptorily reject it, nor dare abſolutely receive it. Not reject it, leſt I come within the compaſſe of the Apoſtles reproofe, 2 *Peter*

---

[1] Satan. [2] *Luther*. [3] latter.

2. 12, *Speaking evill of the things they underſtand not.* Confeſſing my ſelfe not to know the reaſons of their opinions, who though citing for it much Canonicall Scripture, yet their interpretations thereof may be but Apocrypha. Nor dare we receive it, not being ſafe to be familiar with ſtrangers at the firſt fight; and this Tenent is ſtrange, as ſet commonly afoot with theſe few laſt yeares. I am afraid rather on the contrary of a generall defection. Seeing the word is ſo ſlighted, and the gueſts begin to play with their meat, I feare leſt God the Maſter of the feaſt will call for the *Voyder:* that ſo when Chriſt comes to judgement, he ſhall *finde no faith on the earth.* But of things to come, *little* and *doubtfully.* If this opinion of Chriſts corporall comming very ſhortly be true, I hope if we live we ſhall have our ſhare therein: if otherwiſe, *Moſes* hath no cauſe to complaine if dying he commeth not into the Earthly *Canaan,* but into the Heavenly.

34. Meane time whileſt we expect the perſonall comming of Chriſt, let us pray for the peaceable comming back of him, who ſometimes is called Chriſt in the Scripture, *the Lords Annointed.* O the miſerable condition of our Land at this time! God hath ſhewed the whole World that *England* hath enough in it ſelfe to make it ſelfe happy or unhappy, as it uſeth or abuſeth it. Her homebred wares enough to maintain her, and her homebred warres enough to deſtroy her, though no forreigne Nation contribute to her Overthrow. Well, whileſt others fight for Peace, let us pray for Peace; for Peace on good termes, yea, on Gods termes, and in GODS time, when he ſhall be pleaſed to give it, and we fitted to receive it. Let us wiſh both King and Parliament ſo well as to wiſh neither of them better, but both of them beſt. Even a happy Accommodation.

35. Only this I will adde, that his Majeſty in making his Medals hath tooke the right courſe to propagate his promiſes and moſt royall intentions to poſterity, and raiſe it to behold the performance thereof. Seeing Princes memories have beene perpetuated by their Coines, when all other *Monuments, Arches, Obeliſks, Piramids, Theaters, Trophies,* and *Triumphs,* have yeelded to Time, and been quite forgotten. Yea, 'tis probable that the names of ſome ſhort reigning

[1] Emperours had been quite loft, if not found in their Impreffes on their Monies; Coynes having this peculiar priviledge to themfelves, that after they had beene buried many yeares in the ground, when taken up againe, they have life enough to fpeake the names of thofe Princes that caufed them and their Impreffions to be ftamped, either to their eternal fhame or lafting honour.

36. To conclude: let us all provide for that perfect Reformation in the world to come; when Chrift fhall prefent the Church his Spoufe to God his Father, *Without fpot*, comming from mans corruption, *or wrincle*, caufed by times continuance. When we fhall have a *new Heaven and a new Earth, wherein fhall dwell Righteoufneffe*. With judgements reformed from error, wills reformed from wilfulneffe, affections reformed from miftaking their object, or exceeding their meafure; all powers and parts of foule and body reformed from fin to fanctity. *Let us wait all the dayes of our appointed time* [2]*till our change come.* Until this time of Reformation. *Amen.*

---

[1] Roman Emperors.   [2] *untill.*

I approve this Sermon as Orthodox and ufefull.

John Downame.

FINIS.

[The foregoing Sermon was intemperately attacked in a small quarto pamphlet by the Rev. JOHN SALTMARSH, M.A., of Heslerton, Yorkshire, a village on the road between Malton and Scarborough; an account of whom will be found in the notes appended to this volume. The pamphlet (pp. 4 + 12), is here reprinted in full, with the title-page in fac-simile, from a copy belonging to the Editor. There is also added the Imprimatur of the Rev. CHARLES HERLE, the Rector of Winwick, Lancashire, one of the Licensers of the Press; an anonymous advertisement; and the dedication to the Assembly of Divines (all occupying page cccxvi.). There seems to have been a previous edition of these *Examinations,* which may have been called in and suppressed by the Author on account of objectionable epithets in the superscription of the above-named dedication. No copy of this edition is known to exist; but a copy of it was used by FULLER when writing his reply to it, called *Truth Maintained.* In that tract, indeed, FULLER reprinted SALTMARSH's original dedication in full, placing it in as prominent type before his own dedication to the two Universities. It is from this source that we learn that the first form of the superscription was as follows :—" To the Most Sacred, and Reverend Assembly For the Reformation of the Church, now convened by the Parliament.— Most Sacred and Reverend Divines," &c. The amended superscription will be found on the next page but one. FULLER's dedication, *posteà,* page 321 *seq.,* should be read in connection with SALTMARSH's. The Assembly perhaps itself made objections to the epithets. FULLER relates in his *Church-History* that the good success of the Assembly was prayed for by the City preachers, " and books dedicated to them, under the title of the most *Sacred Assembly,* which, because they did not disavow, by others they were interpreted to approve." He adds in his margin, as an instance of the books referred to, " Mr SALTMARSH his book against THO. FULLER " (Book xi. page 200, § iv.). There is no manuscript date to the copy in the British Museum (701. g. 4/6).

FULLER himself, when replying to the pamphlet, reprinted in sections the whole of it (excepting the title-page). His example has been followed in this edition of the Sermons, the *Examinations,* however, being reprinted in small type for the sake of a distinction which will readily enable the reader to peruse the entire pamphlet. Its arrangement in (eleven) "examinations" is according to SALTMARSH's divisions. In FULLER's reprint, the headings there given (viz. " Examiner" and " Treatise,") refer respectively to SALTMARSH and FULLER. The index-letters were inserted by FULLER in SALTMARSH's text for the purpose of referring to his own comments. The pamphlet, both in its original and reprinted form, has been very carelessly printed; but a tolerably accurate text has been obtained from a comparison. Occasionally where FULLER has in his pamphlet varied any important spelling or altered a word, the differences are indicated in the notes; but these variations may in part be due to the other edition of the *Examinations* which has been referred to.]

EXAMINATIONS,
OR,
A DISCOVERY
Of some Dangerous Positions
delivered in
A SERMON
OF
REFORMATION
Preached in the Church of the Savoy last
fast day, *Iuly* 26. by *Tho. Fuller* B.D.
and since printed.

2 Tim. 3. 5.
Having a forme of godlinesse, but denying the power thereof.

By *Iohn Saltmarsh*, Master of Arts, and Pastor of
Heslerton in Yorkshire.

Raptim Scripta.

LONDON,
Printed for *Lawrence Blaiklock,* and are to bee sold at the
Sugar loafe near Temple Barre, 1 6 4 3.

Nihil invenio in hoc libello, cui titulus (Examinations or a Discovery of some dangerous Positions delivered in a Sermon of Reformation, preached by *Tho. Fuller* B.D.) *quin utiliter imprimatur.*

Charles Herle.

An Advertisement returned to the Author by a Reverend Divine, to certifie him touching the Licensers allowance of Mr. Fullers *late Sermon of Reformation.*

SIR, To satisfie you concerning Mr *Downams* approbation of Mr *Fullers* Sermon of Reformation, I can assure you I heard him complaine that he was wronged by him, in that he having taken exception at some passages of that Sermon, Mr *Fuller* promised to amend them according to his correction, but that he did not performe what he promised.

To the Reverend Divines now convened by Authority of Parliament, *for Consultation in matters of* RELIGION.

I HAVE but the thoughts of an afternoon to spread before you, for I examined the same pace that I read; that if it were possible, a truth might overtake an errour ere it got too farre. It is not a little encouragement that I may sit like the *Prophetesse under the Palmetree,* under such a *shade* as your *selves;* and what weaknesse soever may appeare in these my assertions, this ayring them under your *Patronage* will heale them : for so they brought *forth the sick into the streets that at least the shadow of* Peter *might touch some of them.* Thus have I suddenly set up my *Candle* for others to light their *Torch* at ; and I hope you will pardon me, if my zeale to the truth made mee see anothers *faults* sooner than my own.

*Your Servant
in Christ Jesus,*
JOHN SALTMARSH.

Truth Maintained.

Or
POSITIONS DELIVERED
in a Sermon at the SAVOY:
Since Traduced
For DANGEROVS:
Now Afferted
For SOVND and SAFE.

By THOMAS FVLLER, B.D. late of Sidney Colledge in Cambridge.

The Particulars are Thefe.

I. That the Doctrine of the Impoffibility of a Churches perfection, in this world, being wel underftood, begets not lazineffe but the more induftry in wife reformers.
II. That the Church of England cannot juftly be taxed with fuperftitious innovations.
III. How farre private Chriftians, Minifters, and fubordinate Magiftrates, are to concurre to the advancing of a Publique Reformation.
IIII. What parts therein are only to be acted by the Supreme Power.
V. Of the progreffe, and praife of paffive obedience.
VI. That no extraordinary Excitations, Incitations, or Infpirations are beftowed from God, on men in thefe days.
VII. That it is utterly unlawfull to give any juft offence to the papift, or to any men whatfoever.
VIII. What advantage the Fathers had of us, in learning and religion, and what we have of them.
IX. That no new light, or new effentiall truths, are, or can be revealed in this age.
X. That the doctrine of the Churches imperfection, may fafely be preached, and cannot honeftly be concealed.

With feverall Letters, to cleare the occafion of this Book.

I will beare the wrath of the Lord, becaufe I have finned againft him, untill he plead my caufe, and execute iudgment for me; then will he bring me forth to the light, and I fhall fee his righteoufneffe, *Micah.* 7. 9.

Printed at Oxford, Anno Dom. 1643.

[" How euer heauen or fortune caſt my lot,
 There liues or dies, true to King *Richards* Throne,
 A loyall, iuſt and vpright Gentleman :
 Neuer did Captive with freer heart
 Caſt off his chaines of bondage, and embrace
 His golden vncontroul'd enfranchiſement,
 More then my dancing ſoule doth celebrate
 This Feaſt of Battell, with mine Aduerſarie.
 Moſt mighty Liege, and my companion Peeres,
 Take from my mouth the wiſh of happy yeares :
 As gentle and as iocond as to ieſt
 Go I to fight : Truth hath a quiet breſt."
—*The Life and Death of King Richard the Second,*
 Act I. Sc. iii. lines 85-96.]

[Introduction.

THE "occasion" of this comparatively unknown tract is amply "cleared" by the budget of preliminary letters (pages 321-336), —elegant epistles, of which the editor has said elsewhere that their fine satire and manly spirit make them more deserving of recognition as specimens of epistolary correspondence. The treatise itself, which is really an enlargement of the *Reformation-Sermon*, is distinguished for its vigour, its wit, and its fairness; qualities which will give it no unworthy position in the literature of controversy. The spirit which the writer exhibits will be found to underlie the maxims of the Character entitled "The Controversial Divine," and its exemplar Dr. WHITAKER (*Holy State*, folio, 1652, pages 54-62). FULLER's ingenuous way of dealing with his opponent's *Examinations*, viz., by printing them in full before making his own comments, was derived from the example of his learned uncle, Dr. DAVENANT, Bishop of Salisbury, whose *Animadversions* (Cambridge, 8vo., 1641) upon SAMUEL HOARD's Treatise, entitled *God's Love to Mankind*, embodied the whole of the latter work, which was printed in sections in small type preceding the Bishop's rejoinders. FULLER followed the same course in regard to the more famous polemical disputation with Dr. HEYLYN in 1659; and the third chapter of that work (*Appeal of Iniured Innocence*, folio, page 3), which details personal and other arguments whether it was necessary to make an appeal in his own just vindication, ought to be consulted by all who wish to ascertain FULLER's disposition in regard to controversies. The two works named are the only writings of FULLER that fall under the head of polemics, his *Triple Reconciler*, 8vo., 1654, which takes up some of the vexed questions of the time, setting him forth rather as a pacificator than a controversialist.

FULLER's biographer has referred to some personal circumstances attending the controversy with SALTMARSH. "Several false rumours and cavils there are about his carriage and opinion touching that sacrilegious thing [the Solemn League and Covenant] by persons who were distanced as far from the knowledge of those passages as fortunately from being concerned and engaged within the reach of that snare. 'Twas not only easy but most prudential for other Ecclesiastical persons to quit their *Livings*, who were out of the gripes and clutches of those ravenous *Reformists* in order to keep their conscience inviolable; but it was difficult enough of it self for the Doctor to escape and get out of that place, when the next preferment would have been a Dungeon. Some velitations, transcient discourses, he made about that frequent and thumb'd subject of the reformation, the rather to suspend the busie censures of the *Parliament* and their party; wherein though he seemed to comply (but as far as the Rule and Example would allow) and indulge the misapprehension of those men, yet then his charitable disguises could not obscure him from the severe animadversions of several Ministers eminent in those Reforming Times, particularly Mr. SALTMARSH. The Contest between them is so known in print that it will be needlesse to trouble the Reader with it here" (*Life*, pages 18-19).

FULLER himself mentions the tract in his *Appeal* (folio, pt. ii. page 83; ed. NICHOLS, 1840, page 501), as follows: "I appeal to such who knew me in the Universitie, to those that have heard my many Sermons on this Subject in *London* and else where, but especially to my Book called *Truth Maintained*, made against Mr. SALTMARSH, wherein I have heartily (to place that first), largely, and to my power strongly vindicated, *Non licet Populo renuente Magistratù Reformationem moliri*."

The date of the appearance of the tract was perhaps about the end of February, 1643-4. A copy in the British Museum is dated in manuscript, "Mar. 8." FULLER states (page 329 *posteà*) that SALTMARSH's reply reached him at Oxford on 10th September, 1643; and he offers explanations why his own answer was "so late" (page 329). Of all the losses upon which he there pathetically dwells, he was most affected by the loss of his books and manuscripts, which had in 1641 been enriched by the literary bequests of Bishop DAVENANT. He seems, however, to have had access to the Bodleian library during the very careful preparation of the *Truth Maintained;* for the particular editions of most of the works cited in the foot-notes are found in that collection.

The text used for the present reprint has been a copy of the original edition from the Editor's collection; and the proofs have been collated with a transcript made several years ago from a copy in the possession of EDWARD RIGGALL, Esq., of Bayswater. The Editor's copy has, by some possessor in the seventeenth century, been carefully altered in several places, as if for the press; but there is no indication as to who this "corrector" was. The majority of his alterations consist of modernizations of orthography, and there are a few ingenious emendations of language; but care has been taken that none of them have passed into this reprint. The original was very carelessly printed at (perhaps) the over-worked press of Leonard Lichfield, the Printer to the University of Oxford. In the Editor's copy, as well as in others, the London edition of the *Sermon of Reformation* is bound up after the introductory epistles;—a plan that was perhaps followed on account of FULLER's request that, by all the obligations of charity, the *Sermon* should be read before entering upon the *Examination* (page 336). The *Truth Maintained* probably created a further demand for the *Sermon of Reformation*.]

To

the Two moſt Famous

VNIVERSITIES

of

ENGLAND.

I DARE not give you ſuch high Epithites as Maſter *Saltmarſh* beſtoweth upon the *Aſſembly*, to call you the [1]MOST SACRED. Be contented to be Stiled the *Two moſt Famous Vniverſities;* a Title which it is no Flattery to give you, but Injury to deny you.

I have the Studies of ſome whole dayes to ſpread before you. I am not aſhamed to confeſſe ſo much, but ſhould be aſhamed to preſent your learned Conſiderations with leſſe. And will rather runne the hazard of other mens Cenſure, to have ſtudied ſo long to no purpoſe, then to be guilty to my ſelfe of ſo much diſreſpect to *You* as to offer to your Patronage what coſt me but ſleight ſtudying.

Indeed I examined his Examinations of my Sermon with the ſame pace that I read them. But I could not confute his Errors ſo ſpeedily as I could diſcover them, nor could I ſo

---

[1] Quid amplius præpotenti et [ac] immortali Deo tribuimus ſi quod eius. proprium eſt eripimus? Bodin, *De Repub.* l. 1. c. ult. [Ed. Paris, fo. 1586, lib. I. cap. x. pag. 173.]

soon make them appeare to others as they appeared to me; and the Evidencing of his Faults did cost me some Paines, whereof I hope I shall never have just Cause to Repent.

I am altogether out of hope that my Truth should quickly overtake his Error, which had the Advantage of me both at the Starting and in the Speed. And yet I beleeve what I want in the swiftnesse of my Feet, I shall have in the Firmenesse of my footing. And when I overtake it at last, as I am sure I shall, seeing untruths will Tire (as being better at hand then at length), I am confident by Gods Assistance it will get firme and quiet Possession in spight of opposition.

It is altogether Improper for mee to compare You being Two in number to the *Palme Tree* under which the Prophetesse *Deborah* sate: But the Analogie will hold well, if I should resemble You to the *Two Olive Trees* continually dropping oyle in the Presence of God. And methinks Master *Saltmarsh* his Expression to the *Assembly*, VNDER SVCH A SHADE AS YOVR SELVES, making *them in the Assembly* but a Shadow (and then what is the Shadow of a Shadow worth under which hee desireth to sit?) was but an undervaluing and diminutive expressing of their worth.

I honour you as You Deserve, and Counting You a Real and Lasting Substance, so I addresse my Respects unto you:

Humbly requesting you to be pleased to Patronize and defend this my defence: the rather because what doctrines therein I deliver, not long since I suckt from One of you, and in this respect I beleive both Breasts give Milke alike. And therefore as your Learning is most Able, so your Goodnesse will bee willing to Protect the same, not so much because I had them from you as because you had them from the Truth.

Some perchance may blame my Choice in Choosing You for my Protection who in these troublesome times are scarce able to defend your selves: The Universities being now *Degraded*, at least suspended from the degree of their former Honour. And I wonder Men should now talke of *an Extraordinary great Light*, when the two Eyes of our Land (so you were ever accompted) are almost put out. However this short Interruption of your Happinesse will but adde the more to your Honour hereafter.

And here, as it were Store of Pride for me to Counsell you, so it were want of duty not to Comfort you. Know, the only Good Token of these Times is, That they are so extreamely Bad they can never last long. God give you a sanctified Impression of your Afflictions, neither to sleight them nor sink under them; and so, forbearing to be longer troublesome to your more serious Employments, resteth

The meanest of your Sonnes

or Nephewes,

Thomas Fuller.

To the Learned and my Worthy
Good Friend,
Master *CHARLES HERLE.*

SIR,

WHEN I read a Pamphlet of M. *Saltmarsh* written against me, it something moved my Affections, but nothing removed my Judgement. But when I saw it recommended to the world with your Approbation, in this manner,

> " Nihil invenio in hoc Libello, cui Titulus,
> " *Examinations, or a discovery of some dangerous Po-*
> " *sitions, delivered in a Sermon of Reformation Prea-*
> " *ched by Tho. Fuller,* B.D. quin utiliter imprimatur.
> *Charles Herle.*

I must confesse it troubled me not a little, suspecting either my Eyes or my Understanding, that either I misread *your Name*, or had mis-written something in my Sermon. Wherefore fearing Partiality might blind me in mine Owne Book (knowing that *Eli* was not the onely Indulgent Father to his owne Off-spring) I imparted my Sermon to some whom you respect, and they respect you, Men of singular Learning and Piety, to Examine it. These likewise could discover no dangerous Positions in it, except such as were dangerous for a Preacher to deliver, but safe for People to Receive in these Troublesome Times. And I am Confident that their Iudgement was such, They would not be deceived with my Falsehoods: and their Honesty such, They would not deceive me by their Flattery.

And now, Sir, (Love cannot Hate, but it may juftly be Angry,) Confider how your accufing of me to maintaine dangerous Pofitions, might, as the Times ftand, have undone me and mine, and at leaft have intituled mee to a Prifon, now adayes the Grave of men alive. Times are not as formerly, when Schollers might fafely Traverfe a Controverfie in difputation. Honourable Tilting is left off fince men fell to down-right killing; and in vaine fhould I difpute my Innocence againft Souldiers violence, who would interpret the Accufation of a man of your Credit to be my fufficient Conviction.

I have in this *my Defence*, fo well as God did Enable me, more clearly expreffed and ftrongly confirmed the Pofitions I formerly delivered, and requeft you to tell mee, which are the dangerous Points that here I mainetaine. By the Lawes of our Land, the Creditor hath his Choice, whether he will fue the Principall, or the Surety, and difcretion will advife him to fue him which is moft folveable. Your Ability is fufficiently knowne; and feeing you have beene pleafed to be bound for Mafter *Saltmarfh* his Booke, in your Approving it, blame me not, Sir, if I (I will not fay fue you) but Sue to you for my Reparation.

If you can Convince me of my Faults herein (and I will bring great defire, and fome capacity to Learne from you) I fhall owne my felfe your Profelyte, thanke God for you, and you for my Converfion. Yea, in a Printed fheet I will doe publique Penance to the open view of the World, to fhew men that although I had fo much Ignorance as to Erre, I have not fo much Impudence as to Perfift in an Errour, and fhall remaine,

Yours in all Chriftian Offices,

THOMAS FULLER.

To the Reverend and his Worthy good Friend,

Master · *IOHN DOWNAM.*

SIR,

BEING about to read Master *Saltmarsh* his examination of a Sermon of mine, which you (to the Preachers credit, and Printers security) were pleased to approve for *Orthodox and Vsefull*, mine eyes in the beginning thereof were entertained (I cannot say welcomed) with this following note,

> ' *An Advertisement returned to the Author by a •Reverend*
> ' *Divine, to certifie him touching the Licensers allowance*
> ' *of* Master Fullers *late Sermon of Reformation.*

> ' Sir, *To satisfie you concerning* M. Downams *approbation of*
> ' Master Fullers *Sermon of Reformation, I assure you I heard*
> ' *him complaine that he was wronged by him, in that having*
> ' *taken exception at some passages of that Sermon,* Master Fuller
> ' *promised to amend them according to his correction, but that*
> ' *he did not performe what he promised.*'

Conclude me not guilty if I were moved, but senceleffe if I had not beene perplext with this accusation. Had it beene true, I want a word bad enough to expresse the foulenesse of my deed. Yea, justly may my preaching be suspected of falshood, if my practise be convicted of dishonesty. We know how the [1]Corinthians from the supposed breach of

---

[1] 2 Cor. 1. 17, 18.

S. *Pauls* folemn promife were ready to infer the falfity, at leaft the Ievity of his doctrine, till the Apoftle had rectified their miftake. This added alfo to my trouble, that I can privately enjoy my innocence with more contentment to my felfe then I can publikly declare it with fafety to others. For the prefent therefore, all that I will returne is this.

Here is an Accufation without a witneffe, or a witneffe without a name, and both without truth. Would the Inke of this reverend Divine (whofoever he was) only hold out to blot my name, and not to fubfcribe his owne? We know what Court was complayned of as a great grievance, becaufe Men therein might not know their Accufers. If it cannot confift with our mutuall fafety to have my accufers (as [1] S. *Paul* had) *face to face*, yet it will ftand with equity I fhould have them name to name: till when, I account this nameleffe note no better then a Libel both on you and me.

God put an end unto thefe wofull times, before they put an end to us; that all outward hoftility being laid afide we may have more leifure to attend, and comfort to follow, that inward *Chriftian Warefare*, which your paines have fo well defcribed.

Yours in Chrift Iefus,
Thomas Fuller.

---

[1] Acts 25. 16.

To Master *JOHN SALTMARSH*, Minister of *Heslerton* in Yorke-shire.

SIR,

YOU have almost converted me to be of your opinion, that some *extraordinary Light* is peculiarly conferred on men in this age. Seeing what cost me many dayes to make, you in fewer houres could make void and confute. You *examined* (you say) *the same pace you read*, and (as is intimated) wrote as fast as you examined, and all *in one afternoon*. This, if it were false, I wonder you would say it; and if it were true, I wonder you could doe it. However I commend your policy herein: for besides that you have given the world notice of the Pregnancie of your parts (and it is no fault of yours, if you be rather heard than beleeved), hereby you have done me a great disadvantage. For if I at leisure discover some notable errors in your examinations, you have a present Plea that you wrote them suddenly, and I shall only be repaired for the wrong that you have done me with [1] your *raptim scripta*; whereas you had done *God as much Glory*, the cause as much good, more right to your selfe, and credit to me, if you had tooke more time, and more truely.

And now consider you only endeavour to confute some dismembred sentences of my Sermon, of which some are falsely, and more of them imperfectly alleged. You know how in a continued speech one part receives and returns

---

[1] [See page cccxv. and Cicero *ad Atticum*, ii. 9. 1.]

strength and lustre unto another: and how easie is it to overthrow the strongest sentence, when it is cut off from the Assistance of the Coherence before and after it? Alas, this disiointing of things undoeth kingdomes as well as sermons; whilest even weake matters are preserved by their owne unity and entirenesse. I have dealt more fairely with you, and set downe your whole Examinations, thereby not expecting any praise, but preventing just censure, if I had done otherwise.

If you demand why my answer comes so late, seeing so long silence may be interpreted a consent, know, Sir, it was the tenth of September before either friend in love would doe me the favour, or foe in anger the discourtesie to convey your booke unto me.

Whether this proceeded from the intercepting commerce betwixt the City and the Country, or that your Booke was loath to come out of London, as sensible that the strength of your positions consisted in the fortifications thereof.

When I had received one of your bookes, I had not your present parts to answer it. Men must doe as they may doe: I hope, though my credit may, Gods cause shall not suffer by my delay, seeing Truth doth not abate with time. Here I speake not of those many afflictions that have befalne me, as not being so unreasonable as to expect any pitty from others in these dolefull dayes, wherin none are at leisure to bemoane the misery of any private men whilst the generall Calamity ingrosseth all greife to it selfe ; and yet, I may say, such losses could not but disturbe my studies.

When I had finished my answer, I could not so speedily provide to have it printed. And to speake plainely, I was advised by my best friends to passe by your pamphlet altogether with silence and neglect, and apply my selfe onely to enlarge my Sermon, for the satisfaction of others.

However, that you may see I will not decline any thing, I have answered every operative passage in your Examination.

Here I might take juſt exception at the ſentence prefixed in the title page of your booke : 2 Tim. 3. 5, *Having a forme of Godlineſſe, but denying the power thereof.* Out of the whole quiver of the Bible, could you chooſe no other Arrow to ſhoot, and make me your marke? whom if you taxe for a *meere formaliſt,* God grant I may make a good uſe of your bad ſuſpition of me, endeavouring to acquit my ſelfe in Heaven, whom you have accuſed on Earth : I muſt *ſtand or fall to my owne Maſter,* to whom I hope I ſhall *ſtand,* being held up by my Saviour. Remember, remember, we muſt all appeare before *Gods Judgment Seat,* when thoſe things which *have been done in ſecret* ſhall be brought to light. Meane time goe you on as faſt as you can in the high way to heaven; but be not too free willfully to daſh your fellow travellers with foule aſperſions : for if dirt may paſſe for coine, debts in this nature may eaſily be paid you backe againe. So reſteth

Thomas Fuller.

To My Deare Parish
SAINT MARY SAVOY.

MY deare Parish: for so I dare call you, as conceiving that although my calamities have divorced me from your bed and board, the matrimoniall knot betwixt us is not yet rescinded. No, not although you have admitted another (for feare I hope rather then affection) into my place. I remember how *David* when forced to fly from his wife yet still cals her, [1]*My wife Michall:* even when at that time, she was in the possession of *Phaltiel* the sonne of *Laish*, who had rather bedded then wedded her.

This Sermon I first made for your sake, as providing it not as a feast to entertaine strangers, but a meale to feed my family. And now having againe inlarged and confirmed it, I present it to you, as having therein a proper interest, being confident that nothing but good and profitable truth is therein contain'd.

Some perchance will obiect that if my Sermon were so true, why then did I presently leave the parish when I had preached it? My answer is legible in the Capital letters of other ministers miserie, who remaine in the City. I went away [2]*for the present distresse*, thereby reserving my selfe to doe you longer and better service if Gods providence shall ever restore me unto you againe. And if any tax mee as *Laban* taxed *Iacob*, [3]*Wherefore didst thou flee away secretly*, without taking solemne leave? I say with *Iacob* to *Laban*, [4]*Because I was afraid.* And that plaine dealing Patriarch, who could not be accused for purloining a shooe latchet of other mens goods,

---

[1] 2 Sam. 3. 14.   [2] 1 Cor. 7. 26.   [3] Gen. 31. 27.   [4] Gen. 31. 31.

confesseth himselfe guilty of that lawfull felony, that hee *stole away* for his owne safety: seeing truth it selfe may sometimes seeke corners, not as fearing her cause, but as suspecting her judge.

And now all that I have to say to you is this: [1]*Take heed how you heare;* imitate the wise and noble [2]*Bereans,* whatsoever the Doctor or doctrine bee which teacheth or is taught unto you: *Search the Scripture dayly whether these things be so.* Hansell this my counsell on this my booke: and here beginning, hence proceed to examine all Sermons by the same rule of Gods word.

Only this I adde also: Pray daily to God to send us a good and happy Peace before we be all brought to utter confusion. You know how I in all my Sermons unto you, by leave of my Text, would have a passage in the praise of Peace. Still I am of the same opinion. The longer I see this warre, the lesse I like it, and the more I loath it. Not so much because it threatens temporall ruine to our Kingdome as because it will bring a generall spirituall hardnesse of hearts. And if this warre long continues, we may be affected for the departure of *charity,* as the *Ephesians* were at the going away of Saint *Paul,* [3]*Sorrowing most of all, that we shall see the face thereof no more.* Strive therefore in your prayers that that happy condition which our sinnes made us unworthy to hold, our repentance may, through Gods acceptance thereof, make us worthy to regaine.

Your Loving Minister,

THOMAS FULLER.

---

[1] Luke 8. 18.   [2] Acts 17. 11.   [3] Acts 20. 38.

To the unpartiall Reader.

BE not affraid to perufe my Pofitions, though they be accufed to bee dangerous. The Saints did not feare infection from the company of Saint *Paul*, though he was indicted to be a [1]*Peſtilent Fellow*.

To acquaint you with my intentions in this Book (that fo you may proportion your expectation accordingly): Herein I have to my Power vindicated the truth, confulting with my confcience, not outward fafety, infomuch that I care not whom I difpleafed to pleafe *the Bird in my Breaſt*. Yea, when the actions of other men have by the Examiner beene laid to my charge, I have tooke the boldneffe to leave them to their Authors to defend. For though Honeftie commands me to pay my owne debts, yet difcretion advifeth me from [2]*Solomons* mouth to avoid *Sureti-ſhip*, and not to Breake my felfe with being bound for the Errors of others.

I cannot but expect to procure the Ill-will of many, becaufe I have gone in a middle and moderate way betwixt all extremities. I remember a ſtory too truely appliable to me. Once a Jayler demanded of a Prifoner, newly committed unto him, whether or no he were a Roman Catholick. *No*, anfwered he. *What then?* faid he. *Are you an Anabaptiſt? Neither*, replied the Prifoner. *What!* said the other. *Are you a Browniſt? Nor ſo*, faid the man; *I am a Proteſtant*. Then faid the Jayler, Get you into the dungeon: I will afford no favor to you, who ſhall get no profit by you. Had you beene of any of the other religions, fome hope I

---

[1] Acts 24. 5.   [2] Pro. 11. 15.

had to gaine by the visits of such as are of your owne profession. I am likely to finde no better usage in this age, who professe my selfe to be a plaine Protestant, without wealt or garde, or any Addition; equally opposite to all *Hereticks* and *Sectaries*.

Let me mate this with another observation. By the [1]*Law of the twelve Tables*, if a man were indebted but to one creditor, he had no Power over his body; but if he owed mony to many, and was not solvable, all his creditors together might share his body betwixt them, and by joynt consent pluck him in peeces. Me thinks a good Morall lurkes in this cruell Law; namely, that men who oppose one adversary alone, may come off and shift pretty well, whilst he who provokes many enemies, must expect to bee torne asunder: and thus the poore *Levite* will bee rent into as many pieces as the [2]*Levites wife* was.

Yet I take not my selfe to bee of so desolate and forlorne a Religion as to have no fellow professors with me. If I thought so, I should not only suspect, but condemne my judgement: having ever as much loved singlenesse of heart as I have hated singularity of opinion. I conceive not my selfe like [3]*Eliah to be left alone:* having, as I am confident, in England more than seventy thousand just of the same Religion with me. And amongst these there is one in price and value eminently *worth tenne thousand*, even our gratious Soveraigne, whom God in safety and honour long preserve amongst us.

And here I must wash away an aspersion, generally, but falsely cast on men of my profession and temper: for all *moderate* men are commonly condemned for *Lukewarme*.

      As it is true,   *Sæpe latet vitium proximitate boni.*
      It is as true,   *Sæpe latet virtus proximitate mali.*

---

[1] Bodin, *De Repub.* lib. 1. p. 50 [ed. Paris, fo. 1586, cap. v. page 32].
[2] Iudg. 19. 29.   [3] 1 Kings 19. 14.

And as Lukewarmneffe hath often fared the better (the more mens ignorance) for pretending neighbourhood to moderation; fo Moderation (the more her wrong) hath many times fuffered for having fome fuppofed vicinity with lukewarmneffe. However they are at a grand diftance, Moderation being an wholefome Cordiall to the foule: whilft lukewarmneffe (a temper which feekes to reconcile hot and cold) is fo diftaftefull that *health it felfe* feemes fick of it, and [1]vomits it out. And we may obferve thefe differences betwixt them.

First, the Lukewarme man (though it be hard to tell what he is, who knowes not what he is himfelfe) is fix't to no one opinion, and hath no certain creed to beleeve: Whereas the Moderate man fticks to his principles, taking Truth wherefoever he findes it, in the opinions of friend or foe; gathering an herb though in a ditch, and throwing away a weed though in a Garden.

Secondly, the Lukewarme man is both the archer and marke himfelfe; aiming only at his owne outward fecurity. The Moderate man levels at the glory of God, the quiet of the Church, the choofing of the Truth, and contenting of his confcience.

Laftly, the Lukewarme man, as hee will live in any Religion, fo he will dye for none. The Moderate man, what he hath warily chofen, will valiantly maintaine, at leaft wife intends and defires to defend it, to the death. The *Kingdome of Heaven* (faith our [2]Saviour) *fuffereth violence*. And in this fenfe, I may fay, the moft moderate men are the moft violent, and will not abate an hoofe or haires breadth in their Opinions, whatfoever it coft them. And time will come when Moderate men fhall be honoured as *Gods Doves*, though now they be hooted at as *Owles in the Defart*.

But my Letter fwels too great, I muft break off. Only

---

[1] Rev. 3. 16.   [2] Mat. 11. 12.

requefting the reader by all obligations of charity, firft to read over my *Sermon* before he entreth on the *Examination*. To conclude: when I was laft in *London*, it was generally reported that I was dead; nor was I difpleafed to heare it. May I learne from hence with the Apoftle, *To Die daily*. And becaufe to God alone tis known how foon my death may come, I defire to fet forth this book as my *Will and Teftament*, which if it can be of no ufe to the reader, it may be fome eafe and comfort to the writer, that the world may know in this multitude of Religions what is the Religion of

Thy Servant in Chrift Iefus,
Thomas Fuller.

TRUTH Maintained.

Examiner.

THE [a]POLICY OF THE SERMON OF REFORMATION.

[1] THE Scope of the *Sermon* is *Reformation;* but it fo [b]moderates, fo modificates and conditionates the *Perfons,* and *Times,* and *Bufineffe,* that *Reformation* can [c]advance little in this way or method. As our Aftronomers who draw fo many lines and imaginary Circles in the Heavens that they put the [d]Sun into an heavenly Labyrinth and a learned perplexity; Such is the [e]*Zodiack* you would make for the light of the Gofpel and the Sun of Reformation to move in. It was one of the Policies of the *Iewes* [f]*Adverfaries,* that when they heard of their buildings, they would build with them: *They faid, Let us build with you, for wee feek your God as you doe.* But the people of God would have no fuch helpers; there is no fuch [g]Jefuiticall way to hinder our work as to work with us, and under fuch infinuations fet the Builders at variance when they fhould fall to labour; and how eafie is it to reafon flefh and blood back from a good way and good refolutions? I remember the *old* [h]*Prophet* had foone perfwaded even the *man of God* to return when he told him, *I am a Prophet as thou art,* 1 Kings 13. 18.

Treatife.

(*a*) The *Policy of the Sermon.*) Such carnall Policy, wherein the fubtilty of the Serpent ftings the fimplicity of the Dove to death, I utterly difclaim in my Sermon. Chriftian Policy is neceffary, as in our Practice, fo in our Preaching; for Piety is always to goe before it, but never to goe without it.

(*b*) *But it fo moderates and modificates.*) The moft Civill Actions will turne wild, if not warily moderated. But if my Sermon clogges Reformation with falfe or needleffe Qualifications (till the ftrength of the matter leakes out at them), my guilt is great. I am confident of my Innocence: let the Evidence be produced and the Reader judge.

(*c*) *That Reformation can advance but little in this way.*) Know that *Zoar a little one* that is lasting, is better then a great Babel of Confusion. That Reformation which begins slowly and surely will proceed cheerfully and comfortably, and continue constantly and durably. Builders are content to have their Foundations creepe, that so their Superstructures may runne: let us make our Ground-worke good, and no more haft then good speed.

(*d*) *They put the Sunne into an heavenly Labyrinth and learned perplexity with their imaginary Lines.*) This your strong line more perplexeth me to understand it: Onely this I know, that you might have instanced more properly in any other Planet which is more loaden with Cycles and Epicycles; whilst the Sunne hath found from Astronomers this favour and freedome, to be left to the simplest Motion.

(*e*) *Such a Zodiack you would make for the light of the Gospell.*) Were I to spread out the Zodiack of the Gospell, it should stretch from Pole to Pole, and be adequate to the Heavens. There should be no more Pagans in the World then there were [1]Smiths *at one time* in Israel; not that I would have any kild, but all converted; yea, the Sunne of Reformation should not have so much darknesse as a shadow to follow it. To effect this, my wishes are as strong as my power is weake. I will (God willing) pray and preach for it, and therefore doe not slander me to be *an Hinderer of the Word.*

(*f g h*) *Of the Jewes adversaries. Jesuiticall way. The old Prophet.*) What you say is as true in the History as false in the Application to me. You compare me to the *Ammonites* (Adversaries to Gods people), to Jesuits, to the old lying Prophet. I hope the God of *Michael* the Arch-Angell will give me patience, when he that [2]disputed with him shall furnish others railing. And now torture me no longer with your Accusation; come to the proofe.

Examiner.

I finde there are three Principles animates *the Sermon:*
1. *How imperfect a* [1]*Church will be and a Reformation, doe the best you can.*

---

[1] 1 Sam. 13. 19.   [2] Jude 9.

2. *That the light which the* [k]*Fathers had formerly was as full and glorious as the light of these dayes, or rather brighter.*

3. *That none but the* [l]*Supreme authority, or authority Royall, and that alone, ought to begin and act in this Reformation.*

These are your principles; and let [m]any judge if this bee a qualification fit for him that judges or writes of such a truth. For, first, hee that conceits [n]there can bee no *perfection of a Church on earth* will scarce labour to make that Church *better*, which he is sure will be *bad* at all times; nor will hee [o]care for any *new light* while the *old* is in best reputation with him; nor will he seek to advance the work, but stay for a supreme authority alone: a good [p]policie to stay the Reformation till his Majesties return, and then there is [q]hopes it may coole in their hands.

Treatise.

(*i*) *How imperfect a Church.*) I said it, and I say it againe: it was a Truth before your Cradle was made, and will be one after your Coffin is rotten.

(*k*) *That the light that the Fathers had formerly was as full and glorious.*) Shew me such a fillable in all the Sermon and I'le yeeld the cause: Not that this Position is false, but becaufe I never said it; except you collect it from those my words [1]where I say that the *Moderns had a mighty advantage of the Ancients who lived in the Marches of Paganisme and in the time wherein the Mistery of Iniquity began to worke.*

(*l*) *None but the supreame Authority, or Authority Royall.*) I said that the supreame Authority alone in those respective places wherein it is supreame, hath the lawfull calling to reforme.

Thus, of the three Principles which you reckon in my Sermon, The first I said, [and] I will defend it; The second I said not, and doe deny it; The third I said otherwise then you doe alleadge it. And yet even for the two latter (that you may not complaine for want of play) in due time, as occasion is offered, I will fully discover my opinion that so we may eitheir freely agree or fairely dissent.

(*m*) *And let any judge.*) On Gods blessing let any indifferent person who is devested of prejudice, which maketh a bad witnesse and a worse judge: And now we joyne Issues.

(*n*) *For, first, he that conceits there can be no perfection in a*

---

[1] [See ¶¶ 32, 24; pp. 311, 307.]

Church will scarce labour to make that Church better.) If the *He* you spake of be a meere carnall man, this nor any other principle (save Grace and Gods Spirit) can spurre him on to goodnesse. But if this *He* be a regenerate man, this doctrine will make him tire no whit the sooner in his endeavours of Reformation. You say *he will scarce labour*, whereby you confesse he will labour. The Gramarian saith, *Quod fere fit, non fit, quod vix fit, fit.* One *scarce* is better then ten thousand *almosts*. Yet I perceive by the scant measure in your expression that you conceive this Doctrine of the impossibility of a Churches perfection on earth to be but a backe friend to Reformation. Heare therefore what I answer for my selfe.

First, hereby you furnish the papists with a Cavill and with a Colour to enforce the same against the Protestants.

1. The Doctrine of the impossibility of a Churches perfection in this world, being well understood, begets not lazinesse but the more industry in wise reformers.

For we teach and maintaine that the best workes of men are stained with some imperfections. Hence the papists may inferre *That he that conceits there can be no perfection in a good deed will scarce labour to doe one.* And thus our Doctrine shall be condemned for disheartning of holinesse. See, Sir, how you meet popery in your undiscreet shunning of it.

Secondly, though there can be no absolute perfection in a Church, yet *quoad gradum*, in some good degree it is attainable, and all good men will endeavour it. Mariners which make forth for the Northerne Discoveries goe out with this assurance: that it is impossible to come to the pole. Yet have they sought and found out very farre, almost to the eightieth degree of latitude. What covetousnesse or curiosity did in them, sure Grace is as active to doe in Gods Children, who will labour *to draw neere* to a perfect Reformation in obedience to Gods command, though they know they shall never fully attaine unto it.

Thirdly, the Doctrine of the impossibility of a perfect Reformation in this world well understood begets not idlenesse, but the more industry in mens endeavours. For those that beleeve that the perfection of a Church may be attained in this life are subject to this mistake (one errour is procreative of another): to thinke that sometimes they themselves have attained it, and so ending in the midst of their journey may sit downe and take up their rest: Whereas those who conceive the impossibility of perfection are kept in constant doing, having still *plus ultra*, with Saint *Paul*, [1]*forgetting those things that are behind, they reach forth to those things which are before, and presse towards the marke.*

Fourthly, if it be objected that the impossibility of perfection discourageth men to endeavour it, seeing they cannot rationally desire it, *non est voluntas impossibilium*, it is no levell wish aimed at a marke, but a Velleity shot at randome, which desires an impossibility. It is answered that Gods servants endeavouring a perfect Reformation doe not light on a labour in vaine, that which is wanting in them being supplyed in Gods acceptance: If they doe their best, their desire is taken for the deed: The deformities of their imperfect Reformation being pardoned by God in Christ, in which respect *their labours are not in vaine in the Lord.*

Lastly, seeing this point of the impossibility of a Churches perfection is most true (as hereafter we shall make so appeare), if hereupon any grow remisse and large [lagge] in Reforming, it is not the fault of Gods straight Doctrine, but of mens crooked practice: For if men inferre hellish Conclusions from heavenly promises [premises], such bad consequences are not the lawfull Children of Gods Truth, but the Bastards of mans corruption, where they are justly to be fathered for their maintenance. And now I suppose that your exception in those your words *will scarce labour* is abundantly answered.

(*o*) *Nor will he care for any new light whilst the old is in best reputation with him.*) This is grounded on what I never said; but if by the *old light* be meant that which shined from the Ancient of dayes into the Scriptures, and thence through the Fathers to us, I preferre it before any new light whatsoever.

(*p*) *A good policy to stay the Reformation till His Majesties returne.*) It need not have stayed till His Majesties returne, which might have been done before His going away; who so often and so earnestly offered to reforme whatsoever could

---

Phil. 3. 13.

juftly be convinced to be amiffe in our Church; which proffers had they been as thankfully accepted as they were gracioufly tendered, long fince it had been done what we now difpute of, though it matters not for the fpilling of our inke, if other mens blood had beene fpared. And I doubt not when opportunity is offered, His Majesty will make good his word, whom no Vollyes of difcurtefies, though difcharged never fo thicke againft him, fhall drive him from His Princely Promife, whilft he lookes not downewards on mens behaviour to him, but upwards to his Proteftations to God, learning from Him whom he reprefents to be *Unchangeable*. But if (which God forefend: and yet all earthly things are cafuall) it fhould come to paffe that in point of Reformation what formerly was proffered by the Sovereigne and refufed by the Subject fhould hereafter be requefted by the Subject and denied by the Sovereigne, we fhall have leifure enough to admire Gods Juftice, bemoane our owne condition, and inftruct our Pofterity not to outftand good offers, leaft for want of feeing their happineffe they feele their owne mifery. But to returne to your mentioning of His Majefties return: when all is done, for ought I can fee, Reformation muft ftay till His Majefties returne. As for the time and manner thereof, when and how it fhall be done, God in his goodneffe and wifdome fo order it that it may be moft for his glory, the Kings honour, the good of the Church and State. But this I fay againe, that till this his returning the generall enjoyning and peaceable practifing of any Reformation cannot be performed.

(*q*) *And then there is hope it may coole in their hands.*) If by their hands you meane his Majefties (and what elfe can your words import?) it is as difloyall a fufpition as his would be an unfitting expreffion that fhould fay that Reformation would boyle over in the hands of the Parliament. But, Sir, thus farre you have excepted againft my Sermon in generall; now you are pleafed to confute fome particulars thereof.

Examiner.

Sermon, page 9 [¶ 10, page 301].

Withall, we flatly deny that Queene Elizabeth *left the duft behind the doore, which fhe caft on the dunghill, whence this uncivill expreffion is raked up.* The doctrine by her established, and by her successours maintained in the thirty-nine Articles, if declared, explained, and asserted from false glosses, have all gold, no dust or drosse in them.

[2] *Examination.* I will not detract from the Religious [1] housewifery of such a *Queen* of famous memory; but wee know her *Reformation* is talkt [2] on now in a [r] politick reverence, and are commended back into her times only to hinder us from going forward in our own; for I am sure till this engine was contrived, she was not such a Saint in the [s] *Prelates Calender.*

For the *Doctrine established from her times*, though it bee not the businesse so much of our Reformation as the thirty-nine *Articles* where it dwels, yet this wee know: either *the light of the Doctrine* was very dimme, or the eyes of our [t] *Bishops* and *Iesuites;* for [3] one of them would needs spie *Arminianisme*, and the [4] Iesuite *Popery*. And some will make it a Probleme yet, whether their glosse may accuse the Article or the Article their glosse; such *Cassanders* found so much latitude in our Doctrine as to attempt a [v] reconciliation of their Articles and ours together.

Treatise.

(*r*) If there be any so base that they now make Queene *Elizabeths* Reformation their protection, which formerly they disdained (running in raine to that bush for shelter, which they meane to burne in fair weather), shame light on them for their hypocrisie. Let such be stript naked to their utter disgrace, who onely weare the Memory of that worthy Queene to cloke and cover them in their necessity, whose Reformation was signed with successe from Heaven: our Nation in her time being as famous for forreigne Atchievements as now it is infamous for home-bred dissentions. Yet God forbid our eyes should be so dazled with the lustre of her days as not to goe forward to amend the faults thereof, if any such be justly complained of.

(*s*) *Shee was not such a Saint in the Prelates Calender.*) I never saw the *Prelates Calender;* but in the late *reformed Almanacks*, I find neither *Her* nor any other for *Saints.*

(*t*) I expect (and ever may expect) that you would have produced some drosse in our Articles, instancing in some false place or point contained in them; and then I must either have yeelded to you with disgrace, or opposed you with disadvantage. But instead of this you only tell us how some

---

[1] huswifry: *Truth Maintained*, page 8.   [2] of: *ibid.*, page 8.
[3] Bishop Montague.   [4] Fransf. a Sancta Clara.

have feene Arminianifme and Popery in them. I anfwer: So the Papifts doe read every point of Popery where you will fay it was never written in the Scripture. Thofe who bring the jaundies in their eyes doe find yellowneffe in every object they behold; and nothing can be fo cautioufly pen'd but ingaged perfons will conftrue it to favour their opinions.

(*v*) *As to attempt a reconciliation of their Articles and ours together.*) Thus many *Egyptian* Kings attempted to let the Red fea into the Mediterranian. A project at firft feeming eafie to fuch as meafured their neerneffe by the eye, and at laft found impoffible by thofe who furveyed their diftance by their judgment; feeing art and induftry can never marry thofe things whofe bands Nature doth forbid. And I am confident that with the fame fucces any fhal undertak the Accommodating of Englifh and Romifh Articles. Nor can the wifeft Church in fuch a Cafe provide againft the boldneffe of mens attempting, though they may prevent their endeavours from taking effect. For my owne Opinion, as on the one fide I fhould be loath that the Bels fhould be taken downe out of the fteeple and new-caft every time that unwife people tune them to their *Thinke*: So on the other fide I would not have any juft advantage given in our Articles to our Adverfaries. However, what you fay confutes not, but confirmes my words in my Sermon, that the thirty-nine Articles need *declaring, explaining, and afferting from falfe gloffes*. And feeing it is the peculiar Priviledge of Gods Word to be perfect at once and for ever, on Gods bleffing let the darke words in our Articles be expounded by cleerer, doubtfull expreffed in plainer, improper exchanged for fitter; what is fuperfluous be removed, wanting fupplyed, too large contracted, too fhort enlarged; always provided that this be done by thofe who have calling, knowledge and difcretion to doe it.

Examiner.

Sermon, page 9 [¶ 11, page 302].

Againe, we freely confeffe that there may be fome faults in our Church in matters of Practice and Ceremonies; and no wonder if there be: it would be a miracle if there were not. Besides, there be some innovations rather in the Church [1]than of the Church, as not chargeable on the publike account.

[3] *Examination.* These are ʷbut ²ſubtle Apologies and diſtinctions for the ˣſuperſtitions in the Church, and to take off the eyes of our Reformers, and entertain them into changeable diſcourſes ; as if they were faults, and no faults ; and thoſe that were, were irreformable, and could not be made better : and thus, while the errours of our Church ſhould call them to reform, your ʸdifficulties and impoſſibilities would call them off. You ſay, It were a miracle to have none. This is ſuch ᶻSophiſtry as the malignity of your Clergy would caſt in the way of our Reformation. And for the ᵃInnovations, they have been made by your moſt learned, the immediate iſſues of our Church ; our Rubrick and Practice have been called to witneſſe it ; therefore goe not on to perſwade ſuch a ᵇfundamentall integrity, and eſſentiall purity. You know in what a poore caſe that ᶜ*Church* was when ſhee thought *her ſelfe rich, and full, and glorious :* he is no leſſe an enemy to the patient [1]than to the Phyſitian that would perſwade him that all is well, or at leaſt incurable.

Treatiſe.

(*w*) *Theſe are but ſubtill Apologies.*) Truly no ſuch matter : they are even plaine and downeright confeſſions from the ſimplicity of my heart.

(*x*) *For the ſuperſtitions in the Church.*) Sir, lay not your Enditement higher then you are ſure your proof will reach. You might have done well to have inſiſted on ſome particulars ; whilſt now your generals accuſe much, convict nothing.

(*y*) *Your difficulties and impoſſibilities would call them off.*) Not ſo ; for to ſhew wiſe Reformers the true difficulties of their worke will quicken, not quench, their endeavours. Thus the Carpenter, being truly told that the wood is hard he is to hew, will therefore not throw away his Axe, but ſtrike with the greater force. And that the Doctrine of the impoſſibility of a Churches perfect Reformation on earth well underſtood is no hinderer to mens Labours to Reforme, hath been largely proved before.

(*z*) *You ſay, it were a Miracle for a Church to have no faults : This is ſuch ſophiſtry as the Malignity of your Clergy would caſt in the way of our Reformation.*) This ſophiſtry will at laſt prove good Logick ; and whatſoever you pretend

---

[1] then : *Trvth Maintained*, pages 10-11.   [2] ſubtill : *ibid.*, page 11.

of *Malignity*, this is a truth to be confided in: Namely, That no Church in this world can be fo compleat but it will have faults. For the Church being a body confifting of imperfect men the Members thereof, the body muft needs be imperfect alfo. This appears by the conftant neceffity of Preaching, which otherwife might well be fpared, and all our Sermons turned into Pfalmes; as alfo by *the power of the Keyes*, which will never ruft in the Church for want of imployment. Yea, that Petition in the Prayer of Chrifts providing for us, *And forgive us our Trefpaffes as we forgive them that Trefpaffe againft us*, were both needleffe and falfe if men might be perfect in this world. This perchance is the reafon why the Perfection-mongers of this Age quarrell with this Prayer, as having too much pride to confeffe their owne faults and too little Charity to forgive other mens: fo ill doth a Publicans prayer fit a Pharifees mouth.

(*a*) *As for Innovations, they have beene made by your moft learned.*) Concerning Innovations I muft inlarge my felfe. In mixt Actions, wherein good and bad are blended together, we can neither chufe nor refufe all, but may pick out fome, and muft leave the reft.

<small>2. That the Church of England cannot juftly be taxed with fuperftitious innovations.</small>

Firft, they may better be tearmed Renovations then Innovations, as lately not new forged, but new furbifhed. Secondly, they were not fo many as fome complaine. The fufpitious old man cryes out in the Comedy that fix hundred Cooks were let into his houfe, when they were but two. Jealoufie hath her hyperboles as well as her flattery. Thirdly, fome of thefe Innovations may eafier be rayled on then juftly reproved; namely, fuch as concerned the adorning of Churches, and the comlineffe of mens behaviour in Gods fervice, where outward decency (if not garifh, coftly above the Eftates of the parifh, mimicall, affected or fuperftitious) is the Harbinger to provide the lodging for inward holineffe. For fome bodily diftance brings our fouls the neerer to God, with whom fome have fuch clownifh familiarity, they have the leffe friendfhip. Fourthly, if thefe gave offence, it was not for any thing in themfelves, but either becaufe,

Firft, they were challenged to be brought in without law.

This often makes good matters to be ill relished; honest men if wise withall being loath to pay their obedience before it becomes legally due.

Secondly, becaufe they feemed new and unufuall; and we know how in dangerous times every well-meaning stranger may be fufpected for a fpy till he hath given an account of himfelfe. Now few daughter-Churches had feen fuch Ceremonies, though fome of their Mother-Cathedrals could well remember them.

Thirdly, becaufe they were multiplied without any fet number; and thofe Ceremonies which men faw were indefinit they feared would be infinit.

Fourthly, becaufe they were preffed in fome places without moderation. And herein fome young men (I will not fay, ran without fending, but) ran further then they were fent, outftripping them who firft taught them to goe.

Fifthly, becaufe they were preffed by men, fome of whofe perfons were otherwife much diftafted; how juftly, let them feek who are concerned.

Laftly, becaufe men complained that painfull Preaching and pious living, the life of Gods fervice, were not preffed and practifed with equall earneftneffe as outward decency, the luftre thereof; whence their feares inferred that the fhaddowes would devour the Subftance.

Now whereas you fay that thefe Innovations have been made by *our moft learned*, herein I muft confeffe that the fcales of my fkill are too little in them to weigh the learning of great Schollers, and to conclude who have the *moft*. But this I know: that alwayes a diftinction hath been made and admitted betwixt the opinions and practife of the moft eminent particular Doctors (how great foever in place, power or parts) and the Refolutions and Commands of the Church in generall. In which refpect, what hitherto you alleadge to the contrary doth no whit difprove my words, that fuch Innovations are rather *in the Church then of the Church*, by which they were never abfolutely enjoyned nor generally received, as alwayes difclaimed by many, and lately difufed by moft.

Such indeed as ufed them out of Confcience (I fhould

have no Confcience to think otherwife of fome) are not to be blamed if they privately practife them ftill, at their own perill, till their judgements are otherwife informed. Such as took them up for fafhion fake, for fafhion fake have fince laid them downe. Such as were frighted into them defift now their feare is removed. Laftly, thofe who ufed them in hope of preferment, now difufe them in defpaire thereof; not to fay fome of them are as violent on the contrary fide, and perchance onely wait *the Word of command* from the prevalent party to turne *Faces about* againe. In briefe, feeing generally thefe Ceremonies are left off, it feems neither Manners nor Charity alwayes to lay that in mens difhes which the Voider fome pretty while fince hath cleane taken away.

Say not that thefe Innovations are now rather in a fwound then dead, and likly to revive when cherifhed with the warmth of Authority, feeing His Majefty hath often and fully proffered that whatfoever is juftly offenfive in them fhall be removed ; and pitty it is but that the reft fhould by the fame lawfull power be re-enforced. But enough hereof, and more perchance then will pleafe the Reader, though leffe could not have fatisfied the Writer : if I have contented any, well ; if I have difpleafed all, I am contented.

(*b*) *Therefore goe not on to perfwade fuch a Fundamentall Integrity and Effentiall purity.*) Indeed the pains may well be fpared, for all wife men are fufficiently perfwaded thereof already. For if hereby you meane (and I would faine learne what other fence your words are capable of) that the Church of *England* hath not as yet been *Entire* in the Fundamentals, and *Pure* in the *Effentials* to Salvation, we all are in a wofull Condition. Have we lived thus long in our Church, now to dye eternally therein ? Seeing none can be faved therein if it be unfound in the Fundamentals of Religion, muft the thoufand fix hundred forty third yeer from Chrift's birth be the firft yeer of the nativity of the Church of *England*, from which fhe may date her Effentiall purity ? Sir, I could at the fame time chide you with anger, bemoane you with pitty, blufh for you with fhame, were it not that I conceive this paffage fell unawares from your pen, and that you intend to gather it up againe.

(c) You know in what a case that Church was, when shee thought her selfe rich, and full, and glorious.) Good Sir, accept of my service to stay you, or else run on till you be stopt by your owne wearinesse. Our Church never brag'd thus her selfe, nor any other for her; whose faults we have already freely confessed, yet maintained her to be sound in all *Fundamentals*, and pure in all *Essentials*.

Examiner.

Sermon, page 9 [¶ 12, page 302].

A [1] through Reformation wee and all good men doe desire with as strong affections, though perhaps not with so loude a noise, as any whatsoever.

[4] *Examination.* If your [1]thorough Reformation in this page be compared with your pages 14, 15, 16, 17 [¶¶ 18 *seq.*], where you have bound it up with so many ^drestrictions, the fallacy will soone appear. You would ^esmoothly taxe some brethren for clamor and noise in their desires after Retormation: indeed, if you could perswade the Prophets of God into silence or slight endeavours, halfe your designe were finished: but they have a fire which flames into stronger expressions. If the zeale of the Prophets and ^fMartyrs had given no further testimony to the truth then their own bosoms, we had not had at this day such a cloud of witnesses. You know these loud importunities awakens and hastens men into that ^gholy businefs you would so faine retard: if you think it your vertue that you can be silent in the midst of our importunities and loud cryes after Reformation, I am sure 'tis your policy too, for should you make too great a noise after it, you might be heard to ^h*Oxford;* and perhaps you are loath to speak out till you ⁱsee further.

Treatise.

(*d*) *Fourteen, fifteen, sixteen, seventeen pages, where you have bound it up with so many Restrictions.*) Indeed I bound Reformation with Restrictions, but such as are Girdles to strengthen it, not fetters to burthen it; and thereupon no fallacy, but plaine dealing will appeare. And if those pages you instance in be guilty of any such fault, no doubt when your examination doth come to them you will presse it home, and I shall be ready to make my best defence.

(*e*) *You would smoothly tax some Brethren for clamour.*) If any be faulty herein, they deserve not onely to be smoothly

---

[1] thorow: *Truth Maintained*, page 15.

taxed, but sharply reproved. For clamour (as the English word is taken in [1]Scripture) founds in a bad sense, as arguing an ill tempered Spirit with a mixture of pride and impatience. And as Reformation ought to be prosecuted and sought after with holy and zealous importunity (farre from all Lethargicall dulnesse and carnall stupidity,) so it must be done with a quiet and composed soule, a grace commended by the [2]Apostle. Now grant none to be guilty, yet seeing all are subject (especially in tumultuous times) to clamour and passionate extravagancies, my gentle Advertisement by the bye could not be amisse.

(*f*) *If the zeale of the Prophets and Martyrs had given.*) I thanke you, Sir, for mentioning the Martyrs. They were the Champions of *passive obedience*, and the lively Patternes of that holy Temper I now described; Men of a meeke and quiet disposition; not clamorous; though since their death, the noyse and fame of their patience hath sounded aloud thorow the whole world to all Posterity. And I pray God in continuance of time the very Doctrine of Martyrdome be not Martyred.

(*g*) *That holy Businesse you would so faine retard.*) I appeale from your hard Censure to the *Searcher of hearts*, who one day will acquit my innocence and punish your uncharitablenesse, except it be first pardoned upon your repentance.

(*h*) *For should you make so great a noyse, you might be heard to* Oxford.) I care not how farre I be heard, nor which way, to *Oxford* and beyond it, to *Geneva*, or to *Rome* it selfe: Truth is Calculated for all meridians. But speake not slightingly of *Oxford*: it is ill wounding of a Court, and a Camp, and an University, and all in one word.

(*i*) *And perhaps you are loath to speak out till you see farther.*) I see too farre already; namely, that ruine and desolation is likely to follow, except Moderation be used on both sides. If you meane, *till I see farther* into His Majesties pleasure of Reforming what shall be found amisse, his unfained desire thereof doth already plainly appeare. But if you meane, till I see farther into his successe, know, Sir, my Religion

---

[1] *Pro.* 9. 13 : A foolish woman is clamorous; *Ephe.* 4. 31 : wrath, and anger, and clamour.   [2] 1 *Thes.* 4. 11 : Study to be quiet.

obferves not the tides of His Majefties Fortune, to ebbe and flow therewith. Where Confcience is the Fountaine, the ftream keeps the fame height.

Examiner.

Sermon, page 10 [¶ 12, page 302].

But with this qualification, That by thorough Reformation, we meane fuch a one whereof we are capable, pro ftatu viatorum, *made with all due and Chriftian moderation.*

[5] *Examination.* You write of the Reformation of a Church like ᵏ*Bodin*, not like*Bucer:* you make it a work of *Policy,* ¹not of *Piety;* of *Reafon,* not *Divinity.* Such Counfellors had ᵐ*Ieroboam* and *Iehu;* and they made a Church as unhappy as a Kingdome miferable. This *moderation* and *qualification* you fpeak of is not fo confiftent with ⁿ*fpirituall effences* and *operations:* if the fpirit of God fhould ᵒ not work in the foules of unregenerate, but expect an anfwerable compliancy firft, who fhould be fanctified? If God had expected any fuch congruity in our bufineffe of falvation, we had yet been unredeemed. To ᵖ fpeak clofer, What *Qualification* did Queen ᵠ*Elizabeth* expect, when fhe received a Kingdom warme from Popery? What Qualification did ʳ*Henry* the eight expect, in his attempt againft the Supremacy, when all his Kingdom was fo univerfally conjured to *Rome?* Such moderation and qualification is no other but a difcreet taking fo much as will ferve your turne: *to the* ˢ*Law,* faith the Scripture, *and to the teftimony; Mofes* wrought according to the *Patterne:* fo *Solomon* too. Godly ᵗ*Bucer* makes it his ᵗwork to perfwade King *Edward* to build up a perfect Church; and he ᵛprophefies fadly that he was afraid Popery would fucceed, becaufe the Kingdome of *England* was fo averfe to the Kingdom of Chrift; and we know the *Marian* dayes followed. Me thinks we are too like his prophecy, and our ʷ*Marian* times approach too faft.

Treatife.

(*k*) *You write of a Reformation of a Church like* Bodin.) Would I wrote like *Bodin,* though on the condition that I never wrote Anfwer to your Examinations. Would we had fome *Bodins,* fome fuch able Statef-men, that they might improve their parts to advance an happy Accommodation betwixt our Sovereigne and his Subjects.

(*l*) *You make it a worke of Policy, not of Piety.*) I make it, as indeed it is, a work both of *Mofes* and *Aaron,* wherein Piety is to be prefer'd and Policy is not to be excluded.

(*m*) *Such Counfellours had* Jeroboam *and* Jehu.) Sir, fhoot your Arrowes at me till your Quiver be empty, but glance

---
¹ Bucer in lib. 2. *De Regno Chrifti.*

not with the leaſt ſlenting inſinuation at His Majeſty, by conſequence to compare him to *Jeroboam* or *Jehu*, for their Idolatry : He knoweth how to beſtow his Gold farre better, and to leave the *Calves* for others.

(*n*) *This Moderation and Qualification you ſpeake of is not ſo conſiſtent with Spirituall Eſſenſes and Operations.*) This your line is not ſo conſiſtent with ſenſe as to need, much leſſe deſerve a Confutation.

(*o*) *If the Spirit of God ſhould not have wrought in the ſouls of Unregenerate.*) I wonder that, allotting (as you ſay) but one afternoon for the whole work of your Examination, you could ſpend ſo much time (ſome minutes at leaſt) in ſuch impertinencies.

(*p*) *To ſpeake cloſer.*) And truly no more then needs; for as yet you are farre enough from the matter. But I will not confute what you confeſſe.

(*q*) *What Qualification did Queen* Elizabeth *expect?*) She needed not to expect any, when ſhe had all Requiſites to reforme. Thoſe who have ſuch Qualification are not *to expect*, but to fall a working; thoſe that want it are not to fall a working, but ſtill *to expect*. Queen *Elizabeth* as ſupream in her Dominions had a ſufficient calling to reforme ; nothing was wanting in her: Onely her Memory doth ſtill deſervedly expect a more thankfull acknowledgement of her worthy paines then generally ſhe hath received hitherto.

(*r*) *What Qualification did* Henry *the eight expect in his attempt againſt ſupremacy?*) He likewiſe had Qualification ſufficient (and therefore needed not to expect any), as your following words doe witneſſe, wherein you ſay that *All his Kingdome was univerſally conjured to* Rome. If it was *his Kingdome*, then he had a *calling;* if it was conjured to Rome, then he had a *cauſe* to reforme: and being the King was bound to be the Exorciſt to un-conjure his Subjects from ſuch ſuperſtition. Yea, had King *Henry* reformed as ſincerely as he had a lawfull Calling thereunto, his memory had not been conſtantly kept in ſuch a purgatory of mens tongues for his lukewarme Temper; even the moſt moderate counting him too good for to be condemned, and too bad to be commended.

(*s*) *To the Law*, saith the Scripture, *and to the testimony*.) I will treasure up this excellent passage till a convenient time, being confident that before the next Paragraffe is examined I shall appeale to these Judges, and you decline them.

(*t*) *Godly* Bucer *makes it his worke to perswade King* Edward *to build up a perfect Church*.) The book of godly *Bucer* which you cite I have seene, on the selfe same token that therein he makes [1]Bishops to be above Presbyters *Jure divino*. You know *Bucer* wrote this worke (as leading the front of his *Opera Anglicana*) in the very beginning of King *Edwards* reigne, before the Reformation was generally received in *England*, and whilst as yet Popery was practised in many places. And next to this his book followeth his gratulation to the English Church for their entertaining of the Purity of the Gospell; so that what he doth perswade in the book you alleadge was in some good measure performed in that Kings reign, and afterwards better compleated by Queen *Elizabeth*.

(*v*) *And he prophesieth sadly that he was afraid Popery would succeed*.) Herein he took shrewd aime, and it happened he hit right. Such predictions are onely observed when afterwards they chance to take effect: otherwise, if missing the marke, men misse to marke them and no notice at all is taken of them. I know a latter Divine (not the lowest in learning, one of the highest in [2]zeale amongst them) who foretelleth that *Atheisme rather then Popery* is likely to overrunne *England*. Such Presages may serve to admonish, not to afright us, as not proceeding from a propheticall spirit, but resulting from prudentiall observations. But before we take our farewell of this book of *Bucers*, it will not be amisse to remember another passage (not to say presage) in the same worthy worke; that we may see what sinnes in his opinion were forerunners

---

[1] *Ex perpetuâ Ecclesiarum observatione ab ipsis iam Apostolis videmus, visum & hoc esse Spiritui Sancto ut inter Presbyteros quibus Ecclesiarum procuratio potissimùm est commissa, unus Ecclesiarum, & totius Sacri Ministerii curam gerat singularem; eáque curâ & solicitudine cunctis præerat aliis, quâ de causâ Episcopi nomen hujusmodi summis Ecclesiarum Curatoribus est peculiariter attributum.* Bucerus, *De Regno Christi, lib.* 2. *cap* 12 [Scripta Anglicana fere Omnia, Basle, 1577, *pag.* 67.]

[2] M. [Richard] Greenham in his grave Counsels in the word *Atheisme*, page 3 [*Works*, fourth edition, folio, London, 1605].

of ruine in a Kingdome. The margin prefents the Reader with the [1]latin which I here tranflate, though the former part thereof be englifhed already in mens practife, and the latter I feare will be englifhed in Gods judgements:

How horrible an affront doe they doe to the Divine Majefty who ufe the Temples of the Lord for Galleries to walke in, and for places fo prophane that in them with their fellowes they prattle and treat of any uncleane and prophane bufineffe! .... *This fure is fo great a contempt of God that long fince even for this alone we have deferved altogether to be banifhed from the face of the earth, and to be punifhed with heavieft judgements.*

Such I am afraid will fall on our nation for their abominable abufing of Churches (befides other of their finnes) and prophaning the places of Gods worfhip. Not to fpeake of thofe (and yet what man can hold his tongue when the mouthes of graves are forced open?) who, in a place to which their guilty confcience can point without my pens direction, did by breaking up the Sepulchers of our Saxon Chriftian Kings, erect an everlafting Monument to their own facriledge. Such practifes muft needs provoke Gods anger: and now me-thinks I write of the Reformation of a Church like *Bucer*, and not like *Bodin*.

(*w*) *Me-thinks we are too like his prophefie, and our Marian times approach too faft*.) I hope otherwife; trufting on a good God and a gracious King. But if thofe times doe come, woe be to fuch as have been the caufe or occafion to bring or haften them! One day it will be determined whether the peevifh, perverfe and undifcreet fpirit of Sectaries, bringing a generall dif-repute on the Proteftant, hath not concurred to the inviting in of fuperftition and Popery, [which] may come riding in on the back of Anabaptifme. If thofe times doe come, I hope that God who in juftice layeth on the burthen will in mercy ftrengthen our fhoulders, and what

---

[1] *Quàm horrendam illi faciunt divinæ Maieftati contumeliam qui Templa Domini habent pro Deambulacris locifque tam prophanis ut in illis quævis impura & prophana cum fimilibus fuis garriant & pertractent.* .... *Hæc certe tanta eft divini numinis Contemptio ut eâ vel folâ pridem meriti fumus omnino de Terrâ exterminari & quidem fuppliciis graviffimis multari.* Bucerus, *De Regno Chrifti*, lib. 1. cap. 10 [pag. 45, ut anteà].

our prayers cannot prevent our patience muſt undergoe. Nor is it impoſſible with God ſo to enable thoſe whom you tax *to have onely a forme of Godlineſſe* to have ſuch *Power thereof* as to ſeale the Proteſtant Religion with their blood.

Examiner.

Sermon, pages 10, 11 [¶ 12–14, pages 302–3].

Such who are to be true and proper Reformers, they muſt have a lawfull Calling thereunto. Duties which God hath impaled in for ſome particular perſons. Amongſt theſe actions, Reformation of Churches is chiefe. Now the Supreme Power alone hath a lawfull calling to reforme a Church, as it plainly appeares by the Kings of Iudah in their Kingdome.

[6] *Examination.* I had not known your meaning by the lawfull Calling you name, but that you expound it, in the lines that follow, to be the *Calling* of the *ſupreme Magiſtrate*, as if no calling were warrantable at firſt to [x] premove a reformation but that. But you muſt take notice, there is an inward and outward Call. The inward is a [y] ſpeciall excitation from the ſpirit of God, and ſuch a Call is [1] warrantable to be active: I am ſure it hath been ſufficient alwayes to ſet holy men on work. Another Call is outward; and that is either of *Place* and *Magiſtracy*, or *publike relation.* Now though *Magiſtracy* be of publike relation, yet when I ſpeak ſpecifically of *publike relation*, I mean that in which every man ſtands bound in to God and his Countrey. Now all theſe callings are Commiſſion enough, either to [z] meddle as Chriſtianly inſpired or Chriſtianly engaged. In ordinary tranſactions I know the ordinary diſpenſation is to be reſorted to; but the buſineſſe of *Reformation*, as it is [a] extraordinary, ſo God gives extraordinary conjunctures of times and circumſtances, and extraordinary concurrencies, and extraordinary incitations. In the building of the Temple you ſhall ſee in *Ezra* and *Nehemiah, Neh.* 8. 1, ſuch workings of God: *when the [b] people were gathered together as one man, they ſpake to* Ezra *the Scribe to bring the book of the law of* Moſes. Here the [c] people put one [on] even *Ezra* to his duty.

Treatiſe.

Before I deale with the particulars of this examination, I will enlarge (not alter) what I ſaid in my Sermon of this point, promiſing as much brevity as God ſhall enable me to temper with Clearneſſe, and deſiring the Readers patience whilſt at mine owne perill I deliver my opinion.

But firſt, here we premiſe [a] neceſſary diſtinction. Diſtinguiſh we betwixt thoſe Times when the Church liveth under

---

[1] warrantable by God: *Trvth Maintained*, page 23.

Pagan or persecuting Princes, and when God blesseth her with a Christian King, defender of the Faith. In the former case the Church may and must make an hard shift to reforme her selfe so well as she can (for many things will be wanting, and more will be but meanly supplyed) without any relating to a supreame Power, whose leave therein will be dangerous to desire and impossible to obtaine. But withall, they must provide themselves to suffer, offering no violence except it be to drowne a Tyrant in their teares, or to burne him with coales of kindnesse heaped on his head. In the latter case, when the supreame Power is a nursing Father to the Church, suckling it, not sucking blood from it, the Church must have recourse to it before shee may reforme. Reforming of a Church must neither stay behind for *Nero* his leave, nor runne before without the consent of *Constantine*. Religion it selfe must not be deckt with those flowers which are violently pluck'd from the Crownes of lawfull Princes.

Come we now then to shew how in a Christian state all are to contribute their joynt endeavours to promote a Reformation.

In a Church and such a State I consider three degrees thereof. First, meere private men without any mixture of a publike Relation. Secondly, persons placed in a middle posture, with the Centurion in publike imployment over some, yet *under Authority* themselves. Thirdly, the absolute supreame Power, who depends of God alone.

<small>3. How far private Christians, Ministers and subordinate Magistrates, are to concur to the advancing of a publike Reformation.</small>

For the first of these, meere private men, they have nothing to doe in publike reforming but to advance it by their hearty prayers to God, and to facilitate the generall Reformation by labouring to amend their owne and their Families lives according to the Word: this is all God requireth of them and more I feare then most of them will performe.

Next, succeed those persons in a middle posture; and these are either Ministers or Magistrates. Ministers, even the meanest of them, have thus far their part in publike Reforming that they are to *lift up* their *voice like a Trumpet* (though not like [1]*Sheba* his Trumpet to sound sedition), both

---

[1] 2 Sam. 20. 1.

to reprove vitioufneffe in Manners, and to confute errors in Doctrine. And if men of power and imminent place in the Church, then as their ingagement is greater, fo their endeavours muft be ftronger to preffe and perfwade a publike Reformation to fuch whom it doth concerne.

Magiftrates may have more to do in publike Reforming: having a calling from God, who therefore hath fet them in a middle place betwixt Prince and people, to doe good offices under the one, over the other, betwixt both; and having a calling from the King, efpecially if they be his Counfellours, whofe good they are to advance by all lawfull meanes, and rather to difpleafe him with their fpeech then to difhonour him with their filence; and having a calling from their Country, whofe fafety they muft be tender and carefull of.

Firft, therefore, they are with all induftry (both from the Minifters mouth and by their owne inquiry) to take true notice of fuch defects and deformities in the Church or State as are really to be reformed. Secondly, they are with all fincerity to reprefent the fame to the fupreame Power. Thirdly, with all humility to requeft the amendment of fuch Enormities. Fourthly, with all gravity to improve their requeft with arguments from Gods glory, the Princes honour, the peoples profit, and the like. Laftly, with their beft judgement to propound and commend the faireft way whereby a Reformation may as fpeedily as fafely be effected. And if they meet with difficulties in the fupreame Power delaying their requeft, they are not to be difheartned, but after their fervent prayers to God, who alone hath the hearts of Kings in his hands, they are conftantly to renue their requeft at times more feafonable, in places more proper, with expreffions more patheticall, having their words as full of earneftneffe as their deeds farre from violence.

As laft comes the fupreame Power, who alone is to reforme by its own Authority, though not by its owne advice alone. For becaufe it is rationally to be prefumed that Divines have beft fkill in matters of Divinity, they are to be confulted with; and here comes in the neceffity and ufe of *Councels, Convocations, Synods* and Affemblyes. And becaufe

<small>4. What parts therein are onely to be acted by the *fupreame Power*.</small>

there is not onely a conſtant correſpondency, but alſo an unſeperable complication betwixt the Church and State, Stateſmen are therefore to be adviſed with in a Reformation ſo to ſettle it as may beſt comply with the Common-wealth. For God in that generall warrant, *Let all things be done decently and in order*, puts as I may ſay the Cloath and Sheeres into the hands of the Church and Chriſtian Princes to cut out and faſhion each particular decency and order ſo as may ſhape and ſuit beſt with the preſent Time and Place wherein ſuch a Reformation is to be made.

Theſe parts therefore are to be acted in a Reformation by the ſupreame Power: Firſt, he is (either by his owne Motion, or at the inſtance and intreaties of others) to call and congregate ſuch Aſſemblyes. Secondly, to give them leave and liberty to conſult and debate of matters needing to be reformed. Thirdly, to accept the reſults of their conſultations, and to weigh them in the ballance of his Princely diſcretion. Fourthly, to confirme ſo much with his *Royal Aſſent* as his judgement ſhall reſolve to be neceſſary or convenient. Laſtly, to ſtamp the Character of Authority upon it, that Recuſants to obey it may be ſubject to civill puniſhments.

But now all the queſtion will be, What is to be done if the endeavours of Subjects be finally returned with deafneſſe or deniall in the ſupreame Power? In this caſe a publike Reformation neither ought nor can be performed without the conſent of the ſupreame Power: It ought not,

Firſt, becauſe God will not have a Church reformed by the deforming of his Commandement. He hath ſaid, *Honour thy Father and thy Mother*, and requireth that all Superiours ſhould be reſpected in their places. Secondly, the Scripture, rich in Preſidents for our inſtruction in all caſes of importance, affords us not one ſingle example wherein people attempted publiquely to reforme, without or againſt the conſent of the ſupreame Power; and in this particular I conceive a negative Argument followeth undeniably: wherefore ſeeing the Kings in *Judah* (there the ſupreame Power) were always called upon to reforme, commended for doing ſo much, or condemned for doing no more; and the people neither commanded to remove, nor reproved for not removing publique

Idolatry, without the confent of the fupreame Power; it plainly appeareth that a publique Reformation belongeth to the fupreame Power, fo that without it it ought not to be done.

As it ought not, fo it cannot be done without the confent thereof: for admit that the higheft fubordinate Power fhould long debate, and at laft conclude, the moft wholfome Rules for Reformation; yet, as *Plato* faid that amongft the many good Lawes that were made, one ftill was wanting, namely, a Law to command and oblige men to the due obferving of thofe Lawes which were made: So when the beft Refolutions are determined on by any inferiour Power, there ftill remaines an abfolute neceffity that the fupreame Power fhould bind and enforce to the obferving thereof.

For inftance: Some Offenders are poffeffed with fuch uncleane Spirits of prophaneneffe that [1]*none can bind them, no not with Chaines* of Ecclefiaftical Cenfures; onely outward Mulcts in purfe or perfon can hold and hamper them. *Scythian* flaves muft be ordered with whips; and a prefent prifon more affrights impudent perfons than Hel-fire to come. In the Writs, *De Excommunicato capiendo* and *De Hæretico comburendo*, fuch as flout at the *Excommunicato* and the *Hæretico* are notwithftanding heartily afraid of the *Capiendo* and the *Comburendo*. Wherefore in fuch cafes the Church when it is moft perfectly reformed is faine to crave the aid of the State by civill and fecular penalties to reduce fuch as are Rebels to Church Cenfures (fometimes inflicting death it felfe on blafphemous Heretickes); and this cannot be performed by any fubordinate Power in the State, but onely by the fupreame Power. Otherwife Offenders, if preffed by any inferiour Power, would have a free Appeale and no doubt find full redreffe from the fupreame Power, without whofe confent fuch penalties were impofed on them.

Now if it be demanded, what at laft remaines for any to doe in cafe the fupreame Power finally refufeth to reforme, thus they are to imploy themfelves: Firft, to comfort themfelves in this, that they have ufed the meanes, though it was

---

[1] Mark 5. 3.

Gods pleasure to with-hold the blessing. Secondly, they are to reflect on themselves, and seriously to bemoane their own sinnes which have caused Gods justice to punish them in this kind. If a rhumaticke head sends downe a constant flux, to the corroding of the lungs, an ill affected stomacke first sent up the vapours which caused this distillation: And pious Subjects conceive that if God suffer Princes to persist in dangerous errours, this distemper of the head came originally from the stomack, from the sinnes of the people, who deserved this affliction. Thirdly, they are to reforme their selves and Families, and if the supreame Power be offended thereat, to prepare themselves patiently to suffer whatsoever it shall impose upon them, having the same cause, though not the same comfort, to obey a bad Prince as a good one.

By the way, a word in commendation of passive obedience: when men who cannot be active without sinning, are passive without murmuring. First, Christ set the principall copie thereof, leading *Captivity captive on the Crosse*; and ever since he hath sanctified suffering with a secret soveraigne vertue, even to conquer and subdue persecution.

5. Of the progresse and praise of passive Obedience.

Secondly, it hath beene continued from the Primitive Church by the Albigences to the moderate [1]Protestants, unlesse some of late ashamed of this their Masters badge have pluckt their cognisance from their coats and set up for themselves.

Thirdly, it is a Doctrine spirituall in it selfe. It must needs be good, it is so contrary to our bad natures and corrupt inclinations, who will affirme any thing rather then we will deny our selves, and our owne revengefull dispositions. And surely the Martyrs were no lesse commendable for their willing submitting to then for their constant enduring of their persecutors cruelty. And it was as much (if not more) for them to conquer their owne vindicative spirits as to undergoe the heaviest tortures inflicted on them.

Fourthly, it is a doctrine comfortable to the Practisers,

---

[1] *Est hæc pontificiorum tessera crudelitas, aliud est Protestantium symbolum clementia. Isti occidunt, Hi occidunt.* Laurentius Humphreys *in Respon. ad Epistolas Campiani* [*Iesvitismi Pars Secunda*, &c., 8vo. Lond. 1584, verso of ¶¶¶. 4].

bitter, but wholfome. Yet it is fweetned with the inward confolation of a cleere confcience, which is Food in Famine, Freedome in Fetters, Health in Sickneffe, yea, Life in death.

Fifthly, it is glorious in the eyes of the beholders, who muft needs like and love that Religion, whofe profeffors (where they cannot lawfully dearly fell) doe frankly give their lives in the defence thereof.

Laftly, it is a Doctrine fortunate in fucceffe. By preaching of *paffive* obedience *the Dove* hath out-flowne *the Eagle*. Chrift's Kingdome hath out-ftreatched *Cæfars* Monarchy. Hereby the wifdome of the Eaft was fubdued to the folly of Preaching. The Sunne of the Gofpell arofe in the Wefterne parts. The parched South was watered with the dew of the Word. The frozen North was thawed with the heat of Religion. But fince the Doctrine of refifting the fupreame Power came into fafhion, the Proteftant Religion hath runne up to a high top, but fpread nothing in breadth; few Papifts have beene reclaimed, and no Pagans have been converted. Alas! that fo good a Doctrine fhould be now in fo great difgrace; yet will we praife fuch *fuffering*, though we fuffer for praifing it. If we cannot keepe this Doctrine alive, we will grieve becaufe it is dying; being confident that though now it be buried in fo deepe difhonour, God in due time will give it a glorious refurrection. And though I muft confeffe it is farre eafier to praife *paffive Obedience* then to practice it, yet to commend a vertue is one degree to the imitation of it; and to convince our judgements, firft, of the goodneffe of the deede, is by Gods bleffing one way to worke our wils to embrace it: In a word, if this Doctrine of *paffive Obedience* be cryed downe, hereafter we may have many bookes of *Acts and Monuments*, but never more any *Bookes of Martyrs*.

And now thefe things premifed, we returne to *Mafter Saltmarfh* his examination of my Sermon.

(*x*) *As if no calling were warrantable at firft to promote a Reformation but the fupreame Power.*) I never faid or thought fo: But in what manner and by what meanes inferiours may and muft labour to promote it, I have at large declared.

(*y*) *The inward call is a fpeciall excitation from the fpirit of*

God, and such a call is warrantable to be active.) I shall have presently a more proper place to deale with these *speciall excitations* when I come to answer your *extraordinary incitations*.

(*z*) *Now all these callings are commission enough to meddle.*) I am not of so froward a spirit as to quarrell at a word. Otherwise I could tell you that *to meddle* generally importeth an over-businesse in some Pragmaticall person, tampering with that which is either unlawfull in it selfe, or hurtfull to, at least improper for the party who medleth with it; and in ¹Scripture it is commonly used with a prohibition, *Meddle not*. To passe this by, the question is not whether Magistrates may meddle (as you say) in advancing a publique Reformation, but how? and how farre they may be active therein? Therein I report the Reader to what I have largely expressed.

(*a*) *In ordinary transactions I know the ordinary dispensation is to be resorted to; but the businesse of Reformation, as it is extraordinary, so God giveth extraordinary conjunctures of Times and circumstances, and extraordinary concurrences, and extraordinary incitations.*) Now you soare high, give us leave to follow you as we can. First, I confesse that a publique Reformation is an *extraordinary worke* in this sense, as not common or usually done every day (as private amendment of particular persons is or ought to be). But it is a rare worke, which commeth to passe but seldome, and the doing of it is out of the road of ordinary mens imployment. But I deny a publique Reformation to be extraordinary in this acception; as if it were to be ordered or managed by any other rules or presidents then such as are ordinary and usuall in the Bible, where many patterns of publique Reformations are presented; in which respect the ordinary dispensation is to be resorted to in the performance thereof. Whereas you say that in publique Reformations, *God giveth extraordinary coniunctures of Times and circumstances, and extraordinary concurrences:* It is true in this sense, that the great Clock-keeper of Time so orders the coincidence of all things that when his

---

[1] Deut. 2. 5; 2 Kings 14. 10; 2 Cro. 25. 19; Pro. 20. 19, and 24. 21, and 26. 17, and 20. 3.

houre is come wherein such a Reformation shall be made, every officious circumstance will joyfully contribute his utmost assistance to the advancing thereof. Wherefore if men cannot make a Reformation without roving from their calling, or breaking Gods Commandement (according to which it cannot be done without the consent of the supreame Power), hereby it plainly appeares that the hand of Divine Providence doth not as yet point at that happy minute of Reformation, there being as yet times distracted with jarres and disjunctures, not onely in circumstances, but even in substantiall matters requisite thereunto. And therefore seeing Gods good time may not be prevented, but must be expected, men are still patiently to wait and pray for that *conjuncture of Times* and *concurrency of circumstances* whereof you speake.

But whereas you speake of *Extraordinary Incitations*, paralell to what you said before, of *speciall excitations*, and *christianly inspired*: In these your expressions you [1] open a dangerous Pit, and neither cover it againe nor raile it about with any cautions, so that Passengers may unawares fall into it.

For every man who hath done an unwarrantable act, which he can neither justifie by the law of God or man, will pretend presently that he had an extraordinary Incitation for it: a fine tricke to plead Gods leave to breake his law. Nor can we disprove the impudence of such people, except we may use some touch-stones, thereby to try their counterfeit incitations. My opinion herein shall be contrived into three Propositions.

6. That no extraordinary Excitations, Incitations, or Inspirations are bestowed from God on men in these dayes.

First, no such extraordinary incitations are extant now a dayes from God as stirre men up to doe any thing contrary to his Commandements. Indeed, some such we meet with in the [2] Scripture, where the Law-giver dispensing with his owne law incited *Abraham* to kill his son, *Sampson* to kill himselfe, and the Isralites to rob the Egyptians. In such cases it was no disobedience to Gods publique command, but obedience to his private countermand, if the servant varied his practice according to his absolute Masters

---

[1] Exo. 21. 33. 34.   [2] Gen. 22. 2; Judg. 16. 30; Exod 12. 36.

peculiar direction. But such incitations come not now a dayes but from the spirit of delusion.

Secondly, no extraordinary excitations are extant now a dayes from God, seizing on men (as anciently) in *Enthusiasmes*, or any such raptures as make sensible impressions on them. For these are within the virge of Miracles, which are now ceased; and our age produceth things rather monstrous then miraculous.

Thirdly, extraordinary incitations are still bestowed by God in these dayes; namely, such that he giveth to some of his servants a more then usuall and common proportion of his grace, whereby they are enabled for and incited to his service with greater rigour and activity then ordinary Christians. My judgement herein shall not be niggardly to restraine Gods bountifull dealing; but I verily beleeve that he who was so exceedingly liberal in former ages is not so close handed in our times, but that in this sence he bestoweth extraordinary motions, especially on such whom his Providence doth call to eminent Places, either in Church or State. But such motions quicken them to *runne the way of Gods Commandements*, not to start without or beside it. And as hereby they are heightned to an Heroicall degree of Piety, so though sometimes we may say of them in a Rhetoricall expression, that *they goe beyond themselves*, yet they never goe beyond their calling, nor never goe beyond Gods Commandements.

Now if any shall pretend that they have an extraordinary excitation to make a publique Reformation without the consent of the supreame Power to whom by Gods law it belongs, such an excitation cannot come from the holy Ghost: For if the spirit of the Prophets be subject to the Prophets, much more is it subject to the God of the Prophets, and to the law of that God. And truly, Sir, this passage of *extraordinary incitations*, as it is by you rawly laid downe and so left, containeth in it seed enough if well (or rather ill) husbanded to sow all the Kingdome with sedition, especially in an age wherein the Anabaptist in their actions, beaten out of the field by Gods Word, doe daily flye to this their Fort of extraordinary excitations.

And you may obferve when God gave *extraordinary excitations, quoad regulam* (ftirring up men to doe things contrary to the received rule of his Commandements), then fuch excitations were alwayes attended with extraordinary operations. *Phinehas*, who killed *Cofby* and *Zimry*, could ftay the plague with his prayer; and *Eliah* who curfed the Captaines with their fifties, could caufe fire to come downe on them from Heaven. It appeares this his curfe was pronounced without malice, becaufe inflicted by a miracle. It is lawfull for fuch to call for fire, who can make fire come at their call; and would none would kindle difcord on Earth, till firft they fetcht the fparks thereof from Heaven. Neither doe we proudly tempt Gods providence, but truly trye fuch mens pretended extraordinary incitations, if when they wander from Gods Commandements in their Actions, and plead infpirations, we require of them to prove the truth of fuch infpirations by working a miracle.

Now, Sir, you being (as it feemes) an oppofite to Prelacy would make ftrange worke, to put downe one *Ordinary* in a Diocefle, and fet up many *extraordinaries* in every Parifh. And for ought I know, if fome pretend *extraordinary excitations* publikely to reforme againft the will of the fupreame Power, fuch as fide with the *fupreame Power* may with as much probability alleadge *extraordinary excitations* to oppofe and croffe the others Reformation, and fo betwixt them both our Church and State will be fufficiently miferable. And now, Sir, remember what you faid in the laft Paragraffe: *To the law*, faith the Scripture, *and to the Teftimony:* to fuch Judges we may fafely appeale from all your *fpeciall excitations, extraordinary Incitations,* and *chriftian Infpirations.*

(*b*) *In the building of the Temple you fhall fee in* Ezra *and* Nehemiah *fuch workings of God: when the people were gathered together as one man, they fpake to* Ezra *the Scribe, to bring the Booke of the law of* Mofes.) The unanimous confent of fo many we acknowledge to be Gods worke. O that we might fee the like agreement in *England*, where the people are fo farre from being *gathered together as one man* that almoft every one man is diftracted in his thoughts, like the times, and fcattered from himfelfe as if he were *many people*. Well, *they spake to* Ezra *to bring the Booke of the law:* what of all this?

(*c*) *Here the people put on even* Ezra *to his duty.*) And little speaking would spurre on him, who of himselfe was so ready to runne in his calling. But I pray, what was this *Ezra?* who were these people? *Ezra* was indeed a Priest, a learned Scribe of the law, who brought up a party out of *Babylon* to *Jerusalem* armed with a large patent and Commission from *Artaxerxes*. The people here were the whole body of the Jewish Church and State, together with [1]*Zerobabel* the Prince and *Jeshuah* the high Priest, who (by leave from the Persian King) had the chiefe managing of spirituall and temporall matters. And judge how little this doth make for that purpose to which you alleadge it, that from hence private persons may either make the supreame power to reforme, or doe it without his consent. Had you free leave of the whole Scripture to range in, and could the fruit of your paines find out no fitter instance for your purposes?

Examiner.

And whereas you say, Reformation is of those duties that are [d]impaled in for some particular persons; I answer, this were a grand designe, if you could [e]heighten Reformation into such a holy Prodigy as you would of late the Church into the *Prelacy* and [f]*Clergy*, and excluded the [g]*Laity* as a prophane crew, and to be taught their distance. *Luther* will tell you this is [h]one of the [2]*Romish engines* to make such an holy businesse, like the mountaine in the Law, not to be toucht or [3]approached to, but by *Moses* alone. Thus you might take off many good workmen, and honest [i]labourers in the Vineyard, whom Christ hath hired and sent in, and to whom he hath held out his Scepter, as *Ahasuerus* to *Esther*.

Treatise.

(*d*) *And whereas you say, Reformation is of those duties that are impaled in for some particular persons.*) It appears that *publike Reformation* is so impaled; for whereas every man is commanded to observe the Sabbath, honour his Parents;

---

[1] This appeares because in the Prophet he is stiled *Governour of Judah*, Hag. 1. 14, and that at the self same time when *Ezra* came thither. See Luthers *Chronology* in 4o millenario.

[2] Roman: *Trvth Maintained*, page 35.   [3] approacht: *ibid.*, page 36.

and every man forbidden to have other Gods, worship Images, take Gods Name in vaine, kill, steale, &c.; yet the supreame Power alone in Scripture is called on for publike Reformation, and no private person, as Saint [1]*Austin* hath very well observed.

(*e*) *I answer, this were a grand designe, if you could heighten Reformation into such an holy Prodigy.*) I need not heighten it, which is so high a worke of it selfe that our longest armes cannot reach it, though we stand on the tiptoes of our best desires and endeavours, till God shall first be pleased to send us a peace. A prodigy it is not (not long since you tearmed it an *extraordinary businesse*); yet if it be performed whilst warre lasteth, *it is a worke of the Lord, and may justly seeme mervailous in our eyes.*

(*f*) *As you would of late the Church into the Prelacy and the Clergy.*) When and where did I doe this? I ever accounted that the *Cœtus fidelium, the Congregation of the faithfull,* was Gods Church on earth. Yet I often find the Church represented in generall Counsels by the Prelacy and Clergy (who are or should be the best and wisest in the Church), and their decisions in matters of Religion interpreted and received as the resolutions of the Church in generall.

(*g*) *And excluded the Layty as a prophane crew, and to be taught their distance.*) What honest man ever thought the Layty, as Layty, prophane? I conceive our Kingdome would be very happy, if none of the Clergy were worse then some of the Layty. And I am sure that the godly Clergy are Gods Layty, his λαὸς, and the godly Layty are Gods Clergy, his κλῆρος. Yet now a dayes, some usurping Lay--men may well be taught their distance who meddle with ministeriall functions: Nor will a wel-meaning heart one day excuse the unsanctified hands of such *Uzzah's* who presuming to preach hold not our Arke from shaking, but shake our Arke with holding it.

(*h*) Luther *will tell you this is one of the Romish engines.*) Indeed this was a Popish device too much to depresse the Layty. But this engine (thanks be to God) is since broken

---

[1] *Auferenda Idola, non potest quisquam iubere privatus.* Aug. Cont. literas Petiliani, lib. 2. cap. 92 [ed. Basle, 1542, vol. vii. col. 149].

afunder, and it will be in vaine for any to glew the peeces thereof together. And now since the Monopoly of the Popish Clergy (ingrossing all matters of Religion to themselves) is dissolved, it is fit Protestant Ministers lawfull propriety in their calling should justly be maintained.

(*i*) *Thus you may take off many honest Labourers in the Vineyard.*) Farre be it from me, especially if they be skilfull Labourers, such as will prune the Vines, not pluck them up by the roots. But this and what you say of those *to whom God hath held out his Scepter* is nothing to the purpose, except you could prove where God in the Scripture hires or cals private men to make a publike Reformation.

Examiner.

And whereas you tell us, that the *supreme Power* alone hath the lawfull Calling, as appears in the *Kings of Iudah*; I answer, that if so, the [k]Parliament were now in a dangerous *Præmunire;* for you know that is suspended from us, and yet our state goes on in their work, enabled (as they say) by their *fundamentall* power, and constitution. I shall not here dispute the emanations of this power in ordinances, votes, and orders : they have made it appeare in their owne Declarations. Only this : I read of an [l]ordinance made by the Nobles and Elders of Israel, those Lords and Commons, *That whosoever would not come, according to the Counsell* which was taken for Reformation, *all his substance should bee forfeited, Ezra* 10. 8. Here is no King of *Iudahs* hand, nor a *Cyrus* King of *Persia's;* but an ordinance of their own to their own people ; only they have King *Cyru's* writ for their first assembling and consulting. Had Christ and his Apostles [m]waited in their Reformation for the consent of the *Roman Magistrate*, the supreme power, they had not made that holy expedition they did. Had *Luther* and *Zuinglius* and *Oecolampadius* [n]staied for the *Emperours* Reformation, they had not shed halfe that light in the [1]*German Hemisphere.* There was a time when God took part of the spirit of *Moses* and put it [o]upon the *Elders.*

Treatise.

(*k*) *If so, the Parliament were now in a dangerous Præmunire.*) I will not marre a meane Divine of him, to make a meaner States-man by medling with matters in the Commonwealth. I that maintaine that every man must stay in his calling will not step out of mine owne. Let the differences

---

[1] Germane : *Truth Maintained,* page 38.

betwixt our Soveraigne and his Subjects, which confist in points of State, be debated by the Politicians on either side, the questions in law be argued respectively by their *learned Counsell*, and the controversies in Religion be disputed by their severall Divines. But alas! such is our misery, when all is done, the finall decision is devolved to the Souldiers sword on either side; and God send the best cause the best successe.

(*l*) *Onely this: I read of an Ordinance made by the Nobles and Elders of Israel, those Lords and Commons.*) By your favour, it was a compleat act of state, as confirmed by the royall Assent. True, there was no King of *Judah's* hand unto it, because at that time *Judah* had no King; and who can expect that the Sunne should shine at midnight, when there is none in that Horizon? Reasonable men will then be contented with the Moon-shine; and see that here. For *Zerobabel*, shining with borrowed beames and a reflected light from the Persian King (in which respect he is stiled, *Hag.* 1. 14, the *Governour of Judah*), concurred to this Ordinance by his approbation thereof. Besides this, there was also a triple consent of the Persian Kings.

First, the grand and generall grant from *Cyrus*, *Ezra* 1. 3, which still stood in full force, as confirmed by *Darius*, *Ezra* 6. 12, whereby the Jewes being authorized to re-build the Temple, were also by the same enabled to settle Gods service in the best manner, by what wholsome lawes they thought fitting. Secondly, a particular implicite grant, in that the Persian King knowing thereof did not forbid it when it was in his power, had it beene his pleasure; and such a *not opposing* amounts to a consent. Lastly, they had a large expresse command from King *Artaxerxes* to *Ezra*, *chap.* 7, *ver.* 26: *And whosoever will not doe the law of thy God, and the law of the King, let judgement be executed speedily upon him, whether it be unto death, or unto banishment, or to confiscation of goods, or to imprisonment.* And now, Sir, I have the lesse cause to be offended with you for citing mangled and dismembred peeces in my Sermon, seeing the Scripture it selfe finds as little favour from your hand; for had you compared on [one] place thereof with another you could not but have seen the Persian

Kings confent to this Reformation. Yea, fo obfervant were the Jewes of the Perfian Kings that at the firft iffuing forth of their prohibition to that purpofe, they inftantly defifted building the Temple; having their foules fo well managed and mouthed with the reines of loyalty that their Kings *negative voyce* [1]checkt and ftopt them as they were running full fpeed in fo good an imployment: fo little doth the inftance alleadged advantage your caufe.

(*m*) *Had Chrift and his Apoftles waited in their Reformation for the confent of the Roman Magiftrate.*) I anfwer: Firft, Chrift and his Apoftles were Chrift and his Apoftles, I meane extraordinary perfons immediately infpired. Secondly, the Reformation they brought was mainly materiall indeed, being the Gofpell, without which there was no falvation. Thirdly, becaufe they had not the Emperours confent to their Reformation, they pacified his difpleafed fword by preferring their necks unto it, not repining at the dearneffe of the purchafe, to buy the fafety of their foules with the loffe of their lives; all the Jury of the Apoftles (*John* onely accepted) followed their Mafter to Martyrdome: and hence we truly deduced the patterne of paffive obedience.

(*n*) *Had* Luther *and* Zuinglius, *and* Oecolampadius *ftayed for the Emperours Reformation.*) Luther was a Minifter, and fo had his fhare in reforming, fo farre as to propagate the truth and confute falfhoods by his pen, preaching, and difputations. What he did more then this was done by the flat command, at left free confent of *Frederick* Duke of *Saxony*, under whom *Luther* lived. This Duke owing homage, but not fubjection to the Emperour, counted himfelf and was reputed of others abfolute in his owne Dominions, as invefted with the power of life and death, to coine money, make offenfive and defenfive leagues, and the like. And although this wary Prince long poifed himfelf betwixt feare of the Emperor and love of the truth, yet he always either publikely defended *Luther*, or privately concealed him, till at laft having outgrowne his fears he fell boldly to publike reforming. As for the ftates of *Zurich* and *Bafil*, wherein *Zuinglius*

---

[1] Ezra 4. 24.

and *Oecolampadius* lived, as those Cities in one Relation are but members of the Helvetian Common-wealth, so in another capacity they are intire bodies of themselves; and in these states the Magistrates did stamp the Character of civill authority on that Reformation which these Ministers did first set on foot by their preaching. But if any extravagant action of worthy men be tendred us in example, our love to their persons binds us not to defend their practice, much lesse to imitate it. We crave liberty, and if denied, will take it to leave them to themselves, who, if they had any especiall warrant to justifie their deeds, will at the last day produce and plead it.

(*o*) *There was a time when God took part of the spirit of* Moses *and put it upon the Elders.*) I will not dispute the manner how the spirit was taken from [1]*Moses*, perchance added to others without being substracted from him, as a candle looseth no light by giving it to another. But this is falsly alleaged by you to intimate that sometimes inferiour Officers may make Reformations without the knowledge, yea, against the will of the supreame power. For you must know that though the Sannedrin or seventy Elders were a constant Court and standing Counsell; yet when there was a chief Governour, they had recourse to him in actions of Moment: *Num.* 27. 15, 16, 17, *And* Moses *spake unto the Lord saying, Let the Lord the God of the spirits of all flesh set a man over the Congregation, which may go out before them, and which may lead them out and bring them in, that the Congregation of the Lord be not as Sheep which have no Shepheard.* See [so] that notwithstanding the power of the Elders stood still in full force, and determined not at *Moses* his death; yet he accounted Gods people no better than Shepheardlesse till they had a power Paramount placed over them, and a supreame above the Elders to guide and direct them.

Examiner.

Sermon, page 12 [¶ 15, pages 303-4].

Meane time meere private men must not be idle, but move in their sphere till

---

[1] Drusius *in Pentetuchen* [Num. xii. 1], *ex* R. Aben-Ezrah [4to. ed. 1617, pag. 408].

the fupreme power doth reforme. They muſt pray to inſpire thoſe that have power. Secondly, they muſt reforme themſelves and their families.

[7] *Examination.* Still you drive on your defign ¹through many plaufible ᵖinfinuations : you would keep *private men doing*, but ſtill doing in their own ᑫ*circle:* I confeſſe I would not improve their intereſt too high, nor too ſoon ; for the early ſettings forth of *private men* is apt to exceed into a tumultuary motion ; yet I would not put them ſo far behind as they ſhould lie like the *lame* and the *diſeaſed* at the *Poole of Betheſda,* ʳ*wayting* till a ſupream power came down amongſt them. There are many publick engagements which they are capable on, and which providence will often guide them to, as in ˢfinding ²out wayes of facilitation, and advancement for the buſineſſe, beſides ſome ᵗother *arcana* and ſecret *preparations*. We ſee every thing naturally is ſpirited with an inſtinct of ayding the whole : ᵛwater and ayre will part with their own intereſts to ſerve the univerſall, in the danger of a vacuity. The very ʷ*Romans* by a ³morall principle would contend to be firſt in the ſervice of their Countrey ; and it remaines as a crime upon record that ˣGilead *abode beyond* Iordan *and that* Dan *remained in ſhips,* and Aſhur *abode in his breaches,* that is, that they would ſit down encircled with their own intereſts and affaires.

Treatiſe.

(*p*) *Still you drive on your defigne thorow many plauſible infinuations.*) Not infinuations, but pofitions ; and thoſe no more plauſible then profitable. Truth hath a precious infide, and withall a pleaſing face.

(*q*) *You would keep private men doing, but ſtill doing in their circle.*) And good reaſon too ; for if they be out of their circle, they are very troubleſome ſpirits to conjure downe againe.

(*r*) *Not like the lame at the poole of* Betheſda, *waiting till a ſupreame Power.*) If God in his Word will have it ſo, they muſt wait. Better to lye ſtill in the porch, though not cured, then to ruſh headlong into the poole and be drowned.

(*s*) *Providence will guide them in finding out-wayes of facilitation.*) I proteſt againſt all out-wayes if they be any way different from the high-road of the King of Heaven. Reformation, however, muſt come lawfully ; and if it will not come eafily, let it come hardly ; we will tug at it with our prayers (which are alwayes beſt at a dead lift), and will

---

¹ thorow: *Trvth Maintained,* page 41.   ² out-ways: *ibid.,* page 42.
³ morral : *ibid.,* page 42.

sweat, but not sin, to obtain it. Nor can any better *facilitation* for private men be found out then for every one of them to reform themselves. How doth an Army of ten thousand men almost change their postures from East to West in an instant, because every one turneth one; and so soone would the work be done in a publike Reformation, if particular persons would take care for their private amendment.

(*t*) *Besides some other arcana and secret preparations.*) Good Sir, play faire and above board: The surface of the earth is wide enough for us both; creep not into crannies, to put me to the pains of Pioners to mine for your meaning: I know [1]*the secret of the Lord is with the righteous;* but then it is such a secret as being concealed from prophane persons is revealed in the Word. This your expression, if cleer from fault, is not free from just suspition; for hereby you buz into peoples heads (and such tinder, I tell you, is ready to take fire) that there are some strange unknown misteries of Religion lately communicated to some private men. Strange, that others of the same forme with you for learning and Religion should know no such secrets, except you have received from Heaven some expresse packet of intelligence. You might have done well to have told us what these arcana are, unlesse being of Heavens *close Committee* you be bound to secrecy. Meane time I will be bold to tell you that if these secrets differ from Gods will in his Word, they are depths of the Divell and misteries of Iniquity.

(*v*) *We see every thing naturally is spirited with an instinct of ayding; the whole water and ayre will part with their owne interests to serve the universall, in the danger of a vacuity.*) I distinguish betwixt naturall Agents and voluntary, rationall and Christian Agents. Naturall Agents goe the neerest way to their owne home, their Center, except countermanded to avoid a vacuity, which being yeelded to, necessarily inferres a destruction of the whole. In such a case heavy bodyes have from God a dispensation, yea, command to ascend, light bodies to descend, forgetting their particular propensity, to remember the publike good, according to the words of the

---

[1] Pro. 3. 32.

Pfalmift, [1]*He hath made a decree which they shall not passe.* But voluntary, rationall and Chriftian Agents are to regulate their actions by Gods will in his Word; the greateft and onely *vacuity* they are to feare is God's difpleafure, whofe glory they are to preferre before their owne temporall felf-prefervation; and indeed mans eternall good is wrapped up in his obedience to Gods will. Wherefore except you can produce a place in Gods Word wherein private men are commanded to make publike Reformations, there is a meer *vacuity* of all you have alleadged.

(*w*) *The very Romans by a morrall principle would contend to be firft in the fervice of their Country.*) It was well done of them. Their forwardneffe in ferving their Country will one day condemne our frowardneffe in difserving, our rending our native foyle afunder with civill diffentions; but in fuch cafes as this which we have now afoot, (whether private perfons may reform without the confent of the fupreame Power,) we are not to be guided by the practice of the Pagan Romans, but by the precept of the Chriftian Romans, [2]*Let every foule be fubject to the higher Powers.*

(*x*) *And it remaines as a crime upon Record, that* Gilead *abode beyond* Jordan, *and that* Dan *remained in ships.*) Thus it was: *Sicera*, a Pagan generall under *Jabin* a Tyrant and Ufurper, hoftilely invaded *Ifrael*; *Deborah*, a Propheteffe by Divine infpiration, incited *Barach* to refift him. In this cafe each fingle man had a double call to affift *Barach*. One from Nature to [3]defend his Country, another from Gods immediate vocation. Here it was lawfull for all to be active, finfull for any to be idle: *Jael* the woman was valiant; shall men be womanish and cowardly? Now prove that private men have the like calling in point of publike Reformation; and if they be not active, we will not onely confeffe it their crime, but proclaime a curfe againft them with *Meros:* till this be done, this inftance befreindeth not your caufe.

---

[1] Pf. 148. 6.   [2] Rom. 13. 1.
In publicos hoftes, omnis homo miles. Tertullianus [Ed. Rigaltii, fo. 1634, cap. i. pag. 3.]

Examiner.

And [y]though you would put private men upon such duties here as are godly and commendable, the policy is to keep them exercised in one good duty, that they should not advance another; and thus you would cunningly make one piece of Divinity [1]betray another, and make the [2]friends of the Reformation do it a [3]discourtesie in ignorance.

Treatise.

(*y*) I confesse it is an ancient subtilty of Satan, *to keep men exercised in one good duty, that they should not advance another.*) Thus he busieth some men all in praying to neglect preaching; all in preaching to neglect Catechizing; all in prayers, preaching, catechizing, to neglect practising. [4]*Jesabels* body was all eaten up, save onely her *head, hands and feet*. But indiscreet zeal so consumes some that they have neither *hands* nor *feet* left, either to *worke* or to *walke* in their Christian calling: Yea, of all their *head* nothing remains unto them but onely their *ears*, resolving all Gods service into *hearing* alone.

But this accusation is not onely improperly, but falsly here layed to my charge, because I forbid meer private men to meddle with publike reforming, which belongs not at all unto them: That so cutting off the needlesse suckers the tree may be fed the better, and that private men leaving off those imployments which pertaine not to them may the more effectually advance their owne amendment; a taske which, when it is done, the severest Divine will give them leave to play.

And because one dangerous Policy hath been mentioned by you, it will not be amisse to couple it with another device of the Divell, as seasonable and necessary in these times to be taken notice of. Satan puts many meere private men on to be fierce and eager upon publike reforming, thereby purposely to decline and avert them from their own selfe-amendment. For publike reforming hath some pleasure in it, as a Magisteriall act and work of authority, consisting

---

[1] to betray: *Truth Maintained*, page 44.   [2] freinds: *ibid.*, page 44.
[3] discurtesie: *ibid.*, page 44.   [4] 2 Kings 9. 35.

most in commanding and ordering of others; whereas private amendment is a worke all of paine; therein a man, as he is himselfe the judge, so he is the malefactor, and must indite himselfe, arraigne himselfe, convict himselfe, condemne himselfe, and in part execute himselfe, *crucifying the old man* and *mortifying* his owne corruptions. And we can easier afford to put out both the eyes of other men, to force them to leave their deare darling sinnes, then to pluck out our own [1]right eye (in obedience to our Saviours precept), and forsake our owne sinnes, *which doe so easily beset us.* Besides, men may be promoted to publike reforming by covetousnes, to gather chips at the felling of the old Church government; by ambition, to see and be seene in office; by revenge, to wreck their spight on the personall offences of such whom formerly they distasted. Self-amendment is not so subject to private ends, but goeth against the haire, yea, against the flesh it selfe, in making men deny themselves in duty to God.

Yea, at the last day of judgement, when God shall arraigne men, and say, *Thou art a drunkard, Thou art an adulterer, Thou art an oppressor;* it will be but a poore plea for them to say, *Yea, Lord, but I have been a publike Reformer of Church and State.* This plea, I say, will then not *hold water*, but prove a *broken cisterne.* Nor will God dispence with their want of *obedience*, becauſe they have offered him store of *sacrifice.* Such people therefore are daily to be called upon to amend themselves and their Families; which is a race long enough for the best breathed private Christians, though they start in their youth, and runne till their old age.

Examiner.

Sermon, page 19 [¶ 26, page 307].

Lastly, with carefulnesse not to give any just offence to the Papists.

[8] *Examination.* I [2]wonder you [2]should here expresse an indulgence which is not allowable; and the memory of the *Parliament* will be honourable for that; they knew so much Divinity as taught them not to value their offence, and to proclaime to them [a]both in [3]*Ireland* and *England*

---

[1] Mat. 5. 29.
[2] would: *Truth Maintained*, page 46.
[3] *England* and *Ireland:* ibid., page 46.

an irreconcileable war. This carefulnesse and tendernesse you plead for was the first principle which embased our Church so farre as to take up their Altars and Ceremonies to avoid offence. Saint *Paul* was of another spirit, who [b]forbore not a Disciple and Apostle : *When I saw*, says he, *that they walked not uprightly, according to the truth of the Gospel*.

You doe much mistake the Divinity of *Christ* in matter of offence, who never forbore to preach or publish any necessary truth ; nay, when his Disciples were scandalized and said, *Iohn* 6. 60, 61, This *is an hard saying. Doth this offend you ?* [1]sayes he. *What and if,* &c. He [2]goes on and [c]pursues the offence, till they left him and his Doctrine too. And for the *Papists*, they are much of the relation and constitution [3] that the *Scribes* and *Pharisees* were ; *not without*, as you say, *nor within;* and yet see if you can finde our Saviour or his Apostles letting out themselves into your restrictions and moderations and cautions. Those truths which are [d]essentially, universally, alwayes, and at all times holy, ought not to be measured by the *umbrage* and scandall of the *Adversary*. Indeed, in things meerly civill or indifferent, our use and liberty may appear more ; but for such truths as our Reformation [4]brings, they will be alwayes an offence to the Adversary. *We preach Christ,* [5]sayes the Apostle, *unto the Jewes a stumbling block, and to the Greeks foolishnesse;* and yet the [e]Apostle [6]preaches, and layes these *blocks* and this *rock of offence* in the way too.

Treatise.

(z) *I wonder you should here expresse an indulgence which is not allowable.*) I wonder and am sorry withall to see a Protestant take unjust offence at this Doctrine, *that no just offence is to be given to the Papists.* Know, Sir, that besides those Papists in *England* and *Ireland* to whom you say (a) the Parliament hath proclaimed an irreconcilable war, there be also many of their Religion in *Spaine, France, Germany, Italy, Poland,* &c., all *Europe* over, with whom the Parliament hath not as yet any professed open hostility, and to these no offence must be given. The eye of all Christendome is upon us ; the Sea surrounds, but doth not conceale us : Present Papists read the text of our actions, and their posterity will write comments upon them: we cannot therefore be too wary.

7. That it is utterly unlawfull to give any just offence to the Papists or to a[n]y men whatsoever.

Besides, grant that this irreconcilable war you speak of

---

[1] faith : *Truth Maintained*, page 46.
[2] goeth : *ibid.*, page 46.
[3] of the Scribes and Pharisees : *ibid.*, page 46.
[4] shall bring : *ibid.*, page 47.
[5] faith : *ibid.*, page 47.
[6] preacheth : *ibid.*, page 47.

should bind men in a *martiall way* to kill all Papists; yet I pray take notice that in some cases we may justly kill them, whom in no case we may justly offend. Though a malefactor be condemned by the Judge to be executed, yet the Sheriffe is a murderer if he torment him to death, contrary to the sentence of law. Now giving unjust scandall to the Papists, is torturing of them, and tyranny to their souls, which may externally destroy them; and you are the first Divine, and I hope shall be the last, which ever held this to be lawfull.

Whereas you say, *I much mistake the Divinity of Christ in matter of offence*, I should be very thankfull to you, if you be pleased to rectifie my erroneous judgement; to which end I will crave the Readers leave the more largely to expresse my opinion in this point.

I hold that we ought not to give just offence to any man whatsoever: Indeed there is no danger of giving offence to the divell. He who fears to offend Satan offends God with his foolish fear: Because the divels very nature is all mischief and malice, nothing being good in him, save his being which he hath of God; and he is utterly incapable of salvation. But seeing in the very worst of men there is some goodnesse, or at lest a capability of grace here and glory hereafter, through repentance and faith in Christ, we may not give any man just offence, as being against the rules of Piety, Charity, and Christian Prudence.

Against the rule of Piety: because God hath said, [1]*Give no offence to any*. Against the rule of Charity: because thereby we are cruell to them which are our Brethren by nature, and may be by grace. Against the rule of Christian Prudence: because we cannot give any just offence, but also thereby we doe give them a just advantage against us. I beleeve, Sir, were you to dispute in an University against Popish Opponents, you would so warily state the question which you defend as that you would not willingly give any *upper ground* to your Adversaries, more then what they could get for themselves. Wherefore, as the wrestlers in the Olimpian

---

[1] 1 Cor. 10. 32; 2 Cor. 6. 3.

games used to annoint themselves with oyle, not only thereby to supple their joynts, but also to make their naked bodies the more slick and slippery, that so those who wrestled with them might catch no hold upon them, so ought we, who are like to have constant opposition with the Papists, to give them no more advantage then what they can earn; and if we give them more, they will be more ready to jeere us for our folly then thank us for our bounty unto them.

Yea, in this respect it is more dangerous to give just offence, and therby just advantage (for the one cannot be done without the other), to the Papists then to any meer Pagans: For Pagans being rude, dull and ignorant, though an advantage be given them, cannot in point of learning husband and improve it to the utmost. But the Papists whom we doe know and must acknowledge cunning fencers in the School of wit and learning, are so well skild as ever to keep and inforce the advantage we once bestowed on them. And though we need never feare them and all their art so long as we have God and a good cause on our side, so if we betray our cause by giving them just advantage, it is just with God to deliver us over into their hands, to beat us with our owne weapons.

And heare let the Reader be pleased to take notice, as much materiall to our purpose, that there is a grand difference betwixt the Removing of things bad in their owne nature, and betwixt the manner of removing them. If any thing be bad in it selfe, it may not be continued, it must be removed. None can dispence with the retaining thereof, though never so many or great Persons take offence at the taking of it away. If Friers bee offended thereat, let them turne their girdles with all their knots in them behind them, whilst wee neede not care for their causelesse anger. They who were so quick sighted that they could see an offence where it was never given them, let them looke againe in the same place, and their quick eyes will behold there the amends which were never tendered them.

But now, as for the manner of removing of things badd in themselves, when there is a liberty and latitude left unto us after what fashion we will doe it, either this way or that way, we muſt doe it ſo as to give none any juſt offence. For where it is at our choice and pleaſure to uſe variety of waies, our diſcretion muſt pitch on the beſt, whereby God may receive the moſt glory, the action the moſt luſter, wee our ſelves the greateſt comfort, and all others no juſt cauſe of offence. And here once againe let mee requeſt the Reader to obſerve that in my Sermon I never mentioned any tendernes to give the Papiſts offence in removing of thinges bad in themſelves; but this caution of not giving the Papiſts juſt offence was inſerted in the proper place, when we came to ſhew how diſcretion is to appeare in the manner of a reformation.

Yea, the ſame thing for ſubſtance may be done, and juſt offence either may or may not be given according to the different manner of doing it. For inſtance, ſuch Pictures which are in the ſuburbs of ſuperſtition, becauſe the gate of that City is alwaies open, may without any giving of juſt offence be fairely taken away. But to ſhoot off the head of the ſtatue of Chriſt, either to ſpite the Papiſts or ſport our ſelves, giveth juſt offence. Though the Image be nothing, yet ſuch uſage thereof is ſomething; the bullet ſhott at the picture wounds pietie: For to do ſerious worke in a jearing way is inconſiſtent with Chriſtian gravities, and argueth not light of knowledge, but lightneſſe, not to ſay lewdneſſe of behaviour.

Another inſtance. Suppoſe that ſome ceremonies ancient for time, uſed by the fathers, (though abuſed by the Papiſts,) reduced by the Proteſtants, defended by our Engliſh, not oppoſed by forraigne Devines, be practiſed in our Church. And withall ſuppoſe that ſuch ceremonies as they are harmeleſſe, ſo to be uſeleſſe, and not without the ſuſpition of danger, as the preſent times ſtand. In this caſe it will give no juſt offence to the Papiſts to take them away under the Notion of things unneceſſary, and unſuting with our preſent condition. But to remove them as things prophane, Idolatrous, or ſuperſtitious, giveth juſt offence and great advantage to our Romiſh adverſaries, by the diſgrace we put on Antiquity. Beſides, hereby we betray our freinds which have don good ſervice for our Religion, namely ſuch Engliſh Devines who with their penns have learnedly and truly aſſerted the lawfulneſſe of ſuch ceremonies, and this our retreating from them and leaving them ingaged (as *Ioas* ferved *Vriah*[1] at the fiege of *Rahab*, treacheroufly) fhews much bafeneffe in us; and in fuch a cafe the difhonouring of good men is the difhonouring of God himfelfe.

But if I fhould in Courticie yeeld fo much unto you (which I never will) that it were lawfull to give juft offence to grounded and dedicated Papifts, yet know there be fome who in their opinions and affections, the borderers betwixt us and the Papifts, *almoft* Proteftants, *not far from* our Religion, having one foote in it, and the other likely to follow: fuch People when they fee that we take no care and make no confcience to give juft offence to the Papifts, will be ready to retract their refolutions and call back their forward affections: fay not that fuch men are better loft then found. Is this the bowels of Chriftian compaffion, which ought to be in us? If we wilfully blaft fuch bloffomes, we are not worthy of any ripe fruite; and it is both cruelty and profaneffe to caft fuch *doe bakt cakes* to the Doggs, which by ftanding a while longer in the Oven would make good and wholefome bread. Nor herein do I write only by gueffe, but too much by knowledge, fuch as I can neither well conceale nor comfortably relate. For when the Religious paines of fome reverend Devines whom I know have brought fome Papifts to the doore of our Church, the juft offence given them by the moderne extravagances of fome undifcreet Proteftants caufed them to fale backe againe to Popery.

And now to returne to your Examination. All things contained therein are eafily to be anfwered by that which we have premifed.

(*b*) *Saint Paule was of another Spirit, who forbore not a* [1]*Disciple and Apoftle*.) Saint *Paule* perceiving a dangerous error in *Peter*, reproved him, both prefently while the wound was greene, and publiquely, that the plaifter might be as broad as the fore. But in thus doing he gave no juft offence to *Peter*, but blamed *Peter* for giving juft offence to other Chriftians.

(*c*) *He goeth on and perfueth the offence till they left him*.)

---

[1] 2 Sam. 11. 15.   [2] Gal. 2. 11.

This inftance of Chrifts his cariage herein nothing advantageth you. Give me leave to repeate what I faid before: If things be bad in themfelves they muft be removed, though they give never fo many offence, or rather though never fo many or great men take offence thereat; fo alfo if a neceffary Truth bee to be introduced, it muft be preached and brought into the Church, though never fo many be offended thereat. And if there be but one way, and no more allowed us, how and in what manner to do it, according to that one way it muft be don, not valluing the offending of any. But if verity [variety] of way be permitted unto us, God expects that we fhould give the leaft, and if poffible no offence to any. Now to apply the truth which our Saviour heare preached and preffed was of abfolute and neceffary concernment: Namely that he was the true *Manna, Meffiah, and bread from heaven.* Such truths muft bee preached; and if any burne with anger thereat, let not their fire be quenched till it goe out for want of fuell. The cafe is far otherwife in this Reformation, betwixt us and the Papifts. We had all effentiall truths before; and if any ornamentall or additionall truths be now to be brought in, they muft be fo done as to give no juft offence to the Papifts.

(*d*) *Thofe truths which are effentially, univerfally, alwaies, and at all times holy, ought not to be meafured by the umbrage and fcandall of the adverfaries*). If hereby you meane that neceffary truths muft not bee forborne to bee preached for feare of giving any offence, I clearely concurre with you. Onely I fay that all fuch truths are in our Church already, and not now to bee newly brought in (as you intimate) by the Reformation.

(*e*) *And yet the Apoftle preacheth, and layes thofe blockes and this rock of offence in the way too*). The Apoftle preached Chrift, and intended him to be a *rock of defence* to all. As for thofe who perverted him to bee a *rock of offence* to themfelves, this fcandall was not juftly given to them, but unjuftly taken by them. If Papifts take offence at any fuch truth, it fhall affect us no more then the cryes of *Baals* [1]Pro-

---

[1] 1 Kings 18. 29.

phets affected any of whom it is said, *there was none to answer them, nor any that regarded them*. But as for the manner of removing away any errors or bringing in any Truths, we ought to bee wary and circumspect, for our own sakes as well as theirs, to give them no just offence.

To conclude. For mine owne part, Sir, I pittie the Persons of all Papists, and heartily desire their convertion, but hate theirs, and all other errors, *with a perfect hatred*. And this my enmity to all Popish Tenents doth the more plainely appeare to be grounded on my Judgement, not on my passion, because I would have all men so cautious as not to give them just advantage, least our actions fight for them, whilst our affections fight against them. What Frier will not laugh in his Coule at this your opinion, that it is lawfull to give Papists just offence? Well, you never shall have my consent to combate as our Churches Champion against Rome for the Protestant cause untill you have learnt more skill in fencing, and not to lye at so open a guard. And if you hold it lawfull to give Papists just offence, by the next returne you will hold it lawfull to give just offence to all which are termed *Popishly affected*, the Gangrean of which expression is by some extended to taint as sound and hearty Protestants as any be in England.

Examiner.

Sermon, page 24 [¶ 31, page 310].

That it is to be desired, not hoped for, a Plato's *Common-wealth, and* Moores *Vtopia. These phansies are pleasing but unfeizable.*

[9] *Examination.* He that looks abroad shall soone have his sight terminated; but the more he goes on, the more hee sees, and that which closed his prospect opens then into new discoveries: if you see no perfect Reformation as you stand, doe not therefore say there is none; they that stand higher, and on a holier Mountaine, [f]perhaps see [1]further. You that stand in the *Horizon* [g]*of Prelacy* cannot see much beyond it; corruption is deceitfull, and makes us, like *Adam*, see all generations in ourselves. Because we will not be perfectly reformed, let us not argue our Judgements into a beliefe that we cannot; [h]let us think it as possible to be the best as easie to be the worst; let us not think that *Plato's Common-wealth*, or a *Moores Vtopia*, which for

---

[1] farther: *Truth Maintained*, page 53.

ought wee know is reall and exiftent: There is *under the Gofpel a* [1]*Royal Priefthood, an holy Nation, a peculiar People;* and certainly had former Ages [k]lived to fee but the difcoveries of [1]later times, they would have admired their owne ignorance and our happineffe.

Treatife.

(*f*) *They that ftand higher and on a holyer mountaine perhapps fee further*). I deny it not. But if they fee a perfect Church on earth, they fee it in a trance or vifion.

(*g*) *You that ftand in the Horizon of Prelacy cannot fee much beyond it.*) Miffe not the matter, to hitt my perfon. If I ftand in the *Horizon of Prelacy,* I ftand no more for it then it ftands with Gods glory and will in his word. Becaufe you taxe me with dimneffe of fight, I will ftrive by my ftudy to get the beft advantage ground I can; I will begg of God, to animate [anoint] mine eyes with *his* [2] *eyefalve;* I will be carefull to keepe mine eyes from being *bloodfhot* by animating any to cruelty in this unnaturall Warr. And know, Sir, that they who ftand in the *Horizon of Prefbutary* or *Independency* are fubject alfo to Errors and miftakes. As delight in old Cuftomes may deceive fome, fo defire of Novelty may blind the eyes of others. God helpe us all! we are badd at the beft.

(*h*) *Becaufe we will not be perfectly reformed, let us not argue our Iudgments into a beleife that we cannot*). A diftinction or two of perfection and your fallacy will perfectly appeare. Some Saints in the Scripture phrafe are ftiled perfect, but then it is Comparatively, as they ftand in oppofition to [3] wicked men who have no goodneffe at all in them. Or elfe they are called perfect, as fo denominated from their better part (good reafon the beft *Godfather* fhould *name the Child*), *their regenerate halfe,* which defires and delights in endeavoring towards perfection. Or, laftly, perfection is taken for integrity, fincerity, and uprightneffe, oppofite to inward hippocrifie; and in fuch a perfection the Heart may have many defects by the by, but no diffimulation in the maine fervice of God. Such

---

[1] latter: *Truth Maintained,* page 53.   [2] Rev. 3. 18.
[3] *Sanctorum nonnulli perfecti dicuntur refpectu mundanorum, qui negligunt res divinas nec ingrediuntur unquam viam perfectionis.* Amb. *Com. in Epift. ad Phil.* cap. 2. [ver. 15. Ed Paris, 1590, vol. ii. col. 260, ad. fin.]

a perfection as this, men may have, yea, muſt have, in this life; and without ſuch a perfection here, no hope of any happineſſe hereafter.

But as for an exact, legall perfection (ſuch as ſome Papiſts dreame of, and moſt Anabaptiſts doate on), a perfection able to ſtand before Gods Iuſtice without the ſupport of his mercy, it is utterly impoſſible for mortall men to attaine unto it. In which ſence in my Sermon I ſaid that a *Perfect reformation of a Church in this world is difficult to be preſcribed, and impoſſible to be practiſed.*

Yea, let me tell you, Sir, (cautions comming from good-will deſerve to be heard, if not heeded,) if you perſiſt in this opinion of *exact perfection*, I conceive your condition dangerous. *Eliſha* told King *Ioram, Beware that thou paſſe not [1]ſuch a place, for thither the* Aramites *are come downe.* I may friendly tell you, preſſe not one [on] any further in this point, for ſpirituall pride lyeth hard by in waite, and the ambuſh thereof will ſurpriſe you. For my owne part, as I hate my badneſſe, ſo I hugge the confeſſion that I am badd. And Gods children finde both contentment and comfort in knowing they cannot bee perfect. Hence they learne (what ſoule ſo bad which hath not ſometimes *ſome holyday thoughts?*) to loath earth, to love Heaven, to runne from themſelves, to fly to their Saviour, to pittie others, to pray heartily for them, to hope comfortably of them; in a word, this doctrine abateth pride, increaſeth charity, and confoundeth cenſuring.

Yea, I ſolemnely profeſſe that I would not herein change my doctrine for yours, to have much to boote. Should I ſay that I could be perfect, both my head and my heart would give my tongue the lye. And one of the beſt hopes I have to goe to Heaven, is that I am ſure I deſerve Hell. I remember a ſtrange, but true and memorable ſpeech of Reverend Mr. *Fox* [2]to this effect, *that his Graces ſometimes did him harme, whilſt his ſinne did him much good.* A wonderfull thing; yet ſometimes ſo it commeth to paſſe, God making a cordiall for us of our owne wickedneſſe, thereby teaching us humility.

---

[1] 2 Kings 6. 9. [2] Cited by Mr. [Richard] Capel in his Booke of *Temptation.* [*Tentations: Their Nature*, &c., Lond. 1633, 12mo. pt. i. pages 233-4.]

(*i*) *There is under the Gospel a Royall Priesthood, an holy Nation, a peculiar people.*) True, Here these things are sincerely begunne, and hereafter fully perfected; for in this life there is still some basenesse even in the *royall priesthood*, impiety in the *holy Nation*, commonnesse in the *Peculiar people*. And I pray remember you are to prove that a whole Church may bee perfectly reformed in this world. For though it were granted that some men might be perfect, yet it followeth not thereupon that any one Church is existent on Earth, consisting intirely all of perfect members. Hipocrites are of so glutenous a nature they will stick close in every visible Church. They cannot be devided who cannot be discerned: except one could borrow Gods *touchstone of hearts*, such shining drosse will ever passe current in this Kingdome of Grace.

(*k*) *Had former ages lived but to see the discovery of latter times.*) If by former ages you meane the *time of Popery*, I concurre with you. If you understand the times of the *Primitive Fathers*, I suspend my suffrage till the next paragrave. But if you extend it to the age of Christ and his Apostles, I flatly discent. Nor am I sensible of any such late *Discoveries* in Religion, though many *Recoveries*, thanks be to God, there have been in rescuing the faith from Romish superstition.

(*l*) *They would have admired their owne ignorance and our happinesse.*) By our *Happinesse*, I suppose you meane what lately we had before this Warre began, and what we had not the happinesse to keepe, and wee trust in due time God will restore to us againe. Otherwise, as for our present woefull condition, I would not wish our friends or envie our foes such *happinesse*.

Examiner.

Sermon, page 24 [¶ 32, page 311].

There are some now adayes that talk of a great light manifested in this age more than before. Indeed we Modernes have a mighty advantage of the Antients: whatsoever was theirs, by industry may be ours. All contribute themselves to us, who live in this latter age.

[10] *Examination.* If wee had no more light than what you insinuate were seen from the Fathers, why doe we see more and more clearly and

further? Hee that fees farre muft either have a good *fight* or a cleere *light;* and fure in this age we have both: thofe errors which our Fathers faw for dimme truths, we fee for herefies; fo furely both our eyes and our light are better; for the light which our Fathers have in their lamps can difcover but fo much to us as it did to them; and we know our [1]difcoveries are fuch as we are able to fee the fhadow which followed them, even that myftery which was working in their dayes, both in Prelacy and Ceremony. Who will deny but that the cloud of *Antichriftianifme* was thick in their times? and then the light could not be fo glorious as now, when thefe clouds grow thinner, and more attenuated by the Preaching of the Gofpel.

Treatife.

To cut off all occafion and pretence of caviling, wee will fhew, God willing, in what refpect the Fathers for knowledge excelled and exceeded us, and in what refpect wee modernes goe beyond them. They had a threefold advantage above us. 1. Of fight, 2. Of light, 3. and of a nearer object.

8. What advantage the Fathers had of us in Learning and Religion, and what we have of them.

Firft, Of a better fight. Being men of eminent natural parts, improved with excellent learning; and to the Eafterne fathers the Greeke tongue, the language of the New Teaftament, was naturall, fo that it cofteth us much paines and fweat but to come to the place whence they ftarted.

Secondly, Of a brighter light. As their conftancie in perfecution was great, fo no doubt the heate of their zeale was attended with a proportionable light and heavenly illumination, God doing much for them that fuffer much for him. Efpecially in thofe points wherein they encountred hereticks, they were more then men, and went beyond themfelves, as St. *Athanafius* againft the *Arians*, St. *Auguftine* againft the *Pelagians* and *Donatifts* from whom our moderne Brownifts differ no more then the fame man differs from himfelfe in new cloathes.

3. Of a nearer Object. They living clofer to Chrifts times could therefore better underftand the *fence of the Church* in the doctrine delivered to the Apoftles. Here we muft know that Apoftles and Apoftolick men, as they wrote Gods

---

[1] difcovery is: *Truth Maintained*, page 57.

word in their Epiftles and Gofpels for the profit of all pofterity, fo for the inftruction of their prefent age they alfo [1]*traditioned it* in their Preaching by word of mouth to the people of thofe times; not that they delivered anything *vivâ voce* contrary or differrent from what they wrote, or that (as the Papifts ftile for their traditions) they supplyed and enjoyned any thing as neceffary to falvation, which other wife was wanting in the Scripture; but the felfe fame things which they wrote in the New Teftament, they alfo delivered in their Sermons, and in their Preaching delated upon them; wherefore the prime primative age having (as I may fay) two ftrings to their bow, Scripture and Preaching, muft needes bee allowed to have had the cleareft apprehention of the meaning of heavenly mifteries. And as the [2] children of *Ifraell ferved the Lord all the dayes of* Iehoffuah, *and all the dayes of the Elders who outlived* Iehoffuah, *who had feene all the great workes of the Lord which he did for Israell*; in like manner wee may conclude that the greateft puritie and the cleareft light of the Church lafted fo long as any, within fight, hearing, or memory of Chrift or his Apoftles preaching or miracles, did furvive.

Now to hold the fcales even, we in like manner have a three fold advantage over the Fathers. Firft, a degree of experimentall light more then they had or could have, having feene the whole conduct, Mannaging and Progreffe of Religion fince their times, whereby (with a litle helpe of hiftory) a Devine who is under fixtie in age, may be above fixteene hundred in experience.

Secondly, we have the benefitt of the Fathers bookes; a mightie advantage if we were as carefull to ufe it to Gods Glory as we are ready to bragg of it for our owne credit. And here I muft complaine of many mens lazineffe. Indeed a learned man [3]compareth fuch as live in the latter times in refpect of the Fathers to *Dwarffes ftanding on Giants Shoulders*. But then if we will have profitt by the fathers learning, we muft take paines to mount to the tops of their Shoulders. But if like idle *Dwarfes* we ftill do but ftand on the ground,

---

[1] Ἐγὼ γὰρ παρέλαβον ἀπὸ τοῦ Κυρίου ὃ καὶ παρέδωκα ὑμῖν. 1 Cor. 11. 23.
[2] Iudg. 2. 7.
[3] *Nos nani fumus ftantes fuper humeros Gygantum.* Holcott.

our heads will not reach to their girdles : it is not enough to through the bookes of the fathers togeather on an heape, and then making their workes our footeſtoole, to ſtand on the outſide and Covers of them, as if it were no more but VP and RIDE, boaſting how far we behold beyond them. No ; if we expect to gett advantage by their writings, we muſt open their bookes, read, underſtand, compare, digeſt and meditate on them. And I am affraid many that leaſt looke into the Fathers boaſt moſt that they looke beyond them.

Thirdly. Wee have the advantage of a darkneſſe removed by Gods goodneſſe from our eyes, which in ſome matters did dimme the fight of the Fathers : Namely, the miſtery of Iniquity which wrought in their times, and now is taken away in the Proteſtant Church. That Bramble of *Rome*, (ſoone will it prick, which will be a thorne,) which afterwards Lorded it over the *Vine*, *Olive*, and *Figtree*, beganne very timely to play his parte. And the *Man of ſin*, then but an infant (and every thing is pretty when it is yonge) was unawares dandled on the knees of many a devout Monke, and rockt in the cell of many an holy hermit, who litle ſuſpected that then voluntary ſequeſtring themſelves to enjoy heavenly thoughts would by degrees degenerate to be in after ages the cover of Pride, luſt and lazineſſe. Now ſeing this man of ſinne is *dead already* in the Proteſtant Church, and hath a conſumption attended with the Hecktick Fever in all other places, the taking away of Popiſh ſuperſtition may juſtly be accounted the third advantage which our age hath.

By the way, we muſt take heed of a fault whereof many are guilty. For ſome are ready to challenge every thing in the practiſe of the Fathers which doth not pleaſe them preſently to be Popiſh, and pretend they taſt ſuperſtition in whatſoever themſelves diſtaſt. O, ſay they, the Fathers lived when the *myſtery of iniquity did worke*, and hence they infer that it is evidence enough without further tryall to condemne any cerimonies uſed by them, becauſe they were uſed by them. The way indeede to make Short Aſſiſes, but Perjur'd Iudges ; whereas it is not enough to ſay, but to ſhew, that they are ſuperſtitious, to anatomize, and diſſect the Popery conteined in them, demonſtrating where it croſſeth the word of God ;

wheras on the contrary all wife and charitable men ought to efteeme the practifes of the primitive Church not only to be innocent, but ufefull and honourable, till they be legally convicted to be otherwife.

If any object that the Fathers had another difadvantage, that befides the fpreading of Popery other Herefies did alfo fpring and fprout apace in that time to the darkening of the light of the truth, let them know that fuch oppofition only gave truth the opportunity to tryumph, and the teeth of Error filled [filed] it the brighter. Herefies *In eodem feculo quo natæ, damnatæ; quos errores patrum ætas tulit, eos et fuftulit*, condemning them in Synods and Councells. And in this point to be an equall Umpire betwixt the *ancients* and us, we muft confider that we live in the *Later age;* and commonly bad humors which have vifited the whole body, do fettle at laft in the leggs and loweft parts. With us Sects and Schifmes do alfo abound; and fome Herefies firft *fet a broach* in the Primitive times now *runne a Tilt* with all their dredgs in our dayes.

Thus we fee how the Fathers were both before and behind us for knowledge, and wee therein both above and beneath them in feverall refpects. See the wifdome and goodneffe of God, how he hath fweetly *tempered* things together. So good that all have fome, fo wife that none have all. And how eafie may this controvercy be accommodated, *whether ours or the Fathers light were the greateft;* where if the difference be but cleerly underftood, the parties are fully reconciled. And now I conceive, having anfwered you in groffe, I need not apply my felfe to any perticulers of your examination.

Examiner.

The *Gofpel* doth ᵐwork and wind its beames into the world, according to the Propheticall feafons for Revelation. Many Propheticall truths were fealed up, and thofe not unfealed but fucceffively, and as our *generations* after may have a *ftarre* rifing to them, which we have not, fo we may have ⁿ*beames* and *radiations* and *fhootings* which our *Fathers* had not. The *Apoftles* ᵒhad not all their *truths* and *light* revealed at once: fome early, fome late, fome not till the Holy Ghoft was beftowed. Revelations are graduall, and the vaile is not taken off at once, nor in one age. Wee honour the *Fathers* as men in *their Generations* famous; their light was glorious in its degree and quality, but they had not all the degrees attainable;

they had a light for their own times, and we for ours; and who cannot think we are rising into that Age ᵖwherein God *shall poure his spirit upon all flesh; and* ᑫ*wherein the light of the Moone shall be as the light of the Sun, and the light of the Sun as the light of seven dayes?*

Treatise.

You hover in Generalls, and seeme to me desirous that your Reader should understand more then you are willing to expresse. My opinion breifly is this: That no new Revelations, or new infused light in essentiall points of Religion, is bestowed on any now-adayes, but that the same light hath in as plentifull a measure beene given to former ages, especially to the age wherein the Apostles lived, and when *the faith was once delivered to the Saints*, and by them sett downe in the Scripture, and that then so perfectly and compleatly that it needed not the accessions of any future Revelations.

<small>9. No new light or new essentiall truths are or can be revealed in this age.</small>

I confesse that men, by searching the Scripture (that oyle will never leave increasing as long as more vessels be still brought) and diligent prayer to God, may and do arrive daily at a clearer understanding of many places of Gods word which they had not before. These words, *Thou art Peter, and on this rock will I build my Church*; and that place, *This is my body*, are now more truly and plainly understood then they were two hundred yeares agoe, when the Pope's *supremacy* was as falsly founded on the former as Transubstantiation was unjustly inferred from the latter. However these were not Revelations of new truthes, but reparations of ould. For the prime primative Church received and embraced the same. The Saints in the time of Popery ¹*sung as it were a new song*, a Song not new but renewed; not new in it selfe, but perchance to the hearers; and such are many truthes which are preached in our age in the Protestant Church.

They that maintaine the contrary opinion of moderne revelations of new essentiall truths doe a three fold mischeife therein. First, they lay an aspersion of ignorance and imperfection of knowledge on the Apostles themselves; and this is no lesse then *Scandalum Magnatum*.

---

¹ Revel. 14. 3.

Secondly, they much unsettle men in matters of Religion, and produce a constant inconstancy and scepticall hovering in all oppinions; and as the *Athenians* erected an Altar to the *unknowne God*, so men must reserve a blancke in their soules therin to write truths *as yet unknown*, when they shall be revealed. Thus men will never know when their creede is ended, and will daily waver in that truth which they have in possession, whilst they waite for a clearer and firmer, as yet in reversion.

Thirdly, they fixe on the Scripture an imputation of imperfection; and such as talke of new revelations of truth may well remember the passage in the Old Revelation, [1] *If any man shall add unto these things, God shall add unto him the plagues that are written in this booke.* And it seemes to mee all one in effect whether men peece the Scriptures with old Traditions or new Revelations; and thus the Papist and Anabaptist are agreed, like men in a circle going so farre from each other with their faces, till their backes meete together. And I professe I should sooner trust a tradition containing in it nothing crosse to the Scripture, and comming to mee recommended from the primitive times, and countenanced with the practise of the Church in all ages, then a new upstart Revelation. The best is, wee have no neede to trust either whilst we have Gods word alone sufficient to relie on.

The result of all is this: We have now a-dayes no new truths revealed, but old ones either more fairely cleared or more firmly assented to; no new Starres of Revelation arise in any hearts. If any such doe burne and blaze there, they are but commetts which will fade at last. In a word, this age is not happie with any new truths, but guiltie of many old lyes.

Yea, it rendereth it suspitious that some men are going about somewhat, which they cannot justifie by the old knowne lawes of God, because they beginne to broach preparative doctrines Introductorie of new revelations: Distrusting (as it seemes) the Scripture, the old Iudge, as not for their turnes, because they provide for an Appeale to an other Vmpirer; and if those are justly accounted dangerous members in the

---

[1] Revel. 22. 18.

Church, who would bring in Innovations in Ceremonies, then pretenders of new Revelations in Eſſentiall points of Doctrine are ſo much the greater offenders by how much Doctrine is more neceſſary and fundamentall in a Church then ceremonies. But I will anſwer ſome paſſages in your Examination particularlie.

(*m*) *The Goſpel doth worke and winde its beames into the world, according to the propheticall ſeaſons for Revelations.*) Diſtinguiſh we heare betwixt matters *of fact*, and matters *of faith*. Matters of fact being foretold in the Scripture are beſt underſtood when they are accompliſhed: In which reſpect the longer the world laſteth, the clearer men ſee and the plainer they underſtand ſuch predictions. The *Seales* in the Revelations were ſucceſſively opened, the *Trumpets* ſucceſſively blowne, the *Vialls* ſucceſſively powred out, and the things imported in and by them are ſucceſſively performed. Wherefore time is the beſt comentator on the propheticall parts of the Bible: *Dies diem docet*. And to day, which is yeſterdaies ſchoolemaſter, will be Scholler to to-morrow; in which reſpect the [1] Prophets words are moſt true, *Many ſhall runne to and fro, and knowledge ſhall be increaſed*. But now, as for matters of Faith, they were at once, and for ever, fully, and freely, delivered at the firſt to the Apoſtles, and ſo from them to us; and that ſo perfectly and compleatly, they neede no new revelations *quoad materiam;* though *quoad modum* old truths may now have a new meaſure to be more clearely underſtood then in the darke times of Popery.

(*n*) *We may have Beames and Radiations and Shootings which our Fathers had not.*) For *Beames* and *Radiation* of knowledge I have delivered my oppinion; but as for *Shootings*, God knowes wee have many, ſuch as our Fathers never had. God in his mercy ceaſe ſuch *Shootings*, or elſe in his Iuſtice direct the Bulletts to ſuch markes as in truth have been *the troublers of our Iſrael*.

(*o*) *The Apoſtles had not all their truths and light revealed at once: ſome early, ſome late, ſome not till the Holy Ghoſt was*

---

[1] Dan. 12. 4.

bestowed.) All this is most true which you say: The Apostles at first were (as we may say) Freshmen, newly admitted into Chrifts Company. Then they tooke their first degree of knowledge, when sent forth to Preach the Gospel, *Mat.* 10, to the *Iewes* alone in their Masters lifetime. They commenced in a higher knowledge after Christ his Resurrection. And after his Assention, assended yet higher in Spiritual Illuminations. Lastly, after the comming of the Holy Ghost, they proceeded Doctors in deede; I meane, they then had the completion and consumation of all understanding necessary to salvation. Now, Sir, Consider that after this time they wrote the New Testament, and therein all essentialls for us to know and doe for our soules health, so that we now doe deduce and derive our knowledge, not from the Apostles in their infancy or minority of Judgement, but from them having attained to the Top and Verticall point of their perfectest skill in heavenly misteries.

(*p*) *And who cannot thinke wee are rising into that age, wherein God will power his Spirit upon all flesh, &c.*) What proportion doth this beare with what you said not long since, prophesying that our *Marian Times* did approach too fast? When nothing was light but the Bonefiers to burne the Martyrs. I will not deny but this *great sun* may arrise; but the reigning vices of the time are but an ill *Morning Starre* to harbinger the rising thereof. We have taken the *St. Shippe* from those in heaven, but have no more holinesse in our selves here on earth. What betwixt the sins which brought this Warre, and the sinnes this warre hath brought, they are sad presages of better times. Never was Gods name more taken in vaine by oathes and imprecations. *The Lords day*, formerly profained with *mirth*, is now profained with *malice*; and now as much broken with Drummes as formerly with a Taber and Pipe. Superiours never so much slighted, so that what [1]*Naball* said sullenly and (as he applyed it) falsly, we may say sadly and truly, *There be many servants now adayes that breake away, every man from his Master.* Killing is now the only Trade in fashion; and Adultery never more common, so that our

---

[1] 1 Sam. 25. 10.

Nation (in my opinion) is not likely to confound the fpirituall Whore of *Babilon* whilft corporall whoredom is in her every where committed, no where punifhed. Theft fo ufuall that they have ftollen away the word of *Stealing*, and hid it under the Name of *Plundering*. Lying both in word and print grown Epidemicall, fo that it is queftionable whether *Gunnes* or *Printing* (two inventions of the fame Countrey and ftanding) at the prefent doe more mifcheife in this Kingdome. It is paft *coveting of our Neighbours houfes*, when it is come to violent keeping them. He therefore that doth ferioufly confider the Grievoufneffe and Generality of thefe finnes will rather conclude that fome *Darkeneffe of Defolation* then any Great light is likely to follow upon them. God, I confeffe, in mercy may doe much both to pardon and profper us, and can extract Light out of Darkeneffe; but whether he will or no, I (though confident of his power) fee little caufe to hope of his pleafure herein. And though herein I muft confeffe, many of thefe inormities may (though not wholly be excufed, yet) be fomething extenuated by pleading the unavoidable neceffities which warre doth caufe, yet furely wee fhall anfwer to God for caufing this warre by our crying finnes and tranfgreffions.

(*q*) *Wherein the light of the Moone fhall be as the light of the Sunne, and the light of the Sun as the light of the feven dayes.*) This, for ought I can finde to the contrary, was accomplifhed at Chrifts Comming, and [at] the generall giving of the Gofpel to the Gentiles with the fending of Gods Spirit miraculoufly upon them. Sure I am a Parallel place of the Prophet was then fulfilled, by the expofition of Saint [1]*Peter* himfelfe, *And it fhall come to paffe in the laft dayes (faith* God) *I will power out my fpirit upon all flefh: and your Sonnes and your Daughters fhall prophefie, and your young men fhall fee vifions, and your old men fhall dreame dreames.* Thefe words having the advantage of that *Date*, 𝔍n the laſt daies, might with the more colour have beene alleadged by you and applyed to thefe times to prove fome fpeciall Revelations in our dayes, had not the Apoftle marred your Mart and prevented you by applying the prophefie to the primative times.

---

[1] Ioel 2. 28; Acts 2. 17.

Examiner.

But wee fee the policy of [r]commending the *Fathers light* to our Generation; for could you prevaile with us to fet our *Dials* by that, you then might reform our *Church* by the *Canterburian* [1]*gnomen*, and fo fet us back to a *falfly-reputed Primitive Reformation*.

Treatife.

(*r*) *But wee fee the policie of commending the Fathers.*) I proteft before Almighty God I have neither bafe nor by refpect in praifing the Fathers. Saint *Paule* blamed *Peter* at *Antioach*, [2]*becaufe he was to be blamed*. I in the like manner commend the Light of Fathers, *becaufe it is to bee commended*, not for any favour or flattery. *A falfely-reputed primitive Reformation* I abhorre from my heart, and I prefume our Church is too wife to be cofened therewith. If *Canterbury* hath misbehaved himfelfe, his friends for him defire no more, and foes to him fhould grant no leffe, then a legall triall. But infult not on any man's fufferings: Organs, I dare fay, are not fo offenfive in Churches as the making of Muficke on men in mifery. Time was when you fett as much by a Smile from *Canterbury* as he ftill fetts litle by a Scoffe from you.

Examiner.

Sermon, pages 13, 14, 15, 16 [¶¶ 15–25, 303–7].

The Qualification for Reformers. The decent buriall of fuch Ceremonies as are taken from the Fathers. The honourable Refervation to our firft Reformers.

[11] *Examination.* That it may appear I look not onely at the worft of the Sermon, there are excellent truths in it; and it is pitie they are not [s]better [3]fituated: I could alwayes wifh to fee a *Diamond* fet in Gold.

Thefe are good Pofitions; and in their Pages not without their enamill of wit; yet there is a Policy to write faire in one leafe, though you make [t]a blot in another, but I cannot let thefe paffe without fome obfervation.

Treatife.

(*s*) *And it is Pitty they are not better fcituated: I could alwaies wifh to fee a Diamond fet in Gold.*) I cannot blame you, efpecially if the Diamond be their owne. But what

---

[1] *gnomon: Trvth Maintained*, page 67. [2] Gal. 2. 11.
[3] fcituated: *Trvth Maintained*, page 68.

meane you by this Expreffion? Would you have had the Truths in my Sermon to have beene fet in the Gold of rich and glittering language? Truly I could not go to the coft thereof, efpecially on fo fhort warning wherein the Sermon was made. However a Diamond is a Diamond though fet in Horne, whereby the lufter thereof may be fomewhat dimmed, but the worth thereof no whit diminifhed. But in one refpect I muft confeffe thefe Truthes were *ill fcituated:* that they ftood too neere to a captious Reader who tooke caufeleffe exception at them.

(*t*) *Yet there is a policie to write faire in one leafe, though you make a blot in another.*) Shew me, Sir, where thefe blotts bee. For as yet I am more troubled to know my fault then my defence.

Examiner.

Firft, for the *Qualification:* 'I dare fay never age afforded more eminent in this Kingdom; their *Calling lawfull*, their *Pietie exemplary*, their *knowledge radiant*, their *courage experienced* [1]thorow a legion of difficulties, their *prudence* in the conduct of a bufineffe, though oppofed with the Policy and Malignity of a grand and potent Enemy.

Treatife.

(*v*) *For their qualification, I dare fay.*) If you dare fay it, I dare not to gainfay it. Their calling no doubt is lawfull, if the fupreame power concurres with them. Of their pietie, which confifts in their hearts, God alone is Iudge. I will not difpute againft their *radiant Knowledge*, nor fight with their *experienced Courage*, and it were folly in me to oppofe their *Prudence*. Let not the perfections of King *Davids* [2]Subjects be *numbered*. God make their *Knowledge*, their *Courage*, their *Prudence*, an hundred fold more then it is; and may the Eyes of my Lord the King fee the fame, to his comfort and Honour.

Examiner.

And for *the decent buriall of* ʷ*Ceremonies, and fuperftitions of the fathers:* they fhall have a *Parliament* of *Senators*, and an *Affembly* of [3]*Divines* to lay them

---

[1] through: *Trvth Maintained*, page 69. [2] 2 Sam. 24. 3.
[3] Devines: *Trvth Maintained*, page 69.

in their Grave; and, I dare fay, a godly Congregation in the Kingdom to fing a Pfalm at their [1]Funeralls: and will not this be a [x]very decent buriall?

And for *the honourable refervation to the Reformers and their memories:* our [2]*Divines* and *Reformers* now have ever made [3]reforts and appeals to the truths they delivered; and in thofe times when *Beza,* and *Calvin,* and [4]*P. Martyr* were fet loweft, till the *Mafter of the feaft* came lately and bid them *fit up higher;* a *Caietan* and *Bellarmine,* and a *Councell of Trent,* I am fure, had [y]more honour from the [5]Divinitie of the other year or your times: fo farre we admire the *Reformers* as to *love* their *Truths,* and to *pitty* their *errors.*

But I will not fay much: [6]errors may be more provoked than remedied with overhandling; let us be wife in the Colours of good and evill; though it be an honeft, yet it is a dangerous miftake [7]to think [8]too many our Friends, and [8]too few our Enemies.

Treatife.

(*w*) *As for the decent buriall of Ceremonies, and fuperftitions of the Fathers.*) You are cunning to improve your felfe on my words. In my [9]Sermon, I made a double fuppofition: Firft, *If there be found in the Fathers praƐtice any Ceremonies fmacking of Paganifme or Popery.* Secondly, *If the fame can be juftly Challenged to be continued in our Church:* Now (as if two Suppofitions made a Pofition) you flatly infer and peremptorily conclude, fuch Superſtitions are in our Church. I fhould be loth to fell wares to fuch a Chapman, and to truft his honefty in meafuring of them out, who hath fuch a flight in flipping his fingers that give him *an inch* and hee will take *an ell.* You might have don better to have tould us what the perticulers of thefe fuperftitions are.

(*x*) *And will not this be a decent buriall?*) The pleafantneffe of your witt doth pleafe me: fome mirth in thefe fadd times doth well. But you might have been pleafed to have taken notice that by *the decent buriall of fuperftitious Ceremonies* (if any fuch can be proved to be in our Church) I ment the removing of them in that manner as might give no juft offence to any, as I have largely difcourfed of before. How-

---

[1] funerall: *Trvth Maintained,* page 69.
[2] Devines: *ibid.,* page 69.
[3] reforte and appeale: *ibid.,* page 70.
[4] *Peter Martir: ibid.,* page 70.
[5] Devinity: *ibid.,* page 70.
[6] *Nimis remediis irritantur deliƐta.* Tacitus. μέμνης' ἀπιστεῖν Σώφρων ἀπιστία.
[7] *Plures amicos quam funt, arbitratur.* Plin. [lib 3. Epift. xi. *ad calcem.*]
[8] to: *Trvth Maintained,* page 70.
[9] Paragraffe 24 [page 307].

ever, as you say, let but a 𝕻arliament lay them in the ground and I shall not moorne for their death but rejoyce at their solemne and legall Intérment.

(*y*) *Had more honour from the Devinitie of the other yeare or your times.*) The more shame for such, if any, who undervalued such Worthy Men. And blessed be God that they have recovered their former esteem. For my part they have not with me regained any new degree of Honor, but still keepe the selfesame place in my valuation of them whereof they ever were peaceably possessed.

Examiner.

[12] *Conclusion.* If I be now examined what *Reformation* I aime at, I answer, my endeavour here was only to ᶻtake out of the way such rubbish as others would bring in. If we can but clear the passage we go far in the work; and in the meantime let us, like ᵃ*Ioshuas spies, bring no evill report upon the land* we are going to.

Treatise.

(*z*) *My endeavour here was only to take out of the way such rubbish as others would bring in.*) Whether rather you have not brought in such Rubbish which others have taken away, be it reported to the judicious Reader.

(*a*) *Let us, like* Ioshuas *spies, bring no evill report upon the Land we are going to.*) By *Ioshuas* spies, you meane those who accompanied *Caleb* and *Ioshua* to spie the Land of *Canaan;* and these were guilty of a threefold Fault.

First, they spake truth with an ill intent to disharten the *Israelites* in their reporting of the strength of the Country. Secondly, they spake more then truth, raising the walls of the Canaanitish Cities by their Hyperbolyes as high as [1]*Heaven*. Lastly, they suppressed the most materiall point, not incouraging the people (as *Caleb* and *Ioshua* did) by the assured assistance of God against their enemies. But I conceive myselfe (against whome your words are darted) to be innocent in the foresaid perticulers.

---

[1] Dut. 1. 28.

Examiner.

But [b]suppose this *perfect Reformation* or *Church* were [c]among the [1]χρύφια, the [2]τῶν πολιτειῶν σοφίσματα, the *Ragione di sacro dominio;* he were no [d]wise nor faithful *Divine,* who would not preserve that [e]secret for holy advantages; 'tis *Gods* own design and his *Apostles* to hold out a *perfection* to us : *Be perfect as your heavenly father* (and some Pastors) *for the perfecting of the Saints.* I [f]commend *Bodin* and *Tacitus* for their *politicall faithfulness:* they writ far, yet would not [3]sun the [g]Imperiall χρύφια, nor make them [h]popular.

Treatise.

(*b*) *But suppose this perfect Reformation were, etc.*) It seemes you suspect the strength of your outworkes, that you so seasonably retire to your Castle; now at last condemning this doctrine, not as false, but unfitting to be preached.

(*c*) *Were among the* χρύφια.) I thinke you would say Κρύφια, or otherwise, Sir, my learning will not extend to understand this your new greeke.

(*d*) *He were no wise and faithfull Devine.*) So then you conclude me a foolish and deceitful Minister; and I had rather you should call me so ten times then my guiltie conscience should tell me so once, for concealing of a necessary truth.

(*e*) *Who would not preserve that secret for holy advantages.*) First, the question is, whether or no it lay in my power, if I would, to keepe this Point secret. What your people at *Heslertonn* in *Yorkeshire* are, you best know. In this Doctrine I was not the teacher, but the remembrancer of my people at the *Savoy,* from whom had I closely covered it with both my hands, they would have seene it through all my fingers. Besides, what hope can one have to keepe it secret when (as you say) so *great and glorious a light* is shining now-a-dayes?

But if I could, I ought not to suppresse it. Let Popish tenents be shutt in a cloister, and sicke opinions keepe their Chamber : God never lighted this Truth for us to put it under a bushell, it being alwaies seasonable to bee divulged, and now dangerous to bee concealed.

10. That the Doctrine of the Churches imperfection may safely bee preached and cannot honestly bee concealed.

---
[1] Aristotle [see *Politica,* lib. 4, cap. 10, § vii.] [cap. ix.]
[2] Arist. *Politica,* lib. 5, cap. 8 [§ ii.]; *Reip.*[*ublicæ*] *blandimenta.* Liv. lib. 2.
[3] *Non vulgare.* Tacit. *Ann.* [Bk. i. § 6]. *Nec proferre decet in publicum.* Arnol. Clapm.[arius] lib. 6, cap. 19 [ed. Leyden, 1644, p. 333].

These *holy advantages* (I would not count them advantages were they not holy) arise from Preaching this point. First, it awakens men from their Idle dreames of their conceited perfection of a Church here; and too many I feare have made this common-wealth here woefully *militant*, under pretence here to make the Church happily triumphant.

Secondly, to teach all Christians (Majestrates and Ministers most especially) as industry, so patience, daily to doe, and constantly to suffer, no whitt disheartned in their endeavours to perfection. Knowing though things bee badd, after their best labours to amend them, that this proceedes from the inevitable *vanity, to which the creature is subject*.

Thirdly, to weane men from this world, making them to love and long *for the time of the restitution of all things*, when this world as a watch out of tune shall not onely bee taken assunder and scoured, but also have all the wheeles made new and then bee perfectly reformed.

Yea, Sir, let us try whether you or I proceeding on our contrary principles shall more effectually perswade a reformation: you will tell the world that a perfect reformation in this life is attaineable, even to the anticipating of Heaven heare; and this you will presse with all your power and flowers of Retorick, and all little enough to performe so unsavory an untruth. Now see, sir, what mischeifes will follow hereupon.

1. Because one falsehood requires more to support it, you must call in other auxilliary falsities to defend this, and so engage your selfe in a multitude of errors.

2. Seeing slights and shifts can never last long, your forgery will be detected.

3. You are lyable to *Heavens Pillorie* to bee punnished for holy fraud.

4. You will scarce be trusted afterwards, though telling truth, being once convicted and ever suspected of falshood.

As for those whom you have deceived unto the utmost of their endevours of Reformation, on your false perswasion that the perfection thereof may bee had in this world, though their labours therein bee very forward at the first, yet soone will they wither and weaken with the graine in the Gospel that wanted Roote (no Roote and a falfe Roote are the fame in effect); and Gods bleffing cannot be expected on the deceitfull proceedings.

As for mee who have no cunning in fuch hunting, but pleafe my felfe with *Iacob* to bee a plaine man, I would goe another way to worke, and tell them the worft firft: that indeede it is vaine to expect a perfect reformation in this world. However, let them comfort themfelves that wee ferve fuch a Mafter *who accepts of the will for the deede, and knowes whereof we are made: Hee remembreth that wee are but duft.* And therefore let us doe our beft, and ftrugle againft our infirmities, being confident that God in Chrift will pardon what is amiffe, and reward what is good in us. And I doubt not but fuch doctrine by Gods bleffing will both take deeper impreffion in mens hearts, and bring forth better fruits of amendment in their lives.

(*f*) *I commend* Bodin *and* Tacitus *for their politicall faithfulneffe: they writt far, yet would not Sun the imperiall χρύφια nor make them popular.*) I confeffe it to bee unfitting, yea, dangerous to impart *mifteries of State* to private people; for fuch Iewels are to bee lockt in a fafe and fure Cabinet, the bofoms of Polititians. Not fo in neceffary Points of Divinity; for though every private man hath not a *State to governe,* hee hath *a foule to fave,* and therefore muft be partner in all wholfome doctrines.

Indeede in fome cafes Preachers may though not finally fuppreffe, yet feafonably conceale, or rather warily deferre the publifhing of fome points of Religion. Firft, when they are not of abfolute concernment to falvation, and the Minifter by his Chriftian difcretion plainely forefees that all the good which rationally can bee expected to redound from Preaching fuch a Truth will not countervaile the ill which in probability will inevitably follow thereupon. Or elfe, when the Auditors are not capeable as yet of fuch difficult Doctrines. Chrift himfelfe did fitt his *Wines* to his bottles, powring in not what hee could give, but they could take, leaft otherwife hee fhould rather fpill his liquor then fill his veffells.

Neither of thefe cafes now alledged take place concerning the publifhing of the Doctrine of the *Impoffibility of the*

Churches perfection in this world. For we may by Gods blessing justly expect and promise to our selves and others much good and comfort from the preaching thereof, as we have largely proved before. Nor dare I so much to disparage the times we live in (now it being above a hundred yeares since *Luthers* reformation) as to count them to have age so much, and Knowledge so litle, as not yet to be capable with safety and profit of so plaine and true a Doctrine. Some shortly expect *the day of Iudgment,* and sure then the world is already *come to Age* to understand Truths, except shee come not out of her *Mynority* till just shee be ready to die and to be dissolved.

(*g*) *Would not Sunne the Imperiall* χρύφια.) Godly secrets in Religion in some respects may be *Sunn'd.* First, that thereby they may be tryed (all Truths have Eagles eyes) whether or no they can behold and beare the Sunne Beames. Secondly, because our Saviour hath said, [1] *What I tell you in darknesse, that speake in the light; and what you heare in the Eare, that preach you upon the House toppe.* Lastly, that by proclaiming them the Godly may have an opportunity to receive them, and the wicked be rendred unexcusable for refusing them, when such Truths are made generally knowne.

(*h*) *Nor make them popular*). I distinguish on the word *Popular.* If it be taken, as generally it is (use having confined a word, of generall acception in it selfe, to an ill fence), to Court the good will of people for any private or sinester end, it is utterly unlawfull; for *Popularity,* which is necessary love in a Prince, is unlawfull lust in a Subject, who may not Court the Kings wife, for to him alone are the People married in a Politicke Relation. All honest men therefore disclaime to make *Truths Popular* in this fence, to impart them to the vulgar to gaine any vaine applause. Yea, consider herein whether you rather be not faultie in making the Imperiall χρύφια to bee *Popular,* who incite and incourage ordinary *People* to make a *Publique Reformation.*

But Truths in Divinity must be made Popular, that is, bee communicated to all people in true sinceritie for the saving of their Soules.

---
[1] Math. 10. 27.

The [1]Apoſtle calleth it the *Common ſalvation*, and therefore it muſt be preached to all in common: our Sermons muſt as wel be *ad Populum* as *ad Clerum*.

Otherwiſe ſuch Monopolies are illegall and diſtructive to the State of the Church, for any Miniſters to engroſſe any wholſome Doctrine to themſelves, and not imparte it to their Pariſh, except in the caſes afore mentioned.

Examiner.

[13] *Apology*. I have now done (I will not ſay) *refuting*, but *committing* errors: I am afraid my haſte at this time hath made me mend one fault only with another.

Treatiſe.

I will not oppoſe yours, but annex my owne concluſion. If I ſhould deny my owne many Imperfections, my practiſe would confute what my Pen hath maintained. Reader, for the matter of what I have written I require thee, in Gods name, do me Iuſtice. For the manner, method, or words thereof, I requeſt thee, as I am a Man, ſhew mee favour. Thinke not the worſe of the Truths for my ſake, but thinke the better of me for the Truths ſake which I have defended. And conceive me not to be of a brawling and controverſiall diſpoſition, who do deſire and will pray for an Agreement from my Soule, ſo long as my ſpeech ſhall ſerve me. Yea, if I ſhould chance to be ſtricken dumbe, I would with *Zacharia make ſignes for table bookes* and write [that] *the name of that which* I deſire above all earthly things is PEACE. God ſend it, *Amen*.

---

[1] Iude 3.

FINIS.

JACOBS VOW.
A
SERMON
PREACHED BEFORE
HIS MAJESTY, AND THE
PRINCE His Highnesse, at S^t. *Maries* in OXFORD.

The tenth of May, 1644. being the day of Publique Fast.

By THOMAS FULLER B.D.

And published by speciall command.

OXFORD,
Printed by LEONARD LICHFIELD,
Printer to the University, 1644.

[I am fo much a friend to all Church-men that have anything in them befeeming that facred Function that I have hazarded My own Intereft, chiefly upon Confcience and Conftancy to maintain their Rights; whom, the more I looked upon as Orphans and under the facrilegious eyes of many cruel and rapacious Reformers; fo I thought it My duty the more to appear as a Father and a Patron for them and the Church, although I am very unhandfomely requited by fome of them, who may live to repent no leffe for My fufferings then their own ungrateful errours, and that injurious contempt and meanneffe which they have brought upon their Calling and Perfons.—Εἰκὼν βασιλική, § xxiv. pp. 141-2, ed. 1649, in *Reliquiæ Sacræ Carolinæ*, Hague, 1650, 12mo.]

[Introduction.

THIS Sermon and that immediately following it, both preached in places garrisoned by the Royalists, are the only two military Sermons of FULLER of which there is any record, and they form themselves into a distinct group.

The tract against JOHN SALTMARSH was not the only publication that FULLER put forth from the city of Oxford. His reference in that tract to his last will and testament (page 336) refers to his intention to take the field. A sentiment of justice to his Sovereign had prompted this resolve, which had further been encouraged by the martial spirit that animated the University,—a spirit which had turned the "silken hoods" of the collegians into military "scarfes" and the colleges into barracks :—

> " 'Mongst us there's scarce a verse, nay line, without
> Charge to the Front, to th' Reere, and Face about.
> This metamorphosis is strange, but we
> Embrace it as we would our Liberty."

FULLER had, accordingly, become Chaplain in the division of the Royal army employed in the West, under the worthy and religious Lord HOPTON. Upon that general's defeat at Cheriton Down, 29th March, 1644, his chaplain retreated to the bravely-defended garrison at Basing House, and afterwards for the second time to Oxford. During April and May the Royalist generals at the latter place were organising their forces for further operations; and meanwhile FULLER was called upon to preach before CHARLES I., who was well acquainted with his services both in the pulpit and in the field. The last paragraph of the Sermon (page 431), where FULLER speaks of the interest which the King had in the welfare of clergymen, is an indication of personal intercourse.

The Sermon was preached upon the May fast-day. On the day preceding its delivery, Dr. WILLIAM FULLER, Dean of Ely, and divers Doctors and Clergymen, who had been long imprisoned in London, came to Oxford on exchange (Dugdale's *Diary*, page 67). The court was somewhat shorn of its brilliance in consequence of the departure, a few weeks earlier, of the Queen and her attendants to Exeter, and of the dissolution of the "mongrel" Parliament. Amidst the godlessness consequent on the presence of large bodies of troops in the garrison-city, the element of devotion then, as always, was distinctly manifested in the Royal quarters; and to an audience consisting of the King, his family and attendants, of the collegians and townsmen, and of refugees who had passed over the rivers Trent, Thames, and Severn,—FULLER's Sermon was addressed. Prince CHARLES, then thirteen years of age, was also an auditor, perhaps an interested auditor, of this earnest discourse. One may conjecture whether he recalled it when, about eight years afterwards (12th Nov., 1652), "Dr. CLARE preach'd on 28 Gen. v. 20, 21, 22, upon Jacob's Vowe, it being the first Sonday his Majesty came to Chapell after his escape" (Evelyn's *Diary*).

The old Wednesday fast-days " for Ireland," to which allusion has already been made at pp. ccxxxiii.--iv., continued to be zealously observed by the adherents of the Parliament, who intended that the King's appeal to arms should be regarded as an indication of the increase of the displeasure of the Almighty on the nation,—to avert which was the chief intention of the fast. The King therefore ordered (5th October, 1643) that that fast should be discontinued; but the Royalists (who according to TWYNE's *Musterings of the University* kept the fast at least as late as 29th March, 1643) continued for some time to observe the day as a *festival*. In the new Royal proclamation reference was made to the ill-use of the Wednesday-fast by "many seditious lecturers;" and it was commanded that a solemn monthly fast should be religiously observed on the *second Friday* in every month in all churches and chapels, with public prayers and preaching in all places where it may be had, to the end that a happy peace might result (Husband's folio *Collection*, 1646, pages 353-4). WILLIAM CHILLINGWORTH, FULLER's fellow-Prebendary, is said to have preached the first sermon, 13th October, 1643 ; which after his death in the ensuing year was published by royal command (Nichols's *Life of Chillingworth*, page 289; Rushworth, vol. ii. pt. iii. 365). In the Forms of Prayer which were drawn up (4to. 1643) in accordance with the proclamation, the fast was said to begin "on the 10th November next." Its purpose was described to be "for the averting of God's judgements upon us for the ceasing of this present Rebellion, and restoring a happy Peace in this Kingdom." On these two fasts, which were thus each month being simultaneously kept in the kingdom, FULLER penned the following meditation (No. xvii. § iii.) in his *Good Thoughts in Worse Times*, 1647 (pages 137-8) :—

" When the *Iewish Sabbath* in the Primitive times was newly changed into the *Christians Lords-day*, many devout people twisted *both* together· in their Observation, abstaining from servile-Workes, and keeping both *Saturday* and *Sunday* wholy for holy Employments. During these Civill Warres *Wednesday* and *Fryday Fasts* have been appointed by different Authorities. What harme had it been if they had been both generally observed ? But alas ! when two Messengers being sent together on the same Errand fall out and fight by the way, will not the worke be worse done then if none were employed ? In such a *Paire of fasts* it is to be feared that the divisions of our Affections rather would increase then abate Gods Anger against us. Two *Negatives* make an *Affirmative*. Dayes of Humiliations are appointed for men to deny themselves and their sinful lusts. But doe not our two Fasts more peremptorily affirme and avouch our mutual malice and hatred ? God forgive us ! We have *cauſe* enough to keepe ten, but not *care* enough to keep one monethly day of Humiliation."

Jacobs Vow, it ſeems, was a ſuggeſtive title, having relation to a devout reſolution which CHARLES I.—"our religious Jacob,"—had publicly vowed ; and in commemoration of it he had inſtituted a weekly ſervice which had been religiouſly obſerved every Tueſday up to the date of FULLER's Sermon (page 422). The "juſt occaſion" of this Vow, by a ſtrange overſight, has not been put on record in the pages of hiſtory ; nor, indeed, can any notice of the public weekly exerciſe be found in the local annals of HEARNE (in his Twyne's *Account of the Muſterings of the Univerſity of Oxford*, 9th Auguſt, 1642, to 15th July, 1643) ; in the almanack-diaries of Sir WILLIAM DUGDALE, who had been in attendance on the King ſince the latter part of 1642 ; in À WOOD ; or in other contemporary writers. Nothing has reſulted from an examination of *Mercurius Aulicus*, and other news ſheets of the time. There are two or three occaſions in the monarch's life fitted by their ſolemnity for the conception of ſuch a vow, as, *e.g.*, when he broke his word with reſpect to Lord STRAFFORD, "that baſe, ſinful conceſſion," as the King called it.

One important Vow has been aſſociated with Charles I., but the firſt recorded reference to it belongs to a period a little later than the date of FULLER's Sermon ; and if it is the ſame vow as that to which the preacher alluded, certain links are at preſent miſſing. This was the celebrated vow to reſtore to the Church all the cathedral and other impropriations, as alſo the lands, &c., which had been taken away from religious houſes, &c. It was penned at Oxford on the 13th April, 1646, ſhortly before the arrival of the diſbanded troops from Exeter, and of the King's flight into the quarters of the Scotch,—an epoch in the monarch's hiſtory that gave riſe to the juſt reflection of HUME : "As the dread of ills is commonly more oppreſſive than their real preſence, perhaps in no period of his life was he more juſtly the ſubject of compaſſion." GILBERT SHELDON and Biſhop DUPPA alone ſeem to have been acquainted with this vow, and its preſervation is due to the former. It was as follows :—

I, A : B :, doe here promiſe and ſolemnly Vow, in the preſence and for the ſervice of Almighty God, that if it ſhall pleaſe his Divine Matie of his infinite goodnes to reſtore me to my juſt Kingly Rights, and to re-eſtabliſh mee in my Throne, I will wholly give backe to his Church all thoſe impropriacons wch are now held by the Crowne ; and what Lands ſoever I now doe or ſhould enjoy which have beene taken away eyther from any Epiſcopall See or any Cathedrall or Collegiate Church, from any Abby or other Religious houſe. I likewiſe promiſe for hereafter to hold them from the Church under ſuch reaſonable Fines and Rents as ſhall be ſet downe by ſome conſcientious Perſons, whome I promiſe to chooſe w^h all uprightnes of Heart to direct me in this particular. And I moſt humbly beſeech God to accept of this my vow, and to bleſſe Mee in the deſignes I have now in hand, through Jeſus Chriſt our Lord. Amen.

Oxford, the 13th *Aprill*, 1646.   CHARLES R.

This is a true Copye of the King's Vow, wch was preferved thirteene yeares under ground by Mee   GILBERT SHELDON.
Aug. 21*st*, 1660.

The beft account of the circumftances attending the penning of this remarkable paper is to be found in Profeffor BURROWS's *Worthies of All Souls,* 1874, page 179, where the writer, after remarking that the vow had ftrangely enough been loft to hiftory, not being found, as far as he was aware, in any Hiftory of England written during the laft 150 years, fays that his attention " was drawn to it by the mention of certain 'buried papers' in a MS. letter of Bifhop DUPPA's (of 1660) which he found in the [Tanner MSS. vol. xlix. fol. 17, in the] Bodleian Library. A reference to LE NEVE's Lives of the Bifhops fupplied the clue. This book, written in the early part of the eighteenth century [1720], gave in full the paper which follows [*i.e.* the Vow] as having been juft then publifhed for the firft time in the Appendix to ECHARD's Hiftory of England [1718]; and in the Clarendon State Papers (2176 Bodl. Lib.) the authentic copy quoted by ECHARD is ftill to be feen. The exiftence of the Vow was found afterwards to be mentioned in the Biographical Dictionary in the notice of SHELDON. Perhaps, if not wholly forgotten, it has been thought an unimportant fact.' Profeffor BURROWS further remarks upon the light which this document throws on the character and conduct of the King. "If one who preferred to run any rifk rather than facrifice his Church deferves the name of a martyr, that facred name ought fcarcely to be denied him. . . . Nor will the impreffion of his juft right to the title be weakened by difcovering that he had bound himfelf in the moft folemn manner, before a competent witnefs, to perform, if he furvived, an act of juftice to the Church, which no one elfe, it need hardly be faid, has fhown any figns of even meditating."

In my *Life of Fuller,* pages 329-30, I have noted an earlier date for the printing of the Vow,- viz. in 1715, in NELSON's *Addrefs to Perfons of Quality and Eftate,* Append. No. iv. page 24; and have alfo mentioned the document in connection with SPELMAN's *Hiftory and Fate of Sacrilege,* edit. 1853, page 231 ; the Rev. J. M. NEALE's *Hierologus,* 1843, page 25; and fome paffages which feem to bear upon it in JUXON's Sermons in MARAH's *Memoirs* of that Bifhop, pages 185, 190, and in FULLER's *Church-Hiftory,* Book xi. fo. ed. page 236. A *copy* of it was, in 1836, in poffeffion of WM. UPCOTT (*Orig. Letters, MSS., &c.,* privately printed, 1836, 4to. p. 9). One other work may be cited, viz. DISRAELI's *Commentaries on the Life and Reign of Charles I.,* 1851, vol. ii. page 438. The paffage in which this writer refers to the Vow affords—when read in connection with Profeffor BURROWS's remarks—a ftriking illuftration of the curiofities of literature :—

"At this moment [of the King's meditated flight from Oxford with four or five thoufand men, to perifh in the field] the feelings of CHARLES were wrought up to their higheft tenfion ; and it may ferve as an extraordinary evidence of the vifionary turn of his mind, and the awful fuperftition of his foul, that CHARLES entertained fome wayward fancy that should he ever re-possess his throne, he would perform a public penance for the sin, as it seemed to him, which lay heavy on his soul— the death-warrant of his great Minister. At this moment he wrote down a secret vow, solemnly offered to God, of his future resolutions to restore to the Church all the Cathedral and other Ecclesiastical lands formerly held by the Crown, and now, as he conceived, appropriated by sacrilegious hands. This singular document, the effusion of some melancholy and feverish hour, when pressed for farther concessions for the establishment of the Presbyterial Government in England, was buried under ground for security, during thirteen years, by Archbishop SHELDON."

It may be added that the Vow and other "buried papers" seem to be referred to, as Professor BURROWS justly supposes (page 221, as before,) in a letter dated 11th August, 1660, addressed by Bishop DUPPA to SHELDON, then Dean of His Majesty's Chapel. He penned the letter at the critical moment when CHARLES II. was hesitating about filling up the vacant sees, and urged his correspondent to make these papers public, "which can't but have," said he, "a powerful influence upon so dutiful a soul as his" (the King's). The vow was accordingly made known, with SHELDON's attestation, on the 21st of the same month; and early in the following month the sees began to filled.

The prominence given in this Sermon to the subject of tithes (pages 426 *seq.*) lends colour to the opinion that the preacher had been discussing that matter with the King, whose opinion is pointedly given (page 431). A brief but admirable historical treatise on tithes is to be found in a quarto pamphlet entitled *Tithes examined and proved to bee due to the Clergy by a Divine Right*, written in 1606 by GEORGE CARLETON, B.D. A short time afterwards, in FULLER's youth, a great controversy had arisen in ecclesiastical circles through the publication of SELDEN's treatise, *The Historie of Tithes, that is, The practice of payment of them. The positive laws made for them. The opinions touching the right of them*, 1618, in which that eminent lawyer historically proved that tithes were payable *jure divino*, and not otherwise. This was the book of SELDEN that clergymen most disliked (*Worthies*, § Sussex, page 111); and, in consequence of it, it was said that "never a fiercer storm fell on all Parsonage Barns since the Reformation" than what it raised up (*Church-History*, book x. cent. iv. page 70, ¶¶ 39, 40). Many divines applied themselves to answering this work, such as the Rev. STEPHEN NETTLES, Dr. RICHARD TILLESLEY, RICHARD MOUNTAGU, &c.; but the writer of the "late Historie" of tithes, to which FULLER refers (page 430), took his cue from it.

In common with many writers, Fuller laments the prevalence of customs that were injurious to the just disposing of this sacred revenue. When commenting on WILLIAM I.'s charter to the English clergy, which seemed to give the tenth loaf of all the bread of the land into their hands, he says that "the municipal laws, which were afterwards made, did so chip and pare this loaf with their *modus decimandi*, that in many places (Vicaridges especially) a small shiver of bread fals to the share of the Minister, not enough for his necessary maintenance" (book iii. cent. xi.

page 5, ¶ 12). Some of thefe local modes of tithing are referred to in Mountagu's *Diatribæ vpon the firſt part* of Selden's History, p. 106.

Complaints as to the pofition of the clergy in relation to their tithes were common in Fuller's days. From the character of the Good Pariſhioner in *The Holy State* we find it ſtated that while amongſt the Romans *Decimum*, the tenth, was ever taken for what was beſt or biggeſt, "it fals out otherwife in paying of Tithes, where the leaſt and leaneſt are ſhifted off to make that number" (3rd ed. pages 85-6). And he ſays elfewhere that in fome places the *modus decimandi* had "almoſt tithed the Tithes" (*Church-History*, book ii. cent. ix. page 113, ¶ 14). In another eſſay he defcribes the not uncommon cafe at that time of a miniſter of narrow means, whofe neceſſity bolted him out of his own ſtudy, fending him to the barn inſtead of his book; or making him ſtudy his Eaſter-book more than all other writers ("Of Ministers Maintenance," *Holy State*, page 223).

The ancient right of the clergy to tithes began to be re-aſſailed during the fittings of the Long Parliament; and the hiſtorical references to the fubject in the *Church-Hiſtory* are affected by thofe difcuſſions. In the fecond book, which was written when the ſtorm againſt tithes had fpent itfelf, the writer infiſts not, as in the prefent Sermon, on the arguments from the Old and New Teſtament to prove them to be by divine right; fuch arguments, he fuggeſtively fays, might be adduced when all tempeſts of tumultuous fpirits were allayed, and when the queſtion might be debated ἐν τῇ ἐννόμῳ ἐκκλησίᾳ (book ii. *ut anteà*, ¶ 11). He here quotes an anecdote of his uncle, Biſhop Davenant, and an Anabaptiſt who refufed the payment of tithes; and paſſes on to record the folid anfwer of "a moſt eminent Sergeant-at-Law of this Age" to the "impertinent clamours" of thofe who would not pay tithes becaufe only due *jure humano*: "My cloak is my cloak by the Law of Man; but he is a Thief by the Law of God that taketh it away from me" (¶¶ 12, 13). The learned lawyer here referred to was Serjeant Maynard, remembered by Fuller elfewhere as "no lefs eminently known for his ſkill in law than his love for the clergy by pleading fo effeдually for their tithes" (*Appeal of Injured Innocence*, part iii. page 41).

Not lefs earneſt is the preacher in denouncing exemptions and impropriations (page 431) by which tithes, being transferred from one to another, were made open fale of. This praдice was firſt "maintained by the wit of Alexander de Hailes, and after by Thomas of Aquine" (Carleton's *Tithes*, page 34). Of the poverty of the clergy which in confequence enfued, an idea may ɒe formed from the eſſay "Of Miniſters Maintenance" already quoted, and from Heylyn's *Cyprianus Ang.*, p. 115.

This Sermon was publiſhed in 4to., and contains pp. ii. 27, the text being fpread out on the back of the title-page, the fermon beginning on A 3, and the laſt page, viz. page 27, containing 17 lines in fmaller type than the former part of the fermon. The copy now printed is taken from a moſt careful tranfcript of the unique original, kindly fupplied by its owner, Edwd. Riggall, Efq., of Bayfwater, London, who purchafed the Sermon at the fale of the Surrenden Library (Sir E. Dering's).

Iacobs Vow.

Gen. chap. 28. verf. 20, 21, 22.

Then Iacob vowed a Vow, faying, If God will be with me, and will keepe mee in this way that I goe, and will give me bread to eat, and raiment to put on, fo that I come againe to my fathers houfe in peace, then fhall the Lord be my God. And this Stone which I have fet vp as a Pillar, fhall be Gods houfe: and of all that thou fhalt give mee, I will furely give the Tenth unto thee.

WHICH words are the Vowe of that holy Patriarke *Iacob*, who being mortally hated of his brother *Efau* for deceiuing him (as he tearmed it) both of his Birth-right and of his Bleffing, was forced to flie for his life: and by the aduife of his Mother, with the expreffe confent and commandement of his Father in the firft verfe of this chapter, hee trauailed towards *Padan-Aran* vnto his vnckle *Laban* for fuccour; in hope there not onely to have his life fecured from his brothers rage, but alfo to be prouided of a Wife, amongft his owne kindred, which might be a helper and comforter vnto him: yet he went not forth like a Woer, nor like either his father *Ifaacs* fonne, or his grandfather *Abrahams* feruant,[1] with Camels, and Men, and Iewels, and other prouifion for fuch a iourney (for then perhappes hee had neuer made this Vowe); but hee went all alone like a poore Pilgrime, with his ftaffe in his hand; and fo came wearie and late (the Sunne being downe) vnto a

---

[1] Gen. 24. 10.

certaine place neere vnto *Haran,* where he tooke vp his lodging for that night: and as Saint [1]*Chryſoſtome* faith, *Ibi dormiuit, vbi nox eum comprehendit,* He ſlept there where he was benighted, not in any towne or houſe or tent, but *Sub dio,* making the earth his bed, heauen his canopie, and a ſtone (which hee found in that place) the pillow whereupon he repoſed his head: and yet hauing a wearied bodie, and a quiet conſcience (which are two good Engines to draw on ſleepe), he ſlept as ſoundly vpon that hard pillow as if hee had lien vpon a bed of Downe. And in his ſleepe he dreamed of a certaine Ladder reaching vp from earth to heauen, vpon which the Angels of God aſcended and deſcended, and the Lord himſelfe ſtood at the toppe of the Ladder; who made vnto him a large and a moſt gracious foure-fold promiſe, in the thirteenth, fourteenth, and fifteenth verſes. 1. That he would giue vnto him and his ſeed that land vpon which he then ſlept. 2. That hee would multiply his ſeede as the duſt of the earth. 3. That in his ſeed all the Nations of the earth ſhould be Bleſſed. And laſtly, That he would be with him and keepe him whitherſoeuer hee went, and bring him againe vnto that land, and not to forſake him vntill he had performed all that he had promiſed vnto him.

When *Iacob* awoke out of his ſleepe, and perceiued that the Lord was in that place, and he not aware of it, and that that place was *no other but the houſe of God, and gate of heauen,* verſe 17, he was ſtricken with feare and reuerence, as euery one ought to bee that commeth within the gate of Gods houſe; and tooke the ſtone that lay vnder his head, and ſet it vp for a pillar, and powred oyle vpon the top of it, and called the name of that place *Bethel,* that is, *the houſe of God.*

And entring into a ſerious conſideration of this gracious Promiſe, which farre exceeded all that hee could either aſke or thinke, hee did not through vnbeliefe make any doubt of the performance thereof; but certainely belieuing that it ſhould be accompliſhed in due time, like a thankefull Pil-

---

[1] Homil. 54. in Gen. [Ed. Paris, fo. 1721, vol. iv. p. 527; ed. Savile, fo. 1612, i. 423.]

grime or a man euen ouer-ioyed with vnexpected, but yet aſſured hopes, he began to ſtudie with himſelfe what hee ſhould render vnto the Lord for all theſe benefits promiſed vnto him; and not finding any better meanes to expreſſe his thankefulneſſe, he vowed a Vow in my Text, ſaying, *If God will be with me, &c.*

Of which Vow there be two parts. The firſt is, *Petitio*, a Requeſt, which he deſired of God. The ſecond is, *Promiſſio*, a Dutie, which he promiſed to performe to God.

The *Petition* in theſe words: *If God will be with me, and will keepe me in this way that I goe, and will giue me bread to eat, and raiment to put on, ſo that I come againe to my fathers houſe in peace.* The *Dutie* which hee promiſeth to performe in lieu of this benefit is three-fold: 1. *That the Lord ſhall be his God;* 2. *That the ſtone which he had ſet vp for a pillar ſhould be Gods house;* 3. *That of all that God ſhould giue him, he would giue vnto God the Tenth.* Of which points in order as they lie in the Text.

And firſt of the Petition or requeſt, which (as you ſee) is very moderate, and reaſonable: for whereas God had promiſed vnto *Iacob* foure things, *Iacob* doth not deſire all, nor halfe, nor the thirde part of that which was promiſed; but contenteth himſelfe with the laſt and leaſt of all thoſe foure things, and deſireth nothing but only neceſſaries for the preſent: not *Quailes* or *Manna* for delight, but onely bread for neceſſitie, that is, neceſſarie food; not purple and fine linnen for pompe, but onely raiment to put on, that is, neceſſarie cloathes; not the attendance of many ſeruants, but onely the protection and bleſſing of God, without which neither his food, nor raiment, nor anything els could doe him good, nor himſelfe either be well or be.

But what is the reaſon why *Iſaac*, who was exceeding rich, ſent foorth his ſonne *Iacob* (who by Gods prouidence was now lately made his Heire) ſo exceeding poore that he is faine to petition for foode and raiment; whereas *Abraham* his father ſent foorth his very ſeruant vpon the like iourney richly furniſhed and ſumptuouſly attended? Was *Abrahams* ſeruant better than *Iſaacs* ſonne?

To omit the diuers Allegories which [1]Saint *Augustine* and [2]*Gregorie* have obserued vpon this paſſage, the reaſons, as [3]*Theodoret* and others haue well ſummed them vp, might be theſe.

1. *Vt fratris conatus melius declinaret;* that going poorely, and priuately, his brother *Eſau* might not ſo eaſily miſſe him, nor know which way to purſue after him.

2. That this miſerie might mooue his brother to compaſſion and reconciliation.

3. *Vt animus eſſet reuertendi;* that carrying no wealth with him to maintaine or detaine him abroad, he might haue the more mind to returne vnto his father home againe.

4. And laſtly, that hee might haue the better experience of Gods mercie; as indeede he had; for which hee returned thankes vnto God at his returne in the thirty-ſecond chapter.

Iacobs pouertie may teach vs that although worldly proſperitie be the good bleſſing of God wherewith he often enricheth his owne children, yet hee euer, at one time or other, chaſteneth thoſe whom he loueth, and traineth them vp in his ſchoole of affliction, and nurtureth them with his *Ferula* of wants and croſſes. *Virga tua & baculus tuus,* ſaith the [4]Pſalmiſt, &c. They muſt as well be humbled and inſtructed with his rod of correction as ſupported with his ſtaffe of comfort. *Abraham* and *Iſaac, Iob* and *Dauid,* and *Iacob* alſo in my Text, after his returne from *Padan-Aran,* were all rich, and our Lord himſelfe was Lord of all; and yet none of them wanted either their wants or croſſes. And the children of *Iſrael,* Gods owne people, were not onely pinched with wants in the wildernesse, but were pricked with [5]thornes in their eyes and goades in their ſides, euen in the land of Promiſe.

Whence wee may learne that *Aduerſitie* is the bleſſing of God vpon his children, as well as *Proſperitie. Res proſpera donum eſt conſolantis, res aduerſa donum eſt admonentis Dei,* ſaith

---

[1] Aug. Ser[mones] de Tempore, [No.] 79 [Ed. Baſle, 1543, vol. x. col. 760-2].
[2] Greg. Mor. lib. 5, cap. 21. [22, vol. ii. 131, ed. Antw. 1615, fo.]
[3] [Ed. Paris, 1642, vol. i. Interr. lxxxiii.-iv. pp. 60-1].
[4] Pſal. 23. 4.   [5] Ioſ. 23. 13.

[1]S. Augustine: *Prosperitie is the Gift of God comforting, Aduersitie the gift of God admonishing.* Prosperity may bee the more pleasant, but *Aduersitie* many times is the more profitable; which made *Dauid* out of his own experience ingeniously confesse that it was [2]good for him that hee had beene afflicted. And so it is good for vs all to be afflicted sometimes, els we should forget both God and our selues, and bee too much wedded to this world, and say with Saint *Peter*, [3]*Bonum est esse hic,* and begin to build such Tabernacles here vpon earth as would hinder vs from our euerlasting Tabernacles of blisse in heauen. And thus much of *Iacobs* pouertie and want.

But now being in so great want as hee was at this time, why doth he preferre so poore a Petition vnto God, who is so rich in mercie? And whereas God had now lately appeared vnto him here in *Bethel,* and promised the whole land of *Canaan* to him and his, why doth hee desire so poore a pittance as food and raiment, which would onely keepe life and soule together? The very foules of the aire are furnished with these.

And yet *Iacob* desires no more; to teach vs how moderate wee should be in the desire of earthly things. We may and ought to be euen couetous of things spirituall and heauenly: so saith the Apostle, [4]*Couet after the best gifts:* but of temporall and earthly things we may not be couetous more then is necessary for our callings and estates; becauſe, as our Sauiour teacheth, [5]*A mans life doth not consist in the abundance of the things which hee possesseth.* Therefore the Apostles rule is, that hauing but [6]διατροφὰς καὶ σκεπάσματα, onely *food* and *raiment,* wee must be content therewith: for *Victus & vestitus sunt diuitiæ Christianorum,* saith [7]*Hierome: food and raiment are the riches of Christians:* and our patterne of Prayer doth warrant vs to petition onely for our daily bread: that is, as it is excellently expounded in [8]that *Royall Meditation vpon the*

---

[1] [Ep. ccx. ad Felicitatem et Rusticum.]   [2] Psal. 119. 71.   [3] Mat. 17. 4.
[4] 1 Cor. 12. 31.   [5] Luke 12. 15.   [6] 1 Tim. 6. 8.
[7] [Epist. l. ad Paulinum Presbyterum, de Studio Scripturarum, vol. iv. part ii. col. 575, ed. Paris, 1706.]
[8] Written by the kings Maiestie [James I., "for the benefit of all his Subiects, especially of such as follow the Court." Works, ed. Mountagu, 1616, fo. pp. 582-3].

Lords Prayer, onely for such temporall things as are necessary for our *Esse*, or, at farthest, for our *Bene esse*. And they that cannot be content with these, but with the Horse-leaches daughters still cry, *Giue, Giue;* and will needes be rich, fall into temptation and a snare, and into many foolish and hurtfull lusts, which drowne the soule in perdition and destruction, 1 *Tim.* 6. 9. *Iacob* hauing once seene God in *Bethel*, and set his heart vpon him who is the true treasure, neither admired nor much desired (more then was necessary) this worldly trash.

Where we may see that howsoeuer worldlings doe not onely admire, but euen adore riches, and honours, and earthly pleasures, as their sole trinitie, yet the Children of God, knowing that earthly honors and riches are but shadowes of heauenly, and the pleasures of sinne not so much as shadowes of heauenly pleasures, vse these things when God giueth them, but neither abuse nor admire the same. And why should men admire shadowes, painted fires which flame, but warme not? and may fitly be compared vnto Glo--wormes, or peices of rotten-wood, which in a darke night shine like stars, but when the Sunne ariseth and sheweth what they are, the one appeareth to be a poore worme, the other nothing but a rotten sticke: So these glorious outward things shine like Starres in the eyes of the Children of dark-nesse; but the Children of light, whose eyes are purged from those skales of darknesse, doe plainely see that in regard of true content they be *Vanitas vanissima*, wormes and stickes, before which [1]*Solomon* incomparably preferred wisedome; and *Agur* in the *Prouerbs* of *Solomon* prayed expressely against riches (in the thirtieth chapter) aswell as pouertie. *Mendicitatem & diuitias ne dederis mihi: Giue me neither pouertie nor riches, but feed me with food conuenient for me.* And this is the reason why *Iacob* in my Text petitions neither for riches, nor honour, nor any other outward thing, but onely for bread to eat, and cloathes to put on.

And yet one thing more is to be obserued in *Iacobs* Petition out of these words of my Text, where he saith, *If*

---

[1] 1 Kings 3. 9.

God will be with me, and keepe me in this way that I goe, and bring me againe to my fathers houſe in peace: wherein beſides foode and raiment, you ſee hee deſireth the protection and bleſſing of God in his whole iourney going out and comming in; without which, neither his bread could nouriſh, nor his cloathes keepe him warme, nor any thing elſe doe him good. For [1]*Man doth not liue by bread onely, but by euery word which proceedeth out of the mouth of God,* that is, the bleſſing of God vpon bread: For as in Phiſicke a diſeaſéd man is preſcribed to boile certaine medicinable hearbes in running water, and then to drinke a quantity of that water, and ſo is cured of his diſeaſe; and yet wee know that it is not the water, but the decoction or infuſion which cureth the Patient: ſo it is not the bread that nouriſheth, nor the abundance of outward things which enricheth or contenteth, but the infuſion of Gods bleſſing, which is the ſtaffe of bread; without which a [2]man may ſtarue for hunger with bread in his mouth, and die like the children of *Iſrael* with the fleſh of Quailes in their teeth.

Whereas on the contrary, *Daniel* feeding vpon bare pulſe, ſtrengthened by the bleſſing of God, which is the ſtaffe of bread and of all other nouriſhment, was [3]fatter and fairer then they that were fed with the Kings diet: For it is the [4]bleſſing of God that maketh rich; and a little that the righteous hath is [5]better then the great reuenewes of the vngodly. And wee may obſerue in our owne experience many a man, who with a [6]dinner of greene hearbes, as *Solomon* ſpeaketh, that is, ſhort diet, courſe clothes, hard lodging, and a poore eſtate, looketh fatter, liueth merrier, ſleepeth ſweetlier, enioyeth more hearts eaſe and true content, and in trueth liueth better then others that weare a chaine of golde. And therfore wiſely did *Iacob* deſire nothing but food and raiment, and Gods bleſſing vpon them, which hee knew would ſerue his turne. And thus much of the Petition, or Requeſt which *Iacob* deſired of God.

---

[1] Mat. 4. 4.
[2] Leuit. 26. 26; Ezek. 4. 16; Pſal. 78. 30, 31.
[3] Dan. 1. 15.
[4] Pro. 10. 22.
[5] Pro. 16. 8.
[6] Pro. 15. 17.

Now I come to the duties which he promiseth to performe to God, in the next words, *Then shall the Lord be my God, &c.*, wherein *Iacob*, who was afterward [1]surnamed *Israel*, hauing receiued but euen the promise of a benefit, presently voweth the performance of a duetie; to teach all true *Israelites* that *Beneficium postulat officium*; and that the thankefulnesse of the receiuer ought to answere vnto the benefit of the bestower, as the Eccho answereth to the voice: wee doe no sooner receiue the one, but we are immediately bound to returne the other. So doth *Dauid*, [2]*Thou hast deliuered my soule from death, mine eyes from teares, and my feet from falling:* There is the benefite receiued; and then it followeth in the very [3]next words, *I will walke before the Lord in the land of the liuing:* there is the duetie returned. So likewise in my Text, *If God will be with me, and giue me bread to eate, and cloathes to put on:* there is the benefit petitioned for, and promise, *Then shall the Lord be my God, &c.:* there is the returne of a duetie vowed.

Now wee all haue receiued the same or the like benefits, both spirituall and temporall, whereby we are all bound vnto the like thankefulnesse; but where is the performance of the same, or the like duties? We owe as much or more vnto God for his benefits then *Iacob* did; but who voweth or paieth vnto him the like duties that *Iacob* did? What heart can thinke or what tongue can expresse our infinite obligations?

First, for spirituall fauours: Infinitely are we bound vnto God for our Creation; more then infinitely (if more might be) for our Redemption and our effectuall Calling vnto the participation thereof. What shall we then render vnto the Lord for all these benefits done vnto vs? *Totum me debeo*, saith [4]S. Bernard, *pro me facto: quid igitur rependam pro me redempto? I owe every whit of my selfe* (vnto God) *for my Creation: what shall I then render vnto him for my Redemption?* And [5]Saint *Ambrose* saith, *Nihil est quod dignum*

---

[1] Gen. 32. 28.   [2] Psalm 116. 8.   [3] Verse 9.
[4] [Ed. Antw. 1620, col. 949 a.]
[5] Ambr. *super Luc. Ser.* 5. [*Expos. Luc.* lib. vi. Paris, 1686, tom. i. coll. 1389-1390, ¶ 26.]

referre poſſumus pro ſuſcepta carne Maria, quid pro cruce obita, quid pro verberibus, & ſepultura reddemus? We are not able to be ſufficiently thankefull for taking our fleſh of the (Virgin) *Marie,* what ſhall wee then returne vnto him for his ſuffering vpon the Croſſe, for his ſtripes, for his buriall?

And as for temporall benefits, we are farre before *Iacob.* He wandred vp and downe the world like a poore Pilgrime, with his ſtaffe in his hand; he kept ſheepe, and was parched with the heat of the day, and frozen with the cold of the night; and in my Text, the bare earth was his bedde, a hard ſtone his pillow; he had nothing; he deſired nothing but onely bread to eate, and cloathes to put on, and the protection and bleſſing of God vpon him in his iourney; and yet hee, euen for theſe, vowed a Vow vnto God. Wee ſit vnder our owne Vines, and our owne Fig-trees, in peace and reſt; [1]*We lie upon beds of Iuorie, and ſtretch our ſelues vpon our couches; we are clad in purple and fine linnen, and fare delicately euery day; we eat calues out of the ſtalles and lambes out of the flockes; wee drinke wine in boules, and annoint our ſelues with coſtly ointments, and inuent inſtruments of Muſicke* (*like* Dauid): *But who is either ſorrie for the affliction of* Ioſeph, the extreame miſeries of our Brethren in neighbour-Countries, or who is ſenſible of our owne great proſperitie and our incomparable happineſſe, or who for all this voweth one Vow to God?

When our Sauiour CHRIST had [2]cleanſed ten Leapers, there was but one found amongſt all thoſe ten, and he a ſtranger too, that returned to giue God thanks. I feare there is ſcarſely one of an hundred amongſt vs that is but euen ſo thankefull vnto God for all his benefits as that ſtranger was onely for his cleanſing.

When this good Patriarke *Iacob* returned rich from *Padan-Aran* in the thirty-ſecond chapter of this booke, he neither forgate what he was then, nor what he had beene before; and therefore in a thankefull remembrance of Gods great mercies towards him he payed one part of this Vow in that place, and worſhipped God, ſaying, [3]*O Lord, I*

---

[1] Amos 6. 4, 5, 6. [2] Luke 17. 17. [3] Gen. 32. 10.

am not worthy of the least of all thy mercies; for with my staffe 1 passed ouer this Iordan, and now I am become two bands.

Many a one there be in this honourable Court who haue passed ouer, not the riuer of *Iordan*, but the riuer of *Trent*, or *Thames*, or *Seuerne*, with their staues in their hands, that is, poore estates in comparison, and haue beene deliuered from many dangers, and are now euen laden with riches and honours; And yet I doubt there bee not manie, that for all this, haue vowed with *Iacob* to haue the Lord for their God, or to build him an House, or to pay him the Tenth of all that he hath giuen them.

One Religious Vow you see weekely payed in this place by our royall *Iacob*, I meane our Tuesdayes Exercise; which was deuoutly vowed vpon as iust an occasion as euer Vow was made. And hitherto (God be thanked) it hath beene religiously performed. God grant that this our *Iacob* may long and long liue a happie King of this happie Island, euen as long (if it bee his will) as the olde Patriarke *Iacob* did, to pay this tribute and the rest of his Vowes vnto the King of Kings. And can wee that are his seruants haue a better patterne to imitate then the Religious example of so Royall a Master? Therefore I will conclude this point with that zealous exhortation of another King, *Psal*. 76. 11: *Vouete & reddite Domino Deo vestro*: *Vow vnto the Lord your God, and keepe it, all yee that are round about him; bring presents vnto him that ought to be feared.* And thus much of the generall of *Iacobs* Vow.

Now I come to the particular duties vowed; and they are three: First, that the Lord should be his God; that is, that hee would worship the true God, and no other. Secondly, that the stone which hee had set vp for a pillar should be Gods house; that is, he would dedicate that place vnto the publique worship of God. Thirdly, for the maintenance of both these he would giue the Tenth of all that hee had. All which were necessary duties, and euery one of them hath a necessary relation and dependance vpon other: For if God must be worshipped, then must hee haue a place to be worshipped in, which is here called an House, and our SAVIOVR saith, [1] shall of all nations bee called the House of Prayer: And if a House of Prayer, then a maintenance for that House, and them that shall say Prayers in it. Of these in order; and, first,

Of the first: *Then shall the Lord be my God.* To haue the LORD for our GOD is the very summe of the first Commandement, the meaning whereof, as all Interpreters expound it, is to loue God aboue all, to make him our treasure, and infinitely to preferre him and his Seruice before our selues and all other things in the world. A duetie whereunto euery man is bound, as well as *Iacob;* and euery man that is not an *Atheist* will confesse, and professe as much. But how they performe this dutie, or either loue or preferre God aboue all, who so farre preferre themselues, their honours, pleasures and profits, vnto Gods Seruice, that they spend more houres of time, and pounds of money vpon the one, then minutes or pence vpon the other, and bestowe more cost euen vpon points and shooe-strings in one day then vpon the worshipping of God in a whole yeere, iudge ye. *Aures omnium pulso, conscientias singulorum conuenio,* as Saint *Augustine* speaketh. If the Lord be their God, where is his feare? where is his loue? where is his honour? There goeth more to this then the hearing of a Sermon once or twise a weeke, especially as it is vsually heard, which is scarce worth the name of a hearing; and *Iacob* meant more then so in my Text. For to haue the Lord for our God is to loue him aboue all, as I said before, and to serue him *semper, & ad semper,* with an vniuersall obedience, both in regard of time and place; and with *Dauid* to haue respect, not vnto some one, or two, but vnto [2] all his Commandements. They which serue God on the Sundaies, but not on the weeke-dayes; in the Church, not in their Chambers, Closets, Callings, and whole course of life; and that, not for praise, profit, pleasing of men, or custome, but out of a good and honest heart and a conscience of their duties; doe not performe this part of *Iacobs* Vow, to haue the Lord for their God. And thus much of the first dutie.

---

[1] Mark 11. 17.   [2] Psal. 119. 6.

The second followeth in the next words, *And this stone, which I haue set vp for a pillar, shalbe Gods House.* A dutie necessarily depending vpon the former; for if God must be worshipped, then must he haue a place to be worshipped in, here called an House.

Now, some thinke that this place where *Iacob* slept and set vp this Pillar, was *Mount Moria*, and that he called it *Bethel*, or the House of God, Prophetically by a *Prolepsis*, because the Temple should afterwards bee built there: yet there may be two other reasons why *Iacob* calleth this pillar Gods House, as before he called the very place *Bethel*.

1. Because God had manifested his presence here in an extraordinary manner, as he did afterwards both in the wandring tabernacle and in the fixed Temple, where he was therefore said to [1]dwell, as in an House.

2. Because *Iacob* consecrated this place vnto the Seruice of God, and (*chapter* 35, *and verse* 14) set vp an Altar for his worship in stead of this Pillar; and (as may probably be thought) would haue built a House for Prayer, and sacrificed in this place, if himselfe and the Church had beene then setled here, and had opportunitie and meanes to haue done it. But being a Pilgrime, and in his iourney, he did what he could for the present; he anointed a Pillar, erected an Altar for Sacrifice, and dedicated a place for an House of Prayer; whereby we may see what great care this holy Patriarke had of the place of Gods worship. His first care was for the worship it selfe, which hee vowed in the former words; his next care is of the place of his worship, in these words.

To teach vs that as our first care should be of the worship of God, so our second care should be of the place of his worship. The obiect of our first loue must be God himselfe; the object of our second loue must be the House of God. *O Lord, I haue loued the habitation of thy house, and the place where thine honour dwelleth* (saith *Dauid*), Psalme 26. 8. *Thy seruants take pleasure in her stones, and fauour the very dust thereof,* Psal. 102. 14. And Psal. 84. 10: *One day in thy Courts is better then a thousand. I had rather be a doore-*

---
[1] 1 Kings 8. 13.

keeper in the houſe of my God then to dwell in the tents of wickedneſſe: And he rendreth the reaſon why he ſo exceedingly loued the Houſe of God, in the very [1]next verſe; for there *the Lord is the ſunne and ſhield; there hee will giue grace and glorie: and no good thing will he with-hold from them that liue a godly life.* God is in all places by a generall prouidence; but hee dwelleth in his houſe by a ſpeciall preſence. Hee diſtilleth the droppes of his mercie vpon euery part of the earth; but he powreth it downe vpon that holy ground which is dedicate to his Seruice. There he ſhineth like the ſunne; there hee defendeth like a ſhield; hee filled the Temple at *Ieruſalem* with his glorie; hee made many gracious promiſes to them that praied therein, or towards it; and ſtill [2]*where two or three are gathered together in his Name, hee will be in the middeſt amongſt them;* and no good thing will he with-hold from them that worſhip him in the beautie of holineſſe, and wait for his [3]*louing kindneſſe in the middeſt of his Temple.*

Priuate Conuenticles are not to be compared with the publique Aſſemblies of the Church, that is both the throne of Gods glorie and his Mercie-ſeat.

Which euer ſo inflamed the holy men of God in former ages with the zeale of his Houſe that they ſpared neither coſt, nor paines, nor euer affected anything ſo much as the building and beautifying thereof. *I will not ſuffer mine eyes to ſleepe, nor my eye-lids to ſlumber* (ſaith *Dauid*), *vntill I find out a place for the Lord, an habitation for the mightie God of Iacob,* Pſal. 132. 4, 5. The good Centurion in the Goſpel [4]builded a Synagogue at his owne charges. Great *Conſtantine,* that mirrour of deuotion, bare twelue baſkets of earth vpon his owne ſhoulders towards the founding of a Church. And when that noble Captaine *Terentius* had done ſuch ſeruice in *Armenia* that the Emperor *Valens* bade him aſke whatſoeuer hee would, for a reward of his ſeruice, his onely ſuite (as [5]*Theodoret* reporteth) was *vt Orthodoxis vna præberetur Eccleſia:* And when the Emperour tare his petition, and bade him aſke ſomewhat els, hee ſtill perſiſted in his ſuite, and called

---

[1] Verſ. 11. [2] Mat. 18. 20. [3] Pſal. 48. 9. [4] Luke 7. 5.
[5] *Hiſt. tripart.* lib. 8. cap. 13. [*Eccles. Hist.* lib. iv. cap. xxix. Ed. Paris, 1642, fo. p. 702.]

God to record that hee would make no other fuit but that. And how zealous our owne forefathers haue beene in this kind of deuotion, I need not fpeake: the zeale of Gods Houfe did euen eate them vp; the goodly Monuments whereof, yet extant in all our Cities and many Countey-Parifhes (which haue fpared vs both the labour, and charge of building Houfes vnto God), fpeake for them. But fome of thofe Houfes which they haue built, and euen the faireft of them, fince their Butterefſes and Pillars (I meane their maintenance) hath beene pluckt away, begin to droope alreadie, and in time, (if it be not preuented,) will moulder away, and drop downe: And yet who pittieth the ruines of Sion, or repaireth any one wall or window thereof? *Will your felues* [1]*dwell in fieled houfes, and fuffer the Houfes of God to lie wafte?* Shall *Pater nofter* build Churches, and *Our father* pull them downe (as the prouerbe is)? or fuffer them to fall? [2]*O let not that be told in* Gath, *nor publifhed in the ftreetes of* Afkalon, *left the Philiftines reioyce, left the vncircumcifed triumph.*

Therefore to conclude this point: Seeing wee need not with *Iacob* in my Text vow to build, let vs all out of our zeale vnto Gods Houfe vow to beautifie, or at leaft to keepe vp thofe Houfes which are built to our hands. And thus much of the fecond duetie, which *Iacob* vowed in thefe words, *This ftone which I haue fet vp, &c.*

The third followeth in the laft words, *And of all that thou fhalt giue me, I will giue the Tenth vnto thee.* A duetie necef- farily depending vpon the two former, as I faid before: For if God muſt be worſhipped and haue an Houfe, then muſt there of neceffitie be a maintenance: therefore *Iacob* in the third place, for a perpetuall maintenance of the worfhip and houfe of God, and them that fhall attend therein, voweth for himfelfe and all the pofteritie as well of his Faith as Flefh, vnto the end of the world, the paiment of Tithes: *Of all that thou fhalt giue mee, I will furely giue the Tenth vnto thee.*

But what is the reafon why *Iacob* here voweth to giue vnto God rather the Tenth then any other part of his goods? Surely howfoeuer fome other caufes may bee alleadged, yet the

---

[1] Hag. 1. 4.   [2] 2 Sam. 1. 20.

true reason is becaufe *Iacob* knew, either by the light of Nature or by the tradition and practife of his Anceftors, that this *quota*, the very tenth, and no other part, was, is, and for euer muft be as due vnto God as either his Houfe or his worfhip: therefore he ioyneth thefe three together, being all relatiues which depend one vpon another; *Se mutuo ponunt, & auferunt*, and they are all equally due vnto God: And due vnto him, not by any common right, as other things; but by a fpeciall proprietie and right of referuation: whereby Almighty God from the very Creation of the world, and donation thereof vnto the vfe of men, referued vnto himfelfe, and feparated from common vfe vnto his owne Seruice, fome out of euery one of thefe fiue things, which fhould neuer after be alienated or taken away without Sacriledge.

1. A forme of Diuine worfhip, which may neuer be giuen to any other.

2. A time for this worfhip, which is the Saboth day, neuer to be abrogated.

3. A place of worfhip, which is his Houfe, neuer to be prophaned.

4. A Prieft-hood, which may neuer bow knee vnto Baal.

5. And laftly, for the maintenance of all thefe, Tithes, which hee therefore calleth his owne inheritance, neuer without Sacriledge to be impropriated. [1]*De omni fubftantia quam Deus homini donat, decimam partem fibi referuauit*: *Of all the fubftance which God hath giuen vnto man, he hath referued the Tenth part vnto himfelfe*: They be the very words of Saint *Ambrofe*. And S. *Auguftine* faith, [2]*Deus fibi tantum decimam vendicans, nobis omnia condonauit*: *God challenging only to himfelfe the Tenth, hath giuen all things vnto vs*. And that hee referued to himfelfe the tithes for this purpofe, euen from the beginning, as well as any of the other foure things, may appeare by this: That for any thing we know to the contrary tithes were payed euen from the beginning of the world; for fome thinke that *Caine* and *Abel* offered the very tithe as they

---

[1] Ambr. *Ser*. 34, *in feria tertia poft* 1. *Dominicam, quadrages.* in vlt. edit. col. [Serm. xxv. De Sancta Quadragefima ix. § 2 : App. vol. ii. Ed. Paris. 1690, col. 425.]

[2] Aug. *de temp. Ser*. 219. [Serm. 1. De reddendis decimis, vol. x. coll. 1077-8, ed. Bafle, 1543.]

were inftructed of their father *Adam*. But howfoeuer that be, certaine it is that there is no fooner mention made of any Prieft, κατά τάξιν, of an order fit to receiue them, then there is mention of paying of tithes vnto him. For *Abraham*, the father of the Faithfull, no fooner met with *Melchifedec*, a Prieft of an Order, but for an example vnto all his pofteritie, euen all the Faithfull vnto the end of the world, hee gaue him tithes of all the fpoiles, *Gen*. 14. And gaue it him, not as an arbitrarie gift, but as a neceffarie due vnto God; for hee fware not to take fo much as a Shooe-latchet of the King of *Sodoms*; And yet hee tooke the tithe, to offer, not as his, but as Gods due. And *Iacob* in my Text, amongft other Morrall dueties (for here is nothing Ceremoniall), voweth the paying of tithes: and in the twenty-feventh of *Leuiticus*, which is the firft place where tithes are mentioned vnder the Law, God doth not then begin to referue them and to fay, *All the tithes of the land fhalbe the Lords;* but claimeth them as his due of old by ancient inheritance, [1]faying, *All the tithe is the Lords; it is holy vnto the Lord;* not, it fhall be. And fo being his owne of old, he onely affigneth them vnto the Leuiticall Prieft-hood for that time. And thus you fee them due both before and vnder the Law.

Now let any man fhew when and where they were abrogated by the Gofpell. Not by our Sauiour CHRIST, who fpeaketh of them twife or thrife; and fo had iuft occafion to haue abrogated them, if he had had any fuch intent; yet hee abrogateth not, but rather confirmeth them: *Matth*. 23. 23, *Hæc oportuit facere:* Thefe things ought you to haue done. Nor by the Apoftle; for S. *Paul* is fo farre from abrogating that on the contrary he both commandeth and eftablifheth them, and prooueth them due. He commandeth them, *Gal*. 6. 6: *Let him that is taught in the word communicate with him that teacheth*, ἐν πᾶσιν ἀγαθοῖς, *in all good things*. Indeed he nameth not the very *Quotum*, how much they were to communicate, as taking it for graunted that the *Galathians* themfelues knew that to be the trueth, both by the light of Nature, and by the Scriptures, and by the perpetuall practife

---

[1] Verfe 30.

of the Church, and by the practife of the Heathen themfelues who vfed to offer their Tithes to their Idoles.

And 1 *Cor.* 9, hee plainely eftablifheth for a perpetuall ordinance the paying of Tithes; for, faith he, [1]*Euen fo hath the Lord ordained that they which preach the Gofpel fhould liue of the Gofpel.* Euen fo, that is, as appeareth out of the [2]former verfe, *As they that miniftred about holy things in the Temple liued vpon thofe holy things, and they that waited vpon the Altar, liued of the Altar:* Euen fo muft the Minifters of the Gofpel liue vpon the felf fame maintenance. Now, how liued they? Indeed the Priefts of the Law had other emoluments, which were Ceremoniall and temporarie: but their principall, morall, certaine, and perpetuall maintenance was out of thofe ordinarie and annuall Tithes, which are Gods ftanding Inheritance; therefore of them muft the Priefts of the Gofpell liue: Euen fo (faith the Apoftle) hath the Lord ordained: here is no abrogation, but a ratification of this eternall ordinance.

And laftly (which in mine opinion is the moft impregnable place), *Heb.* 7, the Apoftle ftrongly prooueth that the Tithes muft for euer remaine due vnto God: For being to prooue the excellencie of CHRISTS Prieft-hood aboue the Prieft-hood of *Aaron* and *Leui*, hee prooueth it by the perpetuitie thereof, becaufe CHRIST remaineth a Prieft for euer after the order of *Melchifedec;* whereas the Leuiticall Prieft-hood was alreadie ended; and to prooue the perpetuity of Chrifts Prieft-hood, he vfeth no other *Medium* but this perpetuall tithing, *Verfe* 8: *Here men that die receiue Tithes,* that is, *Leui,* who died both both in regard of perfon and office; *but there,* that is CHRIST in *Melchifedec receiued them, of whom it is witneffed that hee liueth:* therefore if Chrifts Prieft-hood be perpetuall, then muft his tithing be perpetuall, or els the Apoftles argument is to no purpofe.

And thus you fee it proued by thefe three places of Scripture, that thefe Tithes, which *Iacob* vowed in my Text long before the Law, are ftill due vnto God and his Church in the time of the Gofpell *iure Diuino:* And this hath beene both

---

[1] Verfe 14. [2] Verfe 13.

the constant opinion of all Antiquitie and the perpetuall practise of the Church, whatsoeuer any late Historie doth report to the contrary. Therefore it is absurde to say that these Tithes were onely Leuiticall, and that there is now nothing but a competencie due by a Morall equitie: For how can they be only Leuiticall, which were vowed by *Iacob* in my text, and paid by *Abraham*, and by [1] *Leui* himselfe in the loines of *Abraham*, fiue hundred yeeres before the Leuiticall Law began? And to speake of a Competencie now is a meere conceit: For who shall presume to prescribe an vncertaine Competencie, where God himselfe hath set downe a perpetuall certaintie which hee neuer yet altered? Or why should any man think that God, who prouided a standing, certaine, and liberall Maintenance for the Leuitical Priest-hood in the time of the Law, which was lesse honourable, should leaue the Ministery of the Gospell, which exceedeth in honour, vnto an vncertaine and beggerley competencie? especially foreknowing and foretelling that in these last dayes Charitie should waxe cold, and men be louers of themselues and their pleasures more then louers of God and his Church. And yet hee requireth Hospitality at our hands too, which he knew the worlds competency could not affoord.

Therefore it must needs follow for a certaine conclusion, wherewith I will end, that all true *Iacobites*, or true *Israelites*, which liue vnder the Gospell, are bound to performe all *Iacobs* Vow in the time of the Gospell, and not onely to haue the Lord for their God, and build or at least maintaine his houses, but also of all that he hath giuen them to giue the Tenth vnto him. And therefore as *Solomon* saith, *It must needs be a destruction for any man to deuoure these things that are sanctified;* the vsurping, and deuouring whereof (as I verily beleeue) hath beene the destruction of many Houses amongst vs. *Noluimus partiri cum Deo decimas,* saith [2] Saint *Augustine; Modo autem totum tollitur: We would not giue our Tithes vnto God, and now all is taken from vs.* And *Malachi* saith, *They are cursed with a Curse, all the whole nation of them, that robbed the Lord of Tithes and Offerings.* And *Dauid* curseth

---

[1] Heb. 7. 9.   [2] *Serm. de temp.* 219, cap. 39 [*ut antea*].

the deuouerers of thefe holy things, with the moft bitter curfe that euer he curfed any creature: [1]*O my God* (faith he), *Doe vnto them that fay, Let vs take the Houfes of God into our poffeffion, as vnto the* Midianites, *as to* Sifera *and* Iabin, *which perifhed at* Endor, *and became as dung for the earth. Make their Nobles like* Oreb, *and* Zeeb: *yea, all their Princes as* Zeba *and* Zalmunna. *Make them like a wheele, and as the ftubble before the wind. As the fire burneth the wood, and as the flame fetteth the mountaine on fire; fo perfecute them with thy tempeft, and make them afraide with thy ftorme, &c.* God keepe all our Nobles and Princes and People from this bitter Curfe! For the auoiding whereof, and obtaining the contrarie bleffing, me thinkes many fhould not onely, with *Iacob* in my Text, vow to giue their owne Tithes, but vow to redeeme thefe captiue-tithes out of the hands of other men who haue vfurped the fame, and to reftore them vnto the Lord againe, who is their right owner; then which they cannot almoft offer a more acceptable Sacrifice or Seruice vnto him.

And yet how thefe houfes of God are taken and ftill helde in poffeffion, and his Inheritance ftill embezelled in thefe dayes, the cryes of the poore Leuites euery where doe witneffe not onely in thofe places where all is gone, and onely a Competency (as it was then fuppofed) of ten pounds a yeere left (which is fcarce a Competency now for a Hog-heard), but alfo in many other places where the tithes are not quite impropriated, but yet fo gelded by pretended prefcriptions and vnconfcionable, nay vnreafonable cuftomes *de modo decimandi, & de non decimando*, and they many times confirmed by prohibitions, that the poore Leuite hath in fome places not the tenth, in fome, not the twentieth part of the tithe. I would to God that the Body of the Honorable Parliament were as willing as the Relligious and Royall Head thereof to take this grievance into their ferious confideration; that this Parliament might have the honour to enact fome wholefome Law for the honour of God, the advancement of his Church, the peace of their owne confciences, and the reliefe of the

---

[1] Pfal. 83.

poore Clergie in this behalfe ; that fo we might all (as we are all bound) pay *Iacobs* Vow unto the God of *Iacob*, and receive from him *Iacobs* bleffing. Which God graunt for his Sonne IESVS CHRIST his fake, who is our eternall Prieft; to whom with the Father and his Bleffed Spirit bee all Honour, Praife, and Thankef-giving for ever and ever. AMEN.

FINIS.

FEARE OF
LOSING
                      THE
            OLD LIGHT.
                      OR,
            A SERMON
            PREACHED IN
                EXETER.

                      BY
            THOMAS FULLER, *B.D.*

                  LONDON,
Printed by *T.H.* for *Iohn Williams*, at the signe of the
        Crowne in *Pauls* Church-yard.   1 6 4 6.

[" More discontents I never had
   Since I was born then here;
Where I have been, and still am sad
   In this dull *Devon-shire*.
Yet justly too I must confesse,
   I ne'r invented such
Ennobled numbers for the Presse
   Then where I loath'd so much."
      HERRICK'S *Hesperides*, ed. 1859, page 25.]

[Introduction.

WITH his patron, Lord HOPTON, FULLER seems to have remained until the Royal cause began to decline. It was to this military employment that the latter was in part referring when he said, in connection with the preparation of his *Church-History*, that during the first five years of the actual civil war (1642-6), he had "little list or leasure to write, fearing to be made an *History*, and shifting daily for my safety. All that time I could not *live to study*, who did onely *study to live*" (*Appeal of Iniured Innocence*, folio ed., part i. page 25). The wearness of an apparently unending war, and the stronger attraction of literary pursuits, led him "betimes" to make the City of Exeter his refuge. There in 1645 he put forth his *Good Thoughts in Bad Times*,—the first book which was printed in that city.

In the descriptions of Exeter, which we find in his own writings, FULLER speaks from personal observation:—"A round city on a rising hill, most capable of fortification both for the site and form thereof. Her walls, though of the old edition, were competently strong and well repaired." Again: "The houses stand sideways backward into their yards, and only endways with their gables towards the street. The city, therefore, is greater in content than appearance, being bigger than it presenteth itself to passengers through the same." (*Church-Hist.*, Bk. vii. sect. i. p. 393; *Worthies*, § Exeter, p. 273.) But we get more details of the position, &c., of the city from another contemporary authority, RISDON, who wrote *circa* 1630 thus:—"It is pleasantly seated upon a hill, amongst hills, saving towards the sea, very beautiful in building, and for quantity, matchable with most cities, which all do meet in the midst of the city, wall of stone by King ATHELSTANE, in a manner circular and beautified with battlements, and many turrets interposed, being before inclosed only with a ditch, and fortified with stakes, whereof an ancient charter maketh mention. . . . . This city hath six gates, the compass of whose wall's measure is a mile and a half, having suburbs extending far in each quarter; well watered is it likewise, being full of springs, and hath certain conduits, which be nourished with waters deduced from out of the fields, and conveyed by pipes of lead under the ground into the same, having four special streets, which all do meet in the midst of the city, called corruptly *Carfox* [*Carfax*, in a MS. copy of RISDON in the hands of the Rev. J. I. DREDGE, Buckland Brewer], but perchance more properly *Quatervoys*, which divideth the city into four quarters, in every of which there be fundry ftreets and by-lanes" (*Survey*, ed. 1811, 8vo., pp. 103-4). The following defcription of it is found in a foreign work of a later date, accompanied with a neat plan : " Locum occupat ad Orientalem Ifcæ partem : foffis & mœnibus cincta validiffimis : adfunt & frequentes interpofitæ turres. MD paffus habent ambitum. Sunt & fuburbia quæ in longum procurrunt. Situs omnino peramœnus in molliter acclivi & clementer edito colle. Incolarum opulentia, magnificentia ædificorum & convenarum commercia hic tanta, ut alibi non fint potiora. . . . Sex ornatur portis" (Hermannida's *Britannia Magna*, 16mo., Amftel. 1661, pp. 351-2). There are fome valuable papers on Exeter during the Great Rebellion in COTTON's *Gleanings from the Municipal and Cathedral Records of Exeter*, 8vo. 1877, pp. 73 feq.

The gates of Exeter to which FULLER (page 442) refers were zealoufly guarded during the military occupations of the place. Dykes and drawbridges were made at each gate to prevent their being blown up.

Exeter at the time when FULLER reached it was an important Royalift garrifon. The part which it played in the civil war may be feen from the following dates and events :—

1642, October. Garrifoned for the Parliament under HENRY GREY, Earl of STAMFORD.

1643, 5 Sept. Capitulated to Prince MAURICE after eight months' fiege ; Sir JOHN BERKELEY made Governor. "Amongft *City-sieges*, remember that of *Exon*, which for the fpace of about fifteen weeks together did faithfully conflict and ftruggle with a double difeafe: partly with a ftrong crafty peftilentiall enemie encompaffing her without, and partly with a malignant putrid fever in her own blood within ; and all this in the loweft and moft hopelefs juncture of time that ever this Parliament did fee, or I hope fhall fee, until our perfect deliverance : and therefore that City, though it be now ravifhed by ftrangers, may truely be faid to have kept her *virgin*-honour and motto (*Fidelis in æternum*) ftill, becaufe fhe cryed out for help, though no man came to her refcue" (John Bond's *Occafus Occidentalis : or, Job in the Weft. As it was laid forth in two feveral Sermons at two Publike Fafts for the Five Affociated Weftern Counties*, 4to. London, 1645, page 63).

21 Sept. Sir JOHN BERKELEY, Knt., admitted a Freeman.

13 Nov. £100 prefented by the City to BERKELEY "as a remembrance from this Houfe," he having then to go out of the city (Act-Book). Another gift of £100 was afterwards made out of thankfulnefs and refpect to him.

1644, 1 May. Queen HENRIETTA MARIA made the city her refuge.

13 June. A fiege threatened by the Earl of ESSEX.

16 June. Birth of a princefs, HENRIETTA ANNE ; baptifed 21 July. She left the city 15 April, 1648, and went to the Queen in France (Herbert's *Memoirs*).

29 June. The Queen's flight from the city.

1644, 26 July. King CHARLES, in purſuit of the Earl of ESSEX, reached Exeter from Honiton; Lord HOPTON being in his ſuite. The King's "coming with his army into the Weſt," welcomed by the Parſon of Dean Prior (*Heſperides*, p. 33). "The *Weſtern-men* were never so well in heart as with their own *Bevile Greenvile, Ralph Hopton, Killigrew, Godolphin*, &c.: when they chang'd theſe for other Generals and Colonels, their Purſes were ſhut, their Courage fell, and their duties were ſlackned" (Hacket's *Life of Williams*, ii. 209).

27 July. The King left the city.

1 Sept. Surrender of ESSEX at Fowey.

17 Sept. The King's victorious return to Exeter, Lord HOPTON then being General of the Horſe.

23 Sept. The King left the city, after ordering the houſehold of his infant daughter. FULLER was made Chaplain to the Princeſs (Anon. *Life*, p. 33).

1645, Jan. "As for the greateſt of all theſe five [Weſtern] Counties, in it one large City, and four great Towns, all accounted as maritime, were ſtrongly fortified and well defended; but that labour hath proved but a labouring in the fire, all thoſe places being now loſt except one poor Plymouth onely" (Bond's Sermon, *ut ſuprà*, page 62).

14 June. Battle of Naſeby. Decline of the King's cauſe. "The ſickneſs or the plague is now rageing in manie places to the greate danger of this Cittie" (Act-Book).

29 Aug. Prince CHARLES viſited Exeter from Launceſton; his coming celebrated by HERRICK. Left on 15th Sept.

Nov. Inveſtment of the city by FAIRFAX.

1646, 27 Jan. The city ſummoned to ſurrender.

Winter. The poor people, "pinched for proviſions" during the inveſtment, were fed by incredible numbers of larks found on the ſouth ſide of the city towards the ſea (*Worthies*, §Exeter, page 273).

19 Feb. Lord HOPTON, Commander of the Royal army under the Prince, defeated by FAIRFAX at Great Torrington, Devonſhire. Surrender of the remnant of his army at Truro, 14 March. Exeter in conſequence more cloſely inveſted.

31 March. The city ſummoned to ſurrender. "Upon the reading of a letter this day received from the Governor, intimating a ſpeciall occaſion of much concernment to this Cittie to conferr with ſome others att his houſe to-morrow morning att eight of the clocke. And his deſire to call a Chamber forthwyth and to appoint two or three of this company to attend that buſineſs. It is agreed that Mr. MAIOR, Sir HUGH CROCKER, Mr. WALKER, and Mr. MALLOCK, ſhalbe deſired to p'forme that ſervice on the behalf of the Cittie, it being by the relation of Mr. Recorder [Sir PETER BALL] from the ſaid Governour concerning hes ſummons

this day fent for the rendering of this Cittie, the managing whereof is left to the difcretions of the faid Committee. .... Upon the further information of the faid Recorder to the faid Governor that in cafe a treatie fhalbe concluded uppon at the faid meeting, that this houfe would name two p'fons for that purpofe on the behalf of the Cittie, they name two Mr. WALKER and Mr. KNOTT and afk that two more may be admitted Mr. KENDALL and Mr. FOARD" (Act-Book. See Cotton's *Gleanings*, &c., page 110).

1646, 3 April. Treaty begun.

9 April. Articles of furrender figned. Of thefe Articles, fays FULLER, "I had the Benefit, living and waiting there on the Kings Daughter at the Rendition thereof: Articles which both as *penned* and *performed*, were the beft in *England*;— thanks to their *Wifdom* who fo warily made, and *Honefty* who fo well obferved them!" (*Appeal of Injured Innocence*, part i. pages 13-14).

18 April. £100 was given to Mr. DANIEL POTTER, who brought the news of the rendition of Exeter. (*Lords' Journals*, viii. 278; *VI. Report Hift. MS. Commiffion*, p. 112.)

It is recorded that FULLER preached conftantly to the "truly loyal Citizens" of Exeter. He entered into relations with the King and with the Councillors of the city. The former, at the fuggeftion of the pious and beautiful ANNE, Lady DALKEITH (afterwards Countefs of MORTON), gave him a place in the houfehold of the Princefs HENRIETTA ANNE, and would have beftowed upon him a benefice at Dorchefter. The Corporation of Exeter gave him a Lecturefhip which was worth £20 per annum. This Lecturefhip had been eftablifhed by Dr. LAWRENCE BODLEY, the brother of the celebrated Oxford Librarian. By his will, 1615, LAWRENCE BODLEY, who was one of the Canons-refidentiary of the Cathedral, bequeathed to the Mayor, Bailiffs, and Commonalty of the city of Exeter the fum of £400 to be invefted for the continual and yearly maintenance of a fufficient preacher within the faid city for ever, to be chofen by the faid Mayor and his Company of the Chamber, and by them to be always appointed to exercife and preach a fermon weekly on the Sabbath days for ever in fuch convenient place or places in the city as fhould by them be procured and thought moft fit and profitable for edification; the faid preacher to be allowed, for his fufficiency and conformity according to the law of the realm, either by the Lord Bifhop of the diocefe or by the Lord Archbifhop of CANTERBURY for the time being.

There are feveral notices of this lecturefhip in the Act Books of the Corporation. On the 23rd June, 1642, it was agreed and ordered by the Chamber that Dr. BODLEY's lecture, which had been continued long in St. Lawrence parifh, fhould be then removed to St. Mary Arches, to be continued there during the pleafure of this Houfe only, and to begin there on the next Lord's day, and that Mr. HENRY PAINTER, the prefent Lecturer, fhould have a copy of the Act.

Mr. PAINTER, who had formerly been in charge of St. Petrock's parifh, was alſo Lecturer of the Rectory of Hennock (*Act-Book of the Chamber*, 21 June, 1642). He and Mr. PEAL, of Dorſet, members of the Aſſembly of Divines, are deſcribed by JOHN BOND ("late Lecturer in the City of *Exon*") as "a paire of workemen that were ſome of the charets and horſemen of the Weſt; both of them were eminent for piety and abilities" (*Occaſus Occidentalis*, 1645, page 69). PAINTER'S conduct as Lecturer diſſatiſfied the Chamber, who, on the 19th November, 1643, reſolved that as he had of late much neglected the performance of Dr. BODLEY'S lecture, as it ought to be done, "and hath alſo left this cittie for divers weeks paſt," he ſhould be "diſmiſte of the ſaid Lectureſhipp from henceforth." Mr. PAINTER was B.D. His death was a recent event when BOND preached the above-quoted Sermon. In it PAINTER is deſcribed as "the Champion and the Oracle of perſecuted Miniſters and people in thoſe parts; yea, the *hammer* of ſchiſmatics, and the *ſalt* of the moſt Weſtern City; which did not only preſerve it (in great part) from the *putrefaction* of Prophaneſſe, but from the *rawneſs* of novelties. In a word, he was ſo publike a good that for him that whole city hath cauſe *to weare blacks*" (page 69).

On the occaſion of the official diſmiſſal of this Lecturer, the Chamber choſe "Mr. WM. FFULLER to p'forme the ſaid lecture from henceforth on the ſabath dayes in the Afternoone during the will & pleaſure onlie of this houſe, the ſaid lecture to be preached on the Sabbath dayes in the Afternoone in his own p'ſon;" and he was to have all the benefit that had been or ſhould be appointed for that ſervice, as Mr. PAYNTER had.

The next entry relating to this Lecture is as follows:—

21 March, 1645-6: "Whereas Mr. WILL^{M} FFULLER Clark, about two years ſince was elected to preach the lecture heretofore founded by D^{r}. BODLIES will [?], who hath now lefte this cittie, It is this daye agreed by xiij. affirmative voices that the grante made to hym ſhall ceaſſe, which is intimated by S^{r}. JOHN BERKELEY K^{t}. our Governour to be the deſire of the ſaid Mr. WILL^{M}. FFULLER. Alſoe this day Mr. THOMAS FFULLER Bachelour of Divinitie [ſeveral words are here deleted], is by full conſent elected to p'forme the ſaid lecture, according to the direccon of the foreſaid Doctor BODLEY, to have and exerciſe the ſame att the will and pleaſure of the Maior and Comon Counſell of this Cittie and noe longer."

The thirteen "affirmative voices" made up the entire number of thoſe who were preſent at that fitting, Mr. JOHN CUPPER, or COOPER, being then "Maior" (his term of office extending from September, 1645, to September, 1646). He with another member of the Chamber was deputed early in 1642 to take a Petition to Parliament touching the injury to their trade by the diſturbances in London, and oppoſitions by Biſhops, &c., in Parliament. He was Sheriff of the City in 1643. The others preſent were: Sir HUGH CROCKER, NICHOLAS SPICER, ROGER MALLACK, ROBERT WALKER, JOHN MARTIN, Sheriff, RALPH GERMAN, CHRISTOPHER BRODRIDGE, THOMAS KNOTT, ALLAN PENNYE, JOHN BUTLER, JOHN PARR, THOMAS PITT, JOHN LAWES. Theſe, therefore, are "all the members of that ancient Corporation" whom FULLER addreſſes in his dedication.

The extracts from the Act-Book relating to the Lectureship thus continue:—

17 June 1646. ".... Alſoe this day Mr. THOMAS FFULLER is diſmiſſed from further performance of the Lecture founded by Dr. BODLEY."

It was on the 1ſt of the ſame month that FULLER, lodging with his ſtationer, WILLIAMS, in London, depoſited his petition for compoſition with the Committee at Goldſmiths' Hall, claiming the benefit of the articles of Exeter, where, as he ſays, he had been attendant on the Princeſs; and he had therefore left Exeter at leaſt three weeks before the date of his ſo-called "diſmiſſal" in the above minute. Colonel HAMMOND was the new Governor of the city; and under his rule ſeveral adherents of the Parliament were re-introduced into the Chamber, in the place of Royaliſts.

On the 25th of June of the ſame year "Mr. FFERDINANDO NICHOLLES," who had been Rector of St. Mary Arches from 1634, was choſen "to perform the lecture founded by Doctor BODLEY, and alſoe to continue the ſame during the will and pleaſure of this houſe;" and he was to have the benefit of the Rectory of Hennock, purchaſed for that purpoſe, to enjoy the ſame as before, and not otherwiſe. There is an account of this Mr. NICOLLS in Calamy, who has related how he rebuked ſome Exeter aldermen who fell aſleep in church. NICOLLS wrote *The Life and Death of Mr. Ignatius Jurdain, One of the Aldermen of the City of Exeter; Who departed this Life July 15th*, 1640, 2nd edit. Lond. 1655, 24mo.; a memoir commended to the reader by THOMAS MANTON.

The ſermon on *The Feare of Loſing the Old Light* was thus preached at the ancient church of St. Mary Arches (or *de Arcubus*, ſo called from its Norman piers), in the ſtreet of that name, on ſome Sunday afternoon ſhortly before the ſurrender of the City,—an event, it ſeems, which had more than once been imminent during FAIRFAX's inveſtiture. From FULLER's quaint apology (pages 457-8) for ſo often in former diſcourſes taking his leave of the citizens, it would appear as if the ſermon was preached when the ſurrender had been determined upon.

The publiſher of the ſermon, JOHN WILLIAMS, who iſſued moſt of FULLER's previous works, was FULLER's hoſt in the year 1646. Royaliſt authors reſorted to his ſhop, "the Crown," in St. Paul's Church-yard. He publiſhed HERRICK's verſes and PEARSON's Lectures on the Creed. FULLER, who was long dependent on the proceeds of the ſale of his books, for ſome time gave up to WILLIAMS everything that he wrote. Mr. NICHOLS, the accompliſhed editor of ſome of FULLER's works, deſcribed WILLIAMS as a man of probity: this was at a time when, in the opinion of a ſhrewd Scotchman, the moſt truſty of the London ſtationers were very rogues (Baillie's *Journals*, ii. 240).

The original ſermon is in 4to. It has never been reprinted. The preſent reprint is taken from a copy in the Editor's hands, pp. iv.+26. A crown and roſe in a floreated ornament is on the title-page. "T. H." of the imprint is perhaps THOMAS HUNT, of Exeter, for whom *Good Thoughts in Bad Times*, 1645, was printed.]

TO THE
Right Worſhipfvl
Mr. *COOPER*, Mayor
of the City of Exeter,

and to all the Members of

that ancient Corparation.

*W*HAT *the ſin againſt the holy Ghoſt is in Divinity, the ſame Ingratitude is in Morality; an offence unpardonable. It argues a baſe Diſpoſition in thoſe who are glad to receive what others give, but loath to confeſſe what they Receive.*

I muſt acknowledge my engagement unto you to bee great: Is not *Exeter* a little one? and my ſoul ſhall live, *where I ſafely anchored in theſe tempeſtuous times. It is a high advancement in this troubleſome Age for one with a quiet conſcience to be Preferred to Life and Liberty: It fared better with me; for whilſt her Infant Highneſſe, (on whoſe Soule and Body God crowd all bleſſings Spirituall and Temporall, till there ſhall be no roome to receive more,) though unable to feed her ſelfe, fed me and many more of her ſervants: other accommodations were beſtowed upon me by your liberality.*

In expreſſion of my gratitude I preſent this Sermon unto you, hoping it ſhall receive the ſame entertainement from your eyes as it formerly found from your eares, and ſtill be read with as much favour as it was once heard with attention. And then, this widowes mite of mine will be made a tallent by your courteous acceptance thereof.

May the shield of Divine providence, which onely is of proofe against the fiery arrowes of his shooting, defend you from the noysome pestilence, and encompasse you with a wall of Help and Deliverance: yea, may God himselfe stand watchman at the Gates of your City to forbid the entrance of any thing that may be prejudiciall unto you, and give full and free admittance to whatsoever may tend to the advancement of your happinesse here and hereafter. So resteth

Your servant in all

Christian offices,

THOMAS FULLER.

Feare of Losing the Old Light.

REVEL. 2. 5.

And will remove thy Candlestick out of his place except thou repent.

1. THIS Epistle was wrote *to the Angel of the Church of Ephesus*; to him *eminently*, not *exclusively*; to Him *chiefly*, not *only*; to Him, yet so to Him as a Letter of Publique concernment, directed to the Prolocutor, with intent that He (according to his office) should acquaint all the Christian Members of the Ephesian Church with the contents thereof. Yea, the very word *Angel* imports no lesse, signifying a messenger, imployed by appointment and intrusted for the benefit of others.

2. Ministers ought not to monopolize the spirituall intelligence which they have received from God, but to communicate it to others. And the more precious the knowledge is which they have, the greater is their obligation to impart it. *David* saith, [1]*Thy word have I hid in my heart, that I might not sin against thee*; and yet the same *David* had said, [2]*I have not hid thy righteousnesse within my heart; I have declared thy faithfulnesse and thy salvation.* Ministers must, and must not hide Gods word in themselves: must, as faithfull Stewards; must not, as crafty Hucksters; must, out of carefulnesse to observe it; must not, out of covetousnesse to ingrosse it.

---

[1] Psal. 119. 11.   [2] Psal. 40. 10.

3. The Epiſtle conſiſts of three principall parts.
   1. A commendation of the Epheſians former Piety and Patience.
   2. A Reproofe of their preſent backſliding, that they had *forſaken* their *firſt love*.
   3. A Threatning of them with future miſery, in caſe they did not quickly amend.

Preachers muſt vary their voices, interchangably uſing frownes, ſmiles, ſwords, ſalves, cordials, corraſives, as occaſion is offered. If *all the Body* of our Sermons be Praiſing, where is reproving? if all be Reproving, where is Comforting? Phyſitians adviſe Nurſes not alwayes to give the ſame receit to their Infants ſick of the wormes, but rather to make uſe of ſeverall Medicines, leſt otherwiſe the Wormes accuſtomed to the conſtant taking of the ſame thing, by degrees turne that Phyſick into their food, and ſo are encreaſed by what was intended for their deſtruction. It is wiſdome in Miniſters to try all wayes to work on the hearts of their Hearers full of ill Humours, and whoſe corrupt Nature, if ever uſed to one Receit, will improve their badneſſe upon it, and bee the more confirmed by what was preſcribed to confute them.

4. See here, no Church in this world can be free from all Faults. Even Epheſus, the beſt of the Seven, had ſomewhat amiſſe in it. As long as there be ſpots in the Moone, it is vaine to expect any thing Spotleſſe under it. The earneſt of Perfection (which is Sincerity) may be received in this life, but the full Payment thereof muſt be expected in another. Such as Fancy a Poſſibility of a Perfect Church here muſt not onely mold a New forme, but make a new matter, cauſe frailty to be firme, folly to bee wiſe, fleſh to be Spirit, Men to be Angels, Saints being too little in this Life, as full of their Infirmities. Witneſſe the Church of Epheſus: For though *He that was* praiſeth them for what they had bin, yet *He that is* reproveth them for what they were, and *He that is to come* threatneth them with what they ſhall be. *And will remove thy Candleſtick out of his Place, except thou repent.*

5. *I will sing* (faith [1]*David*) *of Mercy, and Iudgement.* Of thefe two, *Iudgement* the moft folemne, *Mercy* the moft pleafing Mufick. Behold them both in the Text: Judgment pronounced in the Commination: *And I will remove thy Candleftick out of his place:* Mercy promifed in the Condition: *except thou repent.* Yea, the Text confifts wholly of Mercy, and Mercy, there being Mercy in the very Commination; God not furprifing this Church with fudden Deftruction, but in fome manner arming it againft himfelfe by forewarning it. Satan never barks before he bites, never tels before hee tempts, becaufe he defires and endeavours the ruine of mankinde. But God who intends their Amendment, not confufion, alwayes warnes before He wounds, that fo by tendering them the Opportunity of a feafonable Submiffion they may prevent the mifery of their finall deftruction. *And I will remove the Candleftick out of his Place, &c.* By *Candleftick* is meant not the dull and dead Candleftick, but it quickned and enlivened with a Candle, namely the *Word of God.* Which amounteth to this effect, that God would Un-church *Ephefus,* and deprive it of the Benefit of the Gofpel, which enlighteneth mens Soules in their wayes to heaven. In the Commination three Doctrines are obfervable, whereof this the firft.

6. 1 *Doctrine:* God alone is the manager of the motions of the Candle of the Gofpel. [2]*Hee that caufeth it to raine upon one City, and caufeth it not to raine upon another City: one Piece was rained upon, and the Piece whereupon it rained not, withered:* He it is that vouchfafed the Gofpell unto *un-repenting* [3]*Corazin and Bethfaida,* and denyed it to Tyre and Sidon; beftowed it on unthankfull Capernaum, and withheld it from Sodom, which would have made better ufe thereof. God alone it was that forbad Paul to [4]*preach the word in Afia;* yea, when he [5]*affaied to goe into Bithinia, the Spirit fuffered him not,* but he was diverted with a Vifion, *Come over into Macedonia, and help Vs.*

---

[1] Pfal. 101. 1.   [2] Amos 4. 7.   [3] Mat. 11. 21.
[4] Acts 16. 6.   [5] Acts 16. 7.

7. Nor can any other Reafon bee rendred hereof, fave onely the [1]*Councell of his Will*. This appeareth plainely in the People of the Jews. [2]*The Lord did not fet his love upon you, nor chofe you becaufe ye were more in number then any People (for yee were the leaft of all People); but, Becaufe the Lord loved you, &c.* Feweft of all People: being foone fummed up in Abraham and Sarah, no more then two Cyphers in point of Procreation, without a Miracle. And as their Number was inconfiderable, fo their Nature was intollerable; for when they wandred forty yeares in the wildernefſe, their intricate windings in their Progrefſe feemed ftrait in comparifon of their crooked Conditions, and their wayes towards God were more indirect then their walking on Earth. Yea, in every outward refpect, fome of their neighbouring Nations did furpafſe them. The Ægyptians excelled them in Wit, the Phæniceans exceeded them in wealth, the Edomites in Antiquity, the Perfians in Induftry, the Arabians in Activity, the Syrians in Cunning, the Affyrians in command, the Philiftims in ftrength, and the Anakims in ftature; notwithſtanding all which, the Lord loved the Jews before and above them all: *even fo, Father, becaufe it pleafeth thee.*

8. And blefſed be God that it is in his power alone to order the Motions and Stations of the Gofpel. *Good fuccefſe have He with his Honour.* He that hath the moft might and right holdeth the Candle. It cannot be put into a better Hand. Had fome Envious or Covetous men (fuch as our Age affordeth too many) bin imployed in fo great a truft, abfolutely to difpofe of the Gofpel, when, where, and to whom they pleafed, O what ftrange worke would they have made! Our Saviour faid, [3]*How hardly fhall they that have Riches enter into the Kingdome of God!* But in this Cafe, how Hardly fhould they which want wealth be faved! their Poverty being unable to Purchafe Gods Word for themfelves, and fuch Mifers charity unlikely freely to beftow it upon them. Such Simoniacall Patrons as Sell fo deare their Prefentations to Church-livings, what unconfcionable rates would they. fet on the Gofpel it felfe, if it were in their Power to

---

[1] Ephes. 1. 5.   [2] Deut. 7. 7.   [3] Mark 10. 23.

make merchandife thereof! But this *marres their Mart*, that the giving of the Gofpel to any Place or Perfons, fooner or later, the continuing it longer or fhorter, the removing it flowly or fuddenly, are all and every one only and abfolutely placed in his power and pleafure, who fpeakes in my Text, *And I will remove the Candleftick out of his place, except you repent.*

9. [2 *Doctrine:*] Come wee now to the fecond Doctrine contained in the Commination, which may thus bee propounded: God will not finally extinguifh, but onely remove the Candleftick of his word. The Dove will not wholly flye away, but onely build her a new Neft; the Setting of the Gofpel in one Place will be the rifing thereof in another; what is loft in a Kingdome, will be found in the World; Particular Churches may, the Church cannot fall away. And it is worth our obferving that when the word hath beene fleighted and neglected by fome, immediately it hath bin embraced and honoured by others.

10. Thus the Gaderens: [1]*the whole multitude of their countrey befought Chrift to depart from them.* Strange that this wind fhould blow from all parts of the Compaffe, that Wanderers fhould entreat *the Right Way* to leave them. Sure the Patient is more fick in Minde then Body that is importunate to fend away his Phyfitian. Well, their Sute is granted: *Ask and ye fhall have:* the Gofpel is a Gueft which will not ftay where it perceiveth it Selfe not to be welcome. Away goeth our Saviour to the other Side, (oppofite to the Gadarens in Pofition and Difpofition,) where behold his entertainement: *And it came to paffe that when Iefus was returned, the People gladly received Him, for they were all waiting for him.* Thus Gods word is a Commodity of quick Vent; it will not lye long on the Merchants hand for want of Chapmen, but if one will not, another will have it. Another Inftance is prefented us in the Jews who difpifed the Preaching of S. Paul at [2]Antioch: *And when the Iews were gone out of the Synagogue, the Gentiles befought that thefe words might be preached to them the next Sabboth.* The Leavings, yea, the

---

[1] Luke 8. 37.   [2] Acts 13. 42.

Loathings of the Jews, were the Longings of the Gentiles; the ones fragments, the others feast. They requested not the Apostles to make new Provision for them, (conscience desires not what is novell, but what is needfull,) but would be pleased with the Repetition of what He had formerly delivered; and indeed, a Sermon being newly broached tasteth the best at the second draught. The Result of all is this: Those feet of Gods Ministers, who finding themselves unworthily used, do *shake the dust off from them* (according to Chrifts [1]command) in witnesse against an ungratefull Place; I say, those very selfe-same Individuall feet shall elsewhere bee welcomed as the [2]*Beautiful bringers of the Gospel of Peace, and glad tidings of good things.*

11. And here it will bee neither improper nor unprofitable to observe some Passages concerning the Motions and Postures of the Candlestick in my Text. And first, we may take notice that the Persecution gave the Occasion to the speedy propagation of the Gospel. Had Satan bin contented to suffer the Saints to dwel peaceably in Jerusalem, probably Christianity had not made its Progresse so fast and so far into the world. But it was Death to Him to see Good Men live in quiet, and therefore his malice mustered all his might to [3]disperse them after the martyrdome of *Stephen,* whereby hee scattered the fire of the Gospel instead of quenching it. Infant Christianity, like infant [4]*Christ, encreased in stature, and in favour with God and Man.* Yea, it is uncertaine whether Martyrs which did dye, or Confessors who did flye, contributed more to the advance of Religion; the former by their patient suffering confirming more, and laying the Truth the thicker; the latter by their Painfull preaching converting more, and spreading the Truth the broader. Thus the Devill did the Church an ill office, and God made it a good turne. Wee will pay our thanks where they are due, not to his malice who intended it to our mischiefe, but to his strength, wisdome, and goodnesse who disposed it for our happinesse.

12. Secondly, wee hitherto cannot finde a Countrey, from

---

[1] Mat. 10. 14.   [2] Rom. 10. 15.   [3] Acts 8. 1.   [4] Luke 2. 52.

which the Gospel did totally depart, to which it ever afterwards returned. The *white [1]horse* in the Revelation (which generally is interpreted the word of God) *went forth conquering, and to conquer.* Went forth, still in a Progressive, not Retrograde motion, like the Sun in the Firmament, which [2]*commeth forth as a Bridegroome out of his chamber, and rejoyceth as a Giant to run his course;* his retreating ten Degrees on the Diall of [3]Ahaz being extraordinary and miraculous. Wherefore seeing it seems not to stand with the State of the Gospel, to goe away *animo revertendi*, it will bee our wisest course carefully to retaine what wee have no President to recover.

13. Thirdly, Christendome is *a Zoar*, a little one, in comparison of the Pagan part of the world. Call for a Map, as our Saviour did for *a Penny*, and see how small a circuit thereof hath the Image and superscription of Christ upon it. Thus it is meet that all the Earth being Gods *Demeanes*, his Private Garden should bee lesse then his common grounds about it. There was a place in the city of Jerusalem, called *the Daughter of Zion*, so named, saith an [4]Author, because it was a parcell of buildings which branched or issued out of old Zion, as a Colony thereof; and surely pretty it was to behold this Babe in the arme of her Mother. But, oh that I might but live to see a Daughter of Christendome borne! I meane a Plantation of Piety amongst the Pagans, a Copy like our Originall, (save onely that it be not written with such red Inke,) in matter of doctrines, and knowledge of Religion.

14. Fourthly, Christianity hath beene these last hundreds of yeares little effectuall in converting of Heathen. For, be it reported to Serious Consideration whether those Indians, rather watered then baptised, driven into the Church, as the [5]*money changers out of the Temple*, deserve to be accounted solid Christians. Abate these, and then we shall finde small impression and Improvement of the Gospel in these latter Ages on Paganisme. I have not heard of many fish (understand me in a mysticall meaning) caught in *New-England*,

---

[1] Revel. 6. 2.   [2] Psal. 19. 5.   [3] 2 Kings 20. 11.
[4] Adricomius, *Theatro Terræ Sanctæ*, page 152, numb. 26 [Ed. fo. 1628].
[5] John 2. 15.

and yet I have not beene deafe to liſſen, nor they I beleeve dumb to tell of their Achievements in that kind. I ſpeake not this (God knoweth my heart) to the diſgrace of any *Labourers* there, being better taught then to condemne mens endeavours by the ſucceſſe; and am ſo ſenſible how poorely our Miniſtery prevaileth here at home, on profeſſed Chriſtians, that I have little cauſe and leſſe comfort to cenſure their Preaching for not taking effect upon Pagans. Onely I ſpeake this to the intent that we all ſhould enter into a ſtrict Scrutiny in our owne ſoules, what may be the Reaſon of this unuſuall barrenneſſe of our Chriſtian Religion. Surely it is no infirmity in the Doctrine it ſelfe, diſabled with Age, like *Naomi* that could have [1] *no more Sons in her wombe:* the fault is not in the Religion, but in the Profeſſors of it, that of late wee have beene more unhappy in killing of Chriſtians then happy in converting of Pagans.

15. Laſtly, from Jeruſalem (whence the Goſpel firſt ſtarted) this Candleſtick is obſerved to have a favourable inclination to verge more and more Weſtward. This putteth us in ſome hopes of America, in Gods due time; God knows what good effects to them our ſad war may produce: ſome may be frighted therewith over into thoſe Parts (being more willing to endure American, then Engliſh *Savages*); or out of curioſity to ſee, neceſſity to live, frugality to gaine, may carry Religion over with them into this Barbarous countrey. Onely God forbid we ſhould make ſo bad a bargaine as wholly to exchange our Goſpel for their Gold, our Saviour for their Silver; fetch thence *lignum Vitæ,* and deprive our ſelves of the *Tree of life* in liew thereof. May not their planting be our ſubplanting, their founding in Chriſt our confuſion; let them have of our light, not all our light; let their candle bee kindled at ours, ours not removed to them, as God threatned the Epheſians in my Text, *I will remove thy Candleſtick out of his place, except thou repent.*

16. [3 *Doctrine:*] The third and laſt Doctrine couched in the Commination is this: God never removes the Goſpel from a Nation, untill they or their Anceſtors firſt remove

---

[1] Ruth 1. 11.

themselves from his service. Where the Gospel is given, it is Gods Mercy, not mans Merit; where it is denyed, it is Gods Pleasure, no Injury to man; where it is removed, it is Gods Justice, and mans punishment, who hath beene unthankfull for it, and unprofitable under it. Thus the Jews our elder brethren were disinherited for their Infidelity; at this day wandring in all lands, yet having no Land, *sine Rege, Lege, Solo, Salo*, (I had almost said *Cælo* too,) stumbling at Him that should stay them, unhappy if they knew their condition, and more unhappy because they are ignorant of it.

17. *Objection:* But this is hard dealing, so just that it is unjust, that children for the default of their Parents shall be debarred from the meanes of their Salvation. Will God banish the sound of a [1]*Proverb* out of Israel, and practise the Sense thereof in his owne proceedings, *setting the childrens teeth on edge*, (even to their [2]*gnashing* in Hell fire,) *for the Sowre grapes which their fathers have eaten?*

18. *Answer:* The Day of Judgement wil be the day of the manifestation of the righteousnesse of God, whose actions which now are just shall then appeare so, to the clearing of his wayes, and convincing of others wickednesse. The Damned shall want *a drop of the water* of a colourable excuse *to coole their tongues with*, discontented with their condition, but satisfied with the cause thereof, so that they may blaspheme, but not complaine. Untill then let us be content *to tarry the Lords leasure*, suspending our Censures, and admiring what we cannot understand. David saith to God, *Thy way* [3] *is in the Sea;* and the sense is the same though inverted, *There is a Sea in thy way*, and that a bottomlesse one, (not like the Adriatick, *Acts* 27. 28, wherein the Marriners sounded *and found it twenty fathoms; and when they had gone a little farther, they sounded againe, and found it fifteen fathoms,*) but in this Ocean the farther we saile the deeper we sinke; and therefore let us make what speed to the Shoare, except the Pilot here had more skill, or his tackling more strength.

19. Meane time, how carefull ought Parents to be, lest by

---

[1] Ezek. 18. 3.   [2] Mat. 8. 12.   [3] Psal 77. 19.

their wickednesse they wilfully deprive their Posterity of the Gospel. Here, O let me plead for them who cannot speak for themselves; yea, I know not how to call my Clients, being as yet unnam'd, unborne, unbegot, I meane such little little *Levi's* which as yet lye hid in the *Loynes* of their Grandfathers: Oh let not their Soules be slain before their bodies be borne, by wilfull debarring them, by the prophanenesse of this present Age, from the future benefit of Gods word. Let that sturdy father, carelesse of himselfe, be conjured into Piety by that potent charme,

[1] *Per spem crescentis Iuli.*

Who can reade the horrid History of so many thousand Childrens corpses, drowned (as they say) in one fishpond in Italy by those Votaries, their mothers, and is not instantly ready, if the fact be proved, to arraigne, condemne, and execute the Memory of such Monstrous Murderers? What then shall we say to such Parents as plunge the Soules of Millions in the Pit of Perdition, sacrificing the Spirituall lives of their Sons and Daughters to Devils? so that as they walke on in their wicked wayes, the floore whereon they tread may bee said to be paved with slaughtered Infants, and that they trample on a Charnel-House of childrens Soules of their owne killing, because the candlestick of the Word was removed from them for their fathers offences.

20. See a sad spectacle hereof in the Church of Ephesus, to which God at this Day hath done what hee threatned in the Text. Indeed, some hundreds of years after the writing of this Epistle, Ephesus still continued the Staple of Religion and learning, where some Generall Counsels were celebrated. Till at last, growing notoriously erronious in doctrine and vicious in manners, it is at the present reduced to a miserable condition, shrunke almost invisible in our Moderne Maps, save that some charitable Geographers, in reverence of what she hath beene, allow her a bare remembrance in their larger Descriptions. The few Christians therein and thereabout grow contented vassailes to the Turke, and the soundest of them are infected in the Point of the Progression of the holy

[1 Æneid, Bk. vi. line 364.]

Spirit, with many other grievous errours. Generally in those Parts God hath permitted his Arke to fall downe before Dagon; the Alchoran hath banished the Bible; the Candle of the word is put out, and in the roome thereof the Moone of Mahomet is risen, whose Light is worse than darkenesse it Selfe. All which had beene seasonably prevented, if the Ephesians had beene but as carefull to take as God was kinde to tender the Caution in my Text. *And will remove the Candlestick out of his Place, except you repent.*

21. Now for application, to leave Ephesus and come to England: Know then, in the first place, our Land hath equalled Ephesus in favours received. No Iland in the world so farre distant from Jerusalem saw the Light of the Gospel so soone; yea, it was morning here when it was midnight in Germany; *the last was first;* our Countrey placed in the *Rere of the world* marched one of the formost in receiving the Christian Religion. And since the Word was here once planted, hitherto it was never totally lost, but still grew amongst the barren Mountaines in *Wales;* as Piety hath ever an ambition to keepe company with Poverty. Yea, here Religion hath enjoyed her selfe as purely and plentifully as in any other place; and though often sick of severall Superstitions, yet these were not the Peculiar Diseases of England, but the Epidemicall Infections of those Ages.

22. Secondly, England (what by her sinnes, which have caused this war, and which this war hath caused) hath equalled Ephesus in faults committed. In one particular hath exceeded Her. For, the holy Spirit commendeth Ephesus in the next verse *for hating the Nicolaitans, whom he also hated.* These Nicolaitans were so called from [1]Nicolas, one of the seven Deacons, who (as Ecclesiasticall History reporteth) having a Beautifull wife, and being taxed for being causelesly Jealous of Her, to confute his Accusers prostituted his wife to the unchaste embraces of any, thereby to wipe off the Aspersion of Jealousie. So then, those who evidence their opposition to any Error in Judgement, or demonstrate their distance from

---

[1] Acts 6. 5.

any vice in practife, with fuch violence and furious indifcretion that they fall into the oppofite error, or reele into the contrary Vice, are moft truly and properly, though not Literall, fpirituall Nicolaitans. And in this Senfe, how many wee have of this Sect in our Kingdome, not hated, but favoured and foftered, I am grieved to thinke and unable to number.

23. But now the third Parallel I dare not fpeake, and I dare not conceale. Yet, why fhould I not fpeake it? In Spaine, great rewards are given to fuch as firft are the meffengers of Bad newes, provided they doe not difperfe it to the Difadvantage of the publick, but impart it onely to the State, which may mend ill accidents before they become worfe. Sure then, though I defire no favour, I deferve no frowne, if from the fimplicity of my heart, without finifter intents, I fhew the danger likely to ceafe [feize] on us, if not providently diverted by fpeedy repentance. Plainely tis this: I feare we fhall be like Ephefus in future punifhment, and that the *candleftick will be removed out of his place.*

24. *Objection:* There is no danger of the departure of the Light which now daily encreafeth. Preaching now a dayes is like Silver in the reigne of [1]Solomon, fo plentifull *that it was nothing accounted of.* The Gofpel formerly going afoote now rides on horfebacke. Wherefore concerning the removing of the Word, you fancy caufleffe feares, then fear your caufleffe fancies; it now fhineth brighter then ever before.

25. *Anfwer:* As all is not Gold that glifters, fo all is not light that fhines, for Glowormes and rotten wood fhine in the darke. Firebrands alfo doe more harme with their Smoake then good with their Light. And fuch are many Incendiaries, which without either authority of calling, or ability of learning invade the Minifteriall function. Whofe Sermons confift onely of two good Sentences, the firft, as containing the Text, and the laft, which muft bee allowed good in this refpect, becaufe it puts an end to a tedious and impertinent difcourfe. Notwithftanding all pretended new lights, and plenty of preaching, I perfift in my former Sufpicion. Yet am I not fo much affrighted with all the Prodigies reported to have

---

[1] 1 Kings 10. 21.

appeared in the Ayre as with the portentous Sins which I dayly behold committed on the Earth. And this I say: God commonly moves the candle before he removes it. The light seemes sicke and faint before it dyes. In Mines, before a dampe commeth, candles begin to burne blew, as by instinct mourning their owne funerall before hand. Some such sad symptomes discover themselves in our Candle, in the preaching of the word, if seriously considered.

26. First, it is an ill signe that so many wantonly play with the Word. When children begin to try Conclusions with a Candle, sporting themselves *at in and out with it*, their Parents use to take it from them, leaving them to doe pennance in the Darke for their wantonnesse. I am afraid God will serve us in like manner: so many have dallied with the Scripture, producing it for the maintenance of their upstart monstrous Opinions. Secondly, so many Theeves in the Candle, such variety of Sects and Schismes, which wast and mispend the light, is another ill boding Symptome. Yet whilst others wonder that they are so many, I wonder they be no more; for untill a good Peace be setled, (which God Speed,) and whilst the great *Bond of Discipline is broken*, every stick in the Fagot will be absolute and set up for it selfe. Lastly, if the wax be taken away from the candle, (as in many places it is, and Tithes denied for the Ministers maintenance,) the light must decay; the five foolish [1] Virgins having so much wisdome as to know that their Lamps could not burne when they wanted oyle; except any doe thinke Ministers may be like the miraculous [2] Bush, which did burne and not consume, that so they may alwayes worke, and yet never wast. Put these together, (and others I could instance in,) and though Ministers, Gods Doves, delight not to be Ravens to croake Funerals; though they, Gods fixed Stars, would not be Comets presaging sad Events; though these [3] Ambassadours, *praying you to be reconciled to God*, are loath to bee Heraulds to proclaime war: Yet be these things seriously considered, and may they not amount to make us *Iealous* over England *with a godly jealousie* what for the future will become of us?

---

[1] Mat. 25. 8.   [2] Exod. 3. 2.   [3] 2 Cor. 5 20.

And this I will boldly adde, that an awfull feare of losing the Candlestick is the best Hope we have to keepe it.

27. But I foresee a Posterne Doore ready to be opened, that escaping thorow it my Auditors may decline whatsoever this Day I have delivered. Some will say, what Josiah was [1]promised, we presume on: *the Evill will not come in our Dayes.* The Gospel will last my life in the Land; and if we are not to care for to morrow, much lesse will wee carke for the Day after our Death. Besides, if a generall Judgement should come in my Time, I shall beare but my share, and shift as well as another.

28. Well, Beloved, tis true this inconvenience attends all generall discourses, (such as this Dayes Sermon is,) that as *filius populi* hath no father, so publique reproofes are seldome particularly applyed by any to themselves. But, that I may catch some fish I must weave my net closer, and draw the threds thereof neerer together. Bee it granted what we hope and thou believest, that the light of the Gospel will last thy life, yet how long or little time thy life will last, there is the Question. Nor will it be any violence to my Text, in a secondary Sense, to expound this *Candle*, of the Life of every man, which how long since it hath beene kindled we know, but how soone it may bee quenched God knows. Some wares in England, are usually set to sale *by the candle;* that chapman carrieth them, who giveth the most before the candle is burnt out. Such is all our condition at this time: Heaven now is to be had, Happinesse to be purchased; [2]*Buy the truth, and sell it not,* lose not a good bargaine, bid bountifully; be not body wife, and soule foolish; the candle weares, the candle wasts, casualty may, sicknesse will, Age must extinguish it. If once the light be out it is too late; there is [3]*no worke, nor devise, nor knowledge, nor wisdome in the grave, whither thou goest.*

29. I should now come to the Condition, *except thou repent.* But it is high time for me at this present to leave preaching, and more then high time for us all to begin practising of this point of repentance. *Let us rend our hearts and not our gar-*

---

[1] 2 Chron. 34. 28.   [2] Prov. 23. 23.   [3] Eccles. 9. 10.

ments, and turne unto the Lord our God. The melting of marble, so that it become fusill or runable, is recounted one of those Mysteries which are lost in our Age, though formerly knowne to, and performed by the Ancients. But O let us labour that the Art of melting stony Hearts (such as ours are by Nature and custome of sinning) be never lost or forgotten, but kept in use, and put in daylie practise. That so the Candlestick may remaine amongst us, not onely forty dayes, the time prescribed for [1]Niniveh's Repentance; or fifteen yeares, the lease of [2]Hezekiahs health restored; or terme of our life outright, a gift granted to good [3]Josiah; or for an hundred and twenty yeares, so long was allotted for the [4]amendement of the old world; or for foure generations successively, which Lease of Lives on the Throne of Israel was bestowed on [5]Jehu; but so long as the *Gnolam* the Eternity of this world shall last, as long *as the* [6]*Moone endureth in heaven.*

30. Men naturally decline Death; and the Quick at the day of Judgement desire *not to bee* [7]*uncloathed, but cloathed upon, that mortality may bee swallowed up of Life.* The same is our request, that there may bee no interruption or intermission of our Light; that it may bee not put out, but tooke up; not destroyed, but devoured in the transcendent Splendor of Glory. Then it will be no thrift *to burne Day; and* [8]*there shall bee no night there, and they need no candle,* no use of preaching, Sermons shall cease, and God alone shall bee the Text, the Hallelujahs of Angels and Saints the Comment upon it.

31. And now I am to take my finall farewell of this famous City of Exeter. I have suffered from some for saying severall times, that I thought this or this would bee my last Sermon, when afterwards I have preached againe. Yet I hope the Guests are not hurt, if I bring them in a course more then I promised or they expect. Such would have forborne their censures had they consulted with the Epistle to the Romans. In the fifteenth Chapter, verse *33*, the Apostle seemes

---

[1] Jonah 3. 4.   [2] 2 Kings 20. 6.   [3] 2 Chr. 34. 28.   [4] Gen. 6. 3.
[5] 2 Kings 10. 30.   [6] Psal. 72. 7.   [7] 2 Cor. 5. 4.   [8] Revel. 22. 5.

to clofe and conclude his Difcourfe, *Now the God of Peace bee with you all, Amen.* And yet prefently he beginneth afrefh and continueth his Epiftle a whole Chapter longer. Yea, in the fixteenth Chapter, verfe 20, S. *Paul* takes a fecond folemne *vale, The grace of our Lord Iefus Chrift be with you all, Amen;* and notwithftanding ftill he fpins out his matter three verfes farther, till that full and finall Period, verfe 27, *To God onely wife bee glory thorow Iefus Chrift for ever, Amen.* Thus *loath to Depart* is the tune of all loving friends: The fame I may pleade for my Selfe, fo often taking my farewell, wherein if any were deceived, none I am fure were injured.

Now this is all: The Rabbins have a conceit that Manna relifhed fo to the pallats of the Jews juft as the eater thereof did fancy or defire. Confult with your felves, and wifh your owne fpirituall and temporall conveniencies, wifh what you will, for Body, Soule, both; You, yours, your Private, the Publique; confine not your happineffe with too narrow meafure of your owne making. And my conftant Prayer to God fhall be, that he would be pleafed to be to you all in Generall, each one in particular, that very thing which You for your owne Good doe moft defire. *Amen.*

FINIS.

A
SERMON
OF
ASSVRANCE.

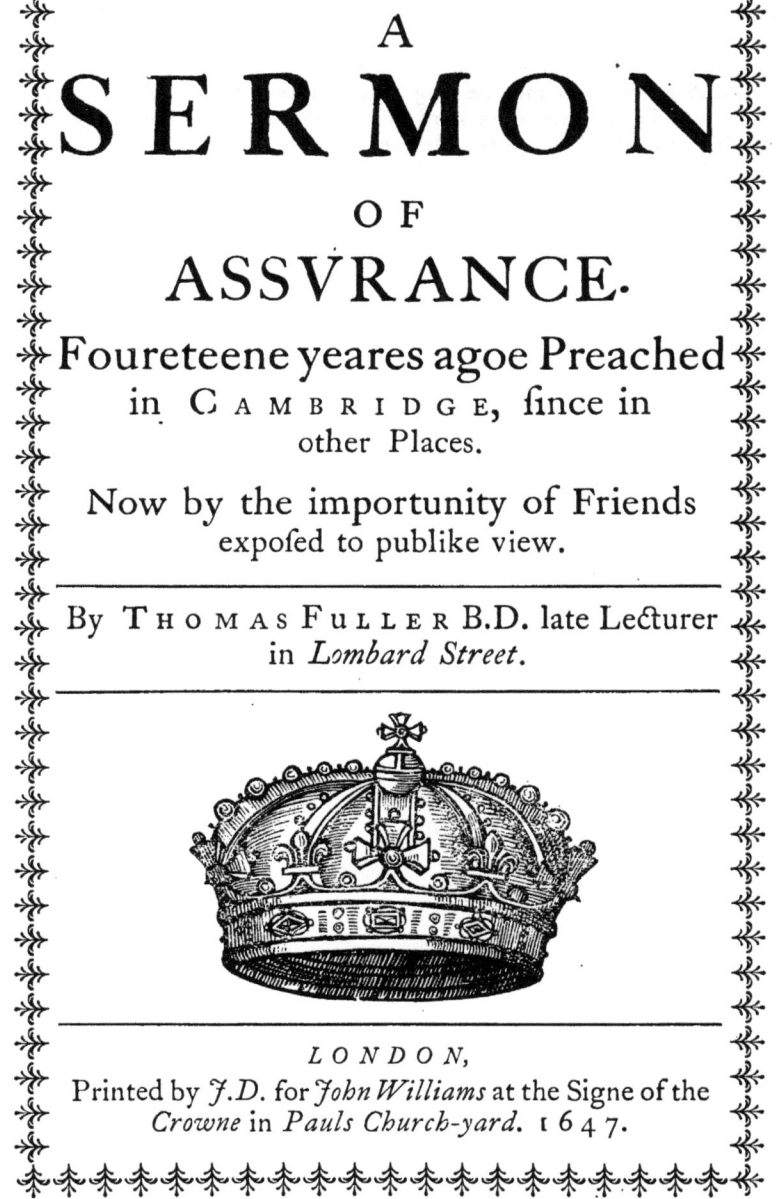

Foureteene yeares agoe Preached in CAMBRIDGE, since in other Places.

Now by the importunity of Friends exposed to publike view.

By THOMAS FULLER B.D. late Lecturer in *Lombard Street*.

LONDON,
Printed by *J.D.* for *John Williams* at the Signe of the *Crowne* in *Pauls Church-yard*. 1647.

["A Soul perswaded of this (assurance of Gods love) may sing merrily with the sharpest thorn at its breast; so David, Psal. 57. 7, *My heart is fixed, my heart is fixed; I will sing and give praise*. What makes him so merry in so sad a place as the Cave, where now he was? He will tell you, *v.* 1, where you have him nestling himself under the shadow of Gods wings, and now well may he sing care and fear away. A soul thus provided may lie at ease on a hard bed. Do you not think they sleep as soundly who dwell on *London*-Bridge, as they who live at *White-hall* or *Cheap-side*, knowing the waves that roar under them cannot hurt them? Even so may the Saints rest quietly over the floods of death itself, and fear no ill."—GURNAL's *Christian in Compleat Armour*, 6th edit. fol. 1679, pp. 14, 15.]

[Introduction.

A GROUP of Sermons now come into notice which FULLER preached as Lecturer in certain churches of London, and as Chaplain in private houfeholds. The Lectureships which were held by him, and which extended over feveral years, divide themfelves into two diftinct periods: firft, fome temporary appointments during the tenure of which he fuffered the penalty of his connection with Royalifm; fecond, more fixed appointments during which, under the toleration afforded by the Commonwealth, he alfo acquired a benefice.

The firft of thefe periods covers FULLER's occupancy of pulpits at St. Clement's, Eaft Cheap, in St. Clement's Lane, near Lombard Street, and St. Dunftans in the Eaft, correfponding with that era of the civil commotions which ends with the Sermons in the prefent volume.

Thefe City Lectureships are not to be confounded with the Incumbencies. The latter were when vacant filled up by the Committees of Religion, and only candidates whofe qualifications CROMWELL's "Tryers" had certified received admiffion. The Lecturers, on the other hand, were directly appointed by the parifhioners at their veftry meetings. As thefe Lectureships gave employment of an independent nature, they were fought after by diftreffed clergymen; and many of the "cavalier parfons" held them. The right of election by parifhioners was derived from an ordinance of Parliament, 8th September, 1641, which had then been introduced to counteract the meafures of LAUD. It was ordered—

"That it fhall be lawful for the Parifhioners of any Parifh, in the Kingdome of *England* and Dominion of *Wales*, to fet up a Lecture, and to maintain an Orthodox Minifter, at their own Charge, to preach every Lord's Day, where there is no Preaching; and to preach One Day in every week where there is no weekly Lecture." (*Commons' Journals*, page 283).

FULLER, who was fhut out from his former pofition at the Savoy, was perhaps one of the firft of the Royalift clergy who thus at St. Clement's, under the decree of his political antagonifts, again fell with huge fatiffaction into the exercife of his profeffion. The addrefs to the reader of this Sermon (page 467), as well as the defcription of himfelf ("late Lecturer") in the title-page, fhows that he did not long hold the appointment. He became, however, very popular with the merchants of the parifh, feveral of whofe names appear as patrons of his *Pisgah-Sight* and *Church-Hiftory*, and whofe memory moreover is perpetuated in the dedication of PEARSON's Lectures on the Creed.

Under the zealous countenance of religious merchants, "who hungered," fays FULLER's biographer, "after the true and fincere word, from which they had been fo long reftrained," the City Lecturefhips benefited the parifhes in which they were held. They alfo proved advantageous to the clergy, who in the year 1647 began to reappear in London, under the protection of the parliamentary order for Lectures above cited. Their labours tended to relieve the fpiritual deftitution of the metropolis.

In FULLER's time St. Clement's was a fmall church void of monuments. Its hiftory may be gathered from the annexed copy of an infcription on a brafs on the north fide of the prefent church :—

"This Church is dedicated to ST. CLEMENT the third Bifhop of ROME. The Benefice was originally in the Gift of the Abbot of WESTMINSTER, but in the firft year of the reign of Queen MARY, was given by her to the Bifhop of LONDON. After the Fire of LONDON the Church was rebuilt by Sir CHRISTOPHER WREN, and was re-arranged in 1872 by WILLIAM BUTTERFIELD, F.S.A. Among the diftinguifhed men formerly connected with the church were Bifhop PEARSON, the Author of the Expofition of the Creed ; Thomas FULLER, the Church Hiftorian ; and as Organifts, PURCELL & BATTISHILL.—W. J. HALL, M.A., *Rector ;* J. S. MARRATT, G. HORSLEY, *Churchwardens,* 1872-3."

The church books were not deftroyed in the Fire. The churchwardens' accounts prove that FULLER was preaching at the church early in the year 1647, beginning in March. In that year one of the firft entries is an item for money paid to their lecturer, as follows :

"Paid for 4 fermons preached by Mr. FFULLER £01. 06. 08."

The extracts from fermons cited in Spencer's folio fhow that FULLER was alfo preaching there in 1648, 1649, 1650, and fubfequently ; the firft-named date fhowing that the preacher's fufpenfion was not of long duration. This preacher would doubtlefs, therefore, have his due fhare of the money referred to in the following entry, occurring in the church-wardens' accounts for 1648 :—

"Paid diverfe minifters for preachinge 22 Sabbath daies, beginiñge the 12 of November, 1648, and ending the 12 of April, 1649, £022. 00. 00."

The *Sermon of Affurance* was a favourite difcourfe of the preacher, who had firft delivered it at St. Bene't's Church, Cambridge. It has, however, been much altered, for it is more mature both in ftyle and fentiment than his earlier fermons on Ruth, preached at the fame place.

Amongft the benefactors whom FULLER met with after his departure from Exeter, during a feafon of actual poverty or diftrefs, was Sir JOHN D'ANVERS (page 465), afterwards one of the Regicides, who feems to have taken him into his houfehold at Chelfea, perhaps as an occafional refident or vifitor rather than as chaplain, and to have given him an annual falary. Thefe, therefore, may be the favours, for the continuance of which FULLER begs in the dedication of this Sermon, page 466. The moft grateful of men, he has himfelf put on frequent record his fenfe of indebtednefs to his benefactor. In former days D'ANVERS, by reafon of the nobility of his birth, had been Gentleman of the Privy

Chamber to CHARLES, when Prince of WALES; and he had been returned for the Univerfity of Oxford in 1621, 1625, 1627-8, and in the Short Parliament of 1639-40. In the Civil War he had, though advanced in years, become a Colonel in the intereft of the Parliament. CLARENDON's account of the Knight (*Hift. Rebel.* ed. Oxf. 1843, book ix. page 696) fhould be read with an allowance, the more fo as it has been fupplemented in the fame fpirit by GEORGE BATE, ECHARD the hiftorian, the author of *The Hiftory of King-killers*, and others. CLARENDON's ftatement is that D'ANVERS, being neglected by his elder brother the Earl of DANBY, had by a vain expenfe in the way of living, contracted a vaft debt which he knew not how to pay; and that being proud, formal, and weak, he had been feduced into the counfels of the Parliament. It was decided in a Parliamentary inquiry, which D'ANVERS himfelf advanced (see his Petition to the Houfe of Commons, *VI. Report Hift. MSS.*, page 93), that his brother, to whom he was heir, and who had died in 1643-4, had by his will deprived him of certain eftates in confequence of his affection to the caufe he had efpoufed;—a decifion which difpoffeffed Lady GARGRAVE his fifter of Noftel, co. York, and Sir PETER OSBORNE, of confiderable property. (*Divifion of Plunder of the Self-Denying Republicans*, 1646.)

The affociation of FULLER with a man about whofe character we have only the teftimony of hoftile pens, is difficult to underftand. It appears, however, pretty certain that in the above-named authorities the Knight's real character has not been given. A very different view of him, at a fomewhat earlier time, is derived from fome pleafing letters from GEORGE HERBERT to him in WALTON's Life of that faintly poet. From thofe letters it appears that D'ANVERS, who had married HERBERT's mother ("for love of her wit") was ever moft kind to his ftep-fon. In one of them, written from college, HERBERT begs for money to buy divinity--books, being then, in confequence of his expenditure in this direction, fcarce able with much ado to make one half year's allowance fhake hands with the other (*Remains*, ed. Pickering, 8vo. 1848, pp. 11, 303–310). D'ANVERS, it is noticeable, was the overfeer of HERBERT's will. DONNE eulogifed the Chriftian difcipline of Lady D'ANVERS's houfehold. Putting afide the fubfequent king-killing propenfities of D'ANVERS, there feems to have been many elements of goodnefs about him; and whatever his hope of gain may have been, he only received out of the ftate fpoils a commiffionerfhip of Delinquents' Eftates. AUBREY relates that he was a faithful friend in the war time to many befides himfelf. Of other Royalifts whom D'ANVERS befriended befides FULLER, an inftance may be mentioned in JOHN THORNBOROUGH, Vicar of Weft Lavington, Wilts; as to whom WALKER (*Sufferings*, pt. ii. page 384) fays that he was "a man of *Eminent Learning*, of a *Sweet* and obliging *Temper*, and beloved of all that knew him and converfed with him. Sir JOHN DANVERS (though a *Regicide*), who was of his [THORNBOROUGH's] Parifh, did, after his expulfion from his *Vicaridge*, get him the *School* there; which yet by the violence of his *Profecutors* and the Iniquity of the Times, he could not long Hold, but was thence alfo *Expelled*. . . . . After which Sir JOHN DANVERS procured him the *Rectory* of *Hilperton* in the fame county; but he (though very *Powerful* in thofe Times) was not able to *Protect* him there." The intimacy of D'ANVERS and FULLER may be one out of feveral cafes that could be cited to prove that the focial intercourfe of families during the Civil War was not greatly difturbed by political or religious differences; party-feeling being marked by an amount of courteous civility which has been too much overlooked by the writers on that age of diffenfion. FULLER had certainly a good opinion of his benefactor, and he appreciated the indirect protection which the connection afforded him.

Such, then, was the "worfhipful" knight who—to ufe the words of the grateful FULLER—by a yearly and ample exercife of his bounty raifed his fortunes at a time when they were, as he expreffively puts it, not only tottering but utterly proftrate. This interefting biographical fact is derived from the engraving of Solomon's Temple in our author's *Pifgah-Sight* (book iii. page 352) in a joint dedication to HENRY D'ANVERS, fon of Sir JOHN, and to FRANCIS ST. JOHN, eldeft fon of Sir OLIVER ST. JOHN, Lord Chief Juftice of Common Pleas. The dedication, which was penned in the year 1649 or 1650, is as follows:—

"HENRICO D'ANVERS, Iuveni generofæ indolis (gratioris quod e pulchre corpore) honoratiffimi patris (qui annua ac liberali largitione, res meas non nutantes modo sed plane jacentes erexit) hæredi: nec--non peregrinatioñ comiti indiuiduo

FRANCISCO de Sᵗ. IOHANNE, Jurisconfultiffimi patris ad togati honoris apicem euecti, primogenito, qui (uti fpero) generis claritatem nouo fplendore illuftrabunt, Templi contra-facturam dedicat. T. F."

A pedigree of D'ANVERS's family, derived in part from the Funeral Certificate of "Old" Sir JOHN DANVERS (ob. 19 Dec. 1594), will be found at page 490. The Sermon following this is alfo infcribed to D'ANVERS (fee page 495), whofe fubfequent hiftory is fketched in the Introduction to the Sermon *Life out of Death*, 1655, in volume ii. of this collection.

There was only one edition of this fermon, which perhaps appeared early in 1647-8. The Editor has a copy dated 1647, whence this reprint is taken. He purchafed it fome years ago in a volume of difcourfes containing VINES's funeral Sermon on the Earl of ESSEX, 1646; CUDWORTH's, before the Houfe of Commons at Weftminfter, 31 March, 1647; GREENE's, before the Houfe of Commons, 24 Feb. 1646-7; and RUTHERFORD's Faft Sermon before the Houfe of Lords, 25 June, 1645. There are copies of the fame fermon dated 1648, which are not fo rare as the few which remain of thofe dated 1647; but thofe of both years, as the collation of them proved, are precifely alike, except in the change of the figure. The fermon was in 4to., pp. viii. + 31. The crown, which is on the title-pages of moft of WILLIAMS's publications, is an exact copy of that on the original fermon. A fimilar crown appears on the title-pages of HERRICK's *Hefperides*, 1648; and a larger form of it is found on the title-page of FULLER's *Church-Hiftory*, 1655, and of PEARSON's *Expofition* of the Creed, 4to. 1659.]

TO

The Honovrable,
and nobly accomplished Knight,
Sir IOHN D'ANVERS, all
*the blessings of this, and a
better life.*

SIR,

1. WEE read how *Zachariah* being struck dumbe called for Table-bookes thereon to write his minde, making his hands to supply the defect of his mouth: It hath been the pleasure of the present Authority (to whose commands I humbly submit) to make me mute, forbidding mee till further order the exercise of my publicke Preaching; wherefore I am faine to imploy my fingers in writing, to make the best signes I can, thereby to expresse, as my desire to the generall good, so my particular gratitude to your Honour.

2. May this Treatise but finde the same favour from your *Eie* as once it did from your *Eare*, and be as well accepted when read as formerly when heard. And let this humble Dedication be interpreted a weake acknowledgement of those strong obligations your bounty hath laid upon me. Well may you taste the fruits of that tree, whose root your liberality hath preserved from whithering.

3. *Sir*, thefe hard times have taught mee the Art of frugality, to improve every thing to the beft advantage: by the fame rules of thrift, this my Dedication, as returning thanks for your former favours, fo begs the continuance of the fame. And to end, as I began, with the example of *Zachariah*, as his dumbneffe was but temporary, fo I hope by Gods goodneffe, and the favour of my friends, amongft whom your Honour ftands in the higheft ranke, the miracle may be wrought, that the dumbe may fpeake again, and as well by words publikely profeffe as now by his hand he fubfcribes himfelfe,

Your Servant in all

Chriftian office,

THOMAS FULLER.

To the Christian Reader.

I SHALL *be short in my addresses unto thee; not onely because I know not thy disposition, being a stranger unto thee; but chiefly because I am ignorant of my owne present Condition, remaining as yet a stranger to my selfe. Were I restored to the free use of my Function, I would then request the concurrence of thy thankes with mine to a gracious God the giver, and honourable Persons the dealers of this great favour unto me. Were I finally interdicted my Calling, without hope of recoverie, I would bespeake thy pitty to bemoane my estate. But lying as yet in the Marshes betweene* Hope *and* Feare, *I am no fit subject to be condoled for, or congratulated with.*

Yet it is, I trust, no piece of Popery to maintain that the prayers of others may be beneficial and available for a person in my Purgatorie condition. Which moves me to crave thy Christian suffrages, that I may be ridde out of my present torment on such tearmes as may most tend to Gods glory, mine owne good, and the edification of others. However matters shall succeede, it is no small comfort to my Conscience that in respect of my Ministeriall Function I doe not die Felo de se; *not stabbing my Profession by mine own lazinesse, who hitherto have, and hereafter shall improve my utmost endeavours by any lawfull meanes to procure my restitution.*

When the Priests would have carried the Arke after David, David *forbad them to goe further,* If *(said hee)* I shall finde favour in the eyes of the Lord, hee will bring mee againe, and shew mee both it and its habitation. But if he thus say,

I have no delight in thee: behold here am I, let him doe to mee as seemeth good unto him. *Some perchance would perswade me to have the Pulpit carried after me, along with me to my private Lodgings, but hitherto I have refrained from such exercises, as subject to offence, hoping in due time to bee brought backe to the Pulpit, and endeavouring to compose my selfe to* Davids *resolution. And if I should bee totally forbidden my Function, this is my confidence: that* That great pasture of Gods Providence, whereon so many of my Profession doe dayly feede, is not yet made so bare by their biting, but that, besides them and Millions more, it may still comfortably maintaine,

Thy Friend and servant

in Christ Jesus,

THOMAS FULLER.

A Sermon of Aſſvrance.

2 Peter 1. 10.

Give rather diligence to make your calling and election ſure.

I. Mans life may not unfitly be compared to a Candle. Curioſity may well be reſembled to the *Thiefe* in the Candle, which makes men to ſpend much pretious time in needleſſe diſputes, the concluſions whereof are both uncertaine and unprofitable. The *Schoolemens* Bookes are ſtuffed with ſuch queſtions, about the diſtances and dignities of Angels, as if men were to marſhall them in *Ranke* and *File*, how that heavenly *Hoſte* doe march in glory one before another. When men heare improbable matters from farre Countries related unto them, it is their uſuall Returne, *It is better to beleeve them then goe thither to confute them.* But let us not credit many unlikely-hoods concerning Angels, which the boldneſſe of Schoolmen have obtruded upon us, but rather labour in Gods due time to goe to heaven, there with our owne happy experience to confute them.

II. Well it is ſaid of *Socrates*, that he was the firſt of the *Grecians* which humbled ſpeculative into morall Philoſophy. How well would the paines of that Miniſter be imployed who ſhould endeavour to bring downe and abate many ſuperfluous contemplative Queries into practicall *Divinity!* It were liberty enough if the *Sermons* of all Preachers were bound to keepe Reſidence onely on ſuch ſubjects which all Chriſtians are bound to beleeve and practice for their ſoules health: Amongſt which the Doctrine in my Text, may juſtly challenge a principall part. When *Naomie* heard but the mention of the name of *Boaz*, the *Man*, said [1]shee, *is neere unto us, and of our affinity :* So no sooner doe you heare this Text read unto you, *Give rather diligence to make your calling and election sure,* but every well affected heart is ready to claime blood and challenge right therein. Questions about Angels are neither *kiffe nor kinne* to my soule; but this a precept of that consequence, of that concernment, we all ought to share a part and interest in the speedy and reall practice thereof.

III. Some difference there is betwixt us and the *Romanists* in reading the Text, who following the vulgar Latine adde *per bona opera: make your calling and election sure by good workes.* A clause altogether omitted in our English Translations, because in the Greeke nothing appeares answerable thereunto. Good reason, therefore, that we should correct the transcript by the Originall, and purifie the streame to the clearenesse of the fountaine. God grant that though on these just grounds we exclude good works out of the Text, wee may admit, embrace, and practice them in our lives and conversations.

IV. My Text may not unfitly bee compared to *Ehuds* dagger, short, but sharpe. And although now it be falne into a lame hand, (the unworthynesse of the Preacher in this place,) to manage it; yet inforced with the assistance of Gods arme it may prove able to give the deadly blow to foure *Eglon sinnes,* tyrannizing in too many mens hearts.

1. *Supine negligence in matters of Salvation.*
2. *Busie medling in other mens matters.*
3. *Preposterous curiosity in unsearchable mysteries.*
4. *Continuall wavering, or Scepticalness concerning our* Calling *and* Election.

(1) *Supine negligence* is dispatched in that word, *Give diligence.* This grace of Assurance is unattainable by ease and idlenesse.

(2) *Busie medling* in other mens matters is destroyed in the Particle *Your.* Each one ought principally to intend his owne *assurance.*

(3) *Preposterous curiosity* is stabbed with the order of the

---

[1] Ruth 2. 20.

words, *Calling and Election*, not *Election and Calling*. Men must first begin to assure their *Calling*, and then *ascendendo* argue and inferre the assurance of their *Election*.

(4) *Continuall wavering* is wounded under the fifth ribbe, in the conclusion of my Text, *Sure*. Wee will but touch at [the] three first, and land at the last, as the chiefe subject of our ensuing Discourse.

v. This *Grace of Assurance* is not attainable with ease and idlenesse. Christianity is a laborious Profession. Observe Gods servants cleane through the Scripture resembled to men of painefull vocations: To *Racers*, who must stretch every sinew to get first to the Goale: to *Wrestlers*, a troublesome emploiment; so that I am unresolved whether to recount it amongst Toiles, or Exercises (at the best it is but a toilesome Exercise): to *Souldiers*, who are in constant *Service* and *dayly Duty*, alwaies on the *Guard* against their Enemies. Besides, we Ministers are compared to *Shepherds*, a painefull and dangerous profession amongst the Jewes; to *Watchmen*, which continually wake for the good of others. So that besides the difficulties of our Christian calling, we are incumbred with others, which attend our Ministeriall function. Let none therefore conceit that Salvation with the Graces accompaning it (whereof this *Assurance* we treat of is a Principall) is to be compassed with facility, without constant care and endeavour to obtaine it. How easily was the man in the Gospell let downe to our Saviour in the house, whilst foure men for him uncovering the roofe thereof let him downe with cords lying quietly on his couch! Some may suppose that with as little hardship they may bee lifted up to heaven, and that whilest they lazily lye snorting on their beds of security (never mortifying their lusts, never striving for grace, never struggling against their corruptions) they shall bee drawne up to happinesse, or it let down to them, merely by the cords of Gods mercy and Chrifts merits. Such men without amendment will one day finde themselves dangerously deceived, and that it is a laborious taske to gaine either the sureneffe or assurance of salvation, wherein, according to the Apostles prescription, *wee must give diligence*.

VI. *To make your.*) Each Chriftian is principally to endeavour the Affurance of his owne Calling and Election. Indeed it were to be wifhed that Parents, befides themfelves, were affured of the true fanctity (fo by confequence of their Calling and Election) of themfelves multiplied, the children God hath given them; of the fecond part of their felves lying in their bofome, their wives, of true grace in their friends and family. How comfortable were it, if Minifters were afcertained of true grace and pietie in the breafts and bofomes of the people committed to their charge! But the beft way to paffe a rationall verdict on the fincerity of fanctity in another, is firft to finde an experimentall Evidence thereof in ones own heart. A Phylofopher complained that it was an exceeding hard thing to find a wife man. *True*, faid another; *for he muft bee a wife man that feekes him, and knowes when he hath found him;* and hence arifeth the difficulty, becaufe two wife men in effect muft meet together, the *Seeker*, and the *Finder*. It is a hard thing in like manner to bee affured of unfained faith and undiffembled Devotion in another mans heart. Becaufe firft, that party muft have a feeling of the operation of grace in his owne foule (otherwife blinde men are incompetent Judges of colours) before he can make his prefumptions of holineffe in another from thofe facred fymptomes and fruits of piety which he findes in his owne Confcience. Let it therefore be every mans maine worke, firft to make a fcrutiny in his owne foule, to make his own *Calling* and *Election* fure.

VII. How contrary is this to the common practice of moft in the world! It is a tale of the wandring Jew, but it is too much truth of too many wandring Chriftians: whofe home is alwaies to bee abroad: Proffeffours in fpirituall Palmeftry, who will undertake to read the *Life-line*, the line of eternall life, in the hands of mens foules; though for all their skill they often miftake the hands of *Efau* for the hands of *Jacob*, approving many hypocrites for their holineffe, and condemning fincere foules for counterfeits and diffemblers.

VIII. *Calling* and *Election*.) Men are not to lanch into the Depths of Predeftination at the firft dafh, but firft foberly to begin with their *Calling* or *Vocation*. Surely the very Angells which climbed up the ladder in *Jacobs* ¹dreame did firſt begin at the laſt and loweſt Round. Firſt, looke to finde thy juſtification and ſanctification; then thy adoption and vocation; laſtly, thy election and predeſtination. But alaſſe! as the *Hebrews* read their letters backward: ſo it is to be feared that too many prepoſterouſly invert the order of my Text, and inſtead of Calling and Election, read Election and Calling; firſt graſping at thoſe myſteries (both in their practiſe and diſcourſe) which are above their reach, as if their ſoules feared to be runne a-ground if ſailing in the ſhallows of Faith and good workes, they never count themſelves ſafe but when adventuring in thoſe ſecrets wherein they can finde no bottome.

IX. We are now come to the youngeſt part in the Text, to which we intend a *Benjamin's* portion. Being to diſcourſe of the certainty of *calling* and *election*, not in reſpect of Gods predeſtination, it being from all Eternity ſure in him (²*from the beginning of the world God knoweth all his workes*), but in reference to man's apprehenſion concerning the aſſurance thereof. And now leaſt our diſcourſe, like ³*Jordan* in the firſt *moneth*, ſhould over-flow, wee will raiſe theſe Bankes to bridle it, and conſider:

1. That aſſurance of *Calling* and *Election* is feaſible in this life to be attain'd.
2. What this aſſurance is.
3. How a Chriſtian buckleth and applieth it to his ſoule.
4. Wee will ſatisfie ſome doubts and difficulties in this behalfe.
5. Wee will conclude with comfortable uſes to all ſorts of Chriſtians.

X. Of the firſt. That aſſurance of ones *Calling* and *Election* may, without any miraculous revelation, be in this life acquired, appeareth plaine in the Text; becauſe the *Apoſtle* in the ſimplicity of the *Dove*-like Spirit exhort's us to the attaining thereof. Now ſurely it had been no better than *holy fraud* (which heaven hath a *Pillorie* to puniſh) to put men upon a *labour in vaine*, to ſeeke that which is not to be found.

---

¹ Gen. 28. 12. ² Acts 15. 18. ³ 1 Chro. 12. 15.

Thinke not therefore that the assurance of *Calling* and *Election* is like the Philosophers *stone*, which so many have searched for, yet all have lost their estates before they could find it out; but no doubt by God's blessing it is in this world attainable. And yet the *Papists* maintaine that whilest wee live in this world and faile in our desires and affections to the rich *Indies* of Heaven and happinesse, no further Land is discoverable beyond the *Cape of good hope*, and that it is arrogancy and presumption (without an immediate expresse by revelation from Heaven) for any to conceive himself assured of his salvation.

XI. For the second, this assurance of ones *Calling* and *Election* is a (separable) fruit or effect, not of every true, but only of some strong Faiths, whereby the party is perswaded of the certainty of his Calling and Election. I say separable, to manifest my dissenting from such worthy Divines who make this Assurance to bee the very Being, Essence, Life, Soule, and Formality of Faith it self. Whence these two Opinions, as false as dangerous, must of necessity bee inferred: First, that every one who hath true faith, and are eternally to bee saved, have alwaies some measure of this Assurance. Secondly, that such who are devoid of this Assurance are likewise deprived of all sincere faith for the present. But God forbid any Preacher should deliver Doctrines so destructive to Christian comfort on the one side, and advantagious to spirituall Pride on the other. Such will prove *Carnificinæ*, the racks and tortures of tender Consciences. And as the [1]carelesse Mother kill'd her little childe, for she overlaid it; so the weight of this heavie Doctrin would presse many poore but pious soules, many faint but feeble infant-faiths, to the pit of Despaire, exacting and extorting from them more than God requires, that every Faith should have assurance with it, or else be uneffectuall to salvation. No; the formality of Faith consists in mans renouncing and disclaiming all sufficiencie in himselfe, casting, rolling, and relying his soule totally and entirely on the mercies of God and merits of Christ, though not assured sometimes of the certainty of his salvation. Like a man in a tempest cast out of the ship, and lying on a planke

---

[1] 1 Kings 3. 19.

or board, placeth all his humane hopes on that planke or board, thereby to escape drowning, though he have no certainty that the same shall bring him safe to the shore.

XII. As for those reverend Divines who have written and maintained the contrary, that Assurance is the very soule of faith, and faith dead and uselesse without it: far be it from me, because dissenting from their opinions, to raile on their Persons, and wound the memories of those which are dead with opprobrious termes. Rather let us thank God for their learned and religious writings left behinde them, knowing that the head of the knowledge of this Age stands on the shoulders of the former, and their very errors have advantaged us into a clearer discovery of the truth in this particular.

In the next place: a Christian thus collecteth this *Assurance* of his *Calling and Election* by composing this practicall *Syllogisme* in his soule.

The Major: *He that truely repenteth himselfe of his sinnes, and relyeth with a true faith on God in Christ, is surely Called, and by consequence Elected before all Eternity to be a vessell of honour.*

The Minor: *But I truely repent my selfe of my sinnes, and rely with a true faith on God in Christ.*

The Conclusion: *Therefore I am truly Called and Elected, &c.*

The *Major* is the *sense of the Scripture* in severall places, the very effect of Gods promises, and the generall scope of the Gospell: so that if Satan should be so impudent as to deny the truth of this Proposition, he may be beaten with that weapon whereat once he challenged our Saviour, *It is written.*

XIII. All the difficulty is in the *Minor*. Happy that man, blessed that woman, who without self-delusion, without flattering their owne soules, can seriously make this Assumption, *But I, &c.* For such I dare be bold to make the Conclusion; yea, it makes it selfe for them without my Assistance. But alasse! many out of fearefulnesse dare not make this *Minor*, conceiving this Assumption to bee presumption in them. And although they might truely doe it (being in a better condition then they conceive themselves), yet overwhelmed with the fenfe of their finnes and Gods feverity they affume the contrary, and, poore foules, often apprehend and conclude their owne damnation in their wounded confciences: whereas others with a more dangerous miftake of common illuminations for difcriminating grace, falfely make the *Minor*, and caufelefly inferre their bleffed condition without juft ground for the fame. Such few as goe rightly to worke doe produce thefe three witneffes, to affert the truth of this *Minor* propofition:

xiv. Firft, the teftimony of their Confcience, that Atturney Generall to the King of heaven, whofe Yea or Nay ought to bee more with us then all the Oathes in the world befide. One knoweth whom it is that he loveth and whom he loveth not, whom it is he trufteth and whom he trufteth not; and in like manner his Confcience tells him whether he doth or doth not truely repent, whether feemingly or fincerely he cafteth himfelfe on God in Chrift.

xv. Secondly, the witneffe of the holy Spirit in their hearts, [1]*which beareth witneffe with their Spirit, that they are the children of God.* Now wee muft with forrow confeffe that this doctrine of the Spirit dwelling in the heart of Gods fervants is much difcountenanced of late, and the Devill thereupon hath improved his owne intereft. To fpeake plainely, it is not the fierceneffe of the Lion, nor the fraud of the Fox, but the mimicalneffe of the Ape, which in our Age hath difcredited the undoubted Truth. But what if the Apes in *India* finding a glow-worme miftooke it to be true fire, and heaping much combuftible matter about it, hoped by their blowing of it thence to kindle a flame; I fay, what if that Animal, γελωτόποιον, that *Mirth-making creature*, deceived it felfe, doth it thence follow that there is no true fire at all? And what if fome Phanaticall Anabaptifts by ufurpation have intitled their braine-ficke fancies to be fo many illuminations of the fpirit, muft we prefently turne [2]*Sadduces* in this point, and deny that there is any fpirit at all? God forbid. We confeffe the Apoftles in the Primitive Church were our elder

---

[1] Rom. 8. 16.   [2] Acts 23. 8.

bretheren, and with *Isaac* carried away the inheritance of the spirit in so great a proportion as to be enabled thereby to miraculous operations: Yet so, that wee, (though the yonger bretheren,) the sonnes of *Keturah*, have rich and precious gifts of the spirit bestowed upon us, which at sometime or other, in a higher or lower degree, sweetly move the soule of all Gods servants, and in many of them testifie the truth of that *Minor Proposition*, namely, the sincerity of their faith and repentance.

xvi. The third and last witnesse we will insist on, is that comfort and contentment the Conscience of the party takes in doing good works, and bringing forth the fruits of new obedience. That though hee knowes his best good works are stained with corruptions and many imperfections, yet because they are the end of his vocation, and the Justifiers of his Faith; because thereby the Gospell is graced, wicked men amazed, some of them converted, the rest confounded, weake Christians confirmed, the poore relieved, Devils repining at them, Angels rejoycing for them, God himselfe glorified by them; I say, because of these and other reasons, he doth good deeds with humility and cheerefulnesse, and findeth a singular joy in his soule resulting from the doing thereof. This joy is an excellent witnesse to depose the truth of his Faith and repentance, and to confirme the *Minor* in the former Syllogisme.

xvii. See here though good works on just ground were excluded our Text, yet in due time and their proper places wee have entertained them in our sermon. If good workes offer to crowd into our justification, let us be so bold as to shut the doore against them. But if wee have any to come into our sanctification, thereby also to averre and attest the truth of our Faith and Repentance, let us say to them as *Laban* to *Jacob*, *Why stand yee without? Come in yee blessed of the Lord.* And this joy, conceived from the good workes men doe, is the more pure the more private, the more sincere the more secretly it is carried. I shall ever commend the modesty of *Elisabeth*, who after long barrennesse finding her self with child did not publish her happinesse to the veiw of the world, but hid her self three moneths. If after too long sterility in goodnesse, thou perceivest thy self at last by God's grace pregnant in pious workes, vent not thy good successe in the Market-place; doe not boast and bragge thereof in discourse to others; but bee contented to enjoy the solid comfort thereof betwixt God and thy owne conscience.

xviii. Soe much for the three witnesses to confirme the truth of the *Minor*. All that I shall adde is this: let us who are or should bee schollars take heed, whom our parents or friends have bred at the Fountaines of Learning and Religion till our portions are almost shrunke into our Education; let us take heed least filly simple people who never read *Aristotle's Organon*, never knew how to mould Argument in mood and figure, make this Syllogisme true in their hearts, by their *supernaturall Logicke*; whilest we, with all our wit and unsanctified learning, make at the best but a Solœcisme, and thereby put a dangerous fallacy upon our owne soules.

xix. *Objections:* But heere wee must propound and answer some objections, the resolution whereof may tend both to our instruction and comfort. The first is this: whether all the servants of God now living and in the state of grace, are for the present assured of their *Calling* and *Election*; so that if instantly arrested to pay their *debt* to nature, they are as confident of their souls mounting up to heaven and happinesse as of their bodies falling downe to dust and corruption.

xx. *Answer:* Wee divide the congregation of God's servants now surviving into rankes. First, [1]*Mnasons* old disciples, seniour professors of piety; [2]*Hannah's*, which have lived many yeares in the Temple, *serving God with Fasting and Prayers night and day*. These by frequent acts have contracted a habit of Piety. Grace by custome is made another nature unto them, especially towards the latter end of their liues; partly becauſe their ſoules do steale a Glymps, Glance, or *Pisgah-*sight of heaven through the Clefts and Chinkes of their Age or ſickneſſe-broken-bodies; and partly becauſe, as all motion is ſwifteſt the neereſt it comes to the Center: So they, the neerer they draw by death to heaven, God's Spirit and all goodneſſe groweth more quick and active in them. Of theſe

---

[1] Acts 21. 16.   [2] Luke 2. 37.

wee fay that it is often obferved, God deales fo gracioufly with them as to crowne their endeavors with an affurance of falvation. To fuch I may add thofe whom I may call *young--old-Chriftians*, whofe profeffion of Chrift, though fhort, hath beene thick; though young in yeares, yet they have not onely done, but fuffered for Chrift. Religion hath coft them deare: they have not only been fummered, but wintered in piety, have not onely paffed profperity, but have been acquainted with adverfity therein. Great travelors in Chriftianity, which have *cut the line*, and have paffed the Torrid Zone of Perfecution, and, which is more, of a *wounded confcience*. Thefe alfo God may admit into the former forme, and out of his undeferved mercy reward them with the Affurance of their falvation.

XXI. But all ftarres which fhine in heaven are not of the firft greatneffe; neither are all of *David's* worthies to bee equalled with the firft three. Other Chriftians there are (who in God's due time may mate the former both in grace and glory), Punies in piety, Novices in Religion: Of fuch I fay, not one of a hundred (whatfoever they may erroneoufly pretend to the contrary) are affured of their *Calling* and *Election*.

XXII. If further it be demanded whether every Saint of God belonging to Election hath not at one time or other in his life, or at his death, this affurance conveyed into his foule, I muft confeffe that heerein the ftreames of learned mens judgements runne not onely in different, but contrary channells. Some are of opinion that God is fo gracious, and magnifies his mercy fo much in his proceedings towards his fervants, that the very meaneft in the *Family of Faith* have fome proportion of this affurance conferred upon them during their abode in this life. Other Divines, no whit inferiour to the former in number, Learning, Religion, and Chriftian experience, maintaine the oppofite opinion: that God fometimes is fo pleafed to try the patience and humble the hearts of fome of his fervants that a continuall feare is a conftant *covering of their eyes: they goe heavily all the day long*, never daring for feare of prefumption to owne and acknowledge any grace in their hearts; alwaies jealous of their owne condition, and sadly suspitious of themselves, least all their holinesse prove hypocrisie, and their Piety be more in profession then sinceritie. Those may be compared unto children in their Mothers belly, which have true life in them, and yet themselves doe not know that they live. For my owne part, I conceive this controversie can onely bee decided betwixt God and a mans own Conscience: no third Person can be privie to the secret transactions betwixt them. The last of these two Opinions (so farre as one may conjecture) hath most of charity, and not the least of truth in it. I am perswaded that many a pious soule, dying in the fit of a temptation, hath instantly expected to sinke from his death-bed into hell-fire, when the same by Gods goodnesse hath beene countermanded a contrary way, and sent to blisse and happinesse. Yea, it is more then probable that many sad and afflicted spirits have beene possessed of glory in heaven before they durst ever owne that themselves had any true *Grace* on earth.

XXIII. The next question which comes to be resolved is, whether this assurance once possessed may not afterwards be forfeited. Here the controversie is not whether once the childe of God may relapse into the state of damnation, totally and finally losing all saving *Grace* in his heart, (which desperate Position cuts asunder the sinewes of all Gospel-comfort,) but it is onely enquired into whether the apprehension or *Assurance of his calling* may not in some cases be lost. Wherein our answer is affirmative; and this usually comes to passe on these two sad Occasions:

XXIV. First, when the Party commits some Consciencewasting sinne, such as *Tertullian* tearmes [1]*Peccatum devoratorium salutis;* and continues in the same some season without repentance. Indeed every surreptitious sinne, or sinne of infirmity, and especially a complication of many of them together, have a good minde to destroy this *Assurance*. But it is seldome seene that their strength is so great (though they frequently fret and dayly nibble at the cordes of our Assurance) as to share or grind them asunder, a thing usually done by the committing of high and heinous offences. There is a whirle-

---

[1] [*De Idolatria*, ed. Lut. Paris., fo. 1641, pag. 104 *c*.]

winde in the *West-Indies* called a *Herricane*, which comes but seldome, and yet too often. For then Rasor-like it shaves downe all levell and flat before it, Trees, and Townes, and Towres; in a word, it is as wild and savage as the Natives of the Countrey. No lesse the impetuous violence and cruelty of a Conscience-wasting-sinne: such as *Lots* Incest, *Davids* Adultery, *Peters* deniall; when they come they make a depopulation of all *Graces* formerly planted in the soule; maiming the hand of Faith, breaking the Anchor of Hope, quenching the beate of Charity, darkning the light of knowledge, and totally taking away for a time the comfortable apprehension of Gods love to them, and their calling to God. This made *David* petition to God, *Restore to me the joy of thy salvation*. Wherein three things are implied: First, that once he did possesse that joy: *Restore it*. Secondly, that now hee had lost it: *Restore it*. Lastly, that the losse thereof was not so desperate but with hope by true sorrow to recover this joy: *Restore to me the joy of thy Salvation*.

xxv. The second way to lose this Assurance is by suffering some great affliction above the standard and proportion of ordinary crosses; seemingly of a sadder hue and blacker complexion then what usually befall other Christians. In such a case a sorrowfull soule is ready thus to reason with it selfe: Once I conceived my selfe in a happy condition, thinking my selfe estated in the favour of God, truely called and by consequence truely elected to grace here and glory hereafter. But now, alasse! I perceive my selfe utterly mistaken. I built my hopes on a false bottome; I am but a meere formalist, a pretender to piety, yea, a reprobate and cast-away; otherwise God would never afflict me in this fashion, with such hideous and horrible crosses, dolefull tribulations, dismall temptations, so that the brimstone of hell-fire may plainely bee sented therein. Thus holy *Job*, when God discharged whole volleys of Chaine-shot of afflictions against him, *one drew on another*, we find him sometimes venting expressions rankly savouring of despaire; and no wonder if hee began to stagger who had drunke so deepely of the bitter cuppes. And now conceiving our selves in some measure to haue satisfied the most important practicall queries wherewith this doctrine of

Affurance is incumbred, we come to make fome profitable application.

XXVI. The *Græcians* had a threefold Song: the *Old men* fung, *We have beene;* the *middle-aged* men, *We are;* the *young* men, *We fhall be.* This *Song* will ferve to divide my Auditors at this time. Some fing, *We have beene.* There was a happy time wherein wee were afcertained of our *Calling* and *Election,* but now, alaffe poore foules! have loft it. Others fing, *We are* for the prefent in the peacible poffeffion of fuch affurance. Others fing, *We fhall bee* in God's due time: when his goodneffe and wifdome feeth fit, fuch an happineffe fhall bee beftowed upon us.

XXVII. Wee begin with the firft that fing, *Wee have beene.* O that it were in my power as well to help as to pitty you, to amend as to bemoane your condition! It is the greateft mifery that one hath once beene happy. All your Song is a *Burthen.* The beft advice I can prefcribe unto you is this: Serioufly confider with your felves which way you loft this affurance of your *Salvation.* Was it by committing a confcience-wafting-finne? No Divine can commend unto you better or other Phyfick than onely [1]*Remember from whence thou art fallen, and repent and doe thy firft Workes.* And although it may pleafe God in his mercy to forgive thy dayly imperfections and manifold infirmities, on thy generall repentance and quotidian prayer, *and forgive us our trefpaffes,* yet the moft comfortable courfe and fureft way to obtaine peace of confcience, after the committing of an hainous offence, is by particular humiliation for it; without which ferious forrow folide comfort is either never given or not long enjoyed.

XXVIII. But if thou haft forfeited thy former affurance thorough the preffure of fome heavy affliction, learne and labour to rectifie thy erronious judgement, who from the premifes haply of God's love, at the worft of his anger, hath falfely inferred a conclufion of his hatred againft thee. Confider how God corrects thofe whom hee loves moft, to the

---
[1] Revel. 2. 5.

intent that all grace may bee encreased and improved in them. [1]Passing by on a night in the streets, I met a youth having a lighted linke in his hands, who was offended thereat, becaufe it burnt fo dark and dimme; and therefore the better to improve the light thereof, he beat, bruifed, and battered it againft the wall, that the wieke therein might be fpread out, and the pitch with other combuftible matter (which before ftifled the light with its over-ftiffneffe) might be loofened; which prefently caufed the linke to blaze forth into a lighter flame. God in like manner deales with thy foul: that thou mayeft fhine the brighter before men hee doth buffet and afflict thee with feverall temptations, which give thee occafions to exercife thy graces which lay hid in profperity. Such corrections will in conclufion greatly adde to thy fpirituall light and luftre. Apply thefe and the like confolations to thy foule, and remember what *David* faith, *Heavineffe may endure for a night, but joy cometh in the morning.* Yea, but you will fay, my night of forrow is like the nights in *Greene-Land*, which laft full four moneths together. A long night I muft confeffe; but day will dawne at the laft, and laft the longer for it.

xxix. Come we now to thofe that fing *Wee are*, who doe not boaft, (that is a bad figne,) but rejoyce that for the prefent they are poffeffed of this affurance. And is it fo indeed? And doeft thou not deceive thy felfe, beholding thy condition through a flattering glaffe or falfe fpectacles? Well if thou affirmeft it, I dare not deny it. It were no manners nor charity in mee to give thy beliefe the lie; and therefore what you fay of your felves, I give credite thereunto. Onely let me ftay a little and congratulate your happy eftate. *Good fucceffe have you with your honour.* God hath not dealt thus with every one, neither have all his fervants fo large a proportion of his favour. And now I will take the boldneffe to

---

[1] [This paffage is to be found in John Spencer's Folio *Storehoufe of Similies*, 1658, No. 890, page 227. *Wick* is fpelled *weike*; "a lighter flame" is printed "a brighter flame"; and the conftruction of the extract is otherwife altered. The paffage is faid by Spencer to be "the obfervation of an *excellent Preacher* yet living," adding in his margin: "T. F. in *A Ser. of Affurance*." He quotes from S. Greg. Mag. in *Moralia Iob*. (on chap. xxxvi. 15, vol. ii. col. 671 *f*, ed. fo. 1615, Antwerp): *Aurem cordis tribulatio aperit quam fæpe profperitas claudit.*]

commend some counsell unto you. In the first place, be thankefull to God for this great courtesie conferred upon thee; and know, that all heavenly gifts, as they are got by Prayer, are kept, confirmed, and increased by Praises.

xxx. Secondly, take heed of insulting over such as want this assurance: upbraid not them with their sad condition. Say not unto them, I am certaine of my *Calling and Election; Ergo,* I am a Saint, a chosen vessell, eternally to bee saved: Thou lackest this certainty, therefore art a reprobate, a cast away, a fire-brand of Hell, eternally to bee damned. Is this the expression of thy gratitude to God, proudly to trample on his servants, and thy brethren? It is hard to say whether that thy inference hath more of profanenesse or falsehood in it. If a Favourite to a great Emperour should say, *All that are not in as high esteeme and credit with the Emperour as my selfe, are so many Traitours;* would not this be accounted not only a vaine-glorious expression, but injurious both to his soveraigne and fellow-subjects? How many thousands of them would be willing, yea, desirous, to adventure their lives in a lawfull cause for their Emperours honour, who notwithstanding never had the favour to bee personably known unto him, much lesse to be preferred by him to places of eminent trust and command? And may not many be presumed on as cordially affected to Gods glory, which from their hearts love and honour both him and his, compleatly loyall to his heavenly Majesty, who have not as yet been advanced so high, and ingratiated so farre with him as to receive the *Assurance* of their *Calling and Election?*

xxxi. Thirdly, walke humbly before God, and know that this Assurance hath a narrow throate, and may be choaked with a small sinne, if God leave thee to thy selfe. There be two kindes of poyson; the one hot, the other cold. Hot poyson makes speedy dispatch; it sends men post to their graves: Cold poyson is not so active and operative, it kills but at distance; and if in any reasonable time it meets with a seasonable Antidote, the malignity thereof may be prevented; yea, perchance without an Antidote, if falling upon a strong and sturdy constitution, may be mastered by natures own Cordiall; not finally to destroy, but onely to stupifie and benumme.

Presumption is hot poyson: it kills its thousands; makes quick riddance of mens soules to damnation. Despaire, wee confesse, is poyson, and hath kill'd its thousands; but the venome thereof is more curable, as more colde and faint in the operation thereof. Take heede therefore of presumption, left the confidence of the *Assurance of thy Calling* betray thee to spirituall Pride, that to Security, that to Destruction.

xxxii. Here take notice that the soule of a Saint consists of sacred riddles, and holy contradictions: *Rejoyce* (saith [1]*David*) *before him with trembling*: if rejoycing, how can hee tremble? if trembling, how can hee rejoyce? Oh, that is an unhappy soule which cannot find an expedient betwixt these extremities! that cannot accommodate these seeming contrarieties: *Rejoycing*, when he lookes on a gracious God; *trembling*, when he beholds a sinfull selfe: *Rejoycing*, when looking upward on Gods promises; *trembling*, when looking downwards on his deserts. Ever *triumphing* that hee shall be saved; and ever trembling lest he should be damned: ever certaine that he shall stand; and ever carefull leaft he should fall. *Tantus est gradus certitudinis*, (saith Saint *Augustine*,) *quantus est gradus sollicitudinis*. He that hath much feare to offend God hath much certainty to continue in his favour: he that feares little, hath little certainty; and he that is altogether feareleffe, whatsoever he proudly presumes to the contrary, hath no assurance at all to persevere in Gods favour. Wee may observe that such as have the shaking Palsie in their heads live to be very aged men: sure I am, that such as have a filiall feare to incurre their heavenly Fathers displeasure hold out to the last, even to that life which hath no end. The heavens themselves are said to have *Motum trepidationis;* and the best and most spirituall servants of God constantly feele such trembling fits in their owne souls. In a word, Assurance to persevere is a sparkle of heavenly fire, fed with the dayly tinder of feare to offend God.

xxxiii. Nor let any confidently presume on the mysterie of predestination, (which like the Lawes of the *Medes* and *Persians* cannot be repealed,) thereon to sinne with indempnity;

---

[1] Psal. 2. 11.

becaufe once and ever Gods fervant, and no feare finally to fall from him. For, befides other anfwers to quell their pride, let fuch ferioufly confider but this particular inftance. God granted *Hezekiah* a Leafe of his life for fifteen yeares longer; and it was impoffible for him to dye till that tearme was expired; fo that had *Hezekiah* fed on Toades and Vipers, on the moft noxious food for mans nature, he was notwithftanding immortall during the time prefixt; becaufe Truth it felfe had promifed it. However if *Hezekiah* proved careleffe in his diet, though certaine of his life, he had no affurance of his health for that feafon. His intemperance might draw fickneffe on him, fo that hee might lofe the life of his life, his liberty of walking abroad, comfort in converfing with company, pleafure in tafting his meate and drinke, to be kept conftant prifoner on his bed, a languifhing as bad as death it felfe. Grant in like manner that Predeftination priviledgeth thee from finall Apoftacie; yet if careleffe to keepe Gods Commandements, thou maift forfeit all thy fpirituall comfort, the *joy of thy Salvation*, have a hell on earth in thy Confcience, having in thy apprehenfion all the beames of Gods favour ecclipfed, one glimps thereof a fervant of God prizeth above millions of worlds.

xxxiv. We come now to thefe that fing, *We fhall be.* It is (fay they) not onely vaine but wicked to feeke to better our conditions by telling a lie. Wee fhould wrong God and our owne confciences to affirme that for the prefent this Affurance is conferred upon us; but are not in defpaire in due time from God's mercy to receive it. Some counfels I have to recommend unto them.

xxxv. Firft, doe not envie and repine at their happines to whom this favour is already confirmed; but becaufe God hath lov'd and honour'd them fo much, doe thou love and honour them the more, and doe defire and endeavour to bee added to their fociety.

xxxvi. Secondly, know to thy comfort that were it not more for Gods glory, and thy good, this Affurance had long fince been beftowed upon thee. And for feverall reafons it is hitherto detained.

1. Perchance becaufe as yet thou haft not fervently fued-to God for it. Thy affections are gold weights, not zealoufly engaged in the defire thereof. Thou feemeft indifferent and unconcern'd whether thou receiveft this Affurance or no. Now God fets fuch an eftimate and valuation on this Affurance, as a grand gift and favour of the firft magnitude, that he will have it fought, and fearched, and fued, and prayed, and preffed for, with holy conftancy and reftleffe importunity, before hee will grant it. *Hannah* called her fonne [1]*Samuel, For* (faid fhee) *I have afked him of the Lord.* Every good thing, temporall, fpirituall, inward, outward, every particular grace muft be a *Samuel,* craved and requefted of God, before the fruition thereof can be fweet to our foules or comfortable to our Confciences. To have a favour before we have requefted it, is the ready way to lofe it, before wee know the true worth and value thereof.

2. Perchance God as yet with-holds this affurance from thee with intent to render it more acceptable when it is beftowed. Never had *Ifaac* beene fo welcome to *Sarah,* but becaufe long barrenneffe and expectation had fet fo fharpe an edge on her affection.

3. It may be God in his Providence forefees, fhould this Affurance be beftowed upon thee, thou would'ft play the unthrift and ill hufband therewith: And therefore God ftill keeps it in his own hand, untill thou beeft more wife and better able to manage and imploy it. The [2]Prodigall Sonne having received his Portion from his Father, riotoufly fpent it amongft Harlots. The fame may be fufpected by thee; and therefore as carefull Parents, jealous of their fonnes thriftineffe, will not deliver unto them all their Meanes at once, but rather confine them for fome yeares to a fmall Penfion and moderate Annuitie, intending to open their hands and enlarge their bounty when they fee caufe; God in like manner will not intruft thee with the groffe fumme of thy Affurance to be paid thee all at once, but retaile it out unto thee, by degrees more or leffe;

---

[1] 1 Sam. 1. 20.   [2] Luke 15. 12, 13.

now a fcruple, now a dramme thereof. And when thou fhalt give good Evidence of thy Chriftian prudence to husband and improve it, the remnant of this Affurance fhall wholly be made over unto thee.

XXXVII. Thirdly, wait and attend the time of God. O *tarry the Lords leafure* (when he will be, he can bee at leafure), who in the moft fitteft minute and moment will confirme this long expected Affurance unto thee. Know this that all the weights and plummets of humane importunity cannot make the Clock of Gods Time ftrike a minute fooner then he hath fet it. No doubt the Virgin *Mary* fhared the greateft Intereft in our Saviour according to the flefh, to obtaine a reafonable requeft of him, and yet could not prevaile for the working of a Miracle before his [1]*houre was fully come.* Wherefore be thou not like to *Hophni* and *Phineas* the Priefts, who contrary to Gods inftitution, when any man offered a facrifice, ufed to fend a fervant, whileft the flefh was feething, with a [2]*Flefh-hooke* of three teeth in his hand, who thrufting it into the kettle, tooke for his Mafters part *whatfoever the Flefh-hooke brought up;* and if any advifed him to ftay till the fat was burnt, according to the cuftome under the law, hee prefently proved impatient; would have no fodden flefh but raw, which if not inftantly given him *he would take it by force.* Now fuch are the ravenous appetites and voracious ftomacks of many men, that when they propound any thing to their defires, they will not ftay till God hath fitted it for them; but by *hooke or by crooke,* by any finifter or indirect meanes they will compaffe their ends. Such will *feed on raw meat* (as if the heat of their ardent defires would roft it enough for themfelves), morfels which perchance fometimes would be pleafant for the Palate to tafte, but never wholefome for the ftomacke to digeft. Thefe are not pleafed, though having what they pleafe, if not alfo when they pleafe: Be not thou of their Diet; know fuch raw meat will occafion crudities in thy ftomacke. Quietly attend till God hath cooked thy meat for thee: thinke not in vaine to antidate; his time is the beft time. Know that gene-

---

[1] John 2. 4.   [2] 1 Sam. 2. 13.

rally the *Watches* of our *desires* goe too faft; and therefore to fet them right, they muft be fet backe according to the *Sunne-dyall* of *Gods pleafure*. Wherefore without any murmuring or repining, doe thou willingly and cheerefully waite the happy time, when God fhall bee pleafed to beftow this Affurance upon thee.

xxxviii. To Conclude with the time. The Schoolemen have a diftinction of a two-fold certainety of Salvation; the one *evidentiæ*, the other *adhærentiæ*: the former is when one evidently and clearely apprehends Gods favour feal'd unto him by his Spirit. This hitherto thou lackeft; but doft diligently labour, dayly pray, and duely wait to receive it. The latter, of adherence or recumbencie, all true Chriftians ought ever to bee poffeffed off which hope for any happyneffe. Namely when a man cafteth himfelfe wholly upon Chrift, clinging about him with *Jobs* refolution, *Though thou killeft mee, yet will I put my truft in thee*. Till we gaine the latter, let us make much of the former, having as much fafety, though not fo much folace in it; and which will with as much certainety, though not fo much comfort, through Gods mercy, bring our foules to heaven and happineffe. *Amen.*

FINIS.

[Pedigree of the Family of Sir John D'Anvers.

SIR JOHN DANVERS, of Dauntefey, Co. Wilts. By right of his Wife, ELIZABETH NEVILL, 3rd dau. and co-h. of Lord LATIMER, he was poffeffed of Danby, Co. York. The granddaughter of his younger brother HENRY became the wife of GEORGE HERBERT. (See Pedigree in *Wiltfhire*: *The Topographical Collections of John Aubrey, F.R.S.,* 1862, p. 217.)

| SIR CHARLES DANVERS, beheaded 1601, for implication in the rebellion of the Earl of ESSEX. | SIR HENRY, Page to Sir P. SIDNEY; Baron DANVERS of Dauntefey, 1603; Earl of DANBY, 1626; K.G.; Died unmar. Jan. 1643-4, æt. 71, the Barony becoming extinct. Left the greater part of his eftates to his nephew HENRY. | (1) MAGDALEN = HERBERT, mother of GEORGE HERBERT. Md. 1609. Buried at Chelfea 8 Jun. 1627. Fun. Ser. by Dr. DONNE. | Sir John Danvers (of Chelfea, Mid., & Weft Lavington, Wilts.), *the Regicide*. Bn. abt. 1574. Dd. 16 or 20 Ap. 1655. Bd. 28 April, 1655. Attainted, 1661. *Sermons*, vol. i. pp. 465, & 495; *Pifgab-Sight*, iii. 352; Aubrey's *Wilts*, p. 226. | = (2) ELIZABETH | = (3) GRACE Hewet. Married 6 Janry. 1648-9. Sole execut x. of her hufband's will. | ELEANOR = THOS. WALMES-LEY, of Dunkelhalgh, Co. Lancafter. Ob. 1640. See Dugd. *Vifit. Lan.* 1665, p. 327. | KATHERINE = Sir RD. GARGRAVE Hunter's *South Yks.* ii. 213. |

daughter and coheir of AMBROSE DAUNTE-SEY, of Weft Lavington. Dd. Apr. 1636.

JOHN, bapt. Chelfea, 10 Aug. 1650.

| CHARLES bapt. at Chelfea, 14 Feb. 1632-3; ob. f.p. 1634. | HENRY, bapt. Chelfea, 5 Dec. 1633; d. 19 Nov. 1654. See *pofted*, p. ccccxciv., and Introd. to Sermon *Life out of Death*, vol. ii. Bur. 12 Dec. 1654. *Pifgab-Sight*, iii. 352. *Cburch-Hiftory*, ix. § 3, p. 101; *Wortbies*, § Wilts, p. 154; Aubrey's *Letters*, &c. | ROBERT (WRIGHT) = ELIZABETH, VILLIERS, alleged fon of VISCOUNT PURBECK; M.P. for Weftbury; took the name of DANVERS. Dd. 1674. | bapt. at Chelfea I My. 1629; coheir of brother HENRY. | Sir HENRY LEE, of = Anne, coheir and fole Ditchley, Oxon. He died before the birth of his 2nd dau. and the mother in childbed of her. M.I. Bur. at Spelfbury, Oxon., 31 March, 1659. | executrix of her brother. Buried at Spelfbury. Oxon. 24 July, 1659. *Cburch-Hift*. Book ix. § 3, 101. |

Earls of ABINGDON.]

A SERMON OF Contentment.

By T. F. *a Minister of Gods Word.*

Phillip. 4. 11.
I have learned in whatsoever state I am therewith to be content.

LONDON.
Printed by *J.D.* for *John Williams* at the Crown in St. *Pauls* Church-yard.
1648.

[*Viator.* . . . . In the mean time *the bleſſing of Saint* Peters *Maſter be with mine.*

Piſcator. And the like be upon my honeſt Scholer. And upon all that hate contentions, and love *quietneſse,* and *vertue,* and *Angling.*

WALTON's *Compleat Angler*, Ed. 1653, page 246.]

[Introduction.

THIS quaint yet admirable difcourfe was, it feems (page 495), preached in the private chapel of Sir JOHN D'ANVERS at Chelfea, where perhaps the former Sermon on Affurance may have been delivered. D'Anvers Houfe, Chelfea (which was pulled down in 1696, the prefent Danvers-ftreet occupying the fite), is faid to have been built on the fite of Sir THOMAS MORE's refidence. AUBREY fays that the chimneypiece in Sir JOHN's chamber was of marble, and that it had formerly been in Sir THOMAS MORE's chamber, "as Sr JOHN himfelfe told me." As was the cafe with the grounds of the Knight's country refidence at Dauntefey Houfe, Weft Lavington, Wilts, his grounds at Chelfea were laid out in a coftly and elegant manner. "Where the gate is now," fays AUBREY of the latter, "adorned with two noble pyramids, there ftood anciently a gate-houfe wch was flatt on the top, leaded, from whence is a moft pleafant profpect of the Thames and the fields beyond: on this place the Ld Chancellour MORE was wont to recreate himfelfe, and contemplate. It happened one time, that a TOM of Bedlam came up to him, and had a mind to have thrown him from the battlements, saying, 'Leap, TOM, leap.' The Chancellour was in his gowne, and befides ancient, and not able to ftruggle with fuch a ftrong fellowe. My L^d had a little dog with him: fayd he, 'Let us firft throwe the dog downe, and fee what fport that will be'; fo the dog was throwne over. 'This is very fine fport,' fayd my L^d, 'fetch him up, and try once more.' While the madman was goeing downe, my L^d faftened the dore, and called for help, but ever after kept the door fhutt." The place has affociations with other celebrated men, a group of whom centred round LADY D'ANVERS and her two accomplifhed fons, the HERBERTS. Dr. JOHN DONNE, 1625, with claffic references to the retired leifure of Cicero, fpoke of the Houfe as his Tufculum. He had been an inmate during a time of general ficknefs not long before Lady D'ANVERS's death. A fecond Lord Chancellor, Sir FRANCIS BACON, often reforted thither. Of him AUBREY thus goffips:—"Sir JOHN told me that when his Lo^p. had wrote the *Hift. of Hen.* 7, he fent the manufcript copie to him to defire his opinion of it before 'twas printed. Qd. Sir John, 'Your Lordfhip knowes that I am no fcholar.' "'Tis no matter,' faid my Lord; 'I know what a fchollar can fay; I would know what *you* can fay.' Sir JOHN read it, and gave his opinion what he mifliked (w^oh I am forry I have forgott) w^oh my L^d acknowledged to be true, and mended it. 'Why,' faid he, 'a fchollar would never have told me this.' ... I remember Sir JOHN DANVERS told me, that his Lo^p. much delighted in his curious garden at Chelfey, and as he was walking there one time, he fell downe in a fowne. My Lady DANVERS rubbed his face, temples, &c. and gave him cordiall water: as foon as he came to himfelfe, fayd he, 'Madam, I am no good *footman*.'" (Aubrey's *Letters*, 462-3, 222, 226). Elfewhere the fame authority gives us to underftand that the purfuit of this favourite "hobby" of ornamental gardening brought on or heightened the extravagance of the proprietor. His brother the Earl of DANBY, in profecution of a fimilar tafte, gave Oxford its Phyfic Garden at a coft of £5,000.

The auditors of this Sermon confifted of D'ANVERS and his houfehold. He himfelf was then a widower, having been wifelefs fince 1636. But he was meditating matrimony with Miftrefs GRACE HAWES, his houfekeeper. The Knight's daughter ELIZABETH was perhaps already married to ROBERT (WRIGHT) VILLIERS, a difreputable man, who reduced his family to want. ANNE, the other daughter, became FULLER's attached friend; and as fuch we fhall meet with her name again in thefe Sermons. HENRY, the only furviving son, already mentioned (page ccclxiv.) as a patron of FULLER's *Pifgah-Sight*, was a youth of a very pleafing difpofition. He died of the fmallpox, 19th Nov., 1654, having juft attained fufficient years to bequeath his large eftates to his fifter ANNE.

The *Sermon of Contentment* is of great rarity. No copy has been preferved in the Britifh Mufeum, the Bodleian, or other large collections; and it has efcaped the notice of Lowndes. The prefent edition is taken from a tranfcript of the copy in Emanuel College, Cambridge, which contains Sancroft's arms, with an infcription: *Ex dono Reverendiss. in Christi Patris WILL. SANC. A. C.* The proof has been compared with another copy, once Mr. PICKERING's, now in poffeffion of E. RIGGALL, Efq., of Bayfwater. The volume is unpaged, the fignatures being A to C in eights, including title D 2 = pp. 52.]

TO

The Honourable
and truly noble
Sr JOHN D'ANVERS
Knight.

SIR,

THIS *smal Sermon may well bee termed* Zoar, *for is it not a little one? Yet it bears good proportion to the short text on which it discourseth, little auditory for which it was composed, and your private Chappel wherin it was delivered. As it is smal, so it desired to be secret, and intended no appearance in publike. Good was the counsel which* Iaash *gave* Amaziah, 2 *Cro.* 25. 19, *Abide now at home, especially in our dangerous dayes, when all going is censurable for gadding abroad without a necessary vocation.*

But seeing such was your importunitie to have it Printed that all my excuses to the contrary which I could alledge with truth, and the delays which I could make with manners, might not prevaile: I have chosen rather to be accounted undiscreet then uncivil, and have yeelded to your desire. Surely, Sir, Heaven can never return a denial to your requests whom I presume, (by proportion of your earnest desiring of so smal a matter,) to be zealous in your desires of hier concernment, that nothing but a grant can give you *satisfaction*. But the *mainest motive, next your importunity, which put me on this publike adventure, was the consideration of my engagements to your noble bounty, above my possibility of deserving it.* The Apostle *saith it is part of the duty of a good servant,* Tit. 2. v. 9. μὴ ἀντιλέγοντας, not answering againe. *I must confesse my selfe your Servant, and therefore it ill beseemed me to dislike or mutter against anything you was pleased I should doe. Thus desiring the continuance and increase of all spiritual and temporal happines on your honour, I commend you to the Almighty.*

T. F.

A
Sermon of Contentment.

1 TIM. 6. 6.

But godlinesse with contentment is great gain.

I. IN the foregoing verse, St. *Paul* sets down the worldlings prayer, creed, and commandements; which is their daily desire, beliefe and practise, and all contained in three words: *Gain is Godlines*. Now in my text St. *Paul* counter-mines their opinion, or raiseth our antiposition to batter down their false conceit, most elegantly crossing and inverting their words: *But Godlines with contentment is great gain.*

II. Take notice of the unaffected elegancy of the Apostle, how clearly and naturally with a little addition, he turns the worldlings Paradox into a Christian truth. Though Sermons may not laugh with light expressions, yet it is not unlawfull for them to smile with delightfull language: Alwayes provided that the sweetnesse of the sawce spoile not the savourinesse of the meat. [1]*The Preacher sought to finde out acceptable or pleasant words*, that so his found matter might be more welcome to his auditors.

III. Well, here wee have two contrary opinions set on foot together: *Gain is godlinesse*, saith the worldling, whose Gold is his god, looking and telling thereof his saying of his prayers. *Godlinesse is great gain*, saith God himselfe, by the mouth of the Apostle. Now as [2]*Peter* in another case, whether it be right to hearken unto man more then unto God, judge yee.

---
[1] Ecclcs. 12. 10.   [2] Acts 4. 19.

IV. 1. The text prefents us with a *Bride*.
   2. *A Bride-maide*.
   3. *Her great portion*.
   4. *The prefent payment thereof*.

(1) *The Bride. Godlineffe*. We need not enquire further into her Pedegree and extraction. She carries her Father in her Name, and relates to God the Author thereof.

(2) *The Bride-maid*. The Virgin her companion that follows her, or her infeparable attendant, Contentment. *Godlineffe with contentment*.

(3) *Her great Portion.* Wherein obferve the rich ware, *Gain*; the large meafure, *Great* gain.

(4) *The prefent payment*. Not in expectances or reverfions; but *down on the naile*, prefently depofited: *is. Godlines with contentment is great gain.*

Wee begin with the Bride; and in the firft place let us put it to the queftion, What godlines is. To which quere feverall anfwers will be made according to mens feverall affections. Afke fome Fryer obfervant what godlines is; and he will tel you, the wearing of a fhirt of hair, girdle of hemp, fafting fo often in the week, praying fo often in the day, with fuch like Canonical devotions. Afk the tenacious maintainer of fome new upftart opinion what godlines is; and he will anfwer: It is the zealous defending with limb and life of fuch, and fuch ftrange tenets, which our fathers perchance never hard of before; yea, which is worfe, fuch a perfon wil prefume fo to confine Godlines to his opinion, as to ungodly all others who in the leaft particular diffent from him. Oh, if God fhould have no more mercy on us then wee have charity one to another, what would become of us? Indeed Chrift tearmeth his own a little flock: [1]*Fear not, little flock.* But if fome mens rafh and cruel cenfures fhould be true, the number of the godly would be fo little, it would not be a flock.

5. It is a true but fad confideration how in all ages men

---

[1] Luke 12. 32.

with more vehemency of spirit have stickled about small and unimportant points then about such matters as most concern their salvation. So that I may say (these sorrowfull times having tuned all our tongues to military phrases) some men have lavished more powder and shot in the defence of some sleight outworks, which might well have been quitted without any losse to Religion, then in maintaining the main platform of piety, and making good that Castle of Gods service and their own salvation. Pride wil be found upon serious enquiry the principall cause hereof. For when men have studied many weeks, moneths, or years, about some additionall point in Divinity, they contend to have the same essentiall to salvation, because it is essentiall to their reputation, least otherwise their discretion be called into question for taking so much pains in vain, and spending so much precious time about a needlesse matter. Hereupon they labour to inhance the value of their own studies, and will have all those mynes gold, which they have discovered; yea all their superstructures must be accounted fundamentall: All their far fetcht deductions and consequential results must be reputed to be immediate and essentiall to godlines; yea, the very life of godlines must be placed in the zealous asserting the same.

6. But it will be the safest way for us to take a description of godlinesse from a pen infallible, impartiall, and unconcerned in our modern distractions. Even from Saint *Iames* himself. [1]*Pure religion* (or godlinesse) *and undefiled before God and the Father is this, to visite the fatherlesse and widdows in their affliction, and to keep himself unspoted from the world.* This setteth forth the practicall part of Religion, and, as I may term it, the heat of godlinesse. To which, if the speculative part, the light of Godlinesse, bee added, [2]*to know the only true God, and Jesus Christ whom he hath sent*, then godlines is made compleat. And godlinesse thus defined admits of a latitude, so that it may consist with some errours in judgement, and infirmities in practise; provided that the godly person persists in Faith, Hope and Charity, which hold out the summe of Religion as to the necessary part thereof.

[1] James 1. 27. [2] John 17. 3.

As for all particular forms of Church Government, Ceremonies and outward manner of divine worship, most of them admitting of alteration upon emergencies, and variation according to circumstances of time, place, and persons, (though these be more or lesse ornamentall to godlinesse, as they neerer or further off relate to divine institution,) yet it is erronious to fixe or place the life or essence of godlinesse therein. Wee conclude this point with the words of Saint Peter: [1]*Of a truth I perceive that God is no respecter of persons; But in every nation he that feareth him and worketh righteousnes is accepted with him:* Yea, in one and the same nation, he that feareth him and worketh righteousnesse of what Sect, Side, Party, Profession, Opinion, Church, Congregation soever he be, is accepted with him, as having true godlines in his heart, *which with contentment is great gain.*

7. Come we now to the Brid-maid attending her: *Contentment*. Contentment is a willing submission of ours to Gods will in all conditions. I say willing; for, if it be patience perforce, *What reward have you? What doe you more then others? Doe not even the Publicans and Sinners the same?* Yea, what doe you more then Mules and Horses, which being kept with Bit and Bridle quietly carry their ryders which they cannot cast off? In all conditions patient in adversity, humble in prosperity, thankfull in both; looking neither above our estates, with the ambitious man, to have it higher; nor beyond it, with the covetous man, to spread it broader; nor besides it with the envious man, repyning at the estate of others: but directly on the Portion God hath given us, and fully satisfied with the same. Even justifying Gods proceedings unto us, though wee receive from him what flesh and blood would count hard measure, namely, if his Divine wisdome should so appoint it, [2]*That with just men we perish with our righteousnesse, whilest wicked men prolong their lives in their wickednes.*

8. Here we must take notice of the conjunction copulative, *with*: Godlines with contentment. Which furnisheth us with two profitable observations:

---

[1] Acts 10. 34, 35.   [2] Eccles. 7. 15.

1. Wherefoever there is true godlineffe there is contentment.
2. Wherefoever there is true contentment there is godlines.

Like *Saul* and *Ionathan*, [1]*lovely and pleafant in their lives, and in their deaths they are not divided.* Thefe twin graces alwayes go together. True it is, that Gods children may often have their fits and qualms of difcontentment, as [2]*Eliah* and *Jonah* had: But this proceeds from the imperfections of grace in them: They are not difcontented as they are godly, but as they have a principle of ungodlineffe in them, the remnant of carnall corruption.

9. On the other fide no wicked man, whatfoever he pretendeth, can have true contentment.

Remarkable it is that in the fame chapter wee finde two brethren laying claim to the grace of contentation, but on different, yea, contrary titles.

Efau faid, *Gen.* 33. 9: *I have enough, my brother; keep that thou haft unto thy felf.* Jacob *faid, Gen.* 33. 11: *God hath dealt gracioufly with mee, becaufe I have enough.* Now *Efau's enough* was indeed not *enough*, being onely a proud and vain-glorious brag, fcorning and difdaining at the firft (till importunity altered him) to receive a guift from his younger Brother, as if it were a difgrace and difparagement to his greatnes to admit of any addition or acceffion of his eftate from his inferiour. *Iacobs enough* was a true and reall acknowledgement of Gods goodneffe to him, refting fatisfied with that portion divine providence had alotted him. Such contentment alwaies gos with godlines, and is great gain.

10. Come we now to the Dowery; and before we defcend to the particulars thereof, take notice in generall of Gods bountifull dealing with his fervants. God might command us to work and give us no wages; and moft juftly enjoyne us to labour all day in his Vineyard, and give us no penny at night. Very good reafon. Why fhould we expect to receive profit by him, who return no profit to him? [3]*When*

---

[1] 2 Sam. 1. 23. [2] 1 Kings 19. 4; Jonah 4. 1. [3] Luke 17. 10.

yee have done all those things which are commanded you, say, Wee are unprofitable servants; wee have done that which was our duty to doe. ¹*Saul* did not give but take a dowry with his daughter; and it is observable that 100 of foreskins onely were required of *David*, but he gave 200 for her. Such was the super-errogation of his valour; love and loyalty, especially when joyned together, never give scant measure. God in like manner might expect that wee should give him a portion for the attaining of godlines: All wee can doe, all wee can suffer, is too little to purchase so precious a grace. Yet see the goodnes of God, who knowing he is to deale with such dull workmen who will take pains no longer then they are paid, whets us on with reward in his service.

11. Here I deny not but it is lawfull to look on those blessings and benefits which God reacheth out to us for his service. Moses *himself had respect unto the recompence of reward.* But two things we must take heed of: First, that wee receive this reward in notion and nature of a meere gratuity, not exactly merited by the condignity of our performances, and onely due unto us by the vertue of Gods free promise, and not our deserts. Secondly, that as we look on the reward, so wee look through and beyond it. It being a good Inn for our desires to bait at, but a bad home for them to lodge in. Let us labour to devest our souls of mercenary thoughts, and learn to serve God for himselfe. Active was the affection of *Sechem* to *Dinah*, as appears by his request to *Jacob* and his sonnes: ²*Let me finde grace in your eyes, and what yee shall say unto mee, I will give. Ask me never so much dowry and gift, and I will give according as yee shall say unto me: But give me the Damosel to wife.* Oh, that our hearts were but wrought to this holy temper, that we should desire godlinesse on any terms, undergo any hardship, though there were neither Hell to punish, nor Heaven to reward. However great is Gods goodnes, who knowing whereof wee are made, and remembring that we are but dust, is pleased to spurre us on in the rase of piety with a reward propounded: godlines with contentment is great gain.

---

[1] 1 Sam. 18. 25.   [2] Gen. 34. 11, 12.

12. So much in generall, That there is a Dowry. Now in particular what is the dowry of godlineſſe? *It is great gain.*

Objection: Great gain? Of what? Let Saint *Paul* himſelf, who wrote this Epiſtle, tell us, when he caſt up his audit, what profit he got by the profeſſion of Piety. [1]*In labours more aboundant, in ſtripes above meaſure, in priſons more frequent, in deaths often.* Where is the gain all this while? Perchance it follows. We will try another verſe: [2]*In journying often, in perils of waters, in perils of Robbers, in perils by mine own Country-men, in perils by the Heathen, in perils in the City, in perils in the Wildernes, in perils in the Sea, in perils amongſt falſe brethren.* Where is the gain all this while? you will ſay: theſe were but the Apoſtles adventures; his rich return (flow but ſure) will come at laſt. Once more we will try: [3]*In wearineſſe and painfulneſſe, in watchings often, in hunger and thirſt, in faſtings often, in cold and nakedneſſe.* The further we go, the leſſe gain we find. *Cuſhai* ſaid unto *David*, [4]May all the Enemies of my Lord the King be as the young man *Abſalom* is! But if this be gain, May all the enemies of God and goodnes have plenty thereof! It will never ſink into a worldlings head that godlineſſe is gain, whileſt the grandees of piety are found ſo poore: *Eliah* begging food of a Widdow; *Peter* without gold or ſilver; our Saviour himſelf not having where to lay his head.

Anſwer: It is confeſt that the doctrine in the text can in no wiſe be made good according to the principles of fleſh and blood. Our Saviour ſaid unto *Pilate*, [5]*My kingdome is not of this world.* So the ſenſe and interpretation of my text is not of this world; is not carnall, but ſpiritual; not temporal, but eternal. This will plainly appear, if theſe two particulars be well weighed:

1. What the world counts gain, is loſſe.
2. What the world counts loſſe, is gaine.

What the world counts gain is loſſe. *For what will it profit a man if he win the whole world, and looſe his own ſoule?* Moſt poore is the condition of thoſe who have plenty of

---

[1] 2 Cor. 11. 23.   [2] Ver. 26.   [3] Verſe 27.
[4] 2 Sam 18. 32.   [5] John 18. 36.

worldly wealth, and are [1]*not rich towards God*. Country people having a peice of light gold ufe to fill the Indentures thereof with dirt, fo to make it the heavier: But wife men wil not take dirt for gold in payment. It feems in like manner that wicked men being fenfible that they want waight in the fcales of the fanctuary ([2]*Tekel, thou art waighed in the ballance and found too light*), of fet purpofe load themfelves with [3]*thick clay*. But all will not make them currant in Gods fight; for [4]*riches availe not in the day of wrath*. They are long in getting with much pains, hard in keeping with much care, quick in loofing with more forrow. Wherefore as the Apoftle menfions [5]*Science falfly fo called*, fo this is gain falfly fo called by men.

13. Secondly, They nicke-name that loffe which is gain in very deed. Such were all thofe fanctified afflictions which Saint *Paul* fuffered. It is confeft that thornes and thiftles had never grown in the world, had *Adam* ftood in his integrity; yet fome of them fince mans fall cannot well be wanted. Holy thiftle (we know) hath a Soveraign vertue, and fweet bryer hath a pleafant fcent. All tribulations are thorns to flefh and blood (the word imports as much); yet as Sanctified to Gods children in Chrift, they become of excellent ufe, increafing their grace here and glory hereafter. Lynnen new wafht though it may dry more by day time, is obferved to whiten more in a fair night: Adverfity fanctified to a Chriftian foule doth more improve the fame in purity and piety then the conftant enjoying of a profperous condition.

14. But we need goe no further for the proof of the great profit gotten by Gods fervice then to the words of the Apoftle: [6]*Godlineffe hath the promife of the life which now is and of that which is to come*. It is reported of *Alexander* that having conquered the World he wept becaufe there was no more left for his valour to overcome: But leaft Gods children fhould have any caufe of difcontentment that their joy may have room enough to dilate it felf in, fee a life and a life, a world and a world, one here and another hereafter, one in poffeffion, another in reverfion alotted unto them.

---

[1] Luke 12. 21.   [2] Dan. 5. 27.   [3] Hab. 2. 6.
[4] Prov. 11. 4.   [5] 1 Tim. 6. 20.   [6] 1 Tim. 4. 8.

15. Come we now to the prefent payment: *is.* Even at this prefent inftant *God hath done great things for us already, whereof we rejoyce.* Excellent is the expreffion of the Apoftle: [1]*Or things prefent, or things to come, All are yours.* Here fome carping curious Criticks may challenge St. *Paul* of impropriety of language; yea, finde both falfe Grammar and Logick in his words: falfe Tenfe, to fay future things are; falf Logick, for how can things to come be ours, which be not? But know, St. *Paul* fpake [2]*with languages more then them all,* and had no need to learn the congruity of conftruction from any other. It is good in law to fay, This reverfion is mine, becaufe the reverfioner is in prefent poffeffion of the right to it, though not of the profit by it; yea, heaven on earth is actually ours already, the poffeffion of a clear confcience, and the fpirit of adoption figns and feals unto us the favour of God, then which, no greater gain.

16. And now as the Eunuch faid to *Philip*, [3]*See, here is water; what doth hinder me to be baptized?* So fay I. Behold, here is a Bride, *Godlines,* ready provided; a bride maid, *Contentment,* ready prepared; the great portion prefently to be paid. What hinders now but the marriage may inftantly proceed, that fo we may be wedded and bedded together? But what anfwered *Philip* to the Eunuch? [4]*If thou believeft with all thine heart, thou maieft be baptifed.* So fay I. If thou loveft this Bride with all thy Soule, counting nothing too dear to obtain her, the marriages folemnities may inftantly goe on. Oh that I had perfwafive eloquence effectually to advance this match! The beft is, what is wanting in mee, the fpokefman, is plentifully fupplyed in her, the bride.

17. But two things we muft beware of. Take heed you miftake not the fhaddow for the fubftance, the picture for the perfon. Saint [5]*Paul* tels us of fome who have the forme of godlineffe, but deny the power thereof. The Poet tels us of many who at firft were fuiters to *Penelope* the Miftreffe, but at laft were married to the Maids which attended her. It

---

[1] 1 Cor. 3. 22. [2] 1 Cor. 14. 18. [3] Acts 8. 36.
[4] Acts 8. 37. [5] 2 Tim. 3. 5.

is to be feared that many who pretend to love godlineffe it felf, fall at laft a courting and woeing of the forme, the meer outfide and garb of Religion, and content themfelves with the fame: wherein an hypocrite may equally, yea, exceed the fincereft Saint and fervant of God.

Laftly, beware leaft thy coveteous heart rather love the Portion then the Perfon, have more minde to the gaine then the godlines. We finde how the next kinfman was very ready to redeem the parcel of *Naomies* land which was his brother *Elimelechs*. But as foon as withall he heard hee muft [1]take *Ruth* to wife, he fell back from his promife and purpofe. Many there be which are very forward to wed the gain, but are utterly unwilling to have the godlines with it. Such a fuiter was *Balaam* himfelfe: [2]*O that I might-dye the death of the righteous, and let my laft end be like his!* who was careleffe to live the life of the righteous. But let us labour to have the fubftance and fincerity of Piety in our hearts, knowing that we are to deale with fuch a God who prefers a dramme of integrity before a pound of profeffion. And if wee acquit ourfelves upright in his prefence, godlineffe with contentment is great gain unto us. I fay godlineffe in generall, not reftrictively ingroffed to fome particular party, but extended according to the dimenfion of charity to all perfons agreeing in the effentials to falvation: [3]*In my fathers houfe there be many Manfions,* as if God had provided feverall repofitaries of happineffe for fuch as differ in fmaller opinions; whileft all agreeing in generall godlineffe may meet in one grand Heaven and place of eternall Felicity.

Amen.

---

[1] Ruth 4. 6.   [2] Num. 23. 10.   [3] Joh. 14. 2.

The
JuST MANS
FUNERAL.

Lately delivered in a Sermon
at
C H E L S E Y,
before several Persons
Of Honour and Worship.

By
THOMAS FULLER.

Printed by WILLIAM BENTLEY, for
John Williams at the Crown in
S. *Pauls* Church-yard.
1 6 4 9.

["Publique Calamities charge every man with a rate of forrow proportionable unto the tenure of his underftanding, put him upon a ferious enquiry of the Caufes and Confequences of them, and exact from him a diligent provifion of meanes to ftop or divert them. Calamity like the *floud* is now *lifted* up above *our Earth*, and hath almoft covered the *higheft Hils* of our temporall felicity. Could our forrow fwell as high as that, the fenfe of our prefent and impending miferies would drowne us. If we fearch into the *Caufes* of them, we fhall find thofe in ourfelves (*our finnes*); their fad Confequences are by fo much the fuperabounding matter of our juft feare by how much they goe beyond our knowledge, nay, even conjecture, and all our power to prevent them: fuch is the inundation of miferies now prevailing over the three kingdoms."—Page 1 of Bifhop Juxon's *Subjects Sorrow: or, Lamentations upon the Death of Britaines Iofiah King Charles, moft unjuftly and cruelly put to Death by His owne People, before His Royal Palace, White-hall.* London, 4to. 1649.]

[Introduction.

A REFLEX picture of the history of the country may be derived from a study of the literary work of FULLER about this time. His *Good Thoughts in Bad Times* was followed in 1647 by his *Good Thoughts in Worse Times*. To this period also belongs his seasonable little book on *The Cause and Cure of a Wounded Conscience*, 1647–49, in which, affected himself with much bitterness of soul, he had, as he says, "written the sweetest comforts I could for others." Then, after an interval, followed *The Just Mans Funeral*, with relation to the death and execution of King CHARLES, on Tuesday, 30th January, 1648-9. It seems that the astounding news of this tragic event reached FULLER when he was preparing his great book on the Worthies of England. His biographer describes his consternation: "Then indeed such an amazement struck the Loyal pious Doctor when he first heard of that execrable Design intended against the King's person, and saw the villainy proceed so uncontroulably, that he not only surceased, but resolved to abandon 'that luckless work,' as he was then pleased to call it. 'For what shall I write,' said he, 'of the *Worthies* of *England*, when this Horrid Act will bring such an infamy upon the whole Nation as will ever cloud and darken all its former and suppresse its future rising glories?'" (*Life*, p. 39). The same authority relates that under the influence of this event FULLER forsook not only his study, but himself also, disregarding his own concerns; "untill such time as his prayers, tears, and fasting, having better acquainted him with that sad dispensation, he began to revive from that dead pensiveness to which he had so long addicted himself" (page 40).

The result of his reflections upon the event was embodied in the present discourse, which is a vindication of Divine Providence in the misfortunes and deaths of the righteous. The event itself is only darkly alluded to, the preacher's relations to the ruling powers, to whom he was indebted for his restoration to the "liberty of prophesying," having led him to speak thus warily. But the references in it cannot be mistaken. The quarto copy of the Sermon noticed page dxii. contains, after the word "Funeral" on the title-page, the words "(vid. K. CHA: 1.)" = (namely, King CHARLES the First), written in a contemporary hand. A pathetic account of the King's death and burial, derived from authentic sources, was penned by FULLER as his "last *devoir* to my gracious Master," in his *Church-History*, Bk. xi. sect. xi. §§ 35 seq., which, in Mr. BREWER's edition, vol. vi. p. 355, is accompanied with Sir THOMAS HERBERT's minute *Memoirs of the last Two Years of Charles the First*.

The call made by the Preacher for "an anniverfary of mourning" (page 528) was perhaps the firft public fuggeftion that was offered for what afterwards became a national faft. The Sermon came from the prefs on the 27th November, 1649, the Britifh Mufeum copy (E. 582. 5) being fo dated. It was perhaps one of the firft of the kind that was printed. Mr. THOMAS CAWTON, fometimes minifter of the Gofpel at St. Bartholomew's behind the Exchange, preached a fermon before the Lord Mayor and Aldermen at Mercers' Chapel, 25 Feb., 1648-9, "not long after the inhumane beheading of His Majefty, for which he was committed Prifoner to the Gate-houfe in Weftminfter;" but it was not publifhed until 1662 (8vo.). JUXON, Bifhop of London, wrote an early (anonymous) fermon, afterwards dated "March 12, 1648," which was (as the very accurate *Catal. of Eng. Writers*, 2nd Ed., Lond. 1668, ftates) printed in "1648." It was entitled *The Subjects Sorrow*, in which "the Divine and Royall Prerogatives, Perfonall Virtues, and Theologicall Graces of his late Majefty are briefly delivered." At the clofe of this difcourfe, the preacher, quoting the faying that the blood of the Martyrs is the feed of the Church, prayed that the Lord would in mercy reftore to His Church "the feed of his Martyr King Charles the Firft unto the Government of thefe Kingdoms, that Religion, Peace, and Liberty, may be reftored unto us" (page 32). In the twelve anniverfary fermons entitled *King Charles His Funeral*, by Dr. THOMAS SWADLIN (4to., 1661), the firft, dated "Anno Dom. 1648" (*i.e.* 1649), was perhaps not then preached or penned. The public anniverfaries grew out of the private obfervance of the day by pious Englifhmen. It is faid of EVELYN that he was ftruck with fuch horror at the King's decapitation that he kept the day of martyrdom as a faft. Neceffarily for a time the fafts were not openly celebrated. On the anniverfary of the event in 1660 PEPYS, before rifing in the morning, fell a-finging Montrofe's verfes on the execution of the King, "and put myfelfe thereby in mind that this was the fatal day, now ten years fince, His Majefty died." Of the next faft, 1661, the fame diarift notes that it was the firft time that the day had been obferved (*i.e.* publicly obferved); and he heard an excellent fermon by Mr. MILLS at St. Olave's, on "Lord, forgive us our former iniquities." On the fame occafion EVELYN mentions that the folemn faft and day of humiliation had been ordered by Parliament to expiate the guilt of the execrable murder of the late King. Dr. NATHANAEL HARDY, in his *Loud Call to Great Mourning*, preached on the anniverfary of 1662 before the Houfe of Commons, fays that fince the event itfelf he had, either upon or near the day, ventured to become a remembrancer of that bloody fact, adding that he had "now lived to fee an Yearly Faft enjoyned upon that doleful day."

Chelfea, which is connected with FULLER's remarkable difcourfe, was at the period in queftion a refort for fome of the London Merchants and members of the Nobility. The Countefs of DERBY, *e.g.*, made it her refidence when the Houfe of Lords gave her leave to dwell there, 9th July, 1647 (*VI. Report Hift. MSS. Commiffion*, page 186). With the ALSTON family, who had a houfe at Chelfea, FULLER was intimate, as alfo with Dr. HAMEY, the pious Phyfician whofe name is connected with its

The Just mans FUNERAL.

Lately delivered in a
SERMON
At
CHELSEY,
before several Persons of
Honour and Worship.

By
Tho. Fuller.

LONDON.
Printed by *J. C.* for *J. W.* and *G. E.*
and are to be sold at the golden
Ball in Aldersgate-street. 1652.

church, and with St. Clement's Eaftcheap. Here, too, as has been feen (pages cccclxii., ccccxciii.), dwelt the family of Sir JOHN D'ANVERS, who in the height of the proceedings againft the King was marrying his third wife. Individuals belonging to thefe and other houfeholds were the "Perfons of Honour and Worfhip" (page 507) to whom the difcourfe was addreffed. According to BOWACK, there were in 1664 not more than thirty houfes in Chelfea. The place had, however, been chofen for that fingular foundation which LAUD derifively called "Controverfy College,",and which the Papifts termed "The Ale-Houfe." It had been ufed as a prifon during the Civil War. The Church, which is dedicated to S. LUKE, was a red brick and ftone edifice fituated near the river.

The Juft Mans Funeral was publifhed *three* feveral times. The prefent text has been fet up from a copy of the firft edition, which was dated 1649, 4to. (pp. ii. + 31), and which is the moft accurate edition. A fac-fimile of the title-page is at page 507. This exemplar-copy, once Dr. BLISS's, is now the property of G. W. NAPIER, Efq., who entrufted it to the Editor. Dr. BLISS has written in it "of THORPE," *i.e.* purchafed from the bookfeller of that name; alfo, "Not in the Bodleian Catalogue, 1843." It has alfo the autograph of "I. BURLEIGH IAMES." Dr. BLISS's ufual marks are found at fignature *B*, before which letter he has added his initial *P*, with "35," *i.e.* perhaps 1835; underneath is "La." The device of the fun and fhield (*poftea*, page 533) is a fac-fimile of the cut at page 31 of this quarto edition.

In 1652 the Sermon was reprinted in octavo, being, it feems, a joint-iffue by two "ftationers," JOHN WILLIAMS, who owned the former edition, and GEORGE EVERSDEN. It was appended (under pp. 193-239, fheets O, P, Q) to the *XII. Sermons* on Chrift's Temptation, which were publifhed by EVERSDEN alone, and which begin the fecond volume of this Collection. The title-page to this edition of the Sermon is fac-fimiled on the former page. The differences in readings are indicated in the foot-notes; but the minor differences, fuch as the *y* termination of nouns, &c., it has not been thought neceffary to note.

In FULLER's lifetime the Sermon was once more iffued by WILLIAMS, viz. in 1660, in the fecond edition of the folio ΘΡΗΝΟΙΚΟΣ· *The Houfe of Mourning . . . in LIII. Sermons*, where it forms Sermon LI., pp. 575-585. It was there printed without careful overfight from a copy of the octavo edition of 1652; and it abounds in errors. Only a few of the variations in reading have been pointed out in the foot-notes (being marked "ed. 1660"); but thefe variations may be quite as much due to negligence as defign. In the 1672 edition of this folio volume of Sermons, *The Juft Mans Funeral* occupies the fame place as before. For FULLER's fecond contribution to this excellent old folio, and for further details of the book itfelf, fee the next volume of this Collection of Sermons under *The Righteous Mans Service to his Generation.*]

The Just Mans Funeral.

Eccles. 7. vers. 15.

All things have I seen in the daies of my vanity: there is a just man that perisheth in his righteousness; and there is a wicked man that prolongeth his life in his wickedness.

1. THE World is a volumne of *Gods* works, which all good people ought studiously to peruse. Three sorts of men are too blame herein. First, Such as observe nothing at all; seeing, but neither marking nor minding the daily accidents that happen; with [1]*Gallio* the secure deputie of *Achaia*, *They care for none of these things.* Secondly, Such as observe nothing observable. These may be said to *weed the world.* If any passage happeneth which deserveth to be forgotten, their *jet memories* (onely attracting straws and chaff unto them) registereth and retaineth them: fond fashions and foolish speeches is all that they charge on their account, and onely empty cyphers swell the [2]vote-books of their discoveries. Lastly, Such who make good observations, but no applications. With *Mary* they do not *ponder things in their heart*, but onely brew them in their heads, and presently breath them out of their mouth, having onely a rational understanding thereof, (which renders them acceptable in company for their discourse,) but never suffering them to sink into their souls, or make any effectual impression on their lives.

---

[1] Acts 18. 17. [2] [note-books.]

2. But *Solomons* obfervations were every way compleat. He mark'd what happened: and well he might, who, advantaged with matchlefs wealth, might make matchlefs difcoveries, and could afford to dig out *important Truths* with mattocks of gold and filver. What he mark'd was remarkable, and what was remarkable he not onely applied to the good of his private perfon, but endeavoured it might be propagated to all pofteritie in the words of my text: *All things have I feen in the dayes of my vanitie: there is a juft man that perifheth in his righteoufnefs; and there is a wicked man that prolongeth his life in his wickednefs.*

3. In the handling of *Solomons* obfervation herein, we will infift upon thefe four parts, to fhew,
(1) That it is fo.
(2) Why it is fo.
(3) What abufes wicked men do } make, becaufe it is fo.
(4) What ufes good men fhould }

Firft, that it is fo: believe *Solomons* eyes, who profeffed that he *faw it*. But here it will be demanded, How came he to behold a *righteous man*? With what [1]care and new *eye-falve* had he anoynted his eyes to fee that which his father *David* (having a more holy, though not fo large a heart) could never difcern? [2]*Enter not into judgement with thy fervant, O Lord: for no flefh is righteous in thy fight.*

4. It is anfwered, Though fuch an one whofe righteoufnefs is Gods-juftice-proof, never was, is, nor fhall be in this life (Chrift alone excepted, being God and man), yet in a Gofpel or qualified fenfe, he is accounted righteous, who, *juxta propofitum jufte vivendi*, is fo *intentionally*; defiring and endeavouring after righteoufnefs with all the might of his foul. Secondly, who is fo *comparatively*, in reference to wicked men, appearing righteous in regard of thofe who have no goodnefs at all in their hearts. Thirdly, righteous *imputatively*, having the righteoufnefs of God in Chrift imputed unto him. Laftly, righteous *inhefively*, having many heavenly graces and holy endowments, fincere, though not perfect, or evangelically

---

[1] rare. [2] Pfal. 143. 2.

perfect *pro hoc statu*, bestowed upon, and remaining within him. Such a *righteous man* as this, Solomon saw *perishing in his righteousness*.

5. But in the second place, it will be inquired, How could *Solomon* patiently behold *a righteous man perish in his righteousness*, and not rescue him out of the paws of oppression? Could he see it, and could he suffer it, and be onely an idle spectator at so sad a tragedie? Did his hand sway the Scepter, and was his head invested with the Crown, contentedly to look on so sorrowfull a fight? Could he onely, as in the [1]*case of the harlots*, call for a sword to kill a child, and not call for it here to defend a *righteous man? He that is not with us* (saith our Saviour) *is against us*. If it hold in private persons, much more in [2]*publick* Officers. They persecute, who do not protect; destroy, who do not defend; slay, who do not save *the righteous man*, who have power and place to do it.

6. It is answered, in the first place, *Solomons* observations were not all confined to his own countrey and kingdom. Though staying at home in his person, his minde travelled into forraign parts, and in the neighbouring countreys of *Egypt, Edom, Syria, Assyria*, &c., might behold the *perishing of the righteous* and long flourishing of the wicked. Secondly, his expression, *I have seen*, relates not onely to his ocular, but experimental discoveries: what *Solomon* got by the help of Historie, Studie, and perusal of Chronicles. He that was skil'd in natural Philosophie from the Cedar to the Shrub, was (no doubt) well versed in all civil occurrences from the Prince to the Peasant, from *Adam* to the present age wherein he lived, so much as by any extant records could be collected. To set humane writers aside, the Scripture alone afforded him plentifull presidents herein. Open the Bible, and we shall find (almost in the first leaf) *just* Abel *perishing in his righteousness*, and *wicked* Cain *prolonging his life in his iniquitie*. To omit other instances, *Solomon*, by relation from his father, might sadly remember how *Ahimelech* the High priest *perished in his righteousness*, with all the Priests, inhabitants of the citie of *Nob*, whilest *Saul* who condemned, and *Doeg* who executed

---

[1] 1 Kings 3. 24.   [2] publike.

them flourished long in their iniquitie. So much for the proof *that it is so.*

Come we now to the reasons *why it is so.* These reasons are of a double nature, some fetcht from Nature, others from Religion. For the present we insist onely on the former, reserving the rest till we shall encounter the *Atheists* in the ¹sequels of our discourse.

7. First, Because good men, of all others, are most envied and maligned, having the fiercest adversaries to oppose them. With the most in the world it is quarrel enough to hate a good man, because he is a good man. ²S. *Paul* saith of himself, ³*I press towards the mark.* And the same is the endeavour of every good man. Now as in a race the formost man who is nearest the mark is envied of all those which come after him, who commonly use all foul play towards him, (justling him on the side, seeking to trip up his heels; yea, sometimes thrusting him forward on the back that so he might fall headlong by his own weight and their violence,) so often cometh it to pass betwixt rivals in the race of honour and virtue. Ill-minded men perceiving themselves quite out--stript by some eminent person who hath got the speed of them, and ⁴dispairing fairly to overtake him, resolve foully to overturn him, by all means possible contriving his destruction.

8. Hence comes those many millions of ⁵devises and ⁶strategems contrived for his ruin, endeavouring either to

Divert him from } his righteousness.
or Destroy him in }

If the first takes no effect, and if his constancie appears such as *without* ⁷*regreet* he will persist in pietie, leaving them no hope to *byass* him to base ends, then dispairing to *bow him from,* they contrive to *break him in his righteousness.* Thus whilest he hath many enemies which conspire his destruction, seeking with power to suppress, or policie to supplant him; the wicked man, on the other side, hath the

---

¹ sequele. ² Saint *Paul.* ³ Phil. 3. 14. ⁴ despairing.
⁵ divices. ⁶ stratagems. ⁷ *regret.*

generalitie of men (the moſt being bad as himſelf) to befriend him: a main cauſe of his prolonging himſelf ſuccesſfull in his wickedneſs.

9. Secondly, *Righteous men periſh in their righteouſneſs*, becauſe not ſo warie and watchfull to defend themſelves in danger, being deaf to all jealouſies and ſuſpitions, over-confident of other men, meaſuring all others by the integritie of their own intentions. This makes them lie at an open guard, not fencing and fortifying themſelves againſt any ſudden ſurpriſal, but preſuming that deſerving no hurt none ſhall be done unto them. Thus *Gedaliah*, [1]governor of the remnant of the *Jews* after the captivitie, twice received the expreſs intelligence of a conſpiracie to kill him, yet was ſo far from giving credit that he gave a ſharp reproof to the firſt diſcoverer thereof. Yea, when *Johanan* the ſon of *Kareah* tendered his ſervice to kill *Iſhmael*, (ſent, as he ſaid, from *Baalis* king of *Ammon* to ſlay *Gedaliah*,) *Gedaliah* rejoyned, [2]*Thou ſhalt not do this thing, for thou ſpeakeſt falſly of Iſhmael*. His noble nature gave no entertainment to the report till he found it too late to prevent it. Whileſt wicked men, partly out of policie, more out of guiltineſs, ſleep like *Hercules* with their club in their hand, ſtand always on their guard, are jealous of their very ſhadows and appearances of danger: a great cauſe of their ſafety and ſucceſs, prolonging themſelves in their wickedneſs.

10. Thirdly, *They periſh* becauſe of a lazie principle which hath poſſeſſed the heads and hearts even of the beſt men, (who are unexcuſable herein,) namely, that God in due time will defend their innocence; which makes them more negligent and remiſs in defending themſelves. As the Prophet makes mention of [3]*a ſtone cut out without hands*, they conceive their cauſe will without mans help hew its own way through the rocks of all reſiſtance; as if their cauſe would ſtand Centinel for them, though they ſlept themſelves; as if their cauſe would fix their Muskets though they did it not themſelves. Thus the *Chriſtians* in their battels againſt the *Turks*, having *wonne the day* by their valour, have *loſt the night*

---

[1] governour.   [2] Jer. 40. 16.   [3] Dan. 2. 34.

by their negligence; which principally proceeded from their confidence that God, interested as a Second in every just cause, was in that quarrel concerned as a Principle, and it could not stand in his justice to suffer it to miscarrie.

11. Whereas, on the other side, wicked men use double diligence in promoting their designs. If their lame cause lack leggs of its own, they will give it wings from their carefull soliciting thereof, and will soulder up their crackt title with their owne industrie. They watch for all tides, and wait for all times, and work by all wayes, and sail by all winds; each golden opportunity they cunningly court, and greedily catch, and carefully keep, and thriftily use: in a word, *they are wiser in their generation [1]than the children of light.*

12. This may be perceived by the parallel betwixt the wife and the harlot: many wives (though herein they cannot be defended) knowing their husbands obliged in conscience to love them by [2]virtue of their solemn promise made before God and the congregation at their marriage, are therefore the less carefull to studie compliance to their husbands desires. They know their husbands, if wronging them, wrong themselves therein; and presuming themselves to deserve love as due unto them for their honesty and loyalty of affections, are the less follicitous to gain that which they count their own already. Whilst the harlot conscious to her self of her usurpation, that she hath no lawful right to the [3]embraces of her paramour, tunes her self to the criticalness of all complacencie to humour him in all his desires. And thus always those men whose cause have [hath] the weakest foundation in pietie, getteth the strongest buttress in policie to support it.

13. Lastly, the *righteous man*, by the principles of his profession, is tied up, and confined onely to the use of such means for his preservation as are consonant to Gods will, conformable to his word; preferring rather to die many times [4]than to save himself once by unwarrantable ways. Propound unto him a project for his safetie, and as *Solomon* promised [5]to favour *Adonijah*, so long as he [6]*shewed him-*

---

[1] then.   [2] vertue.   [3] imbraces.
[4] then.   [5] favour to.   [6] 1 Kings 1. 52.

self worthie, otherwise *if wickedness were found in him, he should surely die*: so our *righteous man* onely accepts and embraceth such plots to secure himself thereby as acquit themselves honest and honourable: such as appear otherwise, he presently dispatches with detestation, destroying the very motion and mention thereof from entering into his heart. On the other side, the wicked man is left at large, allowing himself libertie and latitude to doe any thing in his own defence, making a constant practice of *doing evil that good may come thereof*.

14. Yea, we may observe in all ages that wicked men make bold with religion; and those who count the practice of pietie a [1]burthen, find the pretending thereof an advantage, and therefore be the matter they manage never so bad, (if possible) they will intitle it to be *Gods cause*. Much was the substance in the very shadow of [2]S. *Peter*, which made the people so desirous thereof as he passed by the streets. And the very umbrage of Religion hath a sovereign virtue in it. No better cordial for a dying cause [3]than to overshadow it with the pretence that it is *Gods cause*. For first, this is the way to make and keep a [4]great and strong partie: No sooner the watch-word is given out *For Gods cause*, but instantly GAD, *behold a troop cometh* of many honest, but ignorant men, who press to be listed into so pious an employment. These may be kild, but cannot be conquered: for till their judgements be otherwise informed they will triumph in being overcome, as confident the deeper their wounds got in *Gods cause* gape in their bodies, the wider the gates of heaven stand open to receive their souls. Besides, the pretending their cause is *Gods cause*, will, in a manner, legitimate the basest means in pursuance and prosecution thereof; for, though it be against Gods word *to do evil that good may come thereof*, yet this old error will hardly be beaten out of the heads and hearts of many men, that crooked ways are made direct by being directed to a streight end; and the lustre of a bright cause will reflect a seeming light on very *deeds of darkness* used in tendencie thereunto.

---

[1] burden.   [2] Saint *Peter*.   [3] then.   [4] good [ed. 1660.]

15. This hath been an ancient ftratagem of the worft men (great Politicians) to take pietie in their way to the advancing of their defigns. Thus *Rabfhakeh* pretended a Commiffion from God for all the wickednefs he committed, and complements blafphemie: [1]*Am I now come up without the Lord againft this place to deftroy it? The Lord faid to me, Go up againft this place to deftroy it.* The Priefts of *Bell* were but bunglers, which could not fteal the meat of their Idol, but they muft be difcovered by the print of their foot-fteps. Men are grown more cunning thieves now adays: firft, they will put on the fhoes of him they intend to rob, and then fteal that fo their treadings may tell no tales to their difadvantage. They will not ftride a pace, nor goe a ftep, nor ftir a foot, but all for *Gods caufe*, all for the good and glorie of God. Thus Chrift himfelf was ferved from his cradle to his crofs; *Herod* who fought to kill him, pretended to worfhip him; and *Judas* kiffed him who betrayed him.

16. By thefe arts and [2]devices it cometh to pafs that wicked men prolong themfelves in their wickednefs. Traiterous *Zimri* indeed continued [3]but feven days; that was not long: wicked *Jehojachin* reigned but three [4]moneths in *Jerufalem;* that was not long: ungodly *Amon* reigned two [5]years in *Jerufalem;* that was not long: idolatrous *Ahab* reigned in *Samaria* twentie [6]and two years; that was indifferent long: cruel *Herod* the King, who fought to kill Chrift, reigned in *Judea* wel-nigh fourtie years; that was long indeed; he prolonged himfelf to purpofe in his iniquitie.

17. Seeing therefore (to recollect what hath been faid) the righteous hath moft foes, the wicked many friends; the righteous free from, the wicked full of [7]jeloufies; the righteous too often over-carelefs, the wicked over-carefull in his defence; the righteous limited onely to lawful, the wicked left loofe to any means for his owne advantage: No wonder if it often cometh to pafs that the *righteous man perifheth in his righteoufnefs, and the wicked prolongeth his life in his wickednefs.*

---

[1] 2 Kings 18. 25.   [2] divices.   [3] 1 Kings 16. 15.   [4] 2 Kings 24. 8.
[5] 2 Kings 21. 19.   [6] 1 Kings 16. 29.   [7] jeloufies.

18. Come we now to the abuſes which wicked men make of the righteous mans periſhing in his righteouſneſs. And here the whole kennel of Atheiſts come in with a full crie (oh that there were no more of them on earth ¹than there are in hell, where torture makes them all ſpeak truth!), ſpending their wicked breath againſt God and his attributes. Some bark at his Providence, as if he perceived not theſe things: ²*How doth God know? and is there knowledge in the moſt high?* Others cavil at his juſtice, that he has no mind; others carp at his ſtrength, that he has no power to rectifie and redreſs theſe ³innormities. This world (ſay they) is a ſhip without a pilot, ſteered onely with the winds and waves of caſualtie; it is a meer *lotterie*, wherein the beſt men daily draw the *blanks*, and the worſt run away with the *prizes*. And, as ⁴*Abſolom* boaſted, if he were king of *Iſrael*, how far he would out-do *David* in right managing of all matters: ſo theſe impudent wretches conceive with themſelves the Plat-form of the world had been more perfect might they have been admitted to the making thereof. The moon would have ſhined without any ſpots; roſes grown without any prickles; fair weather ſhould ⁵have never done harm, becauſe rain ſhould onely fall in the night, neither to hinder the pleaſure of the rich, or hurt the profit of the poor. Merit ſhould be made the onely ſtandard of preferment; no *periſhing of the righteous man in his righteouſneſs*, when ſucceſs ſhould onely be entailed on deſert. In a word, ſuch Atheiſts preſume all things by them ſhould be ſo prudently diſpoſed, that nothing, no doubt, in the whole world ſhould be out of order, ſave themſelves.

19. More might be ſpoken to ⁶highten and ⁷improve the objection, but I am afraid to perſiſt further therein. It is not onely dangerous to be, but even to act an Atheiſt, though with intent to confute their errour, for fear that our poiſons pierce further ⁸than our ⁹antidots. But in anſwere to this objection, know that God, without the leaſt prejudice to his juſtice, may ſuffer *the righteous man to periſh in his righteouſneſs*, becauſe

---

¹ then. ² Pſal. 73. 11. ³ enormities.
⁴ 2 Sam. 15. 4. ⁵ never have. ⁶ heighten.
⁷ prove. ⁸ then. ⁹ antidotes.

allow him righteous *jufticia caufæ*, he is not fo *jufticia perfonæ*, the beft man ftanding guiltie of many faults and failings in his fight. God needs not *pick a quarrel* with any man, having at all times matter of a juft controverfie againft him. And feeing God hath oftentimes connived at him being faultie, he may condemn him being faultlefs; for *nullum tempus occurrit Regi*, the King of heaven is not limited to any time, but at his own pleafure and leafure may take an opportunitie to punifh an offender.

20. Secondly, grant that the caufe of the *righteous man* was juft in the primitive conftitution thereof, yet if it branch it felf forth into numerous circumftances appendant thereunto (many whereof may be intricate and perplext); if it be of fo fpacious and ponderous a nature that it requires many heads and hands as fubordinate inftruments in feveral places for the managing thereof: Laftly, if the caufe be fo prolix and tedious that many years muft be fpent in the profecution thereof; the original righteoufnefs of the caufe may be altered with the handling of it, and much injuftice annexed thereunto; for which God may juftly caufe it finally to mifcarrie. For it is [1]impoffible that a caufe confifting of fuch varietie of limbs retaining thereunto, fhould be carried on without many grand [2]errors and miftakes committed therein; and the righteoufnefs of the beft man will not fpread fo broad without fhrinking, ftretch fo long without tireing, applie it felf fo exactly to each circumftance without fome fwerving therein. Efpecially when all the faults of the inferior officers employed under him are chargeable on the *righteous mans* account, the matter of whofe caufe may juftly perifh by Gods juft anger on the unjuft managerie thereof.

21. Yea, God, without the leaft blemifh to his Juftice, may fuffer the righteous temporally to *perifh in his righteoufnefs*, becaufe in the midft of their fufferings his mercie fupports them with the inward comfort of a clear confcience. In the time of perfecution a woman being big with child was imprifoned and condemned to die, which the night before her execution, was (I cannot fay brought to bed) delivered of a

---

[1] poffible.   [2] errours.

child, when her pain (wanting the help of a midwife) muſt be preſumed exceeding great. The Jailor hearing her cry out in her pangs: *If you cry* (ſaid he) *to day, I will make you ſhreek worſe to morrow, when you are to be burnt at a ſtake.* The woman replied, *Not ſo; to morrow my pain will be abated: for to day I ſuffer as an offender for the puniſhment juſtly impoſed by God on our ſex for our diſobedience and breach of his law; but to morrow I ſhall die for the teſtimony of the truth in the defence of Gods glory and his true Religion.* Thus it is ſtrange to see what alacrity a good cauſe infuſeth into *a righteous man*, deriving comfort into his heart by inſenſible [1]conveiances, ſo that he [2]embraceth even death it ſelf with a ſmiling countenance, feeding his ſoul on the continual feaſt of a clear conſcience.

22. Beſides this, it clears divine Juſtice, and comforts the righteous man *periſhing temporally in his righteouſneſs*, that his Cauſe ſhall be heard over again, and rejudged in [3]an other world. If one conceive himſelf wronged in the *Hundred*, or any inferiour Court, he may by a *certiorari*, or an *accedas ad curiam*, remove it to the *Kings-Bench* or *Common-Pleas*, as he is adviſed beſt for his own advantage. If he apprehendeth himſelf injured in theſe Courts, he may with a *Writ of* [4]*Error* remove it to have it argued by all the Judges in the *Exchequer--chamber*. If here alſo he conceiveth himſelf to find no juſtice, he may with an *Injunction* out of the *Chancery* ſtop their proceedings. But if in the *Chancery* he reputeth himſelf [5]agreeved, he may thence appeal to the *God of heaven and earth*, who in another world will vindicate his right, and ſeverely puniſh ſuch as have wilfully offered wrong unto him. And ſo much to aſſert Gods juſtice in ſuffering the *righteous man to periſh in his righteouſneſs*.

23. Now on the other ſide, God may without any prejudice to his juſtice ſuffer wicked men for a time to thrive in this world, and not ſuddenly ſurpriſe them with puniſhment, ſo giving them [6]*a ſpace to repent*, if they would but make uſe thereof. Indeed *David* ſaith, [7]*Evil ſhall hunt the violent man*

---

[1] conveyances. [2] imbraceth. [3] another. [4] *Errour*.
[5] agrieved. [6] Rev. 2. 21. [7] Pſal. 140. 11.

to overthrow him. But God is a *fair hunter:* he might in the rigour of his juftice knock wicked men down as he finds them *fitting in their forms:* But God will give them *fair law;* they fhall for a time run, yea, fport themfelves before his judgements ere they are pleafed to overtake them.

24. Know alfo, to the farther clearing of his juftice, that wicked men, notwithftanding their thriving in badnefs for a time, are partly punifhed in this world with a conftant corrofive of a guiltie confcience, which they carrie about them. The Probationer-Difciple faid to our Saviour, [1]*Mafter, I will follow thee whitherfoever thou goeft:* what is promifed by him is performed by a guiltie confcience, that *Squire of the bodie,* alwayes officious to attend a malefactour. Faft, and *I will follow thee;* and thy emptie bodie fhall not be fo full of wind as thy mind of difmal apprehenfions: feaft, and *I will follow thee;* and, as the [2]*hand on the wall,* bring in the fad reckoning for thy large bill of fare: ftay at home, and *I will follow thee:* ride abroad, and *I will follow thee;* or elfe meet thee in the way with my naked fword, as the Angel did [3]*Balaam:* wake, and *I will follow thee:* fleep, and *I will follow thee,* and affright thee with hideous fancies and terrible dreams, as I did King *Richard* the third, the night before his death.

25. I have read of one who undertook in few dayes to make a fat fheep lean; and yet was to allow him a daily and large provifion of meat, foft and eafie lodging, with fecuritie from all danger, that nothing fhould hurt him. This he effected by putting him into an iron-grate, and placing a ravenous wolf hard by in another, alwaies howling, fighting, [4]fenting, fcratching at the poor fheep; which, affrighted with this fad found and worfe fight, had little joy to eat, lefs to fleep; whereby his flefh was fuddenly abated. But wicked men have the terrors of an affrighted confcience conftantly, not onely barking at them, but biting of them; which disfweetens their moft delicious mirth with the fad confideration of the fins they have committed, and punifhment they muft undergo, when in another world they fhall be called to account.[5] This

---

[1] Matt. 8. 19.   [2] Dan. 5. 5.   [3] Num. 22. 23   [4] fcenting [ed. 1660].
[5] [This paffage, fiom the beginning of the paragraph, is met with, with a few variations, in Spencer's *Things New and Old,* headed "Confcience fpoils the

thought alone makes their souls lean, how fat soever their bodies may appear. And as sores and wounds commonly smart, ake, and throb most the nearer it is to night; so the anguish and torture of a guiltie conscience increaseth the nearer men apprehend themselves to the day of their death.

26. Now not onely wicked men, but even the children of God, because of the corruption of their hearts, too often make bad uses to themselves *of the righteous mans perishing in his righteousness*. These may be divided into three ranks:
(1) Such as *fret at*
(2) Such as *droop under* } Gods proceedings herein.
(3) Such as *argue with*

The first are the *Fretters*: for if the *perishing of the righteous* cometh to the serious observation of a high-spirited man, one of a stout and valiant heart, he will scarce brook it without some anger and indignation, fuming and chafing thereat. Thus *David*, we know, was a man of valour, of a martial and warlike spirit; and he confesseth of himself, that, beholding the prosperitie of the wicked, [1]*his heart was grieved, and he was pricked in his reins*. Nor was it meer grief possessed him, but a mixture of much impatience, as appears by that counsel which in like case in one Psalm he gave himself three several times: [2]*Fret not thy self because of evil doers; and again, fret not thy self because of him who prospereth in his way; and the third time, fret not thy self in any wise*.

27. Our Saviour observeth that there are a sturdy kind of devils that will not be [3]*cast out*, save *by fasting and prayer*. But this humour of fretting and repining at *Gods proceedings herein*, which he understood not, could not be ejected out of *David*, but by prayer no doubt, and that very solemnly; not at home, but in Gods temple: [4]*When I thought to know all this, it was too painful for me: until I went into the Sanctuarie of God, there understood I their end*. O let [5]men of high spirits and stout hearts not lavish their valour and misspend their

---

wicked Mans mirth," No. 1345, page 376. He gives the reference " T. Fuller on *Christ's Temptat.*," *i.e.* the volume so entitled, to which *The Just Mans Funeral* was appended; and he annexes this parallel passage from Ovid's *Amores*, I. iv. 45: *Multa miser timeo, quia feci multa protervè*.]

[1] Psal. 73. 21.   [2] Psal. 37. 1, 7, 8.   [3] Matth. 17. 21.
[4] Psa. 73. 16.   [5] them.

courage, to chafe and fume at such accidents, venting good spirits the wrong way; but rather reserve their magnanimous resolutions for better services, and (besides their private devotions) address themselves with *David* to Gods [1]publick worship in his house, who in his due time will unriddle unto [2]him the equitie of his proceedings.

28. But if men be of low and mean spirits, pusillanimous and heartless natures, and if these narrow souls in them meet with melancollie and heavie tempers, such fall a drooping, yea, despairing at the *perishing of the righteous;* they give all over for lost, concluding *there is no hope;* they rather languish [3]than live, walking up and down disconsolate, with soft paces, sad looks, and sorrowful hearts; all their children they are ready to call and christen [4]*Ichobods, the glorie is departed from Israel;* being affected like the Citizens of *Jerusalem* besieged by *Sennacherib,* their hearts are like the trees of the wood, [5]*moved with the wind.* But let such droopers know that herein they offend God and wrong themselves; and let them gird up their loins and *tie up their spirits* at the serious consideration that God in due time will raise them out of the dust, *maintain his own cause,* and confound his enemies.

29. The third sort of people, are the Arguers or Disputers, who being of a middle temper, neither haughtie nor [6]stomachful, neither low nor dejected, and withal being good men, embrace a middle course, neither to fret nor dispute, but calmly to reason out the matter with God himself. Of this [7]latter sort was the Prophet [8]*Jeremie,* who thus addresseth himself unto the Lord: [9]*Righteous art thou, O Lord, when I plead with thee; yet let me talk with thee of thy judgements: Wherefore doth the way of the wicked prosper? wherefore are they happie that deal very treacherously?* The good man could not conceive Gods proceedings; and although he kept to the conclusion, *Righteous art thou,* O *Lord,* yet *his heart was hot within him,* and he would fain be exchanging an argument with God that all was not right according to his humane capacity. *Job* also was one of these Arguers in the

---

[1] publike. [2] them. [3] then.
[4] 1 Sam. 4. 21. [5] Isa. 7. 2. [6] stomackful.
[7] later. [8] *Jeremiah.* [9] Jer. 12. 1.

agonie of his paffion: [1]*Oh that one might plead for a man with God, as a man pleadeth for his neighbour!*

30. But let flefh and bloud take heed of entering the lifts by way of challenge with God himfelf. If the [2]*Synagogue of the Libertines, and Cyrenians, and Alexandrians, and of them of Silicia, and of Afia, difputing with* Stephen, *were not able to refift the wifdom and the fpirit by which he fpake*, much lefs can frail flefh hope to make good a bad caufe by way of oppofition againft God, the beft and wifeft Anfwerer. Remember the Apoftles queftion, [3]*Where is the difputer?* But if we fhould be fo bold, in humility, to examine Gods proceedings, let us take heed left whileft we difpute with God, Satan [4]infenfible prompts us fuch reafons as are feemingly unanfwerable in our apprehenfions; fo that in ftead of being too hard for God (which is impoffible) men become too hard for themfelves, raifing fuch fpirits which they cannot quell, and ftarting fuch doubts which they cannot fatisfie. Wherefore let not our ignorance be counted *Gods* injuftice; let not the dimnefs of our eyes be efteemed the durtinefs of his actions, being all puritie and cleannefs in themfelves: Let us, if beaten from our out-works, make a fafe retreat to this impregnable caftle, [5]*Jeremie* his conclufion, *Righteous art thou, O Lord,* &c.

31. Come we now to the good Ufes that the godly ought to make of a *righteous mans perifhing in his righteoufnefs.* And firft, when he finds fuch [6]an one in a fwoun, he ought with all fpeed to bring him a cordial, and with the good [7]*Samaritane* to pour oil and wine into his wounds, endeavouring his recoverie to his utmoft power, whileft there is any hope thereof. I muft confefs it is onely Gods prerogative, [8]*according to the greatnefs of his power, to preferve thofe that are appointed to die.* However, it is alfo the boundant duty of all pious people, in their feveral diftances and degrees, to improve their utmoft for the prefervation of dying innocencie from the crueltie of fuch as would murder it.

32. But if it be impoffible to fave it from death, fo that

---

[1] Job 16. 21.   [2] Acts 6. 9, 10.   [3] 1 Cor. 1. 20.   [4] infenfibly.
[5] *Jeremiah.*   [6] a.   [7] Luke 10. 34.   [8] Pfal. 79. 11.

it doth expire, notwithstanding all their care to the contrarie, they must then turn lamenters at the funerals thereof. And if the iniquitie of the times will not safely afford them to be *open*, they must be *close Mourners* at so sorrowful an accident. O let the most *cunning Chyrurgeons* not begrutch their skill to unbowel, the *richest Merchants* not think much of their choicest spices to embalm, the most *exquisite Joyner* make the coffin, most *reverend Divine* the Funeral Sermon, the most *accurate Marbler* erect the *Monument*, and most renowned *Poet* invent the Epitaph to be inscribed on the tomb of *Perishing Righteousness*. Whilest all others, wel-wishers to goodness in their several places, contribute to their sorrow at the solemn Obsequies thereof; yea, as in the case of *Josiah* his death, let there be an *Anniversarie of Mourning* kept in remembrance thereof. However, let them not mourn like men *without hope;* but let them behave themselves at the interment of his *righteousness* as confident of the *resurrection thereof*, which God in his due time shall raise out of the ashes: It is sown in weakness; it shall be raised in power: it is sown in disgrace; it shall be raised in glorie.

33. Lastly, the temporal perishing of the righteous man in this world minds us of the necessitie of the day of Judgement, and ought to edge and quicken our prayers that God would shortly accomplish the number of his elect, consummate this miserable world, put a period to the dark night of his proceedings, that so that day, that welcome day, may begin to dawn, which is termed by the Apostle, [1]*The day of the revelation of the righteous judgement of God.* Five things there are (besides many [2]other) in the primitive part of Gods justice, which are very hard for men to conceive:

First, How the sin of *Adam*, to which we did never personally consent, can justly be imputed to us his posteritie.

Secondly, How Infants, who never committed actual sin, are subject to death, and, which is more, to damnation it self.

Thirdly, How God can actually harden the hearts of some, as he did [3]*Pharaohs*, and yet not be in the least degree accessarie to sin and the authour thereof.

---

[1] Rom. 2. 5. [2] others. [3] Exod. 14. 4.

Fourthly, How the *Americans* can juftly be condemned, to whom the found of the Gofpel was never trumpeted forth, and they by their invincible ignorance uncapable of Gods will in his word.

37. Laftly, How God, as it is in the Text, can fuffer *righteous men to perifh in their righteoufnefs, and wicked men to flourifh in their iniquitie.*

In all thefe, a *thin veil* may seem to hang before them, fo that we have not a full and free view of the reafons of Gods proceedings herein; yet fo as that under and thorow *this veil* we difcover enough in modeftie and fobrietie to fatisfie our felves, though (perchance unable to utter what in part we apprehend) we cannot effectually remove all the fcruples which the pious, nor all the cavils which the profane man brings againft us. But at the day of *judgement*, at the *revelation of the righteous judgement of God*, this *veil* fhall be turned back, or rather totally taken away, fo [1] all fhall plainly and perfpicuoufly perceive the juftice of Gods dealing in the cafes aforefaid. Not that then or there, any new effential addition or acceffion fhall accrue to Gods juftice, to mend or make up any former default or defect therein; but his proceedings (which before wanted not clearnefs in themfelves, but clearing to our eyes) fhall then be pronounced, declared, and adjudged juft, in the prefence of [2]divels, men, and Angels; fo that ignorance fhall not doubt, nor impudence dare to denie the truth thereof.

38. But before we take our final farewel of the words in our Text, know they are alfo capable of another fenfe, *I have feen the righteous man perifh in his righteoufnefs;* that is, I have feen a good man continuing in goodnefs, and fnatched away in the prime of his years, whileft wicked men, perfifting in their [3]profanefs, have prolonged their lives to the utmoft poffibilitie of nature. I confefs [4]S. *Paul* will in no cafe allow the word *perifhing* to be applied to the death of the godly, but ftartles at the expreffion, as [5]conteining fome Pagan impietie therein, pointing at it, as an Atheiftical pofition:

---

[1] that all. [2] devils. [3] profanenefs.
[4] Saint. [5] containing.

[1]*Then they also which are faln asleep in Christ are perished.* However, in a qualified [2]sense, (not for a total extinction, but temporal suspension of them in this world,) the Prophet pronounceth it of a just mans death, [3]*The righteous perisheth, and no man layeth it to his heart;* Yet, as if suspecting some ill use might be made of that term *perishing*, in the next words he mollifieth the harshness thereof, and (who best might) expounds his own meaning: *The righteous man is taken away from the evil to come.*

39. Indeed, when a just man dieth, with *Abraham*, in [4]*a good old age*, he is not properly said to be *taken away*, but, in Scripture-phrase, to *tarrie till God comes*. Thus, when *Peter* was very inquisitive to know how *John* should be disposed of, Christ answered him, [3]*If I will that he tarrie till I come, what is that to thee? John*, of all the *Jurie of the Apostles*, died in his bed, a thorow old man, of *temper* and *temperance*, of a strong and healthful natural constitution, moderate in diet, passions, and recreations: [6]*Abijah* and *Josiah* may be instances [of those who] are cut off by an untimely death; such are properly said to be *taken away*.

40. Now even such men God (not onely without the least stain to his Justice, but in great manifestation of his Mercie) may cause to *perish*; or, if that be too harsh a [7]tearm, may take them away from the evil to come: And that in three several acceptions.

First, To keep him from that evil of sin which God in his wisdom foresees the good man would commit, if living longer and left to those manifold temptations which future times (growing daily worse and worse) would present to, and press on him. True it is, God could by his restraining and effectual Grace keep him, though surviving in sinfull times, from being polluted therewith: but being a free Agent, he will vary the ways of his working, sometimes keeping men *in the hour of temptation*, sometimes [8]*from the hour of temptation*. The [9]latter he doth sometimes by keeping the hour from coming to them, or rather, from coming to the hour; making

---

[1] 1 Cor. 15. 18.   [2] sense.   [3] Isa. 57. 1.
[4] Gen. 25. 8.   [5] Joh. 21. 22.   1 Kings 14. 13.
[7] term.   [8] Rev. 3. 10.   [9] later.

them to fall short thereof, and preventing their approach thereunto, by taking them away in a speedie death. Thus mothers and nurses suspecting their children would too much play the wantons, disgrace them, and wrong themselves; when much company is expected at their houses, haste them to bed betimes, even before their ordinarie hour.

Secondly, from the [1]evils to sin which other men would commit, and he behold, to the great grief and anguish of his heart, *Lot*-like: for that [2]*righteous man dwelling among them, in seeing and hearing, vexed his righteous soul from day to day, with their unlawful deeds.*

41. Manifold Uses might be made of the Just [3]man thus perishing in his righteousness. First, men ought to be affected with true sorrow [4]thereat: yet the Prophet saith, *The righteous perisheth, and no man layeth it to his heart.* Surely his wife or children will (or else the more unworthy), [5]happily he hath none when dying. His kindred will, except (which is impossible) with *Melchisedech*, he be [6]*without father, without mother, without descent.* His friends will, though rather the rich than the righteous have friends whilest living, and leave them when dying. But to satisfie all objections at once: By *none*, are meant very few, inconsiderable in respect of those multitudes that pass the righteous mans death unrespected. Parallel to that place in the *Proverbs*: [7]*None that go to her return again, neither take they hold of the path of life.* Not that adulterie is the sin against the *holy Ghost, unpardonable;* but *vestigia pauca retrorsum.* Be thou, by an holy Riddle, *One* among that *None*; I mean a mourner in Sion for the righteous mans death, amongst those very very few, who lay it to their hearts.

Secondly, Men from hence are seriously to [8]collect and apply to themselves the doctrine of their mortalities, when they see *the righteous man perish in his righteousness.* There is a bird peculiar to *Ireland*, called the *Cock of the Wood*, remarkable for the fine flesh and follie thereof: All the difficultie to kill them is to find them out; otherwise a mean marksman

---

[1] Evil of sin.   [2] 2 Pet. 2. 8.   [3] mans.   [4] thereat *omitted*.
[5] [haply, ed. 1660.]   [6] Heb. 7. 3.   [7] Prov. 2 91.   [8] recollect.

may eafily kill them. They flie in woods in flocks; and if one of them be fhot, the reft remove not but to the next bow or tree at the fartheft, and there ftand ftaring at the fhooter till the whole covie be deftroyed. As foolifh as the bird is, it is wife enough to be the embleme of the wifeft men in point of mortalitie. Death fweeps away one, and one, and one, and the reft remain no whit moved at, or minding of it, till at laft a whole generation is confumed.

[1]It fareth with the moft mens lives as with the fand in this hypocritical hour-glafs: behold it in outward appearance, and it feemeth far more [2]than it is, becaufe rifing up upon the fides, whileft the fand is emptie and hollow in the midft thereof; fo that when it finks down in an inftant, a quarter of an hour is gone in a moment. Thus many men are miftaken in their own account, reckoning upon three-fcore and ten years the age [3]of man, because their bodies appear outwardly ftrong and luftie. Alas! their health may be hollow; there may be fome inward infirmitie and imperfection unknown unto them; fo that death may furprife them on a [4]fuddain.

Thirdly, They are to take notice of Gods anger with that place from which the *righteous man is taken away*. *Solomon*, fpeaking of the death of an ordinarie man, faith, [5]*The living will lay it to heart*: But when a *righteous man is taken away*, the living ought to lay it to the very *Heart of their heart*, efpecially if he be a Magiftrate or Minifter of eminent note. When the eye-ftrings break, the heart-ftrings hold not out long after: and when the *feers* are taken away, it is a fad [6]fymtome of a languifhing Church or Common-wealth.

Laftly, Men ought to imitate the virtuous examples of fuch as are dead. The [7]cloud and pillar at the Red-fea, was bright toward the *Ifraelites*, to guid and direct them with the light thereof: but the reverfe or back-part thereof, was dark [8]towards the *Egyptians*. In the beft men there is fuch a

---

[1] [This paragraph, with a few slight alterations, is to be found in Spencer's *Things New and Old*, fo. 1658, No. 1341, p. 375, entitled "How it is that men are fo much mistaken in the thoughts of long life." He quotes from "T. Fuller, *Fun. Serm. at Chelfey*, 1652;" and he adds in the margin the following: *Nihil ita decipit, quàm cum ignorent homines fpatia vivendi.* Hieron, Ep. 79.]

[2] then.   [3] of a man.   [4] fudden.   [5] Ecclef. 7. 2.

[6] fymptom.   [7] Exod. 14. 20.   [8] toward.

mixture of light and darkness, who with their virtues have many faults, failings and infirmities. Well, let the *Egyptian* walk by his dark side, follow his faults, whilest the *Israel of God*, all pious people, endeavour to imitate his virtues, directed in their conversations by the [1]luster of his godly examples. That so as *Herod*, hearing of the fame of Christ, conceived that [2]John Baptist was risen again from the dead: so let us labour that our virtuous lives may give just cause for others to conceive that those *righteous men* which have *perished in their righteousness*, those *champions* of *Christianitie* and *worthie Heroes of holiness* long since deceased, are revived again, and have in us a miraculous resurrection.

---

[1] lustre.   [2] Matth. 14. 2.

FINIS.

Deus nobis hæc otia fecit.
                Virgil, Eclog. 1.

Passages from
SPENCER'S KAINA KAI ΠΑΛΑΙΑ.
Things New and Old.

[JOHN SPENCER, to whom references have been made *paſſim*, was the learned Library-Keeper of Sion College, in London Wall, a resort which FULLER happily termed a Ramah for the fons of the prophets in London. As a Lecturer in the city FULLER was entitled to take up quarters at the College; and being engaged in the preparation of works of a great scope, he found the books, then the only public collection in the metropolis, an effective source of help. He seems to have been a particular favourite with SPENCER, who regarded him as an excellent preacher (see *anteà* p. 483); and FULLER held SPENCER in regard to the end of his life (see *Worthies*, § Chester, page 189). SPENCER belonged to Uttoxeter, Staffordshire; and though no scholar by profession, had from his childhood conversed with Books and Book-men; and, says his friend, "alwaies being where the Frankincense of the Temple was offered, there must be some perfume remaining about him." He had been placed in the Library by the Rev. JOHN SIMPSON, its Founder. Spencer was Library-Keeper at least as early as the year 1630, when he edited Dr. ROBERT WILLAN's Sermon preached in 1629 at the Funeral of the Right Honourable Viscount SUDBURY, Lord BAYNING, entitled *Eliah's Wiſh. A Prayer for Death*, London, 1630, 4to. The discourse is dedicated by the Preacher to ANNE, Viscountesse of SUDBURY, &c.; and SPENCER adds the following epistle to the reader, dated "From Syon Colledge, Aprill 12, 1630," which explains his own interest in the piece: "Hauing by much importune labour receiued from Noble hands a Coppy of this Sermon; out of a confidence that one paſſage therein, celebrating our first Benefactor *Viſcount Sudbury*, may do good to the Library of *Syon* Colledge, whereof I am Keeper, I have aduentured without consent of the Author to put it vpon thy censure, not doubting if I can procure his pardon, to promerit thy thankes. And so Farewell: Thine, *Iohn Spencer*." The paſſage to which allusion is here made occurs at pp. 40–2 as follows: "He was the firſt Benefactor to the Library of *Syon* Colledge, *Samuel* his *Ramath*, when, by the pious care and zealous industry of that graue and Reuerend

Divine M. *John Symfon* (who, as *Camillus* was called a fecond *Romulus*, merits the title of a fecond Founder (maugre the oppofition of an enuious *Sanballat*), a moft Stately roome is erected for the benefit of the worthy Preachers of this Honourable City of *London*, but wants the Furniture of bookes. [1] Bookes are the Riuers of Paradife watering the earth; the deaw of *Hermon* making the vallies fertile; the Arke preferuing the *Manna* pot and *Mofes* tables; the Monument of ancient labours; the Bafkets keeping the depofited Reliques of time fo as nothing is loft; the Magazine of Piety and Arts. A Souldier without Armes may be valiant, but not victorious; an Artifan without his instruments may be fkilfull, but not famous: *Archimedes* is known by his Spheare and Cylinder. A Preacher without bookes may haue fome zeale, but little knowledge to guide it: S. *Paul* himfelf, although fo infpired, found as much want of his bookes as of his cloake in winter. To ayme at Learning without bookes is with the *Danaides* [2] to draw water in a fiue. What were it for this wealthy City to reare vp a [3] Library equall to that of *Pififtratus* at *Athens*, of *Eumenes* at Pergamus, of *Ptolemy* at *Alexandria*? Were the meanes of your induftrious Preachers anfwerable to their minds, this good and great worke needed no other fupply, for they like *Plato* would give 3000 *Græcian* pence for three fmall volumes of *Pythagoras*, and with [4] *Hieronime* empty their purfes by purchafing *Alexandrian* Papers, and with *Thomas Aquinas* rather haue *Chryfostome* vpon St. *Mathew* then the huge City of *Paris*. O that you knew the fly and cruell Arts of our Aduerfaries in corrupting bookes! fo as if the ancient Fathers were now aliue, they could not know their owne elaborate workes: you would at any rate purchafe true and ancient coppies for your Preachers, that from them you might receive true and ancient doctrine. Remember the lofs at *Heidlebergh*, and feek to repaire it by following his Noble example, who in this particular fheweth what affection hee bare to Religion and Learning."

Things New and Old was publifhed in 1658, being commended to the reader in an addrefs by FULLER himfelf, dated from his chamber in Sion College, 10 January, 1657-8. He eulogifes the compiler's induftry; and remarks that while fome men's books are mere kites'-nefts,—a collection of ftolen things, SPENCER's ingenuity was commendable in that " on the margin he hath entred the names of fuch at whofe *Torch* he hath lighted his *Taper;* and I am confident that by fuch quotations he hath revived the memories of many Worthies, and of their fpeeches, which otherwife had been utterly loft." The full title is as follows: ΚΑΙΝΑ ΚΑΙ ΠΑΛΑΙΑ. Things New and Old. Or, A Store-houfe of Similies, Sentences, Allegories, Apophthegms, Adagies, Apologues, Divine, Morall, Politicall, &c. With their feveral Applications. Collected and obferved from the Writings and Sayings of the Learned in all Ages to this prefent. By JOHN SPENCER, a lover of Learning and Learned Men.
——*Deus nobis hæc otia fecit.* Virgil. Eclog. i. London, Printed by *W. Wilfon*

---

[1] Vide Sixtum Senenf. in proem. Bibliothec.
[2] Haurit aquam cribris clericus abfq; libris.
[3] Affidue repetunt quas perdunt Belides vnda. (Ovid.)
[4] Noftrum marfupium charia Alexandrina euacuarunt. (Hieronim.)

and J. *Streater*, for *John Spencer* at Sion Colledge, MDCLVIII. Fo. pp. xiv., 679, and Table xxxv.

FULLER's writings are more largely drawn upon in this old folio than any other writer. There are eighty-three quotations from his works. The only other authors moſt frequently cited are THOMAS ADAMS, Biſhop ARTHUR LAKE, JEREMIAH BORROUGHS, and Dr. D. FEATLEY. A complete liſt of SPENCER's extracts from FULLER is here ſet down, with extra headings in brackets to facilitate identification, and with full references to the places whence the citations are made :—

NO.	PAGE	
13	4.	Knowledge very uſefull in the matter of Reformation [Drake in '88].—*Holy State* [?] *Anteà*, p. 305.
42	11.	The Grouth of Sin to be prevented [Piſmires and Corn].—*Holy State* [?] See *The True Penitent*. *Poſteà*, vol. ii.
58	14.	God's Infinite Power on the Reſurrection of the Body [Peter Martyr's Wife].—*Ser. at S. Dunſt. Eaſt Lon.* 1647. *Anteà*, p. 182 ; and *poſteà*, p. 543.
81	20.	The Guilt of Innocent blood crying to Heaven for Vengeance [Philip II. and St. Lawrence's Chapel].—*Good Thoughts in Bad Times*.
119	29.	Riches have Wings [The Falconer's Cry].—*Serm. at S. Clem. Lond.* 1647. *Poſteà*, p. 544.
249	60.	Immediate Addreſſes unto God by prayer find acceptance [The Race of Cuſhai and Ahimaaz].—*Obſervat.*
252	61.	The Vanity of needleſs and intricate queſtions [Frobiſher and the Mineral Stones].—*Holy State* [The Controverſial Divine].
256	62.	Careleſſe Churchmen condemned [Tully on Sluggards].—*Holy State* [§ The Good Pariſhioner].
260	63.	To bleſſe God for our memories [Staupitius and the Genealogy of our Saviour].—*Holy State* [§ Of Memory].
264	64.	Many ſeem to be willing, yet are loath to die [A Tomb uſed as a butt].—*Holy State* [Of Tombs].
268	65.	The way to have our will is to be ſubject to God's will [The Shepherd and the Weather].—*Holy State* [§ Of Contentment].
272	66.	Hypocriſie may paſs for a time undiſcovered [Maud, Henry II.'s mother, Two eſcapes of].—*Holy State* [§ The Hypocrite].
279	67.	Others Harms to be our Arms [Lacedemonians and drunken Servants].—*Ser. at K. Inaugurat. at Weſtm.* 1644. *Anteà*, i. 280.
283	68.	National Judgments call for National Repentance [The Irruption of the Sea].—*Serm. at Weſtm.* 1642. *Anteà*, i. 255.
296	72.	Not to continue angry [Grecian Biſhops and the Sun. Lengthened Lawſuits].—*Ser. at S. Clem.* 1627. *Poſteà*, i. 544.

NO.	PAGE		
316	77.	Not lawful to fight for Religion [Mahomet a Warrior] *T. Fuller* [qy. in reference only to the laſt line: " Let Religion sink to Hell rather then we ſhould call to the Devill for help to ſupport it."]	
435*a*	107-8.	A meer Souldier an Enemy to Peace [Demades the Coffin-maker].—*Holy State*. ? See *anteà*, i. 252.	
440	109.	Prayers of the Godly, the unanimity of them [Ptolomy Philadelphus and the Seventy].—*Ser. at Savoy*, 1642.	*Anteà*, i. 258.
509	128.	Conſideration of God's Omnipreſence, to be the Sinner's curb [Camden on Wotton-under-Weaver]. *Poſteà*, p. 550.	
511	128.	Time ill ſpent [Drake's Loſs of a Day].—*Holy State* [§ Life of Drake].	
518	129.	An Orthodoxal Chriſtian hath a like Eſteem of all Gods Ordinances [Rivalry for the mural crown at New Carthage].—*Holy State* [§ The faithful Miniſter].	
562	141.	Miniſter to cry down the ſins of the time [What ſins our Saviour inveighed againſt].—*Ser. at S. Clem. Lond.* 1649. [Cf. *Holy State*, § The faithful Miniſter]. *Poſteà*, p. 548.	
569	142.	The Convenience of Virginity [Simile from the uſe of a church-porch].—*Holy State* [§ The Conſtant Virgin].	
571	143.	Infirmities to be in the beſt of God's children, and why ſo [London merchants and Dunkirk].—*Ser. at S. Clem. Lond.* 1649. *Poſtea*, p. 549.	
579	145.	The Scripture not to be jeſted withal [Edward IV. and the Cheapside Citizen].—*Holy State* [§ Of Jeſting].	
582	146.	God flow to anger and of great patience [The Roman Magiſtrates and the Flagellifer].—*Ser. at S. Dunſt. Eaſt. Lond.* 1647. *Poſteà*, i. 543.	
589	148.	Reſurrection of the body proved by a natural demonſtration [The ſmith's forge and ſparks].—*Ser. at S. Clem. Lond.* 1648. *Poſteà*, i. 547.	
601	151.	The Romaniſts error in the point of the Antiquity of Ceremonies [Miſtaking a ſon for a father].—*Holy State* [§ The True Church Antiquary].	
609	153.	The Great difficulty of forgiving one another [Children's pronunciation of the Lord's Prayer].—*Ser. at S. Clem. Lond.* 1648 [Cf. *Triple Reconciler*, p. 143 orig. ed.] *Poſteà*, i. 548.	
611	153.	The great danger of not liſtning to the Word preached [Cæſar and Artemidorus' petition].—*Obſervat.*	
620	156.	Unworthy Communicants condemned [Children and their new ſhoes].—*Obſervations.*	
623	156.	The danger of looſe Travel into forraign parts [Weeding a Library].—*Holy State* [Of Travelling].	
668	168.	The danger of introducing uſeleſs Ceremonies in the Church [Horſe-hairs turning to ſnakes].—*Serm.* [Cf. alſo *Holy State*: § The True Church Antiquary].	

NO.	PAGE	
677	170.	Sin attendant on the beſt of religious performances [Ovid and his Father].—*Medit.*
708	178.	Moderation little felt by [Men of moderate stature].—*Holy State* [§ The faithful Miniſter].
724	183.	A good ſermon not to be ſo much queſtioned as practiſed [Veniſon at table].—*Holy State* [§ The good Pariſhioner].
726	183.	Strange ſins, ſtrange puniſhments [Sodom drowned].—*Meditat.*[
729	184.	The ſloathful contractedneſſe of our prayers unto God reproved [Alteration of Jubilee years by the Popes].—*Meditat.*[
742	187.	To ſhun ill Company [Nazarites forbidden to eat grapes].—*Good Thoughts.*
747	188.	Man to be ſociable [Contiguity of Iſlands].—T. Fuller, *ut anteà* [ſhould be *Holy State:* § Of Company].
767	193.	Deformity of body not to be contemned [The Emperor of Germany and the miſ-ſhapen Prieſt].—*Holy State* [§ Of Deformity].
778	196.	The ſtrength of Imagination demonſtrated [Children and twig-horſes].—*Holy State* [§ Of Fancy].
782	197.	The danger of Stage-plaies [Zeuxis' picture and the birds].—*Holy State* [§ Of Recreations].
798	201.	Riches, Honour, &c., the Devils bait [Baits for gnats].—*Meditat.*
804	203.	Married men better Common-wealths-men than Bachelers [London merchants and mariners].—*Holy State* [§ Of Marriage].
806	203.	The benefit of keeping cloſe to good principles [The beſt point of obſervation in a fair].—*Holy State* [§
813	205.	Gods Power, Wiſdom, &c., to be ſeen in all the Creatures [Arms of the Duke of Rohan].—*Holy State* [§ The Atheiſt].
817	206.	The encreaſe of Drunkeneſſe in England [The depth of the ſea near Holland and England].—*Holy State* [§ The Degenerous Gentleman].
890	227.	God afflicts his children for their good [The Link in London Streets].—*T. F. in a Ser. of Aſſurance.* Anteà, p. 483.
899	230.	Blaſphemous language condemned [Cato and the Greek tongue]—*Serm. at S. Clem. Lond.* 1647. Poſteà, p. 545.
903	231.	The juſtice of God, what it is, and how defined [Edward I. and the yard-meaſure].—*Serm. at S. Clem. Lond.* 1647. Poſteà, p. 546.
904	231.	Juſtification by Chriſt, the extent of it [The Father of the Prodigal] [?] Poſteà, p. 546.
905	231.	How it is that the proceedings of God in his Juſtice are not ſo clearly diſcerned [The ſtick in the water].—*Ut anteà.* Poſteà, p. 546.
913	234.	God a merciful God [Maiden Aſſizes].—*Serm. at. S. Clem. Lond.* 1650. Poſteà, p. 551.

540   Fragments from

NO.	PAGE	
918	235.	The feveral expreffions of God in his mercies, and why fo [Legal language in conveyances].—*Ut anteà. Pofteà*, p. 552.
920	239.	The generality of God's knowledge [Edward VI.'s knowledge of Englifh coafts].—*Serm at S. Clem. Lond.* 1650. *Pofteà*, p. 552.
957	247.	Recreation, the neceffity thereof [Recreation, fecond Creation].—*Holy State* [§ Of Recreation].
987	256.	The great danger of fleighting the leaft finne [General Norris' wound].—*Serm. at S. Clem. Lond.* 1650. *Pofteà*, p. 553.
1132	302.	The Scriptures not to be plaid withall [The font and the chalice].—*Holy State* [§ Of Jefting].
1334	373.	No Man free from Temptations [The Countryman and the Robber on the plain].—*On Chrifts Temptat. Pofteà*, ii. p. 21.
1341	375.	How it is that Men are fo much miftaken in the Thoughts of long life [The hypocritical hour-glafs].—*Fun. Serm. at Chelfey*, 1652. *Anteà*, p. 532.
1345	376.	Confcience fpoils the wicked Man's mirth [The fat Sheep made lean].—*On Chrifts Temptat.* *Anteà*, p. 524-5.
1346	377.	Sathans fubtilty in laying his Temptations [The affault of a city].—*Ut anteà.* *Pofteà*, ii. 33.
1348	377.	A bleffed thing to have Riches and a Heart to ufe them aright [Thomas Sutton's prayer].—*Church Hift. of Britain. Anno* 1611 [Bk. v. § 20, p. 66].
1154(*fic*)	412.	Knowledge and Learning to be owned wherefoever they be found [Virgil and Ennius' poetry].—*Serm. at S. Clem. Lond.* 1649. *Pofteà*, p. 549.
1353	473.	Graces of the Spirit to be held faft in the midft of temporall loffes [The fhipwrecked man and the ftandard-bearer].—*Serm. at S. Clem. Lond.* 1652. *Poftea*, p. 554.
1371	478.	Wife men dying as well as Fools [Paracelfus].—*Holy State* [§ Life of Paracelfus: merely a reference].
1557	538.	Ranters, Roaring boys, &c., their converfion, not confufion, to be endeavoured [The would-be Donatift Martyr].—*Wounded Confcience*.
1559	538.	Small buddings of Grace in the Soul, an argument of greater growth [Spring Primrofes and Violets].—*Cure of a Wounded Confcience*.
1561	539.	Godly company, the benefit thereof [Slender buildings in London fupporting each other].—*Cure of a Wounded Confcience*.
1565	540.	To be more ftrict in the holy obfervation of the Sabbath than heretofore; and why fo [Superftitious Almanack of the Sunday].—*Cure of a Wounded Confcience* [page 89].
1567	541.	Patiently to wait on Gods Good Will and Pleafure [Elijah on Carmel and his fervant].—*Cure of a Wounded Confcience*.

NO.	PAGE	
1569	541.	Men to pray for others as well as themselves [David's Prayer, Ps. xxv. 2].—*Cure of a Wounded Conscience.*
1571	542.	Prayer for others in the same condition with ourselves, prevalent with God [Beggars Prayers when asking alms].—*Cure of a Wounded Conscience.*
1605	554.	Curious Inquisitors into God's Secrets deservedly punished [Sir William Champney's overlooking his neighbours]. *Posteà*, ii., *Grand Assizes.*
1636	563.	A Great Blessing of God to be gently used in the matter of Conversion [Apprentices and their fathers' trade].—*Cure of a Wounded Conscience.*
1638	563.	The pain of a wounded conscience greatned by the Folly of the Patient.—*Cure of a Wounded Conscience.*
1640	564.	A good man tedious to bad company [Hunted Deer].
1642	565.	Greatness of the Torture of a Wounded Conscience [Adam in Paradise].—*Cure of a Wounded Conscience.*
1644	566.	Patiently to wait God's time for deliverance [Horses broken leg].—*Cure of a Wounded Conscience.*
1764	603.	How to make a right use of the doctrine of Predestination [Cardinal Pool].—*Serm. at S. Clem.* *Posteà*, p. 554.
1903	645.	Ignorance and Wilfulness ill-met [The Jews in England]. *Serm. at S. Brides.*
		Posteà, ii., *Short Tract on the History of the Jews.*

Of the above 83 passages from FULLER's works 28 are taken from his sermons. Out of these 28 passages, which include those already quoted in the *Sermons* of this volume, 19 remain to be cited here, being extracts which belong to discourses delivered in London from 1647 to 1652, *i.e.,* those discourses which in the order of time fall into the present volume. The extracts are taken by SPENCER either from FULLER's manuscript sermons, or from printed copies now lost; and several of them were printed in RUSSELL's *Memorials of Thomas Fuller,* 8vo., 1844, pp. 319-25. Two of the passages (§§ 1, 2) are from a sermon or sermons preached at *S. Dunstan's East;* and the remaining seventeen (§§ 3-19) are from sermons preached at *St. Clement's Eastcheap.* FULLER's relations with the latter church have already been noticed, pages cccclxi. *seq. anteà;* and will again be referred to pages xi. *seq.* of the next volume. As to his connection with St. Dunstan's East, "a parish of many rich merchants," as STOWE tells us, there is only one direct notice of it to be found in our author's works. That occurs in his *Appeal of Injured Innocence,* fo. 1659 (pt. ii. page 49), in reference to a laughable circumstance bearing on his natural powers of *memory;* for even by this time his reputation in this respect was made. His antagonist HEYLYN, in his Animadversions of the *Church-History,* thinking he had found the author in error, had written of him: "If our Author be no better at a pedigree in private Families than he is in those of Kings and Princes, I shall not give him much for his *Art of Memory,* for his *History* less, and for his *Heraldry* just nothing" (*Examen Historicum,* 1659, pp. 75-6). Whereupon FULLER, writing in 1659, thus replied: "When I intend to expofe them to fale, I know where to meet with a francker Chapman. None alive ever heard me pretend to the *Art of Memory*, who in my booke [*Holy State*] have decried it as a *Trick, no Art;* and indeed is more of fancy than memory. I confeffe, some ten years fince, when I came out of the Pulpit of St. *Dunſton's-Eaſt*, one (who fince wrote a book thereof [viz. HENRY HERDSON, and *Ars Mnemonica*, 8vo., 1651],) told me in the Veſtry, before credible people, That he in *Sydney Colledge* had taught me the *Art of Memory*. I returned unto him, That it was not fo; *for I could not remember that I had ever ſeen his face;* which, I conceive, was a reall Refutation!"

In the 19 extracts, which now follow, there is an evident connection between fome of the paragraphs, fhowing that they were taken from feparate difcourfes on fpecial topics. One of the fermons, it is clear, was on Forgivenefs (§§ 1, 4, and 9); another on the Refurrection (§§ 2 and 8); and others on the Juſtice (§§ 6 and 7), Mercy (§§ 14 and 15), and Omnipotence (§§ 13 and 16), of God.]

[§ 1] *God Slow to Anger, and of Great Patience.*
(No. 582; page 146.)

IT is obfervable that the *Romane*[1] Magiftrates when they gave fentence upon any one to be fcourged, a bundle of rods tyed hard with many knots was laid before them. The reason was this, That whilft the Beadle or Flagellifer was untying the knots, which he was to do by [*i.e.* in] order, and not in any other hafty or fudden way, the magiftrate might fee the deportment and carriage of the delinquent, whether he were forry for his fault, and fhewed any hope of amendment, that then he might recall his fentence, or mitigate the punifhment; otherwife to be corrected fo much the more feverely. Thus God in the punifhing of finner, how patient is he! how loath to ftrike! how flow to anger if there were but any hopes of recovery! How many knots doth he untye! how many rubs doth he make in his way to Juftice! He doth not try us by Marfhal law, but pleads the cafe with us, *Why will ye dye, O ye houfe of Ifrael?* and all this to fee whether the poor finner will *throw himfelf down at his feet*, whether he will *come in and make his compofition, and be faved.*—T. FULLER, *Ser. at St.* Dunft. *Eaft*, Lond. 1647.

[§ 2] *Gods Infinite Power in the Refurrection of the Body.*
(No. lviii; page 14) [Cf. *anteà*, p. 182].

IN Queen *Marie's*[1] daies the body of *Peter Martyr's* wife was by the charity of that time taken out of her grave and buried in a dunghill, in deteftation of that great Scholar her bufband, fometime *Profeffour of Divinity* in the univerfity

---

[1] Ludov. Feneftella *de Magiftr. Rom.*

of *Oxford*. But when the tide was once turned, and that Queen *Elizabeth* of happy memory swayed the Sceptre of this State, her bones were reduced to their place, and there mingled with the bones of St. *Fridefwide*, to this intent, that if ever there should come an alteration of Religion in *England* again, (which God forbid,) then they should not be able to discern the ashes of the one from the other. Though Death hath mixed and blended the bodies of men, women, and children, with the flesh of beasts, birds, and serpents; hath tossed, typed, and turned their ashes both into aire and water, to puzzle (if possible) the God of heaven and earth to find them again. But all in vain: he can call for a finger out of the gore of an Eagle, for a leg out of the belly of a Lion, for a whole man out of the body of a Fish. If the devil, or thy corrupt reason, shall suggest that this is impossible, make no other answer but this: *God is omnipotent; God is infinite.*—THO. FULLER, *Ser. at S. Dunst. East,* Lon. 1647.

[§ 3] *Riches have Wings.*
(No. cxix.; page 29.)

IT is a tearm amongst Falconers, that if a Hawk flie high, *she leffens, O she leffens* (saith the Falconer); but if she soar yet higher, then he cries out, *O she vanisheth, she vanisheth!* And it is now found to be true by sad and woefull experience, that *Riches* are upon the wing, and have of late by one means or other taken such a *flight* out of many *men's purses*, that they have *leffened* and *leffened* every day more and more, and are now at present by the continuance of time even as good as *quite vanished.*—TH. FULLER's *Serm. at S.* Clem. Lond. 1647.

[§ 4] *Not to continue Angry.*
(No. 296; page 72.)

TWO *Grecian* Bishops, being fallen out about some difference in point of judgement, parted asunder in great anger;

---

[1] *Acts and Monuments*, p. 1785. Tibi abfit quod at refufcitanda corpora, &c. Auguftin, *De Civitate Dei*, lib. 22. Ex. 9. 6.; Gen. 17. 1.

but the elder of them (for so the wiser is to be accounted) sent unto his Collegue a message, onely in these two words, *Sol ad occasum*, The Sun is about to go down. The other no sooner heard it, but he *reflected* on that of the Apostle, [1]*Let not the Sun go down upon your wrath;* and so they were both friends again. How doth this *amity* of theirs condemn the *enmity* that is amongst many of us at this time? As that deadly feud of the *Scots*, who entailed their Lands on posterity, conditionally, that they should fight against the party that had offended, and never entertain any the least pacification. And such wrangling Law-suits as that of the two noble families, *Barclay* and *Lisle*, which began in the reigne of *Edward the fourth*, and continued to the first year of *King Iames*, full seven score years. It cannot be denied, but that a man may with good qualifications go to *Law* for his own; but the length of time in the *Suit*, when the *Grandchild* shall hardly end that which the *Grandfather* began, may draw on a great suspition in the want of charitable affection.—T. FULLER'S *Serm. at* S. Clem. 1627 [1647].

[§ 5] *Blasphemous Language Condemned.*

(No. 899; page 230.)

CATO being very much struck in years would by all means study the *Greek* tongue, and being asked by one, why in his old age he would set upon such an exotick language; *O* (said he) *I am informed that the Greek is a copious and fluent tongue, and withal such a tongue as the Gods speak in; I would therefore learn it, that I may be able to converse with the Gods in their own Dialect.* This was *Catoes* conceit in those darker times of *Nature;* but there is a generation amongst us in these clearer times of *Grace, Ranters, Roaring boyes,* such as are great proficients in all manner of blasphemous language, such as belch out nothing but oathes, and direful execrations in the very face of Heaven. What can this else be but to practice here on *Earth* what by a sad *Prolepsis* they are sure to come to *hereafter,* that is, to be *roaring boyes and girls*

---

[1] Eph. iv. 26.

in Hell to all eternity.—T. FULLER's *Ser. at St.* Clem. Lond. 1647. [Spencer adds this paffage from S. Auguftine, Non minus peccant qui blafphemant Chriftum regnantem in cœlis quàm qui crucifixerunt ambulantem in terris.]

[§ 6] *The Jusftice of God, what it is, and how Defined*

(No. 903; page 231.)

IN the Raign of King *Edward* the firft, there was much [1]abufe in the *alnage* of all forts of *Drapery*, much wrong done betwixt Man and Man, by reafon of the diverfity of their meafures, every man meafuring his cloath by his own yard, which the King perceiving, being a goodly proper Man, took a long ftick in his hand, and having taken the length of his own arm, made Proclamation through the Kingdom that ever after the length of that ftick fhould be the meafure to meafure by, and no other. Thus *Gods Juftice* is nothing elfe but a conformity to his being, the pleafure of his will; fo that *the* [2] *counfell of his Will* is the *ftandard of his Juftice*, whereby all men fhould regulate themfelves as well in commutative as diftributive Justice, and fo much the more righteous than his Neighbour fhall every man appear by how much he is proximate to this rule, and leffe righteous as he is the more remote.—THO. FULLER, *Serm. at St.* Clem. *Lond.* 1647. [The next fentence, No. 904, "Juftification by Chrift, the extent of it," may be Fuller's out of the fame fermon.]

[§ 7] *How it is that the Proceedings of God in his Juftice are not fo clearly difcerned.*

(No. 905; page 231.)

TAKE a ftreight ftick and put it into the water; then it will feem crooked. Why? Because we look upon it through two mediums, air and water; there lies the *deceptio*

---

[1] Th. Walsingham, *Hist.*   [2] Ephe. 1. 5.

vifus ; thence it is that we cannot difcern aright. Thus the Proceedings of God in his Juftice, which in themfelves are ftreight, without the leaft obliquity, feem unto us crooked ; that wicked men fhould profper, and good men be afflicted ; that the *Ifraelites* fhould make the bricks, and the *Egyptians* dwell in the *houfes;* that Servants fhould ride on horfe-back, and Princes go on foot : thefe are things that make the beft Chriftians ftagger in their judgements. And why? but becaufe they look upon *G*ods proceedings through a double medium of Flefh and Spirit, that fo all things feem to go crofs, though indeed they go right enough. And hence it is that *G*ods proceedings in his juftice are not fo well difcerned, the eyes of man alone being not competent judges thereof.—T. FULLER, *ut anteà*.[1]

[§ 8] *Refurrection of the Body proved by a Natural Demonftration.*

(No. 589 ; page 148.)

I HAVE ftood in a Smiths forge, and feen him put a rufty, cold, dull piece of Iron into the fire, and after a while he hath taken the fame piece, the very fame, numerical, individual piece of Iron out of the fire, hot, bright, fparkling. And thus it is with our bodies : they are laid down in the grave, dead, heavy, earthly ; but at the Reffurrection *this mortal fhall put on immortality ;* at that general conflagration this dead, heavy, earthly body, fhall arife living, lightfome, glorious ; which made *Job* fo confident : *I know that my Redeemer liveth, and that with thefe eyes I fhall fee him,* &c. Chap. 19. 25.—T. FULLER, *Ser. at* St. Clem. Lond. 1648.

---

[1] In the same margin Spencer adds, as a reference to a similar sentiment, "R. WILLIAMS [i.e. Ro. WILLAN's] *Serm. at Fun. of* L. [Sir Paul] Bayning, 1629," entitled *Eliahs Wish*, Lond. 1630, 4to. At page 3 in the following passage : "Our eyes behold all things, yet they see not themselves, but by reflection in a looking glass. Here are two looking glasses : one upon the Hearse, informing us that neither Wisdom, nor Honour, nor Wealth, nor Strength, nor Friends, nor Physicke, nor Prayers, are sufficient Parapets to shelter us from the stroke of death. Here is another looking glass in the text [1 Kings, xix. 4], expressing the miserable condition of our lives."

[§ 9] *The great Difficulty of Forgiving one another.*

(No. 609; page 153.)

IT is worthy obfervation, and fuch as are converfant amongft little children know it to be true, That when they are taught to fay the *Lords Prayer*, they are ufually out at that Petition, *Forgive us our trefpaffes, as we forgive them that trefpafs againft us.* The reafon is, becaufe of the harfhneffe of the found, the reiteration of one and the fame words, the multiplicity of the confonants, and the like. It were to be wifhed that that which they are fo *often out at*, we could be more *frequently in at*; that what is not eafie for their fhallow heads to conceive, may not be too hard for our more experimental hearts to practife. But it is hard indeed. Why elfe did Chrift make a Comment on that Petition, paffing by the other five, when [1] he taught his Difciples to pray? And hence it is that *injuries* are regiftred in fheets of *Marble* to all Pofterity, whilft *benefits* are written in the *fand*, ready to be dafhed out by the foot of the next that paffeth by.— T. FULLER, *Ser. at St.* Clem. Lond. 1648.

[§ 10] *Minifters to cry down the Sins of the Time.*

(No. 562; page 141.)

IT is obfervable that our Saviour never inveighed againft Idolatry, Ufury, Sabbath-breaking amongft the *Jews*; not that thefe were not fins, but they were not practifed fo much in that age, wherein wickednefs was fpun with a finer thread. And therefore Chrift principally bent the drift of his preaching againft fpiritual pride, hypocrifie, and traditions, then predominant amongft the people. Thus it ought to be with the Minifters of the Gofpel: in this thing they are to trace their Mafters fteps; they are chiefly to reprove the raging fins of the time and place they live in; yet with this caution, that in publique reproving of fin they ever whip the vice, and let the perfon go free.—T. FULLER, *Ser. at St.* Clem. Lond. 1649.

---

[1] Mat. 6. 14.

[§ 11] *Infirmities to be in the best of Gods Children, and why so.*

(No. 571 ; page 143.)

THE merchants of *London* petitioned Queen *Elizabeth*, that they might but have liberty to levell the town of *Dunkerk* (a place at that time very obnoxious to the safety of the merchants trade), and they would do it at their own charges. The Queen by the advice of her Councel, returns them an answer in the negative : She could not do it. What ! no suffer them to beat hers and their enemies? Not to fire such a nest of hornets? Not to demolish such a pyraticall town as that was? No; it must not be. And why? She knew well that it would not do amiss that they should be alwayes sensible of so neer and so offensive an Enemy, and so be alwayes preparing and prepared to defend themselves and the State of the whole Kingdom. Which took a right effect ; for hereupon all turn men of war ; hardly a Boat but is man'd out for service, which otherwise might have either rotted in the Harbour, or ridden securely at Anchor. Thus God, when his dear children cry out unto him to be [1]*delivered from the body of sin*, that *sin may not raign in their mortal bodies*, he so far granteth their requests that by the special dispensations of his holy spirit, sin shall not prevail over them. Not but that [2] sins of infirmity shall still cleave to the best of his children here in this world. Why? because they shall be still upon the guard, in a posture of defence, resisting the Devil, quitting themselves like men, who otherwise might live in all security.—T. FULLER, *Ser. at* St. Clem. Lond. 1649.

[§ 12] *Knowledge and Learning to be owned wheresoever they be found.*

(No. 1154; page 412.)

IT is observed, that the *Egyptians* had Idols and very heavy burthens ; these the *Israelites* detested ; but they

---

[1] Rom. 7. 24. [2] Rom. 1. 26.

had withall veffels of gold and filver (*Exod.* 11. 2), and thefe according to Gods command they made a Religious ufe of. [1] One feeing *Virgil* very ftudious in a dull piece of *Ennius* Poetry, afked him What he did with that book? He anfwered, *Lego aurum in ftercore,* I am gathering gold out of a dunghill. Thus it is that Knowledge is to be owned wherefoever or in whomfoever it is found : *fas eft et ab hofte doceri,* a man may learn of his enemy ; nay, *aliena pericula,* another Man's harms may teach us how to beware. Much of Morality may be picked up from the Heathens ; much of the Knowledge of God from Philofophers; much of Learning from the Poets ; and much of *D*ivine truth from fome of our well-read Adverfaries of Rome, of whom it may be faid, as it was fometimes of another, [2] *Ubi bene, nemo melius; ubi male, nemo pejus.* Where they have written truth, as in meer fpeculative points of God, the bleffed Trinity, &c., there no man better; and there it is that as the *Ifraelites,* fo we may go down to the Philiftims forges (1 *Sam.* 13. 19) to whet our fwords and fpears, to be furnifhed with fharp arguments and folid reafons to the confutation of falfe and heretical opinions. But where they have roved from the Truth, as in the doctrine of Merit, Indulgences, &c., where you fhall be fure alwaies to find a Matthew *fitting at the receipt of Cuftome,* there no man worfe ; and there we may and muft forfake them.—T. FULLER, *Serm. at* S. Clem. Lond. 1649.

[§ 13] *Confideration of Gods Omniprefence to be the Sinners Curb.*

(No. 509 ; page 128.)

*C*AMBDEN in his *Britannia* maketh mention of a great high Hill in *Staffördfhire* called *Weever,* under which there is a little Village called *Wotton.* Now this village being feated in fo fad a dreary, dolefome place, the Sun not fhining into it any further then on the tops of the houfes, by

---
[1] Rob. Holcot *in Sap.*   [2] Origen.

reason of the height of the hills over-topping it, the people of the place have been observed to chant out this note:

*Wotton under Weever,
Where God came never.*

This now were an excellent place for a rapacious rich man to make a purchase of, and then to plant a colony there, where *God came never*: a good place for drunkards to swill in, for epicures to surfeit in, for the voluptuous to take pleasure in, for the prodigal to riot in, &c. But let them all know that *God* is at *Wotton*, and *God* is with them all, in all places, at all times, every where included, no where excluded: *whither shall I fly* (said [1]*David*) *from thy presence?*—THO. FULLERS *Serm.* at Clem. Eastch. Lond. 1650. [The following passage from Prosper is added in the margin: Locis præsens simul est Deus omnibus unus.]

[§ 14] *God a Mercifull God.*
(No. 913; page 234.)

THERE happens sometimes in *England* such Assizes as are called the *Maiden-Assizes*, that is, when the offences brought to the bar do not reach to the taking away of life, so that there is not any execution. Whereupon the *High Sheriffe* of the County presents the Judges at their departure with *white gloves*, to wear in commemoration of the *mercies* then shewed to offenders, which perhaps by the strict rule of justice might have been cut off: such an *Assizes* as this God now keeps. We sin daily, we offend hourly, and therefore guilty of death eternally; but God woes and entreats us to come in, promiseth life eternall, nay, binds it with an oath: *As I live,* saith he, *I will not the death of a sinner.* Let us then return unto him, white hands, candid thoughts, clean hearts, and then rest assured that he will look upon us neither black with revenge, nor red with anger; but with a smooth brow and smiling countenance receive us into

---

[1] Psalm 139. 7.

mercy.—THO. FULLERS *Serm. at St. Clem. Lond.* 1650. [In margin, from Chryfoft. *in Pfal.* 50 : Quid eft peccatum ad Dei miferecordiam? Tela araneæ, &c.]

[§15] *The feverall Expreffions of God in his Mercies, and Why so?*

(No. 918; page 235.)

AS Lawyers in this captious age of ours, when they draw up any Conveyances of Lands, or other writings of concernment betwixt party and party, are fain to put in many æquivoall terms of one and the fame fignification, as, *to have and to hold, occupy and enjoy Lands, Tenements, Hereditaments, Profits, Emoluments; to remife, releafe, acquit, difcharge, exonerate of and from all manner of actions, fuits, debts, trefpaffes, &c.*; and all this to make fure work, fo that if one word will not hold in Law another may : Thus God, when he fhews himfelfe to his People in love, he varies his expreffions as he did to the *Ifraelites, Exod.* 34. 6, 7 : *The Lord, the Lord God, mercifull and gracious, long-fuffering, and abundant in goodneffe and truth, keeping mercies for thousands, forgiving iniquity, tranfgreffion and fin,* &c. Here's an *homonomy* of words, all *Synonymaes*. And why fo? To *raife up* the drooping foul, *to bind up* the broken-hearted, that if it chance to ftumble at one expreffion, it may be fupported by another ; if one word will not reach another may. His mind is that the poor foul may rather *leave* then *lack* when it comes to draw comfort out of the breafts of Mercy.—THO. FULLER *ut anteà*.

[§ 16] *The Generality of Gods Knowledge.*

(No. 920; page 236.)

IT is faid of King *Edward* the fixth, that he [1] knew all the *Ports, Havens, Harbours,* and *Creeks,* in and about the

---

[1] *Sir* John Hayward *in vita*.

English Coasts, together with the depth and shallowes of the water ; as also the severall burthens of every ship that could ride there with safety. Yet this was but a *puny knowledge* in that young king, when we look upon the *general knowledge* of God. He *knowes* all things, all creatures ; nothing is hid from his knowledge ; he *knowes* the thoughts of man afar off : he *knowes* what he will think many years hence if he live to it ; he *knowes* the stars by their names. Whereas our eyes are dim, they small, the distance great, yet his infinite essence is a vast *Nomenclator* of them all. Such and so general is the knowledge of our all-knowing God that he knows all things also *Simul, semel, & uno intuito,* all at once, both things past, present, and to come.— THO. FULLERS *Serm. at St.* Clem. *Lond.* 1650.

[§ 17] *The great Danger of sleighting the Least Sinne.*

(No. 987 ; page 256.)

GENERAL *Norris,* one of the Ancients of that noble Family, having (as he thought) received a *sleight wound* in the wars of *Ireland,* neglected the same, presuming belike that the *balsome* of his own body, without calling in for those other Auxiliaries of Art, would have wrought the cure ; but so it was that his arm gangrened, and both arm and life were lost together. Thus it was with him in the body natural, and thus it will be too in the body spirituall ; the least of sin therefore is to be avoyded, the least growth of sinne to be prevented. The Cockatrice must be *crushed* in the egge ; else it will soon become a Serpent : the very thought of sinne, if not thought on, will break out into Action, Action into Custom, Custom into Habit ; and then *actum est de Corpore & Anima,* both body and soul are irrecoverably lost to all Eternity.—THO. FULLERS *Serm. at St.* Clem. *Lond.* 1650. [In margin : *Principiis obsta.*]

[§ 18] *Graces of the Spirit to be held fast in the midst of Temporall Losses.*

(No. 1353; page 473.)

AS it is with a man in a wrack at fea, when all is caft over-boord, the *Victuals* that feed him, the *cloaths* that fhould keep him warm, yet he fwims to the fhoare with his *life in his hand*. Or as it is with a valiant Standard-bearer that carries the banner in the time of battel, if he fees all loft he wraps the banner about his body, and choofeth rather to dye in that as his winding-fheet then let any man take it from him or fpoyl him of it; he will hold that faft though he lofe his life with it. Thus [1] *Job* in all his troubles is faid to hold faft his integrity, chap. 2, verse 4. And fo muft all of us do, hold our *fpirituals* whatever becomes of our *temporals*: when Wife and Children, and Friends, and liberty, and life, and all's a-going, fay unto peace of Confcience, to Innocence and Integrity, as *Jacob* faid to the angel, (whether they be thofe *Summer-graces* of Profperity, as Joy and Thanksgiving; or the *Winter-graces* of Adverfity, as Patience and Perfeverance; or the grace of Humility that is always in feafon,) *We will not let ye go;* for indeed there is no bleffing without them. There's not a man upon the face of the earth, but if he be of an heavenly temper and fpiritual refolution will in the greateft *ftorm*, in the hotteft *affault*, wrap himfelf round about with his *integrity*, and will not let it go until he *go along with it.—* T. FULLER, *Serm. at S.* Clem. Lond. 1652.

[§ 19] *How to make a right ufe of the Doctrine of Predeftination.*

(No. 1764; p. 603.)

CARDINAL *POOL*, a good man, though a Papift, being defired by one to tell him how he might come to underftand the former part of S. *Paul's* epiftles, which are

---
[1] Jos. Caryl, *in locum.*

for the moſt part *Doctrinal Poſtions*, made this anſwer : " *By a careful practiſing of the latter part of the ſame* epiſtles, which conſiſt much in *precepts*, and *directions* how to lead a life in all godlineſſe and holineſſe of converſation. And thus if any man deſire to know *the former part of Predeſtination*, whether his name be written in the book of life, whether he be of the election of grace, whether he be predeſtinated to life eternal, let him but look into *the latter part of Predeſtination*, the means as well as the end of Predeſtination; whether his converſation be in heven ; whether his life be ſuitable to the profeſſion of the Goſpel of Chriſt, and though he meet with many rubs in the way, and through frailty ſtumble and fall, yet riſeth again and preſſeth on to the mark of the high calling of God in Chriſt Jeſus. Thus if a man do, he may conclude himſelf to be within the number of the elect : and this is the right uſe that is to be made of the doctrine of predeſtination. But it is otherwiſe with too too many in theſe all-queſtioning dayes of ours : for whereas S. *Paul* preſents us with a chain let down from heaven, *Rom.* 8, *Election* and *Predeſtination* at one end of the chain, and *Glorification* at the other end thereof ; both which ends God keepeth faſt in his hand. As for the middle links of the chain, *Calling* and *Juſtification*, thoſe he leaves for them to lay hold on ; but they cannot be quiet, but muſt be tugging and labouring to wreſt thoſe parts out of *Gods* hands, and ſo miſſe of the right uſe and comfort that is to be found in the abſtruſe, yet ſweet doctrine of pre-deſtination.—T. FULLER, *Serm. at S. Clem. Lond.*

END OF VOL. I.

The Gresham Press,

437/63

PLEASE DO NOT REMOVE
CARDS OR SLIPS FROM THIS POCKET

UNIVERSITY OF TORONTO LIBRARY

BX   Fuller, Thomas
5133   Collected sermons
F84
1891
v.1

Lightning Source UK Ltd.
Milton Keynes UK
UKHW022017230119
336088UK00014B/550/P